Tourism in Contemporary Society
An Introductory Text

TOURISM IN CONTEMPORARY SOCIETY

AN INTRODUCTORY TEXT

Lloyd E. Hudman, Ph.D.
Brigham Young University

Donald E. Hawkins, Ed.D.
George Washington University

Foreword by Willibald P. Pahr
Secretary General of the
World Tourism Organization

A NATIONAL PUBLISHERS BOOK
PRENTICE HALL, Englewood Cliffs, New Jersey 07632

Library of Congress Cataloging-in-Publication Data

Hudman, Lloyd E.
  Tourism in contemporary society.

  Bibliography: p.
  Includes index.
  1. Tourist trade. I. Hawkins, Donald E. II. Title.
G155.A1H823 1989   338.4'791   89-3294
ISBN 0-13-925447-1

Editorial/production supervision: Ellen Schneid Coleman
  and Nancy Goodman
Cover and interior design: Hudson River Studio

© 1989 by Prentice-Hall, Inc.
A Division of Simon & Schuster
Englewood Cliffs, New Jersey 07632

Printed in the United States of America
10 9 8 7 6 5 4 3 2 1

ISBN 0-13-925447-1

Prentice-Hall International (UK) Limited, *London*
Prentice-Hall of Australia Pty. Limited, *Sydney*
Prentice-Hall Canada Inc., *Toronto*
Prentice-Hall Hispanoamericana, S.A., *Mexico*
Prentice-Hall of India Private Limited, *New Delhi*
Prentice-Hall of Japan, Inc., *Tokyo*
Simon & Schuster Asia Pte. Ltd., *Singapore*
Editora Prentice-Hall do Brasil, Ltda., *Rio de Janeiro*

CONTENTS

FOREWORD

Tourism is one of the success stories of the twentieth century. It would be no exaggeration to place the development of contemporary tourism alongside such achievements as the first man in space, the information technology revolution, and the commercial jet. Yet the tourism "miracle" has, for the most part, not captured the public imagination. It has been a quiet revolution, perhaps because it is concerned more with the satisfaction of the individual than with scientific or technological achievement.

It has been very aptly stated that tourism and leisure are, perhaps, two of the nicest things in contemporary society. It is certain that they promote peaceful coexistence, the happiness of the individual, and the well-being of society.

Tourists are, for the most part, "gentle invaders." They do not—except in the occasional circumstances of accidents, disasters, or hijackings—hit the headlines of the world press. Few newspaper editors would think it of interest to publish a story about the millions of our fellow citizens who were able to enjoy a peaceful holiday without incident or mishap. Yet tourism deserves our attention. While travel is as old as mankind, tourism in its present form is a very powerful economic and social force. Indeed, serious experts believe that tourism will become the world's *number one* industry by the end of the century.

The economic facts speak for themselves. Over the past decade, tourism has emerged as the fastest growing component of world trade. In 1987, according to the latest World Tourism Organization statistics, 355 million international tourist arrivals were recorded worldwide, accounting for expenditures of $150 billion. Tourism is now ranked by the United Nations Conference on Trade and Development as the world's third largest export industry, and annual spending on domestic and international tourism together now amounts to twelve percent of world gross national product—close to $2 trillion per annum.

Tourism is no less important in social terms. It is a powerful instrument of regional development policy. It has, potentially at least, the capacity to provide strong cost-benefit justification for measures of environmental conservation and protection. It is, above all, a people business with tremendous job-creating potential.

Tourism development over the past quarter of a century has spearheaded the services revolution whereby more than fifty percent of employment in the industrialized countries is attributable, not to industry or agriculture, but to the services sector. The World Tourism Organization estimates suggest that twenty out of every one hundred workers today are employed in tourism-related activities. With so many new jobs being created in tourism, education and training are bound to take precedence. Yet, despite the importance the industry has acquired, reliable and authoritative educational material documenting the growth of travel and tourism is surprisingly scarce.

The World Tourism Organization, therefore, for which education and training is a high priority, can only applaud the publication by Lloyd E. Hudman and Donald E. Hawkins of their new book: **Tourism in Contemporary Society.** The book is, I am pleased to see, intended not only for college and university students but also for those already employed in travel and tourism. This is a definite advantage, since the education of those already in the industry will be very important in ensuring constant improvement in the quality of the tourist product, upon which future success so critically depends.

The wealth of information contained in the book has been systematically presented with a view to understanding tourism as both a cause and an effect of life in contemporary society. Few could put down the book without having learned something new and significant about the industry—such as the fact that we owe the concept of travel facilitation to the ancient Greeks!

Tourism, say the authors, should be treated as an emerging profession, representing a significant career opportunity for the 1990s. I thoroughly agree with their judgment. However, the continued success of tourism should not be taken for granted. Tourism does not just happen. Satisfied customers and repeat visitors are the result of patient and intensive efforts by the industry. Expectations of continuing success are well-founded but the necessary investments, especially in education and training, need to be assured.

Increased efforts must be made, for example, to provide more protection and greater security for tourists. It is clear from recent events that whenever travelers perceive a situation as dubious or unsure, they choose to vacation elsewhere. Therefore the establishment and implementation of a worldwide program on security and protection of tourists and tourist facilities (a subject already included in the World Tourism Organization's agenda) should have a tangible, positive impact on tourism development prospects.

Statistics on tourism must be enhanced and developed. They are essential if the progress and trend of the industry are to be properly evaluated. The service sector, of which tourism is a key component, urgently needs an industrial classification reflecting the importance services have acquired and providing the necessary disaggregation for meaningful economic studies to be conducted. Definitions and concepts, in some cases already twenty-five years old, need to be refined and developed, and the travel industry should signal its support for World Tourism Organization initiatives in this regard.

More must be done to satisfy the aspirations of the tourist to enjoy holidays and leisure in a high quality environment. Educated to be aware of environmental and heritage issues, today's tourist is increasingly discerning. The World Tourism Organization, which since its inception in 1975 has regularly included environmental questions in its agendas, is well placed to advise. Demand is steadily increasing for environmentally-respectful tourism products, and it seems certain that the future lies with quality tourism.

All these efforts to expand tourism will, of course, fail if the tourism industry is not allowed to develop unhindered. Individual as well as group travel must be facilitated, while the industry itself should enjoy the benefits of liberalization. Both are basic requirements for future tourism development.

With respect to customs controls and frontier formalities, the members of the World Tourism Organization have already declared themselves unanimously in favor of an international instrument to facilitate tourist travel visits, and stays, which should be adopted soon by a diplomatic conference to be held in the Hungarian capital, Budapest.

Liberalization, which in many spheres has not yet extended beyond North America, will involve all branches of tourism but can be expected to affect the transportation and automation sectors in particular. Following the Ministerial Declaration adopted in September 1986 by the signatories of the General Agreement on Tariffs and Trade (GATT) accords, work is under way to create a multilateral framework of principles and regulations for trade in services, which will naturally include tourism since it represents no less than one quarter of world service trade. However difficult it may be to apply GATT rules to tourism, such an initiative can only be welcomed if the present impetus of the sector is to be sustained. It is time for the industry to familiarize itself with the principles of the GATT system so as to be prepared for changes in ownership, control, and operating practices that might become necessary as a liberalized regulatory framework is established and implemented.

In the space of this Foreword it has only been possible to touch upon some of the issues which will impact upon future tourism development. The authors have set themselves the difficult task of simplifying and clarifying tourism in contemporary society. In the interests of present and future students of travel and tourism, upon whose education and training the industry so crucially depends, I commend them for their dedication and commitment and wish them every success.

WILLIBALD P. PAHR
Secretary General of the World Tourism Organization

Figure 1: CONCEPTUAL FRAMEWORK: TOURISM IN CONTEMPORARY SOCIETY

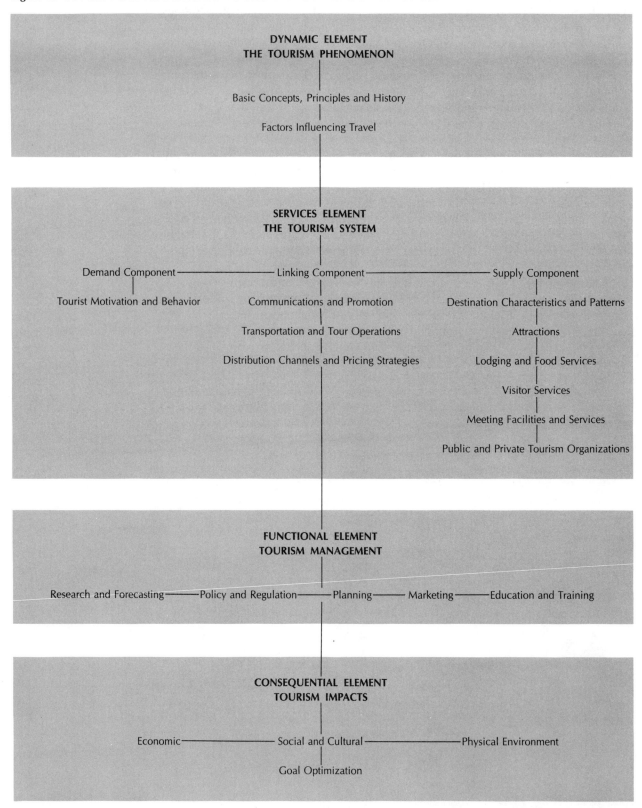

PREFACE

This textbook has been designed as an introduction to tourism in contemporary society, principally for use in post-secondary professional preparation programs and as an in-service training course for personnel employed in the travel and tourism field. The text has been researched and developed with a conceptual framework in mind that is based on our experience in teaching introductory courses at the college level and in in-service situations. Our concept is divided into four parts, each of which we call an element. An element is defined as essential data required to understand tourism as both a cause and an effect of life in contemporary society. The elements which are diagrammed in Figure 1, are used as a basis for forming the four parts of this book. The parts of the book are described as follows:

I. Dynamic Element—The Tourism Phenomenon

The tourism phenomenon is an extraordinary occurrence, which developed historically from an activity of the privileged few to a mass cultural lifestyle, accepted as a basic need of our modern world. It is characterized by constant change, producing personal, social, and physical benefits, that holds great promise for human growth and development in society.

II. Services Element—The Tourism System

The tourism system is an open-ended arrangement of components logically related or practically connected so as to enable people to use tourism resources. These components produce the results or opportunities that are a reflection of the characteristics and behavior of tourists, otherwise called the *demand component*. On the other side is the *supply component*, which includes the destination environment and tourism services. Connecting these two components of tourism is the *linking component*, which includes promotion, transportation/tour operations, distribution channels, and pricing strategies.

III. Functional Element—Tourism Management

Tourism management is the art of successfully accomplishing all the functions required to fulfill a goal, including, but not limited to, the major tasks required to operate and control the tourism system that includes tourists, hosts, business concerns, nonprofit organizations, and governments. The chapters in this part describe the major tasks involved in the process.

IV. Consequential Element—Tourism Impacts
The goal of the tourism system is to achieve outcomes that attain the best and most favorable balance of benefits and costs when all the tourism components are combined. Throughout the process, the essential element of hospitality needs to be preserved and maintained in as culturally authentic a manner as possible. Hospitality is defined as the act, practice, or art of being friendly, kind, and solicitous of guests, with appropriate concern for their health, comfort, security, and overall happiness. The exchange of cultural and human experience through tourism should be provided in the most harmonious manner, so that the needs of both the tourist and the host are met with equal care. When all involved in the tourism phenomenon "think globally and act locally in a responsible manner," this optimum goal is achieved.

Our approach to the study of tourism was based on the following precepts:

1. The study of tourism in modern society requires an analysis of both theoretical and practical considerations, using a conceptual framework that integrates both.

2. Tourism should be analyzed in terms of its global scope, and how it affects both industrialized and developing countries. Increasingly, tourism will be viewed as a vital force for bringing people of the world together to share information, knowledge, and experience, with a view toward creating goodwill, mutual understanding, and world peace.

3. Tourism should be treated as an emerging profession, representing a significant career opportunity in the 1990s. Evidence of the profession's status can be seen by the establishment of professional societies and scientific associations in the field, formed to set down a common code of ethics, a body of knowledge, and the formulation of professional standards and practices. It should be recognized that a variety of organizational linkages have resulted, including travel and tourism curricula which are free standing, or components within such departments as hospitality, parks and recreation, leisure studies, business, human services, and other related fields.

4. Tourism today should be distinguished from other types of movement by its transitory nature. Its essence, from antiquity to the modern era, has been characterized by the friendly, courteous, and respectful treatment of the host and the guest to each other's needs and objectives. Due to the complexity of modern society and the rapid rate of change, host and guest interactions may result in conflict and dissatisfaction, unless good management of the system produces the best conditions for tourists, hosts, and their respective societies.

This book has been designed to simplify and clarify tourism in contemporary society. This is a difficult task in light of the complexity and fast pace of change in the countries that generate tourism and those that receive the tourists. Voluminous charts, graphs, and statistical information are available to study tourism's growth and impact on the world today. We have attempted to provide some of the most relevant sources and predict longer term trends. We advise the student of tourism to maintain an active reference library and to keep current with the expanding body of knowledge made available through more specialized textbooks, trade and professional journals, and relevant information sources.

LLOYD E. HUDMAN
DONALD E. HAWKINS

Tourism in Contemporary Society

An Introductory Text

PART I

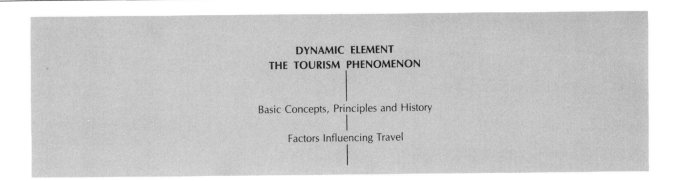

DYNAMIC ELEMENT
THE TOURISM PHENOMENON

Basic Concepts, Principles and History

Factors Influencing Travel

DYNAMIC ELEMENT: THE TOURISM PHENOMENON

CHAPTER 1

BASIC CONCEPTS, PRINCIPLES, AND HISTORY

One of the major characteristics of modern times is the phenomenon of travel and tourism. Almost all inventions and innovations in the world have in some way contributed to the increased ability of people to travel. Today, people talk of visiting capitals and exotic places around the world almost as an everyday happenstance. People from Minnesota, Utah, California, London, or Tokyo meet people they know in such places as Tahiti, Rome, Toronto, Budapest, Cairo, Sydney, and Bangkok. It is seldom one goes to a party or social function without hearing people talking about far off places they have visited or intend to visit soon. Our world has become a world where countries and communities are in contact with each other. One major avenue through which this contact is made is tourism. Today, tourism is at its peak. It is more highly developed than it has ever been.

People have always traveled, but in the first few thousand years of human history only a select few could do so. Most people were concerned with the daily task of living; their idea of a trip was to their neighbor's farm, or to the local town market. The transition from a rural society to an industrial one brought with it the tourist phenomenon. In fact, one characteristic of industrial and post-industrial society is the onset of leisure time associated with travel.

The first major change in modern history came with the Industrial Revolution. Modern machines and techniques brought people into the cities. As we moved to an urban society, changes in religious organizations and in rural kinship systems led to the formation of recreational groups. Leisure pursuits became a new aspect of our society. There was a change from the concept that "the idle mind is the devil's workshop" to the realization that leisure is a human right if not a God-given one. Still, old habits die hard, and whether conscious or unconscious, many people still think of idleness as wrong.

The use of computers in recent years has resulted in what we may call a second industrial revolution. Computers have not only increased our ability to work quickly and produce more, they have given us even more leisure time and better incomes with which to pursue other interests. Although attitudes toward our work ethic and our free time are changing, most people still feel that they must work hard and play hard; that their leisure pursuits, which may be healthy and restful, should also keep them busy.

GENERAL CONCEPTS

The identification of leisure as one of the major influences of an industrial society was explored by Jost Krippendorf. He indicated that man in an industrial society is concerned with three primary things: work, habitat, and leisure. The industrial society can be understood to have four subsystems that relate to these concerns: (1) its values, (2) its economy, (3) its government and (4) its environment or resources. In turn, each of these parts of society can be analyzed further. Its values stress wealth and consumption. The economy can develop into supercompanies and a concentration of wealth. The environment can be treated as having either limited or infinite resources. A government's policies have direct influence on the lives of its people. According to Krippendorf's analysis, people travel so they can better endure their work and home life.

Krippendorf documented a growing feeling among people that society is going through such profound changes that it will no longer be a society known for its work. He stated that the post-industrial society will be one that:

> . . . should put the art and quality of life before the standard of living. Values such as freedom, participation, autonomy, and the desire for self-fulfillment are gaining priority in the hierarchy of needs. The professional careers, security, and salaries are losing importance. One begins to realize that man has an overabundance of money and possessions, but that he does not have enough time. No time for living. People are rediscovering the meaning of time.[1]

He concluded with the statement that, although the character of travel will change as society changes, tourism will contribute to the desire for a better life and help in building a better society.

The study of tourism has become very complex. To understand it better, there is a need to consider the various points of view held by many participants in the field. These different perspectives are held by tourists, businesses, governments of those countries from which tourists come (subsequently referred to as *tourist governments*), host governments, and the host communities.[2]

Tourists: Tourists have a set of needs and wants that travel fulfills. These needs and wants vary depending upon the tourists' time, money, cultural background, and social characteristics. The needs and characteristics of tourists help determine the destinations and activities chosen.

Businesses: The opportunity to provide services and products that meet the needs and desires of tourists, either to assist them in transportation or at the destination, is a market function, referred to as the tourist industry. The tourist industry is divided into its components of transportation, accommodations, shopping, and activities. All these components, from a duty-free store in an international airport through festivals, superbowls, hotels, or rides in horse carriages, are highly organized.[3]

Tourist Governments: Economically and politically governments view tourism as a competitive export—money flows from their country or region to another. To some governments, particularly socialist nations, the flow of money is very important to their economy and stability, and must be carefully controlled.

Host Governments: Host governments enjoy the benefits of tourism—income, jobs, and tax revenues.

Host Communities: It is on the local community level that tourism has its greatest impact, both positive and negative. Tourists not only bring income, jobs, and cultural interaction, but they also bring environmental concerns.

While each of the five groups have differing complex viewpoints that require considerable effort to understand, their interaction increases the complexity of tourism, and together they make the world grow closer and more congenial.

DEFINITION OF TOURISM

Because of the complexity and importance of tourism in the world, there is a need to define it so as to better understand it. A definition would be that tourism is the sum of all the relationships arising from the interaction of tourists, businesses, tourist governments, and the host government and communities.

H. Robinson described a tourist as a person traveling for more than a day to any place other than where he normally lives.[4] Sir George Young utilizes a broader definition, saying that a tourist is someone who travels away from home.[5] Professor W. Hunziker of Switzerland defined tourism in 1942 as "the sum of the phenomena and relationships arising from the travel and stay of non-residents, in so far as they do not lead to permanent residence and are not connected with any earning activity."[6]

In January, 1975, the department of Hotel, Catering and Tourism Management at the University of Surrey in England, adopted a broader view. "Tourism denotes the temporary, short-term movement of people to destinations outside the places where they normally live and work and their activities during the stay at these destinations. Much of this movement is international in character and much of it is a leisure activity."[7]

A. J. Burkart and S. Medlik suggest both the journey and stay, outside the normal place of residence and work, if it is temporary, can be defined as tourism.[7]

All the different definitions of tourism are evidence of how complex this subject is. In 1937, the League of Nations realized the importance of collecting tourism data. It suggested that tourists be considered those people traveling for a period of twenty-four hours or more in a country other than the one in which they usually reside. The committee assigned to the task by the League of Nations regarded tourists as those traveling for pleasure, health and domestic reasons; those traveling to international meetings; those traveling for the purpose of business; and those arriving in a country by a sea cruise regardless of the length of stay, which was in many cases less than twenty-four hours.

People *not* regarded as tourists are those entering a country to work, reside, or go to school. Also not considered tourists are people living near frontiers who work in an adjacent country, or travelers passing through a country without stopping.

This was revised at a United Nations Conference on International Travel and Tourism in Rome in 1963 as follows: the term "visitor" describes any person visiting a country for any reason other than following an occupation enumerated within the country visited. Visitors were divided into two categories.

1. *Tourists* are temporary visitors staying over twenty-four hours in the country visited, whose journey is in one of the following categories: leisure, recreation, holiday, sport, health, study, religion, business, family, friends, mission, meetings.

2. *Excursionists* include temporary visitors staying less than twenty-four hours in the country visited, including cruise passengers.

This distinction between the two kinds of visitors is important, as excursionists require less planning for accommodations, but more with regard to transportation and shopping facilities.

Another term used frequently is travel. In most cases the terms *travel* and *tourism* are used as synonyms, although some writers have tried to draw a fine line between the two. Douglas Frechtling former director of the U.S. Travel Data Center, uncomfortable with both terms, devised a definition for the term "traveler" as one who takes a trip of at least one hundred miles away from home and returns.

The term tourism has become more popular for government agencies. Many states in the United States, the provinces and territories in Canada, as well as various countries, are using the term "tourism" in their agency titles. For example, there is the British Tourist Authority, the U.S. Travel and Tourism Administration, the Tourism Industry Association of Canada, and the World Tourism Organization (WTO). The everyday use of "tourist" is usually associated with some sort of pleasure trip, while "traveler" usually has a broader meaning to include trips for both pleasure and business.

All definitions have three common elements at either the domestic or international level. They are: (1) movement between two or more places (origin and destination); (2) purpose; and (3) time (temporary). Most organizations have established a minimum mileage between two places to qualify as tourism.

The explanations of the word tourist exclude certain types of trips. The U.S. Travel Data Center excludes travel as part of an operation crew on some form of public transportation such as airplane or train, the journey to work, and student travel to and from school. In general, most measurements and definitions exclude migrant workers and other temporary workers, students, and immigrants.

The time element, referring to the length of time that a visitor is in an area, is divided into two categories: less than twenty-four hours and at least twenty-four hours. The basic concept is that tourists or travelers will return to their original residence, having visited an area for the purposes defined as a trip.[8]

THE TOURISM NETWORK

Since most people use the terms travel and tourism synonymously, they will be used interchangeably throughout this text. Similarly, the term "travel industry," which is a tourism network encompassing both the private and public sector, will be broadly used. Gee, Choy, and Makens define the travel industry as "the composite of organizations, both public and private, that are involved in the development, production, and marketing of products and services to serve the needs of the travelers."[9] This definition is illustrated in Figure 1-1, which clearly identifies both the direct and indirect components of the travel industry. The interrelationships within the travel industry affect tourists in three categories.

The first category involves organizations that provide services or products (for example, a hotel room, a meal, an airline ticket, a swimming suit, a taxi) directly to the traveler.

The second category is a little more complex. It provides goods and services for both the traveler and for organizations that sell goods and services directly but not exclusively to those tourists. For example, contract laundry service provides service for hotels as well as for local organizations. Another example would be tour wholesalers who prepare tours and, rather than sell directly to the public, sell the tour through a travel agency. Travel agencies are full of brochures and pamphlets of companies that offer goods and services that can be purchased through the travel agency. Thus, the traveler receives the service indirectly through these support services.

The third category, referred to in Figure 1-1 as tourism development, affects the other two categories, both directly and indirectly, as well as the traveler. A governmental agency or planning board may create a land use plan for a beach and its surroundings, which would allow the development of certain types of retail activities, support services, or both, or they may prohibit any development. This decision would affect both travelers and tourist suppliers. Thus, all aspects of the tourism network are affected by decisions of government agencies and planners.

Not only is the definition of tourism complex, but the tourism industry, that provides goods and services to the

THE DIRECT AND INDIRECT COMPONENTS OF THE TRAVEL INDUSTRY

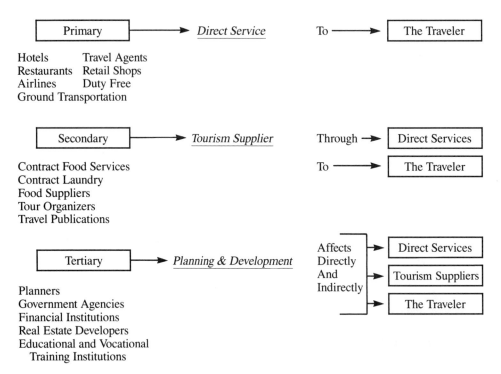

Figure 1-1: Information compiled from Chuck Gee, Dexter Choy, and James Makens, *The Travel Industry,* AVI Publishing Co., 1984.

tourist, is equally complex. Recognizing this fact helps our understanding of the nature of tourism. Mill and Morrison suggest that, for a number of factors, tourism should be considered a system rather than an industry.[10] Their reasons are that there is no industrial classification for tourism; many providers service both tourists and local residents; and, most importantly, tourism is an activity that occurs when someone crosses a border, or travels within their own political unit.

Their concept of a tourist system is depicted in Figure 1-2. The system is divided into four parts—origin, travel, destination, and marketing. The origin is the part of the system where people determine which elements of travel will satisfy their basic needs. After this decision is made, consideration must be given to the *when, where,* and *how* to travel. A number of other factors must be understood here, such as the social, psychological, and economic characteristics. The results of all of these decisions determine travel flow patterns. These patterns are studied to help understand trends in travel.

The third major part of the tourist system is the destination and its development process. This includes the advantages and disadvantages of tourism, the policy to promote it, and the degree of promotion required.

Marketing strategy is the fourth factor. This deals with how travel suppliers sell their services and the effectiveness of their different distribution channels.

APPROACHES TO THE STUDY OF TOURISM

No matter what philosophy and method are used to describe tourism (as a network or a system), it is an extremely complex field of study. Because of this, there are many different avenues of scholarly pursuit involved in tourism research and academic training programs. The two major divisions of study are the tourism phenomenon and the hospitality process.

Figure 1-3 illustrates the varying disciplines involved in tourism research and education, indicating that tourism can be described as a truly interdisciplinary endeavor. Today, with the growth of interest in tourism, both by tourists and by academicians, tourism degree programs in schools, colleges, and universities are growing at a rapid pace. These programs are found in various departments, from geography to business. Some institutions have departments of tourism in their colleges of business, humanities, and social sciences. Research articles concerned with tourism appear in journals for each of the fields illustrated.

The key word in the hospitality process is *hosting*—the ability to make a tourist feel welcome. Professor Philip Nailon, of the University of Surrey in England, has defined professional hospitality as: ''. . . providing psychological and physiological comfort and security for money.''[11] A certain element of the hospitality sector is to provide a bit of the comfort of home. Some of the major fears of potential

MILL AND MORRISON'S TOURISM SYSTEM

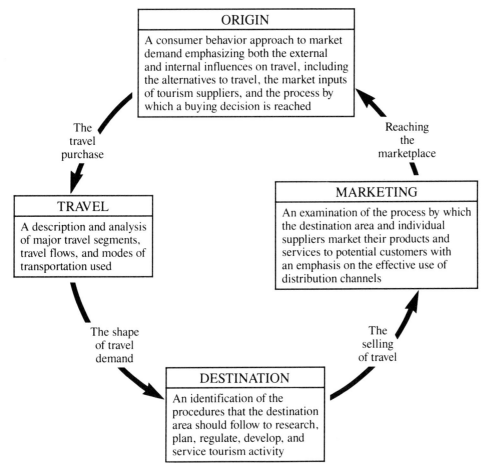

ORIGIN

A consumer behavior approach to market demand emphasizing both the external and internal influences on travel, including the alternatives to travel, the market inputs of tourism suppliers, and the process by which a buying decision is reached

The travel purchase

Reaching the marketplace

TRAVEL

A description and analysis of major travel segments, travel flows, and modes of transportation used

MARKETING

An examination of the process by which the destination area and individual suppliers market their products and services to potential customers with an emphasis on the effective use of distribution channels

The shape of travel demand

The selling of travel

DESTINATION

An identification of the procedures that the destination area should follow to research, plan, regulate, develop, and service tourism activity

Figure 1-2: Source: Robert Christie Mill and Alastair M. Morrison, *The Tourism System: An Introductory Text* (Englewood Cliffs, NJ: Prentice-Hall, 1985). Used by permission.

travelers are the type of food provided, the condition of lodgings available, and the personal comfort to be obtained. The hospitality process provides these. In a document prepared by The Hague Hotel School, the relationship between the traveler and the hospitality provider was discussed. It distinguished three major elements of hospitality. They are the hospitality or tourist product (presenter); the guest or tourist (receiver); and the transfer of hospitality from the presenter to the receiver.

In order to further characterize the hospitality process five elements were isolated, three influencing the presenter and two influencing the receiver. They are:

1. *A material product offered by the presenter*
2. *Behavior of the presenter*
3. *The environment within which the product is presented*

4. *The needs of the guest with relation to safety and comfort*
5. *The objectives of the guest that he wishes to realize within the hospitality situation*

In creating a hospitality situation the presenter is influenced by economic, cultural, social, and technical factors.

Thus the host (presenter) takes into account the social and economic factors of travelers, based on their needs and objectives, to provide a product in a particular fashion and in a given environment to make the user (receiver) feel that it is a "home away from home." Put another way, the host offers a particular product in a specific way (behavior) in a unique environment to meet the needs and objectives of the tourist.

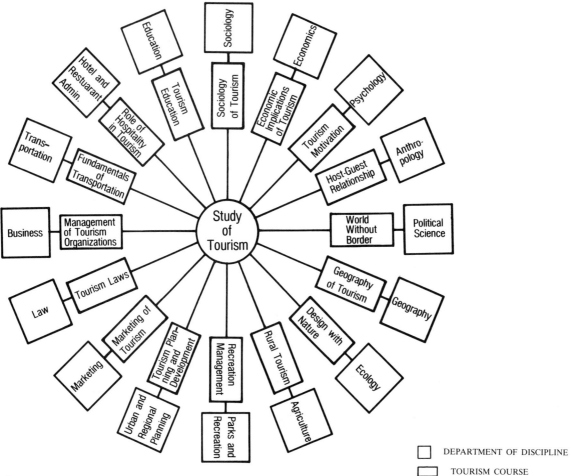

DEPARTMENT OF DISCIPLINE

TOURISM COURSE

Figure 1-3: Source: Jafar Jafari and J. R. Brent Ritchie. "Towards a Framework for Tourism Education: Problems and Prospects." *Annals of Tourism Research*, 1981, VIII (1).

This concept of the hospitality system leads to another set of educational objectives, which include the socioeconomic needs of the receiver, marketing techniques, host/guest relationships, design, planning and development, and the specific talents of the hospitality provider.

The study of the travel industry appears to fall naturally into two camps. The first studies tourism, and the second, the hospitality process. Both represent a systems approach. A system is a set of interrelated disciplines that academicians coordinate to form a unified whole. It provides the background to an understanding of the processes of tourism and hospitality.

HISTORY OF TOURISM

Curiosity, anticipation, and graffiti—yes, graffiti—have characterized travel and tourism throughout history. Curiosity has always led people to explore new environments, seek new places, discover the unknown, and enjoy new experiences. The Bible records an early account of travel for the sake of curiosity when the Queen of Sheba went to see King Solomon in Jerusalem.

The anticipation of what one may find, what one may see, and what one may be able to do has increased the desire to travel to new places. Indeed, the anticipation is so exciting that, in and of itself, it may be the most enjoyable part of the trip. Consider how much time a person puts into planning a trip, poring over maps, reading books and guides, and checking with travel clubs, travel agents, and airlines.

Once a person has made the journey there seems to be a universal desire to leave a mark for posterity. Graffiti are a written record indicating where all the "Kilroys" of the world have been. Prehistoric people left their mark on the walls of caves and rocks to tell stories of their journeys. Ancient Egyptian travelers were impressed with the "Kilroys" of their time, who recorded the fact that they had been to see the great monuments and temples. We still continue to record our names for subsequent visitors to note and appreciate and visit.

Tourism has become tremendously important in today's world. It is the second largest item in international foreign trade and, in some respects, it is a method of redistributing wealth, since most traveling is from the industrialized nations to the less industrialized nations.

The growth and development of tourism may be characterized by the word *holiday*. Originally, the word was derived from two sources. The first, from holy day, a day that was associated with religion. In Christian Europe certain days were celebrated by a few, usually religious, people. The remnants of these early holy days can be observed in a number of countries where a large number of days are recognized as official national holidays.

The second or parallel development of the word holiday is associated with ancient Rome where a public holiday was set aside for feasting and fun. It was such a grand occasion that even the slaves were allowed to participate in it. A glimpse of the activities that might have taken place are illustrated in Taylor Caldwell's book, *Dear and Glorious Physician,* in which Luke was introduced to a Roman festival. During the festival Luke's total being was absorbed in the sensual events of the day. Women dressed in elegant topless gowns and had their bodies covered with oils and perfumes; naked men wrestled; tables were set with many kinds of foods and drinks; all this designed to appeal to the senses.

In 1552, Edward VI of England established certain saint's days for civil servants to have as holidays. On these days, public and semipublic offices were closed. The influence of civil servants on holidays has always been important. In the United States today, for example, holidays are moved from the actual historical date to coincide with weekends. However, it was not until the Industrial Revolution that general public holidays evolved for the masses. The modern concept of holiday is a product of that revolution. The social changes, which came about as a result of changing from a rural society to an urban one, brought about the gradual change of the holiday from a religious day to a day of leisure.

Many of the characteristics of modern tourism were established and developed early in history when only a privileged few were able to enjoy this phenomenon. Today, of course, tourists and tourism have become a basic part of our lives. In fact, in the United States the only activity on which we spend more money is eating!

Of the three key elements in the development of travel, transportation is the most important. The other two, money and the ability to communicate, need little discussion. Can you imagine how difficult it would be to travel under a barter system? Checking into the Marriott Hotel with two pigs and three chickens to pay the bill would create an interesting situation!

The difficulties associated with land travel is an important factor in understanding its early development. Consider that if the average person walks at a speed of two to three miles an hour how long it would take to go even fifty

miles. When Hammurabi, the Babylonian ruler between 1792 and 1750 B.C., dispatched a courier to a destination of 120 miles, he was expected to travel night and day in order to reach the destination in two days.

With the advent of the wheel, even in the days of the highly touted Roman roads, speed was only slightly faster than it was when walking. In most places, paved roads were nonexistent, and bridges even rarer. Today, people complain of poor road maintenance problems and the loss of automobiles in chuck holes, but these problems in no way compare with the poor road conditions facing early travelers.

Records and legends of the ancient world mention some remarkable trips to Asia and the Pacific. The Pacific peoples performed prodigious feats of island hopping. Sea travel was of major importance to China and Japan well before the birth of Christ. There are many early records of travel throughout the world. The early Polynesians, for example, traveled throughout Southwest Asia, Micronesia, and Polynesia. At times they covered over 2,000 miles at sea in dugout canoes, navigating by the stars at night and the sun by day. When we consider the problems of obtaining fresh water and food, we are even more impressed by these peoples. When Alexander the Great visited India from Greece, no small journey in itself, he found a well-developed travel industry. There were carefully maintained roads lined with trees and dotted at intervals with wells, police houses, and rest stops. This trip through history deals with travel and tourism as it relates to Western civilization. This text, too, is concerned with travel and tourism from a Western perspective.

This summary of the history of tourism is divided into six eras according to their contributions to tourism.

The Ancient Era	The Grand Tour Era
The Empire Era	The Transition Era
The Decline and Revival Era	The Modern Era

The Ancient Era

Early peoples did not travel far except to hunt, or to travel with the seasons as nomads. Travel, for any reason, was time consuming, expensive, and dangerous. However, many retained a desire to travel because they were curious about the world both far and near. Three significant features of early travel are: (1) the development of travel for trade and commerce, with the subsequent creation of specific paths and routes; (2) the development of water travel; and (3) the improvement of routes and paths at the same time as specialized, if crude, vehicles specifically for traveling were being created.

The growth of cities in ancient Mesopotamia, clustered along and between the Tigris and Euphrates Rivers, created a need for political and economic contact. Caravans and couriers soon established patterns of travel that provided them with relatively easy terrain to traverse, as well as water, food, and even resting places in some cases. The growth of cities beside rivers and coastlines led to the commercial use of waterways, particularly the Nile and the Mediterranean, for hauling goods from one city to another.

With the increased contact between cities, and a resulting increase in the flow of goods, travel began to change. At first, travelers walked or rode donkeys, then the wagon was introduced to carry goods from one town to another, and specialized carriers developed; other vehicles were created to carry the wealthy and elite.

The development of vehicles led to the improvement of paths between cities. Although the routes eventually established were far from being freeways, they did facilitate movement considerably.

The Empire Era

As empires developed, transportation systems improved, and hospitality lated services grew to serve an increasing number of tra.elers. Tourism reached its highest point under the Romans. This was the beginning of travel infrastructure (roads, hotels, taverns, etc.) development. The first inns and hotels were not for travelers; beds for overnight stays were incidental to the most important business of obtaining drinks and sexual favors. Decent people did not frequent them. They did, however, provide the base for the hotel business as we know it today. This era saw the development of tourism as a phenomenon distinct from travel. Certain characteristics of it have been perpetuated in modern tourism.

The Egyptians

Although travel on official government business occurred earlier in Mesopotamia than elsewhere, it was not until the growth of empires that travel for the purpose of official business became important. Traveling facilitated communication between a centralized government and its territories. Associated with the increase in travel was the development of hospitality centers and hotels (the forerunners of the modern hotel/motel industry), and taverns (the primitive equivalent of today's restaurants). Then, as now, they were located along major routes and in the cities.

In this period we also begin to recognize the seeds of actual tourism for pleasure, to participate in religious festivals, and plain curiosity. Herodotus reported on such excursions to Bubastis, wrote

> some of the women have castanets on which they play, and the men play on the flute during the whole voyage; the rest of the women and men sing and clap their hands together at the same time. . . . When they arrive at Bubastis, they celebrate the feast, offering up great sacrifices, and more wine is consumed at this festival than in all the rest of the year.[13]

The creation of large temples, tombs, and monuments in Egypt gave impetus to travel for curiosity and pleasure. On their walls messages were found, left by people who had made a special trip to see these impressive buildings of their past.

Just as tourists today leave their marks on monuments for future generations, early travelers left graffiti on the walls of these relics. But graffiti is not the only record we have of early travel. Other tourist habits developed at this time including bringing home souvenirs. The habit of seeking bargains in faraway places for oneself, family, and friends began too. Tourism was also seasonal then as it is now. Interestingly, the tourist season in Egypt was from November to April to avoid the hot weather.

At the height of the ancient Egyptian period, we see travel for business, trade, and commerce; official business; curiosity and pleasure; and religious festivals. In turn, travel and tourism created the need for an infrastructure which included roads, hotels and taverns.

The Assyrians and Persians

From early 1100 B.C. and for about the next four hundred years, the Phoenicians were the dominant maritime power. They extended the known world into the Atlantic and around the west coast of Africa.

With the growth of the Assyrian Empire, it is probable that there were no new developments in the existing travel structure. However, this period is characterized by the increased range of travel and the improvement of an infrastructure that greatly facilitated travel within the Assyrian Empire, particularly for military use. The roads were improved to carry heavy materials, equipment, and men. Road markers were established to indicate the distance traveled. In addition, sentinel posts and wells were located every few miles for protection, communication, and water. Roads leading to areas of economic, political, and military importance were paved, and stone bridges were constructed over strategic river crossings. The use of horses helped travel in this period. Horse-drawn chariots remained popular among the military, although "average" travelers remained attached to the donkey as the chief mode of transportation.

The Persians, like the Assyrians, contributed to travel mainly in the expansion of their empire and in improving the travel infrastructure. Roads that had been built by the Assyrians were expanded and refined, and new kinds of wagons were developed. These included classical four-wheeled, closed carriages for the aristocracy.

Thus, by the end of the Near East's domination of Western civilization, the rudiments of travel and tourism were established. Lionell Casson summarized the contributions of this era as follows:

> By this time, the general lineaments of ancient travel had been fixed. On the sea, sailings of merchant craft offered communication between major ports of the eastern Mediterranean. On land, key centers were linked by carriage roads, the best of which might boast bridges and ferries, road signs, way stations, and guard posts. The technique of paving had been developed, although still sparingly used. Travelers had their choice of wagons, carts, donkeys, horses, or camels. Along major routes there were inns, and in towns, inns and taverns. And, among the users of the sea-lanes and roads, the official and commercial travelers, we begin to catch a glimpse of the traveler for travel's sake, the tourist.[14]

The Greeks

With a shift in the domination of Western civilization from the Near East to Greece, and subsequently to Rome, new dimensions to tourism were added. The Greeks became the great traders of their time, extending the known world throughout the Near East and part of Africa. The growth of city-states in Greece, mostly along the sea coasts, developed with less land contact than was required for the grand empires of the Near East. The mountainous terrain was not conducive to smooth, well-developed routes for travel between the city-states. Water travel became the easiest and most important means of moving commercial goods. Most travel was, therefore, by sea.

Several important contributions to tourism were made by the Greeks. Up to this time, the exchange of currency was a serious problem for travelers. Now, the money of certain Greek city-states came to be accepted as international currency. This gave travelers more flexibility, allowing them to travel more easily, since they would not be required to carry goods for both commerce and barter upon arrival at their destinations. A second standardization that eased travel was the spread of the Greek language as the common tongue throughout the Mediterranean area. These two leveling factors greatly facilitated travel. It is in this period that a new dimension of tourism can be traced—travel for participation in festivals of various kinds. Although the main purpose for a journey might still be trade or to conduct official business, traveling to festivals became extremely important. One of these major festivals is still important to travelers today—the Olympic Games. The Olympic Games were the start of traveling to attend sporting events. Some festivals were enacted in local theaters in

many countries. People were attracted to them and, as word spread, the growth of the travel industry accelerated.

As city-states grew, they, themselves, became another attraction. Athens, particularly, became a tourist destination well before the birth of Christ. This led to even greater improvements of the infrastructure. Many hospitality centers offered floor shows, dancing girls, and gambling (the forerunners of Las Vegas or Monte Carlo). Additionally, the Greeks began another custom that continues into today's world of tourism. That was the provision of a *proxemos*, a person whose prime function, like tour guides today, is to assist fellow citizens traveling abroad, particularly those on official business.[15]

The Romans

The height of tourism in early history was reached during the period of the Roman Empire. The Romans' keen sense of military and administrative organization brought under political and cultural control, the greatest empire in Western civilization. The Empire extended from the Scottish marshes in the north of Britain, to the Euphrates River in Mesopotamia, to the south and east. For long periods the Mediterranean was free from strife and, therefore, safe for travel.

The Romans perpetuated most of the basic reasons for travel, which had begun with the Greeks, and refined them considerably to an extent never before achieved in history. The concept of second homes and short-term vacation moves to sea coasts and mountains, by both the wealthy and the growing middle class, was a unique Roman contribution to tourism.

Travel within the Roman Empire was relatively safe

Boboli Gardens, Florence. Photo courtesy of the Italian Government Travel Office.

and easy. Four factors accounted for the improved travel conditions. First, Roman coins were the only medium of exchange the traveler needed to carry. Second, an excellently planned network of good roads and water routes made established paths available for travel. Third, Greek and Latin were the principal official and business languages, enabling travelers to communicate relatively easily in whatever part of the Empire they happened to be visiting. Last, the legal system provided protection from foreign courts and jurisdiction. All of these factors had a stabilizing effect on travel.

The organization and control of such a vast empire also led to economic growth, and so increased the demand for goods and services. A growing middle class traveled for trade, creating an economy that allowed a greater number of people to travel for pleasure, curiosity, or relief from boredom. The political unification of many countries within the Empire facilitated travel to an enlarged world. At the same time, the ability of the Romans to build superior transportation networks shrank the known world for the Roman citizen. Road building reached its height as the Romans designed them to move armies and equipment quickly. Such roads soon became major thoroughfares from Rome to major tourist centers such as Naples, and were much used by the new leisure class.

The purposes for travel in this period were as varied as they are today. The sporting games started by the Greeks, which drew spectators and participants from all over the world, were copied in the Roman Empire. The Romans added to the games by developing contests of gladiators and other spectacles that drew large crowds to the cities. Rome became the focal point of these spectacular holidays.

Sight-seeing also reached its ancient zenith in the Roman Empire. The relative safety of travel, an increase in the wealth of military, commercial, and government leaders, and improvement in travel conditions helped to boost the number of sight-seers. Sight-seeing became as popular (at least among the wealthy) as it is today.

One favorite tour was an excursion through Greece, with its temples, religious sanctuaries, and magnificent art. Other former empires in Western civilization were also major attractions for the Roman tourist. Tourist travel was easy in Egypt since the major attractions were situated close to water routes. Naturally, Egypt was truly a mecca for the curious traveler, who found, not only the magnificent structures and monuments built by the pharaohs, but a completely different environment, both culturally and physically. It was a genuinely exotic experience for the Roman traveler.

The third area of significant travel was Asia Minor, brought into prominence by the Trojan War. And, as is the case in all empires or countries, Rome, the capital of the Empire, was a focal point for tourists who desired to see and visit the old as well as the new. The importance of sight-seeing, and the widespread acceptance of such tourism, can best be illustrated by the development of the idea of the Seven Wonders of the World by an unknown scholar in Alexandria. Many people have traveled just to see those Seven Wonders.

Travel for the improvement of health was an acknowledged reason for travel in the Roman Empire. Mineral springs and shrines became major points of interest for many wishing to improve their health, or merely to rest. The large volume of increased maritime trade gave people of poor health the opportunity to experience the exhilarating air of a sea cruise.

As is the custom today, when travelers arrived at their destinations they were met by guides offering their services. Although travel was strongly oriented to man-made features, the physical features of a country could be an important attraction. Casson described several of these.

> Certain natural features became attractions because of their literary fame, the way the English lake country has for us. A typical case in point is the Vale of Tempe in northern Greece, whose virtues were sung by poet after poet and a replica of which, a triumph of landscape gardening, was one of the wonders of Hadrian's grand villa at Tibur. The ancient tourist also liked to visit rivers which had made a mark in literature—the Nile, the Danube, the Rhine, the winding Meander in Asia Minor.[16]

A final characteristic of tourism during the Roman period, that is similar to tourism today, is that vacations became associated with owning second homes. The construction of roads southward eased the building of villas along the road to Naples, in the hillsides, and in Naples itself. Generally, villas were built near scenic locations—the sea, mountains, or mineral spas.

Today's tourist industry closely follows the patterns established in the Roman Empire. From then to the beginning of modern tourism there are, however, fluctuations in the scope and importance of tourist travel.

The Decline and Revival Era

Travel by the religious bureaucracy and the clergy during the latter part of the Roman Empire under Constantine reflected the elevation of Christianity to a role of major importance. Others continued to travel until the problems associated with the Dark Ages stopped them. Under Constantine, the Holy Land became the focal point for travelers—the Cave of the Entombment, the site of the Crucifixion, the Mount of Olives, the cities of Jerusalem and Bethlehem, the Dead Sea, and the River Jordan were star attractions—not unlike modern tourism to the Holy Land.

As the empire began to crumble, pilgrimages to the Holy Land, became unsafe. Consequently, tourism began to decline.

The Dark Ages

Little can be said concerning tourism for many years after the fall of Rome. The established political and economic structures were destroyed. The middle class was in decline, commerce decreased, and cities declined as the citizens returned to farm the land. The medieval period of history was marked by numerous barbarian invasions, during which trade and city life became almost extinct. There may be some similarities drawn between the barbarian invasions and today's waves of tourists, who bring about change in the pre-existing cultures they visit.

However, to imply there was no travel would be an error. The Vikings were venturing boldly throughout most parts of the Western world. In addition, an Arab Empire came to power between 1,000 and 1,500 A.D. Here, as in previous civilizations, travel was generally for official business, pilgrimages, and commerce.

Medieval Cities

City life is based on economic specialization; its growth is synonymous with the quickening tempo of civilization. The revival of cities throughout Europe in medieval times occurred concurrently with the growth of trade and manufacturing. This revival was largely brought about by the decline of serfdom. An increase in population caused people to create new occupations as industrial areas grew and artisans and merchants began to accumulate wealth. This growing middle class led to the creation of the necessary organizations, both political and commercial, to stimulate travel.

> *After about the year 1000 the principal European roads became relatively safe, largely because of the multitudes that used them. Until carts were used merchants carried their goods on pack animals, jostled by men and women on horseback, horse litters, pilgrims, beggars, minstrels and jugglers, itinerant monks, students traveling in rowdy groups to a university.*[17]

The writer makes it sound as if all kinds of people were busily traveling for a variety of reasons. This growth in travel, cities, and the middle class set the stage for the Renaissance.

The Renaissance and the Elizabethan Age

The Renaissance was marked by a transition from a relatively static culture to a dynamic one. Society, once based on feudal, rural, and monastic ideas, became individualistic, secular, and urban. The growing trade between the West and the East set the stage for travel during the Renaissance. Wealth and leisure, created by growing trade and cities, brought an influx of adventurous travelers into France, Germany, Italy, the Holy Land, and Egypt.

Curiosity, also, was leading people into remarkable voyages of discovery and exploration. An atmosphere conducive to tourism was returning to the Western world. A number of books with essays on travel began to flood England in the sixteenth and seventeenth centuries. It became a widespread custom for young gentlemen of the Elizabethan age to either complete or complement their education by traveling to other countries. During this period, there was some decline in pilgrimages to the Holy Land and to religious shrines due to the spreading religious reformation in many parts of Europe. Two other types of tourists are associated with this time period. One was the vagabond, who traveled for the sake of traveling; the other was the person out to help the world or himself, the knight-errant.[18]

The growth of a new middle class, combined with the achievements in art and thought of the Renaissance, laid a foundation for what eventually became known as the *grand tour,* a tradition that, in turn, was the forerunner of modern tourism.

The Grand Tour Era

The ascension of Elizabeth to the English throne in the sixteenth century marked a pivotal point in the development of English tourism. The growth of commerce through the expansion of trade by the English navy made England the major proponent of the grand tour. However, it was not an exclusively British phenomenon. The French, too, participated in the grand tour, but not with the enthusiasm of the English.

The focal point of the tour (which might easily have lasted three years) was Italy, where the traveler might spend the greater part of a year absorbing the culture and language of the Italian Renaissance. Switzerland, because of the Alps, was regarded as a disagreeable obstruction to be crossed. Other areas avoided on the tour were the Riviera (which was a haven for pirates), Rome, and some towns with overzealous local officials whom the Protestants feared would involve them in the Inquisition.[19] France was the other principal focal point, with Germany and the Low Countries (the Netherlands, and Belgium/Luxembourg) as part of the tour, but of lesser importance.

To serve the wealthy aristocratic tourists and in some cases their tutors, a marked improvement, except in Germany, was made in the hospitality sector.

Guidebooks became popular during the Grand Tour era. They covered such diverse topics as the items to take on a tour, and books on observations and reflections of journeys taken.

The Transition Era

After the 1750s, economic and social structures underwent profound changes that drastically shrank the world to a size that was beyond comprehension at the beginning of the century. The change from a rural society to an urban society completely altered life-styles and travel characteristics. Although, in this period tourism and travel were still enjoyed by a relative few, factors were beginning to emerge that would account for the present-day mass-tourist phenomenon.

Four factors associated with this changing world were: (1) new machinery, which increased the ability to produce goods to a remarkable extent; (2) new kinds of power, which were being developed to facilitate productivity and move a greater number of people over greater distances at less expense; (3) new methods of extracting and using metals, providing a variety of new goods and construction materials; and (4) dramatic discoveries that could be used to provide new methods of production, new occupations, and new goods, some of which would greatly affect tourism.

It was during this period that tourism in the United States began to develop along paths similar to Europe's system and with similar characteristics. The general nature of tourism in the United States is similar to that described in this chapter.

Several factors associated with the economic expansion referred to during this period have greatly affected the nature and extent of tourism. Increasing industrialization caused both population shifts and population increases. Living in urban areas brought new lifestyles with increasing leisure time and the demand for recreational activities. This growing population, occurring at the same time as increased industrial productivity and wealth, added to the number of people wealthy enough to travel, and stimulated the growth of new resorts.

Spas became fashionable places for the wealthy. Many, such as Saratoga Springs in the United States and Bath in England, which became showplaces for socialites, later evolved into centers of amusement and entertainment.

The location of many major urban centers near oceans, seas, and lakes led to the growth and development of seaside resorts. Atlantic City was first opened in 1854. In the 1700s, references were made to the inns on the islands close to New York, and walks and promenades in New Jersey. Sea bathing was first recorded in Brighton, England, in 1736. H. Robinson described those early English sea resorts:

> *English holidays at this time, however, could be, and doubtless often were, dull and dreary. The gentility and snobbery of the "refined" resorts added up to dullness and ennui and Charles Lamb with some exasperation wrote: "we have been dull at Worthing one summer, duller at Brighton another, dullest at Eastbourne, a third, and are at this moment doing dreary penance at—Hastings!" The only interesting diversion seems to have been flirting with the fair ladies and watching the bathers. People at first bathed in the nude and this led to inquisitive onlookers congregating to watch. To discourage such "peeping Toms," bathing machines, which could be trundled into deep water, appeared. But the impolite sightseers were, apparently, not to be outdone and took to using telescopes. The ladies countered this by adopting bathing dress, a costume soon so concealing that the disappointed sightseers were constrained to complain:*
>> *"The ladies dressed in flannel cases*
>> *Show nothing but their handsome faces."* [20]

Seaside resorts, however, did not come into their own until around the 1870s. In both England and the United States tremendous development occurred. The growing resorts were close to large population centers. In addition, improved transportation and communication systems, particularly the railroads, changed the nature of seaside resorts from wealthy playgrounds to large complexes for the masses with improved recreational facilities and amenities. There was a dramatic increase in shops, stores, restaurants, and other amenities. Some resorts, however, still maintained their identity as playgrounds for the wealthy. Atlantic City,

for example, had grown into a year-round resort drawing the wealthy and fashionable from fourteen states by the early 1900s. [21]

Tourism in this era can be characterized by two elements. First, the growing middle class that flocked to resorts in the mountains and seasides close to their urban centers for short stays, and the wealthy tourists going, for extended times, to exotic places like the Mediterranean resorts and the American "Riviera," Palm Beach.

Modern Era

World War I serves as an excellent point of reference from which to date the modern age. The Industrial Revolution set the stage for rapid advances in society and tourism. Both world wars not only sped the process of technological change, but also put many people from various parts of the world in contact with each other. This contact and mixing continued between both wars and increased in intensity following World War II. For fifty years following World War I, there was a considerable and substantial migration of peoples from Eastern, Central, and Western Europe to the United States. Western European countries gained many new immigrants from Eastern Europe, India, Pakistan, East and North Africa. Following World War II, southern Europeans migrated north for short- and long-term employment. Improved technology accelerated this movement of people on a scale never before known.

A capsule review of the changes is illustrated in Figure 1-4. Between the world wars, travel was still mostly a pastime for the wealthy, but the stage was being set for the growth that followed World War II. Van Doren summarized the changes in travel and tourism in the United States since World War II; his summary ties together those changes and this discussion of the growth of modern society.

SIZE OF THE TOURISM INDUSTRY

Tourism is the largest business in the world today, accounting for about twelve percent of the world's gross national product. Total world spending on both domestic and international tourism, to places twenty-five miles or more from home, exceeded $2 trillion in 1986. International travelers spent $115 billion, not including expenditures for transportation. Spending for travel is now more than double the $900 billion spent by the world's military organizations. World tourism generated 64.3 million jobs directly or indirectly, according to the *Travel Industry World Yearbook: The Big Picture—1987*. In every region of the world, tourism continues to grow. Table 1-1 shows growth estimates, for the period 1986–1996, for the world and for the United States. [22]

In the United States, tourism is the single largest retail business, and accounted for over 13 million jobs in 1984 (approximately 12.9 percent of the labor force). The $456 billion spent for domestic and international tourism in 1985 was about twenty-five percent of that spent in total world tourism. At that time, Americans spent some 5.6 billion nights in hotels, motels, campgrounds, and vacation homes. [23]

		TRANSPORTATION	ATTRACTIONS	FACILITIES & SERVICES	INFORMATION-PROMOTION-LEGISLATION	PEOPLE (TOURISTS)	
MASS RECREATION	1946 ↓ 1958	Europe by Ship Cruise Ships on the Great Lakes Greyhound Scenic Cruiser Highway Promotion Assoc.'s-Turnpikes-N.J. Stationwagons **Rental Cars** **Interstate Highways** Air Coach-Tourist Class "Fly Now-Pay Later" **Jet Airliners**	Natural-Scenic Attractions-National Parks Cottage Resorts Vacation Homes Crowded Parks Ski Area Growth Atlantic City Declining **Disneyland-California Mission 66 Operation Outdoors** **ORRRC Study Commission**	Mom & Pop Tourist Courts Tourist Rooms Luxury Hotels-Resorts **Credit Cards Oil Cos. & Diners Club** Camping (Tent) Motel Boom **Frozen Foods-Howard Johnsons** **Franchising-Holiday Inns** Air Conditioning American Express Card	AAA (1902) NATO (1941) State Travel Promotion Magazines Local Regional & Highway Tourist Association Private Business Promotion Guide Books	**Motivations:** Scenery Education Driving for Pleasure Recreational Activities Population Growth **Growth of Middle Class Travel** Suburban Travel	1946 ↓ 1958
MASS MOBILITY & TRANSIENCE	1958 ↓ 1974	Eastern Shuttle Fly-Drive Programs **Recreation Vehicle** Air Conditioning Common in Autos Airports–Cities Themselves **Wide-Body Jets** AMTRAK **Energy Crisis** Speed Limit-55mph Revival of Bus Tours	Miami-Las Vegas Growth Cuba Closed Six Flags-Texas LWCF-Bur. of Outdoor Recreation Hawaii Growth Condominiums Retirement Communities National Seashores Lakeshores-Wild & Scenic Rivers **Disney World-Florida**	Toll Free Reservation Systems Airport Hotels Commercial Campgrounds Budget Motels Franchise Hotel Growth Airport Resort Hotel Center City Hotel Construction Expansion of City Convention Facilities Self-Service Gas Stations	International Travel Act-USTS "SEE THE USA" Promotion State Highway Information Centers DATO Federal Holidays-Mondays Travel a Part of Popular Magazines US Travel Data Center (1973) **Destination USA-NTRRC (1973)** More Travel Guide Books	Civil Rights Youth Movement Rock Festivals "Me" Generation ERA Working Wives Growth of Older Age Group Population Growth Slowed Later Marriages	1958 ↓ 1974
POST MOBILITY ADJUSTMENT	1974 ↓ 1983	Small Cars-High Mileage **Computer Reservations** **Airline Deregulations** **Second Energy Crisis** Airlines Mergers-Failures Bus Deregulation New Generation of Jet Aircraft Bus Expansion in Tours Charters Airline Pricing Peoples Express-New Airlines Intermodal Conncections	Hotel/Motels as Attractions-Atriums **Tourism/Environmental Issues** Historic Preservations Bi-Centennial Gambling-Atlantic City Cruise Ships as Attractions EPCOT-Educational Theme Park Water Parks More Private Development	Travel Agency Growth Time Sharing **Computerized Reservations** Hotel/Motels Lacking Food & Meeting Services-La Quinta Rebirth of Country Inn Bed & Breakfast Lodging UP Scale Lodging/Food Lodging Diversity to Attract Road Business Traveler	Travel Promotion–T.V.-Radio **Last National Travel Survey-1977** Recreation Coalition TIAA Travel Industry Association of America Tourism Caucus House & Senate Replaced by T&T Industry Government Affairs Council 1982 National Tourism Policy Act (USTTA) More Information on Therapeutic Value of Travel	Smaller Families Single Parents Small Town Growth Physical Fitness High Risk Sports New Foreign Visitors Customized Travel Cost Consciousness Quality Experience	1974 ↓ 1983

Figure 1-4: Source: *1985 Annals of Tourism Research,* Carlton S. Van Doren, "Chronology of Travel and Tourism Changes in the United States: 1946–1983," Vol. 12, No 3, p. 470. Pergamon Journals, Ltd. Reprinted with permission.

Today, tourism is recognized as a major source of employment in a world where the growth of service industries is outpacing the growth of manufacturing. To understand its significance and the changes that are taking place, it is necessary to examine not only the cold statistics about the movements of people, but also to observe the shifts in political and economic affairs that will affect the travel industry in the coming years.

TABLE 1-1 TOURISM GROWTH
(Billions)

	1986	1996
International World Receipts	168	248.0
U.S. International Receipts	25	40.7
World Receipts from Domestic	1,874	2,721.0
U.S. Domestic Receipts	467	691.2
Worldwide Accommodations Revenue	141	208.7
U.S. Hotel-Motel Revenue	44	65.1

Source: *Travel Industry World Yearbook: The Big Picture—1988.*

In the study of physics, philosophy, or economics, there are both shallow truths and deep truths. The deep truths allow our minds to perceive vistas that are often hidden by the constant bombardment of shallow truths. For many years, the author of *The Big Picture,* Somerset Waters, has helped open our minds to new vistas that enable us to perceive the profound impact that tourism is making in this fast-changing world.

He points out that in the past several years many governments have elevated their official tourism offices to cabinet level position. His estimates show that tourism is not only the largest business in the world, but that the spending of domestic and international travelers is twice as large as the world's total military spending.

BASIC GUIDELINES FOR TOURISM

Although tourism in the past quarter century has rapidly grown to become a major factor in world trade and an important force in generating people-to-people contacts and improved understanding between them, many governments continue to impose restrictions on the interchange of travelers, both between nations and within their own borders. Political leaders have often ignored the recommendations of their official tourism offices. Even in the most advanced industrial nations tourism is often considered of negligible importance when priorities are assigned in the allocation of budgets, energy supplies, transportation resources, and personnel. During the energy crises of 1973 and 1978, in the United States energy allocation to the travel industry was the first sector cut, although tourism was the largest generator of employment, providing many jobs to the lower income levels.

A number of international agreements have been reached in the past stressing the importance of travel. In 1948, the United Nations General Assembly adopted an article that stated: "Everyone has the right to rest and leisure, including reasonable limitation of working hours and periodic holidays with pay." Again in 1966, the General Assembly recommended that all states ensure everyone's right to "rest, leisure, and reasonable limitation of working hours and periodic holidays with pay, as well as remuneration for public holidays." Another international agreement, the Helsinki Accord, was signed by thirty-five nations "to facilitate free movement and contacts." To date some signees of the Helsinki Accord still fail to provide the basic freedoms expressed in the document.

However, world tourism has reached such a level of importance, involving so many countries, that the WTO needed to face the growing issues of tourism today. In Manila, on September 27, 1980, 107 countries met to review the broad role and progress of tourism during the twenty-five years since the first intergovernmental conference convened under the auspices of the United States in 1954. The outcome of that meeting has been a benchmark for tourism agreements, both between nations and within nations. The accord reached is referred to as the Manila Declaration. It recognized that tourism is an essential life activity, and clearly identified the potential of tourism to enhance the quality of human life in both a national and international context. It recognized tourism as an important part of the social, cultural, educational, political, and economic well-being of the residents of the world and citizens of the various nations. The major principles expressed in the Manila Declaration are listed in Chapter 14.

The Manila Declaration strongly suggests that tourism be considered a basic human right, regardless of political ideology, even though there are recognized economic differences within societies. It stresses that there is a need for the travel industry to allow for those differences. All societies stress the importance of leisure and tourism as an important element of leisure. This document recognizes the importance of domestic tourism and stresses its importance for citizens of all countries. In Acapulco, in 1982, the WTO reaffirmed its commitment to this Declaration. Further meetings of the WTO led to the creation, at Sofia in 1986, of a Tourism Bill of Rights and Tourist Code.

To further emphasize the importance of tourism in the world today, Pope John Paul II reflected on the role of tourism from a religious point of view at the annual meeting of the American Society of Travel Agents in Rome. His major theme was fostering understanding to enhance the philosophy of the world as being a global village.

RESEARCH AND REVIEW

1. What was the importance of the Industrial Revolution as it relates to tourism?

2. What will the major characteristics of tourism be in the post-industrial society of the future?

3. What are some common elements in all the different definitions of tourism?

4. What are the three categories that describe tourism as an industrial network?

5. Why do Mill and Morrison consider tourism a system rather than an industry?

6. Define and describe the two major divisions of tourism study.

7. What is the hospitality process?

8. What is the history of the word *holiday*?

9. Identify the six eras of tourism and outline the major contribution of each.

10. Compare and contrast modern tourism with the Roman period.

11. Describe the Grand Tour.

12. What was the significance of the Helsinki Accord for international travel?

ENDNOTES

1. Jost Krippendorf, "Tourism in the System of Industrial Society," *1986 Annals of Tourism Research,* Vol. 13, No. 4 (1986), pp. 517–532.
2. Robert W. McIntosh and Charles R. Goeldner, *Tourism: Principles, Practices, Philosophies* (NY: John Wiley, 1986), p. 4.
3. Ibid.
4. H. Robinson, *A Geography of Tourism* (London: Macdonald & Evans, 1976), p. 54.
5. George Young, *Tourism: Blessing or Blight?* (Middlesex, England: Penguin, 1973), p. 1.
6. W. Hunziker, (Grundriss der Allgemeinen Fremdenverkehrslehre).
7. A. J. Burkart and S. Medlik, *Tourism Past, Present and Future* (London: Heinemann, 1981), pp. 41–45.
8. Robert A. Chadwick, "Concepts, Definitions and Measures Used in Travel and Tourism Research," in *Travel, Tourism, and Hospitality Research: A Handbook for*

Managers and Researchers, ed. J. R. Brent Ritchie and Charles R. Goeldner (NY: John Wiley & Sons, 1986), pp. 47–62.

9. Chuck Gee, Dexter Choy, and James Makens, *The Travel Industry* (Westport, CT: The AVI Publishing, 1984), p. 12.

10. Robert Christie Mill and Alastair M. Morrison, *The Tourism System: An Introductory Text* (Englewood Cliffs, NJ: Prentice-Hall, 1985), pp. xvii–xx.

11. Nico J. Nanninga and Ruud J. Reuland, *Hotel and Tourism Training in Developing Countries* (The Hague: School of Hospitality Management, Hague Hotel School, 1985), p. 5.

12. Ibid., pp. 4–14.

13. Lionell Casson, *Travel in the Ancient World* (London: George Allen & Unwin Ltd., 1974), p. 31.

14. Ibid., p. 56.

15. Ibid., pp. 65–94.

16. Ibid., p. 232.

17. McIntosh, p. 10.

18. E. S. Bates, *Touring in 1600* (Boston & NY: Houghton Mifflin, 1911), p. 14.

19. William Mead, *The Grand Tour in the Eighteenth Century* (NY & Boston: Houghton Mifflin, 1914), p. 3.

20. Robinson, p. 11.

21. Leslie Dorsey and Janile Devane, *Fare Thee Well* (NY: Crown Pub., 1964), p. 296.

22. Somerset R. Waters, *Travel Industry World Yearbook: The Big Picture—1987* (NY: Child and Waters, 1987), pp. 8–12.

23. Ibid.

CHAPTER 2

TRAVEL IN A CHANGING WORLD

Growth and development in the travel industry is, quite naturally, based on demand. When a service or a product is desired by enough individuals, it is studied and assessed so that the demand process can be better understood.

CHARACTERISTICS AND DEFINITION OF DEMAND

In an effort to define demand, economists have suggested that the term be used to describe the amount of products or services that people are willing to buy, at a specific price range, during a specified period of time. There are two types of demand, elastic and inelastic. *Inelastic demand* means that if prices are increased, demand will not be affected. In that situation, if the price of air fare were increased, there would still be approximately the same number of travelers as before. Inelastic demand is somewhat characteristic of business travel; since the travel is required as part of doing business, the journey will be made whether prices rise or fall within a reasonable range. There are three reasons for this: First, since the company pays for the trip, businesspeople will be less concerned with cost. Second, since time is extremely important to businesspeople, they look for quick, comfortable services. Third, the destination is often chosen by someone other than the traveler. Certainly, if prices rose to extremes even necessary travel might be curtailed.

Elastic demand, on the other hand, dictates that with a given price decrease or increase there will be a proportionate increase or decrease in the number of patrons desiring the service. If air fares are reduced, a greater number of travelers will be attracted to flying. Airlines found this to be true following deregulation; as air fares dropped, the number of travelers reached an all-time high. It was also found, in a cost-benefit study by the Hawaiian tourist industry, that a ten percent reduction in air fares increased the number of visitors to Hawaii by about fifteen percent. The same fare reduction increased the house count in Hawaiian hotels by about nine percent, and increased the length of stay of travelers by about three percent.[1] Conversely, as the American dollar fell in value against most Western European currencies, the resultant real price increase inhibited travel to Europe by Americans traveling for pleasure.

Demand can be divided into two types, actual or potential. For companies or governments to plan and use their resources effectively, it is important that they know the *actual demand* for a particular service or a product. Demand brings income, jobs, transportation links, and communications systems to an area. Not meeting demand effectively through good service or good products will reduce future demand, and change the nature of the business in a given area. Both the public and private sectors have found it important to understand actual demand in order to provide good services and products for those who use them. *Potential demand* makes it possible for companies and governments to increase actual demand through marketing and advertising. One needs only to watch television for a few minutes to see the considerable effort expended in an attempt to create demand.

There are a number of external factors that also influence actual and potential demand. *External factors* are those over which the company or organization offering services or products has little or no control; the factors are outside their spheres of influence. Briefly, these external factors are political, social, environmental, economic, and technological in nature. These factors influence an individual's propensity for travel. A propensity to travel includes an individual's psychological and socioeconomic nature that predisposes that person to travel. The term "born with an itchy foot" is an expression that illustrates this predisposition to travel. The inverse is true also. There are those who lack the desire to travel or to participate in a particular activity. Some factors influencing a person's propensity to travel will be discussed in this chapter. A few that are psychological in nature, are discussed in the following chapter under motivations. The inverse of demand (the propensity to travel) is resistance. Resistance is also caused by a number of psychological and socioeconomic characteristics. This equation can be expressed as follow:

$$\text{Demand} = (\text{Propensity}, \text{Resistance})$$

Propensity depends upon:	Resistance depends upon:
Psychographics	Psychographics
Demographics	Demographics
Socioeconomic Status	Destination
Information and Distribution Systems at Point of Origin	Characteristics (political, economic, physical cultural, etc.)
	Distance and Technology[2]

Psychographics is the study of consumer behavior in the context of three variables and their interrelationships. These variables are predisposition, influences, and product attributes. The first and third are somewhat self-explanatory. However, influences range from the psychological nature of the individual to the family and cultural background that form a person's lifestyle. Some of these influences are attitudes, beliefs, opinions, and personality traits. Thus, the study of psychographics helps identify current and potential demand in order for a company or organization to market and advertise their product to those with the greatest likelihood to use their service or product. Psychographics is also equally important in helping overcome resistance. This can be illustrated by the following example. American Airlines commissioned Louis Harris to conduct a survey of those who travel and those who don't, and what flyers were most "afraid of." Table 2-1 shows the results of this survey.

Among the most vital concerns of the people surveyed were food, rooms, amount of cash to take, and the customs of the area. In other words, most travelers want to know they will be staying in clean rooms, not eating strange food, and being kept informed of the social norms of the area. Also of prime importance in choosing a destination is un-

TABLE 2-1 TRAVELERS' FEARS

What Travelers Worry About in General	Flyers Percent	Non-Flyers Percent
Something may go wrong	38	20
Sickness	21	15
Accidents, safety, crashes	15	11
Delays, not being able to get away	10	2
Weather	16	6
Costs, spending too much money	16	12
Leaving kids at home	8	2
Poor arrangements, no accommodations	8	7
Car trouble	0	21
All other	5	6
What Travelers Worry About Specifically		
Right clothes	54	54
What weather will be like	53	52
Amount of cash to take	40	40
Kind of room will get	36	30
If food will be good	38	35
If will be as nice as expected	32	30
If have too much luggage	31	24
Kind of service will get	25	17
Convenience along way	23	30
If arrangements taken care of	22	18
Unexpected expenses	21	19
If kids will behave all right	16	19
Whether others will be disappointed	20	14
Whether made right choice	16	15
Kind of people will meet	13	9
How much to tip	12	9
If will feel left out	5	4

Source: George G. Brownell, *Travel Agency Management*, Southern University Press, 1978, Appendix II-F.

derstanding the general cost of such a trip well in advance. In fact, the industry does an excellent job of communicating to potential travelers the services and products they offer, which does help to eliminate these fears.

MEASURING AND FORECASTING TRAVEL DEMAND

Although almost every type of organization and business is concerned with some aspect of measuring and forecasting demand, it is difficult to forecast accurately. Two elements are used to measure demand—market forces (which are somewhat easier to measure) and nonmarket forces. Market forces, or actual demand, are measured by the number of visitors or consumers using a given product or visiting a given area, and the length of time they use the product, or the number of days and/or nights they stay in the area. Another critical measure of demand is the amount of money spent by the consumers. Understanding all this information will help in analyzing the nature of demand and what effect changes in the demand have on the organization or area.

It should be recognized that using the information gathered from the variables listed above, an organization would have considerable information upon which to base policy and growth expectations. For organizations that provide products and services, demand measuring and forecasting are extremely critical to their existence. The techniques of forecasting and assessing are covered fully in Chapter 13.

A center such as Disney World translates its statistical records of the number of visitors, their length of stay, and the amount they spent into income per visitor hours. Capacity, amount of advertising, and expansion possibilities can then be estimated. For governments and states in which tourism is a high income-producing industry, various meth-

ods of measuring have been used. Table 2-2 is an example of a national survey form.

In analyzing the tourist trade, a number of methods of counting tourists and gathering information are used.

Frontiers

Many countries record the flow of visitors arriving and leaving the country through passport and immigration controls. This form of data gathering is relatively easy, and can be completed with little additional manpower and cost.

The changing or easing of entrance requirements to many countries may affect data gathering since some countries no longer require visas. Unless a traveler is required to complete a form, travel documents generally provide information concerning the number of travelers and their origin. Information collectors at airports, ports, and on roads provide accurate information at the end of a trip concerning the length of stay, the money spent, and the area traveled while in the country. Probably the most exact information that can be obtained from a traveler leaving a country is the mode of transport used, the type of residence in the country, the main purpose of the trip, and the length of stay in that country.

Hotel, Motel, and Camping Accommodations

Registration information can indicate the number of nights a traveler spends in the country, and the distribution of travelers. When this is combined with information concerning capacity and employment data, the impact on the hotel, motel, and camping sector can be computed readily. One important disadvantage of this system of reporting is that it doesn't account for the many travelers who stay with friends and relatives. It is estimated that in Sochi, USSR, as many people stay with friends and relatives as in the hotels

TABLE 2-2 NATIONAL HOLIDAY SURVEY FORM

Country: _____	Name: _____
1. Breakdown by socioeconomic groups and by income groups of persons having taken a holiday and persons not having taken a holiday.	7. Number of holidaymakers and nights' stays in the country of residence and abroad, broken down according to the form of accommodation most currently used:
2. Breakdown by sex and age groups of persons having taken a holiday and persons not having taken a holiday.	—hotel, model, boarding house; —camping site; —relatives or friends; —youth hostel; —own property;
3. Number of separate holiday trips made in the country of residence and abroad.	—rented house or apartment; —other types of accommodation.
4. Average length of main holiday in the country of residence and abroad (if necessary, in number of weeks).	8. Number of holidaymakers broken down by principal means of transport used when going on holiday in the country of residence and abroad:
5. Main holiday period chosen in the country of residence and abroad.	—motorcoach, motorcar, motorcycle, scooter; —railway; —ship;
6. Number of holidaymakers and nights' stays in the country of residence, and abroad (in all and for the main foreign countries for which the sample is representative).	—airplane; —other means of transportation.
	9. Total holiday expenditure, divided into expenditure in the country of residence and abroad.

Source: Organization for Economic Cooperation and Development, *Tourism Policy and International Tourism in OECD Member Countries*, 1976.

of the region. In many countries, some types of accommodation centers are not required to keep records; in others the recording system is not standardized. A nonstandardized system of information collection requires considerable cooperation from the guests as well as the accommodation industry. In some countries, accommodation registration is seen as government interference in the travel industry with ulterior purposes. In Guatemala, for example, hotels are required to pay a room tax for each guest. Hotel owners feel this is a governmental method used to ascertain the accuracy of the hotel's records. Certainly, in countries with little or no frontier control, hotel records could be an important source of information. An additional question or two, concerning the purpose of the trip, would not be difficult to include on a registration form.

Banking

The exchange of currency through the banking system can be an important method of estimating the expenditures of visitors in the host country, as well as the expenditures of its citizens traveling abroad. However, there are significant problems with this method because all transactions, including black marketing, do not go through the banking system. Private persons in various tourist center businesses will accept foreign currency. This may be their means of exporting money out of the country if they fear change in the political situation and, consequently, a change in the economic system. Travel agents and tour operators often provide services in exchange for services from their counterparts in other countries. Then, only the differences in price are recorded, not the full amount of the transaction. Lastly, it is difficult to keep track of money from other sources such as temporary workers, legal or illegal, or from the stationing of foreign troops. For example, the United States has troops stationed in other countries. These troops are paid in dollars, which they then exchange for the local currency.

Carriers

Public transportation carriers can be a source of statistics on passengers by date and location. This method is helpful when other sources are unavailable and other forms of transportation, such as auto, ship, or train cannot be used.

Visitors

Sample surveys can be obtained from visitors by personal interview, by on-the-spot completion of a form, or by the completion of a form that is returned by mail. Sample surveys have their limitations and weaknesses, however, they can provide more information than the other methods discussed and, when used with some of the other forms of data collection, can provide excellent explanations on the nature of the tourist trade. Surveys at the frontier, of course, would be the most helpful as they would reach the entire traveling population. A final method of survey is conducted only in households to determine their

foreign travel habits. Generally, such surveys are more effective in assessing domestic travel. The United States Travel Data Center conducts an extensive monthly household survey to assess and analyze domestic tourism and travel abroad by United States citizens.

MAJOR FACTORS SHAPING DEMAND

Leisure

Leisure can be defined as freedom from the necessity to labor. We are free to choose how we spend our time when not at work. Since the very earliest societies, a considerable amount of leisure time has been used by people to travel and enjoy the benefits of touring (see Chapter 1).

The development of machinery in modern society, both during and after the Industrial Revolution, has increased our free time considerably. The work week in the United States has been reduced by thirty-one hours since 1850. Additionally, if we consider other fringe benefits that have been introduced, such as sick leave, paid vacations, personal days and holidays, we see that people have a considerable amount of free time today.

Fringe benefits are a recent phenomenon. In the 1920s, only a few wage earners had paid vacations.. The rapid growth of unions just before and following World War II increased the length of paid vacations to two and three weeks a year plus eight to ten holidays a year. Today, in some industries, the steel industry being a good example, workers have thirteen weeks paid vacation annually. Although this is still the exception, there is a strong movement toward increased vacation time. Paid vacations now average between three and four weeks a year, with eight to twelve additional holidays, depending on the state. A comparison of the vacations in eight developed countries can be seen in Table 2-3.

This shows that people in all economically advanced countries have a considerable amount of leisure time. The sum total of leisure time is becoming quite impressive. Given a forty-hour work week, with two-day weekends fifty-two weeks a year, we have a hundred and four leisure days. Adding this to twenty and thirty days of paid vacation and eight to fourteen holidays each year, we find Americans have between 132 and 148 days of leisure time a year. This

TABLE 2-3 ANNUAL LEAVE AND HOLIDAYS

Country	Paid Vacations	Holidays	Total
United States	18–30	8–10	26–40
United Kingdom	15	6	21
Italy	15–20	17	29–37
USSR	30	6	36
France	24	9	33
Belgium	18	10	28
West Germany	28	12	40
Sweden	31	10	41

Source: Lloyd E. Hudman, *Tourism: A Shrinking World* (Columbus, OH: Grid, 1980).

is a little over one-third of a year that an individual has available to spend in leisure pursuits.

The work ethic was not only strong in the United States and Europe, but also deeply entrenched in Japanese culture. The "leisure ethic" has been slow to develop in Japan. Labor ministry figures indicate that the Japanese take only about fifty-five percent of allotted annual level. However, this situation is slowly changing. In an effort to speed this change, the government established a policy whereby banks and government offices began closing for two Saturdays a month instead of one. The overall goal is to cut the number of average annual working hours to 2,000 by 1990 and to add ten more nonworking days. By comparison, the average annual working hours a year are 1,610 in West Germany, 1,900 in the United States, and 1,940 in Great Britain.

The reduction of the work week will continue in all industrial nations. Many firms are operating on a three- and four-day work week. Some firms are experimenting with flexible scheduling, which would allow people to design their work days. The movement of the United States government to tie many official holidays into a weekend means three- to four-day holiday periods, creating new markets for the travel industry.

Retirement age has lowered considerably over the past few years, and as a result has increased the amount of leisure time we may expect to enjoy. With the reduction of the work week, more vacation and holiday time, and earlier retirement, there is now an extensive amount of leisure time available for prospective tourists to enjoy either long or short vacations, and other leisure-time activities.

Distribution of Leisure Time

The growth of leisure time has also brought about competing use of that time. Mill and Morrison have divided leisure into three periods; they are weekdays, weekends, and vacations. Weekday leisure time is the period between the end of work and going to bed. Weekends provide a larger block of free time during which short trips might be taken, while vacation time provides extensive periods for longer trips (vacations). Changes in the amount of leisure time available may be made in any of the three; however, changes in the first would have little direct impact on tourism as it would provide little opportunity for travel. Mill and Morrison pointed out that although the amount of leisure time has increased since 1950, the work week has remained five days.[3] Today, many jobs in developed countries are changing from industrial to service industries. As these changes occur there will probably be greater flexibility in the use of free time. People will be able to work longer days so as to have longer weekends and extra vacation days. As developing nations of the world become industrialized, they will go through the same stages of added leisure time that characterized the western world following World War II. This is beginning to happen in China where, for example, in the 1970s domestic and international tourism were almost nonexistent. Today, as the Chinese have more leisure time, there is a growing domestic market for tourism.

Life Cycle

Our life cycle consists of nine different stages, as identified by the U.S. Travel and Tourism Administration.[4] These are:

1. Young single head, no children
2. Young couple, no children
3. Young couple, young children
4. Young couple, older children (under 46 with child 6–18)
5. Older couple, older children (over 46, at least one child under 18)
6. Older couple, no children
7. Older couple, no children, retired
8. Single head, working
9. Single, retired, may be living with family

The young, single, and newly married have considerable time for leisure pursuits. The travel industry acknowledges this fact by offering special fares and rates for travel and accommodations for people under twenty-six. Throughout Europe, a considerable network of accommodations (such as youth hostels) are available for those who have the time, but lack substantial income, to travel. As family size increases, free time and money become limited. This usually results in choosing places and activities closer to home for leisure needs. In later years, as incomes increase and family members grow older, they are again more able to pursue leisure activities far afield. But now their needs and travel requirements are different from those they had when they were young. Another level of services and products are required from the travel industry. In stages six, seven, and sometimes eight, with today's better health and greater income, people have considerably more free time which they often choose to use in traveling.

Mobility

"I will build a motor car for the great multitude . . . so low in price that no man . . . will be unable to own one—and enjoy with the family the blessings of hours of pleasure in God's great open spaces."[5] Henry Ford made good this pledge between 1914 and 1917. He began a change in America that brought about the transformation of travel in Western society and the greatest revolution in the history of man's way of life. In 1900 there were 8,000 motor vehicles registered in the United States. The number increased to a little over five million by 1917, 61.5 million in 1960, and over 130 million by 1984. World automobile registration has increased from 98 million in 1960 to 148 million in 1984.[6] Interestingly, the first use of the auto was for pleasure. Modern road construction was begun, therefore, with this purpose in mind. The first parkway, the Bronx River Parkway, was completed in 1923 and starting in the 1930s, others soon followed. Today, such an elaborate system of roads has been built in the United States that a person can go from coast to coast or border to border without stopping for one red light. This vast network of roads, plus mass production of the car at a price almost all people can afford, has led to the development of a tourist industry unmatched in the world. Motels, hotels, restaurants, service stations, curiosity shops, entertainment centers, and campgrounds support a phenomenal amount of travel.

The rapid growth of automobile production was followed by monumental improvements in air service. By the 1960s, transportation improvements in speed and comfort had created a society of travelers who could reach the far corners of the country, and even the world, in a matter of hours. Consequently, we now express distance in terms of time rather than miles or kilometers.

Affluence

The transformation to an urban society brought about by technological advancement includes another large factor in developing American travel. Henry Ford served as the catalyst for raising the standard of living of the working person. When he began the mass production of the automobile, he set the wage rate at five dollars a day, which was an unheard-of high rate, double any existing level.

Through the twentieth century, there has been a very sharp increase in both real and disposable incomes. Incomes in constant dollars for the peak years of travel from 1947 to 1976 have more than doubled.

Several factors have influenced this increase in personal income. Smaller family size, and an increase of women in the labor market have made the American family more affluent. As a result of this affluence, increased demands have been made upon the tourist industry. The cost of many tourist services has decreased over the years. This, along with increased affluence, has made travel available to more and more people. Although the cost of auto travel and hotel accommodations has increased, airlines and bus compa-

nies have been able to adjust their fares to new low levels, which created a tremendous new market in the late 1970s. The net effect is that, with increasing incomes, and a relative decrease in the cost of travel, the growth of the travel industry has been tremendous. A combination of increased expenditures in tourism and tourism-related areas, with an increase in money available, has created an age of affluence to finance our leisure-oriented traveling society.

During this same period, Americans have not only been gaining more disposable income, but paid vacations have also added to wealth, and thus increased the opportunity to participate in leisure activities.

Socioeconomic Pressures

Not all individuals have the same propensity to travel. Certain people or age groups make demands on different sectors of the tourist industry. An understanding of these factors can assist those in the travel industry in preparing and presenting special strategies for advertising, and in the selection of transportation, accommodations, and tours.

Age, income, occupation, and sex may all influence travel decisions. Most travel research indicates that the people most likely to travel are professional males between the ages of thirty-five and fifty-five, with incomes over $30,000. By and large, income increases with age until retirement, thus the elderly have the lowest propensity to travel. Two, or possibly three, factors account for this. Increasing health problems tend to keep the elderly closer to home. Incomes have decreased, and there is not as much disposable income available for leisure pursuits at a time in life when it is probably needed the most. Elderly people tend to be more comfortable at home, and less desirous of

1928 Ford Model A

experimenting with new foods and are uncertain of new cultures.

Presently more males travel than females because most travel is for business. As the growing numbers of women in the work force move up in the corporate structure, this may change. The recent National Travel Survey data by the U.S. Travel Data Center suggests that women are more likely to take vacation travel than men. Again, this probably results from the present work structure, where males are more tied to their employment in corporations. The professional group is most likely to travel. Professional people travel both for business and pleasure while blue-collar workers, craftspeople, and laborers usually have little reason to travel for business purposes. Professionals generally have a higher salary, thus more disposable income. In an effort to stimulate travel of the young with limited means, the travel industry offers lower air fare, youth rail passes, and youth accommodations in Europe, making foreign travel extremely attractive for college-age students. In many cases, their travel conditions are more restricted, such as air fares and accommodations that are limited in amenities and, in many cases, dormitory in character. Farmers are the least-traveled group, followed by household and services personnel. Farmers are tied to an agricultural cycle that has little leisure time; people in the household and service sectors are the lowest-paid occupational groups, and have little discretionary money for travel.

Organizations, both private and public, continue to survey and gather data pertaining to socioeconomic patterns and to ascertain changes. The travel industry, to be successful, needs to be aware of these factors and their changing characteristics in order to take them into account when providing service and when conducting advertising campaigns.

Work Patterns

In addition to the leisure patterns discussed above, the clients' working conditions influence their propensity to travel. Flexible time, job sharing, work at home are all trends that suggest a growing opportunity for people to travel.

However, travel associated with business is still the major factor which supports more travel companies and organizations than any other segment of the potential market. Travel by businesspeople will continue to be important to the tourist industry as society becomes more service oriented. In addition, the growth shown by the newly industrializing nations also indicates the probability of more internal travel. Lastly, growing international communication is increasing the demand upon the industry to provide more and greater service to more places in greater numbers than ever before.

With growing economic development and trade, conferences and meetings will also continue to expand and grow. More international organizations will develop, not only along political lines as in the past, but according to professional and other interests that require an exchange of ideas.

There is one cause of concern when future travel by professional people is projected—the influence of new communication technology. With the ability we have to hold conferences, and communicate directly through special hook-ups to telephones and computers, many meetings and conferences can probably be handled more efficiently and with less cost than traveling would allow. However, these would then free businesspeople from many business trips and probably increase their time available for leisure pursuits and travel. On the other hand, there is a certain prestige in having a job that requires a considerable amount of travel. People will continue to select exotic locations for their conferences and meetings or find opportunities to visit branches or other businesses in locations they want to see.

Thus, current work patterns increase the demand for travel. As the developing industrialized nations and the western world change to service-oriented societies and multinational organizations increase, travel can be expected to continue being in high demand.

CURRENT SOCIETAL TRENDS

While the factors discussed above were important to the evolution of the travel industry, current changes and patterns will continue to have not only impact, but long-range implications on the growth of tourism. Two trends in the world today substantially influence the growth of tourism. First, people in newly industrialized countries will increasingly be more able and eager to travel. They will be influenced by the factors discussed earlier in this chapter. Second, in the Western industrialized countries new trends are creating an additional impact on the travel industry. These trends are as important to today's industry and to its future as those discussed previously were to the travel industry between World War II and the present.

Women in the Work Force

One of the significant trends of the 1980s is the growing number of women in the work force, and the movement of women into executive positions. As women continue to move into the business hierarchy, their impact will be felt on the tourism industry. It was estimated that at the end of 1982 there were approximately 48 million women working in the United States. They comprised forty-four percent of the work force. The U.S. Bureau of Labor Statistics estimates that by 1990 there will be 56.6 million working women. This increased movement of women into the work force and executive positions is interrelated with other societal trends and, in fact, is a major contributor to them. Therefore, these trends will be treated as an outgrowth of this movement. The influence of women in the work force is evidenced by the growing number of single people, smaller families, and larger family real and disposable incomes. These all have a significant effect upon society.

These factors do not hold true in the Japanese culture. Although the number of women in their work force is increasing, it doesn't provide them the same opportunity for travel.

Singles

The desire to further their education and to improve their career opportunities has led women to postpone marriage and, in some cases, to divorce. Thus, the number of single people increased slightly more than sixteen percent from 1970 to 1980, to a total of over 53 million single, widowed or divorced people in the United States.

Single people travel more than do married people; they already have a higher propensity to use public carriers and to travel outside the United States. This, combined with their increasing salaries from promotions in the professional hierarchy, will allow them to travel in increasing numbers.

Smaller Families

The inclusion of women in the work force creates pressure to reduce family size. Families with both spouses working tend to be smaller than families with only one working member. With fewer children, smaller families will be better able to travel.

Larger Real and Disposable Family Income

The increase in the number of women working, and the reduction in size of the family unit, will, quite naturally, mean an increase in both real income and disposable income for the family. The amount of real income to the family will increase when both parents work, particularly if the wife moves into an executive position. In addition, the reduction in family size will increase the discretionary income available to the family.

With more money available, combined with smaller families, the demand on public carriers will increase. Most important, however, will be the influence the spouses have on each other. With both parents working, coordination of vacation time will mean more frequent, shorter vacations. The general tendency in the past was to schedule the family vacation around the husband's work schedule, and to take a long trip by private automobile. The trend nowadays is to take shorter vacations, with the intent of reaching the destination as quickly as possible. This increases the demand for fly/drive vacations. It is far easier to arrange and coordinate shorter vacations for multiple-wage earners than to arrange extended vacations.

Security

The industry has become security conscious as a result of the increasing number of women travelers. Many hotels are offering escort service from the lobby, dining room, or parking garages to the guest's room; special tables in the dining room; and more security in the rooms.

Amenities

A number of hotel chains are refurbishing their rooms in brighter colors, installing full-length mirrors, shower caps, skirt hangers, hair dryers, curling irons, sewing kits, and ironing boards. Some are adding telephone monitoring service that cuts off calls after 8:00 P.M. unless the guest specifically asks to receive calls.

These trends will continue to significantly impact the travel industry. The implications are indeed positive for its continued growth. The industry has recognized the importance of the woman business traveler by improving security and amenities. Other changes will continue to occur.

Attitude Change

The influence of all these changes is particularly seen in the hospitality sector of the tourist industry. This is expressed somewhat in the changing vocabulary, for example, referring to people as solo and paired rather than single and couples. The term solo denotes that an individual is traveling alone by choice, while paired can be one of several combinations: father-son, mother-daughter, two men, two women, or man and a woman. The previous connotation of "single" may have implied "swinger." Today, employees in the industry are being trained to recognize that women traveling alone are doing so by choice, and that they should behave towards them in the same manner as they would a man traveling alone. Restaurant staff and hotel desk clerks have been trained to be more courteous and friendly than they were in the past, when they were sometimes aloof and indifferent to the lone woman traveler.

Changing Labor Force

Work discontentment is increasing in the United States. This is occurring for two reasons. First, there are surplus college graduates taking jobs that require little experience and training, and for which they are over-qualified. Second, there are shifts from blue collar to white collar jobs, and from the industrial northeast to the sunbelt; also, there is a loss of industrial jobs, as industries have declined due to foreign competition. This has resulted in many people being employed in positions for which they are neither trained nor suited. If people do not find satisfaction with their work, then they seek leisure time activities to provide that satisfaction. Therefore, there is an increasing desire for leisure time through job "splitting" or sharing, and flextime, in which a worker is allowed to start and leave work at times that best meet a personal schedule. Job splitting and flextime also benefit the working woman who has to care for a family.

The shift from industrial labor to a service labor market gives workers more flexibility in their leisure time and pursuits. People in the service sectors have less structure in their work and more options available to them for working hours.

Population Shifts

Presently there is a higher percentage of people over forty-nine in the population; approximately two out of every five people are over forty-nine and this trend will continue. People in this age group, with older children and higher family incomes, are actively engaged in travel. As children grow older and move from home, parents can increase the amount they travel. The improving health of this segment of the population will increase their ability and desire to travel. With the trend of resort development and time-share plans in attractive areas, the older population will be even more willing and likely to travel.

The shifting and growing populations, particularly in developing nations of the world, has a number of implications for the future demand of tourism. First, as these nations become more urban in character, new jobs will be created, increasing the labor force. This will primarily increase the demand for domestic travel and, to a lesser degree, for international travel. In 1983 the WTO estimated that fifty-nine percent of the world population was of working age. Once these developing countries solve some basic employment issues, they will encourage the growth of the travel industry. This will, in turn, assist in providing even more employment. The shift from agrarian to urban employment will increase the demand for tourism. Data suggests, according to the WTO, that the more urban societies become, the more service jobs there are, increasing the demand for tourism.

Urbanization

The degree of urbanization is also an important factor in determining a country's potential for attracting tourists. As cities grow and draw more international tourists, this in turn provides more jobs in the travel sector. The effect of this, of course, produces more potential clients for both domestic and international travel. In addition, the money generated to other sectors of the economy of developing nations also stimulates tourism. It is a cycle that can only be seen as beneficial to the tourist industry.

DESTINATION BARRIERS INHIBITING DEMAND

It is important to understand what factors reduce demand for a product or service.

Location

How popular a particular destination will be is determined by its accessibility. Put another way, how much time will it take to get there, and how much will it cost? The further away, naturally, the more costly the transportation, and more cost usually means less demand. Take, for example, a trip to the South Pacific. Americans most frequently choose to go to Hawaii, Australians to Fiji, and Japanese to Guam. As the distance traveled increases, so the demand decreases.

Time

The second factor in accessibility or lack of accessibility is time. If we are given distance in terms of miles for instance, we quickly convert it to the length of time it takes to get there. We use time regardless of type of carrier: Washington to New York is three hours by train or fifty minutes by airplane. The question travel agents or airline reservation people must answer is not "how far is it?" but, "how long does it take to get there?"

Economics

Economic activity affects demand for a given area. First, as currency exchange rates change, becoming favorable or unfavorable for a particular country, the number of tourists to that country, will either decline or increase. When the U.S. dollar is extremely low compared to the Japanese yen, Japanese tourists pour into Hawaii, Alaska, and the Western United States. When the British pound drops, travel from European countries to Britain increases. The reverse is also true, when the value of the currency increases the number of visitors decreases.

A second major consideration is the cost/price relationship. Popular destinations, that have a high demand, are those that are perceived by the traveler to offer excellent service and/or goods for the price. Tourism is generally price elastic. This means, as price increases the demand for the goods and/or service decreases. The inverse is also true, as the price decreases the demand for the goods and/or service increases. A boon to Caribbean travel during the 1970s and early 1980s was unlimited travel for a reasonably low fare provided by two major airlines. Most travelers before that time were from the East Coast; those that were closest in time and had the money. The unlimited inexpensive mileage prices attracted those from the West Coast as well.

The third economic factor to consider is the ease with which large companies can expand in different countries, whether they are newly developing or highly industrialized. Nations that have restrictions and limitations on foreign companies, retard tourism. By decreasing the amount of facilities in a country for tourists, they are decreasing demand. Conversely, the growth of multinational companies has enhanced the ability of countries to develop both an infrastructure and superstructure, creating an environment conducive to attracting visitors. A good example of this has been the South Pacific Corporation which has developed hotels, resorts, and cultural centers all over the Pacific, thus increasing tourism to the region. Sometimes the economic climate of a country may discourage development due to high interest rates, increased insurance liability costs, and laws restricting development investments.

Money leaving a country is referred to as leakage. Leakage means that less capital is available for development and expansion. One of the drawbacks of multinational companies is that, while bringing development to a region, leakage is created. A certain amount of money goes for management costs and a return on investment to the parent company in the home country. Another form of leakage is that travelers leaving a country take money with them to other countries. Many countries that have serious financial problems limit the amount of money that an individual can take out of the country. In the past France, Spain, Italy, and Brazil, as well as other nations have all limited the amount of currency that can be taken out.

Industrialized nations provide both money and a climate for easy development and growth. The rest of the world is divided into the newly industrialized countries and the developing countries. The developing countries are those that are the poorest; consequently they have few available resources to allocate for expanding tourist facilities and attractions. Newly industrialized nations are those that have growing economies because they are attaining some form of industrialization. Examples of these countries are Singapore, Korea, and Hong Kong. All have a healthy climate for development, and are well on their way to establishing a good tourism industry to service the traveler.

Politics

A number of barriers to demand are created by either political situations or political decisions.

Many countries limit their accessibility to travelers. Some of the Arab countries allow visas for business or transit, but not for tourism. Some socialist countries have a long and cumbersome visa application process. There is a movement in some countries to reduce the need for passports, visas, and other travel documents. The United Nations' Rome Conference on Tourism in 1963 recommended the gradual elimination (where possible) of all barriers, restrictions, and formalities to facilitate international travel. Some countries have already started this procedure. Many Western European countries have abolished visas, and other countries are beginning to accept identity cards, or even expired passports, as sufficient information to cross borders. The Scandinavian countries check passports or other identification only at the Scandinavian country of entry. As is happening in many countries that have shared frontiers, Canada and the United States do not require passports for travel between them.

Travel to developing countries is a problem for many potential visitors due to health conditions in those countries. When outbreaks of serious diseases occur, they can destroy their potential demand for tourism. The World Health Organization issues alerts and states health conditions around the world that might affect a potential traveler to a particular region.

The biggest barrier to demand is the concern of travelers for their personal safety. This is manifest at two levels. First is the fear of safety within a country due to the degree of criminal activity that occurs normally in that country. Tourism to Mexico has been affected a number of times when reports have been made of tourists being killed, robbed, or attacked either beside the roads or in resorts such as Acapulco. In the past, violence between nations, or civil war within nations, has quickly reduced the demand for travel to that country or region. The *Washington Post* suggested that there were forty-two wars being fought in 1986. It quoted Secretary Casper Weinberger as saying that "one out of every four countries around the globe is at war." A few of the countries listed were India, China, Sri Lanka, Malaysia, Papua New Guinea, Ireland, Colombia, El Salvador, Guatemala, Ecuador, Lebanon, Morocco, Iran, and Iraq.[7]

Today, a second and new concern has developed which has far-ranging impact on demand. That is terrorism or its threat. Tourists feel threatened by bombings and shootings that randomly menace innocent individuals around the world. Yet, it has been shown that more Americans died in terrorist incidents in 1974 (42) than in 1985 (23) or in 1984 (11). The public perception, however, is of increasing danger. In 1986, it was estimated that forty percent fewer Americans visited Italy, thirty percent fewer went to France.

Environment

The physical environment can serve both as an attractor or a detractor to an area. An area's attractiveness is highly related to the quality of the physical environment. What may look beautiful on a travel poster or calendar may not necessarily invite tourists, if the area is known to have environmental problems. Air and water pollution will deter tourists from the most beautiful cities or beaches. Sometimes environmental problems are a result of an overabundance of tourists, destroying the local attraction and thus repelling other potential travelers to the area.

The weather can also serve as a barrier to demand. Too much rain or snow will deter people from choosing a particular resort. Even ski areas that depend upon snow will lose business if there are a considerable number of days without sunshine. The amount of sunshine is one factor in the popularity of the Alps and many resorts in the Western United States. These areas have many sunny days during the winter, and add to the enjoyment of a skiing holiday or vacation.

Social Characteristics

Barriers to demand for a particular location are raised by its social character. Places with large populations, described as "teeming," are often looked upon negatively. Older travelers may choose not to go to areas that attract teenagers because of the activities offered and the noise that results. Social behavior and sex patterns can also affect demand. Probably, the "punk look" in London would be of interest to some travelers, but if the city were dominated by the "punk look," the number of travelers would drop considerably. Associated with social behavior is the crime rate. Areas with high crime rates are avoided by the potential traveler. For many years, New York was regarded throughout the world as an unsafe area. In an effort to overcome this negative image, New York City started the "I Love New York" campaign, which had a positive impact on its travel industry.

Cross-Cultural Communications

One of the strongest fears many travelers have is that they will become sick in a foreign country and won't be able to communicate with medical personnel. Some regions of the world, such as China and the Soviet Union, where written messages and notices are not only in a foreign language but also in a completely strange alphabet, are of little interest to such travelers. A language barrier may retard exploration and movement within a country. This is an important factor in planning group tours sponsored by the travel industry. Tours can provide the security of communication and yet allow the individual to experience the country or region visited. While the desire to participate in cultural experiences is extremely high, some cultural experiences seem "canned" and sterile, and can act as a deterrent to tourism. While initially they may attract tourists, through time the demand will fall. The desire for cultural experiences has resulted in the development of cultural centers around the world similar to the Polynesian Cultural Center in Hawaii. The most successful attractions seem to be those that are along well-traveled highways. Here an ever changing tourist base will stop out of curiosity, or to take a break from the monotony of driving. Unsuccessful cultural attractions are those that display very different values from those of the potential travelers. They will deter tourists, who do not want to be offended or have their value system challenged by the visit. The visit is expected to be relaxing, fulfilling, and beneficial.

Energy

The worldwide energy crises of 1973 and 1978 demonstrated how quickly an area can be affected by either a shortage of energy or a dramatic increase in price. In the United States, the government reduced the allocation of gas; consequently, states that were highly dependent on tourism in their economies were hurt. Employment dropped, tax revenues decreased, and businesses closed during this period. In addition, as the cost of energy increases, it increases the cost of a trip, thus decreasing demand. Shortly after the energy crisis in 1978, when gasoline prices skyrocketed, two significant changes occurred in domestic tourism. There was a shift to the use of public forms of transportation, and a reduced use of the automobile. Second, the length of trips were shortened since states advertised excellent vacation locations close to home. As Americans adjusted to the high cost of energy, travel again increased.

TOURISM INDUSTRY ACTIONS

In an industry that relies very heavily upon drawing visitors to its region, techniques need to develop to stimulate the demand for their particular activity or service. The travel industry has responded with effective methods of creating and increasing demand. To some extent this may backfire, as people's expectations may be greater than the product offered. The language used to attract people sometimes leads them to feel they are going to receive the greatest experience of their lives, when in actuality the product or service may not meet their expectations.

Macro- and Micro-Management Approaches

The Hague School of Hospitality Management has identified the process of selling services to the tourist as a two level process; the levels are identified as macro and micro levels. The macro level is composed of those authorities of the organizations that function on an international, national, or local level, such as tourist boards, hotel associations, and airlines. The focus of these authorities is broad. Their function is to establish policy and programs that affect the area as a whole, as well as to take care of other lesser responsibilities. For example, the Hotel Association in Palma, Spain works to promote tourism and collaborates directly with government officials to be sure that hotel interests are understood and taken into account.

The micro level involves those organizations that work as hosts directly with tourists in providing goods and services. Included are companies offering room and board,

tour operators, bus companies, cultural and tourist attractions, and entertainment.

All organizations at both the macro and micro levels are concerned with increasing demand, and then providing the traveler with the best possible experience. Thus, "the heart of the matter is the art of hosting, because this structures the guest/host relationship in such a way that the guest feels himself to be treated as a guest."[8] The hospitality process, then, is concerned with the comfort and security of travelers (guests) in order to satisfy their physical and psychosocial needs and objectives so that they will feel safe and enjoy themselves. The basic definition of the hospitality process was presented in Chapter 1.

The tourist product at the macro level is the material culture and the infrastructure, such as airports, roads, sewers, and restaurants. The product at the micro level is the room, food, seat on a bus, or local tour. Cultural behavior can be studied on a macro level at special events and ceremonies, such as a Super Bowl or the changing of the guard at Buckingham Palace. On a micro level, behavior approaches can be studied by observing tour guides, waiters, and reservationists in providing the host's services directly to the guests.

The macro level of the physical environment and its importance is covered at length later in this text. It involves all levels of government and industry to ensure a quality environment. On the micro level, the layout of a building and the quality of a bus are important.

Both macro and micro levels are concerned with meeting the needs and objectives of tourists, to provide them with a quality visit that will initiate an increase in future demand for the area in two ways. First, the guest will, in many cases, return for future visits; and second, the guests will serve as a secondary medium of advertising. Guests, if satisfied with their experience, will tell friends and relatives, thus creating a desire in them for travel or increasing their existing desire. It has been found that there is a strong tourist link between some countries and areas of the world. For example, the English have a high degree of destination linkage with Palma and the Costa del Sol in Spain. Such patterns persist through the years and are probably related to the experiences of the guests with their hosts, and are reliving their experiences through conversations with their friends.

Intermediaries

Within a region or country, considerable effort is given by the tourist industry to encourage and stimulate travel. The organizations or companies hard at work to influence travelers are tourist boards, airlines, tour operators, travel agencies, hotels, and cruise lines, all of which want to provide information and create an interest in travel.

There are many considerations to take into account when advertising products and services of the tourist industry. They must be effective in turning potential tourists into actual tourists. It is difficult to turn on a television or radio or to pick up a newspaper without seeing or hearing an advertisement for a trip or a service. The travel industry, by nature, uses such a high degree of stimulating words such as exotic, sensational, and deluxe, that a problem of truth in advertising can arise. The nature of the industry and the expectations of potential clients leads to advertising that allows the making of promises that can be hard to fulfill.

In order to handle a number of fears and concerns of the prospective traveler, the industry provides a considerable number of people specializing in assisting individuals or groups in the decision-making process. In many cases, prospective travelers have not visited the areas they might enquire about. The advice of a knowledgeable person is an invaluable aid in selecting the right vacation. Through the process of referrals and recommendations people can feel more comfortable with their decision. Travel counselors provide a number of services. First, assistance in the reservation and scheduling process. Counselors must be familiar with the areas and facilities they are promoting. Secondly, they should provide information that will improve the perception of an area, overcoming a client's fears or apprehensions. As we've already pointed out, in recent years, increased media exposure of terrorist activities created problems in the tourist industry for many countries in Europe, despite the fact that the risk in the 1980s is no greater than in the 1970s. A travel counselor, who is trusted, can help a potential traveler understand the nature of safe travel within a given area. In 1986, a new service was begun that provides the industry with a listing of potential areas where travel might be risky. With this information a tourist can make better travel decisions and have a safe, enjoyable holiday.

Paris Hilton

Special Interests

Realizing that all people are not alike in their preferred activities or destinations, some parts of the industry specialize in providing a specific service or destination to meet the particular demands of a specific segment of the population. Today, for example, there are tours for photographers, nudists, bird watchers, doctors, and so on. People also have different values concerning money and expenses. Therefore, the industry offers a broad range of service at various prices to meet the "pockets" of travelers. The airline industry, with its complex set of pricing, offers seats at a variety of prices, such as first class, cabin class, economy class, advance purchase, no cancellation, and so on, all on the same plane and to the same place.

Traveler Services

The likelihood of sickness, or the inability of a company to perform a desired service, is felt by some travelers to be a risk. Travel insurance takes this concern out of a prospective trip. It reduces the element of risk that some fear. The travel industry is so well developed that it is easy, and will become easier, for people to make reservations for hotels, airlines, resorts, plays, and other events. The airline industry has developed complex computer reservation systems. Other industry segments, such as hotels and car rental agencies, interface with these systems to provide complete service for a client. These computer systems are readily available to travel agency offices. Almost anyone, anywhere in the industrialized nations, can easily make reservations for numerous travel services. The system will continue to improve as cable television channels and the personal computer revolution bring more of the world closer to "reach out and touch."

Market Segmentation

Although each person is unique with a different set of characteristics and motivations, there are enough people with similar motivations and needs that they can be grouped accordingly in order to provide services for them. Market research has identified a number of variables that allow travel professionals to recognize who likely travelers might be and what they desire. Some of these are age, income, education, race, nationality, family size, family life cycle, gender, religion, occupation, and psychological needs. Demand for services can be increased by understanding the interrelationship of these socioeconomic characteristics and psychological needs of people and the expectations of each group. This is accomplished by identifying those people who would most likely use the services or products being offered, and designing advertising with them in mind.

Travel Decision Process

In order to make a travel decision, travelers first have to decide how they are going to use their discretionary income. People must first budget their income for necessities—food, clothing, shelter, transportation to and from work, and so on. Discretionary income is income that is left after buying these necessities. It is often spent on new cars, better furniture, additional clothes and travel.

The wealthier a family is, the more discretionary money they have, and more possible ways to use it. They often choose to travel a great deal and have a wider choice of destinations available to them. For some travel is becoming so important, that it is considered a necessity of life.

After evaluating personal finances, and making the decision to allocate money for travel, a person begins searching for a destination. Information comes from various channels and in various forms. Everyday experiences (from movies, contact with friends, and fellow workers), provide information about regions or activities. The industry and government organizations create a variety of advertising and marketing strategies to provide consumers with information about their products. Travel counselors and other professionals assist in the information search. Many people know exactly where they want to go, but others need assistance in making a decision. For example, a person may decide the Caribbean would be a good place to visit, but is uncertain about the exact country. A research report at the Travel and Tourism Research Association indicated few people were able to locate individual islands. However, they were able to recognize the names of those islands that had negative news in the press (Cuba and Haiti). While a few islands were well known due to their highly structured travel industry, specific places were difficult to locate. This study indicated that, while many people knew of the Caribbean and some of the countries in the Caribbean, they needed a great deal of assistance in deciding which islands to visit. If people are considering a number of areas to visit, a travel professional will provide information concerning the character of the regions in question and information concerning many of the major attractions in the area.[9]

Once the decision is made to travel and the informational search is completed, potential travelers will then evaluate alternatives. This evaluation will take into account the client's characteristic needs, motivation, and economic considerations such as cost versus the benefit resulting from such a decision.

Organizational Strategies

In order to facilitate travel, the industry, both private and public, has organized itself in a very efficient and effective manner. Many large national and international companies can provide travelers with a broad range of services to take care of their every need. For example, Thomson Travel in the United Kingdom owns its own group of charter airplanes. Japanese companies often own almost all the service they offer. They sell the tours, fly the patrons on their own airlines, and accommodate and feed them in their own hotels. They are continuing to expand and purchase hotels, resorts, and large recreational areas throughout the world, particularly in the United States, in Hawaii and Alaska. Some countries are beginning to wonder about the economic impact made by tours that are bought in one area but receive service by companies in another country. Today, in Europe, a major issue concerns English people working in hotels, in foreign ski resorts, and other popular foreign destinations which are leased by large English companies.

The packaged tours, and other tourist services, are designed to meet a broad range of interests from a simple one-time service, such as buying a hamburger at Disneyland, to a complex tour including air travel, hotels, sightseeing, visits to local events, and so on. To assist the travelers in obtaining passports and visas, governments have simplified what was once a difficult process; also a number of agencies have been created to assist potential travelers in obtaining both passports and visas. Large travel organizations provide the service as they would any other service. Companies have developed to process passports and visas for those wishing assistance or needing fast service.

Health Services

In addition to providing health information, many companies that specialize in programs for senior citizens or others concerned about potential health problems, provide either nurses or doctors, sometimes both, as part of their programs. One reason that cruises are so popular is that a doctor is always available on board; also, there is an environment similar to that of the traveler's home. Another service that has been developed is traveler's insurance. It ensures that travelers have the attention of doctors, who speak the same language as the traveler does, wherever they might go in the world. An additional guarantee, in the case of sickness, is that the traveler would be transported to a facility with specified standards.

Destination Marketing

At the macro level, government organizations and large companies and associations all market their services in the same area. A state such as Hawaii will have both private and public organizations marketing their services and the state. The Hawaii Visitors Bureau advertises in major markets, mostly Japan, Canada, and the continental United States, to encourage visitors to Hawaii. At the same time, the major airlines involved in Hawaiian traffic advertise flights on, of course, their own airlines. Large hotel chains or associations also encourage visitors to the islands. At the micro level, those agencies that provide direct services to tourists advertise both locally and in larger market areas. Large companies advertise widely and constantly. Small companies take advantage of this advertising to provide a broad range of services once the tourist is in the area. Almost all major tourist areas in the world have publications that announce local attractions, services, entertainment, and availability of other organizations that depend on tourists for business.

In the travel business, people sometimes have a problem obtaining reliable travel information. Agencies, at times exaggerate their services. As in many businesses, there are opportunities for unfair practices such as bait and switch, which is advertising an unavailable service for a low price to entice clients, then persuading them to buy a more costly service. A number of methods have been developed to assist in providing reliable travel information. First, there are guide books published for particular audiences; second, there are reports compiled on specific items of interest from visitors and organizations; and third, the expansion of franchising is helpful to the industry. For example, both Holiday Inn and Best Western, as well as other hotel and motel chains, have a very detailed set of criteria to be met by anyone who wants to own one of their franchises. Companies have developed to assist travelers in obtaining reliable travel information.

Internal Transport/Tour Operator Linkages

In order to facilitate travel and provide tourists with the best possible service, the linkage between tour operators in both the origin and destination has been strengthened in two ways. First, tour operators in the destination, who also have strong ties in the client's home area, will provide complete transportation service. This direct contact with the tourist from the beginning helps market demand. Since the tourist will identify their entire experience with one specific company, if it is a good one, they will then want to use that company again. Second, small tour operators generally provide hosts to assist travelers with problems, and help make a trip smoother. These small tour operators do not have the capital or the market to provide many services. Frequently, the demand from one area to another is so small that it does not warrant the commitment of financial resources by multinational tour companies.

Differentiated Hospitality Products

In order to meet the needs and objectives of tourists, the hospitality sector of a destination provides a broad range of accommodations and food services from luxurious high-priced resorts and hotels to small inexpensive bed and breakfasts, with a considerable range of choices in the middle. As discussed earlier, a Louis Harris poll indicated that the two greatest fears of travelers are the quality of food and the standard of the room. The travel industry has become extremely efficient in handling food and accommodations for travelers. The growth of multinational companies throughout the world has helped to increase demand to travel. In and around Leicester Square, a popular London location, one can eat Mexican food at Chi Chi's or Taco Bell, or typical American hamburgers at Burger King; have a Mrs. Field's cookies or one of thirty-one flavors of ice cream from Baskin Robbins, for dessert. A short walk away one can eat ribs at Tony Roma's, pizza at Pizza Hut, "all you can eat" Italian food at several Italian restaurants, and lamb in pita bread from a host of small foreign shops, each of which has its own name for the food, depending upon the country of origin. For lodging, there are a number of Holiday Inns, Hiltons, and Best Westerns for the traveler concerned about having all the comforts of home.

Host-Visitor Relations

Demand has been increased to areas that provide a comfortable, positive experience for travelers. One aspect of that positive experience, and possibly the most important one, is the contact of travelers with local people. Many officials realize this fact, and governments make considerable effort to teach the public the importance of such con-

tact. In Utah, for example, a portion of the budget allocated to the Utah Travel Council and the Salt Lake Convention and Visitor's Bureau was spent on advertising in Utah telling the residents how important tourism was to the state. Utahans were told that they should treat tourists courteously and warmly so that they would either want to return or would recommend a visit to the state to friends.

A major portion of the training programs for employees of travel-related businesses is involved in the host relationship—in providing services in such a manner that tourists will feel like wanted guests.

To further enhance a visitor's stay, governments first provide the climate for businesses to develop in an area serving tourists and, second, maintain visitor's centers, print booklets of information, and so on. These visitor's centers and materials provide tourists with a listing of interesting events and activities in the local area. They assist in making the visit an experience the traveler will want to repeat in the future, and will talk about to friends and family.

Conservation and Protection

The general concern for the environment has also become important to the travel industry. Just as a destroyed or polluted environment decreases demand, an attractive environment encourages visitors. Many countries and states are developing natural areas as added tourist attractions. The government of Majorca, Spain has established a natural area for bird watching. National parks have been designed to maintain an attractive physical environment for the traveler, and wilderness areas have been created where public and private development is not allowed. There are no facilities or services provided for visitors to these regions. Governments at all levels have provided economic incentives for the management of fish and wildlife in both the private and public area which are major tourist attractions. They have also given greater thought to land use and environmental planning than in the past. Laws have been passed and funds made available to clean up the environment and to create standards for states and local governments to maintain.

PREDICTING THE IMPACT OF WORLD EVENTS ON TOURISM

Given the current trends, tourism will continue to grow in importance in the future. As more countries develop industrially, more citizens of those countries will want to travel. In addition, leisure time will increase in the industrial countries as the type of work changes and average retirement age is lowered. The changing patterns of the school year (year-round schools, for example) will increase the demand for travel at different times of the year so that it will be less seasonal in character. Transportation will continue to improve to allow tourists to travel further, more quickly, to have more destination choices, and to stay longer than previously. Tourism will be seen as both a basic right and a necessity as single people and families formulate their annual budgets. Table 2-4 lists major world events with potential impact on tourism over the next decade.

TABLE 2-4 WORLD EVENT STATEMENTS BY ENVIRONMENTAL CATEGORY*
(50/50 Likelihood of Occurrence Over the Next Ten Years)

Physical and Built Environment
1. Effective programs in most countries establish economic incentives to private industry for the protection of wildlife, scenic beauty, and natural environments.
2. Regional areas of the world establish and enforce programs to monitor and reduce pollution.
3. Reliable short-term weather predictions of one week or less are the norm.
4. Limited access to natural resources is achieved by (1) rationing, (2) drawing lots, or (3) residential qualifications.
5. Completely new frontiers and adventure opportunities are open to tourism (sea and underwater, underground, polar, desert and space environments).
6. Visitors are responsible for preserving ecological habitats of the host country.
7. Artificial environments are commonly used as substitutes for outdoor recreation areas and facilities to provide tourism opportunities.
8. Urban and regional population centers are overcrowded throughout 75% of the world.
9. Agriculture and light manufacturing are integrated with tourism in developing countries.

Economic Environment
1. An international currency is used for monetary exchange among nations of the world.
2. The number of developed and newly industrialized countries increases to 50% of the world's countries.
3. Skyrocketing insurance liability rates result in business closings and unaffordable pricing situations.
4. Labor shortages and value shifts require major organizational changes by employers—e.g., flexible work schedules, personal growth opportunities, and ownership options.
5. A major oil crisis causes major supply disruptions and gasoline price increases of 300%.
6. Real estate value boom pushes purchase prices up and encourages investment in rental properties.
7. The dollar continues to decline dramatically against major foreign hard currencies.
8. The prime interest rate increases to 20% and more.
9. Vertical and horizontal consolidation/integration of travel and tourism industry components and suppliers increase dramatically.
10. Worldwide spending for international travel doubles by the year 2000 as compared to 1986 expenditures in real terms (i.e., without inflation).
11. Major "flag" franchisers, management contractors, and developer/operator companies penetrate both traditional (hotel, motel, resort, inn, etc.) and nontraditional forms of accommodation (camping, timeshare, cruise ship, etc.).
12. A network of international travel routes for most of today's national air carriers is established.
13. Worldwide stock market crashes reoccurrence reduce travel spending and inhibit industry expansion.

Political Environment
1. Restrictions on foreign ownership of land and transnational companies inhibit economic expansion.
2. The escalation of terrorism throughout the world significantly reduces international travel.
3. Border formalities (e.g., requirements, visa, customs) of most countries are increased.
4. Mandatory retirement age in OECD countries is increased to 75.
5. The public and private sectors work together through education and cultural projects to reduce hostility toward tourists.
6. Energy saving 55 mile speed limit raised to 70 plus miles per hour in most developed countries including the U.S.
7. Global efforts to coordinate tourism-related environmental protection, consumer protection, multinational cooperation, regulation, and facilitation intensify and produce a widely accepted Tourist Bill of Rights, Code of Ethics, and widespread international cooperation.
8. Deregulation of commercial transportation carriers becomes the norm in developed countries with market economies.
9. Unfair competition becomes a major political action issue of the private sector designed to limit commercial involvement of nonprofit and public agencies.
10. Liberalization of international airline agreements makes travel movements between East and West almost as easy as within the West.
11. Tourists involved in human rights and political action contribute measurably to world peace.

Personal and Social Environment
1. The two-income family is predominant in developed countries.
2. Most people travel on other continents as commonly as in their own country today.
3. Half the urban working population throughout the world work primarily for life fulfillment rather than economic necessity.
4. The 30-hour work week and annual month-long paid vacations characterize the normal work patterns in developed countries.
5. Biochemical developments and wellness programs retard aging and extend the average human lifespan to 90 years.
6. Two separate holiday periods (summer and winter) and frequent shorter trips are dominant in developed countries.
7. Industrialized countries experience increasing resistance to travel due to cultural insularity, home/leisure substitutes for travel, saturation of tourist destinations, etc.
8. Increasing weekend travel to longer-haul destinations, 500–1,000 miles and more.
9. Nontraditional work lifestyles like telecommuting—i.e., work at home with advanced communications/computer capabilities—and other home-based compulsive time uses (chores, shopping, etc.) increase demand for travel.
10. AIDS becomes major risk factor inhibiting travel to some countries.

TABLE 2-4 (*Continued*)

Technological Environment

1. Fully automated data retrieval systems are developed on a global basis to provide travel information on a real-time basis.
2. Automation replaces most labor-intensive administrative and industrial jobs in urban areas of developed countries.
3. Major technological advances lower international travel costs to affordable prices on a middle-class budget.
4. Computer-based voice messaging systems (*i.e.*, a voice mail box) are commonly provided as a basic hotel service.
5. Inexpensive long-haul (over 100 miles or 167 KM) mass transport by water is feasible.
6. Fifty percent of the world's cash transactions occur through computerized credit, audit, buying and billing systems.
7. Air taxis to destination locations within 200 miles are integrated with major metropolitan airports in developed countries.
8. An international reservation system and data bank with video realtime communications are established for tourist information and attractions.
9. *Compunications* (integration of telecommunications and computing)—and fiber-optic cable technology will result in "postal pricing"—*i.e.*, every telephone call will be a local call.
10. Super conductor technology produces magnetic trains and energy transmissions resulting in cost-effective access to remote destinations.

Events are listed in random order.

RESEARCH AND REVIEW

1. Identify and define the two types of demand. Give an example of each.

2. Define psychographics.

3. Describe the two elements in measuring demand.

4. Identify five methods of counting tourists and gathering information. What are the strengths and weaknesses of each?

5. Discuss the characteristics of leisure and its role in tourism.

6. Describe the major factors shaping demand.

7. What are the socioeconomic factors characteristic of a person most likely to travel?

8. Discuss three societal trends and the impact they are having on travel.

9. What are eight factors in reducing demand?

10. What is discretionary income and how does it affect tourism?

11. Outline three world events and show how they will affect tourism.

ENDNOTES

1. "The Visitor Industry in Hawaii's Economy, A Cost Benefit Analysis," *Mathematica* Vol. 27–29 (1970), pp. 187–203.
2. McIntosh and Goeldner, p. 244.
3. Mill and Morrison, p. 49.
4. "Development: Assessing Your Product and the Market, 1978," *Tourism USA* (Washington, DC: U.S. Travel & Tourism Administration).
5. David L. Lewis, *The Public Image of Henry Ford* (Detroit: Wayne State Univ. Press, 1976), p. 43.
6. *Travel Industry World Yearbook—1987*, p. 7.
7. "What Do 42 Wars Add Up To?", *Washington Post*, Apr. 27, 1986, p. c5d.
8. Nanninga, p. 5.
9. Lloyd E. Hudman, "The Mental Image of Tourist Destination Region—Caribbean." Unpublished paper presented at the annual meeting of the Travel and Tourism Research Association, 1987.

PART II

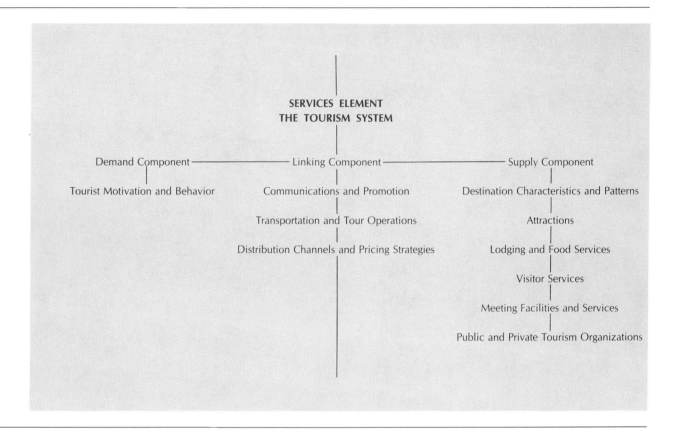

SERVICES ELEMENT
THE TOURISM SYSTEM

Demand Component ——————— Linking Component ——————— Supply Component

Tourist Motivation and Behavior ———— Communications and Promotion ———— Destination Characteristics and Patterns

Transportation and Tour Operations ———— Attractions

Distribution Channels and Pricing Strategies ———— Lodging and Food Services

Visitor Services

Meeting Facilities and Services

Public and Private Tourism Organizations

SERVICES ELEMENT:
THE TOURISM
SYSTEM

CHAPTER 3

TOURIST
MOTIVATION
AND BEHAVIOR

Tourism motivation research has generally been concerned with the concept of *push* and *pull*. The push element is composed of those factors that are sociopsychological, and have been helpful in explaining the desire to travel and to take vacations. They are referred to by some travelers as the impulse that caused a trip to take place. Thus, reasons that motivate us are push factors. This motivating process is heightened by the pull that attractions exert. The pull factors are those characteristics of a destination that draw the tourist to it. Most research in tourism and motivation is concerned with the pull aspect. The industry wishes to identify those factors which cause travelers to select specific destinations. The two forces, push and pull, operating together account for local, national, and international travel patterns. It is, therefore, important for those working in the travel industry, and students alike to understand these factors. This knowledge is necessary to develop facilities and promotional programs that will intensify the appeal of specific areas for the potential tourist. Consequently, this chapter is concerned with the characteristics of motivation and behavior.

CULTURAL DETERMINANTS OF TRAVEL

Why do people travel? Is traveling an inherent need that must be fulfilled? Each person is part of a social group, which influences behavior and instills attitudes about others. These social groups form a cultural reference point from which we gain much of our information of other people and places. For example, consider the sources that provide us with information. They are our family and friends, government, school, ethnic jokes (which in many cases are derogatory), and direct contact through visits. Visits can be very short and so limited that they may not provide enough input to change misperceptions or may reinforce them.

Culture can be defined as a set of beliefs, values, attitudes, habits, and forms of behavior; a way of life shared by a society and transmitted from generation to generation. Mill and Morrison have indicated four ways in which culture affects society. First, the overall values of the culture determine the goals and behavior that will be either socially acceptable or unacceptable to others. Second, the social culture is defined in the types of institutions formed. Third, acceptable behavior in the consumption of food at home, or away from home, is culturally determined. Fourth, the ways we communicate within our society (oral language, gestures, facial expressions, body language) affect our use of space and interaction with others. Often, our uncomfortable feelings, when in another culture, are caused by different methods of communication; yet we seldom consciously discern the origin of our discomfort.

An understanding of the role culture plays in travel is an important part of consumer behavior research. The following list identifies some important factors in analyzing a culture for developing marketing strategies aimed at people from different cultures.

Checklist for Analyzing a Culture

1. Determine relevant motivations in the culture. Which needs do people seek to fulfill?

2. Determine characteristic behavior patterns. How often are vacations purchased?

3. Determine what broad cultural values are relevant to the purchase of the product. Are vacations, leisure, and recreation thought of in positive terms?

4. Determine characteristic forms of decision-making. Who makes the vacation purchase decision? When is it made? What information sources and criteria are used in making the decision?

5. Evaluate advertising methods appropriate to the culture. What kinds of promotional techniques, words, and pictures are acceptable or unacceptable to the people of this culture?

6. Determine appropriate institutions for this product in the minds of consumers. Do people tend to purchase vacations directly from suppliers, or are retail travel agents used? What alternatives, acceptable to the consumer, are available for distributing the product?[1]

D. Louden and A. J. Della Bitta identified many common characteristics of Americans. They make simple, concise judgments, such as people are either right or wrong, good or bad. They believe "all men are created equal." There is a constant search for new technology. Americans tend to be materialistic and competitive. Most think "time is money." They admire youthfulness and products geared to it. People in the United States are always developing new products and services, whether needed or not. They are generally moral and religious.[2]

These characteristics set Americans apart from others in a number of ways, especially with respect to leisure. An article in the *Wall Street Journal* compared Europeans and Americans. The paper indicated that Europeans regard work as a means to a better family life and more vacations. However, it said that Americans consider work a basic need and a means to increased material wealth. In Europe evenings, weekends, and holidays are sacrosanct in that the people leave work at work; Americans take work home with them, or frequently call the office while on vacation. Further, it indicated that in Europe there are more restaurants, taverns, and other attractive places to spend time than in the United States; eating is considered a social event in which two or three hours is not considered unusual.[3]

Further, within a culture, subcultures exist that, with other differences, have different views on travel and use of leisure time. These subcultures can be ethnic (Spanish, Black, Jewish) or regional (southern, western, etc.).

HIERARCHY OF NEEDS

Maslow, Herzberg, and others have suggested that there is a hierarchy of human needs. According to Maslow, high up on that list is the need to travel. The reasons given are for self-preservation and the "love-romance-adventure" need. The former need is to relax—to have a change of pace, of climate, of environment, and so on. The latter need, quite naturally, is an important part of almost all vacations and travel. High self-esteem, another Maslow-defined need and an important motivating factor in travel, involves recognition and admiration by neighbors, friends, and co-workers. Even "self-actualization," the need at the pinnacle of Maslow's hierarchy, may be achieved in the culmination of a long-held dream—a specific trip.[4]

TRAVEL MOTIVATIONS

Using the clues these basic human needs provide, a model can be developed to identify the purposes and the motivating factors that cause people to travel (Table 3-1).

It should be recognized that many people travel for more than one purpose. Certainly, people living in Hawaii, San Francisco, or New Orleans may well have more visits from friends and family than if they lived in North Dakota or the panhandle of Texas. A visitor to a skiing area may select that area over others with equal or better facilities for a host of reasons. Many skiers obtain their information about ski resorts by word of mouth, which may indicate factors, other than those in the model, are at work in the selection process. However, it would not be wise to carry this argument too far, for the main purpose of the vacation, in this case skiing, is still the chief factor in deciding where to go.

Health

As noted in Chapter 1, the original motivating forces in the development of waterside resorts were the recommendations of doctors that the sick and feeble partake of

TABLE 3-1 MOTIVATORS OF TRAVEL

Health	*Spectator*	Religious headquarters
Physical	Football	Historical sites
Mental	Baseball	Drama and musical
Curiosity	Track and field	productions
Cultures	Horseracing	**Professional and Business**
Politics	**Pleasure**	Scientific expeditions
Society or public	Travel	Conventions
figures	Art	Business travel
Physical features	Music	Education
Disasters	Entertaining	**Friends and Relatives**
Sports	Gambling	**Roots Syndrome**
Participating	Honeymoon	Homeland
Hunting and fishing	**Spiritual or Religious**	Family research
Golf and tennis	Pilgrimages	**Esteem**
Team competition	Meetings	

Source: Lloyd E. Hudman, *Tourism: A Shrinking World* (Columbus, OH: Grid, 1980).

health-giving waters at spas or seaside resorts. Davos, an important winter sports center in Switzerland, began as a health resort. In the socialist countries, a considerable amount of tourism is health oriented. Indeed, the purpose of vacation travel in those countries is to restore the body and mind of the tourists so they can be productive members of society. Consequently, in the Soviet Union, there are numerous sanatoriums in the foothills of the Caucasus Mountains and along the Black Sea in towns such as Sochi, Pitsami, and Yalta. Physicians in some countries recommend a variety of environments to cure various problems. Asthma and other bronchial problems, arthritis, rheumatism, and paralysis are some common ailments that trips to certain areas help relieve. Warm Springs, Georgia and Hot Springs, Arkansas are two noteworthy examples of health resorts in the United States. President Roosevelt found the waters at Warm Springs relieved him of some health problems. Famous resorts such as these still serve their original purpose, that of restoring health. Specialized health resorts for the overweight are a modern development, particularly in the United States. Carefully planned menus and physical activities are used to slim and tone the body. The only occupation we engage in more than traveling is eating; it certainly shows on our waistlines!

However, it appears that most people choose to travel because of their mental attitude. Many people have a great desire to "get away from it all." Modern society moves at a very rapid pace; stress and strain on most people have created a need to relax, to rest. We have come, as a society, to accept the notion that a change is the equivalent of rest and relaxation. A change either in the environment, or activities, or both, provides people with that rest and relaxation. Yet the change in environment and activities needed vary from person to person. Rest to some may involve lying on a beach or fishing for most of the day. To others, it may be a day of golf, water skiing, or tennis, followed by a visit to a late night disco. Whatever the type of rest and relaxation engaged in, many travelers find a return to the "rat

race" of job and community activities often as restful as the vacation after time away.

Curiosity

Curiosity leads travelers to search for different kinds of experiences in many parts of the world. To visit other people and places or to experience other cultures and political systems are prime motivational forces for travelers. The desire to have new experiences in new places has been fueled by modern communications media such as television, which finds its way into every corner of the world. Wars, which bring diverse cultures into violent contact, also fuel curiosity. World War II and the Korean and Vietnam Wars tended to create an American awareness of those places and people. The art, way of life, folklore, music, literature, sports, and drama of other cultures have served as the focus of interest to prospective tourists. Few advertisements of Hawaii neglect to include the Polynesian Cultural Center; a trip to Guatemala is not complete, according to travel folders, without a visit to the Indian market town of Chichicastenango.

Interest in famous people or high society prompts some people (usually from the lower income bracket) to travel to certain places. Tours in large cities often include visits to the homes of movie stars, rich people, and political leaders. At the other end of the spectrum, people of middle- and higher-income groups tend to be curious about low-income environments. Harlem, South Chicago, and East Los Angeles are places of interest to some tourists. Memphis, Tennessee is currently capitalizing on the curiosity seeker's desire to see, hear, and feel the Elvis Presley "mystique."

Today, the interplay of the two dominant political systems in the world, socialism or communism and capitalism, have heightened political interest as they relate to tourism. Travel to socialist countries has increased yearly for the past five years. Travelers are eager to test a set of preconceived notions concerning the opposing political system. Nations receiving tourists from competing political ideologies perceive the influx of tourists as an opportunity to promote the virtues of their own system, and, therefore, encourage those activities and itineraries that best express their most attractive attributes.

A desire to see certain natural phenomena generates many trips. Volcanoes, high tides (such as at the Bay of Fundy), lakes, and other sights perk the interest of travelers. Many go to see the fall colors in the Ozarks or New England, climb Mount Vesuvius, or see what an Alaskan glacier is like.

Natural disasters, also attract tourists to an area. Although they affect tourist patterns only temporarily, there are some people who prolong a visit because they have a great desire to see the after effects of the disaster. (The motivation is the same as that which attracts crowds to scenes of fire, suicides, or car accidents.) For instance, some curious people traveled to Guatemala in 1976 to see what the earthquake had done.

Sports

Sports interest is one of the fastest growing generators of travel. Tourists either participate, or watch, or both. Hunting and fishing have long been popular activities in the United States. More recently, skiing, golf, and tennis have become prime motivators for travel. These industries have grown rapidly, since the key element in participation sports is the desire to obtain a healthy body. Resorts specializing in golf and tennis have sprung up all over the country, although the southeastern and southwestern states have the greatest proportion. Golf or tennis vacations may be taken all through the year. While those who travel to hunt and fish come from a broad socioeconomic background; skiing, golf, and tennis are more often played by those with higher incomes, particularly those with professional occupations.

In the United States, the interest in traveling to watch a sporting event began at the turn of the century, first with baseball, then basketball and boxing. Since that time, the preoccupation with spectator sports has grown quite spectacularly. Little has changed today or is likely to change in the foreseeable future. Most major newspapers have a section for sports. With cable television becoming increasingly common there are many channels allocated only to sports. The motivating force behind spectator sports is threefold. First, there is the desire to "get away from it all." Athletic events allow us to escape for a few minutes or hours and become absorbed in experiences that allow us to vent a variety of emotions.

Second, many sports gatherings become social events that, to the participants, may be more important than the game itself. For example, just sitting in the bleachers at a baseball game is an experience apart from the game. There are people from all social levels engaged in a variety of activities, none of which is directly related to the game. Baseball probably is the greatest class equalizer in the United States today. The importance of this identification can be explained by almost every college athletic director or alumni director in the country. When a school's team is doing well, donations flow into the university's coffers much more easily than when they are not.

Third, there is the element of fantasy. Sports allow people, young or old, to dream of the role they would fulfill if they were playing. Rare are the men who have not pictured themselves striking out the opposing side in a crucial world series game, or hitting a game's winning home run, or sinking the final basket at the buzzer, or throwing the winning touch-down pass in a football game.

All three—escape, identification, and fantasy—are important motivational forces that cause Americans to become involved in spectator sports. The old baseball song, "Take Me Out to the Ball Game," embodies the three forces. Sports make an important contribution to our way of life.

Pleasure

The importance of pleasure as a tourist motivator was expressed by McIntosh and Goeldner when they wrote

Perhaps uppermost of all individual travel motivations is simply the motivation for satisfying a person's need for pure pleasure. . . Travel has the unique quality of being able to satisfy that desire.[5]

It is the pleasure principle that the travel industry focuses upon most of all in its effort to promote services and tours. The development of Las Vegas, Lake Tahoe, Monte Carlo, and Atlantic City has been a response to the public's desire for pleasure. The national parks were, in part, developed because of this same desire; scenic areas, mountain, and lakes are thrilling to see and give considerable pleasure. People are drawn to entertainment centers such as New York, London, Los Angeles, and other capitals.

The cruise industry has grown increasingly popular as more and more people search for new avenues of pleasure. Cruise advertising focuses on sun, fun, and relaxation, with a touch of romance for spice. In 1986, revenues for the cruise industry were an estimated $4 billion, more than five times the amount spent in 1970.

Honeymoon travel is another expression of the pleasure-seeking trend. A sizeable honeymoon market exists today in spite of changing family mores.

The planning of a trip is important to the pleasure principle in many, if not all, cases. The hours spent in looking through travel folders, magazines, and newspapers, and in studying maps and other informational sources, or talking with friends and neighbors are a large part of the fun. The anticipation of the event is part of the excitement of a vacation.

Crompton, in a research project to determine the nature of pleasure motivation, found that almost all the respondents in his study felt that the principal motivator for a pleasurable vacation was a break from routine. This idea can be viewed in two ways. First, the continuation of routine (lifestyle), but in a different place gives pleasure. Second, a change in the routine (increasing or emphasizing certain elements of the lifestyle rather than changing them) to incorporate different activities, is also a pleasure motivator. For example, if people enjoyed sports such as tennis, golf, and the like, they are likely to increase that sport's activity during their vacation.[6]

Crompton's research further indicated that the motivator is important in creating a desire to travel, rather than a desire for a specific location. The people in the study were not looking for a destination to fulfill their needs, rather a need existed before a destination was sought. Motivators that caused pleasure-seeking, Crompton referred to as *sociopsychological behaviors*. The sociopsychological motivators were divided into seven categories: escape from perceived mundane environment; exploration and evaluation of self; relaxation; prestige; regression; enhancement of kinship relationships; and facilitation of social interaction. By regression, Crompton meant the participation in behavior in one's own environment.

Spiritual or Religious

Religion also gives rise to travel. There are four, or maybe five, broad categories of such travel: pilgrimages, meetings, visits to religious headquarters, visits to historical sites, and attendance at religious dramas and musicals. There are differences between these categories and within them. There is a difference between travelers of one faith visiting the headquarters of another faith and people visiting their own church headquarters. For the former, the prime motivation is curiosity, while the latter is usually spiritually motivated. In addition, there is fine line between a pilgrimage and a visit to religious headquarters, though for prac-

tical purposes they may be the same. The difference in this case might be defined as a difference in the level of spiritual involvement on the part of the traveler. A pilgrimage is associated with deep spiritual experiences and miracle. A trip to Lourdes or Fatima to be cured of an illness may be a pilgrimage. Visits by people in Central America to the Black Christ in Guatemala, or those in southern Europe to Guadalupe, Spain to worship at the statue of Mary and the Christ child (reputed to have been found by a miracle) are pilgrimages. The special trip to Mecca by peoples of the Arab world has a spiritual significance that transcends a simple visit to church headquarters; this, therefore, would be considered a pilgrimage.

Travel to visit the headquarters of a church is a very important motivator for travel. Catholics travel to Rome, Jews to Israel, and Latter-Day Saints (Mormons) to Salt Lake City. Travel to attend meetings such as church conferences, revivals, and so on are other examples of travel for religious purposes.

Another area of religious travel involves trips to see dramas, plays, and historical sites. Such activities serve as faith-promoting experiences that enable travelers to draw closer to their own faith. The Passion Play in Germany draws travelers of many faiths, as do the historical sites associated with Christ in Israel.

Professional and Business

Business travel is the third most important reason given for travel in the 1986 National Travel Survey. It was also listed as the third most important reason for international travel from the United States on passport application blanks. Since business travel is relatively inelastic, it is especially

Fatima Shrine. Photo courtesy of the Portuguese National Tourist Office.

significant. Businesspeople tend to stay in the best hotels and eat at expensive restaurants. In addition, they use a variety of transportation options including car rentals. Business travelers accounted for eighty-five percent of all air travel in 1985. The auto rental industry is highly dependent on the business traveler. Water's survey indicated that sixty-five percent of all car rentals are leased by business travelers.[7]

There are at least four categories of business travel: scientific expeditions, conventions, company travel, and educational travel.

Scientific expeditions account for a relatively small proportion of the total amount of business travel. Since research projects are included in this type of travel, scientific expeditions are broadly defined. They range from *National Geographic* expeditions to the Amazon River to individual studies of market towns in Africa.

There is a vast amount of convention travel. An estimated $34.6 billion was spent in the United States in 1986 for off-premises corporate meetings, association meetings, and conventions.[8] Resorts and large cities are favorite meeting places for conventions.

Business travel is important in the United States, and will remain so as the white-collar labor force grows and corporate headquarters expand into the suburbs. The continued practice of building airports in easily accessible locations will help maintain the business market. The mixing of business travel with pleasure is well known. In 1982, 16.9 percent of the respondents to a survey stated that they traveled with a spouse according to *Travel Market Yearbook* indicators.[9]

Travel for educational purposes includes travel programs offered by high schools and colleges to students and teachers.

Friends and Relatives

The most important motivation for travel, as indicated by respondents to a United States national survey in 1986, was the desire to visit friends and relatives. Most of this traveling is by private automobile. Traveling by road puts more emphasis on the route than it does on the destination. Motels and campgrounds are designed specifically for the traveler who is passing through an area. A chief concern of the travel industry are those people who are visiting family and friends. Indeed, many stay with the friends and relatives they are visiting. These travelers are "lost" to the travel industry unless the friend or relative lives in an exotic or interesting place.

Roots Syndrome

A desire to visit a homeland (the country from which a traveler's ancestors came) is another strong motivation for travel. Since vast numbers of United States immigrants from past centuries came from European countries, there are many descendants of those peoples who wish to visit the land of their forebears. Many travel agencies specialize in certain ethic areas providing specialized tours to visit "the old country."

"Going home!" The words can have a particularly sweet sound for people who have been raised in the United States, but are going back to trace their roots. Many of these Americans find travel agents specializing in such trips, in newspapers circulated in ethnic communities throughout the country, especially in those New York City neighborhoods to which many immigrants first came.

When visiting Poland, one can see a large number of tour groups at the Holiday Inn in Krakow. Almost all of these specialized tours were arranged by agencies in Chicago, Milwaukee, and Toronto, Canada where there are large numbers of Polish descendants living. Part of this traveling is to identify family lines through genealogical research. The surge in this type of traveling was sparked when Alex Haley's *Roots* was published and, later, televised. Many people have developed a strong interest in tracing their family genealogies.

Esteem

There are those who travel for the express purpose of impressing others ("keeping up with the Jones's"). This is characteristic of "jet-set" travel. The implication is that there are some places that only "special" people go; therefore, those who would like to feel that they are equally special go to those same places. Birds of a feather flock together— and those who want to be like them, travel like them. To be the first to go to an exotic place, or to go where certain types of other people go, offers some excitement, and creates an illusion of sophistication for the envy of one's friends. Club Mediterranee visits may be tinged with a little snobbery. In many cases, even a simple tour of Europe, the Caribbean, or Hawaii is a prestige builder. This behavior occurs at all levels of society. In fact, there is probably just a little snob appeal in all travel. It is a positive experience that creates a special aura, and makes one the center of attention when sharing memories with others.

Summary

People's reasons for travel are wide and diverse. Although nine basic motivating factors have been identified, it is often difficult to isolate a single specific reason for any given trip. In fact, most trips are motivated by more than one factor, since we unconsciously tend to choose vacations that satisfy a combination of needs. There is a certain degree of curiosity, pleasure, and prestige in all trips. For example, the Olympics in Moscow combined an interest in sports with an interest in a socialist political system. The Soviet Union understood this, and prior to the Olympics gave Moscow a face-lifting unequaled in history. When television rights were sold for the Olympics, they also included the right to broadcast programs about the country and its political advancements.

SOCIAL AND PSYCHOLOGICAL CONSIDERATIONS

Man is a unique species with attributes that make it possible for an industry such as tourism to develop on an extremely large scale. Man is a social animal, with desires beyond the basic needs of shelter, food, safety, and comfort. This combination of needs and desires has given impetus to one of the largest industries today—the travel industry.

Human beings are dependent upon others, and seek to establish social contacts. Often people escape the crowded conditions of the city only to deliberately choose a vacation spot in the middle of other high-density areas. "Getting away from it all" finds us at crowded beaches, amusement parks, restaurants, and the like. Vacation centers and resorts, like Club Mediterranee, have grown in response to this need. A knowledge of people's needs helps the travel industry plan and establish tours, activities, and places to visit. Group tours provide people with companionship, as well as the necessary shelter and food.

As we've said, many tourists feel more at ease when they can obtain familiar food, communicate with fellow travelers, and sleep in accommodations maintained by a familiar organization. How many areas of the world now boast a Kentucky Fried Chicken, a McDonald's, a Burger King, or a Holiday Inn? They also feel more secure if they can speak their native language in foreign countries.

An advertisement in Torremolinos, Spain, for employment in travel and tourism indicated that if prospective employees spoke only in Spanish they need not apply.

Many tourists appear to want new experiences, if they can take along a little bit of home.

DETERRENTS TO TRAVEL

There are those who refuse to travel. There are a variety of reasons for this. Most of them concern health, finances, security, isolation, time, and family.[10]

Some people, particularly the handicapped and elderly, have physical limitations that impede travel. The handicapped, with physical impairments that require the use of wheelchairs, walkers, and the like have been somewhat overlooked by the travel industry until recently. While modern, technologically advanced nations are responding to the need for facilities that accommodate the handicapped, many countries still have barriers, that inhibit the handicapped travelers.

The elderly, who have a higher incidence of health problems that require constant medical care, have traditionally been reluctant to travel. The age group over sixty-five, not only travels the least, but also has the highest proportion of nontravelers. Slower motor responses, tiring more easily, as well as special dietary needs, make travel less inviting for the elderly.

There are some people who lack the necessary financial resources to travel. The ratio of nontravelers to travelers is the highest for those with incomes under $10,000 per year, almost three nontravelers for every traveler. The lower the net income, the lower is the disposable income available for traveling.

Many people have psychological reasons for not traveling. Some feel very uncomfortable in strange surroundings, are afraid of not being understood because of language differences, and are unwilling to meet and mix with new people. They may fear that the food (whether familiar or new) and water will make them sick, or that traveling by either air or water, or both, will be hazardous.

These nontravelers are happy and quite comfortable with their surroundings, and have no wish to experience the delights of tourism. They make a conscious choice to spend their disposable incomes on activities near their homes. Their leisure pursuits are within close range—golf, tennis, movies, parks, lakes, and hobbies at home. Special local interests consume the time that might have been spent traveling. McIntosh reported a survey in which twenty-nine percent of the respondents stated they would rather stay at home than take a trip.[11]

Some people do not have the opportunity to travel because of lack of time. Small independent businesspeople often find themselves so bound to their businesses that they are unable to take a vacation. Some small grocers, for example, operate twelve to fourteen hours a day, seven days a week. They generally have family stores which they are unable to close because there is no other source of income.

Some people are simply workaholics! They choose not to take a vacation because they feel they are so important to the job, or the job is so important to them.

Other people do not travel for family reasons, perhaps because a family member requires constant care. If the family is unable to make arrangements for that person's care, they will not take a vacation. Some families with young children are unwilling to undertake the perceived inconvenience of traveling with them. Also, families with several children might not have the finances to travel.

The industry has responded to these last two problems by developing campsites, mobile home parks, and tent trailers that allow for easier, more comfortable, and in some cases, less expensive family vacations. Major motel chains now offer rooms on a family plan—they charge the regular rate for two adults, but the children stay free.

The two basic human needs of safety and comfort and the desire to travel are at opposite poles. Therein lies the task of the travel industry: to provide a service that fulfills the need for safety, comfort, and well-being, while offering the excitement and stimulation that come from visiting places, meeting people, and having new experiences.

In many cases, people don't admit to an outright fear of travel, but they do express concerns pertaining to trips. Louis Harris and Associates conducted a survey for American Airlines of some deterrents to travel. The results suggest the importance that the industry should place on assisting people in their traveling. Travel agents, tour operators, hotel and motel chains, and restaurants can help alleviate tourists' fears. The standardization of rooms and food throughout the world encourages people, who would like to take a little bit of "home" with them. The more assurances travel agents can give their clients, the less anxious they will be. In addition, agents and tour operators can provide travelers with information about clothing and cash, as well as making arrangements for the trip. Of course weather and family problems cannot be controlled by the f travel agencies, but in most other areas they can relieve the anxieties that some travelers have.

INFLUENCE OF MOTIVATORS—DETERRENTS TO TRAVEL

The travel industry and travelers are influenced both negatively and positively as they respond to motivating forces. As a result of recognizing and using this knowledge, the travel industry has grown.

For many travelers, the pleasure derived from one trip becomes a motivating force to plan future trips; for others, if their trip is frustrating and unenjoyable, this lessens the desire for future trips. Psychiatrists and psychologists refer to this latter group as those with "vacation blues syndrome."

Some people return from a vacation feeling tense and depressed because it did not meet their expectations. They complain about high gasoline prices, incompetent hotel employees, and poor airline schedules. They appear convinced that many situations were beyond their control, thus the fun they had planned to have did not materialize. Some characteristics contributing to "vacation blues" have been identified as resulting from family stress, choosing the wrong type of vacation, misusing time, and the magnification of existing family problems.

Days spent in close contact in some instances, will create friction, no matter how loving the family's normal relationship, especially in unfamiliar surroundings. Frequently, the breadwinner and head of the household suddenly becomes disposable because he or she becomes just one of the family. Decisions become family decisions—with each member having the same amount of input. The breadwinner may react negatively.

There are those in our industrial society who still view leisure time as a negative experience. They are unable to relax, enjoy new sights, form new friendships, learn something new, improve a skill, pursue a hobby, or just get a tan. In many cases, they expect too much from a trip; they can't cope with all the free time. In addition, if they have planned an active time and bad weather or other problems interfere, they then become bored.

Some people take the wrong kind of vacation; either their own interests do not match those provided at the vacation site, or they choose the wrong season. People who prefer tennis or golf vacations will not be happy on European tours visiting museums and churches, or sitting on a bus for long stretches of time. Those who prefer mountain climbing will feel they have wasted their time on a Caribbean cruise.

In general, the most likely victim of vacation blues, regardless of age, sex, or race, is the hard-driving achiever who feels guilty about spending time on frivolous leisure pursuits, or on anything other than work. Some do justify their vacations, but on the pretext that the experience is not related to rest and relaxation; that getting a tan is good for the complexion, that bicycle riding tones up the leg muscles, or that visiting museums improves the mind.

TOURIST BEHAVIOR

People are motivated in different ways by different stimuli, and not all people react the same way to the same stimuli. For example, there are those who take trips for social approval or social status, while others may do so out of curiosity. People normally spend a large portion of their income on necessities: food, shelter, medical expenses, clothing, etc. What is left of the income is used with discretion, according to the strength of their motives. This discretionary income can be used in a number of ways, one of which is to travel. Once the initial choice has been made, there are many other kinds of choices to make. The motives for all the choices are important factors in the selection of a particular travel experience. Those involved in the industry know of this behavior pattern and use it to create different forms of advertising. The goal of any company or industry is to identify those people most likely to use their products, then to attract them with persuasive advertising.

Psychocentric and Allocentric Types

A number of efforts have been made to classify people according to types in order to identify those most likely to be motivated to select a particular type of service. One such study, by Stanley Plog, categorized people as either psychocentrics or allocentrics. Allocentric people were described as being outgoing, self-confident, curious, and willing to experiment and seek adventure. Psychocentric people were described as being concerned with themselves and small problems; they were, in general, anxious, unadventurous, and inhibited. A summary of Plog's study describing the differences between the two types is illustrated in Table 3-2.

This classification can be diagrammed along a continuum from allocentric to psychocentric. However, few people are either entirely psychocentric or allocentric; most lie between the two extremes on the scale. Figure 3-1 illustrates the type of vacation destination chosen by psychocentrics and allocentrics.

The scale indicates that people with psychocentric personalities usually are attracted to destinations that are well-known and familiar such as Coney Island or Miami Beach; while allocentrics, who are adventurous, curious, outgoing, and energetic, will usually be attracted to off-beat destinations such as those in the South Pacific, Africa, and the Orient. Those in the middle of the scale, who comprise the bulk of the population of the United States, are attracted to destinations such as those in Hawaii, the Caribbean, Europe, and Mexico.

Plog, in his research, found a relationship between the extremes and income.[12] He found that families with lower incomes tend to be psychocentrics, and people at the upper end of the income levels tend to be allocentrics. However, a number of other factors need to be taken into account. College students, who have a high propensity to travel, but little income, may not choose vacations consistent with

TABLE 3-2 PSYCHOCENTRICS AND ALLOCENTRICS

Psychocentrics	Allocentrics
Familiar travel destinations	Nontourist destinations
Common activities at destinations	New experiences
	Sense of discovery
Sun and fun spots	Visit before others
Relaxation	New and unusual destinations
Prefers driving	Prefers flying
Heavy tourist accommodations such as hotel development, family-type restaurants, and tourist shops	High activity level
	Tour accommodations should include adequate to good hotels and food, not necessarily modern or chain-type hotels and few tourist attractions
Family atmosphere (e.g., hamburger stands), familiar entertainment, no foreign atmosphere	Enjoy meeting and dealing with people from a strange or foreign culture
Complete tour packaging with heavy scheduling of activities	Tour arrangements should include basics such as transportation and hotels and allow considerable freedom and flexibility

Source: Stanley C. Plog, "Why Destination Areas Rise and Fall in Popularity," *The Cornell Hotel and Restaurant Administration Quarterly* (Nov. 1973).

their types due to financial constraints. Also, people change. Travel itself changes people's attitudes toward travel.

Once people begin to travel, the experience often leads them to expand their destination field, and they become more allocentric. In addition, over time, the attractiveness of some destinations will change, becoming more or less acceptable to the masses. A successful destination area will attract tourists in greater and greater numbers until it is no longer a prestigious place to visit. The French Riviera and Acapulco, in Mexico—resorts that began as "musts" for the jet-set—are examples of this reversal. The destinations have become so commercial, offering more of the amenities and recreation facilities that delight those in the middle of the scale, that people at the upper end of the social scale no longer go there. Today, Acapulco vacationers can spend a week in a Holiday Inn or other hotels, along a highly developed beach. They may watch people para-gliding, surfing, or sunbathing on the beach or at the poolside; they may take a jeep ride or a tour to a nearby village to discover something new and different. Much around them will be familiar, with the possible exception of the language. It is important to note that the uniqueness of Acapulco disappeared as it became highly commercialized in order to attract more tourists. The area changed to attract those in the middle section of the psychographic types; there was

PSYCHOGRAPHIC TYPE AND POPULATION CHARACTERISTIC

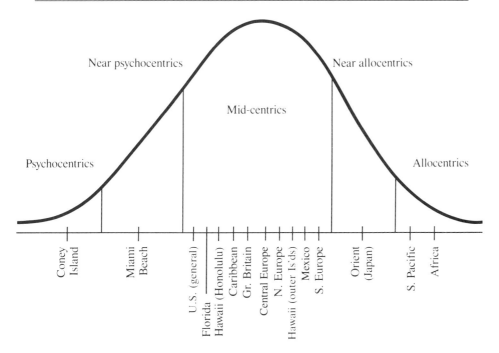

Figure 3-1: Source: Stanley G. Plog, "Why Destination Areas Rise and Fall in Popularity," *Cornell Hotel and Restaurant Administration Quarterly*, Nov. 1973.

a standardization and Americanization of accommodations, food, activities, and entertainment.

It would be unwise to assume a direct linkage between the two types of tourists and the destinations they choose. Since the travel industry provides facilities to make people feel safe and comfortable while traveling, a psychocentric may choose a well-planned, fully-escorted tour, while an allocentric may choose a resortlike complex close to home. What must be kept in mind is of twofold importance to the industry. First, travel counselors must understand the prospective traveler's psychological and demographic profile to provide services and travel experiences that are worthwhile and satisfying to the client. Second, a knowledge of psychological profiles and motivating forces, as they relate to the promotion and marketing of the various products, is important to the travel industry. The industry has recognized these two important facts and spends considerable time and money identifying those people who would be most likely to use their specific services in order to create the appropriate advertising.

Market Segmentation

The question most often asked by the various organizations who market tourism products is, "Who are the buyers?" Market segmentation is an attempt to identify those most likely to be motivated through advertising to become a buyer of a particular tourist product. Of prime interest to the tourist marketer are sex, age, location, marital status, size of family, education, occupation, and income level; therefore, tourist buyers are grouped (segmented) according to these variables. Each market segment identifies the characteristics of a specific group (the market target) who are most likely to use a particular product or travel service. Table 3-3 provides a listing of segmentation categories describing behaviorial characteristics of trip activity.

In a study made to determine the effectiveness of advertising and proper advertising methods, the Hawaii Visitor's Bureau concluded that the profile of a typical mainland tourist was the following:

> The visitor is a female, in her middle forties, from California. She has arrived by plane, stayed for ten days at a hotel. She came for pleasure and visited one or more of the neighbor islands. She was highly satisfied with her visit to Hawaii and plans to return.[13]

When considering that the typical advertisement was of a young woman wearing a skimpy swimming suit in an attractive tropical Hawaiian setting, there was concern about whether this advertisement was instrumental in attracting the typical visitor as described above. Interestingly, it was found that the advertisement did reach that market.

One marketing strategy to attract a particular segment of the population can be *not* to advertise. An example of this can be seen at Caesar's Palace in Las Vegas, where they want to attract "high rollers." High rollers are those who will win or lose approximately $20,000 or more during a short visit. The management of Caesar's Palace determined not to buy advertising space to attract customers, so there has never been a Caesar's Palace magazine, nor a television, radio, or newspaper advertisement. However, they do advertise specific events and entertainers who appear at their hotel.

To attract these large bettors, Caesar's Palace set out to create an attractive environment through personalized service, architecture and design, a sensitive credit policy, and the holding of special events that sets it apart from the other hotels in Las Vegas. During championship fights and other sporting events, the casino is packed with both high rollers and others wanting to be in on the action.[14]

The industry is divided into many market segments as each sector of the industry—hotels, airlines, restaurants, states, cities—has a different market to which it appeals. In addition, within each of these sectors, different companies have different market targets. Different airlines, for example, target different areas of the population for their principal market, such as business travel or vacation travel.

The most basic type of segmentation is finding out who travels and who does not. In Chapter 2, we identified the people most likely to travel. It was shown that there is an association between income and education and the likelihood for travel. Consequently, little effort is made by companies to reach either people with low incomes or those with little education. By further restricting their markets, companies can create the kind of advertising that would be most effective for those markets. Some other examples will further illustrate this point. In a study for the state of New York, Doyle listed the characteristics of various psychographic profiles. (See Table 3-4.)

In addition to the socioeconomic and psychographic segments, other segmentations can be made according to a host of variables such as business, leisure travel, group travel, individual travel, ethnic, young or old travelers, outdoor enthusiasts, photographers, ad infinitum. The market segments determine the product to be sold.

Psychographic research identifies market objectives in order to develop research that will identify the most likely people to use a particular service or product (target market). *Tourism USA* summarizes the importance of target marketing as follows:

> One certain way to fail is to try to please everyone. Everyone is not an equally avid tourist and, therefore, everyone is not equally important as a potential tourism visitor. Markets can be defined in a number of ways. Geographic segmentation, for example, might allow the tourism promoter to focus on a particular city or group of cities or, perhaps, only on locations within a specified distance of the site. Similarly, the age of tourists or the stage in family life cycle may provide a very good basis for market segmentation. By examining past research, you might find, for example, that a heavy incidence of travelers to a particular site are families with children aged six to fifteen. Similarly, you may find that few young unmarrieds or visitors under age twenty-five visit that particular site.

TABLE 3-3 TRAVEL SEGMENTS

1. **Purpose of Trip**
   A. Pleasure—e.g., touring, city, theme park/special event, friends and relatives, tournaments/sporting events
   B. Personal—e.g., health, investment, social obligations, education, volunteerism
   C. Business—e.g., government, commercial, nonprofit
   D. Convention meetings—e.g., government association, corporate, social functions
   E. Incentive

2. **Distribution Channel Utilization**
   A. Vendor/supplier direct sales—e.g., airlines, hotels, rental cars, attractions
   B. Travel agent intermediaries
   C. Tour operators or wholesalers
   D. Electronic reservation and booking system
   E. Government marketing organizations

3. **Socioeconomic and Demographic Characteristics**
   A. Age
   B. Education
   C. Sex
   D. Income
   E. Family size
   F. Life cycle stage
   G. Home ownership (primary and second home) or rental
   H. Race (ethnic group)
   I. Handicapped/mobility impairment
   J. Occupation

4. **Psychographic Characteristics**
   A. Personality traits
   B. Attitudes, interest, and opinions
   C. Motivations and expectations
   D. Lifestyle typologies
   E. Activity and experience preference/patterns

5. **Service Requirements**
   A. Accommodation—e.g., hotels, motels, B&B, friends and relatives, boat charter
   B. Transportation modes, origin to destination and at destination—e.g., airlines, rail, bus, rental, auto
   C. Recreation facility and equipment use—e.g., ski, marina, camping
   D. Business facility (equipment—e.g., telex, telefax, computer)

6. **Destination/Product-Related Preference/Use Patterns**
   A. Brand-loyalty
   B. Method of booking
   C. Advertising and promotion reach—e.g., advertising, direct mail
   D. Length of stay
   E. Frequency of use
   F. Participation in frequent user programs—e.g., frequent flyer
   G. Satisfaction level
   H. Pricing—e.g., market, discount, upscale
   I. Response to position statements (image campaigns)

7. **Geographic Factors**
   A. Trip origin—e.g., city, county, state, country
   B. Statistical unit—e.g., SMSA, zip code
   C. Residence characteristic—e.g., degree of urbanization, population density
   D. Transportation hubs, routing, and access points

8. **Trip Characteristics**
   A. Individual or group itinerary
   B. First time or repeat visitor
   C. Season-peak, shoulder, off-season

Source: Developed by Donald E. Hawkins.

TABLE 3-4 PSYCHOGRAPHIC SEGMENTS

Outdoor Enthusiasts	Sun Resorters
Who they are:	
Mostly married with children	Mostly married with children highest incomes
Cross-section by age and income	Fewer are college educated
Fewer have college education	Women and large-city skew
Majority are men	
What they look for:	
Country vacation	Resorts on seashores
Beautiful scenery, mountains lakes, parks	Well known, exciting, "in" places.
Unspoiled beauty	Hot climate in cold months
What kinds of facilities:	
Not preoccupied with quality	Top quality, modern resorts
Little interest in luxury or extras	Comfort, luxury, extras
Many go camping	Top-name entertainers
Little interest in packages	Planned activities
Spend less than others	Good value, packages
	Spend above average
What they like to do:	
Focus on nature and the outdoors	Beach, swimming, sunbathing
Fishing or hunting, sailing, hiking	Having fun, lots do to
Less interest in beach, swimming	Good nightlife
Low interest in golf, tennis	Golf, tennis
Little interest in nightlife	
Where they go:	
Majority vacation in the North	Almost half vacation in sun states
Favor New England and New York	Florida a favorite
Least likely to go to a city or go overseas	Favor Caribbean when going overseas

Source: William S. Doyle, Joseph Pernica, Martin Stern, "Some Technical Aspects of a Recent Study of Tourism in New York State," *The 80s: Its Impact on Travel and Tourism Marketing* (Salt Lake City: Bureau of Economic and Business Research, Univ. of Utah, 1977).

Other ways for segmenting tourism, which may be even superior, are available. Some of these are sociodemographic/economic and psychobehavioral. Among them are activities, equipment, skill levels of benefits wanted, psychographic factors, and volume of use. Care must be taken to identify good market descriptors so that a few specific markets can be actively cultivated, while others may be entirely passed over. Seldom are budgetary resources so abundant that promotion can use a shotgun approach to market development. Moreover, it is virtually impossible to write advertising copy that will motivate everyone. It is much more effective to carefully study your major market segments or a specific potential market that has a good probability of being developed.[15]

RESEARCH AND REVIEW

1. What is the definition of culture and how does it affect society?

2. Compare and contrast common cultural characteristics of Europeans and Americans.

3. Identify and discuss five motivators of travel.

4. What are four different types of religious travel?

5. Identify and discuss five types of deterrents to travel.

6. What are three causes of vacation blues?

7. How does the concept of allocentric and psychocentric help in understanding travel motivation?

8. What is market segmentation? Give some examples of different types.

ENDNOTES

1. David L. Louden and Albert J. Della Bitta, *Consumer Behavior: Concepts and Applications* (NY: McGraw-Hill Book Co., 1979), pp. 135-139.
2. Ibid.
3. Susan Carey, "Joie de Leisure," *Wall Street Journal*, Ap. 21, 1986, pp. 9D and 14D.
4. A. H. Maslow, "A Theory of Human Motivation," *Psychological Review*, Vol. 50, No. 4 (July, 1973), pp. 370-396.
5. McIntosh and Goeldner, p. 176.

6. John L. Crompton, "A Systems Model of the Tourists Destination Selection Process with Particular Reference to the Roles of Image and Perceived Constraints," Diss. Texas A & M Univ., 1977.
7. *Travel Industry Yearbook,* 1985, p. 118.
8. *Travel Industry Yearbook,* 1987, p. 15.
9. *Travel Market Yearbook,* (NY: Ziff Davis Publishing Co., 1982) p. 90.
10. *The Changing Travel Market,* 1964, p. 11.
11. McIntosh and Goeldner, p. 174.
12. Stanley C. Plog, "Why Destination Areas Rise and Fall in Popularity," *The Cornell Hotel and Restaurant Administration Quarterly* Vol. 14, No. 4 (Feb. 1974), pp. 55–58.
13. Evelyn K. Richardson and Ernest J. Donehower, "Tourism Marketing Research and Its Applications—The Hawaii Case," *Report of Proceedings* (Honolulu, HI: Sixth PATA Travel Research Seminar, 1978), p. 12.
14. Bill Weinberger, Jr. "Marketing for the Premium Gaming Customer—Caesar's Palace Experience," (Salt Lake City: Univ. of Utah: XII Annual Conference, Travel and Tourism Assn., 1981), pp. 23–26.
15. *Tourism USA: Guidelines for Tourism Development* (Washington, DC: U.S. Dept. of Commerce, U.S. Travel & Tourism Admin., 1986), pp. 120–121.

CHAPTER 4

DESTINATION CHARACTERISTICS AND PATTERNS

Tourism is an interaction between people of two unique places. People with a propensity to travel, travel from one region, with distinctive characteristics, to another region, with its own set of distinctive characteristics. Considerable research has been conducted to understand the character of both the region of origin and the destination region. Volumes of statistics are published by various agencies at international, national, and local levels, which provide information concerning the amount and degree of interaction that occurs at each level.

Chapter 2 was concerned with the factors that influence the demand that exists in the regions from which tourists originate. This chapter is concerned with tourism destination characteristics, beginning with development (or potential development) and continuing through the evolution of an area as a destination. It will briefly describe the patterns that exist on an international level between demand (origin) and destination regions.

GEOGRAPHIC AND ACCESSIBILITY FACTORS

The potential degree of tourism development of a destination is associated with its geography and accessibility. The three major components of a tourism development model are the *resource base, market,* and *physical and cultural characteristics.* (There are other lesser criteria such as population and infrastructure.) These three factors interact and indicate the potential for tourism development of a destination area.

The Resource Base

The foundation for potential tourism development has to be the resource base—everything else is built on it. Good transportation facilities and the infrastructure will not de-

50

velop in an undesirable location. Ferrario suggested that the study and assessment of this basic component should be undertaken by those who have a strong desire to develop an area, since all further development will depend upon it. He suggested that studies of areas are often little more than unevaluated, detailed lists of all possible attractions.[1]

The resource base includes both physical and cultural characteristics. The physical characteristics of an area can be generalized as natural scenery, climate, and the environment. The natural scenery is a composite of the general topography, flora, and fauna; proximity to lakes, rivers, sea, islands, and islets; hot and mineral-water springs; caverns; waterfalls; absence of water; etc. The greater the variety and uniqueness of the scenery, the more appealing it is. Consequently, it has a greater potential for tourism development. The appeal can be increased if the area has a "comfortable" climate. A comfortable cold climate is determined by the wind chill factor—a term used to express how temperature feels to the exposed skin. A comfortable warm climate is determined by a combination of humidity, temperature, and wind. Thus, the Caribbean is an excellent example of the latter because, although many of its islands are in the tropical zone, the wind currents make it more comfortable than the temperature and humidity would indicate. Sometimes when a climate is uncomfortable, particularly beautiful vistas can make up for some of the discomfort. The fjords of Norway are more impressive in a rain storm. The flow of waterfalls into the fjords is increased. Despite the intense cold outside, Glacier Bay, in Alaska, is most enjoyed from the deck of a ship where you can hear and see the glaciers breaking up into the bay.

Given the appealing characteristics of climate, resources, such as water, are needed to support development. Potential environmental problems of pollution and waste disposal must be evaluated, so that the development of an area won't destroy its natural beauty. In other words, if development were to occur, would the location still be scenic and draw tourists? Another issue concerning site development is whether there is sufficient land with appealing characteristics available. Some problems can be overcome with development. Miami Beach was a swamp in its natural state; Cancun was set in a scenic waterscape, but sand had to be brought in to develop a beach. Both have been developed into major tourist attractions. The aesthetics of a site can add or detract from its potential.

The suggestion here is that destination development can occur at two levels. First the macro level (the broad, general characteristics of the area), with its climate, scenery, water, etc. that form the primary basis for developing an area. The second level is at the micro level; it is the character and quality of the actual site that can be developed. Thus, the location available for development can either enhance or detract from the general area. For example, a very scenic coastal cove with a small beach may only have a location suitable for development that would exclude a good view of the coastal cove; or it might have a beach too small to support the number of guests at a hotel; or it might detract from the general environment of the area. On the other hand, a facility built to provide easy

and quick access to the views, or to offer easy access to the beach, would be in high demand. The Stralheim Hotel, in Norway, built in the grand hotel style on a level mountainside location at the junction of two major valleys, offers visitors breathtaking views of deep valleys cut by glaciers. Because the hotel is so popular, and accommodations are limited, many travel companies only include the hotel as a short stop for tour groups, just to admire the scenery.

Switzerland, recognizing the importance of the building environment as part of the landscape, formulated some rather stringent regulations for development that accomplish two objectives. The first is concerned with the protection of the environment. Developers must assure the government that the development will not detract from nor degrade the natural environment. The second concern is for the aesthetic character and size. A developer who built a large hotel, which was not in keeping with Swiss regulations for chateau architecture, was required to destroy the completed building. He had to rebuild to bring his facility into conformity with the environment and the aesthetic standard required by the Swiss government.

The second major element of the resource base is the availability of culture in the region, which either can be a major attraction or can be developed into one. Among these are plays, dramas, or museums.

Combining factors, such as the cultural and physical, increases the potential for development. For example, Chichicastenango, Guatemala, a famous Indian market town high in the mountains, often appears on travel posters, and is visited by over eighty percent of the visitors to Guatemala. Its attributes that are important to tourism are:

1. The high, scenic mountain environment.
2. The architectural characteristics of the town with its white-walled buildings, red-tiled roofs, and colorful plants in the courtyards and planter boxes on homes and businesses.
3. Colorful Indian markets, where many of the women wear typical highland clothing.
4. Folk Catholic worship and its traditions including use of idols and the waving of smoke-filled small buckets on the steps of the principal church.
5. Special Indian dances performed at the entrance to another church facing the town square, commemorating the arrival of the conquistadors to Central America.

These factors led to the development of Chichicastenango. They were there when a local travel company decided to arrange tourist trips to it, and have since made Chichicastenango an important destination center for tourism in Central America.

Market-Related Factors
Once the resource base has been identified and evaluated, those locations with a high quality resource base for tourism can then be studied to ascertain if they can be developed. Identification of the market region and its location relative to the destination is of prime importance.

Proximity to markets refers to the geographical distance expressed in time, or money, between the destination and the tourists it will attract. Harold J. Nolan, Jr. stated that

> If an attraction is to meet the needs of tourists, a fundamental requirement is that it be strategically located to draw various populations from different locations. In judging the location of the tourist attraction, it is important to appraise any significance in terms of the number of persons that the resource can serve and the type of geographic areas from which they come, as well as any unique scenic, scientific, or historical values of the resource itself. The concern then surrounds such particulars as size, aggregate gross area, strategic location, accessibility, and proximity to areas of large populations.[2]

As suggested above, distance can be measured in either actual mileage or in the amount of time or money required to reach a destination. There may be a difference between real and perceived time, or actual versus cognitive distance. Cognitive distance is based on memory, belief, or perception. It can be affected by topographical barriers, political boundaries, or ethnic differences. As age and education increase, they have positive effects on reconciling cognitive with actual reasoning.[3]

According to Mayo and Jarvis, tourists have perceptual maps in their minds, where they organize elements as they do in geometric space. The resulting perception, in terms of distance involved in time and money required, can act as deterrent factors.[4] Thus, it is easy to understand that some countries, such as Switzerland, which shares its borders with five countries, and West Germany, which shares its borders with eight countries, attract a large number of tourists.

Once major market areas are established, transportation and facilities become of paramount importance in determining their potential. Tourists need easy access to various forms of transportation, such as road, rail, air, and water. Thus, the amount of time from major population centers via each mode of transportation is important. For example, road analysis should include the average driving time and distance between major centers in miles, kilometers, and hours; transportation carriers that use rail, air, and water generally express travel times to destinations in their analyses. It is important to have convenient access and quality service. The cost of reaching the destination and staying there must also be considered. This should include special needs such as road tolls, gasoline, repairs, parking, car rentals and charter and scheduled bus services. Internal access and linkage with facilities and attractions must be available.

Thus, the location of the destination region is important. The Pocono and Catskill Mountains can attract large numbers of tourists from nearby population centers in New York, New Jersey, and Pennsylvania; while more spectacular ranges such as the Himalayas or the Alaskan Rockies,

by virtue of their more remote locations, are less frequently visited.

A region also must have a good infrastructure (the existence of a network of highways, roads, railways, water, sewage, and electrical facilities; public transportation systems; and air transportation facilities) if it is to be developed. Where these are not fully developed, the area must have access to resources that can be developed. Some form of transportation must be provided to allow tourists to travel in the destination locality. When public transportation, or some alternative, is poorly developed, travelers are bound to a limited area; other attractions and opportunities then become inaccessible to them. Transportation services include gas stations, repair services, taxi/limousine and mini-bus services, parking, and car rentals. The transportation system, in many cases, does not have to be elaborate. Any good, local transportation that can be used by the tourist would be adequate. In fact, Tahiti has open-air trucks which tourists enjoy using. The trucks add an element of fun to the atmosphere. They contribute to the character of Tahiti that is so appealing to many of its visitors.

In addition to the infrastructure, it seems that all tourists like to spend money, and enjoy being close to shopping centers and some of the other urban amenities. These shopping centers should include malls, convenience and grocery stores, and souvenir and gift shops. In addition to these urban amenities, there need to be accommodation facilities, such as hotels, motels, cabins, campgrounds, trailer parks, guest houses, condominiums, and convention facilities. Some destinations may only appeal to certain travelers who want specific types of accommodations. But with mass marketing, destination areas are improving their ability to attract a variety of people who don't all want the same type of accommodation. The same is true of the dining services.

As part of the urban amenities, the services of banking, medical facilities, realtors, laundry, retail stores, information centers, and such are all considered in the evaluation of a potential area to draw and support tourists.

There must be enough land to develop and support tourism. Mass tourism accounts for the movement of a vast number of people who must be housed and entertained. At times, an area will be built up and promoted as a prime tourist location; then, through overdevelopment, either due to insufficient space or lack of proper controls, reach a saturation point. No more room for future expansion results in problems. This happens in many beach resorts, where commercial developments have been constructed without regard for proper planning or a concern for complementary open space, resulting in lack of sufficient beach space as well as blocked ocean and waterside views.

Tourism requires space to create a healthy, aesthetic, and workable environment for present success and future visitor growth. In the Netherlands, the local population is already crowded into a small area; prime land is in demand from all sectors of the economy including housing, agriculture, and industry. With tourism, the country's available land is developed even further. The Netherlands has now reached a point where any new tourism development may infringe upon other essential activities, and the land area it needs to function properly.[5]

Similar conditions may also exist in other small countries, in microstates such as Monaco and Hong Kong, or in other land-restricted areas such as Hawaii. Even in larger nations, some specific regions may become subject to overdevelopment. London, Paris, or Los Angeles may, to some degree, lie within this category.

Other Physical and Cultural Characteristics

Other important considerations in studying potential tourism development are knowing the manpower available for both skilled and unskilled jobs, and understanding their wage rates; knowing local labor laws, existence of training facilities, and employment agencies; knowing zoning laws, legal regulations, and political characteristics of the area. These studies should include the seasonal character of labor needs, the community industrial mix, competition from other industries for workers, average area earnings, and level of schooling available.

While many of these factors are directly related to providing the tourist with services, the social and political characteristics of the area will influence the decision of whether travelers visit there or not. Political considerations have been important in the past, and are becoming even more so. These consist of, not only the ideology of the government in power, but the stability of the political situation and the absence of civil strife and disruptions.

Tourists will avoid areas where the government is unstable or civil contentions are overt. The decline of travelers was especially evident in Europe in 1986, following a year of terrorist activity, and in the Middle East due to terrorism and unstable political events. Tourists are rather quick to change their preferences from one country to another; thus the travel industry is continually subject to changes based on government action.[6]

The current situation concerning apartheid in South Africa is detrimental to its international tourist trade, even more so today with the increased violent outbursts in cities and provinces. Political instability in Argentina, El Salvador, Guatemala, and Nicaragua have posed problems for travelers to those areas. These political troubles have often affected other countries in their regions where hostile factions may not even be present. Tourism has suffered in Costa Rica because the political situation of its neighboring countries is unstable.[7] In 1986, Canadian and Alaskan tourism benefited from the problems in Europe.

Social, economic, and political stability at local, regional, national, or international levels affects the demand and supply of tourism; consequently, they influence the success or failure of destination areas. Thus, an evaluation must be made of the degree of stability in each area.

Philippos Loukissas has indicated that additional factors, such as the local capacity to absorb development, the potential interaction between locals and tourists, and the integration of the tourism industry with the rest of the economy, should be considered more heavily than they may have been in the past. In a study of two Greek islands, one

large and one small, Loukissas concluded that while the inhabitants of the large island could derive economic and other positive external benefits from tourism development, the small island needed to restrict the type, location, and availability of facilities, particularly room rentals in private homes.[8] What all this suggests is that tourism marketing for destinations has become very complex, and that a number of variables must be considered when assessing potential destination development.

TOURISM AREA DEVELOPMENT CYCLE

Most tourist destinations evolve through a series of stages. An area is first discovered by a few people who, in many cases, are the jet set. These early arrivals are those that have access other than mass transportation. In other words, some effort is required to visit the destination. This can be studied in the early development of the Cote d'Azur (Riviera). First, it became fashionable as a therapeutic spa because of its clear Mediterranean air. The scenic beauty of the Mediterranean coast, and the mild climate in the winter, soon attracted rich, leisure-seeking visitors. It then "took off" as a resort when a fast, comfortable form of transportation was introduced with the establishment of the railroad line from Marseille in 1860. This was soon followed by improved rail connections with Paris; the journey now took only eighteen hours when once it took thirteen days by coach. With this increase in accessibility, more and more people vacationed in coastal resorts such as Nice. Hotel accommodations were developed rapidly to meet the increased demand for first-class restaurants, ballrooms, game rooms, gardens, and sports facilities. In 1884, gambling was introduced; this, of course, not only brought gamblers, but others as well. Robert Rudney reported one observation of the then "elite class" toward the new visitor:

> The class of people who are attracted by the unparalleled gambling facilities now offered on the Riviera, is fast driving away the solid members of various foreign colonies, who annually passed six months in their own villas, and spent money freely in entertaining, and in the shops of various kinds. These no longer come, the new element bewilders their more steady and old-fashioned ideas; they find prices advancing by leaps and bounds, and the class of society distinctly deteriorating; so they come no more.[9]

The Riviera was thus discovered and developed. This early development was as a winter resort. It was not until the outbreak of the First World War that seasonal problems were noticed. Probably, with development restricted to the winter season, the Riviera would have leveled or begun a decline. The idea of a summer season following World War I, brought a new fad. It became fashionable to revel in the sun and frequent the local night spots. An increase in mobility in the 1920s with the introduction of the automobile, and continued improvement of the public transportation systems, combined with societal changes in the use of leisure, vacations, and work introduced France to modern tourism. Consequently, the Riviera continued to grow.[10]

This exploration, involvement, and development has been a common pattern throughout the world. While it has occurred mostly through chance in such resorts as the Riviera, Costa del Brava, Waikiki beach, Atlantic City, etc., the process can be started by the government working through the three stages of exploration, involvement, and development—then the tourists will follow. A good example of the latter process is Cancun. The government, looking for the best place to develop a resort to increase Mexico's market share of international tourism, found that Cancun was accessible to most United States population centers in a reasonable amount of time, and had most of the resources necessary to be a major destination. They then developed the infrastructure, and even brought in sand to have an attractive white beach to go with the beautiful blue sea. They established accessibility and started an advertising program to bring the area to the attention of the potential tourist. Thus, Cancun was made one of the most outstanding winter destination areas for North America travelers.

Once a destination, resort, or attraction has been visited by large numbers of people over several years, it begins

Reggio Canal, Venice. Photo courtesy of the Italian State Tourist Office.

to age. In some cases it wears out, but in others its population density becomes too large for the other attractions within the destination region. Therefore, the next stage is more questionable. In some cases it will, if left alone, begin to decline; or with some effort, maintain its present level of activity. This is done somewhat by freshening major attractions in the area. However, to continue its growth, the destination needs to be revitalized and other attractions added. Revitalization is the replacement of some of the attractions with new, more exotic ones; the new attractions provide more activities for current visitors, and generate additional visitors to the area.

Kenya may be a good example of a destination that is at the capacity level, and needs to weigh alternatives to decide its tourism future. For years, Kenya has been a popular destination, principally for photo safaris through the game parks and reserves. Growth has been minimal, but a steady flow of visitors has allowed the government to develop programs and facilities to meet the small, but steady demand. Following the film *Out of Africa*, demand increased dramatically and existing facilities became saturated. Complaints about the state of tourism in Kenya resulted. A resolution concerning the future is still to be determined. Orlando, Florida is a good example of a destination where continued growth of facilities and attractions brings additional tourists to Florida's central region. Once Disney World was established, tourism to central Florida increased rapidly. Development of Epcot Center and other attractions continues and with a concomitant increase in hotels and restaurants, the area continues to grow. There are times when the destination region can do little to change tourism trends as other destinations are developed and tourists' tastes change. When this happens the only future is stagnation and decline.

IMAGE OF TRAVEL DESTINATIONS

People react to the world as they perceive it to be, not necessarily as it is; thus, image is extremely important to destinations. Choosing a destination, or a vacation package, is extremely subjective. It is based on individual likes and dislikes, interests, attitudes, and motives. While visiting with a university professor who was trying to encourage a lady to join a university tour he was conducting, the lady noticed a picture of the professor with pigeons sitting on him. She asked where the picture was taken. His response was "Seville," but he also stated that similar scenes could be observed in London and Venice. As she left his office she was heard muttering, "I hate birds." Needless to say, she did not participate in the tour.

For ten years, students in an introductory geography class at Brigham Young University have been asked to list the three most preferred states and the three least preferred states in which they would like to live once they graduate. Every single person has listed New York as the least desired state. Discussion usually indicates that their concept of New York is centered on New York City, as being big, unsafe, and unfriendly. These students are not alone in this view.

When the people of New York realized that the state had an image problem, they instituted the "I love New York" campaign in 1977. As part of the promotion, they advertised a variety of opportunities for tourists from dude ranches to Broadway shows. The program was successful. It brought more tourists to New York City, and initiated business in many other destination areas. Bumper stickers and tee shirts can be seen throughout the United States and the world, sporting "I love _____," following the New York example.

In a study of the negative images of the United States by tour operators from other countries, Robert McLellan and Kathryn Foushee found that the three major potential problems perceived by these tour operators were (1) personal safety, (2) cost, and (3) the lack of information available to foreign visitors to the United States.[11]

Ireland, in American minds, has an image problem. The problems of Northern Ireland have been identified in the minds of most Americans as belonging to Ireland in general. Second, the American media, through news articles and travel guidebooks, has expressed many negative comments about the Republic of Ireland. Jane Ehemann, reviewing articles listed in indexes and review guide books found that, for the period of January 1974 to March 1975, eighty-seven percent of the news articles and sixteen percent of other references were negative. This is further compounded by the fact that thirty-seven percent of the tour guide references were negative![12] Thus, in all forms of media, a highly negative view of Ireland was given to the American people.

Perceptions of other places or cultures are formed mostly by the externalities in our lives—by others rather than our own direct contacts. In some cases, our direct contacts are so limited that they may have the tendency to reinforce existing perceptions. Some external influences that affect our perceptions are

Media	Direct contact through travel
News	School
Friends and family	Government
Ethnic jokes	

Out of the seven influences identified thus far, six are external. When we are exposed to them our attitudes and perceptions are formed by forces outside our own experiences. The students' image of New York was created, in part, by the media—mainly television, and especially news, which has a tendency to stress the negative aspects of life. By the same token, the media can contribute considerably to positive perceptions of a place. Many millions of first time visitors to Hawaii expect to see mammoth waves, surf boards, bikinis, Diamond Head, boulevards lined with palm trees, and bronze-skinned Hawaiians as a result of "Hawaii Five-O" or "Magnum P.I."

Our friends and relatives form reference groups in which we receive sanctions for our actions; they also help develop and reinforce our perceptions. The higher class you are economically, the more you tend to travel and be willing

to explore. Very early in life, parents influence their children through their attitudes, and their reaction to world events. The family's selection of vacation areas, and the experiences gathered from them, will affect the younger members and reinforce the family view of an area and culture. Friends and social groups provide the same kinds of experiences. Any of the linkages that are established between origin and destination regions, such as Britain and the Spanish coast, Finland and the Black Sea, or France and Tahiti, are due to the positive experiences that friends and relatives carry home. They portray an image of the place for those who have not visited it, and instill either a positive or negative attitude about it, which are hard to overcome. This can be illustrated through a study abroad program. A group of forty-three students were living in London for six months during the winter of 1987. On one occasion, one of the girls had an opportunity to visit the Netherlands with her fiance's family for two days. Upon her return, she expressed rather negative comments about Amsterdam. Later, when the other students had an opportunity to travel independently, nine of them chose not to visit Amsterdam. Six of the nine were close friends of the girl who expressed negative comments about that city.

The interest in world travel leads people to investigate potential destinations, and to gain some understanding of other places, mainly from travel magazines. Travel magazines are relatively popular sources of information—*Traveler, Travel and Leisure, Travel Holiday, Town and Country, Departures, Gourmet, Arizona Highways, Yankee,* and *Southern Living* are just a few. People read them to gain information about interesting places. From this experience, they form their own images. Each magazine is designed for a particular market, a particular set of readers. *Traveler,* for example, concentrates on areas accessible to most North Americans; consequently, most articles are about the United States and Canada. Others, such as *Outside,* are designed for those who enjoy wind surfing and rock climbing—a select audience. Probably more than any other magazine, *Traveler* tries to provide the reader with an intimate feeling for the place being researched. Some of the information given will be new to the reader, and some will change images the reader may have. The magazine is concerned with the physical aspects of the place—the climate, topography, location, attractions, and culture expressed in architectural details and street scenes of people and activities.

DESTINATION SATISFACTION PATTERNS

In 1979, a news article entitled "Vacation Blues Syndrome Strike," reported that three out of every five people are disappointed by the way their vacations turn out.[13] While many of the problems are caused by people taking the wrong type of vacation, their inability to relax, or family problems, some are due to the wrong choice of destinations. The Canadian government, recognizing these problems, started a project in the early 1970s to develop a system that would enable the Canadian Government Office of Tourism to develop a product/market matching system in order to be more selective in targeting areas in which to market Canadian tourism. The goals of the system were:

1. To find the locations that best met the requirements of certain market segments with the existing tourism plant.
2. To find the markets that are most likely to be attracted to a particular location given its existing plant.
3. To find and identify attitudes, perceptions, and preferences of specific market segments.

The results of this project, if successful, will attract individuals who will enjoy their experiences and take home a positive image to share with friends and relatives, thereby increasing the effectiveness of Canadian advertising.

Researchers, in an effort to provide assistance to governments and others interested in visitor satisfaction, have been seeking methods of measurement. R. Neil Maddox wrote an article illustrating this effort. His desire was to present some methods that might be useful in identifying the degree of satisfaction that would be obtained from a visit to a particular destination.[14] This objective is similar to the Canadian effort, to ascertain which experiences were worthwhile and which were not. From this information, researchers can determine, for example, whether an experience in the destination region or the destination region itself caused dissatisfaction. If it is the destination region itself, then studies can indicate exactly why visitors were dissatisfied. If the problem can be overcome by creating a new product to give visitors a more pleasurable visit, then the visitors' will continue to consider that destination as a choice, and influence friends and relatives positively. If the wrong group was targeted in the region's advertising, the campaign can be changed.

Abraham Pizam, Yoram Neumann, and Arie Reichel defined tourist satisfaction as ''the result of the interaction between a tourist's experience at the destination area and the expectations he had about that destination.''[15] They used Cape Cod to illustrate a technique for studying tourist satisfaction. The results of their study suggest that tourists were fairly well satisfied with Cape Cod as a destination. More specifically, the items that received the highest ratings were natural assets such as the scenery, natural attractions, the environmental quality and beaches, and the tourist facilities, which included hotels, motels and restaurants. The items they identified as receiving the lowest ratings were high costs, poor traffic conditions, and the extent of commercialization.[16] The most important fact here is that the visitors liked and enjoyed Cape Cod. The second item, traffic conditions, is an issue that can be handled by the local authorities, through better planning. At this point, it is probably too late to do anything about commercialization, but it can have planning implications for other areas, especially when redevelopment becomes necessary.

Sadrudin A. Ahmed, in an effort to assess visitors impressions of the strengths and weaknesses of the Sri Lankan tourist product, in 1982, studied three hundred international tourists and one hundred and fifty middle and up-per-middle class Sri Lankans. The conclusions of the visitors were that the principal assets of Sri Lanka are its natural beauty and beaches, and that the lack of adequate transportation, sports facilities, and nightlife were the principal deterrents. These results are not unusual for developing nations, but describe their common characteristics. The implied question is whether improvements would result in more tourists. In the case of Sri Lanka, the answer would probably be no, since Sri Lanka is not very accessible to the major industrial countries from which most tourists originate. Most of the current visitors probably come for the beauty and cultural experiences; the lack of sports facilities and nightlife are obviously not determining factors in their visit. Interestingly, the Sri Lankans responded somewhat the same way as the foreign tourists. They recognized that the sports facilities and other recreational opportunities were poor, but felt that tourists came for reasons other than these. They did feel, however, that added nightlife would improve the visitor's experience and bring added revenues. The author's conclusion was that the basic assets of Sri Lanka—scenic beauty, beaches, historical sites, wildlife, and climate—were the strengths of the country and that amenities such as highways, traffic, nightlife, sports facilities, improved cleanliness and, to a lesser extent, shopping and restaurants, need to be improved to give a more favorable image to Sri Lanka.[17]

INTERNATIONAL TRAVEL PATTERNS

In 1986 over 340 million tourists were recorded by the WTO. This is a fifty-eight percent increase since 1975, and continued growth is projected.

Destination Countries

The relative position of a region's tourist arrivals has remained the same over the past twenty-seven years. Europe, as a region, dominated the international arrivals in the 1950s, 1960s, 1970s, accounting for sixty-six to seventy-five percent. In 1986 it accounted for 66.9 percent of the visitors and the WTO projects it will account for nearly sixty-six percent in 1990. Europe dominates international arrivals because of its considerable intraregional travel. Europe, in fact, has the highest intraregional travel in the world, eighty-four percent. The high number of visitors to European countries can be accounted for by three factors. First, a large number of tourists are from Europe itself. Second, the historical ties of North America with Europe serve to stimulate travel between these two major areas. Third, the relatively strong economies of Europe help promote tourism.

The Americas are dominated by North America. Canada and the United States account for over eighty percent of the international arrivals to the Americas. Canada receives a little over ninety percent of its visitors from the United States. This is the highest percent for any country. Both are very wealthy nations and major population centers are close to the border between them. A slight increase in arrivals to Asia and the Pacific can be attributed to the opening of China to the western world.

It appears certain that for the long future, Europe and the Mediterranean will continue to be the principal tourist destinations, but with the increased popularity of China, Kenya, and tropical islands, the percentage of total arrivals may decline a bit. For as long as the American dollar remains low, travel to North America will remain high.

Seasonality

The strongest seasonal fluctuations are in Europe. The number of arrivals in the region during the summer months almost triple those of the low season, which is the first quarter of the year. North Africa and North America have a seasonal fluctuation, although not nearly as pronounced as Europe's. Arrivals to Latin America, the Caribbean, and South Asia peak in the first or fourth quarter coinciding with summer in the southern hemisphere. There are small differences in the rest of the world.

Purpose of Visit

Throughout the world the major purpose for travel is holidays. This is particularly so in East Asia and the Pacific, Europe, South Asia, and the Americas (Table 4-1). Travel for business purposes is far above the international average in the Middle East and Africa. Some middle eastern countries only issue business or transit visas and have no desire to promote vacation traffic. Also, the political situation of the Middle East is not stable enough to attract the vacation traveler.

Average Length of Stay

Table 4-2 charts the average length of stay by region. Oceania has the longest. While the data doesn't cover more recent years, it does illustrate a pattern that, like arrivals, is relatively the same over the years. The lengthier stays in Oceania can be accounted for by the greater distances between islands and the degree of difficulty of going from one to another. North and Central America rank second in length of stay, due largely to their distance from the major tourist generator, Europe. Europe's average of 6 days reflects an average of the longer visits of those from North America and the shorter visits of tourists from other European nations who, because of proximity, can come for a short period of time.

TABLE 4-1 PURPOSE OF VISIT

Region	Main Business (percents)		
	Holidays	Business	Others
Africa	63	20	17
Americas	76	12	12
East Asia and the Pacific	71	12	17
Europe	68	13	19
Middle East	45	25	30
South Asia	73	14	13
World	71	13	16

Source: WTO Economic Review of World Tourism, 1982.

TABLE 4-2 AVERAGE LENGTH OF STAY

Region	1985
Western Europe	6.9
Eastern Europe	5.1
North and Central America	8.9
South America	5.2
North Africa and Middle East	4.6
Africa	4.4
Far East	5.2
Oceania	14.4

Source: 1985 estimates from WTO Yearbook of Tourism Statistics, 1988.

Income Per Tourist Arrival

Table 4-3 indicates the amount of money spent in each of the major regions. It is significant to note that receipts per arrival have increased for all regions at a rate much faster than that of inflation. The largest increases in receipts per arrival are for the Middle East, South Asia, and the Americas—regions where the length of stay is longer or, in the case of the Middle East, are more expensive regions in which to travel.

Tourism Generating Countries

The areas that generate the most tourism are Western Europe, North America, and Japan. These countries accounted for over seventy percent of total foreign travel expenditures. Again, this reflects the importance of the advanced economies of the world on tourism. It should be noted, however, that this is a five percent reduction since 1975. It would, to some extent, suggest a transfer of money from the developed to the undeveloped countries. Although Eastern Europe generates a large number of tourists, its percentage of total expenditures is an insignificant 1.9 percent. (See Table 4-4.)

The only noteworthy change in the past thirty years, has been the emergence of Japan as a high tourism generating country. Its dramatic economic advances since World War II have made this possible.

Africa and the Middle East, other than Israel and South Africa, generate little tourism, as the income levels in these

TABLE 4-3 TOURISM RECEIPTS PER ARRIVAL—INTERNATIONAL TOURISM (in U.S. Dollars)

Regions	1977	1980	1983	1985	1986	1987 (estimates)
Africa	286	323	335	263	330	343
Americas	270	379	218	201	501	471
East Asia and the Pacific	330	452	250	293	316	544
Europe	204	318	344	373	292	372
Middle East	298	455	212	175	660	600
South Asia	332	588	196	156	588	666
World Total	227	342	298	310	338	

Source: The Travel Industry World Yearbook: The Big Picture—1986, Travel & Leisure's World Travel Overview 1987/1988, and Current Travel and Tourism Indicators (WTO: Madrid, 1988).

PERCENT OF WORLD ARRIVALS
1981, 1986, & 1990
data and projection

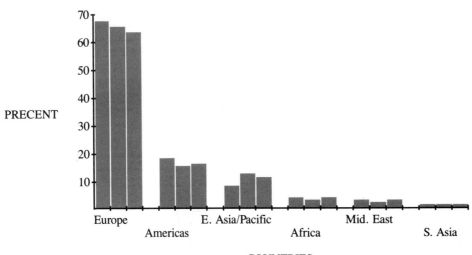

WORLD ARRIVALS
1981 & 1986
and estimates for 1990

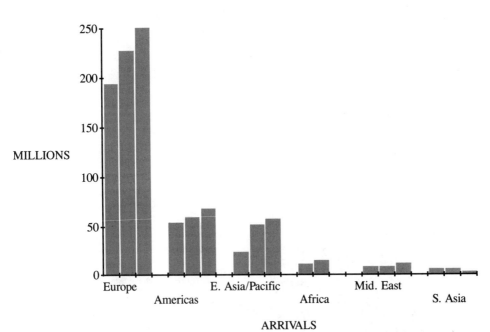

Figure 4-1 Source: *Travel & Leisure's World Travel Overview 1987/1988.*

TABLE 4-4 PERCENTAGE OF WORLD TOURISM EXPENDITURE
FROM MAJOR ORIGIN COUNTRIES

	1966	1974	1980	1983	1985
West Germany	12.5	—	21.9	15.8	13.8
United States	21.6	16.9	10.9	14.3	15.5
France	10.6	6.7	6.3	4.4	3.0
Canada	6.8	4.6	3.2	3.8	4.9
United Kingdom	6.8	4.5	6.8	6.2	6.0
Japan	1.0	3.9	4.8	4.5	4.5
Netherlands	3.2	3.8	4.8	3.3	3.0
Italy	2.1	3.5	2.0	1.8	2.2
Belgium/Luxembourg	2.6	3.2	3.5	2.1	1.9
Austria	1.4	2.5	3.3	2.9	2.2
Sweden	2.0	2.2	2.3	1.6	1.8
Switzerland	2.3	1.9	2.5	2.3	2.3
Denmark	1.5	1.5	1.6	1.2	1.1

Source: *Travel & Leisure's World Travel Overview 1987/1988* and WTO annual reports.

regions are quite small. Australia, which generates slightly more than one-half the number of tourists that Japan does, has easy access to other countries in Southeast Asia. The Philippines, a country with a low standard of living and geographically remote, ranks as one of the lowest of the reporting countries. Thus, Europe, Canada, the United States, Japan, and Australia are the major source regions of tourists. (See Figure 4-1.)

Travel Flows

Although major upheavals in politics, economics, or physical terrain of the world will affect tourist flows, there seems to be a stable pattern over periods of years. Certainly, a few bad experiences in any of the three categories will alter the opportunities of any given country to attract and keep the tourist trade. Research by Williams and Zelinsky demonstrates a number of strong flows and connections between various countries. (For example, they found that the strong flow of Dutch tourists to the United Kingdom was accounted for by strong trade ties.) They suggested a few factors that account for the patterns they found, including proximity; presence or absence of international connectivity, including business, political, military, and other ties; general attractiveness of a country to tourists from another; cost of traveling; influence of intervening opportunities; the national character of the source country; and the mental image of the target area held by potential visitors. Another factor is the type and degree of services offered. Costa del Sol is a good example. A number of British and other European enclaves have been established in various parts of the Costa del Sol. These separate con-

centrations of each group allow visitors to communicate with other members of the same group and enjoy common foods and recreations.

Hotels there can also be identified by the groups they cater to—such as the English, Dutch, Swedish, and German's—who tend to cluster together. Transportation systems reinforce these patterns. Charters and low fares are directed to areas of perceived demand. The low fares, in turn, draw additional tourists to an area, thereby perpetuating the travel-flow patterns.

These factors, then, are important once a pattern or connectivity is established. They tend to deepen the existing trend and encourage further travel.

As standards of living rise and disposable income increases, particularly in developing countries, the number of international tourists should continue to increase. This has been true in countries such as Yugoslavia and Spain, where increased well-being at home has led to increasing numbers of tourists traveling abroad.

Although there has been a shift toward some of the developing areas such as China, Europe and North America will still dominate in tourism, both as a destination and as a generator.[18]

RESEARCH AND REVIEW

1. Identify and describe the three major components of tourism development.

2. What are three transportation concerns that improve accessibility?

3. Discuss two political considerations that influence whether a destination will have large numbers of tourists or not.

4. Discuss the development cycle of a tourist area.

5. What impact does the following statement suggest as it pertains to tourism? "We react to the world as we perceive it to be, not necessarily as it is."

6. What is America's image of Ireland?

7. What are five external influences that affect our perception of other cultures?

8. Why are people disappointed with their vacations?

9. What three factors account for Europe dominating international arrivals?

10. What is the average length of stay for each region of the world? Why?

11. What three regions of the world generate the most tourists? Why?

12. What are three factors that create stable tourism patterns once they are established?

ENDNOTES

1. Franco F. Ferrario, "Inventories as a Tool in Regional Tourism Development," paper presented at the XIV Travel and Tourism Research Assn. (Banff, Canada, 1983), pp. 1–11.

2. Howard J. Nolan, "Tourist Attractions and Recreation Resources Providing for Natural and Human Resources," *Tourism Planning and Development Issues,* ed. Donald E. Hawkins, et al. (Washington, DC: George Washington Univ., 1980), pp. 277–282.

3. Robert L. Cook and Ken W. McCleary, "Redefining Vacation Distances in Consumer Minds," *Journal of Travel Research,* Vol. 22, No. 2 (1983), p. 31.

4. Edward J. Mayo and Lance P. Jarvis, *The Psychology of Leisure Travel* (Boston: CBI, 1981), pp. 38–42.

5. Martinus Kosters, "Holland and Tourism in the Next Decade," *Tourism Planning and Development Issues,* ed. Donald E. Hawkins, et al. (Washington, DC: George Washington Univ., 1980), p. 48.

6. Mario D. Zamora, Vinson A. H. Sutlive and Nathan Altshuler, eds. *Tourism and Behavior* (Williamsburg, VA: William and Mary, 1978), p. 42.

7. *Travel Industry World Yearbook—1987,* p. 94.

8. Philppos J. Loukissas, "Tourism Regional Development Impacts: A Comparative Analysis of the Greek Islands," *Annals of Tourism Research,* Vol. 9 (1982), pp. 523–541.

9. Robert Rudney, "The Development of Tourism on the Côte d'Azur: A Historical Perspective," in *Tourism Planning and Development Issues,* p. 215.

10. Ibid., pp. 213–224.

11. Robert W. McLellan and Kathryn Dodd Foushee, "Negative Images of the United States as Expressed by Tour Operators From Other Countries," *Journal of Travel Research* (Summer, 1983), pp. 3–4.

12. Jane Ehemann, "What Kind of Place is Ireland: An Image Perceived Through the American Media," *Journal of Travel Research,* Vol. 16, No. 2, (Fall 1977), pp. 28–30.

13. Charles W. Bell, "Vacation Blues Syndrome Strike," *Salt Lake Tribune* (July 1, 1979), p. 2W.

14. R. Neil Maddox, "Measuring Satisfaction with Tourism," *Journal of Travel Research* (Winter 1985), pp. 2–5.

15. Abraham Pizam, Yoram Neumann, and Arie Reichel, "Dimensions of Tourist Satisfaction with a Destination Area," *Annals of Tourism Research,* Vol. 5, No. 5 (July/Sep. 1978), p. 315.

16. Ibid., p. 319.

17. Sadrudin A. Ahmed, "What Attracts Tourists to Sri Lanka? An Empirical Analysis of Sri Lanka's and Tourists' Belief," unpublished paper (Ottawa: Univ. of Ottawa, 83–69), p. 29.

18. S. E. Williams and W. Zelinsky, "On Some Patterns of International Tourist Flows," *Economic Geography* (Oct. 1970), pp. 549–567.

CHAPTER 5

ATTRACTIONS

In previous chapters we have studied some of the shared characteristics of successful tourist areas: accessibility, natural environment, culture, climate, the activities offered, and amenities. This chapter concerns itself more specifically with the "pull" factors that influence travelers.

Throughout history certain attractions have become famous. The Seven Wonders of the World were once much extolled (the celebrated Hanging Gardens of Babylon, the Great Pyramid of Egypt, the Statue of Zeus at Olympia, the Temple of Artemis at Ephesus, the Mausoleum at Halicarnassus, the Colossus of Rhodes, and the Lighthouse at Alexandria). More recently, Rand McNally has published a book on travel attractions and has increased the seven wonders to the one hundred and one wonders of the world. The five hundred top attractions in the United States have also been listed.

Today, small countries such as Ireland may have their own seven wonders. The Irish Tourist Board considers (1) Newgrange (a prehistoric burial ground), (2) Great Skellig (a small rocky island off the southern coast), (3) Clonmanois (center of learning), (4) Bunratty Castle and Folk Museum, (5) Kilkenny City (an ancient medieval city), (6) Trinity College in Dublin, and (7) Cultra (another folk museum), to be the seven wonders of Ireland.

An attraction is a destination that pulls or entices a person to it. John Jakle indicates its setting is either manmade or natural. It may also be social. He writes "An attracting force, is what Dean MacCannell calls a 'sight' and its interpretation, is what he calls a 'marker,' [they] combine to form an attraction."[1]

Attractions are different for different people. Jakle adds:

Many tourists prefer places that are exaggerated for their attractiveness; places that are clearly distinctive and perceptually undemanding; places, that facilitate superficial touristic role playing. More sophisticated travelers, offended by the obvious, seek subtle attractions in the everyday world. They contrive to get behind the scenes of important places, and even to participate in activities ongoing there, and they seek chance encounters with places. Although they travel to validate place expectations, like other tourists, they do so by retaining the important element of surprise. They may even seek to comprehend "personality of place" or to identify "spirit of place" as ways of communing with the landscape on abstract levels.[2]

What Jakle is saying is that people are different and as such have differences of opinion about the types of attractions they enjoy.

Having a combination of attractions helps to create strong tourist appeal. However, sometimes an attraction is so outstanding that the industry of an entire region depends on and promotes this one feature. It is important to note that since the needs and tastes of tourists vary considerably, an attraction may have strong appeal to a relatively limited group. Also, the tourist industry is susceptible to change, what is a key attraction today may not be considered worth a second look tomorrow. These two significant factors will be discussed later in the chapter.

CLASSIFICATION OF ATTRACTIONS

The Built Environment

Man, both ancient and modern, has left an impression upon the land, in his work, play, and religious activities. Ancient structures and artifacts remind us of our historical past, and exert a major "pull" on tourists.

How ancient civilizations functioned is a matter of increasing interest to people today. In many cases, little is known about early civilizations other than what is garnered from structures and artifacts that have survived the centuries. These remnants of civilization have sparked the curiosity of many people about the level of knowledge and technology obtained in some of these early cultures. Stonehenge in England, Tikal in Guatemala, Chichen Itza in Mexico, or Machu Picchu in Peru have features that defy modern explanation; they are so impressive that they attract multitudes of tourists who explore and wonder about people of long ago.

Industrial Archeology

The Industrial Revolution ushered in a major change in technology. Early industrial locations have been renovated to attract tourists who want to see how the work "used to be done." In many industrial areas, such as the docklands in London and waterfront area in Sydney, the docks are being renovated to offer major attractions. Old sugar mills in Hawaii have been restored, as have former textile plants in such places like Lowell, Massachusetts, and Wales, Great Britian.

Historical

Societies and individual people have always been interested in their past. It is not surprising, therefore, that historical monuments, buildings, and places have become prime tourist attractions. Washington, DC, Mount Rushmore, Runnymede, Waterloo, and the Arc de Triomphe are examples of attractions in this category.

Historical buildings are those that have special significance in relation to historical events or people. The Liberty Bell in Philadelphia, Faneuil Hall in Boston, and Appomattox Courthouse are American examples of such buildings. Restored villages throughout the United States such as New Salem in Illinois, Williamsburg in Virginia, and Sturbridge in Massachusetts attract many tourists who want to understand what colonial American life was like.

Historical places often are significant attractions. Old battlefields such as Gettysburg, Chalmette (the site of the battle of New Orleans), and Yorktown, where Lord Cornwallis surrendered to Washington, are but a few of the numerous examples of such sites.

Museums

Museums have been, and still are, important in helping us understand history by preserving objects of the past, including art and everyday cultural artifacts. Some museums have displays that help us understand the modern world in which we live. For example, it is possible to observe a working coal mine in Chicago; you can walk inside a giant replica of an eye in Munich to find out how it works. A trip to Paris is not complete without a visit to the Louvre; in Munich, to the Deutschemuseum; in Chicago, to the Museum of Science and Industry; in London, to the British Museum.

Folkway Customs

Folkway customs are extremely interesting to tourists. A drive through the Pennsylvania Dutch and Amish areas of Pennsylvania is an exciting and interesting part of any tour of the eastern United States; a trip to Spain is not complete without a drive through La Mancha country southeast of Madrid. Some governments have tried to recreate or preserve the folkways by creating small villages to display housing styles and folk culture.

Political

Capital cities around the world draw many tourists. The Kremlin in Moscow, Buckingham Palace and Parliament in London, and the White House, the Bureau of Engraving and Printing, the Capitol, and the Supreme Court Building in Washington, DC are of major interest to many tourists.

Religious

The Vatican in Rome, Westminster Abbey in London, Chartres Cathedral in France, Washington National Cathedral in Washington, DC, Sophia in Turkey, the Great Cathedral in Guadalajara, modern (Mormon) Latter-Day Saint temples in Hawaii, Washington, DC, and Salt Lake City, and the many pagodas of Southeast Asia are only a few examples of the numerous religious structures that attract a considerable body of tourists.

Architecture

Modern civilizations have created new landscapes in cities with their high-rise buildings. The Sears Building in Chicago or the World Trade Center in New York offer spectacular views of the urban skyline. Modern buildings, with their unique and dramatic architectural styles, fascinate many people. Agricultural and rural areas can also be impressive. A drive through the horse farm area of Kentucky, or along large single-crop fields of corn, sorghum, and cotton also fascinate tourists.

Many manufacturing companies offer tours through their plants to large numbers of tourists who are inquisitive about the manufacture of their products. Considerable variety can be offered on a tour program which will measurably increase the success of any given tour. For example, a trip through the Pennsylvania Dutch and Amish areas can be augmented by a trip to the H. J. Heinz Company, a steel-producing company in Pittsburgh, or the Hershey candy company in Hershey, Pennsylvania. A trip to Michigan could well include a trip to the Kellogg plant and an automobile assembly plant in Detroit, as well as a visit to Dearborn, and the tulip fields in Holland, Michigan.

Many cities have redeveloped their downtown areas, not only for the local residents but also to attract tourists. Many older areas have been restored to their original state. Old San Juan, the old cities in Albuquerque and San Diego, and the wharves in San Francisco and in Seattle are among those that have been turned into unique shopping areas for the pleasure of visitors and local residents. Many redevelopment projects have changed the character of the areas considerably. In Baltimore's inner harbor the historical Power Plant building has been turned into a state-of-the-art entertainment theme park center by the Six Flags Corporation.

Shopping Centers

Many major cities now have shopping centers that are well known; visitors generally feel that no trip is complete without having bought something. Harrods in London, Neiman Marcus in Dallas, and Rodeo Drive in Beverly Hills are such world-class shopping centers.

Cultural Activities

Cultural traditions and activities arise from the collective history and customs people share as a cultural whole.

Festivals

Tourists flock to festivals for excitement, fun, and games. The Mardi Gras in New Orleans, the Carnival in Rio de Janeiro, Oktoberfest in Munich, Pierre de Grotta in Naples, and Fias in Valencia are but a few of the many festivals that attract throngs of people to join in the festivities and fun. On a smaller scale, state fairs generate the same spirit of fun that makes them festival attractions.

Arts

Tourists commonly visit places that either display art such as paintings, sculpture, graphics, and architecture, or places where art is being produced. Art festivals are becoming increasingly more important to the tourist industry particularly in seasonal resorts. An art festival held in the off-season attracts people at a time when they would not ordinarily visit.

In addition, art festivals assist in attracting tourists to large cities. The Edinburgh Festival in Scotland attracts local and international tourist traffic to its art and crafts, displays, musical performances, and pageants.

Handicrafts

Residents of many areas are beginning to take advantage of an increased interest in native handicrafts, and are including demonstrations of their skills in addition to selling the arts and crafts they make. Several Indian tribes, such as the Cherokee in North Carolina and the Navajo in Arizona, have been successful in such endeavors. Travel in many foreign areas now includes stops at ceramic, wood-carving, and other craft centers. A tour to Guatemala, for instance, is not complete without a visit to Chichicastenango on market day. The demand for handicrafts from this little market town has created an income of over $2 million a year for its people. At some periods during the day there are more tourists in the market than native Indians!

Mardi Gras in New Orleans. Photo courtesy of the Louisiana Office of Tourism.

Music and Dance

Probably music and dance are among the most entertaining and appealing cultural attractions for tourists. Hawaii, Tahiti, Mexico, the Caribbean, Spain, and Russia are excellent examples of places where music and dance are major components of the tourist trade. The dances performed in the Polynesian Culture Center in Hawaii, the performances of the Ballet Folklorico of Mexico, Thai dancing, the folk dancing of the Eastern European countries, and the Kabuki dancing of Japan are excellent examples of a high standard of folk dance.

Native Life and Customs

This category includes the customs and way of life of unique groups. For example, in America the Amish form a distinct group with many unique customs. Tours might focus on the reasons for those customs, and the effect of outside pressures on traditional Amish mores.

Customs don't always have to be different to attract tourists. People from Germany, for example, generally associate with "average" Americans on an American tour. Foreign tourists can observe customs in farming, foods, business, social life, recreation, and so on, which would probably be common to society as a whole.

Language

Today, many tourist agencies specialize in "learning the language" tours to foreign countries. Tour operators in Spain, for example, provide opportunities for Spanish people to learn English in England. Their students use this experience to assist them in obtaining jobs in the travel industry. Other Spanish schools teach Spanish to foreigners. Many American high schools, colleges, and universities provide similar services. High school students go on educational group tours to Europe. Colleges and universities provide language study programs in foreign countries.

Religion

A variety of religious groups, traditional as well as nontraditional, have been important stimulators of tourism. St. Mark's Cathedral in Venice is as full, if not more full, of tourists as it is of the faithful on Easter Sunday.

Politics

Tourists make political trips for one or two reasons. The first is to observe political processes in operation. Visiting a session of Congress in the United States or Parliament in Canada is popular among tourists. Americans also visit their state representative or observe a branch of the government in session. Visits to houses of government in state, national, and international capitals are interesting to many tourists. Much interest is expressed in watching the General Assembly of the United Nations in New York City.

Second, an interest in opposing political systems also draws a large number of tourists. Travelers are often attracted to countries with a political system different from their own to compare and to see how effective or ineffective it is.

Science

Scientific centers such as the John F. Kennedy Space Center in northeastern Florida, or the Space Center in Houston, provide information about space and travel to the curious traveler. In addition, scientific exchanges between countries provide access to new and different scientific ideas, which give impetus to travel for scientific reasons.

Physical

Nature's effect on tourism and patterns cannot be overstated. Many people travel simply to experience the beauty of nature. Few tours, therefore, omit the contribution of Mother Nature to a vacation.

Ideal vacations always end
  In lovely memories. . .
When souvenirs have long been lost,
  The heart remembers these;

The quaint and dusty country road
  One chanced to come upon. . .
The shaded pond where willows bent
  To kiss a graceful swan.

The sunlit, gilded meadow where
  The buttercups were found,
Where goldenrod and primroses
  Did cheerfully abound. . .

The mountains reaching toward the sky
  Half hidden in a cloud. . .
The stalwart pines along their sides
  So stately, tall and proud.

The rocky shore one stood upon
  As day drew to a close
To watch the sunset tint the sea
  In tones of gold and rose.

The friendly smiles and greetings that
  One met in ev'ry town. . .
The hillsides turned by autumn's touch
  To russet, gold, and brown.

The babbling brook that led one to
  A mossy, wooded glen;
The perfect peace that one found there
  and often sought again.

No photograph or souvenir
  Can ever quite impart
The warmth such mem'ries kindle in
  The confines of the heart.[3]

Climate

Climate is important to tourism for two reasons. One, is simply that climate itself is an attraction. People from the American northern states flee south and west for the winter to Florida, Georgia, Arizona, and California. Northern Europeans flock to the Mediterranean countries to soak up the sun's rays. San Diego's advertisements are created to attract tourists to experience its temperate, perfect year-round climate. Cruises to the Bahamas are most popular during the winter. Also, in the winter, hordes of people travel to the Alps of France, Switzerland, Austria, southern Germany, and in the United States to the Rocky Mountains to ski. The promises of sunny, clear, cold days is the rule rather that the exception on the ski slopes. To be sure, not many winter ski resorts would exist if winter vacations were spent mostly looking out of windows at clouds and blowing snow. To talk about a holiday is to talk about the weather, to brag or complain about its effect upon the vacation.

The second reason that the climate of an area attracts visitors involves health. Some resorts have capitalized on the medical benefits of certain climates by developing facilities (spas) to "cure" people with poor health.

Scenery

Dramatic scenery is a fascinating attraction. Scenery can be classified broadly as landforms, water, and vegetation. In a large part, the American national parks system was established in order to preserve America's rich scenic resources. The more recent movement to establish wilderness areas is further evidence of the value society places on scenic areas.

Landforms such as mountains, canyons, cliffs, volcanoes, coral reefs, and plains are some of nature's great wonders that never fail to awe the tourist. Crater Lake in Oregon, Mt. McKinley in Alaska, the Grand Canyon in Arizona, Canyonlands in Utah, the coral reefs of Australia, the Himalayas, Ras Muhammad on the Red Sea, the Amalfi Drive in Italy, and the Flint Hills of Kansas are among inspiring views that attract a considerable number of tourists.

Water, like mountains, has a special appeal for most people. It is, therefore, no coincidence that the majority of the great resorts are along the oceans and seas. The Riviera in France, the Black Sea in Russia, Cancun in Mexico, Costa del Sol in Spain, and the islands of the Pacific and Caribbean are proofs of the drawing power of water. Lakes and rivers are also major attractors of tourism. Lake Nasser is as spectacular as the Pyramids. The Lake District in England is well worth a visit. Every American state has lakes for recreational use that are important to their economies.

Little needs to be said about the importance to tourism of Niagara Falls, Yosemite Falls, or Victoria Falls. Glaciers and geysers also contribute significantly to the tourist trade. Glacier National Park, Old Faithful in Yellowstone, and the geysers of Iceland underline the attracting power that water has for tourists.

Vegetation is often a tourist attraction. Temperate forests, tropical jungles, grasslands, moors, and deserts all offer dramatic scenery for travelers. Tours to see the fall leaves in the Ozarks and New England are popular; South America and Africa have resorts set in the tropical rain forests; the moors in England attract single tourists and tour groups.

Wildlife

Wildlife attracts two kinds of tourists: those who observe and those who hunt.

Observation

There are a wide variety of wildlife attractions including animals in natural habitats in national parks, forest, and wilderness areas; game parks such as those in East Africa where the emphasis has shifted from hunting to photography and observation trips; game reservations and safari parks where people remain in their cars and drive through, watching the animals in a natural, if restricted, environment; and zoos and aquariums, where the animals and sealife are kept in very confined and restricted habitats for a viewing audience.

Hunting and Fishing

A more active pursuit of wildlife can be important to the tourist industry. In the United States over thirty-five million participate in hunting and fishing. The income derived by some states from these sports is considerable. In 1987, Utah, with a population of a little more than one million residents, had over 220,000 hunters in the field on opening weekend. This explains the importance of hunting revenues to a state.

Outdoor Recreation and Sports
Sports

The desire to participate in sporting events was discussed in the chapter on travel motivation. Therefore, only a brief comment will be included here. The drawing power of sports, to participant and spectator alike, is thoroughly exploited by the travel industry. The Olympic Games attract millions of people, American Super Bowls over 100,000. College football games also have large audiences.

Participation

Major resort centers and areas wishing to attract physically active tourists offer a variety of sporting options. These range from archery to beach combing, bird watching, body surfing, mountain climbing, nature trails, golf, scuba diving, skeet shooting, water skiing, and trap shooting. Furthermore, the desire to be active, or adventurous, has led to hiking and exploration tours. People like to run with the bulls in Pamplona, kayak in rough waters, climb mountains, ride bulls, and so on. Outdoor adventure is a growing industry in the United States.

Others prefer less vigorous physical activities such as observing birds and other animals, and tours are planned to accommodate them also.

Hallmark Events

During hallmark events, such as the Super Bowls and Olympics, people charter buses, fly in private aircraft, and in many cases, create a need for between two to three hundred extra commercial flights. For the 1982 Super Bowl in Detroit fans rented 6,600 cars and 23,000 hotel rooms. The average fan spends $200 to $250 per day—nearly four times as much as the average tourist. The Los Angeles Super Bowl in 1987 brought in an estimated $100 million to the area.[4] ABC contracted with Calgary to televise the 1988

Olympics for $309 million. The fee paid not only increased the possibility of economic success, but drew the attention of thousands of potential travelers to Calgary as a ski area, that many may never have thought of before.

When Alabama played the University of Southern California in the fall of 1977, nine charter aircraft, in addition to the normal commercial flights, were flown from Alabama to southern California. Travel agents and tour operators are quick to schedule tours in conjunction with athletic events to take advantage of the extra business engendered.

Resorts that specialize in golf and tennis tournaments cover the warmer sections of the United States.

Entertainment

The use of entertainment to fill leisure time is characteristic of the modern urban world. The entertainment industry is, therefore, very important to it. Since a variety of activities have been developed to provide entertainment, resorts and tourist agencies stress the entertainment features of their resorts in advertisements.

Theme and Amusement Parks

Disney is a household word, not only for his movies, but for his two theme parks, Disney World in Florida and Disneyland in southern California. Both are major attractions for foreign, as well as American tourists. Scattered throughout the world, especially in the United States, are a host of other successful parks. Opryland USA in Nashville, Six Flags Over Texas in the Dallas-Fort Worth area, Tivoli in Copenhagen, and Magic Mountain in southern California are only a few of the many examples of popular theme parks.

Cinemas and Theaters

Some cities have a well-established tourist trade chiefly because of the theaters and cinemas available. The outstanding ones are in capitals such as Paris, Vienna, Washington, New York, London, and Moscow. In addition, Los Angeles is a major tourist center because of its television and cinema industry.

Nightlife

Cinemas and theaters are a part of nightlife. However, nightlife is in a special category because certain cities and resorts have such unique and interesting activities that attract large numbers of tourists. One of the major factors in the selection of convention sites is the amount and form of nightlife available. New Orleans, San Francisco, Toronto, Las Vegas, and Miami are good examples of cities in the United States that are famous for their nightlife.

Cuisine

Some resorts and cities have excellent, and even unique, food. Although food alone is not a major pull factor for most tourists, it does exert a strong secondary influence. The popular French Market in New Orleans is as well known as Paris for its cuisine. Many who appreciate good eating

and cooking go for the gourmet Cajun meals at such places as the famed Café Brulot.

Gambling

There are some towns and cities that owe their very existence to gambling; the cuisine and entertainment offered are of secondary importance. Las Vegas, Monte Carlo, and now Atlantic City are attracting large numbers of tourists. To enlarge their tourist centers, many states have actively pursued the tourist dollar with gambling. Southern Florida, feeling at a disadvantage in attracting tourists, has twice placed the issue of gambling on the election ballot. Every state but two now offer some form of gambling. Those states, which have little or no gambling, such as Utah and Idaho, have a steady flow of traffic through them to Nevada and Wyoming, that do.

World's Fairs

Major expositions, such as world's fairs, draw people from everywhere. They make it possible for travelers to see the industry, products and art of other countries that they would probably otherwise not. The Eiffel Tower in Paris was erected as part of a world's fair. The waterfront area of Vancouver, Canada, was renovated to accommodate the 1986 World's Fair. Not only did large numbers of visitors attend the fair, but they also toured the Northwest. It was very difficult to book a cruise directly to Alaska since most included a stopover in Vancouver to visit the fair.

Health and Spas

Historically, traveling to spas to restore one's health has been an important tourist activity. Bath in England, Davos in Switzerland, and Baden in Austria have always been renowned spa centers. Japan's highland area is full of recreation centers which have spas as their main attraction.

Harvey's Casino in Lake Tahoe, Nevada.

Lastly, areas that have been historically significant in the treatment of diseases have become tourist attractions. Kalaupapa, Hawaii, a famous leper's colony will after its remaining patients die or move away, be put under the control of the National Park Service. The discovery of a cure for leprosy means that Kalaupapa will not longer be needed to provide medical services.

ENHANCEMENT OF ATTRACTIONS

Two major elements enhance the desirability of an attraction for tourists. They are accessibility, discussed earlier, and the provision of amenities, including infrastructure and superstructure.

Amenities

The amenities are those additions to an area that enhance its potential value for the tourist trade. Tourists, for example, may want to visit a scenic bay, but, if there are poor accommodations with few services and no facilities for recreation other than swimming in the ocean, they will probably not stay very long. A good example of such a place is the Great Salt Lake. Tourists to Salt Lake valley Utah stay only about a day. The usual pattern, if they are not visiting the Canyonlands area, is to stop in Salt Lake City for part of a day, then visit the Great Salt Lake. However, there are few other attractions there, so, after seeing the lake, there is nothing to do but to return to Salt Lake City or drive on to the next destination.

Tourists want variety and "action." Piers, promenades, parks, pools, putting greens, discos, theaters, and cinemas, are the kind of amenities that a resorts need to attract and keep them. It also means there is a need for a well-developed infrastructure and superstructure.

Infrastructure

The infrastructure is the organization and development of utilities and services in an area. It consists of water supply systems, sewerage disposal systems, gas and electric lines, communication systems, drainage systems, highways, roads, parking lots, parks, lighting, airports, marinas and docks, bus and train stations, and other transportation facilities. These are generally provided by the government.

Superstructure

Superstructure facilities are those that provide direct service to the tourist such as resorts, hotels, restaurants, shopping centers, places of entertainment, museums, stores, airports, and rail and bus terminals. These are usually provided privately, or by companies.

Both the infrastructure and superstructure require large investments of money, and one is not fully effective without the other. Both require a great deal of careful planning to offer a quality, comfortable environment for the tourist—indeed for everyone.

RESORTS

Resorts are formed by combining attractions and amenities together for the express purpose of attracting and serving large numbers of tourists. They have developed in a variety of ways. Some grew from small beginnings, such as a small spa, or a hotel by a lake or on a beach. Others were begun when a government or private agency decided to develop a particular location which had outstanding physical features like Cancun and Miami Beach. A third resort development takes place when towns or cities started for one purpose and then changed character to become resorts. Nazare, Portugal, once a fishing village, and Park City, Utah, once an old mining town, are two towns that have made this transition to resorts.

The early development of resorts was related to the growth of railroads, which made them accessible to the masses. Until then, resorts were almost exclusively for the wealthy.

Attributes of Resorts

H. Robinson has suggested that most resorts have certain characteristics in common. He identified six attributes (the authors add one other element) which characterize resort communities. These are:

1. Lack of manufacturing. If factories exist, their activities are small and unobtrusive. The major employer is the service sector.

2. A high proportion of the population is elderly. This is true of many resorts in the United States with the possible exception of ski resorts.

3. A large commuter population. Many resorts that grew up close to large cities have become bedroom communities for those cities. They offer an environmentally pleasant setting with the recreation amenities typically available in a resort.

4. Employment demand and tourist flow are seasonal, which means there is a season of idleness depending on the location and type of resort. Winter ski resorts are fairly idle during the summer, while lake and forest resorts in the northern United States and Canada have their slack periods in the winter. Southern locations, such as Miami Beach, the Caribbean, and the Mexican Yucatan have their slack season in summer. Many resorts offer discount rates and sponsor special programs in the off-season to attract tourists, business meetings, and conventions.

5. Second home investors are attracted to resort areas. The English, for instance, have purchased many homes along the coastal areas of Spain for second and retirement homes. Many Americans have purchased vacation homes in the ski areas of Colorado and Utah.

6. Resort towns tend to be small unless they are located near, or are part of, a large city with multiple economic activities.

7. Successful resorts have excellent facilities and amenities. Some of the more important items necessary for success are

—Accessibility and good transportation to the areas
—Comfortable and clean accommodations

—Accommodations for a wide economic range
—Adequate parking facilities for both long-term and
  short-term visitors
—Excellent internal transportation facilities
—Open spaces: parks, recreation areas, beaches,
  walks, promenades
—Gardens and flowers
—Amusement facilities such as theaters, cinemas,
  theme parks, and fairs
—Sports facilities such as boats, water skiing, paddle
  boats, golf, miniature golf, tennis, and bowling
—Shopping centers
—Eating facilities: restaurants, cafes, snack bars,
  cafeterias
—Lounging areas and facilities
—Information and tourist centers
—Medical services[5]

There are many different types of resorts. There are mountain and sea resorts, health and beauty resorts, sports resorts, ranches, and religious retreats. Each has its own unique characteristics. However, to be successful, each must include many of the services suggested above. The increase in worldwide leisure time and income will continue to stimulate the growth of resorts. In underdeveloped regions of the world, resorts are an excellent way of developing a tourist trade which has minimum impact on most of the local cultures.

COMMUNITY DEVELOPMENT

Proper planning accomplishes two major tasks. First it assists in the correct development of an area to maximize its use and maintain a comfortable physical and social environment for both tourists and local residents. Second, it assists in the continuous process of improving the attraction to either maintain its momentum as an attractor, or to improve its quality in order to increase demand. The planning process can be done either from the top down, or it can be started at the local level. In the former process, assessment is made of the potential for tourism, and the possible attractions to "pull" them, at the regional or country level. Then development is encouraged, and assistance given in marketing. The latter process creates an impact locally before affecting the state, region, or country.

Tourism has provided an economic stimulus for developing nations. Some projects have developed quickly and made a noticeable impact on the economy; others have developed slowly and it has taken years to realize economic benefits. One factor that caused Sadat to enter into a peace accord with the Israeli government was that Egyptian economic conditions required a reallocation of resources from military to domestic spending; sudden increase of income was required to accomplish the task. Since Israel was the largest generator of tourism in the Middle East and Egypt was a neighbor, tourism could be increased rapidly if their joint borders were open and political conditions were more favorable.

Egypt began the development and promotion of a variety of areas. The common interest which Egypt and Israel had in the Sinai and Red Sea became important to Egypt's development strategy. The coastal areas along the Mediterranean underwent development first; current marketing refers to El Arish as the Palm Springs of Egypt.

Mexico has developed some world-famous resorts through top-down planning. The Mexican government, realizing the importance of tourism to its economy, developed a model to determine which area was the one to transform into a coastal resort. After considerable research, several locations were chosen; the government then developed them into world-class resorts which have become household names for travelers particularly from North America. As we mentioned before, Cancun was developed in this way. Ixtapa, on the west coast of Mexico, was a mango grove until it was developed as a resort.

Many times local events grow to such a size that they make an impact on the state, region, or country. The Spoleto Festival for example, was taken to Charleston in 1977. Since that time it has grown so that it attracted 85,000 people in 1985; it will probably be even larger in the future. In the fall of 1986, the Festival was featured on the "Today" show as an example of a significant attraction on the Atlantic coast. Almost eighty-seven percent of the visitors to Charleston came specifically for the festival. Their presence was more significant than that of the average traveler to South Carolina because they stayed longer and spent more money. Further, a study by the Department of Parks, Recreation, and Tourism found that six percent of all the visitors to South Carolina, other than festival visitors, were attracted to the state because the festival was located there. This is not a unique phenomenon as many areas and states can point to similar success stories.

PLANNING

Planning is discussed in depth in Chapter 15. For now, we will only introduce the concept and make a few comments about its relationship to attractions. All attractions, natural, cultural or social, require careful planning both to preserve them as part of the state or national heritage and to properly develop them with visitor organization and facilities for tourism. Good planning improves the host/guest relationship and alleviates some of the problems that can occur. Planning strives to create a balance between the conserving of the attraction feature and providing facilities and organization for visitor use and enjoyment of the features.

Edward Inskeep, a WTO consultant, has identified the nine stage process as follows:

1. Survey and analyze the site or feature, and determine conservation needs.
2. Identify particularly important conservation areas.
3. Determine the carrying capacity of the site.
4. Determine the market for the attractions.
5. Project visitor demand and reconcile it with the carrying capacity to arrive at projected visitor use.

6. Formulate a plan including consideration of alternative plans.
7. Prepare the final plan.
8. Analyze environmental and sociocultural impact.
9. Implement and manage the plan.[6]

Stage one is the inventory stage which provides an assessment of an area to establish the major and ancillary attractions that will appeal to the general public.

Stage two, the identification of the features that need conservation is important to good planning and enhancing the attraction. Things to be considered are repair and maintenance, restoration, and so on—things which will make the attraction more appealing and preserve it better.

Stage three is critical to the host/guest relationships and maintaining the site's attractiveness. This involves determining the optimum number of visitors that would not be detrimental to either the area or the attraction itself.

Stage four is the analysis of those attractions and the market segment which they would most likely attract. Once a market segment has been identified as the likely user of an attraction, further assessment needs to be made as to the origin and destination of the travelers. Certainly, if a market segment was identified that would be unable to receive adequate information about an area, or if the area were inaccessible to the prospective user, there would be little purpose in its development. Furthermore, consideration of the area must include some evaluation of the quality and character of those attractions inventoried. The authenticity/value ratio is a key element in the evaluation. The greater the authenticity of the experience, the greater the value is to the traveler.

It is important for the attraction to provide some sense of individuality. It is the unique quality of a place that initiates interest. Many times the uniqueness disappears when the attraction draws large numbers of tourists who unconsciously destroy it. Then a void is left to be filled by the shifting market to other attractions. A good example of an area that has retained its individuality is Lancaster County, Pennsylvania—the land of the Amish. The Amish have maintained their culture and religious beliefs in a modern world, despite the demands of tourism. In fact, they have capitalized on their uniqueness by constructing an Amish farm so that tourists may get a feel for the Amish way of life. The Kutztown folk festivals, which draw visitors from all corners of North America, use the customs and norms of the Amish as their central theme.

As discussed earlier, different attractions draw different people, either allocentric or psychocentric. These different types are attracted to different destinations. The outgoing, highly educated allocentric, looking for a new adventure will normally select an attraction less known, in order to be one of the first there, and to keep away from the crowds. The gregarious psychocentric will normally opt for popular attractions where there are crowds of people and where they will be close to home in terms of time and distance.

The final five stages identified by Inskeep are relatively self-explanatory and are discussed in depth in Chapter 15.

Table 5-1 illustrates an overall criteria for touristic attractiveness, summarizing the requirements for success.

PLANNING PROBLEMS

Overload of Attractions

Throughout the world, many of the great attractions are closing, or limiting access, due to the large numbers of tourists who are destroying the very attractions they come to see. People don't vandalize the sites intentionally, but the large number of tourists visiting them are wearing them out. For example, England's Canterbury Cathedral has had to be renovated because the solid stone floors, which were once five inches thick, have been worn down to a fraction of an inch. Stonehenge, which for centuries was open for tourists to wander thorugh and admire, now must be viewed from a path that circles the site. Visitors were wearing away the turf around the stones, exposing them to gravel being kicked up, that was chipping them away. The Parthenon, on the Acropolis in Athens, can only be visited by scholars and restorers. The famous Altamira caves in Santander, Spain were closed in late 1977 because chemical action, caused by breath and perspiration of visitors, was damaging the paintings. To see the facsimiles of the cave paintings, tourists have to visit a museum in Madrid. Tourists who wish to see the mysterious Nazca lines, ruler-straight markings and giant figures etched into the desert of Peru, must either climb a viewing tower or hire a small plane.

All through the world, from South Africa's huge Kruger game park to the Palace of Versailles, government officials are planning ways to control the number of visitors to their most important historical, cultural, and tourist resources in order to preserve them.

Life Cycle

Many within the field of tourism research, development, and planning feel that most attractions go through a cycle. First, the pristine beauty of an area or high-quality attraction becomes soiled and run-down due to improper care, or lack of further development. Next, "highbrow" tourists are replaced by those less refined. Third, residents initially enamored with the tourism industry become disenchanted. Last, tourism, with all its inherent promises, self-destructs.[7] (See Figure 5-1.)

Planning can do a number of things to change this cycle and keep the region from self-destructing. First, would be to simply hold development to a particular level in order to maintain the integrity of the area; or second, would be to have a rigid development plan to which developers must conform. Third, would be to develop new attractions, such as introducing gambling to Atlantic City, to stimulate new growth. Atlantic City was in a state of decline before gambling was introduced; now it is in another growth period.

CURRENT ISSUES AND TRENDS

Claire Gunn has identified some of the variables that are important in current issues pertaining to attractions. These,

TABLE 5-1 CRITERIA FOR TOURISTIC ATTRACTIVENESS

Criteria	Considerations
Natural Factors	
1. Natural beauty	General topography; flora and fauna; proximity to lakes, rivers, sea; islands and islets; caves; waterfalls
2. Climate	Amount of sunshine; temperature; winds, precipitation; and discomfort index
Social Factors	
3. Festivals, fairs, and exhibits	Music and dance festivals; sports events and competitions; concerts cultural events; commercial fairs
4. Attitudes toward tourists	Local congeniality and treatment of tourists; Aloha Spirit
5. Distinctive local features	Folk dress; folk music and dances (not organized); local cuisine; folk handicrafts; specialized products; Polynesian Culture Center; luaus; local architecture; churches; monuments; art museums
Historical Factors	
6. Ancient ruins	Existence, condition, accessibility of ancient ruins; heiaus; petroglyphs
7. Religious significance	Religious importance, in terms of present religious observances and practices
8. Historical prominence	Extent to which a site may be well-known because of important historical events and/or legends; Pearl Harbor is an example
Recreation and Sports	
9. Land sport facilities	Golf; tennis
10. Ocean-related sports	Swimming, surfing; snorkeling; scuba diving; fishing; boating
11. Facilities conducive to health, rest, and tranquility	Health spas; hot-water spas; hiking trails; picnic grounds
Infrastructure, Food and Shelter	
12. Infrastructure above "minimal touristic quality"	Highways and roads; water, electricity, and gas; safety services; health services; communications; public transportation facilities
13. Food and lodging facilities above "minimal touristic quality"	Hotels; restaurants; condos; resorts; camping facilities
Shopping, Educational, and Evening Activities	
14. Shopping facilities	Souvenir and gift shops; handicraft shops; department stores; boutiques; duty free shops; groceries and necessities
15. Nighttime recreation	Night clubs; discotheques; theaters; dinner shows; and cruises
16. Educational facilities	Archeological and ethnographic museums; zoos; botanical gardens; aquarium; commercial parks

Source: Juanita C. Liu and Jan Auyong. "The Attractiveness of Hawaii Tourism." *Travel and Tourism: Thrive or Survive* (Salt Lake City: Travel and Tourism Association, Bureau of Economic and Business Research, Univ. of Utah, 1987), p. 207.

DESTINATION TOURISM EVOLUTION

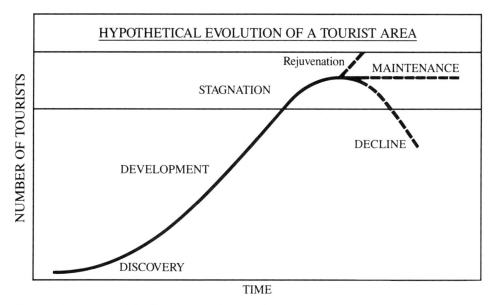

Figure 5-1 Source: Michael K. Haywood, "Can the Tourist-Area Life Cycle
Be Made Operational?," *Tourism Management* (*Sept. 1986*).

as well as some less important issues, help us focus on the nature of attractions in the travel industry today.

Information Explosion

In today's world there has been an information explosion through mass media, the use of personal computers, widespread advertising, visitor's centers, and an increasing supply of travel books. On one hand we seem to have a surfeit of information; on the other we appear to lack information. The United States Conference of Mayors created a National Tourism Data Base to promote American cities by pooling and distributing tourism information for the travel industry and traveling public. This seems to indicate that cities and towns throughout the United States lack tourist information to give to the public. Whatever the situation, despite the amount of material that is available, it is important to understand that people learn most about attractions from friends and relatives. This should not be surprising since they add a personal touch to the decision-making process. Formerly, the lack of information was not important because there were few places to choose from, but today we have so many places and attractions, and so much information to sift through, that it helps the potential traveler to seek personal input into the decision-making process.

Much of the information we are exposed to however, may be detrimental to an attraction. An oil spill in the Gulf of Mexico depressed tourism. As we've discussed, all the media attention on terrorist activities in Europe in 1985 and 1986 had a dramatic impact on tourism from the United States.

The tourist industry, though, can use the media to its advantage. Disney, for example, received considerable publicity in its pursuit of a location in Europe. The final selection of a site in France, despite publicity uncovering negative feelings, was negotiated smoothly. The negative feelings were engendered by the knowledge that American cultural practices concerning fast foods, different forms of labor relations [flexible working hours, few guarantees against dismissal, etc.], and other customs would be imported into France. Positive advertising helped the French people see that the benefits of having Disneyland on French soil far outweighed the costs.

Another important factor in this information explosion is the ability to sort out the difference between information and promotion. As attractions become larger and more commercialized, more and better advertising will be used to promote them. Tourism is an industry that uses glamorous words and pictures to attract people and induce them to use the service or product or visit the attraction.

Although modern technology has improved our ability to take photographs, we don't learn much about the places depicted. Some people seldom have the opportunity to personally participate in the experiences that led to those photographs being taken. They may never even go to the exact same location. But photographs can leave a lasting impression. They have the ability of drawing tourists by the atmosphere or mood they evoke. On the other hand, tourists visit places, take a few pictures, go home and show their friends what a splendid trip they took, but still know little of the area they visited.

Attractions as Independent Entities

Synergy (which means a combined or cooperative action) in the travel industry is expressed as an "attraction." Although each attraction may be owned and managed by

---

a corporation or government agency, and is situated in a specific area, it cannot be separated from the tourist network as a whole. The travel network of tour operators, marketing experts, sales people, middlemen, owners, etc. combine to present a package of services and attractions to the traveler, both to enhance the pleasure of the trip and to increase the likelihood that the attraction will continue to draw tourists. Attractions are combined into a package (network) to enlarge the experiences of travelers and to increase their potential draw.

Management Difficulties

The increasing complexity of the world is mirrored in the development and management of attractions. While newcomers can enter the field and develop an attraction or a service on a small scale, the complexity of today's world sets the stage for failure of "amateur" entrepreneurs if they endeavor to expand. Not only is management far more complex, but major issues are also far more complex than they once were. Gunn pointed out that fewer large theme parks will be developed in the future, due to both the lack of capital and the type and combinations of management skills needed to complete and manage the project. Today, conflicting priorities have been focused on preservation, environmental, and restoration issues. On the one hand we have the purist who wants to have buildings and the environment maintained in their original states; on the other we have the interpretive user, who wants to modify building interiors and environments to meet the needs of a modern industry. To illustrate the complicated nature of such issues, Gunn raised a number of questions that need to be asked when considering the building that would be a historic attraction. These questions are:

1. How pure must the restoration be?
2. Can the outside be restored to that of an earlier period and the inside be renovated for contemporary use?
3. Are visits even to be allowed inside?
4. If so, will the building need to be air conditioned?
5. How can this be done so that the building will retain its historical context?
6. Are the artifacts so fragile and valuable that they will be destroyed by visitor use?
7. Who can be hired to design visitor flows so that the resource can be protected?
8. Where will the conveniences be positioned, and how will they be designed to meet the needs of forty-passenger busloads?
9. How much interpretation should be introduced?[8]

Increased Interest in Cultural Tourism

While American interest remains high for trips to Europe and Asia and countries such as Mexico, there is an increasing desire to see and participate in the daily life of the people. This new trend is expressed in a number of ways—the matching of professional interests such as physicians visiting other physicians, local health centers and/or hospitals; farmers and farm organizations visiting their counterparts; teachers visiting schools and organizations associated with teaching; and government employees assessing the social problems of city governments in other areas. Of course, some of this interest may have been influenced by tax laws that allow a part of professional travel expenses to be tax deductible. However, the interest does go beyond that of the Internal Revenue Service. More and more programs and tours are including experiences that allow tourists to interact with the local culture in activities such as visiting with families in private homes, staying overnight in a traditional Mongolian tent (called a yurt), or visiting in a Bedouin tent. A number of university programs have become popular because they emphasize that the tour host will be a professor from the university faculty; one who is familiar with the region to be visited, and who can offer considerably more insight than a hired tour guide. Many university programs to the Holy Land include a number of lectures concerning the culture and religious significance of the Holy Land, which are given before the group arrives in Israel. These lectures are generally attended by many of the participants.

The growth of cultural centers throughout the world is another indication of the increasing interest in the culture of an area. The popularity of the Epcot Development Center is an excellent example.

The Evolving Nature of Attractions

A major characteristic of the evolving nature of tourism has been discussed in the nature of the life cycle of a specific attraction. The second characteristic is the continued development of new attractions. The limiting factor in the development of new and lasting attractions is the human mind. Product creativity and innovation change the nature of the attraction landscape. Many developing nations have areas or sites that would make significant attractions and draw large numbers of travelers if developed. Time, capital, and advertising will bring these attractions to the forefront of the travel industry and to the traveling public. For example, Turkey is just starting to be discovered and beginning to provide an infrastructure and suprastructure that will support a growing tourist market. It offers the uniqueness similar to that of Greece or the Middle East, combined with the safety and proximity of major European markets.

Existing attractions can be changed to further enhance the attraction. Putting the Epcot (Experimental Prototype Community of Tomorrow) Center next to Disney World in Florida offers an excellent example of a way to enhance the quality of an already excellent attraction in an area. The development of the new Disney theme park near Paris, France will encompass many of the ideas of the Epcot Center, which contains super high-tech exhibits such as robots, computers, giant television sets, as well as historical exhibits sponsored by companies who wish to advertise on a grand scale (General Motors, Exxon, Sony, and Honda). In France, Euro-Disneyland will offer a tribute to French history and culture.

The growth of animation is another example of how modern technology can be used to create new attractions. Animation presently focuses on three types of attractions, shows, museums, and amusement parks. It now enhances major theme parks such as Disney, Six Flags, MCA, Inc., Busch Gardens, and Fantasyland; animation is also used in the West Edmonton Mall in Canada.

Today, in an effort to make better use of attractions, greater attention is given to advertising in off-peak and shoulder periods.

Seasonal Variations

One of the salient characteristics of the travel industry is its seasonal demand. Demand for tourism varies by season, by month, by week, and by day. In some tourist regions, there is a distinct *high season,* and an equally distinct *low season.* Air travelers have seen a marked difference in the number of people flying, as well as the amount of the fare charged, depending on the day of the week. Visitors to recreation centers and golf courses find that they wait a long time before beginning an activity on certain days of the week, while on other days they can start at once. Most tourist data on arrivals and departures show considerable fluctuation from month to month due to seasonal demand; some show fluctuation from day to day. Raphael Baron has identified two types of seasonal demand. He uses the terms *natural seasonality* and *institutionalized seasonality.* Natural seasonality is the change that occurs in the climate and weather throughout the year, and includes such aspects as hours of daylight, extremes in temperatures, rainfall, snow, and so on. This seasonal change affects agricultural production, transportation, commerce, and the construction industry as well as tourism. Institutionalized seasonality includes recognized holidays, school vacations, and festival days. Some of these institutionalized holidays and events such as Easter are variable—they come on different days and in different months from year to year. The fiscal year, which affects budgets and taxes, also creates seasonal change and demand, not only economically, but also in the availability of free time for vacations as well. These seasonal changes, whether natural or institutionalized, have considerable influence on the tourist industry. In addition, different types of travelers are common to each season. In Europe, for example, a high proportion of young people travel in the summer, while there is a higher proportion of conference and business tourists in the other seasons. This results in lower tourist expenditures in the summer.

In Mexico, for example, there is a seasonal difference in hotel/motel/camping occupancy rates in various areas. The coastal areas, relying on sun and fun, have their peak tourist season during the warmer months; while inland areas such as Mexico City and Merida, have peak seasons coinciding with institutional seasonality.

In addition there are differences in the times that Americans are likely to travel. Monthly departures to Europe are heaviest in the summer—June, July, and August—and command peak fares. This is associated with both natural and institutional seasonal changes when free time and good weather coincide.

Seasonality changes from country to country. For example, Israel has strong peaks in the spring (associated with the Passover festival and Easter), and in the winter (associated with Christmas). Spring is the principal peak season for tourists in Germany, Scandinavia, and South America, while December is the peak for tourists in South Africa, Australia, and New Zealand. Summer is the best season for touring France. In the United States, in such places as Florida and the ski areas of Utah, Colorado, and other western states, the heaviest tourist trade is in the winter. The United Kingdom is invaded by tourists during June, July, and August, when good weather patterns tend to prevail, and most free time is available.

Seasonal international and domestic tourism is characterized by the following traits:

1. Summer tourism, with its emphasis on sun and swimming, has a short season—July and August—in the northern hemisphere, and longer seasons farther south, with a corresponding summer season in January and February in the southern hemisphere.

2. Most long vacations for the majority of the working population and students are in the summer months.

3. Cultural tourism can take place throughout the year, but peaks during specific cultural or religious festivals.

4. Business and conference travel takes place throughout the year; but peaks at times other than popular vacation seasons.

5. Vacation areas specializing in particular activities will enjoy peak business during periods that climatically favor that activity.

The industry has tried to establish methods of extending the seasons and attractions of vacation areas to draw people at different times of the year. The airlines offer lower fares during their off-season; hotels charge lower room rates; resort centers hold special entertainment presentations in an effort to attract tourists out of season. The Costa del Sol in Spain offers special packages to retired people who have free time all year. Moab, Utah, a small town with a large summer tourist population drawn by Canyonlands National Park, conducts a late-year baseball tournament in order to use their tourist facilities over a longer period of time.

There is also a weekly cyclical side of tourism, which affects the airline industry. They have tried to adjust this travel imbalance by offering special fares for travel during the week. For instance, a trip from Salt Lake City to Hawaii on an excursion fare during the week is approximately $20 less than a weekend excursion fare. Many special fares at outstanding savings are available only on weekdays. This has created a balancing of air traffic to Hawaii. The tourist industry has taken advantage of the lower weekday air rates to encourage tourist travel then, particularly on Thursdays and Mondays, in an effort to match the high amount of traffic on Saturdays.

Vulnerability of Attractions

The development of tourist attractions is vulnerable to external factors. The problem of terrorism and the influence it has had on tourism has already been discussed. Not only has it reduced the number of visitors to various areas, but it has also caused a shift in the sponsoring of new events. The Philippines and South Korea have also had internal strife that troubles tourists. The increased need for protection has created higher insurance costs that could prohibit or restrict the future development of tourism. Although United States airlines have only one death per five million air miles and theme parks one death per sixty-five million visitors, insurance rates have skyrocketed, making new developments in these two industries more difficult. Land values in areas of potential major attractions have also increased tremendously, making it too expensive to be developed. The land near Santa Clara, which was to be the site of the Great American Park, sold for $200 million. In order to pay for the land, the cost of development, and maintenance after the park was built, millions of tourists would have had to pass through its gates.

RESEARCH AND REVIEW

1. What were the seven wonders of the ancient world?

2. What is an attraction?

3. Identify and give examples of the nine major classifications of attractions?

4. What are amenities?

5. Describe five of the seven attributes of resorts.

6. How important is time-shares to a resort?

7. What two major tasks does proper planning accomplish?

8. What role does planning play in attraction development and maintenance?

9. How has the information explosion been helpful to both the visitor and the destination?

10. What are three examples of cultural tourism experiences?

11. What are some differences between developing and industrial counties in the evolving nature of attractions?

12. Define the two types of seasonality.

13. What are three ways the industry tries to adjust for seasonality?

ENDNOTES

1. John A. Jakle, *The Tourist* (Lincoln, NE: Univ. of Nebraska, 1985), p. 24.
2. Ibid., p. 23.
3. Taken from "Vacation Memories," *Ideals* (Milwaukee, WI: Ideals Publishing Co.), Vol. 25, No. 4, July 1968. Used by permission of Peggy Milcuch.
4. *USA Today* (Jan. 20, 1987), p. C1.
5. Robinson, pp. 157–158.
6. Edward Inskeep, "Interdisciplinary Study Cycle: Planning of Cultural Tourist Attractions" (Granada, Spain: WTO, 1987), 3.3.
7. Michael K. Haywood, "Can the Tourist-Area Life Cycle be Made Operational?" *Tourism Management* (Sept. 1986), p. 158.
8. Claire Gunn, "Getting Ready for Megatrends in Travel Attractions," *Tourism Management* (June 1985), pp. 138–141.

CHAPTER 6

LODGING AND FOOD SERVICES

Lodging and food services are two of the biggest businesses in industrialized countries. Both lodging and food services offer a wide range of jobs, from the relatively unskilled to highly technical and skilled positions. The amount of income and number of jobs available are most impressive. In developing societies, both services offer considerable opportunity for jobs, since most don't require highly skilled people and are labor intensive. These latter facts make these two services of great value where employment is scarce.

THE LODGING INDUSTRY

Since the beginning of history, there has been some form of lodging industry. Early inns were not particularly inviting, and in many instances the wealthy avoided them by carrying their own tents and cooks. During imperial Roman times most inns offered a bed and a candelabra; one's own servants did the cooking.[1] The early and classical reference to an inn is found in the Bible. Christ's earthly father, Joseph, was told, "There is no room at the inn." However, it was probably in the sixth century that lodging began to develop significantly. Although money was used earlier, particularly by the Romans, the sixth century seems to be the pivotal time for its use in the lodging industry. With the growth of lodging, the food industry grew accordingly. During the Industrial Revolution (at its height in the late 1700s and early 1800s), the need for lodging and food became much greater as people poured into the cities to work. Businesses and the travel industry grew together. The Industrial Revolution and the development of spa and ocean side facilities (primarily for health reasons) aided a fledgling hotel industry. By 1750, Brighton, Blackpool, Southend, and other English seaside resorts were attracting bathers to the shores to drink mineral waters, and immerse their bodies in the sea. Similarly, in the United States, Atlantic City and Saratoga were becoming household names for the same purpose.

In the seventeenth century, English inns were offering food, drinks in private parlors, and lodging at a reasonable price. The French had establishments called *hotels*, which meant mansions. Throughout Europe, palatial buildings were available to transients, sometimes on a paid basis, but only with royal or high governmental sanction.

In the United States, the first hotel was the Union Public Hotel, built in Washington, DC in 1793. The second, in 1793, was in New York City and called the City Hotel. In 1794, New York had a population of 30,000, and the hotel was one of the biggest buildings in the city. It consisted of a total of seventy-three rooms. About this time, a deluxe (first class) hotel called Tremont House, was built in Boston. It was the largest and costliest building that had ever been erected in America. Tabel 6-1 with extracts from the book *Fare Thee Well* lists the amenities developed in hotels during the 1800s. At the same time, hotels in the western parts of Canada and the United States were still rather primitive. Table 6-2 is a list of the house rules for a room at the Macleod Hotel in Canada in the late 1800s. Development in lodging closely followed that of transportation, particularly the development of railroads both in Europe and the United States. Rail service advanced towards the end of the Industrial Revolution and helped increase the movement of people to the cities; it was a symbol of business growth. This led to many more business travelers and more people with time to travel. The railroad's contribution to the hotel industry was not only as an agent in society, but also as a builder. Early railroad companies

built large terminal hotels which were an important part of that industry for the following one hundred years. Not only did the railroads build these large hotels, but they also acted as generators which fed smaller hotels built near the stations to offer accommodations for weary travelers. By the late 1800s, hotels were well established in large and growing cities like San Francisco and Chicago. The Palmer House, Briggs House, Sherman House, Grand Pacific, and The Pick Congress are still recognized as first-class hotels in Chicago.[2]

The forerunner of our motel industry did not offer the same amenities or luxury to the traveler as did the large hotels in resort areas and large cities. These early "motels," or taverns as they were called in the 1800s, were built along the newly-developing road system. The forefather of today's interstate system had its inception in 1806, created by an act of Congress. Construction began in 1811. The purpose of the road system was to connect Cumberland and Maryland on the northern bank of the Potomac with the state of Ohio. As this road was laid, taverns were built along it. However, these early motels were probably not the type in which we would normally have reserved rooms. These first taverns were built of logs and had one or two rooms and a fireplace in front of which the guests slept on the floor. Of course, meals were not yet certified by the Diner's Club or Duncan Hines, and generally consisted of game, fish, potatoes and/or cereals, indifferently cooked.

The lodging industry became so well developed by the twentieth century that in 1910 the American Hotel Protective Association was formed with sixty important hoteliers at the initial meeting. They were concerned about protecting themselves from the receipt of bad checks. By this time

---

TABLE 6-1 HOTEL DEVELOPMENTS IN THE 1800s

1829—First bellboys (the Tremont called them Rotunda Men).

1829—First inside water closets (Tremont) signaling disappearance of the old outhouses.

1829—Debut of the now ubiquitous hotel clerk, complete with company smile (Tremont).

1829—A matter of some dispute is the appearance of the French cuisine on Yankee menus, but historians give the nod to the Tremont.

1829—No argument here; the Tremont had the first menu cards.

1829—Annunciators placed in Tremont rooms.

1829—Room keys to give Tremont guests a degree of privacy.

1829—Start of permanent residency in hotels—Tremont again showed the way.

1829—Mostly for the ladies, the Tremont set aside a quiet Reading Room.

1817—[1830] A disputed date. Nobody quite agrees about the first hotel to have gaslight, but since Baltimore, Maryland had the first public gasworks in the U.S., Barnum's City Hotel, in that city, lays claim to having gaslight first.

1836—New York's City Hotel was the first to offer clubs a regular meeting place.

1836—House rules first defined by the Astor House and posted in guests' rooms.

1836—Washington Hall in New York first instituted the European Plan.

1846—Eastern Exchange Hotel, Boston, had first central heating system.

1848—The New England Hotel, Boston, offered first safe deposit boxes for the protection of cash brought in by the merchants who were staying there.

1875—Floor clerks installed by the Palace Hotel, San Francisco.

1888—Electric lights first dazzled guests in New York's Hotel Everett.

Source: Excerpt from *Fare Thee Well* by Leslie Dorse and Janice Devine. Used by permission of Crown Publishers, Inc.

TABLE 6-2 HOTEL REGULATIONS

Macleod House - 1882

1. Guests will be provided with breakfast and dinner, but must rustle their own lunch.

2. Spiked boots and spurs must be removed at night before retiring. Dogs are not allowed in the bunks, but may sleep underneath. Only one dog allowed to a room.

3. Candles, hot water and other luxuries charged extra, also towels and soap. Towels changed weekly.

4. Insect powder for sale at the bar.

5. Crap, Chuck Luck, Stud Horse Poker, and Black Jack games are run by the management.

6. Two or more persons must sleep on one bed when requested to do so by the management.

7. Baths furnished free down at the river, but bathers must furnish their own soap and towels.

8. Only regularly registered guests will be allowed the special privilege of sleeping on the Bar Room floor.

9. Guests without baggage must sleep in the vacant lot and board elsewhere until their baggage arrives.

10. No cheques cashed for anybody. Payment must be made in cash, gold dust and blue chips.

11. To attract attention of waiters, or ball boys, shoot a hole through the door panel. Two shots for ice water, three for a deck of cards, etc.

12. All guests are requested to arise at 6 a.m. This is imperative as the sheets are needed for table cloths.

13. No tips must be given to any waiters or servants. Leave them with the proprietor and he will distribute them if necessary.

14. Every known fluid (except water) for sale at the bar.

15. No more than one dog allowed to be kept in each single room.

16. No kicking, regarding the quality or quantity of the meals will be allowed; those who do not like the provender will get out or will be put out. Assault on the cook strictly prohibited.

17. Quarrelsome or boisterous persons, also those who shoot off without provocation, guns or other explosive weapons on the premises and all boarders who get killed will not be allowed to remain in the house. When guests find themselves or their luggage thrown over the fence, they may consider that they have received notice to quit.

18. In case of Fire, the guests are requested to escape without delay.

19. Guests are forbidden to strike matches or spit on the floor or sleep in bed with their boots on.

20. Everything cash in advance. Following Tariff subject to change; Board, $25.00 per month: board and lodging, $50.00 per month with wooden bench to sleep on. Board and lodging $60.00 per month with bed to sleep on.

there were two types of travelers: those seeking rest or relaxation at a resort, and those on business who traveled to city centers to visit their clients and customers. Travel was still mostly by train, and would be so for the next fifty years. In 1886, the United States Hotel Directory contained 708 pages listing all hotels in the country at that time. By 1910, there were probably 10,000 hotels employing over 300,000 people and totaling about one million rooms.

With the development of the automobile and the improvement of roads, the motel industry began to grow in earnest. Near Douglas, Arizona, in 1913, workers erected six wooden structures on a vacant lot that had been used as an "auto camp." It was a place where drivers could park their cars for the night and sleep in them; some would pitch tents. This service was copied around the country until, by 1920, there were thousands dotting the landscape. The term motel was first used on a California facility erected in 1925. The camps and early motels continued to spread on the edges of cities until the end of the Second World War. Entrepreneurs took advantage of cheap land to build one-story, frame structures. In comparison to the hotels of the time, with their formal atmosphere and expensive service, motels provided clean, safe inexpensive accommodations. By the 1960s there were over 50,000 establishments with over 800,000 rooms and a

combined income of over $2 billion. Most were independent and locally owned.[3]

Following the Second World War, with improvements in roads and other societal changes, mass tourism began. There was a subsequent sudden rise in the construction of hotels and motels. Their number peaked in 1958 with over 70,000 establishments. Since that time, the number of hotels and motels has decreased while the number of rooms and employees have increased. A 1982 census indicated half that number of establishments with triple the number of rooms. In addition, from 1930 to 1970, motels represented an increasing percentage of the hotel room inventory, but beginning in 1972, their peak year, they too began to decline.[4]

As the interstate highway system neared completion in 1972, a change in the pattern of hotel/motel locations occurred. Small towns were bypassed; travel time between major cities was reduced considerably; thousands of small family-run and chain motels closed because of their locations. At the same time, the increasing use of airlines as a means of transportation, particularly for the business traveler, increased the demand for accommodations in the cities. The growth of resorts and hotels at major attractions and destinations also pulled the industry to cities, which were themselves attractions. The major hotel growth recently has been around airports, in downtown areas, and in resorts.

CLASSIFICATION OF HOTELS AND MOTELS

Hotels/motels can be categorized in four different ways depending on their locations. They are commercial, resort, transit, and special interest or groups. Commercial hotels are those that cater to businesspeople, and are located either near the airports or in downtown areas, while resorts and destination hotels are for vacation visitors. The commercial hotels offer many amenities to businesspeople including stores, restaurants, lounges, and some shopping areas. Stays in these hotels are usually short (one to three days), while stays in resort hotels are longer (five to ten days). The resort or destination hotels offer considerably more amenities, shops, and recreation opportunities (tennis, golf). Some of these hotels are the most luxurious of all.

The third type, transit accommodations (e.g., economy motels), are those located along major routes; their primary purpose is to provide a clean bed and an inexpensive stay, generally for one night. They are normally used by travelers en route to a major destination, and the night's stop is for rest rather than enjoyment. Historically, vacationers in the United States placed major emphasis on travel to and from a destination. For example, if a family had two weeks vacation they would generally spend about ten days traveling to and from the destination point, enjoying the journey along the road, sight-seeing, and relaxing at night by the motel pool. On the other hand, Europeans are more point oriented; they go to a destination as quickly as possible, then take side trips from there to surrounding attractions. People in the United States are slowly beginning to change to the European pattern. They now want to spend less time traveling to their destinations, and more time at them, in more luxurious settings than previously. The president of Quality Inn, during a Travel and Tourism Research Association meeting, discussing the movement of Quality Inns into the economy market with a new chain, the Comfort Inns, quoted his barber's concise statement as representative of the changing market—"I go like the devil staying as cheaply as possible until I get to Las Vegas, Disneyland or the destination; then I want to be pampered." The fourth

category, is comprised of a broad range of hotels for special interest groups. Youth hostels, "fitness" farms, and castle hotels, are examples of hotels/motels in this group.

WORLDWIDE LODGING TRENDS

With the development of mass tourism on an international scale, lodging is the main concern of travelers. With adequate lodging, the rest of the tourist infrastructure can be put in place rather rapidly. Since what may be considered quality lodging differs from one place in the world to another, a major concern is to develop a standardized classification of hotels. The main purpose would be to establish certain operational standards, which guarantee a homogeneous level of service delivered by the hotel establishment, within each of the proposed categories. Thus, with standardization, it would be easier for tour operators, travel agencies, tourist enterprises, and tourists themselves to know exactly what standard of service is offered by each hotel in a given country. The classification system would be divided into five categories depending upon the level of service offered, sanitary and safety standards, common areas, rooms, amenities, and so on.

As we can see in Table 6-3, hotels, like airlines, rely heavily on business travel. The North American market has a much higher percentage of tourists, and the lowest percentage of business travelers, than other areas. This is probably because it is relatively isolated from the other continents and has a highly developed domestic market. Many of the developing nations have a greater number of business travelers arriving rather than departing; businesses and governments in the industrialized countries have invested heavily in developing countries, and send representatives to conduct their business affairs. Industrialized nations are also far more complex than developing ones and there is much greater interchange within the countries leading to more domestic travel. North Americans have either less opportunity or ability to travel outside the continent because of the long distances and consequent costs.

PRODUCT DIFFERENTIATION

Table 6-4 illustrates the many options available to today's traveler.

TABLE 6-3 CHARACTER OF WORLD'S LODGING INDUSTRY—1986

Characteristics	All Hotels	Africa and the Middle East	Asia Australia	North America	Europe	Latin America and Caribbean
Percent Occupancy	64.6	55.9	67.9	68.4	62.9	63.4
Percent Double Occ.	36.2	21.8	45.6	46.6	31.6	70.4
Aver. Room Rate	$56.72	$58.72	$51.65	$61.40	$51.99	$55.56
Composition of Sales						
Rooms	56.0%	53.1%	50.8%	60.1%	50.3%	55.4%
Food	24.6	21.6	27.7	21.8	29.2	22.8
Beverage	10.7	8.3	10.3	8.6	14.7	9.6
Telephone	3.7	7.1	3.8	2.5	2.9	4.2
Other	5.0	9.9	7.4	3.2	2.9	8.0

Source: *Travel and Leisure's World Travel Overview 1987/1988.*

TABLE 6-4 TYPES OF LODGING ACCOMMODATIONS

Type	Characteristic	Cost
Hotels		
Luxury	Considerble amenities	Expensive
First Class	Comfortable	Moderately priced
Economic	Basic	Inexpensive
Hostels	Minimal facilities for youth	Inexpensive
Campground	Generally for families	Inexpensive
Pensions	Small hotels	Inexpensive
Bed & Breakfasts	Lodging in private homes	Inexpensive in Europe— More expensive in U.S.
Motels	Convenient for auto tourist	Expensive to inexpensive
Condominiums	Generally in resorts and destination locations	Moderately expensive
Castles, Chateaux and Mansions	Excellent accommodations	Expensive
Health Spas	Exercise options	Expensive to very expensive

Source: Compiled by the authors.

Hotels

Within the hotel sector of the lodging industry there are many options. Hotels have been designed and built to meet almost any kind of budget or comfort level that the traveling public might want. As you can see from Figure 6-1, the largest part of the hotel market is business and government. This can be further divided. Under business and government, convention travel and business is extremely important, particularly in city locations perceived as exciting or exotic destinations.

The most recent development has been in the luxury and economy hotel/motel segments. Deluxe hotels at out-standing destinations (in both cities and resorts), offer considerable comfort and opportunity to relax. They offer a full range of shopping and luxurious services. Hilton, Hyatt, Marriott, Radisson, and Stouffer have become popular names in deluxe hotel development. In many cases, the hotels themselves have become attractions because of their use of open space, atriums, glass elevators, and so on. This is carried over into their food services. These hotels, located in major cities, are much frequented not only by tourists but by local people as well, delighting in both excellent food and an attractive environment.

Since the vast majority of the population is in the mid-

COMPOSITION OF MARKET

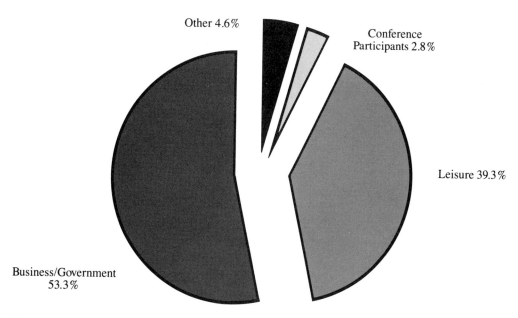

Other 4.6%

Conference Participants 2.8%

Leisure 39.3%

Business/Government 53.3%

Figure 6-1 Reprinted with permission from *U.S. Economy/Limited - Service Lodging Industry 1986,* a publication of Laventhol & Horwath.

TABLE 6-5 TOP 25 HOTEL/MOTEL ORGANIZATIONS

Total Number of Rooms		Total Number of Hotels	
1. Holiday Inn/H.I. Crowne Plaza	352,893	1. Best Western	3,364
2. Best Western	171,847	2. Holiday Inn/H.I. Crowne Plaza	1,832
3. Ramada Hotel Group	136,894	3. Quality International	892
4. Sheraton	136,495	4. Ramada Hotel Group	778
5. Marriott Hotels & Resorts	104,670	5. Days Inns	595
6. Quality International	104,366	6. Accor International	544
7. Hilton Hotels	96,788	7. Super 8 Motels	491
8. Days Inns	85,323	8. Sheraton	479
9. Accor International	67,443	9. Forte Hotels International	455
10. Howard Johnson	55,682	10. Howard Johnson	454
11. Hyatt Hotels	48,777	11. Motel 6	432
12. Motel 6	48,750	12. Econo Lodges	417
13. Radisson	37,500	13. Marriott Hotels & Resorts	367
14. Hilton International	37,456	14. Hilton Hotels	273
15. Inter-Continental Hotels	37,325	15. Budget Host Inns	223
16. Forte Hotels Int'l	35,407	16. Red Roof Inns	178
17. Westin Hotels & Resorts	34,291	17. Radisson	158
18. Econo Lodges	33,733	18. Hampton Inns	152
19. Super 8 Motels	31,139	19. Prime Motor Inns	131
20. Meridien Hotels	21,176	20. Friendship Inns	130
21. Embassy Suites	19,621	21. Inter-Continental Hotels	99
22. Red Roof Inns	19,550	22. Hilton International	95
23. Hampton Inns	19,129	23. Hyatt Hotels	89
24. Prime Motor Inns	18,324	24. Embassy Suites	81
25. VMS Realty Partners	17,346	25. Crest Hotels	71

Source: *Travel and Leisure's World Travel Overview 1987/1988.*

dle socioeconomic range, two types of hotels have been developed to serve this large market. The first type, full-service hotels/motels made popular by such chains as Holiday Inn, Quality Inn, Best Western, and the like, located at both destinations and along major paths, have become a common sight on the landscape. They offer a clean room, some recreational activities (usually a swimming pool and a game room), restaurants, and some in-room amenities such as color television, king-size beds, water beds, relatively large rooms, and, at destination points, more extensive room service than along the roads. Table 6-5 is a listing of the largest hotel/motel organizations.

However, in the late 1970s, it became apparent that there were a vast number of travelers who wanted to spend less of their travel budgets on lodging than in other areas; thus, the growth of the economy/limited service industry began. Large chains recognizing this trend were quick to act. Quality Inn introduced the Comfort Inn and Holiday Inn's Hampton Inn are examples of lodging adapted to this change. The trend started in the 1960s with a number of new chains—Imperial 400, Motel 6, and Econo Lodger—that recognized the demand for inexpensive lodging.

Historically, this market had been filled primarily by the small "mom-and-pop" owners, many of whom were rated and advertised by such organizations as AAA and Best Western. This was a service made available to the public to assist them in the selection of a night's lodging. It was designed to provide information about the level of cleanliness and service offered. In the 1970s, Best Western became a franchising organization. Franchised chains are an

indication of the growth being made in this sector of the industry.

These early economy motels lacked amenities such as restaurants, cocktail lounges, and meeting rooms; televisions were provided, but usually for an extra charge, rates were standardized and rooms were constructed and maintained alike throughout the nation. Their major location has been along highways and in the highly-populated centers of the north central United States.

Today, there are well over sixty chains that consider themselves to be in the economy sector. Many have expanded their amenities to include color television, swimming pools, playgrounds, small meeting rooms, and, in some cases, limited food services.

The future of the economy market appears to be bright for existing organizations. The general business patterns of mergers, acquisitions, and consolidations is a strong trend in the economy lodging segment. Dennis Fitzgerald suggested six reasons for continued optimism. They are:

1. From an economic standpoint, there is a much larger portion of the population willing and able to pay $30 a night for accommodations than $100 plus per night.

2. Travel habits are changing with more time being spent away from home and annual vacations now considered a necessity rather than a luxury.

3. More gas efficient automobiles, coupled with stable gasoline prices, means more Americans will make use of their cars by taking shorter (average two to three days), but more frequent trips throughout the United States. This, in turn, will require overnight accommodations.

4. A larger portion of the business and commercial market is being attracted to the economy segment of the industry in an effort to cut their travel costs. This could have a significant impact on government travel and the maintenance of existing per diem rates.

5. The facilities offered today by the economy properties are comparable to the accommodations offered by the midpriced segment of the market only ten years ago.

6. Well-educated consumers will no longer be lured merely by a brand name or extra amenities that they do not need. Cost effectiveness and the best value for the dollar will become top priorities.[5]

These factors and the fact that major hotel chains such as Marriott have responded to the changing trends, even though they have considerable investment in the luxury market, will cause others to invest in that market, too. Market growth is limited though. City properties are becoming very expensive and difficult to obtain. Future expansion for economy chains may have to be done internationally—particularly in Europe, the Far East, and Australia. Days Inn and Super 8 have done well in Canada. Days Inn is also negotiating with Chinese authorities to develop some twenty properties there.[6]

Further market division is occurring for a special segment of the market. In addition to providing for the economy-minded traveler, it has been shown there is a need for quality hotels with fewer amenities such as pools, restaurants, valet and laundry services, saunas, and free in-room movies. The response to this has been the all-suite hotels that emerged in the 1980s. The emphasis of the all-suite hotel is on the unit rather than the public area so important in much of the hotel industry. The units are almost twice as large as those in the standard hotel, and usually incorporate a combination living/parlor area, sleeping area, and kitchenette.

These units are designed for the business traveler, who wants spacious accommodations with a homelike atmosphere yet with functional work areas for displays, interviewing, entertaining, and relaxing. The pleasure market for these hotels is largely a weekend one, since many of these hotels offer free rooms to children traveling with parents on weekends. They also offer the advantage of separate rooms and a kitchen, reducing the expense of eating out. These hotels are located in major business centers of the United States. Since many do not offer food or beverage services, they must be located near restaurants and places of entertainment. These suites are available in a range of price levels from budget to luxury, and are available for either short or long stays. They are more profitable than other accommodations because they have higher occupancy rates, and are less labor intensive; also, they do not have the money-draining amenities of food services on the premises.

There are still a number of smaller, mainly family-run

properties that offer more personal service, although the chain, combined with interstate development drove most out of business. Some people who travel frequently enjoy these because they become well acquainted with the owners. They are recognized and, to some degree pampered with personal service such as a newspaper delivered to the room, birthday recognition, and free coffee. Most small establishments that are developed in the future will be in destination locations, or near major attractions. Much of this development will occur on the property already owned by the existing small hotel owner.

Resorts

The growth of resorts accelerated in the 1980s as Americans changed their vacation patterns. As suggested earlier, the trend to place more emphasis on destinations has accounted for this growth. During the late 1800s, the railroad development process included the building of grand hotels in scenic regions of the country. The Pocono and Catskill Mountains, and Banff in Canada became major resorts for the wealthy. With the advent of modern travel for the general public, resorts were needed to accommodate them, and soon began to dot the landscape around the world. Acapulco, Costa del Sol, Atlantic City, Waikiki Beach, and Miami Beach have become household words. Not only has easier transportation made this possible, but the development of additional lodging modes has been a contributing factor. Following the European pattern, second homes and apartments also grew in the 1950s and 1960s. With an increase in disposable income, residents of the industrialized nations had more money for residences that would only be used on a limited basis. Many wealthy industrialized nations of Europe are in the cold north, while many of its poorer nations border the warm waters of the Mediterranean. While disposable incomes of the industrialized north are growing, the economies of the south welcome the investment being made in apartments and homes along their coastal areas. These investments provide much-needed employment in the construction and service industries and bring capital into the countries concerned.

In addition to the second home market, resorts have become popular retirement centers. Their attractiveness is not only important to the short-term visitor, but highly important to those who wish to settle there. In 1983 there were 900 United States resorts that sold timeshares to 525,000 people. In 1984 there were 1,500 resorts worldwide, providing vacations to 750,000 purchasers.

Bed and Breakfast

Another form of lodging originating in Europe and brought to the United States is bed and breakfast. The original idea was to provide overnight lodging, food, and beverage in a private home. "Bed and Breakfast" signs can be seen in windows of quite a few homes in Britain; while on the continent the traveler will see signs such as "Zimmer Frei," "Chambre d'hote," and "Szoba Kiado," all indicating a bed for the night and breakfast the following day. It was not until the 1970s that the idea was brought to America; most in the United States are more expensive than their counterparts in Europe, where they are considered low-cost lodging. While there are a number in the low-cost range in the United States, the average price range, according to Bernice Chesler in *U.S. New and World Report*, is $30.00 to $50.00 a night. Naturally, prices are higher in cities and resorts and less in small towns and suburbs.

The growth of the bed and breakfast phenomenon in the United States is largely the result of Americans who had been in contact with the system in Europe. To them, it became a more acceptable alternative form of travel lodging. Apparently, retired and semi-retired people with large homes, have been major contributors to the growth in these establishments.

While the travelers most likely to use a bed and breakfast establishment in the United States are a couple traveling for pleasure, some studies have indicated that between twenty to thirty percent of rooms rented are by business travelers.

More business people are turning in their hotel room keys for the chance to bunk in a spare bedroom and be served breakfast in another person's home. The accommodations often are cheaper than at major hotel chains and they offer corporate travelers a home away from home.[7]

The industry started in earnest under Sally Reger during the bicentennial year, 1976, in the historical town of Charlottesville, NC. She organized a few homes and acted as a representative in bringing the hosts and guests together. She started with ten homes and an initial investment of $800, by placing "guesthouses" advertisements in magazines. She established a system for making advance reservations. For these services, she charged the host homes twenty-five percent of the night's lodging. In eight years, her registry increased to 200 homes, and, in 1984, her earnings were in excess of $50,000. This was the beginning of a Reservation Service Organization (RSO) which has now developed into over 200 such organizations offering services to the public. Some of these organizations have expanded their services to include an inspection to insure minimun standards.

Two of the major problems facing bed and breakfast development have been laws governing zoning and health standards. Most city zoning ordinances do not cover bed and breakfast residences. Sometimes they are considered under special use permits or restricted to certain zones. The health codes were also developed before the advent of the bed and breakfast; consequently, many states inspect them as commercial kitchens and require them to comply with a long list of regulations, some of which are not applicable to bed and breakfast.

Campgrounds

Camping is another alternative very popular on both sides of the Atlantic. The Organization for Economic Co-operation and Development, composed of the industrialized nations of Europe, North America, and Asia, provides statistics on campgrounds as well as hotels. In the United States, more than sixty million Americans, owning more than sixty million recreational vehicles and millions of tents

enjoy camping. According the the National Campground Owners Assocation, the 1982 economic analysis of the American campground industry estimated there were 7,300 campgrounds, employing over 80,000 people, and generating approximately $1.7 billion in revenue. This, too, is an industry that depends on national advertising of its standards to attract travelers. One of the leaders in the field has been Kampgrounds of America (KOA). KOA had its beginnings in Billings, Montana in 1962 on the banks of the Yellowstone River. The largest association is the National Campground Owners Association, which provides an annual economic report.

The range of services offered in campgrounds today is expanding, and some can be considered full-service establishments. Most now include stores, dumping stations, firewood, showers, vending machines, laundry equipment, and propane gas. Some, in addition, offer babysitting services, meals, cable television connections and have a nurse/doctor available. They also have a whole range of recreation facilities, from swimming pools and playground equipment to horses for riding and trail bikes and guides for excursions into the countryside.

Other Types of Lodging

The lodging sector provides as many varieties as there are reasons to travel. A traveler wanting to experience many forms of recreation or leisure pursuits can find someone who is willing to offer a service and a night's rest. Those who like to backpack, trail ride, or river run can find a company offering the service. Travelers need only bring themselves and the clothes they are wearing. Campsites, in some cases, are laid out in advance and are readily available for the use of the traveler. The organizers of river runs will provide tents and meals of high quality and variety. There is little left for the traveler to worry over.

Even the various forms of public transportation are offered with facilities for a night's rest. Trains have sleepers in a variety of sizes and quality; ships offer anything from crowded cabins to luxurious suites; first-class travelers on airlines are offered comfortable sleeping arrangements; even passengers on some special motorcoach tours are provided with sleeping arrangements. One bus introduced in the American market, not yet seen extensively, is patterned after the train. It is a double decker where the top is a lounge and the bottom sleeping quarters.

Other accommodations have developed around a specific need or desire of the public, such as health and fitness. A number of "fitness farms" offer not only a good night's lodging, but also assist clients in improving their health or shape. In these establishments foods are selected according to the specific needs of each person and a rigorous course of exercise is designed to shed fat and increase well being.

It is also possible to rent the home of a well-known person. Rex Harrison's villa on the French Riviera or Princess Margaret's four bedroom villa on Mustique are two such examples.

Timeshare

The concept of timesharing originated in Europe, but quickly spread to the United States, where it has become an accepted element of the travel industry. Timesharing is the selling of vacation lodging, usually condominiums, for a specific week or weeks over a given number of years or in perpetuity. Originally, condominiums in resorts were purchased and marketed as either a second home or primary home depending upon the purchaser's needs. The resort would then rent the units during periods that the owner was not in residence, providing an income to assist with the payments. It became evident that a new marketing approach would sell more lodging facilities at a higher return to the developer. First, by selling weeks instead of a permanent residence, the total asking price can be much higher. For example, in Acapulco, a unit which sells for $100,000 as a residential structure would sell for $15,000 per week. Thus, in bringing a total sales price or return of over $500,000. Timesharing also increases the number of potential buyers since the average person, who is restricted by both time and money, would then be able to afford a week at a resort, and still receive the benefits of having made an investment in property.

Hawkins estimated that timeshare in 1985 represented less than a fifth of one percent of the market and was growing faster than the industry as a whole.[8] While resorts, which help account for this rapid growth, have become more popular, a new market is beginning to develop. This is an urban landscape, which is still largely untouched by timeshare developers. For example, in Salt Lake City, in 1986, an apartment house in the process of being renovated for a condominium project, was redesigned as a timeshare condominium once it was seen to have considerable potential: First, there are two annual conferences conducted in Salt Lake City by the center of the Mormon church. In addition, the church has one of the largest genealogical centers in the world. Many people frequently visit Salt Lake City to do genealogical research. There are also many ties between the residents of Utah and other states, particularly California, where many Mormons have moved. Lastly, just south of Salt Lake City, a forty-minute drive away, lies the large church-run school, Brigham Young University, with many students from all over the world. A number of high-rise apartment buildings in the area have clientele who live and work in other regions of the United States. All these factors indicated a market for a timeshare condominium.

Two basic types of timesharing programs have been developed. First, interval or fee-simple programs (probably the most widely sold) provide the purchaser with both an occupancy and ownership right to a specific resort unit for a fixed period of time annually. This unit can be sold or leased, and used for tax purposes like any other real estate purchase. Second, right-to-use programs guarantee an annual occupancy right for a specified period, but do not convey ownership interest in the property. Both types of timeshare ownership require payment of a pro-rata share of the annual maintenance costs of the entire property.

A later development, which has increased the attractiveness of timeshares, is a system of exchanges. This allows a person who purchases a timeshare in a particular resort to trade for another timeshare in another resort. There are several companies that provide computerized trading services for owners. Membership in one of these companies allows a timeshare owner to select another location and obtain an equal amount of time in that resort, while another person, at the same time, can then reserve and use the original timeshare unit.

ORGANIZATION OF THE LODGING INDUSTRY

The hotel is both capital and labor intensive. Hotels provide both a diversity and a considerable number of positions. Naturally, the plan for any particular hotel depends on a wide range of variables such as property location, clientele, services offered, structural layout, type of ownership, etc. Figure 6-2 is an organizational chart typical of a large hotel. From it you can see that a hotel organization can be large and complex.

This chart illustrates seven major divisions. The personnel division provides a central and coordinating office responsible for recruiting new employees and administering policies and employee benefits for the company. The engineering and maintenance staff is reponsible for making necessary repairs and implementing the hotel's energy management program, an item very important to the cost effectiveness of a hotel. The accounting division is responsible for handling the financial activities of the operation, including paying the bills, sending out statements, payroll, and compiling monthly income statements.

The security division provides protection for both the employees and guests. They attend to the common concerns of personal safety as well as large disasters, such as fires, that may occur.

The food and beverage division is the second largest generator of income in many hotels; in others it is not profitable at all. It is responsible for all the food and beverage products provided and served in the hotel dining rooms, lounges, room service, special banquet functions, hospitality suites, and employee food service.

Marketing and sales is responsible for selling the rooms and food service. It is involved in the development of promotional material and advertising, and making direct contacts with prospective clients. The importance of this staff should not be underestimated. To understand the divisions of the marketing and sales staff Figure 6-3 should be read carefully.

The room division is responsible for the front desk, telephone, reservations, uniform services, and housekeeping department. The front office, in this instance, is considered to be the front of the hotel where services that directly effect the clients generally are handled—day-to-day registration, message services, client accounts, and, in many cases a concierge who provides special guest services.

TYPES OF OWNERSHIP

A vast majority of hotel ownership today is in some form of equity ownership. Equity ownership occurs in a number of ways. The most popular are the franchises and consortia as can be seen from hotel chains listed in Table 6-5. All are one or the other of these two types of organizations. Although the nature of the hotel business can be attractive to people, many need access to management and market-

ORGANIZATION CHART OF TYPICAL HOTEL

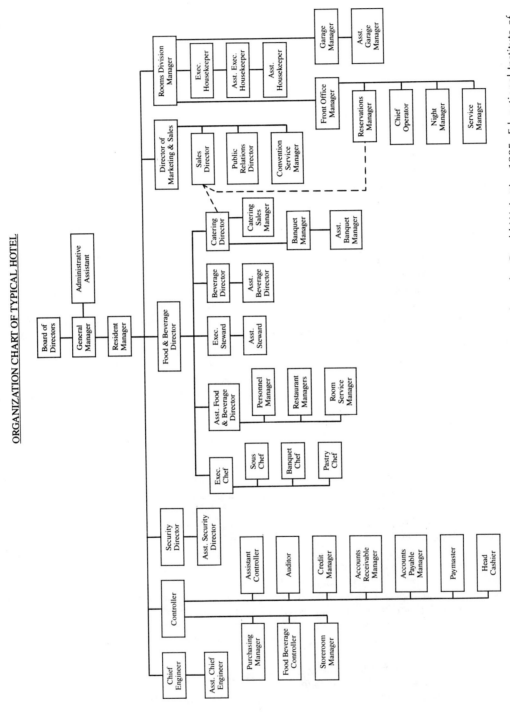

Figure 6-2 Reprinted with permission from *Lodging and Food Service Industry* by Gerald W. Lattin, 1985, Educational Institute of the American Hotel & Motel Association. All rights reserved.

84

ORGANIZATION CHART OF A TYPICAL MARKETING AND SALES STAFF

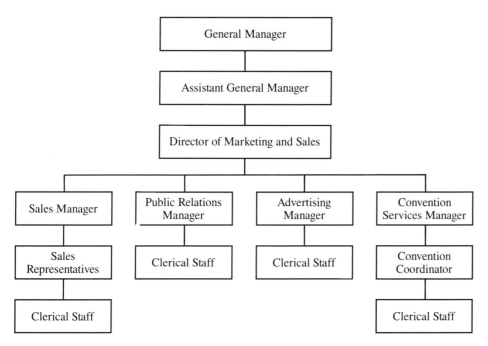

Figure 6-3 Source: Orachorn Kunopasvorakul.

ing assistance, both of which a franchise or consortium can offer. Some of the large companies such as Hilton or Holiday Inn have a franchise plan for regions, but do have some hotels that belong solely to the parent company. The early development of both franchises and consortia was individually motivated, but it became apparent that neither could expand or provide the necessary economic resources to maintain all the hotels of a large chain.

A number of advantages can be gained by franchising:

1. They provide a central reservation system through a toll-free number.
2. They provide regional, national, and international advertising.
3. There is a standardization of product which establishes the public's quality recognition.
4. They provide specialized assistance in development and management of the property.
5. They provide standard manuals of procedure and inspection.
6. The advantages of collective purchasing power provide considerable savings on products and supplies.[9]

Equity ownership can occur either through the issuing of stock (a public company), or by partnerships. Partnerships can either be two or three people combining resources to own a hotel/motel, or are part of an investment team partnership. In an investment partnership, the members place their money with a management company which is not involved in any way in the operation of the hotel. It is, to them, simply an alternative investment opportunity.

Independent ownership of a small percentage of the

market is difficult today due not only to the capital investment needed but also because of the management knowledge and skill needed. In the United States, there are over 125 management companies operating. Independent management companies can provide hotels with more control over daily operations and access to professional staff to supervise the operation of a hotel than others can. A management contract can provide some of the same benefits as franchising.

RATING SYSTEMS

In an effort to rate hotels/motels to assist both the travel industry and the traveler in making decisions, a number of companies have devised some form of rating system. The WTO has undertaken the development of a system for rating of hotels at a world level. Many countries have devised their own schemes. A number of independent rating guides have been published commercialy by individuals, automobile associations, and travel organizations using various combinations of stars, dots, and alphabetical indicators.

Most rating systems are concerned with the quality of the physical structure, furnishings, maintenance, housekeeping, and overall service. The better rating systems have experienced individuals inspect the hotel or restaurants annually. Many are regional field representatives who submit detailed reports to the appropriate office. The raters are anonymous to the facility being rated. *Mobil Travel Guide* uses the following to rate hotels, motels, inns, resorts, and guest ranches:

1 star = Good, better than average
2 stars = Very Good

3 stars = Excellent
4 stars = Outstanding – worth a special trip
5 stars = One of the best in the country

ISSUES AND TRENDS

Vertical or Horizontal Integration

The increasing complexity and high degree of competition in the business world today has led to two types of integration in the hotel industry. The first is a vertical integration where much of the travel package for the client is under one ownership. To date this has only been marginally successful. Some airlines, such as United, which owned the Westin chain, have purchased hotels and car rental firms, and planned to offer a full package of services all controlled by the same company. However, today most United States airlines are selling their travel-related companies. This has been more common in Europe, where the leasing of hotels by large firms that own planes and travel agencies, is accepted practice. The potential of vertical integration is yet to be realized in the United States.

Horizontal integration is conducted mainly through the development of chains concentrating on specific services such as lodging as seen in Holiday Inn and Hilton. This has been far more popular in the United States than vertical integration.

Occupancy Rates

Historically, the occupancy rate has been around sixty percent for the hotel industry to reach the break-even point. Even with a growing population and increasing numbers of travelers, the occupancy rates have remained at sixty percent or slightly above for the past few years. This, in part, is due to the increase in hotel construction. Even when problems of overbuilding developed, construction continued fueled by tax incentives and low-cost financing. This caused the number of hotel rooms to outpace the population growth. A factor in the decline in hotel occupancy is jet travel, which permits more single-day trips, and increases the probability of people having second homes and timeshare facilities. While the general trend has been toward lower occupancy rates, some sectors of the hotel industry, such as the all-suite hotels, are still doing well.

As a result of declining occupancy rates, many hotel chains have begun to turn to a stronger marketing program through market segmentation, brand proliferation, and product differentiation. The growth of major chains, Hampton Inns by Holiday Inns and Comfort Inns by Quality Inns, is one effort. Other methods have been seen in the development of a strong "frequent user" program such as that begun by Marriott. Marriott has reduced its advertising budget and allocated more financial resources to its "Honored Guest" program since business travelers are its most important clientele. Some of the extras that hotels offer their frequent guests are illustrated in Table 6-6. Other marketing approaches have been the off-peak pricing on weekends, in slow seasons, and in market competition.

Technology Explosion

Technologically, the hotel industry has improved rapidly in order to minimize its costs, and to improve its marketing and services to the general traveling public.

The worldwide computer and information explosion has been mirrored in the hotel industry. In the 1960s the industry began to take computers seriously and so began a number of technological changes. Sheraton established a computerized central reservation system and pioneered the use of an 800 toll-free number for reservations. IBM attempted to install a turnkey system at the newly-opened New York Hilton, but it settled on an NCR electro-mechanical machine at its front desk and back office. Finally, near the end of the sixties, a comprehensive computer system was established for the hotel industry. By the late 1970s, more than half of the multiproperty companies indicated they had some in-house data processing capabilities. In 1979, Holiday Inn installed the first of its satellite earth stations. Microcomputers for spread sheets and word processors are now common in hotels. Phone call accounting systems, smoke and fire detectors with central communications, and security technology are all improving hotel operations rapidly.[10]

Guest Services

In an effort to provide a little extra that might make the difference, some guest services have been added or improved; some of these have been brought about by the needs of increasing numbers of women business travelers. Some of these improvements are better security in the parking areas and escort service from the parking lot to the hotel lobby and to the room.

One important service that is spreading is the use of a concierge. A concierge's primary function is to answer questions and assist guests to move about the hotel and community. The concierge will arrange tours, provide maps of the area, and identify key people in the community and hotel that the guest might need to contact. Originally, in the United States, many of these functions were done by the head bell boy, but increasingly the trend is to have a special person providing this service. The economy hotels have begun offering a continental breakfast (a roll and a cup of coffee or tea) in the mornings.

Amenities

Hotels still strive to improve their environment by providing a "bit of home away from home." Again, the increase in women business travelers has had a noticeable impact on this change. The rooms in many chains have been brightly redecorated; blow driers, more skirt hangers, and full length mirrors are provided.

The physical fitness trend has been attended to by the hotel industry; jogging tracks and workout rooms are now standard in many hotels. *USA Today*, on May 20, 1987, reported that between thirty percent and forty percent of hotel guests are using fitness facilities. Many guests ask if fitness facilities are available before they make reservations. The resort hotels have instituted elaborate fitness programs.

TABLE 6-6 FREQUENT HOTEL GUEST PROGRAMS

Holiday Inn:	Accumulated bonus points for each visit. Awards include hotel, car rental, and air fare discounts, $50 cash and free room upgrade.
Hyatt:	Corporate room rates, room upgrades, express check-in and check-out, free newspaper, $250 check cashing, bonus awards including free weekends.
Inter-Continental:	Priority reservations, $250 check cashing, special gift, newsletter.
Marriott:	Hotel accommodations, free Hertz car rentals, air fare on Eastern, TWA, Delta, Continental, priority reservation, 10% gift-shop discount, express check-in and check-out, check cashing.
Ramada:	Preferred rates, automatic room upgrade, free newspaper, $100 check cashing, guaranteed reservations, spouse stays free, discount on Hertz rentals.
Sheraton:	Guaranteed room rates, upgraded rooms, express check-in and check-out, toll-free reservations number, children under 17 stay free in same room, free newspapers.
Stouffer:	Room upgrade, use of fitness center, wake-up service, bonus awards range from $25 American Express gift certificate to free weekends at Stouffer hotels.

Source: Compiled by authors.

Many hotels have also added nutritional dishes to their restaurant menus.

To assist the business traveler, special rooms are equipped with computers and other special services. In addition, hotels will offer tele-communications, tele-conference, secretarial services, and the *Wall Street Journal*.

Research

With an increase in competition, and the increased sophistication of travelers, research has become more important to hotels' ability to stay competitive with each other. An active research program assists in indicating the effectiveness of marketing programs and the likely changes needed to increase the number of guests. It also identifies the new markets and trends in travel patterns, lifestyles, technology, and legislation, all having a considerable impact upon the industry. The need to stay current with these trends is central to the success of an organization.

FOOD AND BEVERAGE SERVICE

Early in history there is considerable evidence that certain groups of people cooked together in large groups and that primative inns provided a crude menu. Although, early travelers carried almost all their food and lodging requirements with them, by the Roman era there were a number of establishments offering sausage or roast meat, a hunk of bread, and a cup of watered wine.[11] The forerunner of the modern restaurant that provides hot food and drink developed in Rome. Most early "restaurants" were in cities, near temples or government houses. After the fall of the Roman Empire it was the manors and castles that carried on the function of providing large numbers of people with food. The early inn, serving pilgrims, gave them straw pallets on the floor for sleeping and bread and wine for food.

Public cookshops were opened in London about 1200 offering precooked take-out food. The royal families of Europe were the source of new innovations such as eating utensils, linen, crystal glasses, new foods such as turkey and the potato, and the roadside tavern. A short list of important food service dates follows:

1670 —The first coffee house in Boston
1740 —The first stagecoaches departed from Boston
1800s—Harvey Parker of Boston offered the first a la carte menu
1803 —The first ice refrigerator
1815 —Robert Owen established a large eating room for workers and their families—the first industrial food service
1820 —The first American restaurant (Sans Souci, Hiblo's Garden, or Delmonico's in New York)
1825 —First gas stove
1834 —Bowery Savings Bank of New York instituted an employee food service program
1853   The first food service in a school
1860 —Dishwashing machine
1860s—First martini was made in San Francisco's Occidential Hotel
1860s—George M. Pullman developed railroad dining cars
1860s—H. J. Heinz opened his food business
1860s—The hot dog was introduced to America by Antoine Feuctwanger
1890 —Cafeteria by John Krueger developed from Swedish smorgasbord[12]

Early in American history it was the tavern that was, not only the birthplace of American hotel industry, but was important in the evolution of the American food industry.

Major events important to the food industry occurred in the early 1900s. The hamburger was first served in 1904 at the St. Louis World's Fair. It also saw the founding of a root beer stand by Roy Allen and Frank Wright, who pioneered the franchise concept in the food service industry. The trends in the early 1900s set the "table" for modern restaurants in the United States. Speakeasies, brought about by Prohibition in 1920, began to serve customers sandwiches and meals with their drinks. Some famous restaurants, such as Club 21, Lindy's, and El Morocco, evolved from the early speakeasies.

The Second World War, brought considerable change to the American public. People were becoming more affluent, the automobile was making them more mobile, and population movements were shifting to the suburban areas of cities. By the 1960s, establishments selling fast food and convenience foods were well ingrained in the landscape.

Today, the diversity of food available in the United States is remarkable. Modern popular cuisine, including French, Chinese, Mexican, and Japanese, has become common in most cities. The role food plays in tourism may not be a direct attraction, but it does help to give a place character (an indirect attraction). Some research has indicated that food is of little importance in people's choice of destination, indicating that attractions such as nature, types of resorts, different people, sporting events, historical sites, etc. are more important than the type of food in the area. A number of factors may account for food's lack of importance. First, the domestic traveler is familiar with the food of his/her own country and, consequently, feels that although there are regional variations, the basic diet would be similar in each region. Also, in many countries there is the possibility of obtaining fast food at franchises such as McDonalds, Wendy's, Pizza Huts, etc. which provide the American traveler with familiar food. Secondly, the travel industry has done a good job in meeting the food expectations. Travelers can expect good food on cruises, tours, and at major destinations.

The expectation of the traveler may be twofold. Certainly, major destinations such as resorts, heavily impacted sea coast areas, large cities, and cruises provide a considerable range of quality and quantity of food. The second consideration is the food needs of the traveler while in the process of reaching the destination. Today, with the growing emphasis on destinations, the quality and quantity of food may encourage travel to a destination. In fact, food may be a major factor in the developing of linkages between origin and destination areas. We've discussed the patterns that develop between origin and destination areas where a large number of travelers from an area go to a specific region. The role of food appears to enhance or deepen these tourist patterns over time. Once a resort or area such as the Costa del Sol begins to develop, it attracts other visitors, in this case English, Germans, Scandinavians, and Americans. With the advent of these tourists, restauranteurs begin to provide the kinds of foods that these tourists are familiar with and like. Torremolinos has reached a point where it can provide such a variety of restaurants that travelers can choose foods associated with different countries during their visits. This will, then, act as a further attraction for future tourists and continue the process of Torremolinos becoming one of the major resort destinations for tourists from England, Germany, Scandinavia, and the United States.[13]

FOOD SERVICE ORGANIZATIONS

The food service industry has many ways to make food available to the public. The transportation sector, whether airplanes, trains, or even long distance buses in Europe, provides food service. Cruise ships are noted for their cuis-ine; it is, in fact, a major attraction for cruises. Ships, restaurants, coffee shops, and cafeterias can range from luxurious food service to fast foods.

The fastest growth in food services has been in the fast-food area with the onset of franchising. Fast food, pioneered by McDonald's, offers a limited menu and quick service. Technology, which enabled the mass production of the hamburger, has led to mass production of chicken, pizza, tacos, and so on. The specialization of the menu and the use of throwaway materials has reduced labor costs considerably.

Franchising has been intensively developed in both the fast foods establishments and in "sit down" restaurants with specialized menus such as Big Boy's, Chi Chi's, and Denny's. Franchising is the most frequent method used in the fast-food industry to provide food to the public. It provides beginning help, professional management, buying power, and advertising. The seven largest chains (Table 6-7) account for over half of all fast-food service.

The industry has a rating system similar to that of the lodging sector. However, fast-food chains are not rated, but do have a reputation for quality control and certain standards. One problem McDonald's is having in negotiating with some of the developing countries, such as China, is the lack of a quality product. There are a number of rating services for restaurants throughout the world. One of the most prestigious is Michelin's *Red Book*. It has been reported that one owner committed suicide when he was dropped from the *Red Book's* top rating.

ISSUES AND TRENDS

Trends

The food industry, like the lodging industry, has to be aware of the changing trends in society, in order for it to respond to them. Two important trends affecting the industry are the aging population and the health movement. The fast-food industry, led by McDonald's, has approached these issues by changing the character of its advertisements to suggest that they offer a well-rounded diet and that their menu is suited to all age groups.

Research by the Nestle Corporation has indicated another trend introduced by the "Yuppie" generation of people on the go and the two-wage earner family. This has led to what Nestle's defined as "grazing" at conferences, workshops, and business lunches. Rather than providing a full course, sit-down menu, small bite-sized food is placed on plates and either served or set around a room. People then sample the various foods. Drinks can vary from fruit juice to alcoholic beverages. People conduct their meetings while they eat. The foods served provide a balanced meal, filling the requirements of good nutrition. This and nineteen other trends have been identified by the industry. Briefly, they are:

1. East meets west with all forms of new pan-Asian menus including Chinese, Japanese, Korean, Thai, and Vietnamese.
2. Eating a la carte in the grazing pattern described above.

TABLE 6-7 TOP 25 RESTAURANTS

Rank	Organization	Business	Sales in 1987 ($ millions)	No. of units (1988)
1	McDonald's	Fast food	14,330	9159
2	Burger King (Pillsbury)	Fast food	5,000**	5179
3	Kentucky Fried Chicken (PepsiCo)	Fast food	4,100	7522
4	Pizza Hut (PepsiCo)	Full service	2,918.4*	5394
5	Wendy's	Fast food	2,870	3816
6	Hardee's (Imasco USA)	Fast food	2,181.9*	2959
7	Domino's	Fast food	1,980	4279
8	Dairy Queen	Fast food	1,900	5005
9	Taco Bell (PepsiCo)	Fast food	1,621.6*	2696
10	Denny's	Full service	1,251	1221
11	Big Boy (Marriott)	Full service	1,096.8*	914
12	Arby's	Fast food	980	1881
13	Red Lobster (General Mills)	Full service	977	464
14	Sizzler (Collins)	Full service	754.3**	574
15	Long John Silver's (Jerrico)	Fast food	746.9	1451
16	Dunkin' Donuts	Fast food	726	1669
17	Little Caesar	Fast food	725	1820
18	Shoney's	Full service	718.6	614
19	Ponderosa	Full service	704	789
20	Jack In The Box (Foodmaker)	Fast food	655.1	897
21	Baskin-Robbins	Fast food	624.7	3372
22	Friendly	Full service	572.4	840
23	Roy Rogers (Marriott)	Full service	566	556
24	Church's Fried Chicken	Fast food	533.9	1422
25	Bonanza (USACafes)	Full service	529.5	605

*R&I estimate; **company est.:
Source: *Restaurants & Institutions,* a Cahners Publication. July 8, 1988.

3. The American bistro with its eclectic, a la carte menu, informal but stylish decor, no dress code, moderate prices, long continuous hours of operation.
4. Homey food with an emphasis on regional flavors.
5. A growing movement for professionalism among waiters, with service charges added to the bill rather than voluntary tipping.
6. A second French Revolution with less formality and more imaginative dishes, both country classic and *au courant.*
7. Culinary patriotism with American chefs cooking that which is raised and grown in America.
8. Different pastas, hot and cold, with designer shapes.
9. Diet-conscious menus of eating for fitness' sake.
10. Vegetables steamed, stir-fried, marinated, skewered, grilled, broiled, battered and fried.
11. Increased delivery service with the growing use of VCRs and microwave ovens.
12. Grown-up grains such as couscous, risotto, and polenta.
13. New smoking techniques for unique and highly flavored food.
14. Wine by-the-glass will increase its popularity.
15. New types of seafood, such as dogfish, barracuda, croaker, dolphin, eel, shark, and sheepshead, growing in popularity.
16. After Yuppies, the Ultras are the next high-profile group of customers. They are over forty-five, with more than $40,000 annual income, and paid-up mortgages. Ultras join health clubs, eat new foods, travel, and are more demanding than any other group.
17. Development of new uses for food from other areas such as peanuts, coconut milk, fish sauce, and strange fruits such as sapote, cherimoya, carambola, cardoons, and ramp.
18. Open-faced kitchens complete with television cameras for demonstrations and performances.[14]

Consolidation and Merger

Again, following general patterns in business, the food service industry is active in consolidation and mergers. One of the best examples has been the Marriott Corporation. In addition to their own hotel restaurants and food service for the airlines, they originally developed the Big Boy chain of coffee shops. It was designed to bridge the gap between the fast-food and upper-scale establishments. The company had both its own and franchised restaurants. They also developed the Roy Rogers fast-food restaurants as an additional branch into the fast-food business, thus giving them restaurants in all three market segments. In 1985, Marriott purchased 350 Howard Johnson restaurants; in 1986, it also purchased the Saga Corporation, a major competitor in institutional food service.

This trend of mergers has increased the market share of the large companies. In 1965, the top 400 companies controlled thirty-two percent of the market, while by 1986 the market share for the top 400 companies had risen to fifty percent.

Fast-Food Industry Matures

The fast-food industry, which started with McDonald's, represents a nearly $50 billion business in the United States with over 113,000 outlets. The three largest companies, McDonald's, Burger King, and Wendy's are quick to adjust to changing tastes and trends.[15] McDonald's is offering McPizza, chicken, and lettuce and tomato sandwiches. Breakfasts at fast-food restaurants have increased sales and extended their day. Many, again led by McDonald's, are now moving overseas in large numbers. The industry feels that is where most future growth will take place.

RESEARCH AND REVIEW

1. Outline the history of the lodging industry.

2. What three changes have occurred in motel patterns as a result of the interstate system?

3. Define the four different categories of hotels/motels.

4. What are the major differences in the hotel industry in developing and industrial nations?

5. Describe the six different accommodation options available to the traveler.

6. What are three advantages of franchising?

7. Why is the lodging industry both capital and labor intensive?

8. Describe the various types of accommodation ownership.

9. Outline the history of food and beverage service.

10. What is the role of food in tourism?

11. What are the major trends in the food industry?

12. Why are liquor sales declining?

ENDNOTES

1. Maxine Feifer, *Tourism in History: From Imperial Rome to the Present* (NY: Stern and Day, 1986), pp. 10–13.
2. Jim Pearson, "Great Moments in Lodging," *Lodging* (June 1985), pp. 81–82, 121.
3. John D. Lesure, "1910–1985: Years of Economic Impact," *Lodging* (June 1985), pp. 71–73.
4. Jim Pearson, "The Economics of the Lodging Industry," *Lodging* (Sept. 1985), pp. 68–73.
5. A. Dennis Fitzgerald, *Lodging* (June 1985), pp. 126–127.
6. Daniel W. Daniele, "The U.S. Budget Lodging Industry Yesterday, Today and Tomorrow," *U.S. Budget Lodging Industry* (Philadelphia: Laventhol and Horwath, 1986), pp. 2–6.
7. Mark Kestigian, "Bed and Breakfast: Kind of Like Home," *USA Today* (Feb. 25, 1985), p. B3.
8. Donald E. Hawkins, "Timeshare Trends and Issues Worldwide," *Tourism Management* (Dec. 1985), pp. 252–271.
9. Gerald W. Lattin, *The Lodging and Food Service Industry* (East Lansing, MI: The Educational Inst., 1985), p. 56.
10. Larry Chrvenak, "Technology: Achieving Inroads," *Lodging* (June 1985), p. 80.
11. Feifer, p. 14.
12. Lattin, pp. 113–115.
13. Lloyd E. Hudman, "The Travellers' Perception of the Role of Food and Eating in the Tourist Industry," *The Impact of Catering and Cuisine Upon Tourism*, (Vol. 27, AIEST, St.-Gall [Suisse], 1986), pp. 95–105.
14. *Restaurant & Institutions*, Vol. 97, No. 1 (Jan. 1987), pp. 154–166.
15. *Travel Industry World Yearbook—1987*, p. 123.

CHAPTER 7

VISITOR SERVICES

There are two types of visitor services. The first type is that provided by the home country which gives travelers information and support that will help make the trip a good one. The second type is that provided by the destination area. These are the normal services governments provide for all people within their political boundaries, such as police and fire protection, health and sanitation and public utilities—services that are enjoyed by travelers even though designed for local residents. Areas that lack some of these services do not receive many tourists.

HOSTING

The University of Missouri developed a program for visitor services which was published in *Tourism USA*. In that document, hosting was identified as the service of paramount importance among those services with which the public had direct contact. Hosting was defined as

> . . .one of the functions of communication. It provides information for visitors on where to go, how to get there, what to see, and what to do to enjoy their visit. It includes being hospitable, knowledgeable, and caring on the part of all members of a community, whether or not they are actually involved in tourism activities. It is an attitude that pervades the community, making the tourist-visitor feel comfortable as a guest of the community. Being a good host will bring visitors back to the community because they will talk to their friends and neighbors about their experience, urging them to visit the community to receive these same satisfactions.[1]

Attitude, although an attribute of service, is considered important by most who receive tourists. The state of California uses advertising to inform residents of the economic benefit tourists are to the state. Other states have, from time to time, adopted similar advertising. A few of the many visitors' services available are discussed and illustrated in this chapter.

INFORMATION AND DIRECTION

Travelers can receive considerable information in both their home areas as well as the areas in which they are traveling. Even before leaving home, reading travel magazines and guidebooks is a popular method of gaining information about a region. Familiarity with travel guidebooks will help you use them more effectively and enable you to provide proper travel counseling to clients.

As there are all kinds of reasons for traveling, there are all kinds of reasons for guidebooks. To pick one randomly from the shelves can be a costly mistake, for it can provide little of the desired information. There are four broad categories of guidebooks. These are general, sight-seeing, restaurants and/or hotels, and special interest. Each has a special purpose.

General guidebooks are designed to provide a lot of data and opinions on sight-seeing, restaurants, hotels, and land transportation in an area. They are a shotgun approach to tourism. They may cover a city, a country, or in some cases, a whole continent. The cities covered are usually major tourist areas. The books range in advice from expensive to economical facilities and tours. Books such as *Let's Go: Europe*, Fodor's *Europe*, and Fielding's *Europe* are good examples of this group, as they cover a range of interests for various socioeconomic groups. *Let's Go: Europe* is written by a group of Harvard students particularly for university students seeking an inexpensive way to visit Europe, and bases its information on the experiences of students traveling, sight-seeing, and lodging in Europe.

Some books specialize in sight-seeing, giving details of major attractions. The Michelin books, for example, provide detailed information on major attractions. Besides Michelin, Nagel's *Encyclopedia* is an example of guidebooks specializing in sight-seeing.

Guides that specialize in restaurants and/or hotels may also include some information on sight-seeing. The most famous is Michelin's *Red Book*. Some restaurant owners feel their Michelin ratings are a matter of life and death. It is a news event when Michelin drops a restaurant's ratings. As is the case of Michelin's *Green Book* on sight-seeing, three stars imply that a trip or meal is worthwhile. Other books, such as *AAA Tour Book* and Mobil's *Travel Guides*, are primarily hotel and restaurant advisors, although they include some sight-seeing information.

Many books are written for special purposes. A number of titles that fall within this category are *A Literary Guide to the United States, Tennis Resorts, Guide to Archaeological Mexico,* and *Made in America (Workshops, Mines, and Industries)*.

The guidebook selected depends on the interests of the traveler. Probably the best strategy is to use excerpts from various sources.

It must be kept in mind that material frequently becomes obsolete, particularly on restaurants. They go out of business or change ownership rapidly. This, combined with price fluctuations, makes it hard to be accurate. In addition, many are not inspected on a yearly basis, and in some cases the inspection does not include eating the food! Changes can be quite dramatic even in hotels. A hotel in Genoa was listed as a budget hotel in 1983, which three years earlier had been part of an American Express deluxe tour.

It is important to keep in mind the background of the traveler. Age and socioeconomic differences are reflected in various books. As stated earlier, *Let's Go* is written for college students, while Fielding's is for the middle class. Myra Waldo's guide is for the more sophisticated middle class.

Many local areas, states, and nations have established visitor centers to provide a wealth of information to a tourist. In many states, information centers can be found at some rest stops along the highways. Almost all cities have visitor centers to help tourists. They generally provide a considerable amount of information concerning local attractions, restaurants, and lodging places, for both groups and people traveling alone.

Large cities and towns not only publish pamphlets and general information, but small booklets providing complete information about events, restaurants, theaters, movies, and other social organizations in the local area. *In-Britain,* a London version of such a booklet is over one hundred pages long; published weekly, its table of contents lists every type of information or service needed while visiting there.

GUIDE SERVICES

Major cities and scenic areas in the United States have developed and standardized tours for their locality. There is still, however, considerable opportunity in the travel field to develop guided tours of local areas. This is becoming more and more important, not only for traveling Americans, but for foreign travelers too. This has become one of the fastest growing sectors of the travel business.

Almost all tourist interests have certain things in common. For example, most tours seem to include such attractions as historical sites, combined with a short discussion about the history of the area, including either visits to or rides past some of these significant places. Generally, standard tours give the best over-view of an area. They give travelers an insight into the culture and highlight the attractions. For example, a tour of Providence, RI would certainly include a visit to the first Baptist church in America. In the 1960s and '70s, tours of San Francisco included a trip through the hippie villages in the heyday of that movement. Government buildings including capitals and city halls are almost always included. Buildings and organizations housing cultural activities of the community are also emphasized. Music halls, theaters, symphony halls, and convention centers are pointed out by the local host.

Special industries are indicated. A tour of New York City is not complete without a trip to the garment district. A tour of Detroit will include at least a pass by one of the automobile plants. Unusual physical phenomena are also focal points of interest for the tourist. Churches of a unique character and important architectural value are highlighted.

Finally, the principal ingredient for a successful tour is the host, and the quality of experience which he or she provides the group. Hosts should be well versed on the local area, and be able to handle most questions that arise. In addition, the host must be able to cope with unusual situations and a variety of people. They should be very friendly, firm, and helpful. When problems do arise hosts should not over-emphasize them, but should commiserate with the client, and explain the difficulties in such a way that the traveler realizes that the host tried his or her best. The traveler will usually empathize with you and generally not hold it against you or your company.

Certainly the organization most people are familiar with in local tours is the Grey Line Company and American Sightseeing. The Grey Line offers tours throughout the world and publishes a booklet about them explaining fares and commissions so travel agents can assist clients.

LANGUAGE ASSISTANCE

One of the greatest problems perceived by many would-be travelers is the inability to understand and communicate with foreigners. They fear the possibility of having medical problems, and being unable to communicate the problem with a person who does not speak the same language. A number of travel insurance programs provide such medical assistance. There are also a number of measures that a traveler can take, such as carrying extra eye glasses and adequate supplies of prescription drugs, along with duplicate prescriptions of both eye glasses and drugs. Avoiding tap water, fresh vegetables, cold plates, undercooked meats and dairy products will help protect them from illness in many developing nations. A number of American organizations have been created to minimize health risks and encourage people to travel. Table 7-1 is an abbreviated version of a bulletin that appeared in *USA Today* concerning aid that is available to American travelers going abroad.

The second major problem of communication concerns itself with all kinds of daily activities, such as driving, walking, using a hotel room, or understanding menus. International symbols are being used more and more frequently in public facilities throughout the world.

Travelers need to be able to ask a few basic questions and understand the answers in order to travel comfortably. Information pertaining to toilet facilities, trains, hotels, restaurants, and directions are often needed. Fortunately, most guidebooks provide a brief vocabulary of important words and phrases. A number of companies specialize in phrase books, dictionaries, and guidebooks. There is even an American/English dictionary to assist in communicating in Britain. For long-term visitors, countries that have many

TABLE 7-1 TRAVEL AID AVAILABLE

Access America Inc.: Provides health insurance for travelers and other emergency assistance.

HealthCare Abroad: Provides health insurance and evacuation for travelers.

Immunization Alert: Provides health reports on countries.

The International American: A newsletter for U.S. citizens living and working abroad.

International Association for Medical Assistance to Travelers: A free directory of English-speaking doctors.

International Legal Defense Counsel: Provides legal assistance and seminars for travelers working or living overseas.

International SOS Assistance Inc.: Offers a medical referral and evacuation services.

Near Inc.: Provides health and other travel insurance and assistance.

Resources International: A consortium of 11 companies that provide services on schools abroad, cross-cultural training, health and research for U.S. citizens overseas.

Travel Assistance International: Provides medical and personal emergency assistance.

WorldCars Travel Assistance Association Inc.: Provides health insurance and assistance for travelers who are in emergency situations.

Source: Copyright 1986, *USA Today*. Excerpted with permission.

tourists offer private schools where courses have been developed to help travelers learn the native language.

FINANCIAL SERVICES

Two major financial concerns of travelers are whether they have enough money and, second, how to keep that money safe. Financial services have relaxed some of these worries a little.

Credit Cards

Credit cards and traveler's checks have become common. Shop windows the world over display symbols of Visa, MasterCard, American Express, Diners' Club, and other credit cards, indicating the shop owners' willingness to accept these cards as payment for goods and services. Much business can be conducted over the phone by the use of a credit card. One of the fastest growing businesses in the United States is credit card television retailing. Along with this, the use of credit cards in the travel business has become almost indispensable. Hotels and car rentals can be reserved with payment guaranteed. One's car and room will be waiting even if arrival is later than originally planned. Many car rental agencies will only accept credit cards as a form of payment. Credit cards are popular with business organizations since travel expenditures can be billed directly to the company; and, since it will be thirty to sixty days before payment is due, the traveler has more flexibility to use the funds allocated for travel. Another advantage of credit card use is safety. A traveler can carry less cash, and cancel the card quickly if stolen. A traveler can also meet unexpected travel costs and other emergency expenses with a card. Additional services provided by credit card companies for the traveler is free insurance when purchasing an airline ticket with the card, check-cashing service in many hotels, a worldwide 800 reservation number, and some travel magazines.

Many are predicting that the industrialized countries will become a "cashless society" in which money will no longer be used. The use of credit cards is a step in this direction.

Traveler's Checks

The second form of monetary assistance to the traveler is the traveler's check. The traveler's check market has become very large. A number of banks compete with American Express and Cooks, both early leaders in the field. In fact, American Express' original name was Wells Fargo. Wells Fargo's specialty was handling money; it only ventured into the travel business because it had many customers at outlying branches who wanted information about the areas they were going to visit. At one time a figure of $2 billion was postulated as the amount of money American Express had issued travel checks for, but had not yet been redeemed. With checks continually being sold and used, this amount will remain about the same or grow even larger. Two billion dollars is a considerable interest-free financial bonanza for any company. It is little wonder that a number of large banks have rushed into the field. Today, traveler's checks can be purchased at banks, travel agencies, hotels, car rental firms, and vending machines at airports. Although there is a fee for their purchase of one percent to 1.5 percent, the ability to replace the checks if they are lost or stolen is a small price to pay. Safety alone is worth the cost of the checks. The acceptance of traveler's checks is not as widespread as a credit card though. In many countries, only a few retail outlets will accept a traveler's check in a foreign currency for the purchase of goods or services. Instead, they need to be cashed at banks, exchange facilities, or some large stores.

Currency Exchange

Trips that extend across national boundaries create monetary problems for travelers. A rather common expression by visitors to a new country after receiving a handful of bills and coins, is "What is this in real money?" To many travelers, the handling of foreign currency is a strange experience. American Express, in an effort to assist in the money exchange program, provides traveler's checks in several European currencies such as French francs, British pounds, and German marks. In some countries, a higher rate of exchange can be gained with traveler's checks. Tourists can obtain currency of the country they are going to visit from their local banks. However, the exchange rate received is a bit less than can be obtained in the country to be visited.

Most countries assist travelers by having exchange and banking facilities available at major ports, airports, and train stations, where tourists first enter the country. This allows visitors to obtain local currency quickly and easily; it enables them to move about quickly within the local area and purchase goods and services, such as taxis, food, and lodging. In countries that have a large number of foreign visitors, local banks and hotels have monetary exchange services. Some countries have established currency exchange booths that function separately from the banks. Thus, in local areas heavily frequented by foreign visitors money exchange is no problem. Just around Leicester Square, a major tourist area of London, there are more than a dozen exchange booths and four banks; also, American Express and Cooks Travel Agency have agents within the area who offer currency exchange services.

Many socialist countries, such as the Soviet Union, Hungary, and China, have very restrictive currency exchange systems, with only a few official exchange places. Some, such as Hungary and Romania, make it difficult to reconvert excess funds to the original currency.

DUTY-FREE SHOPS

In an effort to encourage visitors to spend money and purchase food and products, many nations have stopped charging them tax. Some countries, such as those in Europe, have high value-added taxes of twenty percent or more. The argument for removing taxes for visitors is that taxes go into social programs for the local residents and travelers do not benefit from them. The second argument, which is probably more logical, is that lower prices increase demand. Consequently, sales, employment, and business increase. For items produced locally, both arguments are valid, and encourage the use of duty-free sales. However, when items are imported, neither argument is sufficient. In these cases, to be competitive and bring in more business, local merchants must reduce their prices. This can be done by reducing the tax. Since it is visitor's money rather than local money being spent, it does not drain the economy but adds to it. Additionally, more sales and better business boosts the local economy even further.

In addition to duty-free shops, many countries in Europe allow stores to reduce the tax on their sales if the goods are shipped out of the country for the visitor. Alternatively, visitors may keep their sales receipts, and complete a duty form at the border. Later, a refund check will be sent to the traveler for the tax portion of the purchase.

Most countries establish duty-free stores at airports or train stations where a considerable number of tourists arrive and depart. These stores offer all forms of retail merchandise at a lower price. The taxes are either partially or wholly removed from the price of the goods. Chuck Gee has identified four benefits of duty-free stores.

1. *They serve as the last chance to obtain revenue from travelers before they leave the country.*
2. *They may serve as a means of producing income from in-transit passengers. Airline passengers who are in transit from one nation to another often have an hour or more to wait in a terminal before making connections. If in-transit passengers are allowed to visit duty-free stores in the terminal, several million dollars in income can be*

Kokeshi dolls on sale in Japanese craft store. Photo courtesy of Japan Air Lines.

> produced through the sale of items to persons
> who, in fact, were just passing through.
> 3. They provide employment opportunities for sales
>   personnel, clerical workers, and warehouse
>   people.
> 4. They serve as excellent sources of hard currency.
>   "Hard currency" is the money from industrialized
>   noncommunist nations that have relatively
>   stabilized economies. Hard currency is in high
>   demand throughout the world. The British pound,
>   the German mark, the Swiss franc, the U.S.
>   dollar, and, lately, the Japanese yen have
>   commonly been regarded as hard currency. . . .
>   Nations need hard currency for trading purposes.[2]

This last reason explains why socialist nations try to control currency exchange so strongly.

Common locations of duty-free stores are cruise ships, near cruise ship docks, airports, international convention centers, and on airplanes. Some countries allow duty-free shops to operate within general retail stores of popular tourist cities.

Busy international airports, as in Copenhagen, Frankfurt, and London, have large duty-free stores comparable to large shopping centers. Popular items in these shops are cigarettes, liquor, perfume, electronic equipment, silver goods, cameras, jewelry, watches, and local products.

Duty-free shops are in restricted areas of the airport, and are not accessible to anyone other than the traveler and those working in the stores. In a second method used, the shopping is not restricted to travelers. Customers leaving the country are given a receipt for goods they purchase. When they either check in at the flight gate or prepare to board the plane, their goods are then handed to them upon presentation of the receipt.

Most duty-free stores do not include low cost items as part of their inventories. They are only concerned with high-priced, high-profit items. They discourage cheaper merchandise that would diminish the amount of direct sales and increase the number of browsers. They encourage last minute, spur of the moment buying.

Some socialist countries such as China and the Soviet Union have established special retail outlets (which they refer to as duty free) in which they require that all goods be purchased with foreign currency. This allows "hard currency" to be brought into the country, and controlled directly by the government. These stores have a broad range of goods from Coca-Cola to typical native crafts. The imported products are used mainly by tourists since they are expensive; the higher prices charged for them brings revenue without an added loss in the balance of trade benefits. The familiar drinks and food make the trip more enjoyable for some visitors.

SHIPPING SERVICES

Another tourist service is shipping or holding baggage. All major forms of transportation have shipping facilities. They also provide some form of short- and long-term baggage storage. These can be quite expensive however. Companies specializing in shipping are usually cheaper and better. They have special crates and packing materials to prevent breakage. In London, for example, baggage left at the railway station costs £1 per bag per week while a company specializing in shipping and storing bags and other materials charges £1 for two bags per week.

Many large retail stores, that often sell to travelers, offer shipping and handling as a service to improve sales. This relieves people of the hassle of carrying packages, particularly breakables. With the airlines becoming more concerned about the size and amount of carry-on baggage that people have, use of the shipping and handling service should continue to increase over the years.

OTHER VISITOR SERVICES

Other organizations and community services involved with tourists are state and national park systems and city and town organizations.

Parks

The most important information tourists receive about parks is the layout. Not knowing one's way around is extremely frustrating to a visitor. In the late 1970s, a study was conducted at Rocky Mountain National Park in Colorado to determine what its users need most. A most important element was information about the park layout (Table 7-2). Thus, many major parks have visitor information centers at their entrances to provide information about their attractions and maps of their location. Lectures, movies, and displays are provided for travelers allowing them to fully utilize the parks, and to gain as much pleasure and recreation from the experience as possible.

Local Communities or Cities

The University of Missouri in *Tourism USA* identified a number of important elements in a community's visitor service program. The first was identifying visitor service needs (other than those for attractions) and hazards. Tourists get sick; they have accidents; they cause disturbances and fires. The local community must be prepared to deal with these problems efficiently and effectively. Consider the following situation:

> . . . a special event, a sailboat regatta, being planned in your community for the 4th of July. Inquiries, reservations, and tickets sold indicate that this one event could attract in excess of 70,000 persons.
>
> It will be a long weekend and those attending will have probably driven 100–300 miles on a 90 degree day. By the time they arrive, they will be hot, tired, thirsty, adventurous, fun seeking, careless, anxious, and impatient!
>
> How does one prepare for all of the possibilities of things happening, that may not only affect the success of this event, but which might also destroy much of the goodwill and community image building your community has worked so hard to develop? How do you prepare for this on-rush of humanity so that each visitor will feel that he is being treated hospitably? How do you look out for, comfort and protect, manage and control, all of these forces, and make it appear orderly, convenient, organized and efficient?[3]

Tourism USA also identified the people who needed to be trained to provide an effective visitor service program in the community. They are: (1) those who render personal

Table 7-2 VISITOR RANKINGS OF INFORMATION PRIORITIES

Rank	Information About
1	Major attractions
2	Park layouts
3	Camping
4	Trailheads and hiking
5	Wildlife
6	Nature displays and interpreting
7	Park rules and regulations
8	Organized park activities
9	Visitor centers
10	Back country use
11	Fishing
12	Horseback riding

Source: *Parks and Recreation*, March 1984, p. 60.

services directly to the tourists in hotels, motels, restaurants, and service stations, along with those who give out information through tourist information booths or offices; (2) those who perform specialized services for the community as well as for tourists, such as fire fighters, police, security guards, etc.; (3) people in the general community itself who need to be aware of the importance of tourism, and who need to develop a spirit of friendliness towards visitors; and (4) the persons staffing the tourist information center.[4]

TRAINING VISITOR SERVICE PERSONNEL

The University of Missouri's suggestions for training personnel in these areas are detailed below. They offer an insight into the importance tourism is to a community, and the methods a community can use to help everyone work together.

Personal Services

Because personal services personnel are in frequent contact with tourists, their training program should be wide-ranging. The impact of tourism on their jobs and on the community should be discussed. The more they realize how important tourism is in terms of dollars, jobs, and community betterment, the more they will develop a respect for the need to be hospitable and to give good service. They should receive hospitality training, learn to answer questions, how to be polite and friendly toward strangers, and how to make strangers into friends.

Some will need training in personality development so they will automatically show their best side. Visitors get a poor impression of a place if they are ignored, or if they are confronted with rudeness or sullenness. Service personnel should learn how to do their own jobs with greater efficiency and effectiveness. They should develop an attitude of "professionalism" about what they do and say, and how they act.

They should be aware of their general appearance and impressions that are created by being clean, well-groomed, appropriately dressed, and well-spoken.

Personnel should become informed about the community and area in which they work. They should know the highway system and know about the natural resources, history, attractions, special events, and places of interest so they can answer tourists' questions.

Specifically, they should be given a one-day tour through the community that highlights its attractions and services. (Employers should be willing to grant this one day with pay to improve their employee's ability to interact with tourist customers.)

Emergency training is important whether it be for fire, robbery, or illness. They should know whom to call first as well as how to, and how not to, react in an emergency situation.

Specialized Services

In addition to knowing their own specialized jobs, service personnel should receive additional training as it relates to tourism and to the individual tourist.

Here again, the training should emphasize the impact that tourism has on their job or business. They should welcome tourists as they would any other guest. Their hospitality training should emphasize "doing extras" that tourists like, but may not expect, such as giving directions, explaining the nice things about your community, and specific things that tourists should do while visiting.

Members of the Community

Community training programs may be accomplished by normal communication channels, such as press releases, public meetings, and progress reports. Special presentations to community interest groups by tourism personnel or by the community's leaders may also be made.

What instruction should the members of the community receive? The most important training should tell citizens about the economic and social impact of tourism. They should know how tourism affects their taxes and where these dollars go in schools, hospitals, street repair, and community beautification. The community members also must be taught the importance of civic pride, clean-up campaigns, and maintaining a good community image.[5]

Other Services

One additional service, available to travelers, can be found in newspapers used by people who travel abroad. AT&T has established a *Traveler's Assistance Directory* to help the traveler. They offer use of a phone, business assistance, medical assistance, and other services. Table 7-3 summarizes some of the services available to travelers.

ISSUES AND TRENDS

There are a number of issues concerning visitors or prospective visitors to foreign countries that need to be resolved to make traveling easier and safer.

Travel Restrictions

Many countries have restrictions on travel. These vary from not accepting tourists at all to having lengthy visa application processes. *USA Today* reported that while the number of American tourists to Europe had increased dramatically over the previous year, France was receiving far fewer of those tourists than other countries. The major contributory factor was the new requirement for visas from non-European Community residents.[6]

Consumer Practices

In September, 1981, the WTO published a report pertaining to consumer protection and information for tourists. A survey of consumer associations was conducted in both the developing and industrialized countries interested in knowing about tourism and travel problems. One purpose of the project was to identify major problems encountered by tourists taking packaged holidays. In general, the responses obtained from the surveys indicate problems such as overbooking, noise in hotel, service and poor quality food, incorrect information in brochures, and delays and unsatisfactory guides. Complaints are frequent and, apparently, at a reasonably high level.

Brochures and Advertising Material

For many, brochures are the only source of information from which tourists make their decisions to go on a tour. In many cases, the travel agents will also rely heavily upon the brochure when they have little direct knowledge of the offering. Brochures have dual functions. One is to promote the holiday, and the second is to provide information about the trip. The brochures of most cruise companies do both extremely well.

A Belgian consumer magazine's survey of packaged holidays completed by their readers showed that about thirty-five percent of the respondents were disappointed either by their holidays, or because the location did not match their expectations gained from the brochures.[7]

The nature of advertising is to use adjectives freely in order to sell a product. Brochures are excellent examples of an advertiser's skill in using words to persuade people to spend money. Words often have different meanings to different people. A refreshing cool breeze might evoke a different response in a person from Germany than a person from Spain. Words such as modern, deluxe, outstanding, attractive, all mean different things to different people.

One feature many complain about is the price quoted in brochures. Many consumer organizations claim that:

—Booking conditions are often hard to understand.
—Booking conditions are often written in small print.
—Information is spread over many pages.
—There is confusion about what is and is not guaranteed.
—Exclusion clauses are not given due prominence.[8]

Many obscure messages may be contained in a brochure. The supplements such as balcony, a view, or full board are mixed with the hotel descriptions and confuse the readers, or leave them with an impression these supplements are normally available when in fact, they must be specially reserved.

Many brochures, although they are improving, are ambiguous in their descriptions of hotels and resorts. One of the biggest loopholes in the law is the right to substitute information. Photographs, too can be misleading; when they are combined with vague information and factual inaccuracies, ordinary hotels can be made to appear deluxe or superior.

Booking Conditions

Purchasing a packaged holiday is a binding contract upon both the seller and the buyer, yet the general feeling is that contracts are one-sided in favor of the tour operator because of the insertion of many clauses that try to limit their responsibility. Tour operators regard themselves as intermediaries between vacationers and those who actually provide the services—airlines, hotels, and so on. This is made clear in the booking conditions, which exclude these services from responsibility for any problems that might arise. However, the courts are beginning to hold tour operators and travel agents responsible for some of the actions, if they, the providers, have a history of not meeting their obligations.

TABLE 7-3 QUICK TRAVEL TIPS

Dialing the USA. Making a direct-call to the USA is actually quite simple. All you need is the access code of the country you're dialing from. After that, it's the same as dialing a long distance call from within the USA.

Use Your AT&T Card. Now you can use your AT&T card to call the USA from most countries. You won't have to worry about the right change, and AT&T card calls are more economical than collect calls.

Beware of Hotel Surcharges. Many foreign hotels add a hefty telephone surcharge to the cost of international calls made from a guest's room. These surcharges are rarely published, so be sure to check out your hotel's policy before you place your call.

Business Assistance Abroad. American chambers of commerce abroad (AmChams) are voluntary associations of business executives concerned with U.S. trade and investment and local community services. AmChams operate in cooperation with host country governments, business firms, affiliates and individuals.

    Through a wide spectrum of activities, AmChams works to:

    —Develop economic, social and commercial relations between business and industrial interests and those of host countries.
    —Foster and communicate abroad the beneficial concepts of U.S. private enterprise.
    —Promote local economic and social contributions for the benefit of host countries.

USA Customs Information: Here are a few facts from *Know Before You Go,* published by the U.S. Customs service.

    Making a declaration. In most cases, you will only need to make a written declaration of items acquired abroad if their total value exceeds $400, otherwise an oral declaration will do. Remember to keep all your receipts.

    Duties. As a resident of the USA, your first $400 worth of merchandise may be brought back into the country duty free provided that:
    —You have been outside the USA for at least 48 hours.
    —You have not already used this exemption within 30 days.
    —Your purchases are for personal use or gifts.
    —You bring your purchases into the USA with you.

Your next $1,000 worth of items is dutiable at a flat rate of 10 percent, while duty rates above $1,400 worth of merchandise vary. U.S. residents who do not meet the 48-hour or 30-day requirement may bring back up to $25 worth of items duty free.

Medical Assistance for Travelers. If you should need a doctor while abroad, the International Association for Medical Assistance to Travelers (IAMAT) has set up centers in 125 countries with English- or French-speaking physicians who are on call 24 hours a day. IAMAT publishes an annual directory of medical centers, along with the names and addresses of associated physicians who have agreed to set payment schedule for IAMAT cardholders. In addition, IAMAT provides its members with a number of charts and brochures with information on weather and health conditions throughout the world.
    There is no cost to join IAMAT, but a donation is requested.

Source: Copyright 1986. *USA Today.* Excerpted with permission.

SOCIAL AND ENVIRONMENTAL CONCERNS

The public has become more aware of the problems of the disabled. To date, provisions for disabled people are still poor. While disabled people prefer to be integrated into the typical holiday programs, many of these organized holidays are not adequate. The problem lies with both the information that is available and the lack of facilities and services for the disabled person. General guidebooks to accommodations or restaurants have little information for the disabled. In 1977, twenty major airlines were surveyed by a consumer review to see if they would allow a collapsible wheelchair into the cabin of the aircraft; only two airlines responded that they would.[9]

In the 1980s, the public became aware of the problems of hotel fires because there was an outbreak of so many throughout the world. Fire safety legislation varies considerably from one country to another. Some countries provide general guidelines that have no legal force, while others have model codes to follow, and regulations that are more stringent.

Of growing concern is the issue of pollution. For example, pollution in the Mediterranean has become a source of international concern. The problem of waters that border more than one country are more difficult to approach, as international agreements are needed to help solve them. There are eighteen countries bordering the Mediterranean; some are industrialized countries and some are developing countries, and each has its own priorities. Although a treaty has been signed by eleven of the eighteen countries in an effort to limit certain toxic pollutants and create water safe enough for bathing, the problem is far from solved. Without an effort by all involved in tourism, pollution will continue to have an impact on tourism throughout the world.

RESEARCH AND REVIEW

    1. Describe the two types of visitor services.
    2. How do guidebooks differ from each other? Describe four different types.
    3. What four general attractions do all local tours usually cover?
    4. Describe two methods host countries use to provide tax-free shopping for tourists.
    5. What are four benefits of duty-free shops?
    6. Discuss two important fears tourists have while visiting other countries and describe how the tourism industry overcomes these fears.

7. What two major financial services are offered to tourists to make travel more worry-free?

8. What kind of visitor services do state and national parks provide?

9. What are the problems facing the disabled traveler and how is the travel industry dealing with them?

ENDNOTES

1. *Tourism USA: Guidelines for Tourism Development* (Washington, DC: Univ. of Missouri, Dept. of Recreation & Park Admin., 1986), p. 147.
2. Gee, Dexter and Makens, pp. 263–264.
3. *Tourism USA,* pp. 147–148.
4. Ibid., p. 153.
5. Ibid., pp. 153–154.
6. *USA Today* (June 10, 1987), p. 131.
7. WTO (Madrid, 1981), p. B3.2.2.
8. Ibid., p. 16.
9. Ibid., p. 27.

CHAPTER 8

MEETING
FACILITIES
AND SERVICES

One of the most rapidly growing segments of the travel industry is conventions and business meetings. In the United States, it has grown to an industry of over $25 billion. Most research projects continued growth into the early 1990s. The international convention and business meeting market has also had considerable growth; most are held in Europe. Richard Henry found that eighty percent of all international associations were located in western Europe mainly in France, Belgium, Great Britain, and Switzerland, with fewer in the Netherlands and Scandinavia; and even fewer in Italy and Spain.[1]

Travel sales from meetings and conventions are so important to the economy that all levels of government have organized, advertised, and provided services specifically to attract these groups. The United States, for example, has offices in six major industrial countries to assist organizations with travel arrangements to the United States. Each state allocates a considerable portion of its budget to advertising to encourage conventions and business travel to their state. Most cities and counties with a population of about 200,000 have visitor and convention centers designed to entice and support meetings and conventions.

MARKET SEGMENTS

There are many businesses and organizations that hold meetings for a variety of purposes. These organizations can be divided into a number of groups.

Associations are formed by organizations with mutual interests such as professional, trade, scientific, educational, civic, etc. Almost all the professions have associations through which they communicate and share new ideas, and assist each other in issues of concern such as politics, health, and retirement.

Businesses have many reasons for holding meetings. Both national and international business organizations need to bring their staff together for a number of reasons. Corporate meetings of boards of directors, management, and regional office stockholders are important for communication and understanding the goals and procedures of the company. Many companies hold sales representatives' meetings at least twice a year to introduce new products, set goals, devise sales strategies, and teach new sales techniques. Many companies that specialize in products have meetings to demonstrate the products either to their sales staff, prospective clients, or businesses that sell their product line. It is quite common for the automobile industry to bring together its dealers to introduce new lines and models. Many of these meetings are not only held in the city of the industrial plant or home office, but also major tourist destination regions. The secondary purpose of the meeting is to express appreciation for the sales efforts and to generate positive attitudes between the dealers and industry.

Annual stockholders' meetings provide stockholders an opportunity to meet management and receive firsthand reports on their successes or failures.

Exhibitions and trade shows are generally designed to introduce new products and innovations to a particular client. For example, medical companies or travel wholesale companies will host shows at convention centers in various cities. In the case of pharmaceutical and medical companies, they will host trade shows for physicians, pharmacies, and companies that specialize in medical sales. Sporting goods companies, such as Nike and Adidas, will hold large trade shows in major cities for the retail sporting stores in that city or region.

Other organizations, whether business or charitable and benevolent societies, are involved in this sector of the industry. The London phone book lists seventy-nine charitable and benevolent societies. These all have local, regional and, in many cases, national meetings. A listing of trade and professional associations may be found in *National Trade* and *Professional Associations of the United States and Canada.*

Religious organizations hold conferences and regional meetings. Religious organizations throughout the world hold retreats and special meetings. Many in the United States hold special summer educational weeks which have become known as "Chautauqua meetings."

Political conventions have become similar to sports super bowls—noted for high pressure, parties, and attractions. Large cities vie (through wining and dining) to host the selection committee; they also offer millions of dollars of benefits in an effort to lure conventions to their cities. Convention goers are big spenders; the impact of a major party's convention will generate over $200 million for the local economy.

Governments at almost all levels conduct meetings. There are international organizations, national, regional, state, and multicounty regions within each state. At all levels, people are brought together to analyze policy, communicate to create new legislation, and administer the territory for which they are responsible.

The list of organizations is long—there are hobby clubs, insurance clubs, sports clubs, and many more. There are as many varieties of possible combinations of organizations as there are varieties of interests shared by people.

GEOGRAPHIC CONSIDERATIONS

A number of choices for convention location are available to organizations. International organizations, associations, and businesses generally conduct meetings in different countries annually. However, there are certain areas that are more likely to be favored. Richard Henry, while working with the U.S. Travel Service, was concerned with bringing more international organizations to the United States (particularly those with affiliations in the United States). He reported that many American associations were not excited about bringing their international counterparts to the United States. The United States affiliate preferred, for example, to go to Singapore rather than Chicago or New York City. Most people would rather hold their meetings in places outside their national boundaries.

Companies that provide travel incentives for their sales force prefer to hold conventions outside their national boundaries as it adds an exotic appeal and indirectly stimulates sales by providing a few more amenities for their employees. Associations holding their annual conventions in exotic locations will draw more participants as long as it lies within a reasonable price range. Hawaii, Mexico, and the Caribbean are all within a reasonable travel distance from the United States mainland to draw an extensive variety of meetings and conventions. Even after the tax laws were tightened to discourage associations from holding their meetings abroad, companies and organizations continued to do so. This indicates that attendance at the convention and the benefits to the work force outweigh the loss of tax deductions.

National locations are important for both businesses and associations for many of the same reasons as those indicated for international locations. There are fine convention facilities in the United States. Some organizations choose to go abroad once every few years, and remain in the United States for the others. There are cities that are very popular for national meetings in all countries. In Canada and the United States, Toronto, Montreal, New Orleans, San Francisco, New York, Washington, and Seattle, to name a few, are considered attractive locations for meetings. They offer a wide range of services and activities to keep meeting or convention goers busy during their stay.

Since most regional meetings are concerned with regional topics and issues, they usually take place at the regional office, or an attractive location close to it. As on an international or national scale, regions also have those locations that are considered attractive. In the West, Jackson Hole, Phoenix, Albuquerque, Salt Lake City, and Boise are a few such attractive centers for conventions. Some of these western cities attract national and, in some cases, international meetings, but generally they are used by smaller organizations with fewer attendees, since these cities lack the facilities of larger cities.

States, provinces, and areas within the United States and Canada generally do have locations for small meetings and conventions. A state teachers association, for example, will generally hold its annual meetings in the state capital, or other large city within the state. They may also look for a traditional tourist location such as Jackson Hole in Wyoming, or Sun Valley in Idaho. Many ski areas have suitable facilities, and encourage conventions and meetings in their off season to increase business. These areas are often very attractive to local and state associations and businesses. Many make good retreats for management assessment meetings.

MEETING PLANNING ESSENTIALS

Each market segment, from conventions through business and exhibits to trade shows, has a unique set of needs to be identified in order to plan and conduct a successful meeting. These needs can be categorized as follows:

Accessibility and Attractiveness

Two elements are important in site selection—accessibility and an attractive destination, be it a city or a resort. A place has to be both easy to reach by the participants and also within the budget of either the organization or the person who is "paying the bill" for the trip. Accessibility also includes time. If a trip will take people away from work for long periods of time, the rewards will have to be considerable for the potential attendee. People prefer to go to places with good entertainment, shopping, and a quality environment. New Orleans, San Francisco, or London come quickly to mind as do resorts in the Caribbean, Mexico, Spain, or the Pacific.

The so-called Sun Belt cities such as Atlanta, New Orleans, Houston, Dallas, San Antonio, Phoenix, Denver, San Diego, and Anaheim are important sites for conventions and meetings because of the climate. They have all built large convention centers, new hotels, and promoted their advantages of climate, friendly citizens, and low crime rates. For trade shows, they offer lower labor costs and freedom from some of the work rules dictated by unions in the larger cities.

Housing and Reservations

Hotels must be first-class, convention-oriented, with good bedrooms and suites, and a proficient, professional staff, knowledgeable in handling convention people. The mix of good bedrooms and suites is important because a number of the participants will host hospitality sessions for smaller groups in business-like suites to provide more personal contact. During the 1970s, a number of hotels were built with convention business as a primary target. These new hotels have a large number of rooms with a smaller group of suites (breakout), large meeting halls, and recreational and sports facilities.

Communications between participants and the hotel is very important. Difficulty both in obtaining information about reservations and actually making the reservation can reduce convention participation, thus lowering the potential of a hotel or region to be selected.

Transportation

In addition to accessibility, transportation can be further categorized by the type and number of flights, trains, or buses to a particular area. Internal transportation is as important as local transportation. Once participants arrive in a city or at an airport, they need easy, fast transfers to their hotel, and good transportation in and around the local area. Both Chicago and London have railway systems extending to major airports; both provide easy, quick transportation to the center of town and, in some cases, close to the hotels. Transportation between the hotel and convention center and to major attractions is also important in the selection process.

Registration and Information

The ease with which a participant can register, and the amount of information given, both about the meeting and the area help make a meeting enjoyable. Once at a meeting or convention site, participants usually have a host of questions about the weather, taxi service, bus routes, movies, events, and important persons in the area. Consequently, most hotels and cities with convention centers offer preregistration and registration assistance. They provide a package of material concerning registration, tours, major attractions, and places to shop.

CONVENTION BUREAU FUNCTIONS

The convention bureau functions somewhat like a national tourist office. It helps promote tourism and conventions, and provides services to visitors. Convention bureaus act as agents for convention and business groups, or as a middleman between the convention management and all the elements of the visitor product that make up a successful meeting. Most convention and visitors bureaus belong to the International Association of Convention and Visitor Bureaus (IACVB), a professional association with about 150 members, including an increasing number of overseas convention bureaus such as the London Convention Bureau and the Philippine Convention Bureau—mainly nonprofit organizations that, in most cases, receive some government funds.

The conventions and visitors bureaus' job is sales, promotion/publicity, and service (the traditional components of marketing). It is the marketing arm of the visitor industries of the areas represented. All the components of the visitor industry, such as hotels, restaurants, carriers, tour operators, and attractions, join together to give the agency the coordinating role of carrying out a unified, comprehensive marketing program for the destination. While most of the visitor industry components have their own individual marketing program, the bureau ties the package together so that there is a cohesive and complete community product. Large convention bureaus have several departments—convention tourist development, visitor services, promotion and publicity, and membership solicitation—to provide a full range of services. The convention bureau has a housing department that assists in locating space, assigning rooms, and acts as a middleman between the participants and the hotels. The bureau, through its convention services department, provides registration services, typists, messengers, cashiers, and other special services, as needed, to assist with the conventions. They also arrange special programs for the spouses, such as sight-seeing tours and other special events.

The convention and visitors bureau assists all types of meetings/conventions held in the convention centers or in hotels, for exhibits, trade shows, and corporate meetings. Obviously, hotels have their own sales staff and get considerable business directly, including exhibits and smaller trade shows. But they work closely with the convention bureau, which is not in competition with them. The convention and visitors bureau is selling the total package. It is the ultimate expert on the city or area.

Solicitation: Sales managers solicit conventions and conferences through

—Active solicitation of associations
—Personal contacts
—Promotion and advertising
—Publicity about the city and area and the facilities in the area
—Familiarization (FAM) trips for meeting planners
—Maintenance of a convention sales calendar listing future meetings
—Maintenance of comprehensive files on associations

Travel Marketing: Tourism promotion of the city and area takes place through advertising, trade expositions, FAM tours, and contacts with tour operators and national and international travel agents. Visitor information centers, FAM tours for travel writers and travel agents, and trade and travel shows all help promote a destination to the business and convention world.

International Promotion: In recent years cities have been increasingly interested in international business—international associations, incentive travel groups, corporate meetings, etc.

Package Tour Promotion: It arranges for production of package tours to the city and area including special tours such as honeymoon packages, golf, tennis, ski, medical, dude ranches, camping, fishing, whitewater trips, hang gliding, and others, limited only by their own capabilities and ability to attract customers.

Public Relations: It prepares brochures, newsletters, deals with media, produces and maintains a photo library.

Membership: Convention and visitor centers solicit new members, maintain members in the bureau, and provide advisory assistance to members on effective ways of approaching potential convention customers.[2]

TYPES OF CONVENTION AND MEETING FACILITIES

There are a number of different types of structures designed to hold conventions or other specialized meetings. Some are a part of a large structure, while others are designed with a particular type of market in mind. They are:

Convention Centers

Most cities of any size have built convention centers in an effort to encourage meetings. Not only have the large cities of New York, Frankfurt, Toronto, New Orleans, London, Tokyo, Los Angeles, and specialized tourist cities like Las Vegas built convention centers, but so have mid-sized cities such as Nashville, Salt Lake City, Columbus, Providence, and Richmond. Convention business is considered to be so important by many cities that any losses accrued by convention centers are absorbed by the cities' budgets. The benefits of a convention center are twofold. Many are built in decaying areas of cities to serve as catalysts for bringing new business and money to the region. This income generates further income to the area and adds to the tax coffers in greater amounts than any losses which occur from time to time. The combination of jobs, income, and area development more than offset any loss.

In addition to meetings, convention centers are used for sporting events, concerts, rodeos, and other indoor activities requiring large space. Many cities have used these centers to attract major league sports teams, which, in turn, helps to attract conventions.

Conference Centers

Conference centers are similar in nature to convention centers though usually smaller, and are naturally found in smaller towns and cities—often near or on university campuses. They provide much the same services as the larger ones. Many meetings of an educational nature are drawn to conference centers. The religious, adult education, special programs for youth, and small academic meetings are important target markets.

Hotel Meeting Facilities

Most major hotels in large cities have their own meeting facilities to attract and support conventions and busi-

Suite at the Marriott. Photo courtesy of Marriott Hotel and Resorts.

ness groups. They convert ballrooms into large meeting rooms, and reserve smaller rooms for small groups. They are also able to offer banquet and cocktail food services. By and large, they provide most of the services that convention bureaus do but on a smaller scale.

Function Rooms

Many convention and conference centers and hotels have special function rooms, specially equipped for presentations or for groups with special needs.

Exhibition Centers

A number of organizations need an area to exhibit either a product or a service. For example, a teachers' meeting, will have many publishers display their books; a physicians' convention will have drug companies and hospital supply companies displaying and demonstrating their products and services. These exhibition areas can also be used by the community for a travel trade show, or a Christmas tree decorating display, camping equipment, new trends in automobiles, and other local exhibits.

Trade Centers

Cities that have large regional or international markets may host a trade show, for which they need either special facilities in the convention center, or a trade center designed particularly for the display and demonstration of those products. Exposition markets have similar requirements to trade shows.

Teleconference Facilities

Current technological advances with satellite communication and super-sophisticated television are begin-ning to change the nature of meetings. They have opened the way for multisite meetings at which people in several different cities talk with each other as they would on a telephone conference call; they watch one another on projection screens or television monitors. This is called two-way, full-motion video with interactive audio. The sporting world is taking advantage of this technique by broadcasting major sporting events live into convention and conference centers, thereby increasing the revenue for both the sporting event and the center. This extends the use of those centers. Interactive audio permits audiences to ask questions which are heard at all other sites, but are answered by someone at the main meeting in the central location. This still requires people to gather together, but it cuts down the long travel distances. Interactive video conferences have three advantages. They increase conference attendance because more people can travel shorter distances; they place more emphasis on smaller more personal conferences in smaller cities with smaller convention centers; and they open up new markets.

Food and Beverage Operations

Meetings and conventions require a wide range of food and beverage service from very formal large banquets to informal coffee breaks. Hospitality bars also play an important part in meeting and convention centers. Currently, trends in drinking laws are presenting major problems for the hotel and convention business. Many states and cities are writing laws that make bartenders responsible for accidents or problems arising from someone drinking too much alcohol on their premises. Utah, for example, which has a rather rigid liquor law and is perceived as a dry state, often has problems promoting meetings in Salt Lake City, even

An exhibit at the Las Vegas Convention Center.

though the state has passed liquor laws with consideration for tourists in mind.

Audiovisual Resources

Convention centers, conference centers, and hotels that host meetings are required either to have, or have quick access to, necessary audiovisual equipment such as tape recorders, record players, television with VCRs, overhead projectors, movie projectors, and charts and graphs. A quality public address system is essential for large groups. A multimedia capability and lighting control for special presentations is often required for large meetings. Conference centers are well equipped with media equipment for meetings and conferences.

PROGRAM PLANNING AND IMPLEMENTATION

Central to the success of a meeting are the program and its implementation. Program planning and implementation are divided into four categories: education and learning, speaker's bureau service, entertainment, and spouses'/children's programs. The formal part of the meeting, the educational and learning part, is the primary purpose of any meeting. The facility must be able to provide structure and support to fulfill this purpose. However, if a city or facility only offered the services associated with the educational and learning segment of the program, it would not be successful in the convention and meeting business. Conventions also provide opportunities to convention-goers to learn about the locale and its special attractions. Thus, most regions and cities have a speakers' bureau as part of the service they provide that identifies the needs of the participants and matches them with those in the local area who can fulfill those needs.

All meetings provide some form of entertainment. It gives participants an opportunity to meet, become better acquainted, and exchange ideas in informal settings. It also allows participants to relax and unwind after formal educational sessions.

Many participants at meetings and conventions invite family members to travel with them. While meetings are in progress, the spouses and children tour the local area, and socialize with the family members of other participants. Shopping trips, skiing trips, coffee or tea functions are planned for them.

PRINTED MATERIAL, ADVERTISING AND PROMOTIONS

The hotel, convention or conference center will work with the client organization to assist in advertising and promoting the conference by providing information about the facility and area. Many meetings prepare an information package which contains all forms of material and advertisements, from both the organization and the host facility. The conference schedule and room assignment is also coordinated between the facility and the client organization.

FEES, CHARGES, GRATUITIES, AND FINANCIAL MANAGEMENT

The relationship between the client association and the host requires considerable financial negotiation. Since costs are high, many host organizations offer benefits to attract conference participants. Some of the benefits are in the form of contributions to the client organization (such is the case with the Democratic and Republican national conventions), or perquisites, known as "perks," (such as a specific number of free rooms for the association leaders or hospitality suites). The registration fees required to attend the meetings reflect the cost to the sponsoring organization for the service rendered by the hosting organization. Gratuities must also be paid for services rendered.

CONTRACTS AND INSURANCE

Contracts should be carefully drawn up between the buyer and the seller (host, hotel, convention center, or meeting place). The contract should cover the days on which the rooms can be used, the rent to be paid and method of payment, and other obligations on the part of the lessee concerning heating, lighting, cleaning, possible building changes, furniture use, etc. If there are other unused rooms in the building, the stipulation could be made that they cannot be rented without express approval of the association. If conditions are such that the rented area is not sufficient for the meetings, additional space should be made available at the usual rent.

Should the meeting have to be shifted for legitimate reasons only a few weeks before its scheduled period, indemnification by the owner may be avoided if there is a good prospect that the convention or meeting will be held at a later time. If, however, a meeting is cancelled and it is impossible to reschedule at a later date, indemnification will have to be paid. This must be stated in the contract.

To the extent that the insurance policies of the lessee do not cover all possible damage, it will be necessary to take out additional insurance against theft, water damage, and accidents to cover participants as well as employees for the duration of the meeting. In addition, other insurance is vital:

Liability insurance to protect the organization from claims on the part of employees, participants, and visitors. Such claims can result if stands collapse, if accidents occur during official sight-seeing trips, or if damage is suffered within the halls and rooms of the convention.

Accident insurance for employees who suffer loss of life, limb, or health resulting from accidents at work. Group accident insurance should also be provided for participants for the duration of the convention/meeting.

Exhibitors' insurance for the protection of exhibition goods being transported to and from the event, and during the event. This insurance should cover theft, fire, pilfering, riot, and damage from visitors.

Both the contract and insurance should cover every possible contingency or potential liability. Both parties, respectively, must understand their accountability and responsibility.

EMERGENCIES, FIRE, SECURITY, AND CONTINGENCIES

Not only are the normal concerns about fire and security important to consider when preparing contingency plans, today's planners must consider situations that may arise due to the state of the world. International meetings and some national meetings, now draw considerable media attention. The presence of important people often make them targets for groups wanting to call attention to their cause or make political statements. In some areas of the world, natural hazards such as earthquakes, floods, hurricanes or tornadoes increase potential problems, and increase the responsibility for good planning to handle all emergencies that might occur.

CONVENTION AND MEETING PLANNER'S ROLE

A meeting planner is the person responsible for planning, coordinating and evaluating the meeting. Everything from site selection and negotiations to solving problems during the convention are the meeting planner's responsibility. A few years ago the job was just a simple task. Today, it has become rather complex, and many large companies and associations now employ a meeting planner specialist. Below the things for which the meeting planner is responsible are reviewed.

Program Design

First and foremost the objectives of the meeting must be established; then a budget and dates are set. Two important considerations in budget and dates are location and season. United States tax law changes in 1980 permitted meetings in Canada, Mexico, Jamaica, Bermuda, Costa Rica and other Caribbean nations under certain conditions. This business deduction, as well as reasonable transportation rates to some of these locations, gave meeting planners greater flexibility. The meeting date is important since tourism is very seasonal. A convention held during the off-season or shoulder season costs considerably less because of lower rates for both transportation and hotels.

The program should be prepared well in advance so the planner will know how many meeting rooms to rent and how large or small they should be. These special requirements might limit the selection of sites available.

Site and Facilities Selection

The selection of a site has to meet two general criteria. First, it has to fit within the corporate budget or, in the case of an association, be reasonable for its members or their sponsoring organization. In all cases, budget is primary; thus a meeting planner will establish a price range and see which locations fall within it.

The facilities are either the hotel or the convention/conference center or both. In selecting a hotel, the most important factors are the quality of food service, types of dining areas, and its ability to set up coffee breaks on time. Second and third in importance are the number, size, and caliber of meeting and sleeping rooms. A meeting planner also needs to be certain that the billing and check-out procedures will be handled efficiently.

To help, the planner should visit the hotel being considered. The planner sends a checklist to the hotel's director of sales to be filled out before arrival. The efficiency of the hotel may be gauged by the promptness and efficiency with which the sales manager completes the checklist and returns it. Speaking with hotel guests is also useful to ascertain how a hotel handles a medical emergency, or to see if beds are turned down at night. Further, a meeting planner can have a checklist concerned with the quality and character of the hotel.

In the event the meetings will be held in a convention or conference center and not the hotel, it is important to know the distance to and from the hotel, and if transportation is available.

Meeting/Exhibit Equipment and Furnishings

The planner is responsible for determining the meeting needs for audiovisual equipment, public address system, special lighting, tables, exhibit areas, furniture requirements in the exhibit area (tables, backdrops, bookcases, and other special needs of the exhibitors and participants).

Negotiations and Purchasing

Once the design and dates of the program have been established, a number of locations may be considered. The negotiations then help the planner in recommending a site. Some locations may provide some of the services needed less expensively than others, or they may have better amenities, thus providing a more comfortable meeting. In addition, travel arrangements to and from the meeting site can be negotiated. In today's competitive world, negotiation is an important element of meeting planning.

Financial Considerations

A conference budget outlining the essential and optional expenses of the meetings has to be prepared, as the actual program will have to be adapted accordingly. Table 8-1 illustrates the budget costs of a convention. Most associations rely upon registration fees as their major source of income, but that is usually not the only source. Some indirect sources are foundation grants, industry sponsorship, revenues from souvenirs, badges, etc. For those meetings that rely on the registration fee, budgeting should be done by dividing the costs of the function and services by the expected minimum number of participants.

Some professional meeting organizers have suggested that association meeting planners should be more concerned about the quality of the program than the amount of the registration fee. The higher the quality of the program, the higher the number of participants. Consequently, the total amount of registration fees will be high. Potential participants look at the program first and the fee later. They suggest that the break-even point, where expenditure balances income, should be set as low as possible. They stress that it is better to have a high caliber program with dedicated participants (even though fewer in number) than a mediocre program with many participants at a lower fee.

Social functions should be included in the fee since they are conducive to the intellectual exchange and en-

TABLE 8-1 BUDGET DOLLARS FOR MEETINGS

Corporate	Percent
Food and Beverage	22.5
Hotel Rooms	22.4
Travel to Meetings	21.7
Programming (includes a-v, speakers, entertainment, recreation)	15.1
Promotion	8.6
On-Site Transportation	3.2
Other	6.5
Association	
Food and Beverage	33.6
Programming (includes a-v, speakers, entertainment, recreation)	16.9
Promotion	14.0
Staff Member Living Expenses	7.5
Hall Rental	7.2
Contracted Expo Services	5.6
Badging and Registration	5.3
Other	9.9

Source: *Meeting News*, November 1985.

hance the atmosphere of the conference. All other functions should be optional. It is wiser to spend money on speakers, the planning of sessions, and preparation for the participants.

Promotion

For corporations, promoting the meeting is not a concern since they (the corporations) are paying for attending, and most participants work within the corporation and are required to attend. However, associations and other organizations rely on their membership for success. Richard Henry has suggested the following checklist:

1. *Initial Notice:* The time the initial notice is sent depends on the extent of the organizational period. It can be up to three years ahead if the convention site requires international travel. The purpose of an initial notice is to stimulate potential attenders into thinking positively about visiting the convention city and attending the convention. The format and content of the initial notice, he suggests, should be a three- or four-page folded leaflet to fit into a 9" × 4" envelope.

Color should be used whenever possible. It should include information about the conference program, whether it be scientific or technical, in general terms, with the theme, purpose and likely subject areas outlined. The social events, excursions, pre- and post-convention tours available during the period of the convention should also be listed. It should concentrate on the attractions of the convention city. An intention card should be sent with the initial notice, and a self-addressed card to be returned by those interested. This card should include a space where the prospective participants can indicate if they wish to participate and note the subject.

2. An *advance program booklet* should be sent about nine months prior to the event to

(a) define all aspects of the program in as much detail as possible.
(b) describe in detail the costs of social events, excursions, etc.
(c) assist registrants with instructions to complete the registration forms.
(d) assist registrants to plan their trip and to provide information pertaining to special requirements regarding customs, health, visas, etc., and arrange for pre- and post-travel.
(e) define for registrants policies concerning the convention, e.g. refunds for cancellations, etc.

3. *Call for papers* (if applicable): Information about the deadline for receipt of abstracts, file papers, and so on should be provided. This should include specific and clear instructions to authors of papers, preferably with a model sheet on which abstracts are to be typed. In some cases this can be included with the advance program booklet.

4. A *registration form* that includes all the information required to make adequate preparation for all aspects of the convention should be sent with the advance program booklet. This form should include spaces for: personal information—name, address, etc; travel arrangements; accommodation requirements or accommodation reservation request.

5. *Program choices* if applicable; social events included in registration fee; optional events, excursions, etc., for which payment is expected, and an advance registration form; and payment for fees, events, etc.[3]

Evaluation

When the meetings are complete an evaluation should be made. The more comprehensive the better, including a self-evaluation by the planner. Many associations include an evaluation in the registration material covering all areas of the convention from presentation of papers to social events. Some associations require some evaluation by the guests and speakers. Evaluations are important to suggest avenues and methods for improving future meetings.

CONVENTION AND MEETING SERVICE PROVIDERS' ROLE—THE SELLER

The seller, or provider of service, can be a visitors' bureau, a convention center, individual hotels or hotel chains, airlines, travel agents, tour operators, ground operators, bus companies, and rent-a-car services. These are the organizations that have a strong interest in getting business associated with conventions, business trips, incentive travel groups, exhibits, trade shows, and other types of meetings. In the case of international associations, the government tourism offices (GTOs) are a key factor. They can be the catalyst bringing together all other elements in the travel and convention industry to help win and service the meet-

A meeting room at The Sheraton Centre, New York City. Photo courtesy of The Sheraton Corporation.

ings wherever they are held. In fact, national and international associations find the GTOs of invaluable assistance. Buyers should go to GTOs or convention bureaus, within the various ministries of tourism, as a first call. On the other hand, the convention bureaus of the GTOs must vigorously research and seek out international business associations.

Some of the elements that are an important part of the functions of providing conventions and meeting services are as follows:

Product/Services Competition Analysis

Providers of meeting services should evaluate their services to determine the products, scenic areas, entertainment, and support elements present in the community, etc. This is an inventory of characteristics and resources they offer or that can be obtained in the local area. This kind of information can then be packaged into brochures, newsletters, media presentations and the like, which identify the strengths and assets of meeting locations for potential clients so they can research and identify the most likely target market. Some organizations may be too big for a particular convention center or city; others may have certain characteristics or limiting restrictions concerning location that may make them unlikely candidates for a particular site.

Target Market Selection

It is important to identify the right market because even the most sophisticated, colorful, best-designed literature will be of little use if it does not reach the right people. Accurate, updated mailing lists are essential. Time should be spent developing these because they are fundamental to the whole exercise. Mailings with information about the

meeting facilities, the area, local affiliates of the targeted groups, and noted people to contact help to sell the area as a potential meeting site. In addition, many locations offer familiarization trips to meeting planners and key personnel to demonstrate firsthand the quality and strength of the site for a potential meeting location.

Sales Presentation

Once an organization has been identified and targeted as a potential customer, a presentation can be prepared especially for that client. It should include an analysis of the client's needs and clear statements as to how the site or area can best fill those needs. The seller should provide a well-prepared document identifying the benefits that an organization can obtain by meeting in that facility, or city. The second step is to overcome any objections that the organization may have concerning the facility or area. Some of the objections may be easy to overcome or can be offset by a benefit. Many large cities, such as Houston and Detroit, have to overcome negative press concerning safety on the streets at night by providing safe travel between hotels and convention centers.

After all the promotion and overcoming of objections, the most important task is to close the sale and finalize a contract with the corporation or association. It is important to obtain some level of commitment—a letter of intent or other document that positively establishes an obligation; joint news releases, or announcements to association members that a particular place has been selected are all helpful in closing the sale. An anouncement to its members by an association that it will be holding a meeting in a few years in Nashville indicates a commitment, even if final contract has not yet been signed.

Customer Services

Customer satisfaction is one of the most important elements of a meeting. Satisfied customers will return. They also spread the word and this is another method of promotion. Most importantly, customer services make a convention or meeting a successful one, and that is the goal of all convention/meeting providers. The services that are necessary are:

1. *Pre- and post-conference tours:* One of the attractions to an area is not only the area itself, but the additional travel opportunities available. Many participants bring spouses who are also interested in the surrounding area. International programs always offer an opportunity for participants to visit other places as they either go to or from the meetings.

2. *Simultaneous interpretation:* Some meetings or conferences are attended by people who speak different languages. If this is the case, a translation service will be needed because the quicker and easier the communication, the more professional and satisfying a conference will be.

3. *Transcription service:* The messages and speeches given at a meeting will have a stronger impact if, after the conference, transcripts of the speeches are made available to the participants. Arranging the service is considered part of the provider's task.

4. *Theme parties:* Social functions in various forms may be built around a theme. A theme may be provided by the local area. Special food and presentations may be chosen. Themes give a purpose to the social functions, and add to their attractiveness; they bring the participants together informally and provide a way for them to become better acquainted. They gain a better sense of belonging in the organization.

5. *Sight-seeing and events:* The local area often has a number of attractions which many of the participants would like to see. They may even want to see something in the area that is not normally available to the average tourist but can be specially arranged by the conference provider. Sight-seeing programs are arranged for both the participants and their spouses or other family members. An industrial plant not usually open to the general public may be of such interest. Arrangements to visit, to observe the process, and to be briefed by a member of the company would be welcomed. Also, such trips with members of the association, rather than with the general public, leads to a sense of comradeship among participants, especially since the experience is more relaxed than the conventional business meeting.

6. *VIP services:* Generally, it is possible to meet local VIPs at conventions and special meetings. The provider is responsible for either obtaining a VIP, or assisting the organization in inviting one. VIPs are invited to either the conference, or to welcome the participants to the area.

7. *Other services:* A number of general services are provided by the facility, whether it is a hotel or a convention center. These provide a good environment in which to hold the meetings. Some are additional amenities, premiums, hosts and hostesses, and specialty items such as a cash bar, buttons, flags, etc. Decorations and signs are designed to identify the organization and make the facility colorful. Specialty graphics are used to make the signs required to provide information and assistance for the participants. Exhibits are designed to display the materials and presentations for the meetings in a meaningful strong manner.

ISSUES AND TRENDS

A number of issues and trends can be identified that have considerable influence on convention/meeting business.

Insurance Liability Crisis

People in today's society are quick to take legal action for almost anything. The law suit against a travel agent for booking a client on a ship that was highjacked is illustrative of the problems faced by the industry. As a result, insurance rates have skyrocketed causing a concomitant increase in the cost of holding a convention or meeting. Money once used for traditional services, now goes for insurance.

Expansion of Convention Centers

It seems that almost every major or secondary city with convention centers reports that the current facility is too small for the size and kinds of groups they could attract with a larger one. Most problems result from certain types of meetings that need considerable exhibition space. Trade shows require large convention centers, limiting them to only a few large cities such as Chicago's McCormick Center or the popular tourist city of Las Vegas, which is currently expanding its facilities. Today, the political climate makes it even more difficult to expand. Many convention centers are losing money. However, convention center administrators argue that an analysis should be made of the amount of money brought into the local community. They feel that most conventions generate tax revenue far in excess of the costs involved in operating the center. Taxpayers, however, are more difficult to convince about the worth of a complex that shows a net operating loss.

Tax Reforms

As is widely known by now, there is a major effort to overhaul the tax code in the United States. This may have a negative effect on the meetings trade. Tax deductions for business luncheons and business travel will continue to be discussed. In addition there is a proposed ban on income tax deductions for meetings on American-flag cruise ships (which is hard to understand as there are few American-flag cruise vessels).

Presently, conventions in Mexico, Canada, and some Caribbean islands (such as Jamaica and Barbados) are deductible. Under the Caribbean Basin Initiative, countries can claim exemption for tax-deductible convention expenses, if they meet certain United States requirements for exchanging tax information. Presently the major stipulation for attendees from the United States at foreign meetings is that the individual must show why it is reasonable to hold the meeting outside North America. The laws are changing and will continue to do so.[4]

Legal Problems

In addition to those that involve insurance, three major issues have come to light. First is the deregulation of both the airline and bus companies. Indications at the beginning of deregulation were that convention and meetings would benefit from the lower airfares and the considerable leverage for bargaining that the lower rates would give them. There are more bus companies in the field now, but their number has increased the difficulty of being certain of finding a reliable company. The impact deregulation will have on conventions and meetings is somewhat clouded.

The second problem is developing a contract. Because of the increased number of lawsuits, contract preparation has become tedious. Contract law, although always important, has become even more complex, thus increasing the costs of meetings.

The third issue of concern is union agreements. This is especially true in areas that have strong unions, specified working conditions, and operational functions for each worker.

Other Issues

A number of issues that need to be considered are multisite meetings, media coverage, protection of privileged information, and telecommunications advances. Many large conventions may use several sites in a city, presenting additional problems of communication, coordination, and transportation. Media has become more central to communication in our society and presents both advantages and disadvantages to a meeting. The exposure given to material in meetings may, at times, represent problems if it is privileged information. Telecommunications growth has certainly been of major concern to the industry, and may change the very character of meetings.

CONFERENCES OF THE FUTURE

The only thing absolute about life is change; conferences and conventions too will change. Some changes will result from the telecommunications boom; there will be smaller more localized meetings, using telecommunications systems to reach more people over a wide area. The future appears bright.

RESEARCH AND REVIEW

1. List the major market segments of businesses and organizations.

2. What are three important considerations when selecting a convention site?

3. What are the essentials meeting planners consider in order to hold a successful meeting?

4. What are the functions of a convention bureau?

5. Name six major types of facilities for conducting meetings.

6. What are the four concerns involved in good program planning for a meeting or convention?

7. What are the three major tasks of a meeting planner?

8. What important customer services help make meetings and conventions more successful?

9. Discuss the insurance, tax, and legal concerns of today's business conventions.

ENDNOTES

1. Richard Henry, "Conventions and Meeting Facilities," unpublished paper, pp. 1–4.
2. Ibid., pp. 1, 28–29.
3. Ibid., pp. 4–6.
4. Ibid., p. 12.

CHAPTER 9

PUBLIC AND PRIVATE TOURISM ORGANIZATIONS

The travel industry is an important and diverse industry which is, for a number of reasons, of interest to all levels of government in most countries. First, because tourism allows interaction of people from one region or country to another, problems are sometimes created by those same people, or by the organizations, whether private or public. Therefore, each level of government has engaged in research to develop methods of promoting, marketing, and regulating tourism, and of encouraging cooperation between countries and between regions of those countries. The agencies created as a result of this research are diverse and complex, involving a multitude of organizations at international, national, regional, state, and local levels. Second, since travel and conducting travel business is such an important and vital element of a nation, it is considered to be of public interest. Therefore, at a domestic level, providing a good infrastructure for health and safety of tourists, and maintaining a strong transportation sector, encourages the government to take an active role in the field.

In addition, since tourism is so diverse and has so many different segments, the need to interrelate and share knowledge and information has led to a host of private and semi-private tourist organizations

INTERNATIONAL ORGANIZATIONS

In 1982 there were over 180 international nongovernmental and intergovernmental organizations dealing directly or indirectly with tourism. The oldest intergovernmental organization that is still active today is the Central Commission for the Navigation of the Rhine (CCR); its creation having been agreed upon at the Congress of Vienna in 1815. Following this, a number of organizations were formed in the nineteenth century; some were specifically concerned with the technical, economic, or cultural interactions of people throughout the world.

The last half of the nineteenth century brought some international development on a bi- or trilateral basis as a few nations began to realize the importance of working together. After the First World War, as tourism began to increase in importance, new offices and tourism administrations were created in European countries. The Netherlands invited other European nations to an International Congress of Official Tourist Traffic Associations in May, 1925. Representatives from nine European countries attended the meeting. The meeting dealt with a number of issues such as representation and distribution of tourism material in each other's country; how their offices functioned; the exchange of publications concerning accounts, statistics, and so on; and governmental affairs concerning passports, visas, and immigration.

During the early part of the twentieth century a tourism organization existed within the framework of the League of Nations. Another international organization was developing—the Atlantic Conference, which dealt with the growing trade between the United States and Europe across the Atlantic. The meetings between nations continued until the outbreak of the Second World War.

World Tourism Organization (WTO)

The World Tourism Organization came into being in 1975 with headquarters in Madrid, Spain. It was an outgrowth of the International Congress of Official Tourist Traffic Associations which met in May, 1925. The idea of international organizations even then was not a new idea.

Following the war, in 1946, the Travel Association of Great Britain and Northern Ireland called a World Conference of National Tourist Organizations, which was attended by representatives of forty-one different countries. The achievement of this conference was:

> . . . recognizing the importance of an international organization of the official technical tourist bodies, [the Conference] therefore recommends that a committee should be set up to study the problem, and to recommend whether the pre-war International Union of National Tourist Propaganda Organizations should be revised and revived, or whether a new organization altogether was necessary. Membership of the Committee should be seven, and the Committee should consider in what way the international organization can co-operate with the United Nations.[1]

This led to the development of the International Union of Official Travel Organizations (IUOTO), which later became the World Tourism Organization. During that time the IUOTO offices were established in Geneva. The organization began to take shape, creating a number of regional commissions such as the Regional Commission for Tourism in Europe, the Regional Travel Commission for the Americas, African Travel Commission, and others. Technical commissions dealt with specific problems such as travel barriers and travel development.

With the continued growth of international tourism and the need for greater international cooperation, the WTO was created through transformation of the status of IUOTO and became operational in January, 1976. The WTO has the same legal character as the United Nations and its specialized agencies, that of an international public law body. WTO has three important legally functioning bodies; the General Assembly, the Executive Council and the Secretariat directed by a secretary-general.

The General Assembly, which meets once every two years, is the supreme organ of the WTO. It is composed of representatives from all the member states. Each member has the right to vote in the decision-making process. However, the Assembly resolutions are not binding on the member states, they are simply recommendations. The Executive Council, which meets at least twice a year, is composed of members elected by the Assembly for a four-year term based on a fair and equitable geographical distribution. The function of this council is to implement the decisions of the Assembly and prepare for future sessions. The Secretariat, headed by a secretary-general, carries out the decisions of the General Assembly and the Executive Council. The secretary-general is elected every four years by the General Assembly on the recommendation of the Executive Council.[2]

The fundamental aim of the WTO is to promote and develop tourism with a view to contributing to the economic development, international understanding, peace, prosperity, and universal respect for human rights and fundamental freedoms for all without distinction as to race, sex, language, or religion. In pursuing this aim, the Organization pays particular attention to the interests of developing countries.

In order to establish its central role in the field of tourism, the WTO establishes and maintains effective collaboration with the United Nations and its specialized agencies. It seeks a cooperative relationship with participation in the activities of the United Nations Development Programme, as a participating and executing agency. In order to accomplish these objectives, the WTO:

1. Monitors and identifies trends in world tourism.
2. Studies travel demand, marketing, trends, tourist motivation, and alternative approaches to marketing.
3. Surveys the environmental effects of travel growth and makes recommendations for the protection of natural and cultural resources.
4. Provides services for developing and organizing tourism for countries.
5. Serves as a clearinghouse for tourist information.
6. Informs members of tourism development.
7. Conducts vocational training programs.
8. Works for the elimination or reduction of governmental measures for international travel, and the standardization of requirements—this includes passports, visas, police registration, and frontier formalities.

9. Assists and develops technical cooperation projects.
10. Works to standardize equipment, terms, phraseology, and signs as an aid to easier travel and understanding for foreign visitors.

The official publications of WTO include *International Travel Statistics,* and "Travel Abroad—Frontier Formalities," "Economic Review of World Tourism," technical bulletins, special publications, and manuals.

International Civil Aviation Organization (ICAO)

At the conclusion of the Second World War, it became necessary for nations to reach an agreement pertaining to air transportation. The Chicago Conference, held in 1944, foresaw the necessity for technical agreements relating to safety and operations in air transportation. The most noteworthy achievement of that Conference was the establishment of the International Civil Aviation Organization, that today consists of some 134 governments, to promote civil aviation on a worldwide scale. The objectives of the ICAO are to:

1. Adopt international standards and to recommend practices for regulating air navigation.
2. Recommend installation of navigation facilities by member countries.
3. Set forth proposals for the reduction of customs and immigration formalities.
4. Plan for the safe and orderly growth of international civil aviation throughout the world.
5. Encourage the improvement of the art of aircraft design and operation for peaceful purposes.
6. Seek the development of airways, airports, and air navigation facilities for international civil aviation.
7. Provide for safe, regular, efficient, economical air transportation.
8. Discourage unreasonable competition.
9. Insure that the rights of contracting countries are fully respected, and that every member has a fair opportunity to operate international airlines.
10. Discourage discrimination between contracting countries.
11. Promote the development of all aspects of air transportation.

The concern of the ICAO and the magnitude of the problems plaguing it are similar to that of an aircraft crew in an emergency. The crew need details of their position, information and instructions concerning nearby aircraft, local weather conditions and services. In order to provide some form of coordination on these matters and to ensure the safety, regularity, and efficiency of international civil aviation operations, adherence to rules and a common understanding of them is an absolute necessity. Just think of the problems these issues present from only a language

point of view without the addition of other governmental and ideological problems.

International Air Transport Association (IATA)

The International Air Transport Association was established in 1945 in Havana. It was composed of airline operators attached to the national delegations of the ICAO conference in Chicago. Today membership includes over 112 scheduled airlines. Their declared intentions are to promote safe, regular, and economical air transport, foster air commerce, and study problems connected with the industry. IATA serves as the agency through which airlines seek jointly to solve problems that cannot be solved individually. It is involved in standardizing tickets, prices, weighbills, baggage checks, and other such documents. This helps to make travel uniform throughout the world.

Although setting rates is the most significant aspect of IATA's work, the final responsibility rests with individual governments. The most serious problem in fare determination is the sheer size of the task. Over one hundred airlines, sometimes representing their governments and sometimes their own concerns, must agree unanimously on all rates and fares set within a conference area. In IATA, every member airline holds a single vote and, given the unanimity requirements, also holds veto power. With current deregulation, the status and function of the organization is changing, and only time will tell its final role, which certainly will be less influential than in the past.

The first serious attempt to formulate regulation occurred at the Chicago Conference in 1944, which set forth five freedoms they hoped would be accepted multilaterally. These included provisions (1) to allow flights through national airspace by peaceful commercial aircraft of any country; (2) to allow landings of such aircraft for noncommercial purposes; (3) to allow a foreign airline to land and to discharge passengers and cargo from its country of origin to the granting country; (4) to allow a foreign airline to load passengers and cargo in the granting country and to transport these to the country of origin; and (5) to allow an airline traveling from (to) its country of origin on one side of the granting nation to (from) a third country on the opposite side of the granting nation, to pick up and discharge in the granting nation passengers to be discharged or who had embarked in the country of ultimate destination.[3]

These five freedoms were not ratified. Therefore, it became necessary to establish a set of bilateral agreements between affected countries to arrange for, and exchange, routes. The first agreement to be signed was the Bermuda Agreement of 1946 between the United States and the United Kingdom. This agreement became the model for subsequent agreements between nations.[4]

The principal elements of the Bermuda Agreement stated that:

1. Routes are to be exchanged, and the exchange shall be negotiated between governments.
2. There shall be no restrictions placed on the frequency of the scheduled services nor any other

limitations on the capacity offered on the agreed route.

3. Fifth-freedom traffic shall be negotiated between governments subject to the proviso that the capacity operated shall be related to:
   a. traffic requirements between the country of origin and the country of ultimate destination of the traffic;
   b. the requirements of through-airline operation;
   c. the traffic requirements of the area through which the airline passes after taking account of local and regional services.
4. Rates are to be controlled.

Agreements like these, and the development of IATA, led to the current airline route and pricing system. There is a complex system of pricing; for example, the mechanism for developing the price structure divided the market into a number of categories within which different prices were charged. The categories were based upon the season of the year, the duration of the journey, weekday or weekend status of flights, differing types of group programs, and reservations versus standby fares. This pattern is illustrated by the various fares charged on the basis of length of stay. An excursion to Europe, from non-European countries required a visitor to remain in the country at least twenty-two days, but not more than forty-five days. Receiving countries were eager for tourist money; therefore, they provided an incentive to keep the tourists longer. The countries from which the tourists came did not want to permit unlimited stays, feeling that they would be a drain upon their money flow, therefore, they set the forty-five day limit.

The entrance to Tivoli in Copenhagen. Photo courtesy of the Danish Tourist Board.

This manner of rate setting presents a multitude of options to the traveler and the assisting travel agent. In 1978, there were sixteen different airfares for the trip between New York and Paris; in addition there were first class (one or both ways), standby fares, charter fares, and many other choices available to the traveler. The nations of the world are relaxing the rate control element (function).

REGIONAL ORGANIZATIONS

Some countries and regions felt it was, and still is, important to band together to strengthen their respective tourism programs. The resultant organizations have become excellent sources of information. Some of the most important ones associated with the United States are discussed below.

The Organization for Economic Cooperation and Development (OECD)

The Organization for Economic Cooperation and Development was set up under a convention signed in Paris on December 14, 1960. It provides that the OECD shall promote policies designed to achieve the highest sustainable economic growth and employment and a rising standard of living in member countries, while maintaining financial stability and contributing to the development of the world economy; to contribute to sound economic expansion in economically developing nonmember countries; and to contribute to the expansion of world trade on a multilateral, nondiscriminatory basis in accordance with international obligations.[5]

The members of OECD are Australia, Austria, Belgium, Canada, Denmark, Finland, France, Germany, Greece, Iceland, Ireland, Italy, Japan, Luxembourg, the Netherlands, New Zealand, Norway, Portugal, Spain, Sweden, Switzerland, Turkey, the United Kingdom, and the United States.

Tourism is an integral part of these objectives. Recognizing this, OECD established a tourism committee responsible for coordinating studies, organizing meetings of member countries to improve statistical methods of monetary exchange and accounting, and assessing the policies of member countries and their impact upon tourism.

Pacific Area Travel Association (PATA)

The Pacific Area Travel Association (PATA) was organized in Hawaii in 1951 and is composed of over one thousand organizations including governments, air and steamship lines, wholesale and retail travel agencies, ground carriers, hotels, publishers, advertisers, public relations firms, and travel associations with major interests in the Pacific area. Its purpose is to develop, promote, and facilitate travel in the Pacific area (including Pakistan, the United States, and Canada). This is accomplished by a wide range of conferences, reports, advertising, training programs, and seminars. Following is a list of some of PATA's publications:

Pacific Travel News
Annual Statistical Reports
Travel Market Study

Meetings Pacific (a country-by-country facilities guide)
PATA Trade Manual
Tourism International Research-Pacific (quarterly)

Caribbean Tourism Association (CTA)

The Caribbean Tourism Association was founded in 1951 to encourage and assist in the development of tourism throughout the Caribbean area by:

1. Providing an instrument for close collaboration among the various territories and countries concerned;
2. Augmenting and assisting local promotional and development efforts of the members of the association and acting as liaison between the members;
3. Providing a liaison between the member governments, government agencies active in tourist development and promotion, travel and transportation industries, and organizations active in tourism and regional development;
4. Carrying out advertising and publicity measures calculated to focus the attention of the traveling public upon the Caribbean as one of the world's outstanding vacation areas;
5. Encouraging the promotion of adequate passenger transportation services to and within the Caribbean area and assisting in the establishment of such services. The promotion and development of intra-Caribbean travel is also a particular concern of the association;
6. Carrying out statistical and research work relating to travel trends and tourism development for the benefit of the members;
7. Negotiating with governments either directly or through the appropriate bodies for an easing of regulations and formalities which tend to be barriers to tourist travel.

In an effort to carry out these objectives the CTA publishes brochures, films, reports, newsletters, and other information about the countries size, languages, currencies, and so on.

Organization of American States (OAS)

The main purpose of the Organization of American States is to strengthen relations between American states by providing advisory services and training programs in many fields, including tourism. Like OECD, although the principal organizational motive was to promote economic growth, tourism is, naturally, an important component. OAS, therefore, conducts a number of travel studies and tourism development programs.

Others

These are only four of a large number of regional travel associations. Others include the South American Tourism Organization (SATO), the European Travel Commission (ETC), and the Common Market Travel Associations (CMTA), all of which have been established to cooperatively coordinate tourist activities between and within member countries. Similar bodies exist around the world.

ROLE OF NATIONAL ORGANIZATIONS IN TOURISM

Government plays an essential role in formulating policy to guide tourism development and promotion in concert with other national economic and social objectives. The WTO Manila Declaration provides the basic foundations and guidelines that assist governments in defining their tourism role.

In terms of supply, governments can play a decisive role in:

Planning: attracting foreign investment and funding infrastructure development.

Employment and Training: determining manpower needs, developing of tourism training programs, etc.

Coordinating Public and Private Sector: determining roles in mixed economics.

In order to proceed with national development, government needs to clearly delineate its policy with reference to tourism and other development options.

The following section outlines some issues and problems confronting governments as they formulate policy. These issues influence both the demand and the supply of tourism.

Tourism Policy Development

Tourism development is too often considered low priority on a list of national development goals; there is a lack of direction to policy decisions because the necessary infrastructure is either not established or is not well defined. A systematic planning process requires trained personnel at all levels and a decentralized mechanism to resolve coordination and cooperation problems. Citizens throughout each country and the region should be motivated and involved in the tourism planning and decision-making process. Design of data collection systems with standardized nomenclature and management controls is essential.

Fiscal/Monetary Controls

Indexes, statistics, and tables can give some indication of whether or not a country has been able to make the most of the net value received from tourism, hard currency earnings, balance of payments, costs/benefits, and the return on investment. Problem areas include tourism's impact on inflation, conflicts which result from attempts to increase revenues while maintaining competitive prices, and control of the black market in currency exchange. By the nature of its operations, tourism and its related businesses need to be regarded as a service industry with compatible standards. Once these factors are considered, it would be possible to determine the most effective private sector and investment incentives (e.g., tax holdings, low interest loans, public participation, or equity/debt ratios).

Environmental Conservation

A national tourism policy would be very beneficial. It could determine tourist population capacity at many natural and historical areas, so that they would not become overcrowded and run down. In areas that have become neglected, investments should be made to upgrade the area and reattract the tourist. At the same time, though, decisions must balance development/use and preservation/conservation of resources of land, energy, water, and food facilities.

Public Education and Human Resource Development

A lack of understanding of the importance of tourism contributes to the poor image some jobs and occupations in the hotel and tourism business have. A career education system would reduce the need to import trained personnel. It is equally important that workers in other areas—agriculture, fishing, etc.—not be displaced. Job creation can be an effective means for income redistribution to poorer areas of the population.

Travel Facilitation

Many travel barriers involving visas, customs, duties, and similar issues can be resolved through bilateral agreements. Increased travel, however, brings other problems such as airport congestion and insufficient international and domestic air, water, and land transportation. Many countries lack the resources to install telecommunications equipment for a reservations system, electronic mail, and other functions of modern businesses. Their outdated business modes all too often furnish inaccurate, unreliable data.

Destination Development

Often, a lack of development priorities for urban or remote areas results in excess capacity, with under or over utilization, crowding, and a decline in quality of the tourism experience. An inadequate infrastructure and organization can lead to ill-chosen priorities for development prospects. A decision to make more effective use of modern technology should also include a decision to use local material, supplies, and personnel. The question remains—is it better to stimulate demand through the promotion of existing attractions or to respond to the demands of tourists seeking familiar resorts and accommodations that meet international standards?

Safety, Security, and Health Actions

Overcoming problems of crime, vandalism, terrorism, and other social disruptions associated with greatly increased tourism is a major challenge to tourism management in popular areas. Education alone may not be enough to ease tourists' concerns on security matters. Special security police forces may be necessary, but an information program on special health concerns can help significantly.

Foreign Affairs and International Relations

Tourism's contribution to improve international relations, peace, and a sense of brotherhood has not been widely recognized. There is still a need to stimulate international business cooperation and to assist tourists in understanding the culture and customs of the countries visited. Also, a more effective means to increase cooperation between developed and developing countries is desirable. Embassies and consulates could be more effective in facilitating tourism exchanges.

Consumer Protection

Inspection and quality control standards not only vary, but too often they are inadequate insofar as land use, zoning, hotel construction and maintenance, and health sanitation measures are concerned. Tourists, as consumers, could benefit from more effective and binding contractual commitments with tour operators. Competitive bidding practices could help resolve some of the problems in the selection of consultants and contractors in all facets of the tourism industry.

Integrated Marketing

Tourism promotion and marketing efforts by public and private organizations need to be more coordinated and integrated. While there is a need to encourage regional cooperation, a competitive environment must be maintained. The matching of specific market segments to existing tourism products is inadequate; better targeting would mean a better use of resources. The travel trade's internal and external distribution channels should become more involved in marketing/promotion efforts. Familiarization tours represent one means of doing this.

Transportation Access

Tourism requires all types of effective transportation, however, it competes with business and commerce for freight and trade. Tourism also requires coordination among air, water, and land-based transportation systems.

Assistance to Tourist Enterprises

Tourism throughout the world may be characterized as a major business comprised of smaller enterprises. As such, government's role can be to assist them in obtaining financing, and to provide standards which assure that quality services are provided to the consumer.

Some governments have developed quasi-public organizations to assist these enterprises to function more effectively at the regional level. The National Society of Area Development for La Petite Cate (SAPCO) in Senegal and the Bali Development Corporation in Indonesia, are examples of such organizations.

In some countries, national level corporations provide assistance to regional and local development projects in areas such as promotion, research, and planning, manpower development and training, protection of tourist resources (e.g., museums, antiquities), infrastructure, construction, financing, and licensing/control/classification of tourist enterprises (e.g., Kenya Tourist Development Corporation, FONATUR (Mexico), Colombian National Tourism Corporation).

Champlain Valley Fair, Essex Junction. Photo courtesy of the Vermont Travel Division.

NATIONAL TOURISM OFFICE
ORGANIZATIONAL PATTERNS

General Guidelines

All countries that have tourists have an official organization that regulates and stimulates tourist activities. Its location within the government, and relative importance, varies from country to country. In some countries, tourism organizations are at the full ministry or cabinet level, while in others it may be on a subcabinet level, or be a consul or information post. In some countries, the tourist office is not officially part of the regular governmental structure. A list of national tourism organizations is included in Appendix A. Given the variety, Michael Peters has said:

> . . .the degree and form of government interest, the responsibility for development and the extent of government financial aid depends on many factors. The extent of state responsibility for tourism varies widely from country to country, and depends on the political structure of the country, the government's assessment of the potential value of tourism to the economy, the degree of private interest and the availability of public and private capital for tourism projects.[6]

These organizations may be highly structured, centralized, and controlled as in the Soviet Union and many of the socialist countries or Spain, or they may be a laissez-faire, decentralized systems such as in the United States

and the United Kingdom, where the government's primary role is statistical, analytical, and consulative.

Most tourist organizations are responsible for the promotion of tourism to their respective countries, and indeed, participate in the overall development of the tourist industry. Wahab, Crampon, and Rothfield have suggested that the objectives of a national tourist office should be to

1. Achieve tourist's satisfaction within the available, and possible, resources;
2. Provide the tools for implementing tourist marketing strategies concerning the country as a whole;
3. Coordinate the various efforts aimed at development of the tourist industry sectors;
4. Carry out research programs aimed at improving existing tourist products and developing new products that should meet market requirements and tendencies;
5. Enhance tourism consciousness among appropriate sections of the public;
6. Develop an adequate, appropriate, and constant communications system with selected markets; and
7. Contribute, through studies and research that yield constant information about tourist markets, to the formulation of a sound and well-received tourist policy.[7]

**Example: United States Travel and
Tourism Administration**

Although there are some fifty federal bureaus and
agencies in the United States involved in some aspect of
tourism, the official government organization is the U.S.
Travel and Tourism Administration under the umbrella of
the U.S. Department of Commerce. Its director is an under-
secretary of commerce for tourism. Its predecessor, the U.S.
Travel Service was created in 1961 in response to a growing
deficit in the travel account brought about by a large flow
of American travelers to other countries. The United States
is exceeded only by West Germany in the number of its
citizens who travel abroad, but Americans spend more
money.

The original charges given to the U.S. Travel Service
were to promote and develop tourism to and within the
United States in order to reduce the travel deficit, and to
promote a better and friendlier attitude toward the United
States. In addition, it was to act as spokesperson to the
world community on tourist matters. In 1975, an additional
charge promoting domestic tourism and the coordination
of tourism within the country created a full-fledged national
tourist office with six field offices representing the United
States travel industry in major European countries, Mexico,
and Japan.

The agency's name was changed and its role redefined
by the National Tourism Policy Act of 1981. The creation
of the U.S. Travel and Tourism Administration (USTTA) was
designed to upgrade the status and functions of the office.
Although it mandates tourism's importance to the nation's
economic and social well-being, its actual impact remains
to be seen.

For example, the act increased federal involvement in
promoting the United States as a destination for international tourists, yet the Reagan administration reduced the
budget of the office. In the past, one problem associated
with the travel industry has been the lack of any governmental agency to assess the impact of broad governmental
decisions and concerns such as the energy crisis of 1978
upon tourism. At that time there were over fifty governmental agencies making decisions concerning tourism.
Therefore, a Tourism Policy Council, headed by the Secretary of Commerce, was conceived to coordinate governmental policies, issues, and programs that affect tourism. It
does have representatives of the Office of Management and
Budget and the U.S. Departments of Transportation, Interior, Labor, State, and Energy.

The office was also upgraded to under-secretary level
in an effort to emphasize the importance of tourism to and
in the United States. The USTTA provides

—Current research and marketing intelligence for the
   private sector.
—Technical guidelines on international tourism
   marketing opportunities.
—Organization and cooperative advertising
   opportunities in the international market place.
   The USA advertising umbrella, aimed at tourism
   audiences, provides a forum for the small business
   or community advertiser.

—Distribution of United States public and private
   tourism sector markets.
—Distribution of materials published by the United
   States public and private sectors to the
   international markets through USTTA's foreign
   consumer information centers.
—Workshops and training programs for tourism
   industry staff in markets abroad.
—Organization of, and technical assistance for,
   travel shows which take place in the markets
   abroad.
—Technical assistance in the planning and
   organization of United States product
   familiarization trips for the travel trade and
   journalists.
—Professional counsel in response to trade inquiries;
   the giving of technical assistance in tour planning.
—Basic reference materials, guides, and library
   services for the travel trade.
—Technical assistance for the trade in the
   management of travel missions from the United
   States.

Other National Agencies

A number of agencies have programs that relate to
recreation and tourism. Agencies concerned with some aspect of tourism may have programs affecting

—natural resources
—recreation
—historical attractions
—cultural attractions
—business development
—community development
—community facilities
—labor and training
—transportation[8]

STATE AND PROVINCIAL ORGANIZATIONS

Forty-eight of the fifty United States, some territories, and
Canadian provinces have governmental offices responsible
for promotion and development of tourism. The responsibilities and structure of these organizations vary widely,
from strictly promotional, to research and development.

Most states have slogans which emphasize the importance of tourism, and offer some characterization of their
state they feel will attract visitors to it. These slogans are
shown in Table 9-1. To assist state and local governments
with finances to organize tourism offices and promote tourism, many states have written a statute creating special use
taxes such as room tax and use of sales tax.

Many countries have organized tourist authorities at
the lower levels of government—the cantons in Switzerland, the shires in England, and the provinces in Canada
are a few areas with local tourist authorities. The province
of Ontario, for example, gained income from tourism in
excess of $8 billion in 1981; tourism represented the sec-
ond largest industry after automobile manufacturing. Recognizing the importance of tourism, the government of

TABLE 9-1 STATE TOURISM SLOGANS SAY IT ALL

State	Slogan
Alabama	Alabama the Beautiful
Alaska	Alaska! Where have you been all my life?
Arizona	Arizona. . . Do it all!
Arkansas	Arkansas. . . is a natural
California	(no slogan)
Colorado	(no slogan)
Connecticut	Better yet, Connecticut
Delaware	In the first place. . . the first state
Florida	Florida: When you need it bad, we've got it good
Georgia	Georgia: This way to fun
Hawaii	The Hawaiian Islands: Where the world wants to be
Idaho	Idaho, the great get away
Illinois	Magnificent miles of Illinois
Indiana	Wander Indiana
Iowa	Try Iowa
Kansas	Kansas. . . Land of ah's
Kentucky	Oh! Kentucky. . . You'll come to love it!
Louisiana	Louisiana, a dream state
Maine	Maine invites you
Maryland	Ooh the state I'm in! Maryland
Massachusetts	Make it Massachusetts
Michigan	Call on a neighbor—Call on a friend
Minnesota	Minnesota: Lakes, and a whole lot more
Mississippi	It's yours in Mississippi
Missouri	Missouri is for kids just like you
Montana	Montana—last of the big time splendors
Nebraska	Nebraska. . . Discover the difference
Nevada	You've been making fun of us for years
New Hampshire	We're better natured
New Jersey	New Jersey's got it
New Mexico	Where the Southwest began, land of enchantment
New York	I love New York
North Carolina	Variety vacationland
North Dakota	North Dakota: historically a good route
Ohio	Ohio's for you
Oklahoma	On to Oklahoma
Oregon	Oregon: One big surprise after another
Pennsylvania	You've got a friend in Pennsylvania
Rhode Island	Biggest little state in the union
South Carolina	Come see S.C.
South Dakota	Imagine your vacation in South Dakota
Tennessee	Let's go Tennesseeing (in-state)
	Follow me to Tennessee (out-of-state)
Texas	Texas—come live the legend
Utah	More vacation per gallon
Vermont	Vermont, a special world
Virginia	Virginia is for lovers
Washington	(no slogan)
Washington, DC	Washington, DC is a Capital City
West Virginia	Wild, wonderful West Virginia
Wisconsin	Escape to Wisconsin
Wyoming	Wyoming is what America was
	Wyoming. . . a natural pleasure

Territories

Puerto Rico	It takes a great island to deliver a great vacation
Virgin Islands	Beyond the blue horizon

Ontario devised a four-pronged development strategy for the province in order to maintain and enhance its strong tourism market. This included the development of high caliber, year-round destination resorts in the province. They developed a full range of attractions and events, catering to the new price and income constraints, as well as the new preferences of travelers. Ontario improved accessibility to tourism products including promotion, information services, reservations, and travel modes.[9]

CITY AND COMMUNITY ORGANIZATIONS

Many levels of government are involved in tourism, among them cities, states, and counties (in the United States) and cantons, provinces, shires (in Europe). Some of these organize to encompass the towns or cities in their regions. However, the major emphasis is at the city level. Most cities and metropolitan areas have organizations to promote and attract conventions to the local area. This was fully discussed in Chapter 8.

The broad extent of tourism is well illustrated in Figure 9-1, which clearly outlines the involvement of local governments in tourism.

QUASI-PUBLIC, TRADE, AND PROFESSIONAL ORGANIZATIONS

Tourism is so important that, along with the government organizations that have developed, a number of other related organizations have developed to bridge the gap between government and industry. By working together, they foster an excellent tourism climate. In addition, groups of interested people, with a common purpose and interest in tourism, have joined together to provide information to both industry and the public and exchange ideas. A few of these organizations which operate in the United States are described below.

The United States Travel Data Center

The U.S. Travel Data Center is an independent, nonprofit research and educational organization, devoted to improving the quality and range of statistical data describing travel and tourism. It is financed by grants and membership fees. The members come from institutions, corporations, the private sector, and governmental agencies. The Data Center is located in Washington, DC. A number of studies such as *A National Travel Survey, Impact of Travel on State Economies,* and *Travel Outlook Forum,* are all published to provide information pertaining to the travel industry in the United States.

Travel Industry Association of America (TIA)

The Travel Industry Association of America is a nonprofit association of companies and government organizations formed earlier under the name Discover America Travel Organizations (DATO), to promote travel to and within the United States. It is a Washington-based organization with a membership of over one thousand organizations, firms, and other agencies. Members from the private sector include domestic and international businesses, corporations,

TOURISM ORGANIZATIONAL STRUCTURE (SAMPLE)

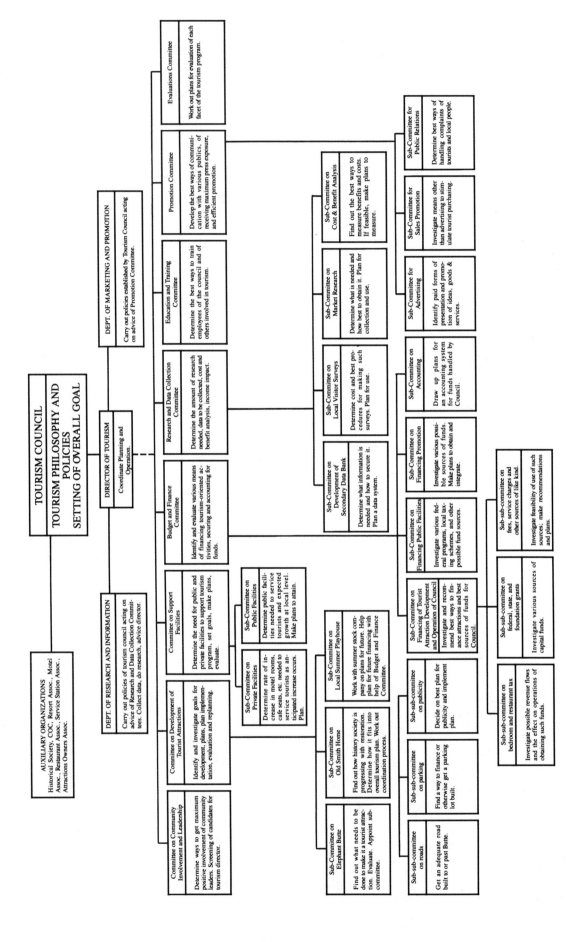

Figure 9-1: *Source: Tourism USA, p. 32.*

120

and associated tourist agencies—accommodations, tour operators, travel agents, and transportation. The public sector members include city, state, and federal government agencies, such as visitor centers, convention organizations, state government travel offices, area and regional tourism organizations. The organization derives its funds from its membership.

Its primary objective is to develop and implement programs that benefit the travel supplier and consumer. It concentrates its activities on those programs that clearly represent a national industry need, but which no single industry component could be expected to carry out. The programs fall into the following categories:

1. *Marketing facilitation:* Promotes and facilitates travel to and within the United States through special promotions and travel marts.
2. *Tourism research:* Works with USTTA and the U.S. Travel Data Center in an effort to promote an understanding of the economic and social well-being of the nation as a result of travel.
3. *Governmental affairs:* Active in legislation issues on Capitol Hill in Washington in an effort to represent the travel industry's views. Also, it assists the government in the development of tourism programs, policies, and legislation.
4. *Educational programs:* Provides a communications network, serving consumer, trade, and membership, for travel-related information for educational purposes.
5. *Travel promotion:* Encourages and promotes reciprocal travel between nations, and acts as a watchdog on programs that would restrict travel.

Travel and Tourism Research Association (TTRA)
A third organization, which includes both private educational institutions and government agencies, the Travel and Tourism Research Association is concerned with travel research, particularly in improving the quality and effectiveness of research in the travel industry. Through a series of conferences, reports, and a journal, the association tries to maintain current communications in travel research developments and methodology occurring in the field. It is concerned with the teaching of tourism and has established communication procedures to support education.

American Society of Travel Agents (ASTA)
One of the largest travel association in the United States is the American Society of Travel Agents. It includes travel agencies and tour operators from both the United States and Canada. Allied memberships are available to other sectors of the travel industry such as airlines, railroads, bus lines, car rental firms, hotels, and government and educational institutions. ASTA is subdivided into eleven areas defined as chapters. The society publishes the *ASTA Travel News, ASTA Notes, Convention Daily Newspaper, ASTA Roster, ASTA Travel Correspondence Course.*

Other Organizations
There are numerous other domestic and international organizations, among them International Federation of Travel Agencies, the Association of Travel Marketing Executives (ATME), the Universal Federation of Travel Agents Association, and the World Association of Travel Agents. The objectives of the Universal Federation of Travel Agents Association are to act as a negotiating body for the various branches of the tourism and travel industries on behalf of travel agents, to give professional and technical advice and assistance to travel agencies on the world economy and tourism, and to improve the prestige and public recognition of travel agents. The World Association of Travel Agents acts to promote and protect the economic interests of its members throughout the world.

A considerable number of professional and scientific organizations also exist. At the international level the World Association for Professional Training in Tourism is concerned with tourism vocational training. Associations range from the Society of Travel Writers to Woman Executives in Tourism Administration. Appendix B, listing some of the associations concerned with tourism, demonstrates their variety and some of their interests.

PRIVATE SECTOR

The travel industry is so encompassing that not only are there organizations and companies directly involved in tourism, but a whole host of other businesses are involved too. At both the national and international level, organizations have developed around specific interests, such as hotel and restaurant associations. To provide an understanding of the depth of the industry and types of businesses involved in the travel industry, Appendix C lists some of the standard industrial codes for related business firms that are involved in the travel industry in the United States.

MAJOR ISSUES

The two major issues facing the travel industry are unfair competition and the integration of the public and private sectors. The first is somewhat self-explanatory. The fact that one or a few companies can dominate the market is a major concern to segments of the industry such as airlines and bus lines. When this occurs, it is possible for some to institute practices that will drive competition from the field and create monopolies.

The second, the integration of the public and private sector is important and again emphasizes the need for the coordinated efforts. Two organizations, the U.S. Travel Data Center and the Travel Industry Association of America, recognized this need for partnership. Since the United States government, under the Reagan administration, has decreased its role in tourism, the added responsibility has fallen on the private sector. Yet the need is there for the government to be involved and work with the travel industry. In the age of high trade deficits, tourism could well assist in alleviating this problem.

One only has to look at all the problems concerning the airlines today (scheduling, delays, and near accidents) to understand the need for tourism and business to work together. In 1987, the number of complaints related to plane service reached an all-time high within the industry. Instead of taking a more active role in working out solutions for passenger service and safety, the government has downgraded its responsibility.

RESEARCH AND REVIEW

1. Why are there so many public tourism organizations?

2. Describe the history and formation of the WTO.

3. What role does the WTO have in international travel? List some of its duties.

4. What was the importance of the five freedoms?

5. What was the significance of the Bermuda Agreement?

6. Identify three international organizations and state the purpose of each.

7. Why is tourism development too often considered low priority in national development goals?

8. What are the two major purposes of national tourist offices?

9. What is the function of the USTTA?

10. Describe three major results of the National Tourism Policy Act of 1981.

11. Outline the various levels of government involved in tourism.

12. Discuss the role of three quasi-public, trade, and professional tourism organizations.

ENDNOTES

1. Robert Lanquar, "The Organizational Development of the World Tourism Organization: A Case Study," *The Travel Journalist*, Vol. 31 (Jan. 1985), p. 3.

2. Ibid., pp. 1–5.

3. John H. Fredrick, *Commercial Air Transportation*, 5th ed. (Homewood, IL: Richard D. Irwin, 1961), pp. 279–291.

4. *Air Service Agreement—U.S. and U.K.* (Bermuda, Feb. 11, 1946) Dept. of State Publication No. 2565, Treaties and Other International Act; Series 1507.

5. "Tourism Policy and International Tourism," OECD (1976), pp. 7–9.

6. Michael Peters, *International Tourism* (London: Hutchinson, 1969), p. 212.

7. Salah Wahab, L. J. Crampon, and L. M. Rothfield, *Tourism Marketing* (London: Tourism International Press, 1976), pp. 176–177.

8. *Tourism USA*, 1986, p. 178.

9. S. Gordon Phillips, "Organizing a Tourism System: The Ontario Example," in *The Tourism System: An Introduction* (Englewood Cliffs, NJ: Prentice-Hall, Inc., 1985), p. 347.

CHAPTER 10

PROMOTION

Promoting tourism means stimulating sales through the dissemination of information. It means trying to persuade existing and potential customers to travel. This is accomplished through advertising. Good promotion is good communication. The words can be used interchangeably. According to Salah Wahab, the objectives of promotion are:

1. *To make the tourist product as widely known as possible.*
2. *To make it as attractive as possible, so inducing the largest possible number of people who are aware of it to try it.*
3. *To make the message attractive without being dishonest. Gilding the lily merely creates high expectations, followed by disillusionment, followed by a high rejection factor. The result is that repeat buying is minimized rather than maximized.*[1]

All three of these objectives refer to communication—in particular, persuasive communication. The communication system is a sender, a receiver, a message, and a channel. The sender (the travel organization) hopes to transmit certain information that will change people's attitudes and create a desire to use the product or service. The receiver is both the travel intermediaries (travel agents, tour operators, and so on) and the potential traveler, who the sender is trying to persuade into action. The message is carried through a channel. Many times, the type of message will dictate the type of channel. In some cases, there may be choices of channels for the same message. The two, messages and channels, interrelate to attract the attention of the customers. The messages can be (1) verbal (friends, family, radio); (2) visual (press advertising, television, film shows, exhibitions, periodicals, and so on); or (3) written (periodicals, brochures, press advertising).

Wahab suggested that persuasion works through what he termed a hierarchy of trust as follows:

	Source	Method
1.	Intimate family	Verbal
2.	Extended family	Verbal
3.	Personal friends	Verbal
4.	Professional colleagues	Verbal
5.	Respected opinion-former	Written
6.	Retailer's representative	Verbal
7.	Producer's representative	Verbal, written, or visual

Naturally, those closest to us are those we trust most. This fact has been important to repeat business; many advertisements invite buyers to "tell your friends." This is one of the major factors forming the linkages between origin and destination regions (the English to Costa del Sol, or the Finns to the Black Sea) that persist over extended periods of time and that have been the focus of some geographical research.

The type of communication is associated with the character of the message (to inform, to persuade, or to remind). Owners of new resorts and other attractions that are in the early stages of their lifecycles will seek promotional outlets to inform the public of the facilities and amenities that would make a vacation experience worthwhile. When an attraction is in its early stages of growth its owners put considerable promotional effort into devising persuasive messages and sending them through a variety of channels. Upon reaching a mature stage, owners will then want to remind people of positive experiences they have had by keeping the product in the public's mind.[2]

DESTINATION/MARKET MATCH

Segmentation has been a recurring theme in this text, and will continue to be in this chapter. However, as we've discussed, there are linkages between origins (markets) and destinations that indicate that certain geographic regions have a higher concentration of the targeted population, and, therefore, promotional efforts in these areas would be more effective than in others. Regions with high Catholic populations are interested in advertisements about the Vatican, and important pilgrimage sites. Northeastern residents are more receptive to advertisements for a vacation in the Caribbean or Florida than residents from the Northwest.

RELATIONSHIP TO MARKETING

Whereas marketing is a total process including all elements, from production and product improvement to the final exchange of a product or service for something of value, promotion is one of the major elements in the marketing mix. Many use the two terms marketing and promotion synonymously, yet most recognize that promotion is one of the major tools used in marketing a tourist product. It is the task of promotional people to devise methods of communication that will make the greatest number of potential consumers (those most likely to purchase the product or service as determined through accurate market segmentation) aware of their products.

As one variable in the marketing mix, promotional channels and types of messages will vary depending on the characteristics of the other variables (price and products). In the United States, few potential travelers have heard of Cosmos, Lindblad, Tauck Tours, Travellers, or Unitours. Most of these are large tour operators that many Americans have traveled with, yet they are not the household words that Hilton, Holiday Inn, or Sheraton are. Promotional activities from these companies have mostly been geared to, and conducted through, the travel intermediaries. An expensive, exclusive resort with a high profit margin will not promote through mass media, since their potential customers are a very select few.

PROMOTION PLANNING

Planning is as important for promotion as any other segment of tourism. Planning is conducted to determine the objectives and goals the organization should pursue; then a plan of action is devised to meet those goals and objectives. According to G. A. Schmoll, five decisions result from the planning process. They are: (1) The objectives of promotion that are consistent with the general marketing plan; (2) The identification of the market group to which the promotion is targeted; (3) The identification of the specific advertising, sales support, and public relations programs to be instituted; (4) The budget allocation to the various market segments and target groups; and (5) The methods to be used to control and assess the effectiveness of the promotion.[3]

Goals

Goals are central to developing promotional strategies. They should be quantitative so that they can be measured to determine if the outcome is achieved. Goals should have a specific time period in which they are to be completed. They should be written clearly and concisely, and be as specific as possible. It is more important to state the communicative purposes of the goals rather than the expected revenue gained over a period of time.

Tourism USA listed the following goals as illustrative of communication goals:

—*To create and measure the awareness of a particular tourism attraction in a specific market*
—*To communicate a specific tourism appeal in your promotion to a specific market and then determine how many people can recall it*
—*To communicate a basic campaign theme to a specific market and then determine how many people can restate the premise without aided recall*
—*To communicate a particular image or try to create a particular attitude about a tourism site and then*

determine if the message registered in the potential prospect's mind creates the correct image
—To measure the effectiveness of promotional materials by tracking inquiry coupon responses from regional advertising efforts.[4]

Goals can be written even more specifically so that measurement can be made before and after. Assume that fifty percent or 500,000 people in a region with one million people were potential clients for a theme park, but only half, or 250,000, of them could identify it by name. A goal of a promotion campaign might be to increase the people's awareness of the theme park by twenty percent to bring the total number of people aware of the park to 300,000. This is a measurable goal (statistics can be gained both before and after the promotional period), which helps the promotional planners to focus on the type of advertisements best suited to meet the goal.

MARKET TARGETS

A common theme is important in establishing a market target. Promotion would be wasted if the plan assumed a homogeneous group of people, or that all people had the same travel wishes. It is equally important to understand that many travel companies cannot provide services for the total population; therefore, it is imperative that a promotional plan recognize both characteristics of marketing.

Figure 10-1, developed by WTO illustrates how travel decisions are made. Segmentation identifies people according to their socioeconomic status, social influences, certain personality features, attitudes, values, and the motivations and expectations they have.

Schmoll suggested that not only does segmentation establish the necessary guidelines for isolating target markets, but that a market segment may not be considered a suitable target for promotion. He felt that certain markets are not compatible for the same destination. For example, a business traveler desiring a good night's rest would not want to be booked into a hotel that was hosting a large convention group. Some markets have a competitive advantage over others and no amount of promotion can offset that advantage. Other markets may require far more development funds than the available promotion budget can allocate for that market segment. Finally, the market segment may have a limited life and therefore not justifying the necessary promotional effort.[5]

In 1977, Schmoll stated that "tourism promotion is still at an early stage of development." Although there has been a marked improvement in the use of segmentation for tourism promotion since that time, promotional activities can still improve on specialized, distinctive promotion plans for different segments within a market.

SPECIFIC OBJECTIVES

Objectives delimit the details of reaching a goal. An objective designates the path by which goals are reached. The previous example about increasing the awareness of a theme

park indicates some specific objectives leading to a goal. By identifying the goal of a thirty percent increase in awareness requires a detailed set of objectives. If, for example, the target market for the theme park is a family one, an objective might be to create interest for the children who then, in turn, generate awareness in their parents.

For example, one of the goals of the U.S. Travel and Tourism Administration is to stimulate travel to the United States; an objective of theirs is to increase the number of tourists to the United States by eight million visitors in 1990. Another objective is to reduce the red tape, or eliminate the need for a visa, and to let potential travelers know of the change. Many advertisements focus on this issue. Mill and Morrison have identified a number of objectives that would help many national tourist offices meet their goals:

—To increase the availability of the tourist product(s) of its country by helping to increase the number of tour operators' programs and the capacity of existing ones, or to maintain at targeted levels the number and capacity of such programs.
—To secure maximum promotional exposure for the product mix of its country.
—To promote a favorable image of its country as a tourist destination, and to maintain or enhance such an image.
—To stimulate and increase demand for the tourist product(s) of its country.
—To familiarize the travel distribution channels with its tourist product mix and stimulate them in order to facilitate and increase sales.
—To increase and make more effective the supply of information on the tourist product mix of its country.[6]

THE MESSAGE

The message selected for the advertisement follows the goals and objectives of the promotional plans. It generally is expressed in an overall theme (such as "A Family Affair" for a family theme park). The message is then promoted in a variety of ways to keep it publicly visible until it becomes very familiar to the potential market. Its purpose is to create an awareness of the attraction, and to supersede all other messages that potential customers are receiving. In tourism, the message is often for two groups; first, the tourist, or ultimate buyer, and second the intermediate buyer, the travel agent or tour operator. A problem arises when the interests of the two are not the same. Recognizing this, Wahab listed the priorities of these two groups:

Intermediary Buyer	Tourist
Profit	Personal satisfaction
Minimal risk	Value for the money and efficiency
Long selling period	Convenient and safe
Prestige (gives good image)	Novelty[7]

While both are interested in the stimulus (the dream)

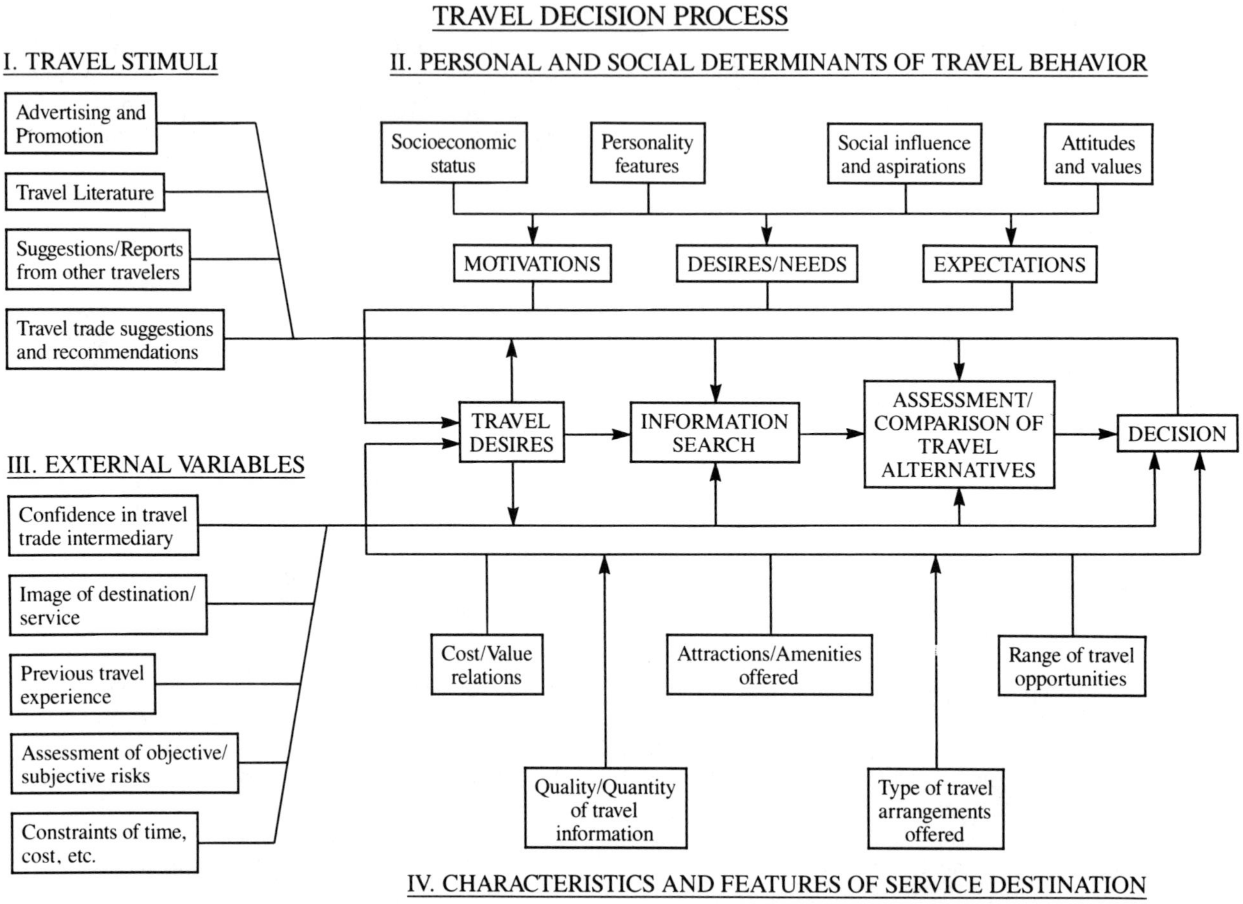

TRAVEL DECISION PROCESS

I. TRAVEL STIMULI   II. PERSONAL AND SOCIAL DETERMINANTS OF TRAVEL BEHAVIOR

Figure 10-1 Source: World Tourism Organization.

for travel intermediaries to catch the attention of the potential tourist they will also need more information and facts on how the product will help make money and maintain their good image as companies with which to do further business.

PROMOTION MIX

Promotion mix refers to the absolute and relative amounts of effort or dollars put into each of the major promotional categories of advertising, personal selling, sales promotions, or public relations. These types are defined as:

Advertising: Any form of paid-for, nonpersonal presentation and promotion of ideas, products, or services by a specific sponsor using some form of mass media.

Personal Selling: An oral presentation to one or more prospective customers on a "face to face" basis (includes telephone solicitations).

Sales Promotions: Those activities, other than advertising and personal selling, that stimulate purchasing. Sales promotions are geared either toward the ultimate consumer (contests, giveaways, and/or drawings, featuring free tickets to attractions or destinations, exhibits, and displays) and/or toward channel intermediaries (trade show participants, exhibits, hospitality training).

Public Relations: The presentation of ideas, goods, or services about an organization using mass media. However, unlike advertising, it is not paid for. It is designed to create a favorable image of the company that is involved.[8]

Advertising

Advertising uses a number of forms to attract attention, arouse interest, convey information, and to induce the potential traveler to act in a specific manner. Some forms of advertising are newspapers, direct mail, television, magazines, radio, Yellow Pages, outdoor advertising, novelties, directories, and display material (e.g. posters, cardboard stands, window displays, dispensers for sales literature, and so on).

Newspaper advertising has six advantages: (1) It facilitates geographic segmentation since markets for distribution can be defined clearly. (2) The cost of newspaper advertising is relatively low. (3) Most newspapers are daily. (4) Newspapers have extensive coverage (it is estimated that approximately eighty percent of the adult population in the United States read at least one newspaper daily). (5) It is quick and easy to schedule an ad in a newspaper. (6) Most Sunday editions have a travel section. The major disadvantage of newspapers is the quality of the ad and the short life span.

There are a number of different types of newspapers, each with advantages and disadvantages. First, large city dailies have wide coverage, but are expensive for small travel companies. Second, small town newspapers are effective for the local tourist services offered, since the price of advertising is inexpensive. Third, the suburban weekly, which is good for travel agents, for example, have offices in those same suburban areas where the potential tourists live. Fourth, ethnic newspapers provide a direct way to reach that segment of the market. This also includes many people who like to travel together. Fifth, club and organization newspapers are beneficial for those tourist services that are assisting the sponsor with a specific trip.

Direct mail, although potentially expensive, ranks high as an advertising medium. Direct mail material consists of sales letters and/or brochures sent to people most likely to become users of the service offered. Names are gathered from mailing lists of magazines devoted to travel such as *Golf, Holiday, Ski, Wheels Afield,* or *Better Camping;* from passport applications; mobile home owners; tour operators; airport flight insurance companies; frequent flyer program participants; and so on. In the United States, over 30 billion pieces of direct mail are sent out each year, which means that every person, (man, woman, or child) receives over 140 pieces of direct mail advertising annually.[9] Direct mail's effectiveness can be measured, in part, if it requires a response by return mail or phone.

Brochures, leaflets, travel catalogs, and sales letters are often used in direct mail. Brochures are less voluminous publications than a travel catalog and offer more information than a leaflet or folder. Brochures, especially for cruise companies, can be very expensive and are used as a sales tool by travel agents, since they provide detailed information on cabins, prices, schedules, and so on. Illustrated travel catalogs present an entire travel program with lists of numerous destinations, services accommodations, activities, excursions, options, and information about the destinations. They, too, are used by travel agents as sales tools, but are usually not used as much for direct mail because they are expensive to publish. Travel catalogs for large companies are usually issued twice a year—for the summer and winter seasons respectively. Some of them contain up to two hundred pages, offering a wide choice of destinations and arrangements.

Leaflets or folders are usually single sheets providing a minimum amount of information; they are used as stimuli to further action. Sales letters are similar; however, they offer a bit more flexibility since they are sometimes used in combination with travel catalogs, brochures, or folders in an effort to personalize the mail contact.

Television is a very effective audio and visual medium when large coverage is required. It is an expensive medium however, which only large organizations use. While the average person spends considerable time watching television, recall of the commercials seen is small. This is one reason why television advertisements at times seem rather outlandish. It is an effort to strengthen memory retention.

Magazines offer high-quality print and graphics, are kept longer than newspapers, are used in waiting rooms, and inserts and coupons are easily added. Magazine audiences are segmented according to the kinds of magazines they read; thus, they facilitate advertising to a specific interest group. Appendix A provides some national and international publications that are classified as travel or travel-related magazines.

Radio has the advantage of being very flexible and relatively low cost, compared with other mass media. It also does allow for some interest segmentation, since radio stations have segmented their own markets according to the music they air. Many have special programs that attract certain types of listeners who might be in the targeted population. Radio advertising can also be useful in destination regions, so that messages can reach tourists already in the area, or those traveling to the area. Visitors driving to Las Vegas are bombarded with ads for many kinds of eating, lodging, casino, or show information.

The Yellow Pages are valuable sources of information for those who know they want a service, but are unsure of where they'll find it. In other words, it is a good place for an organization to advertise when trying to attract shoppers in both the origin area and in the destination area. A tourist in the area might use the Yellow Pages to find a service such as a restaurant or other tourist-related retail outlets.

Outdoor advertising is generally seen in three areas: first, in areas of high visibility (on public transportation vehicles such as buses and taxis); second, on benches (particularly along public transportation routes); and third, billboards (used extensively along highways to create an awareness of the hotels, motels, service stations, restaurants, and campgrounds that are ahead). In cities billboards and signs are seen along major transportation routes to and from airports, and other major arteries traveled by local residents.

All outdoor advertising is subject to city, state, and federal laws, in regard to location, spacing requirements (to avoid sign congestion), distance from highway, and the length of time the advertisement can exist. Since outdoor advertising usually holds attention for a very brief span of time, the message it conveys must be short and clear. Much of the communication in outdoor advertising is through symbols and pictures rather than words; it is not at all suitable for long and complicated messages. It usually serves as a reminder to supplement advertising in other media such as the press, television, or radio.

Point-of-sale advertising commonly uses windows, floor displays, counter displays, and literature racks. One major value of this form of sales advertising is that the prospective customers come in contact with it when they are in the process of making travel decisions. The main purpose of point-of-sale advertising is to remind customers or potential customers of the advertising messages and themes communicated in the media. It offers opportunities for variety in artwork, size, color, and material used. It is similar to outdoor advertising in that point-of-sale advertising usually only holds the attention for a short time; therefore, the message must be short and clear.

Personal Selling

Personal selling occurs in direct contact with a prospective tourist, either face to face or by telephone. Oral presentations take place in travel agencies, in large or small meetings, formally and informally.

Sales Promotion

Sales promotions have become very common today with free tickets to special events, trade shows, exhibits, and for trips. Hardly a week goes by without seeing or hearing of a free trip being offered. A common sales promotion available for the travel intermediary is the familiarization visit. These are used by airlines, hotels, and destination regions to draw attention to their services or the development of a new service.

Travel shows are a common form of sales promotion, and they take in many forms. Travel agencies and tour operators will gather travelers together to promote a specific tour or cruise. Food, from simple refreshments to formal dinners, are served. Fairs, and other events such as conferences and conventions, bring together a large number of prospective tourists for a specified time; displays, visuals (such as slide shows and short films), posters, brochures, leaflets, are available. Films featuring travel destinations, cruises, and other forms of travel are a basic element of travel shows. Films are available from large companies, governments, and film distribution organizations for companies that are too small to develop their own.

Other sales promotions are local contests, parades, receptions, open houses, reunions, seminars, special events, speeches, and joint offers between banks and department stores.

Public Relations

The purpose of public relations is to build a strong positive image of an organization for the public. Schmoll identified three principal characteristics of public relations: (1) The purpose of public relations is communication to potential customers in methods other than normally paid advertisement channels or direct sales effort; (2) It recreates a public awareness in order to enhance advertising and sales; and (3) Public relations creates a positive image for a product, service, or destination in the minds of those who make public opinion such as journalists, travel writers and those who act as intermediaries such as travel agents and tour operators.[10]

The major form of public relations is news releases; in addition there are public appearances on radio and television talk shows. However, since the publicity is not paid for, there is no guarantee that it will be carried in the media or that it will be in the form that the company has requested. Print news releases are more readily acceptable to newspapers, local ones in particular, than magazines.

Public relations and sales promotions overlap where free tickets and special familiarization trips are handled and distributed through public relations efforts.

BUDGETING

Table 10-1 shows the general division of the tourist promotion budget for various segments of the travel industry. It can be seen that the majority of the promotional budget goes into advertising.

The key costs in the budgeting process are the cost per message, the cost per reader, and the cost of repeated messages. It is rare that a single message has sufficient impact; thus, a television or radio spot must be aired several times. The number of times a message needs to be shown to have impact is considered part of this cost.[11] The major consideration in constructing a budget is the effectiveness of the advertising. This takes into account impact, appeal, retention, readership, and costs.

The following case study illustrates that effectiveness does not always have to be expensive. It also combines many of the issues discussed in this chapter.

Case Study: Emily Post Summer Camp

The "Emily Post Summer Camp," developed for The Breakers in Palm Beach, Florida, is an example of a successful national promotion. . . . The promotion of an etiquette camp for children was created in support of the resort's stated marketing goals, to: increase summer season business, traditionally the slowest of the year, by creating an exciting image for the property; attract/appeal to family vacationers; overcome the image of The Breakers, as "old, stuffy and an anachronism," and appeal to a younger, family clientele; accomplish all this without jeopardizing the image of the resort as offering old world elegance and a tradition of gracious hospitality.[12]

It was the first program of its type in the country endorsed by the Emily Post Institute, and the first time The Breakers ever presented such an unusual family-oriented program. Since the summer camp was especially designed for The Breakers, only registered guests of the hotel were ecable to enroll their children in the etiquette school. (Residents of Palm Beach could also send their children to the camp on a daily basis.) However, the experience could not be duplicated by hotel guests in Palm Beach who did not stay at The Breakers. In addition, the promotion highlighted the comprehensive resort/recreational facilities and amen-

TABLE 10-1 TOURIST PROMOTION BUDGETS

Type	Advertising	Sales Support	Public Relations
Travel Trade (Travel Agents, Tour Operators)	60%	35%	5%
Air Carriers	65%	25%	10%
Hotels, Motels	70%	20%	10%
National Tourist Offices	70–80%	15–25%	5–10%

Source: G.A. Schmoll. *Tourism Promotion* (London: Tourism International Press, 1977).

ities of this Five Star/Five Diamond resort, without threatening The Breakers "traditional, conservative image."

Since The Breakers already offered a structured, six-day-a-week supervised activities program for children, the "Emily Post Summer Camp" did not affect resort operations in any serious or overburdening way.

Finally, the camp promotion was staged on a minimal budget, totaling just $4,000. Included in the budget were such items as two round-trip airline tickets for the camp's etiquette instructor, local advertising, the design and printing of collaterals, including a course instruction workbook, and a direct-mail leaflet sent to five hundred former visitors, the printing and mailing of press releases describing the program, and other fees and honorariums.

The following shows how the program was organized and implemented, and what results were achieved.

Program Description

The Breakers' first annual "Emily Post Summer Camp," an etiquette instruction camp for children ages eight to fourteen was offered during two week-long camp sessions in August, 1983.

The camp provided morning classes for children on poise and posture, the art of conversation, good sportsmanship, table manners and table settings, grooming and hair care, clothing coordination, telephone manners, writing thank-you notes, and dancing. Following lunch, campers participated in the hotel's regularly scheduled supervised youth program. A wrap-up session was held at the conclusion of each day. At the end of the week-long camp, each student received a signed certificate of completion, as well as a gift of The New Emily Post's Etiquette. While campers were happily occupied learning "social and survival skills," parents enjoyed numerous opportunities to play tennis, golf, swim, and relax.

To help promote the program to travel writers and sell it to guests, an "Emily Post Summer Camp" package was developed. Based on a stay of eight days/seven nights, it included accommodations for two adults and one child in two connecting rooms; camp enrollment fee; green fees and tennis; a welcome reception; and, on three other evenings throughout the week, a big band dinner-dance, a family cookout, and a graduation banquet.

Implementation

A press release, "The Breakers Presents Country's First Emily Post Summer Camp," was drafted and sent to national and regional newspaper travel editors; to the Society of American Travel Writers; to news editors of top television and radio stations; and to directors of special interest programs, including those oriented towards "families" and "education," in the country's major metropolitan areas.

A letter, suggesting coverage of the camp under the umbrella topic of "art of parenting" was sent inviting editors to report on the camp in session. The mailing went to travel, family, and lifestyle editors of high-circulation national consumer magazines; to nationally syndicated travel writers and columnists; and to producers of selected national and local television and radio programs.

The Breakers produced a program brochure, containing a schedule of camp events, a tariff schedule and registration form, and provided it to any who requested information on the camp.

Three weeks before the first camp session, The Breakers ran one black-and-white, digest-size ad, offering the special day-rate for local children, in the "neighborhood" section of The Miami Herald.

A press conference was held for local media to announce the camp at The Breakers, two months prior to the opening session. Florida-based travel/lifestyle writers and the news media attended this conference.

Editorial coverage of the program was increased by suggesting to the public relations agency of Elizabeth Post, director of the Emily Post Institute, that they encourage her to mention the camp in all her media interviews.

Finally, follow-up coverage of the camp appeared in the resort's quarterly newsletter, which was placed in guest rooms and mailed to clients.

Results

From a publicity standpoint, the "Emily Post Summer Camp" was an overwhelming success. Highlights of that coverage were a Newsweek cover story; a live interview on the "CBS Morning News"; a spot on the nationally-broadcast "ABC World News Tonight"; as well as exposure on local television news programs. Feature articles appeared in USA Today; the New York Times "Style" section (syndicated in eight papers across the country); The Washington Post; the Boston Globe; the Philadelphia Inquirer; the Miami Herald, and other major metropolitan dailies; and in numerous weeklies. Both AP and UPI ran wire stories that added to the coverage.

Most importantly, the enormous and sustained visibility of The Breakers in the news and consumer media during the summer of 1983 had a great impact on the hotel's summer business in 1984. Because of this promotion, groundwork was laid for the future positioning of The Breakers as a resort for family vacations.

COOPERATIVE PROMOTIONAL EFFORTS

The ability of the travel industry to use several different services and intermediaries lends itself well to cooperative promotional efforts. There are three major types of cooperative promotions. First, intercommunity, where two or more communities pool their promotional budgets and abilities to advertise in a wide area, so as to increase the total number of tourists. Second, is cooperation between the various private companies and sectors of the travel industry; and, third, between states, and between states and the federal government. Tourism USA indicated the advantages of cooperation as:

—Better utilization of promotional funds.
—Less dilution of promotional effect of individual community effort.
—More matching monies that will allow more promotional "clout."

—Encouragement for tourists to spend more time in an area, resulting in more total tourist expenditures.

—Area-wide improvement of resources and facilities that make for a better total sales package.

—More opportunities to create large attractions and events.

—Better clarification of community and area image.[13]

The single most important reason for a cooperative effort is that it will stimulate more business for all—whether they are private or governmental agencies. A very common form of cooperation is that between travel agents and major suppliers, such as between airlines and cruise companies. Cruise companies will financially support sales promotions (travel shows) and joint advertising ventures. Airlines will provide brochure jackets and posters for travel agencies. Cruise lines and tour companies will run large advertisements in the Sunday travel section of newspapers, and make arrangements for local agencies to insert logos, addresses and telephone numbers, indicating they are agents for the cruise or tour company.

In the United States, cities and counties work together to form travel councils and jointly advertise their area. *Tourism USA* provides several good examples. One of their examples is as follows:

Fall River, Massachusetts is a pleasant little community nestled in the southeastern corner of Massachusetts, an area rich in early American history. Although Fall River had some attractions, such as a marine museum, the battleship USS Massachusetts, and the home of Lizzie Borden, it did not receive much tourism business. Tourist traffic tended to move along routes fifteen miles southeast of Fall River, to New Bedford.

It was not until 1965 that tourism development began to occur in Fall River because Fall River and Bristol County community leaders decided to extend themselves beyond the local market and create something that would lure tourists throughout Bristol County. They met with community officials from Mystic, Connecticut to Plymouth, Massachusetts, and created the American Trail: 350 years of history in 119 miles. *This cooperative effort brought $2.5 million into Bristol County in slightly less than eight years. Bristol County had a tourism development budget in excess of $300,000 and the Bristol County Development Council coordinated the individual community promotion efforts for four cities and sixteen townships.*[14]

The states of Colorado, Wyoming, and Utah combined to advertise in Europe. They suggested that a visitor fly into Denver, an international airport, rent a car and follow a suggested route through the three states; leave the car in Salt Lake City, then return to Europe from there. The combined effort provides all three states the opportunity to reach

Salem, Massachusetts: The House of Seven Gables, setting for Nathaniel Hawthorne's famous novel. Photo courtesy of Massachusetts Department of Commerce and Development.

the travel-minded European market. None of them would be able to do this effectively alone.

OTHER FORMS OF PROMOTION

In addition to these forms of promotion (advertising, personal selling, sales promotions, and public relations), there are a number of other sales gimmicks worth mentioning briefly. They are the sale of souvenirs and other mementos, the purpose of which is also to promote or stimulate sales and generate revenues. Souvenirs and mementos help remind tourists of a pleasant vacation and good experiences.

MAJOR ISSUES

The major considerations of promotion are accuracy and reliability of information on the one hand and false and misleading advertising on the other. Promotion techniques use words that evoke emotion and create awareness and action. Typical promotions will use superlatives—exotic, tremendous, outstanding, deluxe, superior, largest, and best—all designed to elicit an emotional response. In many cases the travel industry may be its own worst enemy by creating such a high expectation of an attraction that it oversells it, thereby creating problems. People in the industry realize that there are some expressions that are known as travel "double talk." The vignette on "Eight Fun-Filled

Days and Glorious Nights" illustrates some of these communication problems.

False, deceptive, and misleading advertisements can lead to legal action by both state and federal governments. Consumer protection has become an extremely important concern of government. Most consumer protection legislation considers unfair or deceptive practices as:

1. False, falsely disparaging, or misleading oral or written statements, visual description, or other representation of any kind which has the capacity, tendency, or effect of deceiving or misleading consumers and which is made in connection with the offer for sale, lease, rental, loan or bailment of consumer goods or services.
2. Representation that consumer goods or consumer services have a sponsorship, approval, accessory, characteristic, ingredient, use, benefit or quality which they do not have; a merchant has a sponsorship, approval, status, affiliation, or connection which s/he does not have; consumer goods or consumer services are of a particular standard, quality, grade, style or model which they are not.
3. Failure to state a material fact if the failure deceives or tends to deceive.
4. Disparagement of the goods, services, or business

... EIGHT FUN-FILLED DAYS AND GLORIOUS NIGHTS

Ever get the feeling that the creators of travel brochures have never even seen the subject of their puffy prose? Here a reformed writer of travel double-talk teaches you how to read between the lines.

by Richard Douglass

For over 20 years, I have been subjected to a barrage of travel magazines, Sunday travel sections, lurid brochures, and jam-packed itineraries. Using these as a reference, I have contributed to the confusion myself, cranking out hundreds of titillating film scripts and tantalizing full-color mailings extolling the virtues of more destinations than I'll ever see.

Everything was going well until a few years ago, when I started traveling, actually visiting the places and experiencing firsthand the "never-to-be-forgotten adventure-of-a-lifetime."

Traveling has opened my eyes. I confess I have been careless with the truth.

I'm sure you've seen my work. I'm the guy who told you how your transatlantic flight to Europe would end: "As the morning sun filters gently through your cabin window, you are awakened by the delicate aroma of freshly brewed coffee being served by your smiling attendant." Something closer to the truth might have read: "Exhausted and queasy from too much liquor and too little sleep, you are startled awake by the blinding sun and acrid smell of coffee mixing with the brewery atmosphere of the cabin."

No more double-talk. No more "racing the sun across the Atlantic" to describe the irreparable damage done to your body clock on returning to the United States. No more "specialty of the house" to cover the fact that you can't order from the menu. No more "cozy" for tiny, "stately" for over-the-hill, or "relaxing" for boring.

Here for your edification—or to confirm your worst suspicions—are some of the most widely used euphemisms in travel literature today, together with what I have determined to be their best approximate English translations. I offer them as a public service—and in expiation for my past transgressions.

Travelese expression	**English equivalent**
all the amenities	free shower cap
aristocratic	needs renovation
gentle breezes	gale-force winds
picturesque	theme park or mystery house nearby
airy	no air conditioning
brisk	freezing
carefree natives	terrible service
bustling metropolis	thousands of hostile locals
open bar	all the ice cubes you want
plush	top and bottom sheets
spacious quarters	sparsely furnished room
surprising bargains	save on hollowed-coconut bird feeders
motorcoach	bus
deluxe motorcoach	bus with clean windows
unique	no one else would do it like this
quaint	run-down
warmed by the Gulf Stream	cold
cooled by the Humbolt Current	hot
off the beaten path	people have stopped coming here
standard	substandard
deluxe	standard
superior	free shower cap
undiscovered	not worth discovering
convenient	bring busfare
playground of the stars	Regis Toomey once stayed here
if you like being pampered	you can get waited on
exquisite cuisine	limited menu
tree-lined boulevards	no sight-seeing
old-world charm	no bath
carriage trade	no kids or pets
sun-drenched	arid wasteland
tropical	rainy
panoramic vista	a long way from town
authentic native dishes	inedible but cheap
options galore	nothing is included in your itinerary
secluded hideaway	impossible to find
. . . too numerous to mention	the writer has never been there
preregistered rooms	already occupied
leisurely transfer	tedious bus ride
explore on your own	pay for it yourself
knowledgeable trip hosts	they've flown before
nominal charge	outrageous charge
"thieves' market"	thieves
dare to be different	ignore your common sense
no extra fees	no extras
steeped in history	old and backward
tipping is considered an insult	they love to be insulted
. . . and much, much more	that's about all there is

Source: ©1984 by Barrington Publications, Inc. Reprinted by permission of Richard Douglass.

of another by false or misleading representation of material fact.

5. Advertisement or offer of consumer goods or consumer services, without intent to sell them as advertised or offered.[15]

Questions have been raised regarding: airline pricing of inexpensive seats that are sold based upon availability because of the perception travelers have that they can "never obtain one"; brochures that suggest a hotel has rooms fac-

ing the Taj Mahal, or the scenic beach, etc. when in fact, it is only the hotel, not the rooms that have the view; statements such as, "after dinner we will go to the theater" are ambiguous. Is it part of the tour or is it optional? However, the industry as a whole does have a good reputation and represents itself well. It is an industry that relies strongly on repeat business and strong recommendations from others, thus its strength is its service. But a few "bad apples" can and do create problems that require careful analysis by both travel intermediaries and potential travelers.

RESEARCH AND REVIEW

1. Define promotion.

2. Describe three distinct market segment areas.

3. What are five decisions arrived at by the planning process?

4. Explain the five communication goals quoted from *Tourism USA*.

5. What is promotion mix? Describe four types.

6. List the advantages of at least eight different types of advertising.

7. Is there a difference between sales promotion and public relations? How are they similar?

8. What are five advantages of cooperative promotion efforts?

9. How does false advertising affect the tourism industry?

ENDNOTES

1. Wahab, Crampon and Rothfield, p. 107.
2. Mill and Morrison, p. 379.
3. G.A. Schmoll, *Tourism Promotion* (London: Tourism International Press, 1977), p. 81.
4. *Tourism USA* (1986), p. 121.
5. Schmoll, p. 65.
6. Mill and Morrison, p. 391.
7. Wahab, Crampon and Rothfield, p. 107
8. *Tourism USA* (1986) p. 119.
9. Robert T. Reilly, *Travel and Tourism Marketing Techniques* (Wheaton, IL: Merton House, 1980), p. 155.
10. Schmoll, p. 77.
11. Wahab, Crampon and Rothfield, pp. 195–201.
12. *MSMAI Marketing Review* (Winter 1985–86) pp. 33–34.
13. *Tourism USA* (1986), p. 143.
14. Ibid.
15. Jeffrey R. Miller, *Legal Aspects of Travel Agency Operation* (Wheaton, IL: Merton House, 1982), p. 120.

CHAPTER 11

TRANSPORTATION AND TOUR OPERATIONS

"Getting there is half the fun" is an oft-quoted expression that indicates a basic element of tourism. How often do travelers select motels with swimming pools and other pleasurable amenities, bypassing less costly places without them? Even economy motel chains like Motel 6 and Scotchman offer more than a room with the essentials for overnight lodging.

Travel and tourism are difficult to separate and, in many cases, are used interchangeably although a traveler, in the strict sense, may not be a tourist. All travelers quite naturally seem to have some tourist inclinations. How much easier it is for a businessperson to go on a business trip, or a convention-goer to decide to go to a convention, if the area is a major tourist attraction. Many companies schedule meetings of their sales forces in New Orleans, San Francisco, Toronto, and such places, not because they are major cities, but because of the pleasurable activities associated with them. Convention-goers can take advantage of the arts and entertainment and shopping of these metropolises.

The desire to travel is encouraged with the improvement of transportation. Indeed, as discussed in the first chapter, the history of transportation improvement has paralleled the history of tourism. Before World War I it took four days to travel from coast to coast; the steam locomotive was able to complete the journey in seven days; by 1950 travelers could go from coast to coast in two and one-half days by train. By 1938, airplane speeds up to 400 miles an hour made possible a nonstop coast-to-coast flight of slightly less than eight hours. However, with the necessity of refueling en route, the actual trip took twelve hours. By the 1950s travel time from coast-to-coast was reduced to four hours. Now the Concorde can make the flight in two and one-half hours.

134

THE DAWNING OF THE JET AGE; OCTOBER 1958

by Joseph Cassen

Even before the first jet airplane takes to the skies on its first scheduled flight, the very term Jet Age is in danger of becoming a platitude.

It is natural that others in the travel industry should think of the Jet Age as primarily an airline affair, but it requires no deep analysis to recognize that it will affect all other components of the travel industry as well.

Thus, eager pronouncements of the potential blessings of the Jet Age lose their meaning if the others who will benefit, such as hotels, travel agents and tour operators, cling to old concepts, routines and prejudices.

The full development of the Jet Age will be influenced by the progressive thinking and actions of everyone in the travel industry, including the airlines.

The big and welcome challenge in the Jet Age will be to generate a sufficient volume of new passengers to pay for the larger and faster planes which will be in operation.

The important thing is that these must be passengers who have never flown before, who have never stopped at hotels before and who have never visited travel agents before.

. . . In the final analysis, the only domestic competitors of the travel industry, individually or collectively, in the Jet Age are the private automobile, the private swimming pool, the motorboat and the mink coat.

It is far better to take the broad view and unite to introduce these people to the joys of air vacation travel, than to take the narrow view of regarding creative vacation promotion by anyone as competitive within the industry. This is the real meaning of Jet Age thinking.

Source: *Travel Weekly's 25th Anniversary,* May 31, 1983

Table 11-1 illustrates historical changes in transportation. The tremendous technological breakthroughs of the past one hundred years are particularly dramatic.

These developments in transportation, which have been paralleled by improvements in communications, have made the world a much smaller place. This has had a very powerful effect on tourism. It is now possible to take a week or two of vacation and spend it at some faraway place. A few years ago, just before or after the Second World War, a vacation in Hawaii, the Caribbean, or Acapulco, (let alone more exotic islands of the Pacific such as Bali, or the countries of South America) was almost unattainable for the majority of Americans. Now transport can be made quickly and efficiently to almost any place in the world. This accessibility depends first on cost, and second on whether there is enough time to go. Air fares to South America are higher than air fares to Europe, therefore more people go to Europe. Although it takes the same amount of time, more people choose Europe over South America because it is less expensive.

As we've discussed, in recent years it has become common to express distance in terms of time rather than mileage. In terms of time, the world has shrunk dramatically. However, if an attraction is close with respect to time, yet is very costly, it becomes inaccessible to many people.

Modern tourism is based on the movement of masses of people (economics of scale). This implies that there are many vacations and opportunities available to people because of short travel times and because a relatively greater

TABLE 11-1 HISTORICAL DEVELOPMENT OF TRANSPORT SYSTEMS

Year	Mode of Transport	Speed (Miles per Hour)
6000 BC	Camel caravan	8
1600 BC	Chariot	20
1784 AD	First English mail coach	10
1825	First steam locomotive	13
1890	Improved steam locomotive	100
1931	Land speed record (Bluebird: Sir Malcolm Campbell)	246
1938	Land speed record (Napier-Railton car: John Cobb)	350
1938	Piston aircraft	400
1952	Liner *United States* from New York to Le Havre	41
1958	Jet fighter aircraft	1,300
1958	Boeing 707 and DC-8 aircraft	600
1961	Space ship (Vostok I orbiting)	17,560
1967	Rocket plane	4,534
1970	Fighter bomber (Mirage IV)	1,450
1970	Commercial aircraft—Concorde	1,320
1970	Boeing 747	625

Source: James Reason. *Man in Motion: The Psychology of Travel* (London: George Weidenfeld and Nicolson Limited, 1974), p. 3.

amount of money is available to these people to spend on recreational and leisure pursuits. The improved standard of living and improvements in transportation increase the public's opportunity, willingness, and ability to travel. With dramatic decreases in air fares that began with airline deregulation in 1978, many more people are traveling.

There are man-made barriers to transportation accessibility. They include inefficient terminal facilities that inhibit traffic flow on the ground, on the water, and in the air. The international airport in Tokyo illustrates this point. The trip from downtown Tokyo to the new airport takes two hours. Many air trips are now shorter than the time it takes to reach the airport. Trans World Airlines perceives the distance between the airport terminal and downtown as an important element in the selection of an airline. They advertise that in New York they have their own terminal through which they can process the traveler quickly and easily. Many travelers bypass certain airports because they feel they are too time consuming and complicated.

Convenience and accessibility are very important considerations for tourists. They willingly substitute one attraction for another if there are less hassles getting there. Thus, a family may dream of a vacation in Jamaica but settle on a trip to southern California, or to a nearby national park, if getting to Jamaica is too much trouble.

TYPES OF TRANSPORTATION

The type of transportation chosen depends on a number of factors including the length of the trip, the number of people in the travel party, and the income of the traveler. These factors, as well as the availability, frequency of trips, cost, time spent in traveling, and comfort in traveling to the destination are important in the decision-making process.

Jagdish Sheth developed a theory to identify transportation variables and the values of travelers. He indicated that travelers choose a travel mode based on their psychological weighing of five factors. They are functional, aesthetic/emotional, social/organizational, situational, and curiosity. The first, functional, is simply the expected likely performance of differing transportation for a specific purpose. Departure and arrival times, safety records, the directness of the trip or the number of required transfers are all considered. Second, aesthetic/emotional, relates to such aspects as fear, social concern, style, luxury, comfort, and other personal attitudes that the form of transportation might evoke. Third, social/organizational, indicates that the dominant users of certain kinds of transportation are stereotyped according to sex, racial origin, income, price/cost, and education. Those who take bus trips are generally perceived to be female—either young or old; while bus tours and cruises have been seen as popular tours for empty nesters (retired people). Fourth, situational, refers to how conveniently located the particular mode of transportation and its terminal facilities are for the traveler's perceived need.[1] In this chapter we will analyze different types of travel and the characteristics of each.

The automobile dominates travel (see Table 11-2) as the major means of transportation in developed countries,

TABLE 11-2 TYPE OF TRANSPORTATION

Type	Percent			
	1977	1982	1985	1986
Auto-truck	85.2	78	68	75.0
Air	11.7	18	25	22.6
Bus	1.8	3	3	1.6
Other	0.8	1	2	0.4
Train	0.4	1	1	0.4

Source: Bureau of Census, U.S. Department of Commerce, *1977 National Travel Survey; Travel Data Center, 1982 (1985) National Travel Survey* and *Travel & Leisure's World Travel Overview, 1987/1988.*

regardless of the driver's purpose. Air travel is proportionately greater for persons traveling to attend conventions and conducting business, but it is still clearly second to the automobile. The heavy-use patterns of the automobile are simply an extension of current United States lifestyle. The development of freeway systems and relatively inexpensive fuel has led to this high usage of the automobile. However, in the United States, the percentage of total passenger miles by automobile dropped from ninety percent of all total trips in 1960 to seventy-five percent by 1986. The number of air miles continued to increase; by 1986 they accounted for twenty-five percent of the total passenger miles traveled.

International travel is dominated by air travel, with the exception of travel between the United States and Canada, which is still predominantly by automobile. Air departures by United States citizens to countries other than Canada exceeded fourteen million people in 1986.[2]

Rail

With the advent of the first steam locomotive in 1825 until after World War II, travel by rail became the dominant means of movement within the United States. During the latter part of the 1800s and the first part of the 1900s, the train linked major population centers and fashionable spas and resorts such as Saratoga, Niagara Falls, Long Beach, New Jersey, and Las Vegas. In fact, railroad companies built resorts along the East Coast from New England to Florida. This reliance on the train is demonstrated in the development of Las Vegas. The early large hotels were located downtown, a short distance from the railroad station; they radiated out from that point. This gave tourists arriving by train quick and easy access to hotels and casinos. These events in America were paralleled in Europe. Thomas Cook, who organized the first travel agency, began excursion specials between Leicester and Loughborough in England on July 5, 1841.[3]

Long-distance rail travel was given a boost in 1863 when G.M. Pullman developed the Pullman coach, a luxury first-class sleeping and dining facility. In 1868 the diner car was introduced on the Chicago and Alton line. Within ten years, an elaborate meal could be obtained on all trains.

The popularity of the train lasted only for a brief period after World War II, when heightened demand for travel began to erode its popularity. By the late 1950s, staggering losses led the United States railroad companies to begin trimming the passenger system. Two factors were important in the development of new forms of transportation for tourism. The Federal Aid Highway Act of 1956 enabled states to construct the interstate highway system; that same year jetliners began domestic routes in the United States. From 1958 until 1966 rail travel continued to decline. The final blow came in 1967 when the post office announced that it was discontinuing nearly all of its railroad post office cars. Trying to salvage a dying industry, the United States government took over rail passenger service with minor exceptions. In an effort to eliminate the most unprofitable runs and improve the ones that were still authorized, Amtrak began operating in 1971. It is governed by the National Railroad Passenger Corporation. It has a fifteen-man board with eight representatives selected by the president of the United States, three by the railroads, and four by private, preferred-stock holders. Amtrak cut out many routes and has tried to upgrade the system with better equipment. Reservation and ticket-issuing systems have been modernized, similar to airlines. The most popular routes are now between the cold north and warm, sunny southern states. Retired people with more spare time, comprise the bulk of the rail travelers.

With increased urban growth and new airports being constructed farther and farther from city centers, with the increased need for speed and comfort, and with the central location of terminals, there could come a revival of the golden era of trains. This is especially true along the eastern seaboard and in major cities in close proximity to each other, such as Kansas City and St. Louis, or San Francisco and Los Angeles. Travel patterns may also become a plane/train combination, similar to the fly/cruise combinations that have developed in the cruise industry. A vacationer from the West Coast could fly to a major city, then transfer to rail travel between Boston, New York, and Washington, returning to the West by air.

Train travel has continued in Europe and Asia more than in the United States, particularly for long-distance travel. The EuroCity network (formerly the Trans-Europe Express [TEE] network) as well as other national lines, has provided excellent rail service between major cities in ten countries. This system is being improved. As of May 31, 1987, the TEE has been replaced by a new system which includes high speed trains, with both first and second class accommodations. The development and construction of the Eurotunnel between England and the continent will further improve travel within Europe. Once the tunnel is complete, it will reduce travel time between England and other European countries by two hours. It will create the single biggest unified rail network in the world. Europeans believe that the train is a more efficient form of transportation from city center to city center on most trips up to 300 miles.

Although the relative importance of rail travel has given way to the automobile and airplane in many countries, railroads are working to improve facilities to accommodate supertrains with speeds between 150 and 250 miles per hour. At the present time Japan has the best railroad system in the world, with 26,000 fast and efficient trains scheduled a day. But even here improvements are being made. Japan

has plans for trains traveling at speeds of 300 miles per hour. Among Europeans, the Germans have a test track designed to carry passengers at a cruising speed of 180 miles per hour, with short sprints to 240 miles per hour. Both the French and Italians have been working with high-speed train systems. There are at least three plans for similar train systems in the United States.

The popularity of the train system in Europe has increased, not only because of their quality and efficiency, but because of the use of the Eurail pass. A number of European countries, Austria, Belgium, Denmark, France, West Germany, Italy, Luxembourg, the Netherlands, Norway, Portugal, Spain, Sweden and Switzerland, introduced the first Eurail pass in 1959, permitting an individual up to two months of unlimited second-class travel on any of the countries' respective rail systems. Later, it included unlimited first-class service over varying periods (fifteen day, twenty-one day, one month, and three months) with access to many ferry and steamer routes. In addition, they developed a student Eurail pass for second-class travel, and included Finland, Greece, and Ireland in the system.

Automobile

From 1768 to 1770 a French engineer, Nicolas-Joseph Cugnot, experimented with a steam-powered artillery tractor, which had a single driven front wheel. In Cornwall, England, on Christmas Eve, 1801, Richard Trevithick drove the first workable steam carriage up Camborne Beacon with seven or eight people clinging to it. Then in Switzerland, in 1807, Isaac de Rivaz built the forerunner of the internal-combustion engine automobile, a crude trolley jerked along by a device known as a "Voltaic pistol" in which gas was exploded in a cylinder by an electric spark. In Britain, from about 1820 to 1840, steam-powered carriages flourished briefly, even operating scheduled passenger services on the streets of London.

The growth of the stationary gas engine industry in Germany during the 1870s paved the way for the development of the first truly practical internal-combustion horseless carriages. Four inventors, all working independently, without knowledge of the others, developed gasoline cars in the 1880s. However, the real inventor of the automobile was Carl Benz, of Mannheim, Germany, who in 1885–86, combined two great Victorian inventions—the bicycle and the internal-combustion engine. He designed the complete vehicle (engine, chassis and transmission). The industry grew rapidly. Then came Henry Ford! Ford produced his Model T car in 1908, built with an assembly-line technique for mass production. The price of the Model T dropped from $825 in 1908 to $260 in 1925. This was a revolution that changed the face of the American landscape. People were free to live far away from their jobs and commute to them. Families were able to take drives in the country; travelers could plot new routes for travel.

However, it wasn't until after World War II that the popularity of the auto increased dramatically. The development and marketing of mass-produced automobiles and plentiful gasoline sources created a low-cost form of travel that was available to large numbers of middle-income people. Today, the automobile is the most popular method of vacation travel in the United States. The car provides travelers greater freedom in choice of route, destination, and timing of the journey. Family auto travel is also the most inexpensive and convenient form of travel within the United States.

The participation of the United States federal government in the construction and maintenance of roads started in 1916 when an act was passed, matching state appropriations for new roads, dollar for dollar. It was climaxed by the 1949 interstate act which planned for nonstop, coast-to-coast travel. The first turnpike was built in Pennsylvania in 1940. In 1954, the federal government, in an effort to encourage road construction, increased its share of the highway construction program to ninety percent. This facilitated the shift to the use of the automobile. The service industry—restaurants, fast-food places, motels—associated with the American highway system became a significant part of the economy. The creation of interstate roads, which bypassed many towns, dramatically altered the economy of small communities in the United States. Dependence on the automobile for travel was shown very clearly when the 1973 Arab embargo on oil, and subsequent increases in gasoline prices, only temporarily changed travel patterns. The United States is an automobile nation; some catastrophic events would have to occur to alter this habit.

The automobile has served to stimulate tourism by creating a need for services along tourist routes. Attractions have been developed along these routes that normally would not have because they are inaccessible by other forms of transportation. Civil War battlefields, the homes of historical figures, such as Daniel Boone or Abraham Lincoln, and scenic areas of the West, such as the Painted Desert and the Petrified Forest, have become more accessible. Creativity, or lack of it, has been expressed in a variety of roadside business developments. "See the Seven States," see the "Two-headed Dog," see "The World's Largest Prairie Dog," and "Discount Indian Jewelry" are testimonies to the use of the highways by vacationers and, consequently, the importance of the automobile.

Despite high gasoline prices, improved rail systems, and long traditions of mass transit, the use of the automobile has been on the increase in Europe and Asia for much the same reasons as in the United States.

Related to the growth of the automobile has been the growth of the car rental market. The idea of car rental was believed to have started in Omaha in 1916 when two brothers, the Saunders, who needed a car for a short term, borrowed one from a salesman in return for a fee. The Saunders thought others might sometimes be in similar situations, so they bought a car and left it on the street as an advertisement for people to borrow it for a fee. They were soon out of the real estate business and into car and truck rental. In 1942, the founder of the Yellow Cab Company, John D. Hertz, bought a Rent-A-Ford company that had been started in Chicago in 1918.[4] Like the use of the auto for private recreation and travel, car rentals became one of the fastest growing service industries in the world, in the late 1950s.

Bus

Bus transportation is the most flexible form of mass transportation. Airlines serve some 650 airports and trains 490 cities, while buses serve over 15,000 cities, towns, and small communities throughout America.

Bus travel is also an economical form of transportation. In the United States buses were first used to carry passengers intracity in the early 1900s. There was little intercity travel before the 1920s. In 1928 the Greyhound Company, which today is the largest privately-owned bus company in the world, was organized. By then buses were traveling from New York to Los Angeles in a little over five days. Just prior to the Second World War, with improvement in buses and roads, the time of a cross-country trip was reduced to ninety hours. The peak for bus usage came in 1949. The number of passengers has continued to decrease from then until the 1960s when the number of passengers carried per year leveled out.[5]

For the past few years bus passenger volume has been slowly rising in the United States reversing the long downward trend. A number of factors have been important in reversing this trend—the end of cheap, abundant gas following the oil crisis of 1979; the fast growth of the bus charter and tour sector; the increasing demand for motorcoach transportation by foreign travelers; the redistribution of some routes; Amtrak and air fare increases. It is important to note the increase in the number of new companies has been faster in the bus charters and tours area than in intercity traffic.

Two companies, Greyhound and Trailways, dominated the intercity traffic, with Greyhound accounting for sixty percent of the market. Like the airlines, the motorcoach was a highly regulated industry until 1982. On September 20, 1982, President Reagan signed into law the Bus Regulatory Reform Act. The few restrictions that bus companies do have are concerned with public safety rather than route selection and fares. For tour brokers there are no entry requirements for licensing, bonding, or insurance. This lack of licensing may result in problems caused by inexperienced or unprincipled people who enter the business, offering shoddy operations and services. In 1987 Greyhound purchased Trailways, giving it a monopoly in the bus market. Deregulation has also lead to the reduction of service to small communities, with many losing their service completely.

The increasing demand for motorcoach tours in the United States, coupled with the improvement of the buses, could result in future large expansion of the bus charter and tour segment of tourism. Today's coaches are wider, offer more leg room, more baggage space, lavatories, climate and noise controls, better lighting, more sophisticated public address systems, and tinted picture windows. In addition, bars and kitchen facilities are available in smaller luxury coaches, used by groups traveling to private destinations and for special events or attractions.

Air

As with the automobile, widespread air travel is a postwar phenomenon. Man began his exploration of sky travel on December 17, 1903, when the Wright brothers took a flight on a beach in North Carolina that lasted twelve seconds and covered all of 120 feet. It wasn't until 1927, in the United States, that the air industry developed regularly scheduled passenger trips, with service between Boston and New York. Other governments aided this growth in the 1920s by subsidizing air companies.

In the United States, almost all early airlines started by carrying mail for the post office. One of the first was Varney, begun in April, 1926, which later became United Airlines. The first passenger service began on April 17, 1926, when Western Airlines carried a woman passenger along with the mail. She paid $90.00 for a six- and one-half hour journey from Los Angeles to Salt Lake City. Pan American Airways had the first international flight in 1927, when it carried mail from Key West, Florida to Havana, Cuba.

During the 1930s there was considerable improvement in the equipment used for air travel, although stewardesses still relied on railroad timetables in case of problems with the airplane. The Second World War helped to further improve planes, by accelerating technological research to improve both their size and their speed and by using the knowledge gained from thousands of servicemen who became familiar with planes and air travel.

The factors associated with a recent boom in air travel include the world economy, rising standard of living, and the quality of air service.

Growth in the airlines has been at an annual rate of five percent since 1959. The industrial nations, which account for the majority of air travel, had a growth rate of seven percent from 1960 to 1970. The standard of living in the world improved at a rate of five percent, with per capita income rising three percent. The industrial countries' per capita constant-dollar gross domestic product (GDP) has increased faster than has the GDP of undeveloped countries. While the United States economy grew at an average rate of 3.3 percent from 1950 until 1960 and four percent from then to 1970, the GDP of other major industrialized nations grew at a faster rate, with Japan enjoying a remarkable growth of almost ten percent per year for these two decades.

The growth of the 1970s did not match previous growth because of economic downturns and inflated fuel-prices. However, by that time air travel was no longer considered a luxury but a necessity.

In addition, air fares throughout the world dropped by nine percent between 1960 and 1970. By adjusting to consumer prices, the average air fare in constant dollars decreased an average of twenty-six percent a year during that period and still continues to decrease, but at a slower pace.

The advent of charter-only travel has stimulated the industry to promote a whole series of new rate breakthroughs that are further pushing the prices of air fares down. Charter services, as an alternative to regularly scheduled services, were authorized by Congress in 1962. Charters were offered at lower fares for two reasons. They did not require the large personnel investment required of an airline with regularly scheduled flights, which has to maintain offices and services in the cities on their routes. In addition,

by flying with a full load of passengers, the charter companies were able to fly their planes for less cost per passenger. The growth of charter companies was impressive; by 1974, one-third of all air traffic from United States to Europe was by charter flight. With deregulation the regularly scheduled airlines have been selling seats at special prices with the same characteristics, such as fixed dates and heavy penalties for changes or cancellation, or charters. This has resulted in a reduction of charter flights, other than for large special groups such as football teams. Freddie Laker, a British entrepreneur, originated a London-New York standby route, selling for one-half the normal air fare. Other countries and airlines were quick to follow, with economy fares from several United States cities to and from England and other European cities.

In summary, since 1950, incomes have increased rapidly, while air fares have declined, making air travel more attractive than ever. While the price of an airline ticket has been dropping, the quality of service with respect to speed, size, and comfort has improved.

Airline Deregulation

The Civil Aeronautics Act, in 1938, was created to provide protection for, and regulation of, the fledging airline industry. This act created the Civil Aeronautics Authority, later renamed the Civil Aeronautics Board (CAB) in 1940. The growing air industry was regarded as a public utility and, as such, CAB was responsible for the safety of airlines, both domestic and foreign, operating in the United States. In 1958, the Federal Aviation Act was passed creating the Federal Aviation Administration (FAA). Most of CAB's safety-related functions were transferred to the new FAA. However, the CAB continued to investigate aircraft accidents until 1967, when that function was transferred to the National Safety Board. At that time, the CAB was established as an independent regulatory agency, as it had been under the Department of Commerce. The CAB maintained its economic regulatory function of allocation of routes, the regulation of air fares, and some operational and commercial aspects of aviation. The basic purpose of the economic regulatory activities was to provide all citizens of the United States access to airlines at a fair price. The Airline Deregulation Act of 1978, passed as the Cannon-Kennedy-Pearson Air Transportation Act, called for the gradual phasing out of the CAB and most airline regulatory functions. The concern of those who wrote the Airline Deregulation Act was the creation of competitive market forces to provide the needed air transportation system. Air routes were available, and new carriers were encouraged to provide a variety of low-priced service.

Some of the major changes and implications of the Air Deregulation Act of 1978 are being felt. Before 1978 air carriers had little, if any, pricing freedom. Fare changes, which had required the CAB approval, were slow and cumbersome. The simple fare structure was based on a three-tiered pricing structure: economy, coach, and first class. From 1978 until January 1, 1983 the airlines were free to set fare prices anywhere within a "zone of reasonableness" without formal approval by CAB. After December 31, 1982 air carriers were free to set fares. One result has been an increase in the complexity of the fare structure, expanding the simple three-tiered arrangement of the past. The result is confusing to the traveling public, who now is able to choose between special fares and regular fares, while weighing the pros and cons of the constantly changing variables.

Prior to 1978, airlines wanting to begin services to one or more new cities had to apply to the CAB. Deregulation procedures were planned as a gradual three-year process in order to protect existing routes, while allowing carriers to enter one new market a year. However, since new route certification was able to be granted quickly and easily, many carriers developed several new routes a year. Today, there is little to keep a carrier from entering a new city other than the capacity of the airport to handle it safely.

Before deregulation, airlines wishing to discontinue service to a city had to apply for formal approval from the CAB, ninety days in advance. The CAB, in turn could require the airline to continue service until an alternate carrier was found for that city. For those routes that would be unprofitable to the carrier, the government, under an "essential service guarantee" is required to subsidize a program providing air service to that city. The competition for major access has led to many problems, ranging from flight punctuality to passenger safety. The FAA tried to force the airlines into readjusting their flight schedules to correct the inequities, but until 1987 little progress was made.

In addition to these problems above, a number of other issues were raised and resolved. Airlines may now function as tour operators providing packaged tours directly to the public; they may own and operate travel agencies; and they may develop new methods of selling tickets other than through the existing travel agency system.

On January 1, 1985, the CAB lost all of its remaining authority. All necessary regulatory responsibilities were transferred to either the Justice Department or the Department of Transportation. The final impact of the Deregulation Act of 1978 is still to come. The industry is still undergoing tremendous changes and feeling pressure from them. Some of these are (1) new airlines entering the market (e.g., Midway, New York Air, Jet America, Muse Air, Air Niagara, American International Airways); (2) finding commuters to fill the gap created by the loss of services to small communities and to providing low cost transportation between certain points, thus competing with the major carriers; and (3) the merging of airlines leading to concerns that the industry might become monopolistic, thereby controlling the market and drastically increasing fares. In addition, other changes have caused financial stress, a restructuring of employment contracts, and bankruptcies (over two hundred from 1984 to 1987).

Deregulation is spreading worldwide. In Europe the movement is called liberalization.

Consumer Issues

Most airline reservations are conducted by travel agents using computer systems developed by the various airlines. American, United, Delta, and Eastern have developed computer reservation systems that can be used to book flights on other airlines as well. However, American and United dominate this market. This is a major concern of both the airlines and governmental agencies concerned about consumer protection and equality of access to the market. The computer systems of the major airlines are programmed to list their own flights first. If the route is a high frequency one, there might be many flights listed. It requires considerable research by a travel agent to check additional screens to find alternative flights, if the customer does not want to fly with the parent airline. One company publishes a monthly book of all current flights and has developed a computer program that is not biased to any airline, and can be used by any travel agency. To date, it has had little success in selling the program since airlines provide a number of incentives for travel agents to use their own machines. The airlines claim to have responded to the problem by developing their own unbiased systems, but none of the airlines agree that the systems are truly unbiased. If airlines merge, the super company formed will have one computer system, which may help resolve the problem. However, marketing the computer system will create other problems since American and United already dominate the market.

Another major concern relating to fares is ensuring that those special fares advertised are indeed available, and not simply used as a bait to attract customers, who are then persuaded to buy seats at a higher price. This "bait and switch" technique is not common in the transportation field, but deregulation does provide the potential for it to occur. The most serious concern for the public is overbooking of flights. It is a well-known fact that airlines overbook. This is done, in part, to protect themselves. In 1986, American Airlines, for example, had seven million customers who did not claim their seats. Research by airlines indicates the percentage of customers who can be expected not to claim their seats. This information is used when plane reservations are made. The planes are usually overbooked so that the companies will be sure of flying full planes.

Federal regulations require airlines to make amends to passengers denied boarding because of overbooking. Normally cash compensation is given. In recent years, however, airlines have become more adept at persuading passengers who have been "bumped" off an overbooked plane to accept ticket vouchers instead of cash. One of the proposals to assist consumers is to require airlines to state, at the time of sale, the number of tickets sold to that date and the number of seats available on a given flight. This would give travelers some idea of whether there is a potential seating problem, and time to decide on alternative flight times or carriers.

Airlines after Deregulation

Michael Derchin characterized the industry in 1987 as it reacted to deregulation as follows:

—*It was a period of rapid hub expansion, a period when hubs sprang up seemingly overnight around the country. . . . Before deregulation there were only half dozen full-fledged hubs. Now there are 49 hubs serving 31 airports.*

AIR TODAY, GONE TOMORROW, BUT IT'S ALWAYS ROY COOPER

by Ben Kemin

Cleveland—not long ago, I presented myself to an agent at the New York Air counter. This was hardly unusual, since my plane ticket was tucked inside a bright-red folder marked "New York Air." But I was in a tentative mood, so I asked, "Is this New York Air?" The ticket agent eyed me with suspicion. What planet did I live on. Solemnly he answered, "Sir, there is no such thing as New York Air." My caution had been misplaced.

I had heard something about mergers and takeovers. But the gravity with which the agent had vaporized New York Air concerned me. "Is there," I asked, "A New York City?" He allowed there was.

In time, I boarded a Continental Airlines flight while holding a New York Air ticket from which protruded a boarding pass marked People Express. Inside the generic jet, I was handed a red bag marked "Flying Nosh," with New York Air napkins and salt packets from Texas Air. The cheeseball was Swiss. Curious to know who it was I was flying with, I awaited the captain's announcements.

"Good afternoon, ladies and gentlemen. This is your captain, Roy Cooper." (For as long as I can remember, the pilot on domestic flights is always Roy Cooper.") "We want to welcome you aboard our Big Apple Flight 397 to New York."

It is the late 1980's in the United States, which produced the Wright Brothers, Amelia Earhart and Mileage Plus. You used to get dressed up, board a plane with delightful nervousness and be asked if this was your first time by an interested, or at least animated, flight attendant. Now even the attendants seem uncertain about the identity of their employers. Seasoned travelers know not to ask a living soul which plane is going up in what landing space. They consult the monitor.

Not long ago, for example, I was waiting for a colleague at the airport. TWA Flight 612 was about to land. I began to watch for a TWA jet among the landings. American, United, two private Cessnas, Ozark, Midway, USAir. An announcement came: "Ladies and gentlemen, Flight 612 has landed and will appear at the gate momentarily." But I had not seen a TWA airliner make an approach.

"Excuse me," I said to an agent at the ticket counter. "Is there anywhere else the planes land?"

"No sir," he replied cheerfully. "You can see it all from these windows."

"So where is Flight 612?"

He did not look up: "612 is already disembarking."

Baffled, I returned to the window. There at the gate was TWA Flight 612. The plane was green, and marked "Ozark." Silly me, expecting aviation verisimilitude. Why, TWA and Ozark had mated, and I never even knew! There had not even been a monitor overhead to give me the news

At this writing, of course, everything may be changing again.

Source: *International Herald Tribune*, Mar. 31, 1987. Copyright 1987 by The New York Times Company. Reprinted by permission.

—It was a period of price experimentation. Airline managements learned that price could be an effective marketing tool to generate lots of new business. At the same time, managements learned that price could be an effective weapon to take on the weak airlines which didn't have the balance sheet strength to survive prolonged fare battles.

—It was a period when new entrants—with low costs and low fares—at first flourished, then fell by the wayside, victims in many cases of their own overexpansion plans.

—It was a period of confrontation between organized labor and management, with all managements attempting, with various degrees of success, to become low-cost producers to keep them in the competitive game.

—It was a period of marketing innovation which gave the innovators an edge until, that is, their competitors reacted and came up with marketing programs of their own. Programs like Computerized Reservations Systems, Frequent Flyer, Commuter Alliances, and Senior Citizen Fares are now household names.

—It was a period of Darwinian struggle.[6]

Ships

There has been a significant change in patterns of tourist travel by ship. In its early stages, and during the heyday of ocean travel, transoceanic cruise vessels left the cold, damp, northern climates of the United States and Europe for the sun and fun spots of the Mediterranean, the Baltic, the Caribbean, and Hawaii. Now, the more usual pattern involves a fly/cruise package. In the 1950s, a cruise to the Mediterranean for Americans would begin in New York. Today, most tourists fly to the Canary Islands, Greece, or a Mediterranean port, and begin their cruise from that point. Cruise Lines International Association (CLIA) estimated that its members carried 2.7 million passengers from North America in 1986. CLIA estimates that the fastest growing segment is the two- to four-day cruises.[7] Their popularity is largely due to two factors. They can offer fun, sun, and relaxation, with several ports of call that offer a wide variety of cultural contact. They also allow tourists to take a little bit of home with them. (They know they will sleep in a comfortable bed and eat familiar food for the time they are on board the ship.)

In effect, cruises very effectively combine the two characteristics of a good trip. Travelers can satisfy their desire to experience new environments and see new cultures, and still take along the comfort, safety, and convenience of home. In addition, there will be little changing of hotels, airports, food, and beds, which may cause sleeplessness and other problems.

Although many Americans traveled abroad before the 1860s, travel for pleasure probably started in the 1860s with voyages to the Mediterranean and the Holy Land. The heyday of ocean travel came in the 1920s, when 511,814 people traveled to Europe and 743,618 traveled to North America.[8]

Although the Depression and World War II slowed travel in the 1930s and 1940s, there were still a considerable number of inexpensive cruises available. Following the war, until the 1960s, when transatlantic liners fell on hard times as a result of growing airline competition, ocean travel was quite popular.

Today, the cruise industry is booming, with annual sales in excess of $2 billion. Major United States cities that serve as ports for cruises are Miami, New York, Port Everglades, Los Angeles, San Francisco, and Seattle. Most cruises from these ports go southward to Mexico, the Caribbean, and the Panama Canal, or northward to Alaska.

While these destinations will continue to be popular, the expanding cruise industry is seeking fresh, exotic ports to improve its market. These new destinations will be both domestic and international. Domestic routes will grow as cruise lines such as Delta Queen, American Cruise Lines, Eastern and Western Cruise Lines, and Clipper Cruise Lines float along the Mississippi and Ohio rivers, the Chesapeake Bay, and coastal waters in the east and west.

International routes are growing with cruises available to Greenland, Belawan and Sibolga in Indonesia, Padloping Island in Canada, Bay of Bengal and Seychelles on the Indian Ocean, Borneo in the South China Sea, Manaus on the Amazon River; Leningrad, USSR; Kobe, Japan, and Honningsvaag, Norway. Most of these destinations will have prospective cruise passengers rushing to their atlases and geography books in preparation for the "cruise of their lives!" The cruise ships and companies, like the airplanes, are making the world smaller and more accessible.

Unlike many other forms of transportation, there is no group of companies that dominate the cruise trade; there are between thirty-five and fifty different ones. There is, however, a considerable overcapacity resulting from a spurt in ship construction, which still continues. From 1986 to 1990 it is expected that at least seventeen new ships will be added.[9]

MOBILITY ASPECTS OF TOURISM

There are three aspects of tourism—point, path, and transit—that have a unique association with the type of conveyance chosen for travel.

Point

The greatest demand for services, hotels, restaurants, and attractions is at the point of destination. In this category, business travel and tours are the most common types. Public transportation, particularly airlines and ships, is most often used for this type of travel. The major objective of today's traveler is to arrive at the destination quickly, and, when it is time to return home, return as quickly as possible. Tours and cruises are considered components of this category because they include a series of points within a given time period that are clearly and specifically programmed and marketed. Business travel, particularly for meetings and conventions, makes the same demand on transportation networks—transportation to and from destinations quickly, comfortably, and safely.

The major difference between business travel and tourism for pure pleasure is that the former is inelastic while the latter is largely elastic.

Path

Private forms of transportation are more important in the area of tourism associated with paths or routes. The demand for services (hotels, motels, restaurants) is greater during the trip than at the destination. The purpose of the trip may be to visit friends and relatives, or for personal business. The travelers who have their own transportation will be more flexible; they will be able to change their paths to visit attractions that may not be their final destination. Many path-related tourist industries have sprung up around the country, taking advantage of locations near major travel routes. Chimney Rock in North Carolina, the Whitney Western Art Museum in Cody, Wyoming, Rock City in Tennessee, and similar attractions are good examples. In addition, some questionable tourist attractions have been developed. These include quick-step "fantastic" attractions such as snake pits, prairie dog villages, roadside geysers, and such.

Transit

Transit tourism revolves around a point of change, whether it is a change in type of carrier or a major change in route. It also may be an assembly point for tours. It encompasses all major forms of transportation. A number of countries and airports have recognized the monetary value of this type of tourism. Major cities of Europe, which are assembly or disembarkation points for major airlines, offer tours, large duty-free centers, and other services to tourists, who are waiting for their next flight. Luxembourg, which is a point of departure and arrival for inexpensive travel, has profited from this. In the past, it has taken advantage of its location by offering rental cars at a less expensive rate than other countries. Amsterdam offers tours of the city while the traveler awaits a scheduled transport change. Reykjavik takes advantage of the inexpensive travel provided by Icelandic Air and offers a one- or two-day stopover in Iceland. Athens benefits from its location on travel routes into and out of the Holy Land and the Near East.

Copenhagen, Paris, Madrid, and Helsinki benefit from their location in the European railway network. Copenhagen is a clearinghouse for travel to and from Scandinavia; Helsinki serves as a jumping-off place for travel into the Soviet Union both by rail and boat; Paris is in the center of Western Europe, and Madrid filters travel to and from the Iberian Peninsula.

St. Louis, El Paso, and Chattanooga in the United States, Bristol in England, Ljubljana in Yugoslavia, and Salzburg in Austria are positioned on highway networks that accommodate large numbers of transit tourists. Increasing numbers of tourists take advantage of the attractions available, thereby creating a demand for more travel-related services.

TRANSPORT TERMINALS

There are wide differences in the quality and services provided for the traveler at various terminals. For some modes of travel, such as air and ship, the terminals are considered part of the infrastructure and an economic benefit to the community. Even where communities are too small to have the resources to develop their own terminals, the federal government will provide grants. The development of airport and ocean terminals are considered vital to the economy. Airport development is funded by federal and local monies together—the federal money is in the form of grants used in the initial stages; the local money comes from a variety of sources, one of which is landing fees imposed on airlines that use the local airport facilities. Master plans for future growth are developed locally in conjunction with airport authorities.

Table 11-3 illustrates the relative size of the major airports in the United States and the rest of the world. There are a variety of reasons that account for these figures. Large population centers, naturally, have the largest airports. Some locations are transit points for either a change in travel mode or a connection with other carriers. International airports connect domestic lines with international carriers, or connect international carriers with each other. These airports are large and are almost cities in and of themselves.

New York has three of the largest airports in the world. Their size is due not only to the size of New York, but also to the fact that New York is the major link between the United States and countries across the Atlantic, which includes most of the industrialized world. On the West Coast,

TABLE 11-3 WORLDWIDE AIRPORT TRAFFIC AT THE TOP 50 AIRPORTS—1986

Airport	Total Passengers
1. O'Hare, Chicago	53,338,056
2. Hartsfield, Atlanta	45,191,480
3. Los Angeles	41,417,867
4. Dallas/Ft. Worth	39,945,326
5. Stapleton, Denver	34,685,944
6. Heathrow, London	31,315,300
7. Newark	29,433,046
8. San Francisco	28,607,363
9. Kennedy, NY	27,223,733
10. Tokyo International, Japan	27,217,761
11. La Guardia, NY	22,188,871
12. Miami	21,947,368
13. Logan, Boston	21,862,718
14. Lambert, St. Louis	20,352,383
15. Frankfurt/Main, West Germany	19,802,229
16. Orly, Paris	18,543,670
17. Honolulu	18,235,154
18. Osaka, Japan	17,694,649
19. Detroit Metropolitan	17,604,583
20. Toronto, Canada	17,136,147
21. Minneapolis-St. Paul	17,073,605
22. Gatwick, London	16,309,300
23. Greater Pittsburgh	15,989,507
24. Charles de Gaulle, Paris	14,427,026
25. Washington National	14,307,980
26. Houston Intercontinental	13,996,015
27. Sea-Tac, Seattle	13,642,666
28. Sky Harbor, Phoenix	13,274,015
29. Philadelphia	12,780,306
30. Orlando	12,495,346
31. McCarran, Las Vegas	12,303,400
32. Fiumicino, Rome	12,241,145
33. Charlotte/Douglas International	11,987,339
34. Mexico City	11,310,871
35. Stockholm, Sweden	10,599,000
36. Kingsford Smith, Sydney	10,114,958
37. Salt Lake City	9,990,986
38. Copenhagen, Denmark	9,971,012
39. Athens, Greece	9,599,651
40. Zurich, Switzerland	9,250,967
41. Tampa	9,198,139
42. San Diego	9,084,438
43. Dulles, Washington, DC	8,962,346
44. Changi, Singapore	8,912,233
45. Memphis	8,725,359
46. Baltimore/Washington International	8,670,506
47. Dusseldorf, Federal Republic of Germany	8,493,402
48. Vancouver, Canada	8,385,000
49. Kansas City	8,309,567
50. Amsterdam Schiphol, Netherlands	8,207,969

Source: *Travel Industry World Yearbook: The Big Picture—1988.*

Los Angeles is the largest city; it is the connecting point for many carriers serving countries in the Pacific.

Within the United States, some airports are larger than would be expected from the size of the surrounding population. The current trend is for airlines to develop a "hub and spoke" type of service instead of a series of direct flights to all the areas they serve. Aircraft are extremely expensive; to be cost effective they should be kept in the air as much as possible. The "hub and spoke" concept accomplishes this goal. The establishment of a hub increases the size of that airport and, in turn, improves the communication of that town with the rest of the United States. This link can be beneficial when the area is competing with other towns for new businesses. Many hubs are located in large cities, central to the region they serve. Atlanta, for example, is the hub for at least two major lines, Eastern and Delta, and is one of the busiest airports in the world. It services the southern region of the United States, including such major industrial cities as New Orleans and Miami, which in turn connect the United States with Latin America, and are major jumping-off points for the cruise industry.

The decision by an airline to make a city a major hub for its network significantly increases the airport traffic and creates an extensive expansion program in that city. In addition, business around the airport grows to fill the needs of both the travelers staying overnight and those in transit.

Cruise ports, while important, are far smaller in proportion to the number of people who pass through them than airports. This is mainly because there is little waiting for passengers and few interconnections. Tourists arrive just before departure time and leave quickly upon arrival. The destination and service are sold well in advance in the tourist's hometown.

In the United States, rail and bus terminals do not fare as well. Terminal development is the responsibility of the various companies; even Amtrak, which is government run, must develop its own terminal facilities with little help from the federal government. They are old and decaying, since rail service is not expanding. Most investment money is allocated to improving the on-line service of new equipment and providing better service. One notable exception is the restoration of Union Station in Washington, DC as a major downtown entertainment, dining, and specialty shopping facility. In Europe most train terminals are very utilitarian, providing few of the amenities offered by the airports.

Bus companies, too, are responsible for their own development. Most bus travelers have lower income levels than other travelers, yet bus terminals are generally somewhat better than railway terminals, though far less impressive than the airports. Major cities with a large clientele have terminals which are large, and, in many cases, well-developed.

Today, most intermodal networks are designed to provide either service between airport terminals, or to connect the airport with the city. Major airports, such as Atlanta, have become so large that train service is provided to connect one terminal with another. In New York, the intermodal network connects the three major airlines by bus. Rail and bus services are the two most important intermodal services. Chicago, Washington (National Airport), and London have made the airports part of their metro system while most cities have established some form of connection between the city center and their airport.

A few international airports, Frankfurt being the best example, have developed intermodal connections between the air, train, and bus terminals for easy transfer to other destinations. From the airport, one can either take another plane, or proceed to the rail terminal in the same complex, and depart on trains to major European destinations. Those airports that serve as transit points for travelers will continue to improve their intermodal services.

Traveler services are very different from each other at the various terminals. By far the most elaborate and complex set of services is offered by airports. Major transit airports, like those in Amsterdam and Frankfurt, are in fact small cities in and of themselves. They offer hotel accommodations, health and fitness facilities, duty-free shopping in mini-department stores, newsstands, candy shops, fast food and full-service restaurants. They also serve as centers for other forms of travel. Some airports are expanding their services to include dayrooms, business meeting rooms, and computer services. The type of waiting rooms in airports may equal the types of services offered by hotels and other businesses. Luxury services for frequent fliers and first-class travelers include comfortable lounges and bar services.

As mentioned before, ocean terminals have fewer travel services. Bus companies usually offer food services, but lack the options available at airports, probably because the airport traveler is usually a businessperson or a more affluent tourist than the bus traveler.

TOUR OPERATORS

The transportation sector is a top concern for tour operators. Most use the motorcoach. There are two kinds; one outgoing and the other incoming. Each has different markets and offers different kinds of services. Outgoing tours might include the use of other forms of transportation. A grand motorcoach tour of Europe, for example, will use a plane or ship to reach Europe, then embark on a program by coach for a given number of days.

The tour-marketing industry can be divided into two components. The retailer or travel agent sells directly to the public. They sell airline and railroad tickets, cruises, independent travel, and group tours—either tours they themselves prepare or tours that a wholesaler has put together. The second element of the travel industry involves the selling of tours by a tour operator or a tour wholesaler. A considerable proportion of tours are sold through them directly or by travel agents. In many instances wholesalers are well acquainted with certain regions and are thus able to provide a number of choices and opportunities for the prospective client. These tour operators then have their tours booked through a travel agent. Somewhere in the neighborhood of sixty to seventy-five percent of all tours sold in America are sold through travel wholesalers or retailers.

Wholesalers are important for a number of reasons. Most importantly, they sell tours to exotic places that may not be in enough demand to justify a travel agent's time in preparing, marketing, and selling them. Therefore, an individual walking into a travel office and asking for a tour to a more unusual location would probably be booked on a tour prepared and marketed by one of these tour wholesalers. In addition, a number of the tour wholesalers specialize in certain areas of the world, and they offer high-quality tours that travel agents and counselors can feel justified in selling their clients.

Efficient travel agents become familiar with the cross-section of escorted tour operators and independent tour wholesalers. They know who sells the U.S.A. and who sells the Caribbean, Central and South America, Europe, Africa, the Near East, the Pacific, and around-the-world tours. The agent knows whether these tours are economical or whether they are for the luxury trade. They have an idea of whether

the operator specializes in tours of two, three, or four weeks' duration, or even longer.

There are many types of tours available. Certainly, when an individual enters a travel agency and glances at the brochure racks and folders, considerable choice in both variety and content is revealed. There are sports tours, holiday tours, and music tours. Recently an individual in Los Angeles was preparing a tour, designed for baseball fans, to visit thirteen major league baseball areas in twenty-two days. There are as many types of tours as there are interests and people. In addition, the range of tours include an individual taking a simple trip as well as the group tour, which is very comprehensive with everything provided.

Tour group in the courtyard of medieval Turku Castle in the city of Turku, former capital of Finland. Photo courtesy of Finnish Tourist Board.

TYPES OF TOURS

It is necessary to delineate the various types of tours available. The first types are independent tours referred as FITs (Foreign Independent Tours) and DITs (Domestic Independent Tours). Whether it be a FIT or a DIT, an independent tour is for those clients who enjoy traveling by themselves; they provide flexibility and freedom to tailor a program to the client's own specific needs. It allows clients to set their own dates, their own time and their own itinerary, without the restrictions which might be imposed by a group. They can select certain services and reject others. Many travel agents overlook the importance of their point-to-point or airline ticket sales as a source for developing independent travel.

The second category of tours is the group tour, sometimes called "conducted tour," "guided tour," or "escorted tour." The particular characteristics of these depend upon the type, the quality, and the client for whom the tour was arranged. Tours are arranged for more than one person and are designed to provide almost all services that an individual or group will need in visiting an area. These services generally include hotels, food (to some extent), transportation, shipping, luggage, and admissions to attractions designated by the tour operator or travel agent.

Group tours have a number of advantages. The most important, of course, is knowing the cost of a trip before departure. In some cases group tours provide companionship and can be less expensive than an individual tour for equivalent accommodations and amenities. Certainly, a package tour is easier for the travel agent to sell and provides a steady income to the agency for a minimum of paperwork.

The independent tour is designed for an individual rather than a group. The advantages of an independent tour are twofold: First, the agent who is preparing an independent tour receives a larger commission on the air fare as well as a commission for most of the services accompanying the fare, such as hotels, sight-seeing, and transfers. Second, the client has the advantage of a complete package for a specific destination. It is tailormade for the client. They do not have to carry as much cash and are assured of the accommodations and sight-seeing they want.

An independent tour is recommended for a number of clients. Here are some examples:

1. A client with an unusual itinerary or interests that cannot be met by an escorted group. Visiting relatives or friends along with regular touring is one common occurrence.

2. A client who may go on a business trip to Washington DC, but wants to visit historical attractions along the way in Philadelphia, Boston, and New York. Such clients may want to take advantage of an independent tour. A client may wish to visit a number of places within a fixed amount of time that cannot be covered by a specific tour. Such clients, too, can best proceed independently with their own itinerary.

3. A client who does not want to risk not having hotel rooms, or who doesn't want to haggle with taxicab drivers at the airport, and wants everything neatly planned before s/he arrives in an area is a prime candidate for the FIT, where reservations are confirmed, airport transfers arranged, and nothing is left to chance.

4. A traveler who has special needs or desires, such as certain hotels or rooms, and demands individualized service for sight-seeing from certain guides and is willing to pay extra, may want to travel independently. Of course, changing the schedule and making decisions from day to day will require additional expenses. However, some people are willing to pay extra for this additional service, and FITs are a very profitable activity for the travel agent.

Of course, certain individuals do not want independent travel, and would rather join a fully escorted group tour. It certainly is important for the travel agent to recognize these clients and provide them with information so that they can make a reasonable decision on the difference between escorted and independent tours. In some cases, people appreciate a fully-escorted tour when traveling alone on a first trip to a specific area. There are certain destinations in Central Africa or South America for which it is best to recommend an escorted tour, since travel is, at best, difficult, and in some cases hazardous.

There are some travelers who are truly explorers by nature, but the vast majority recognize the difficulties encountered in offbeat destinations. The advantages of an exclusive tour, with safe and comfortable travel appeals to most. Sometimes certain events are so heavily attended that it is difficult for either an individual or a travel agent to make the necessary arrangements. For example, each spring, in Spain there is a large fiesta in Valencia ("the Fires") and it is completely sold out years in advance to travel wholesalers. Anyone who wants reasonably good accommodations will find it necessary to join a tour in order to participate in this outstanding event. People who want to see the Passion Play (it occurs once each decade) in Oberammergau have also found it necessary to book themselves on group tours.

THE TOUR ESCORT OR MANAGER

Probably the most important person for the success of the tour is the escort. The functions of a tour escort are to:

1. Pay the bills, including tipping.
2. Coordinate the sight-seeing and maintain the schedule.
3. Handle all tickets and documents for the group.
4. Anticipate problems and double-check in advance to be sure services are ready.
5. Make room assignments.
6. Keep track of luggage.
7. Socialize as a host would at a party.

8. Act as a counselor on services, free time, and clothing.
9. Handle a multitude of seemingly insignificant problems.

A tour escort must have a number of characteristics that bring a group together into a cohesive unit and provide an exciting experience for all the participants. The first and most important characteristic is common sense. A tour escort must adjust quickly to situations and make decisions that are reasonable and that can be accepted by everyone in the group. Certainly, a commonsense approach will assist in alleviating the emergencies that do arise. Second, the tour escort should have the ability to cooperate with others and gain the cooperation of each member of the group. There are always a few individuals who are difficult, and it is important for the escort to handle them in such a way that s/he makes such people an effective part of the group. Third, a great deal of patience and understanding is essential. Fourth, a sense of humor is invaluable. Above all things, a tour escort must be able to recognize situations and make the best of them. Fifth, firmness is required to make the decisions needed.

A tour escort is like a party host with greater responsibilities. The host's job is to create a cohesive group, each member enjoying and gaining some benefits from the experience. A good tour escort certainly cannot be a tourist too. Some activities that the tour escort must be involved in before, during, and after the tour are:

1. *Tour manager's information log.* Tour managers or escorts should maintain a log of the starting times, the stopping breaks and information pertaining to these, not only for their own benefit, but for future tours.

2. *Wardrobe and packing.* Tour escorts must be familiar with the characteristics of the trip and the required clothing. As you recall, clothing is a major concern to tourists.

3. *Reconfirmation.* Wherever possible, escorts should confirm transportation, hotels, meals, and special activities in advance, so that they will not be surprised by changes in the itinerary. In most cases it is not necessary or advisable to tell clients in advance if there is a problem. The problems should be handled when they arise and, if the problem continues to exist, then the clients should be made aware of it. There is no need to create tension and apprehension over what might or might not occur.

4. *Tickets.* In most cases it is necessary to keep vouchers on hand for sight-seeing and hotels. Tour escorts carries such vouchers, and give them to the appropriate individuals or organizations.

5. *Customs procedures.* Tour escorts should be aware of customs procedures and have a copy of the customs statement in order to counsel and advise their group. It is always important to inform the group members never to carry a stranger's gifts for other people from one country to another.

6. *Border crossings.* Tour escorts should have the necessary paperwork completed in advance, where possible, for border crossings, and should have them organized to facilitate the process. Border crossings in some countries can create anxieties, and everything that hosts do to alleviate the stress is helpful to the tour.

7. The final important activity of tour escorts is to maintain group identity on the tour bus.[10]

RESEARCH AND REVIEW

1. Why are air fares to South America higher than to Europe?

2. What are the advantages and disadvantages of five different types of transportation?

3. What are two advantages of charter flights?

4. Discuss the history of airline deregulation through the sunset of CAB.

5. Describe three major consumer issues relating to airlines.

6. List five characteristics of the airline industry after deregulation.

7. Describe three aspects of mobility as they relate to tourism.

8. What are the two factors that account for the wide differences in quality and service between terminals?

9. What are the advantages of the hub and spoke system used by many airlines?

10. What is the difference between a tour operator and a travel agent?

11. Describe the advantages of the two principal types of tours.

12. Discuss at least four important responsibilities of a tour escort.

ENDNOTES

1. Jagdish N. Sheth, "A Psychological Model of Travel Mode Selection," in *Advances in Consumer Research*, Vol. 3 (Proceedings of the Assn. for Consumer Research, 6th Annual Conference, 1975), p. 426.
2. *Travel & Leisure's World Travel Overview* (NY: American Express Publishing Co., 1987), p. 29.
3. John A. R. Pimlott, *The Englishman's Holiday* (Salem, NH: Faber, 1947), p. 91.
4. Jay Ferguson, "Competition Heightens for Car Rental Market," *Travel Weekly's 25th Anniversary*, Vol. 42, No. 46 (1983), p. 228.

5. National Assn. of Motorbus Owners, 1974.
6. Michael Derchin, "1987 Outlook for Airlines," *1987 Outlook for Travel & Tourism* (Washington, DC: U.S. Travel Data Center, 1987), pp. 89–97.
7. *World Travel Overview*, p. 68.
8. *The Travel Agent*, April 19, 1971, p. 30.
9. *World Travel Overview*, p. 68.
10. Robert T. Reilly, *Handbook of Professional Tour Management* (Wheaton, IL: Merton House, 1982), pp. 71–94.

CHAPTER 12

DISTRIBUTION CHANNELS AND PRICING STRATEGIES

The travel industry is not only a very large one, but it is also an extremely complex one. Even the sale of a travel service to one person requires the work of a complex group of people and organizations, and the process is repeated each time a tourist selects a travel agency that has a trained staff prepared to give assistance and counsel. Travel choices may have been made because of promotional sales presentations in the media, or word-of-mouth information from a friend who has either been on a similar tour or is pleased with the service received from that particular agency. The tourist then joins a group of other people and is transported smoothly and efficiently by one of several forms of transportation—air, rail, bus, or boat—and by one of several different companies. The traveler is then shown the sights, housed, fed, and guided by either a representative of the original travel agency, or by a tour operations wholesaler, or a local guide in the area of destination. The tour operator will use the talents of many—unskilled porters and clerks, highly skilled accountants, guides, and managerial personnel from restaurants, hotels, and attractions. Again, one or several forms of local transportation will be used. Finally, the tourist will return home by one or several forms of transportation operated by one or several different companies. Generally, this process will involve overlapping government agencies (at various levels with different degrees of regulation and control), which are either of a general nature (e.g. business licenses, taxes), or a specific nature (e.g. air fares, routes), or both. All of which demonstrate the complexity of the travel industry.

DISTRIBUTION CHANNELS

The process detailed above is referred to as the distribution channel. The distribution channel creates the link between

149

the suppliers of travel services and the consumer. Robert McIntosh defined the tourism distribution channel as "an operating structure, system or linkage of various combinations of travel organizations through which a producer of travel products describes and confirms travel arrangements to the buyer."[1] This definition points out that most organizations providing tourist services do not sell directly to their customers. Prospective clients usually live far away in another city, state, country, or region; thus, tourist service companies must rely on sales intermediaries such as travel agents, tour operators, reservation services, hotel and air charter, or air group brokers. In most industries, other than tourism, the supplier or producer has full or at least decisive control over the product, its pricing, its quality, and the manner in which it is distributed and promoted. Tourist service providers are an exception. The distributing sector of tourism is much stronger; those same intermediaries just mentioned have a far greater power to influence and to direct consumer demand than their counterparts in other industries. The distributors control so much demand, and also have so much bargaining power in their relations with suppliers of tourism products, that they are in a position to influence pricing, product policies, and promotional activities, particularly if the tourism provider is in a developing nation.

The success and profitability of tourist service providers depends upon their ability to promote and advertise, and their ability to gain access to the appropriate distribution channels (the intermediaries). The WTO has identified the benefits these distribution intermediaries provide for the producers of tourism services and the functions they, the intermediaries, perform on behalf of the producers:

—It is in the producer's interest to be able to concentrate on furnishing the services he specializes in, to control and improve their quality and to use his marketing expertise first and foremost to make sure that the service he offers corresponds to the needs and expectations of his customers.
—Intermediaries can, again through specialization, achieve better results in the field of distribution and selling than the producer himself; they have direct contact with the markets and potential customers which would be difficult and more costly for the producer.
—Intermediaries assemble the heterogenous service of different producers into a "package" of services that is meaningful and attractive to the customer.
—Intermediaries not only create a complete package of tourist services, although this is their most important function, but from the point of view of the tourist, they also serve as sources of information about destinations, types of services, and their advantages and disadvantages; thus confronting the potential tourist with a range of choices and alternatives.[2]

Figure 12-1 illustrates the functions of distribution. The complexity of the travel industry, with several levels of primary and intermediary suppliers all having a number of choices, can be clearly seen. For example, the airlines can work with the tour operators, or travel agents, but also have the option of going directly to the consumer or tourist. Their tour operators sell their products with the assistance of a

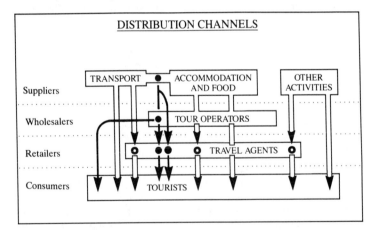

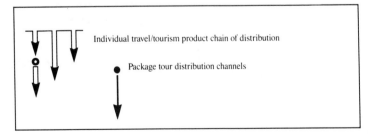

Figure 12-1 Source: World Tourism Organization.

travel agent or go directly to the consumer. In England, Thomson Travel, one of the biggest tour operators, offers its program to the public, directly and indirectly through travel agents. Travel agents offer them more access to the market. This suggests there are three distribution channels. They are

The Product Supplier—Consumer Channel: This is direct distribution without going through intermediaries. It is the direct selling of airline tickets, hotel rooms, restaurant meals, and other retailers available to the consumer. Airlines, hotels, and franchised restaurants do considerable advertising to encourage people to either use their product directly, or to purchase the product through an intermediary. They are able to generate considerable direct sales from travelers.

The Product Supplier—Travel Agent—Consumer Channel: The most popular form of purchasing services and products in the travel business is through an intermediary in the form of a travel agent. The travel agent represents the industry as a whole to provide services and products to the consumer.

The Product Supplier—Tour Operator—Travel Agent—Consumer Channel: While the travel agent makes travel arrangements in response to demand from the consumer, the tour operator (wholesaler) strives to anticipate and, in some cases, create demand; arrangements are made with the suppliers (block booking on airlines, hotels, restaurants, and attractions) to produce a travel package, which is sold through the travel agent or directly to the customer. Demand can be generated by tour operators purchasing, or assuming an obligation to purchase, blocks of a service or product and selling a reduced-rate package. The bulk purchases generate a lower rate than an individual purchase; a tourist traveling with a group pays less than a lone tourist buying each component of the trip separately. In some instances, the combination of hotel, meals and air fare will cost less for a group than the air fare alone for an individual. The package trip is an attractive bargain to consumers.

The primary distribution functions of the system are to provide information, suggest combinations, and make travel arrangements. Other than airlines, hotels, and franchised restaurants, travel as a product does not fit well into the standardized, mass-produced style of selling and merchandising. Consumers receive a vast amount of information from various sources, but are not given precise information about trips, tours, or the companies offering a specific service in one piece of information. They need to receive this information in complete, readily understandable form, covering a wide range of travel alternatives and combinations with the names of the companies offering the alternatives. A WTO report suggests three reasons for the high degree of need:

1. Travel, especially to far away destinations, involves a considerable amount of money. It is, therefore, unlikely that customers will make a decision on where they will go before they have compared alternatives and make an assessment of the satisfactions likely to be derived from visiting one destination rather than another.

2. Nowadays, prospective travelers are faced with a wide range of choices, all of which are presented in an attractive, interesting way. They are able to choose among them only if they are given sufficient information.

3. Unlike routine purchases of small items and even major purchases of durables (home equipment, automobiles, etc.), travel decisions are considered "high risk" decisions; an unsatisfactory washing machine can be returned or repaired, a holiday spoiled by bad service, illness, or other untoward events is irretrievably "lost."

In all cases, the importance of skilled professional assistance is demonstrated.

RELATIONSHIP TO MARKETING

The distribution system is a part of marketing; that fact must be taken into account when choosing a method of distribution. A number of options are available to suppliers, both at the producer level and the wholesaler level. These options range from mass marketing to the general consumer to marketing solely through travel intermediaries. Large companies can offer both as part of their services. For most companies, unless they are either large or integrated or both, market coverage and costs are the major factors to be considered when choosing direct marketing options or the use of intermediaries. An extensive market distribution system provides maximum exposure of a travel product. For example, a number of airlines, in an effort to control the quality of offerings by tour operators, established a consolidated tour program and created a manual called the *Consolidated Air Tour Manual* (CATM). They established a number of criteria for listing packaged tours to the Caribbean. A tour operator or producer can package a product, receive approval, and place a listing in CATM for a fee. This publication is sent to all providers and travel agents in the United States. Thus, for a small fee, a producer can have an advertisement placed in over 26,000 offices.

The marketing of a product, for large companies that have the resources for mass promotion and advertising, can be facilitated through the use of intermediaries. The cost of establishing a distribution system is fixed; however, travel agents, acting as intermediaries, reduce the cost of marketing. If, instead, each airline and hotel chain had a sales outlet for the public in all reasonably-sized cities that now have travel agencies, the cost of marketing tickets and rooms would increase dramatically; consequently, the price of the product to the consumer would also increase. The salaries of the office staff and sales force, in addition to office expenditures, would require considerable generation of income to justify such an operation. In addition, the expense of selling products through an intermediary does not occur until the product has been sold, further reducing expenses to the company are lower.

The characteristics of the tourist product being sold will indicate the appropriate distribution strategy. Those products that are high priced, or purchased infrequently, are best suited for intensive or exclusive distribution, since they will be scarce, and competition would have little affect on the price or availability.

Some companies have chosen to restrict the distribution channels through exclusive, selective, or personal distributing. Vertically integrated systems are those that are either owned or controlled by a single enterprise. A tour operator may control the complete distribution of a product by owning both the tour operator and the retail travel agent business. Thomson Holidays, in the United Kingdom, and American Express, in the United States, are vertically integrated companies, although American Express also sells its products through other travel agents. Thomson Holidays owns its own charter airline company and retail outlets; however, most of its business comes through the travel agent community as a whole. A less stringent form of integration is through the use of franchising by contractual commitments. The franchise is restricted from selling the products of competing agencies, and so market a particular product exclusively.

A second advantage of vertical integration and selective distribution is that power is concentrated in the hands of a few large companies, which can exact concessions from the providers, thus offering the product at a lower rate. The producer, working with a large group of intermediaries, can charge high process fees since arrangements for a large group require more time and labor than a smaller group.[3] Before deregulation of the airline industry, this latter method was not commonly practiced in the United States. In West Germany this practice is quite common. Indeed, Germans traveled all over the world in the 1970s and 1980s as a result of these distribution patterns. Coastal areas in Spain are filled with small communities of Germans and English who have taken advantage of trips sold at half the price of the apex air fare. Their trips include board and room for a week, in addition to the price of air transportation to and from home. The United States companies have been encouraged by the economic climate of deregulation to emulate vertical integration.

In the 1960s and 1970s significant changes occurred in the merchandise distribution system of the industrialized countries which are now being followed by the travel industry. Self-service stores and supermarkets have almost entirely replaced conventional over-the-counter stores, discounters and cash-and-carry outlets have achieved significant market shares through a low-price, no-service policy. Large mail order houses have grown; formerly-independent retail stores have been absorbed into chain stores; and cooperatives and shopping centers, located at the periphery of large cities, have drawn business away from downtown areas. The WTO has identified three significant influences these trends have had on merchandising distribution:

—Larger size of the average retailing unit; floor space, sales volume, and sales per employee have consistently increased.
—New forms and methods of retail merchandising; self-service, discount stores, shopping centers, rack jobbers, and mail order selling have, to a large extent, replaced conventional forms of retailing.

—Integration; concurrently, retail chains and cooperatives have replaced the small independently operated retail stores.[4]

These trends raise a number of questions for the travel industry:

1. Traditionally, travel agencies used to be the main distribution channel for travel services, especially of international travel. Which changes have taken place in the travel agency business? Have travel agencies lost market shares to other distribution intermediaries? Will the number of travel agencies increased? Is there a significant trend towards concentration in the travel agency business?
2. What is the real importance of new sales methods (sales by correspondence or "mail order," travel sales counters in supermarkets and department stores, travel services offered by banks, etc.)?
3. Has the emergence of large tour operators or travel wholesalers been due to significant changes in the distribution system and the sales techniques used in the travel business?[5]

In many industrialized countries the answer to many of these questions has been and still is, "yes"; resulting from the deregulation of the airline industry in the United States, and the economic changes caused by alteration of the characteristic general merchandising distribution pattern. Before deregulation, in the United States, there was such a high degree of standardization in the transportation sector that the only difference between many of the intermediaries was service.

TYPES OF DISTRIBUTION CHANNELS

While the channel, as depicted in Figure 12-1, remains much the same as it did twenty years ago, the internal variations are changing dramatically. Large companies are growing larger; emphasis is being placed on integration; several large companies are conglomerates, which contain all three levels of the distribution channel (producers, wholesalers, retailers).

Retail Travel Agent

The independent, owner-managed travel agency is still the most common form of organization, although it is changing rapidly. It should be noted that travel agency chains, operating on a national or international scale, frequently have a larger share of the market in relation to the number of independents than their number of outlets would indicate. Travel business in the United States can be characterized as a pyramid, with the most business being conducted by small agencies. The revenue generated per agency is represented by an upside down pyramid, a small number of large agencies generate the most revenue.

The first travel agency in the United States, once known as Wells Fargo, was American Express. Although it was not a travel agency in the 1890s, American Express started two services that have become almost indispensable to travelers—the money order and American Express Traveler's Checks. When American Express opened offices in Europe to increase its express business worldwide, it became a focal point for travelers and was soon thrust into the travel business.[6] By 1912, despite the protest of its president, J. C. Fargo, American Express became a travel organization issuing tickets for rail and sea, offering services such a traveler's checks, mail, communications, and organized sightseeing tours in Naples, Berlin, Paris, and London. When Fargo retired in 1914, American Express continued its expansion into the tourist business.[7]

The beginning of travel as a business probably started with Thomas Cook over one hundred years ago. In 1841 Cook chartered a train to carry people to a temperance convention from Leicester, in England, to Loughborough twenty-two miles away. Today, the travel agency counsels potential tourists on alternative opportunities, modes of travel, and routes to be taken for a particular trip. It also makes the necessary arrangements once a choice has been made. The arrangements may include accommodations, transportation, transfers, and restaurant meals. Generally these arrangements are made at no additional cost to the traveler. This is a unique feature of the travel industry, since most other professional agencies charge a fee for all their services.

Travel agents serve as professional travel counselors to their clients in all phases of travel. The bulk of the agent's income comes from other companies—airlines, car rental agencies, tours, and hotels they arrange for their clients' use—in exchange for the services rendered.

In 1976, approximately 12,000 travel agencies produced total sales of $14.9 billion. During 1976, United States airlines paid travel agents $703 million in commissions, which was a twenty-nine percent increase over the previous year and a 161 percent increase over the fees paid five years before. The increase continued in 1978, with a fifty-two percent increase in sales over the previous year. By 1986, there were over 28,000 travel agencies producing over $32 billion worth of sales.

Despite the growing complexity of air fare prices, travel agents have been important sources of help to the public and should continue to grow in importance. Some airlines rely heavily upon travel agencies to write and sell tickets for them. Approximately eighty-five percent of all sales are through travel agents (see Table 12-1). An advantage of the travel agency is that it is not tied to any particular carrier or destination. Therefore, agencies can serve their clients easily and quickly, according to their changing needs. This is a unique feature of retailing in the travel business. The agent does not have to dispose of products the client may not want, a fact that is particularly important in establishing a good permanent clientele. Agents report that sixty-five percent of their sales is from repeat business. The key to this service is the flexibility of the travel agent in meeting a client's travel needs in addition to providing good service and consumer satisfaction follow-up. It is a business in which the adage "success breeds success" is, indeed, important and true.

TABLE 12-1 U.S. TRAVEL AGENTS BOOKINGS (PERCENT OF SUPPLIERS TOTAL BUSINESS)

Type	Estimated Percent of Volume Booked by Agents
Airlines	80% of International
	67% of Domestic
Hotels	79% of International
	18% of Domestic
Cruise Lines	92%
Rail	23%
Bus	Less than 10%
Rental Cars	40%
Packaged Tours	90%

Source: *Travel Industry World Yearbook: The Big Picture—1987.*

Another trend, in addition to increasing sales, has been the increase in the quantity of business for the average agency. Business has almost doubled in the past ten years. Large agencies, with sales over $1 million, account for sixty-seven percent of total earnings in the travel agency business. Table 12-2 illustrates twenty years of travel agency growth.

Historically, travel agencies were primarily sellers of steamship tickets and foreign tours. With the advent of air travel, it was quite natural to use their existing structure and experience. Today, the majority of ticketing is for air travel, for either business or pleasure, or both. Although most agencies provide services for all types of travel, some agencies specialize in particular clientele such as corporate, incentive programs, ethnic, or other special groups. Travel agents reported that forty-four percent of their total bookings came from commercial accounts. Corporations use travel for incentive programs, as prizes for outstanding work or sales, in addition to the normal business travel required.

Most travel agencies are small, with an average number of 7.6 employees, 5.8 full-time employees and 1.8 part-time. One of the most serious problems of travel agencies is the high rate of employee turnover. This is due, in part, to disillusionment. Employees often expect a glamorous, exciting job, which would allow them to visit exotic places;

TABLE 12-2 GROWTH OF TRAVEL AGENCIES AND SALES

Year	Approved Travel Agencies	Agency Sales (Billion)
1966	5,972	$ 1.2
1969	7,119	$ 2.0
1972	9,127	$ 3.0
1975	12,437	$ 4.5
1978	16,628	$11.4
1980	17,339	$18.0
1982	20,962	$21.8
1986	28,933	$32.6
1987	30,169	$37.9

Source: *Travel Weekly's 25th Anniversary: "Twenty-five Years of Jet Age,"* Vol. 42, No. 46, May 31, 1983 and *Travel Industry World Yearbook: The Big Picture—1987 and 1988.*

BURSCH TRAVEL BEGINS IN A GREYHOUND DEPOT

by Alan Fredericks

Pete Bursch is a born salesman.

In high school in Alexandria, Minn, when they needed to sell tickets to a football game, it was Pete who sold the most. He even sold the free one they gave him in recognition of his achievement.

After school, in the depths of the Depression, he worked for Montgomery Ward, traveled the Midwest in the wholesale appliance business and, because he liked having people around, ran a restaurant in South Dakota.

In 1956, after 21 years away, he came back to Alexandria, a town of 12,000 in the lake country northwest of Minneapolis, and bought the Greyhound depot.

That was to be the beginning of a travel agency career that got its official start two years later. In 1958, the year *Travel Weekly* began, Bursch Travel became the first ATC-appointed agency in the area.

Today, as Pete, now 70, and his 21-year-old son, Fred, preside over a $6 million business with one office in Alexandria and two in St. Cloud, Minn., he says the agency business has given him and his family more than financial rewards. It has allowed him to make people happy.

"When I started at the Greyhound depot, it was just a rest stop for the buses with a cafe. We no sooner began selling bus tickets than this woman came up and wanted to know how to fly someplace, I forget where.

"Most people 25 years ago hadn't taken their first flight, but I had flown quite a bit in my past businesses and at least I knew how to proceed.

"So I wrote a letter and made some reservations for her. Frankly, I didn't know there was such a thing as a travel agent.

"The woman told her neighbors and they started to come in and ask me to do this for them. Finally, it became a nuisance and I started charging a dollar or two dollars to pay for my time.

"I would write to people like Bill Balfour, who was with Western Airlines in Minneapolis, and John Strauss at American Express. Soon, someone suggested I should apply for a travel agency appointment."

In the late 1950s when Bursch applied, the need clause was still in effect and apointments could be denied simply because someone decided there was no need for that agency. Bursch was turned down twice, but on Feb. 28, 1958, the approval came through.

"I had no idea we could really make a living at it. We were doing it mainly as a service to the community and still depending on the depot for our living. But I remember one day I was in the hospital with a minor problem and my sister, who works with us, called to say she had just sold a ticket to Frankfurt.

"I took a look at that and I could see that this one ticket to Frankfurt was the equivalent of 10 or 12 tickets to Chicago. I thought, 'Maybe we have us something here.'"

Minnesota, with a large population tracing roots to Europe, seemed fertile ground for travel to the Continent. Soon, Bursch, working with his friend, John Strauss of American Express, was traveling to Europe to set up tours.

It took a while for the travel agency to generate meaningful income. In its first year after appointment, Bursch Travel grossed $12,000. It was three years before the volume reached $100,000.

In 1962, four years after getting his appointment, Bursch decided he'd had enough of the bus depot business.

"I had come back to Alexandria about five years earlier and I hadn't increased my worth one penny with the bus depot and a little travel business so I decided to give travel a full shot.

"I must say the community raised its eyebrows, wondering who the hell I thought I was to think I could make a living selling travel."

Source: *Travel Weekly's 25th Anniversary,* May 31, 1983, pp. 96–98.

the reality can be a shock. Also, salaries are relatively low, and in many agencies there is little opportunity for advancement.

In addition to assisting the traveler with the type of air travel desired, the agent can assist in booking hotels, car rentals, sight-seeing trips, and in arranging a specific tour. Some of the choices that a travel agent can help a traveler make in choosing a tour were explained in Chapter 11.

As stated earlier, the travel agent does not usually charge the client. The airlines, hotels, car rental firms, and tour wholesalers pay the agent a commission for the booking. The commission varies among the different segments of the industry, and for the different services reserved. Table 12-3 indicates the different types of commissions available to the travel agent. This table also shows that the profit margin is rather low. Such a slim rate of return requires professionalism and efficiency to retain clients.

In order to maintain a high degree of control and professionalism in tourism, there are specific requirements for starting a travel agency. To be able to sell airline and other transportation tickets, it is necessary to obtain an appointment (e.g. the International Air Transport Association, the International Passenger Ship Association, and the Pacific Cruise Conference). These appointments are concerned with financial standards, bonding, personnel, and location of agencies. The personnel requirement, for example, directs that at least one member of the agency must have had previous experience in the sale of transportation tickets. The owner, officer, or manager of the agency must have had two years full-time experience in transportation sales and services, and this person must also be devoting a full workday at the location of the agency for which the appointment is sought.

An excitement for traveling and a high standard of professionalism to build and maintain public trust in the travel industry are paramount. Irresponsible or dishonest people with "get rich quick" schemes would be able to move in and out of the profession rather easily, if there were not organizations and methods for controlling their entry.

With the growth of franchising and vertical integration we must not assume that travel agencies will become extinct in the near future. With such a diverse industry, and the difficulty that some specific producer organizations have in getting their products to the markets, travel agencies are needed. They are one of the most effective instruments for product marketing. This is, in part, due to the fact that no payment is made by the producer until after a sale is made. A number of factors account for this pattern continuing. The WTO has identified a number of them:

—*Selling directly to the final customer requires sales offices in carefully chosen locations, trained sales staff, and sales managers.*
—*The cost of sales offices, salaries and other selling expenses will have to be borne even if the sales volume is not sufficient to cover them.*
—*It would be necessary to cover a more or less important number of markets, often located far*

away. This creates additional problems of planning, coordination, communications and control.
—*Different market conditions, customer habits and competitors will have to be taken into account, thus further limiting the possibilities of applying a uniform sales and distribution policy.*
—*Tourist services are complementary in nature and most customers require various services at the same time and hence prefer to deal with sales outlets that can meet several related needs rather than just one requirement.*[8]

Even before these changing times, there were some weaknesses in the travel agency sector of the distribution channel. Among them are

Passive Selling: Many producers of tourist products, and tour operators, feel that travel agencies act merely as passive acceptance points for travel reservations and do not make a sufficiently strong effort to provide useful information and advice to potential travelers. This is probably one factor for the relatively low wages paid in small agencies, apart from the economics of a small profit margin. Many entrepreneurs purchasing travel agencies for the first time look upon agents as technical people who make reservations and write tickets rather than professionals with counseling abilities.

Reluctant Innovation: Most important innovations in marketing, especially in distributing tourist services of package tours, special interest travel, vacation clubs, new selling techniques, etc., did not originate in the travel agencies, but with outsiders who recognized the existing potential for development and had the marketing and management "know-how" to exploit the ideas.

Insufficient Specialization: Most travel agencies, owners, and managers believe that they can operate economically only by providing as wide a range of service as possible, rather than by capitalizing on the advantages of specialization. This may also be the trend of the new economic order following deregulation.

Absence of Well-Managed Incoming Services: Few agencies in travel doing significant outgoing business are involved in the incoming traffic, although they have an understanding of the industry and a background in negotiating with suppliers. It would seem that developing incoming services would be a natural extension of their skills.

Limited Cooperation: With the exception of travel agencies affiliated on a national or regional basis or organized in chains, cooperation between independent agencies, including joint market research, joint promotion, and common use of management and accounting facilities, is still the exception rather than the rule. The smaller and medium-sized, individually-owned agencies could, without doubt, benefit from a pooling of certain functions.

Limited Sales Coverage: Small independent agents have limited sales coverage; they need to develop new ways to reach out to a new market. One that may have some merit for the small individual companies in rural areas and small

TABLE 12-3 COMMISSION FOR TRAVEL AGENTS' BOOKINGS

Domestic air	Advertised air tour	11%
	Independent air tour	11%
	Incentive air tour	10%
	Round-trip excursion fares	10%
International air	Point to Point	8% and bonus, volume incentive and group override
Car rental		10% to 20% with bonus based on volume
Railroads	Amtrak	10%
	European	8% to 10%
	National Railroad	8%
	French	8%
Bus lines	Continental Trailways	10%
	Greyhound Lines	10%
	National Trailways Bus System	10%
Shipping Lines	Cruises, transatlantic, and interport	5% to 11% with discounts and overrides for volume
Tour operators		10% to 12% with overrides

towns is to have commissioned sales representatives cover potential customers in an assigned area.

Some of these problems are beginning to be addressed by the industry. One of the most popular methods is the consortium. A consortium is a group of agents connected by common marketing and service interests. The various ways of cooperating and working together is illustrated in Table 12-4. There will certainly be some significant changes in this segment of the distribution channel, but travel agencies will still be viable into the twenty-first century.

Tour Wholesalers and Operators

By definition, a tour package is any combination of two or more travel service components, put together and sold as a single unit. Historically, before the development of packages, travel agents would make individual arrange-

ments with each service supplier for each client. For overseas destinations, agents would establish foreign independent tours (FITs); for domestic destinations the agents established domestic independent tours (DITs).

With the development of the jet plane and middle-class people traveling in large numbers came the need for easy-to-sell vacations for the traveler. Destinations wishing to encourage the development of tourism (e.g., Caribbean islands, Hawaii, Europe) created inclusive programs that were easy to advertise, promote, and book. Travel agents handling the new wave of travelers needed programs that were easier to explain to prospective tourists than FITs and DITs, and also priced lower than the custom-tailored independent program. The packaged tour developed to meet these needs.

Today, most overseas tours are arranged by tour

TABLE 12-4 WHAT ARE AGENCY GROUPS ALL ABOUT?

Trade Groups. Organizations that create forums at which issues important to the trade or group may be addressed, ideas exchanged, and information gathered pertaining to those issues. They also sponsor educational programs and encourage professionalism. Some require some association with the industry as the group acts both as educator and as advocater for the travel industry.

Marketing Associations. Entities which create collective buying power or market positions, which individual agencies would not otherwise have, such as override commissions and other preferred vendor relationships. The banding or grouping together of a number of companies increases the purchasing power and gains added benefits from the suppliers.

Consortia. Organizations that offer travel agencies both a unified buying program and extended customer service opportunities. Hotels, belonging to corporations are good examples. Membership is exclusive with territorial rights for the individual locations.

Franchises. Agencies that group together under a common trade name or definition such as "Ask Mr. Foster." The benefits mainly are combined purchasing programs and public image through advertisement and previous association with clients. Most franchises include territorial and exclusive rights to its members.

Local Groups. Two or more agencies in the same community will form collective organizations to bulk purchase travel services and share advertising. Membership is generally non-exclusive, although some groups limit participation by competing agencies within different districts or areas of the same community.

Source: Extracted from *The Travel Business Manager* Vol. 3, No. 6, March 27, 1986

wholesalers. They arrange packaged tours at different prices, and for a variety of purposes, by working with airlines, shiplines, hotels, restaurants, and governments. They then sell these tours through travel agencies, which act as the retail agency. The travel agent receives a commission from the tour operator or wholesaler. Although many travel agencies operate tours themselves, they often do not have enough business to provide tours to all parts of the world. Therefore, they provide and operate tours that are popular in their particular area where they are able to draw enough clients to support them. Travel agents sell a packaged tour organized by a tour wholesaler for those who wish to travel to parts of the world that are likely to draw only a few clients.

The services offered by a tour operator may vary from basic air fare, transfers, hotels, meals, and sight-seeing, to entertainment, and even ceremonies upon arriving and leaving the area.

Today's tour operator began with ship and rail tours. In the United States there are over five-hundred firms providing tours that are sold through travel agencies to the public. However, the majority of tours that are sold through travel agents are sold by forty to fifty major tour operators. Cartan Tours, one of the largest companies today, began business by offering Mississippi River trips in 1899. It expanded in the 1920s and 1930s, offering tours to Canada, Hawaii, and Mexico. American Express began wholesaling tours in the 1920s with offerings to Bermuda and grand tours of the United States.

Other major companies began offering wholesale tours following the Second World War, particularly in the 1950s. Most followed the general pattern of first offering domestic tours in the United States, then offering transatlantic trips for grand tours of Europe. The 1960s saw considerable growth, with the development of special air fares that allowed the tour operator to offer mass-produced tours at prices that were enticing to the large middle class. The improvements in air transportation, which reduced travel time, provided many people an opportunity to participate in grand tours of Europe within their normal vacation times.

Thus, today's large companies package a variety of travel service components. The programs are described in detail in brochures, often elaborately printed in an array of colors. The brochures are distributed to travel agents and airlines for use in soliciting travelers. These folders and brochures have become essential for selling travel, and most prospective travelers expect them. The brochures help make an intangible service more tangible.

Tour packages are marketed in all sizes and shapes, and in all price ranges. The package may be a one-day sight-seeing tour, a city or resort package including hotel and transportation, or a long escorted tour with many features to several cities. Costs may range from a few dollars to thousands of dollars. Several items are common to all. The package will be designed for a target market segment; it will be described in reasonable detail in a brochure; and it can be booked with a single phone call to a tour operator, airline, or travel agent.

Extensive advertising and promotion has given the general public the belief that tour packages, in general, are bargains, providing more for the travel dollar. Many vacationers often ask their travel agent: "Do you have a program to . . . ?" Package tours are not automatically bargains, or even the best value, while many are priced at less than the sum of the individual parts if purchased separately. Thus, if a couple bought a Caribbean island package with hotel, ground transportation, and sight-seeing tour, they would be getting the best value they could. Sometimes, however, packages cost more than the sum of the parts. Special events packages such as the Super Bowl, or the Rose Bowl, or Mardi Gras offer large profit margins, but sell well because of the large demand. Other packages include "development" or operational costs.

The WTO compared the tour operations businesses in the United Kingdom and Germany. They are significantly different in structure and style. Four major differences are:

1. In the United Kingdom (U.K.) tour operating companies grew out of, or are closely linked with, charter airlines or, in the case of Thomson, out of a large publishing group. In Germany, the majority of tour operators are linked to large retailing establishments and banking interests.

2. In the U.K., competition between tour operators is intensive—to the point that two major firms (Horizon and Clarkson) collapsed in 1974. In Germany, a process of concentration and horizontal integration began in 1968 with the formation of TUI (Turistik Union International), which by 1974 had led to an almost complete integration of four tour operators: Tourapa, Scharnow, Hummel, and Dr. Tigges.

3. Virtually all U.K. tour operators sell exclusively through conventional travel agents, although a few of them own small chains of "retail outlets." Tour operators in Germany use both travel agents and their own outlets for distribution. This applies in particular to those tour operators that are linked to department store groups or mail-order houses.

4. U.K. tour operators rely on extensive distribution and cooperation, in principle, with all member firms of ABTA (Association of British Travel Agents). Marketing services as regular sales support are, however, more restricted. In contrast, tour operators in Germany apply a policy of selective distribution, by restricting their sales support to a relatively small number of outlets.

Speciality Channels

In addition to the major channels described above, there are a host of other types of channels within the distribution system. One that has grown rapidly in the past few years, as a result of deregulation, is the travel club. Before deregulation, travel clubs were designed to provide services; they took advantage of their bulk purchasing power at destination points. However, with deregulation of the airlines, they now have the same opportunity for bulk purchasing power as a large group. In addition, a new segment of travel clubs associated with the under capacity of the industry has developed. In most cases, the hotels, airlines, and cruises, are not fully booked; therefore, organizations have developed, under the title of travel clubs, that allow members to purchase unused spaces at the last minute.

They are heavily discounted and are basically designed to cover the line costs of the additional service needed. The fixed costs are the same, regardless of the number of clients; the industry prices a program or trip based on the fact that the trip or hotel will not be sold out completely. For example, the break-even point for airlines is approximately sixty-two percent. Thus, if a flight between New York and London is seventy-five percent booked, additional clients who book seats at a reduced rate will still reap revenue and profit for the company. This has become another marketing option available to the industry, in addition to the various pricing structures for economy, special fares, and first class seats.

Other channels have developed based upon specialization—incentive travel firms, corporate travel firms, and meetings and convention planners, to name a few. There are two methods of handling a corporate travel account. One is for a corporation to work with a travel agent. An outgrowth of this has been that some travel agents specialize in corporate travel. It offers not only an established market, but increased worker productivity, since once a business relationship is established, calls are made for a purpose and little shopping is done; thus, one agent can handle far more business. The second corporate option is to establish its own travel agency within the corporation. In the past, this latter option was not very advantageous, since company travel agencies would not receive a commission as travel agents did. However, convenience and service are the two major reasons for a corporation to have its own corporate travel department. Deregulation allowed corporations to be able to negotiate discounted fares for large amounts of travel with the various airlines.

Historically, incentive travel has been for those members of a sales force who reached their quotas and received bonuses in the form of travel. Incentive travel requires a much greater knowledge of destinations and services available, than does business travel, which primarily deals with hotels and transportation facilities. Therefore, a number of agencies were formed to address this special need, even though other agencies also provide the same service.

The offer of a trip invariably acts as an exciting bonus to stimulate sales. A certain percentage of each sale is set aside for the incentive travel program. A new innovative form of incentive travel, tailored for individuals, has been introduced. There are always some people who are unable to participate in a company program for a number of reasons. Sickness, work, school (for some working in summer sales) may prohibit participation. A disadvantage of group trips for a company is that it takes all the best people away from the office at the same time. In some cases, a disaster such as a fire, plane crash, or overturned bus could destroy a small business corporation. Incentive travel reduces some of the liabilities of a company, such as taxes, social security and unemployment benefits, whereas paying a bonus does not. Individual travel developed slowly until the 1980s, when some companies developed the concept of giving vouchers or special travel checks, which could be redeemed by certain hotels, airlines, resorts, car rental companies, travel agencies, and even campgrounds. These in-

centive travel checks are issued in $10 to $60 denominations with the purchasing company paying from three to ten percent service charges above the total amount of checks they buy. The individual incentive travel awards give winners the opportunity to travel when, where, and with whom they want.[9]

DIRECT SUPPLIER SALES

Most scheduled airlines, car rental services, hotel chains, and cruise lines maintain their own network of sales and ticketing or reservation offices in important cities, in addition to selling their services through travel agents. Two reasons for this are, first, since there is intense competition between airlines operating the same routes with the same type of equipment and similar timetables, direct promotion and sales services to potential clients are necessary; and, second, each airline's sales offices need to maintain contact with their own authorized travel agents to assist their sales effort by providing them with information, brochures and schedules, and by keeping them aware of new routes, services, and so on.[10]

Car rental companies are less dependent on travel agents because a considerable amount of their business comes from direct rentals, both business and individual. The decision to rent a car is a relatively easy decision to make because there are few choices available, and there is little counseling needed, when compared with choosing air routes and fares. There are also spur-of-the-moment rentals within the leisure market at destination centers.

OTHER DISTRIBUTION SUPPLIERS

Mail order selling of tours began in Germany in the early 1960s with the three large companies of Quelle, Neckermann, and Reisen. In the United States, Sears Roebuck has considered establishing travel agencies, and the next step for them could well be to sell tourism through catalogs or electronically.

The computer revolution is also taking place in the distribution system. Several data base services for people who want to book airline flights, hotels, and other services have developed. Future travel planning using computers may allow clients to suggest a destination, such as Athens for two weeks, and the price they are willing to pay, and then receive a complete itinerary in return. To date, the cost of equipment for such a service is quite expensive, but with development and mass public response, the price will soon go down. Table 12-5 presents an overview of some of the systems on the market in 1987.

In order to encourage repeated use of travel services by companies, frequent flier programs have been developed by most airlines. They are designed to capture repeat business and a greater share of the flying market.

The distribution system will continue to evolve and change in this deregulated climate. Some changes that have already taken place are:

Newspapers as Travel Distributors: In Germany, a number of regional newspapers have offered their readers special travel arrangements.

TABLE 12-5 PERSONAL COMPUTER ELECTRONIC
TRAVEL SERVICE

Compuserve. Compuserve Information Service Inc., Columbus, Ohio offers TWA Travel Shopper with flight schedules from most airlines, excluding United and Southwest. Also includes *Official Airline Hotel Guide* with 20,000 hotels worldwide. Worldwide Exchange, international swapping of homes, apartments, yachts, and recreational vehicles. Travel advisory services from the State Department and TWA. Book flights through TWA Travel Shopper and OAG; hotel and rental cars booked through link with American Express.

Official Airline Guide. The Dun & Bradstreet Corp., Oak Brook, IL. gives the *Official Airline Guide* (OAG) airline schedules, but no booking capabilities.

The Source. Source Telecomputing Corp, McLean, VA has the OAG and AIRSCHED airline schedules. Guide to 16,000 hotels and good restaurants with ratings by *Mobil Travel Guide*. Guide to 22,000 hotels with no ratings which are frequently updated and is linked to travel agency.

Travel Scan Videotext. Travel Scan Video Text Ltd., New York, NY provides flight guide through Pan Am with major and regional airlines. Guide to 10,000 hotels, mostly domestic. Car rental rates for seven companies, including Hertz and Avis. Frequent Buyer Club rebate program; fees paid can go toward travel discounts. On-line bookings.

Viewtron. Knight-Ridder Newspaper Inc, Miami, FL provides OAG airline schedules. Moment's notice last minute travel specials. Car rental with Alamo only. American Express tie-in for flight bookings, hotel reservations, tours, archive of travel stories.

Health Food Outlets as Travel Distributors: Travel itineraries and programs have been distributed exclusively through some chains of health food stores.

Door to Door Travel Sales: In Germany, organizations selling books and magazine subscriptions to private households include a selection of packaged tours.

Shop Committee: In France and Germany, trade unions have both distributed tours and established their own tour operator companies to provide direct benefits to their union members.

It is very possible that large insurance companies, with large sales organizations in both the rural and city areas, will offer some travel services—particularly package tours. This would work well in rural areas with small populations. Distribution channels could be linked directly with travel agencies and producers (insurance companies).

PRICING STRATEGIES

Service makes tourism an exceptional product in the business world. The truly unique character of tourism is that it is many things—a composite product of hotel, transportation, food, and attractions. This adds to the complexity of pricing. It is more than a single product, such as Coca-Cola or an automobile, where inventory can wait to be sold. Tourism is intangible and its service is perishable. When hotel rooms or airplane seats are not sold or occupied, they are lost; they perish, just as fruit or vegetables not purchased are perishable. This is the character of a service

industry, and it is particularly true of tourism, and must be constantly considered in the tourism planning process. Another characteristic is the product's inseparability. This means that the person who delivers the service is the person who actually creates the service. A brain surgeon, for example, both creates and delivers the product, just as a restaurant or car rental firm does. The next characteristic of tourism is its heterogeneous nature. A product such as noodle soup or a candy bar is all the same product, food. In a service industry such as tourism, each product is different. Two people can take a trip to London or Portugal and it will be different for each person. There is no homogeneous element in the tourism service industry.

The characteristics of tourism products as a service are important to pricing strategies. Those items that go together are complementary. Complementary is bread and butter, peanut butter and jelly. Complementary in the tourism industry means that when a trip is taken other things such as hotel, a friend to visit, a family person to stay with, and a means to get to the destination are complementary. The last characteristic is price flexibility. A reader of any travel section of the local newspaper will find hotel advertisements giving weekly and special weekend rates. The Hilton

American Airlines reservations facility.

may charge $75.00 for weekdays, but drop the price to $50.00 for the weekend. This flexibility, the ability to adjust the price up or down, makes tourism not only unique but able to work well. These elements (compositeness, perishibility, inseparability, heterogeneity, complementary, flexibility) identify a service product.

The types of pricing fall within three basic categories. There is market pricing, discount pricing and premium pricing. The latter two are somewhat self-explanatory. Market pricing is the selling of goods or services at a specified market price, which was the character of the airline industry before deregulation. The differences between two companies before deregulation were advertising and the quality of the products sold, but not the price. Since all prices on all routes were the same, the only difference between one travel agency and another was the service. The second, discount pricing, is selling the product below market level. Peoples, American West, and PSA entered the market for this purpose. Those companies that offer premium service offer it at premium price or above the market level.

A number of other pricing practices are intuitive pricing (your hunch as to what the market will bear); differential pricing (when hotels reduce prices for weekends); loss leader pricing (when free wine is given); and trial-and-error pricing (try it, and if it works all is well and good, if not, it is not used again).

In the travel field, price is determined by the quality and distinctiveness of the service, competition between suppliers, profit margin objective, seasonal effects, and buyer resistance. As a product becomes higher in quality and more distinctive, there is less competition. The costs will be higher, and there will also be a higher profit margin. Mass tourism is based on lowering profit margin and lowering costs through mass purchasing. Almost all sectors are affected by the seasons, which increase and decrease demand. Thus, travel to the coasts of Spain in the winter, or to the coasts of Mexico in July, are considerably less expensive than in the peak seasons of summer in Spain and winter in Mexico.

Tourism as a product is sensitive to price changes and price levels. The demand for a product or service can be classified as elastic or inelastic. Elastic refers to the fact that as price increases, the demand will decrease. Mass tourism and vacation travel is based on this concept. As price decreases, more people will travel. However, inelasticity has the opposite effect. Whether price increases or decreases it will not influence demand. Much of business travel is inelastic. Most business trips are required regardless of the price. The airlines have tried to establish their pricing policies to take these two elements into account. Advance purchases can be sold at considerable savings. Business travel, where plans often change from day to day and trips are scheduled at the last moment can be sold at a higher price. The new policy of reductions in fare depending upon the amount refundable is often oriented to the leisure traveler who makes plans in advance and is free to travel at a specified time.

Break-even analysis is designed to find that point of sales at which profit will be shown. Airlines, hotels, and restaurants realize that it would be highly unlikely, if not impossible, to operate at full capacity all the time; therefore, the decision to enter a market or establish a price will depend on the amount of sales, or capacity levels of the equipment or facility. Airlines consider about fifty-eight to sixty-eight percent occupancy as a break-even point. Routes that constantly have less than this will be dropped as being unprofitable.

MAJOR ISSUES

Two major concerns of the industry are deregulation and currency rate fluctuations. The latter is a constant problem because much of tourism is international; pricing and selling tours sometimes up to a year in advance can be hazardous. In 1987, the dollar dropped rapidly, losing over twenty percent of its value in a three month period. Tours priced for sale earlier that summer were seriously hurt by the drop.

The full effect of deregulation is yet to be seen. One of the first changes was the increase in commissions to ten percent for domestic travel. American, TWA, and Frontier tried to reduce this percentage but other major carriers refused to follow their lead. Additional changes in the commission structure have evolved. While the standard rate is ten percent, overrides (increased commissions) are paid for two types of business. When a large group is taking a trip, the individual travel agency can negotiate either a lower fare or a higher commission of from twenty to thirty percent. The second form of override is the airlines' method of rewarding those agencies that produce large amounts of business throughout the year. Some airlines will pay a small percentage, such a two percent of the year's gross sales, to those agencies that have been large producers.

Considerable pressure has been put on the industry by the Justice Department of the United States to allow net fares. Net fares are based on the assumption that a ticket purchased from the airlines could be sold for less than the commission given to the travel agents for selling it. The Justice Department looks upon the distribution of airline tickets as a retail/wholesale type of sale; while the industry considers the procedure as that of a professional agent contracting to provide a service for which they, the agents, receive a commission.

The second major element affecting the distribution channel is the ruling by the CAB to eliminate agency exclusivity. This, combined with the changing commission structure and pressure from the Justice Department, makes possible some new distribution systems. Newer ones will continue to evolve. Exclusivity is the appointment of travel agents as the sole agents, other than the airlines themselves, to sell airline tickets. No other form of sales are possible, other than appointments to cooperate to operate a business travel department without commissions. In 1984, the CAB ruled that this should no longer continue, but granted antitrust immunity for the remainder of the year allowing the industry to develop new systems. After January 1, 1985, airlines were able to appoint, or were free to establish, any form of sales they so desired. This has led to major corporations negotiating directly with airlines for reduced rates based upon large amounts of business, the use of ticket machines for direct connections which can be placed in shopping malls, supermarkets, and at airports, and the likelihood that banks will be selling tickets in the future. Any airline is free to negotiate with any form of intermediary it desires.

The primary producers—airlines, cruise companies, and tour operators—are developing a concept of preferred agency status. Prior to deregulation, airlines and all other vendors provided equal service and "freebees" to all agencies regardless of size, product mix, or anything else. The notion of a preferred vendor simply means that an agency has chosen to give a predominate portion of its business to a certain vendor in return for favorable rates and service. Some advantages the agent receives from the producers are overrides, unlimited free tickets, bulk fare deals, special treatment on group space, top priority on waiting lists, free or reduced payments for automation, co-op advertising, and guaranteed super saver space on flights where only full coach space exists.

This changing fare structure and loss of exclusivity is bringing about the second major change in the distribution channel. Franchises and mergers of agencies have become commonplace and their ultimate size is now important. Franchising in travel under deregulation has offered the same benefits that are found in other businesses (name recognition, preferred supplier programs with overrides, cooper-

ative advertisement programs, a range of training options, and additional promotional tools). It also provides easier ways for small agencies to gain the benefits that larger agencies have.

The profound changes distribution channels are undergoing due to the continued pressure brought about by deregulation and the computer revolution may well have been hard to conceive of in the late 1970s.

RESEARCH AND REVIEW

1. Define the distribution channel.

2. Describe four benefits of distribution intermediaries.

3. Describe the three distribution channels.

4. What are three factors the WTO points to as requiring a high degree of need for distribution?

5. Discuss five types of distribution channels.

6. What are three changes in the distribution system that have evolved as a result of deregulation?

7. Indicate and give examples of three pricing strategies.

8. What impact will deregulation and eliminating agency exclusivity have on the distribution system?

9. Using your local newspaper's travel section, identify which level of the distribution channel each advertisement represents.

ENDNOTES

1. Robert W. McIntosh, "Definitions," unpublished paper, 1979. (Quoted in Mill and Morrison, p. 400).
2. WTO (Madrid, 1976), p. 3.
3. Mill and Morrison, pp. 400–406.
4. WTO, p. 5.
5. Ibid., p. 6.
6. Peter Z. Grossman, *American Express: The Unofficial History of the People Who Built the Great Financial Empire* (NY: Crown Publishers, 1987) pp. 108–132.
7. Ibid., p. 112.
8. WTO, pp. 10–11.
9. Ann Hughes, "Incentive Travel: Tailored for Individuals," *Successful Meetings* (Dec. 1984), pp. 35–38.
10. WTO, p. 24.

PART III

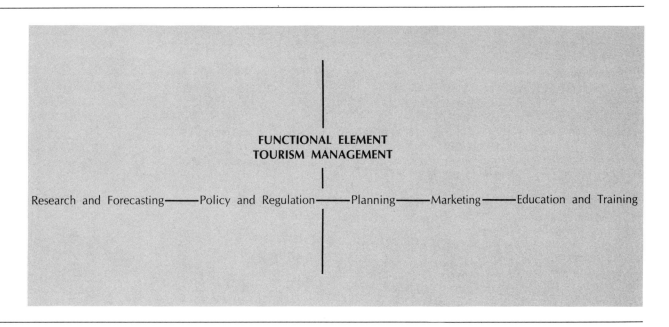

FUNCTIONAL
ELEMENT:
TOURISM
MANAGEMENT

CHAPTER 13

RESEARCH AND FORECASTING

Central to the success of either government or private organizations is good research and forecasting. Every organization involved in tourism requires a certain level of research, measurement, and forecasting, whether it is a surfboard outlet on the beach, a family-run hotel, an airline corporation, or a town, city, state, province, country, or region. Research helps to plan for the future in determining markets and the affect tourism will have on the organization, whether private or public. Research helps assess the success of promotional and marketing strategies, and the affect tourism has had, or is having, on the organization, region, or facility.

Tourism has grown remarkably, and will continue to grow both domestically and internationally, making research and forecasting even more essential. Its impact upon the land, for example, is both serious and long lasting. Some of the great lessons learned from tourism, teach us the importance of controlling land development.

Research helps stimulate tourism by identifying targets as potential tourist generators. Government assistance in direct advertising is well within the realm of proper planning and research for tourism.

Tourism research cuts across many categories of study. Because of this, the formulating of policy and programs requires considerable input from a number of planning teams. From its planning stage to implementation, the process is quite complex.

Research needs are no less important in the private sector. An investment of $500 for a stand on the beach selling ice cream cones and a multimillion dollar investment in a resort complex require the same understanding of the market and its location. Government and public research needs overlap. They both need market researchers. Paul Hall of the U.S. Travel and Tourism Administration

(USTTA) suggested that market research attempts to find out what consumers want, or need, and develops a plan to meet those wants and needs, so it can be sold to them. A marketing plan requires research. Hall has identified a series of steps needed to create a marketing plan. The importance of research in the development of the plan can be seen.

1. Assessment of the current situation or "Where am I now?" The assessment includes

    a. Demand analysis both present and future
    b. Supply analysis including present and future competitive activity
    c. Future economic and technological developments
    d. Inventory of resources
    e. Analysis of products' strengths and weaknesses. (See Figure 13-1.)

2. Next, market research must answer the question, "Where do I want to be?" Large corporations will plan their growth strategies over an extended period of time, while a smaller enterprise may only be able to plan one or two years ahead. Forecasting is essential in determining the future direction of the business.

The identification of alternative future paths, and the possible consequences of those paths, is part of this task. The research should be able to indicate what will happen as a result of acting on certain decisions, or of a change in policy.

3. This step accepts the decision of where an organization is going, and determines how best to get there. A series of long term goals, such as to increase the rate of return on the tourist product, or to increase the average annual number of tourists by a certain percent, or to attract tourists who will spend more money per trip, may, in part, be achieved by the construction of a new tennis court or golf course, or a change in the advertising campaign.[1]

These are all the steps that outline what good planning and research studies involve.

RESEARCH NEEDS AND APPROACHES

Good research follows certain traditional patterns and procedures. The elements of research are to define the problem, to establish research procedures and methods, to use

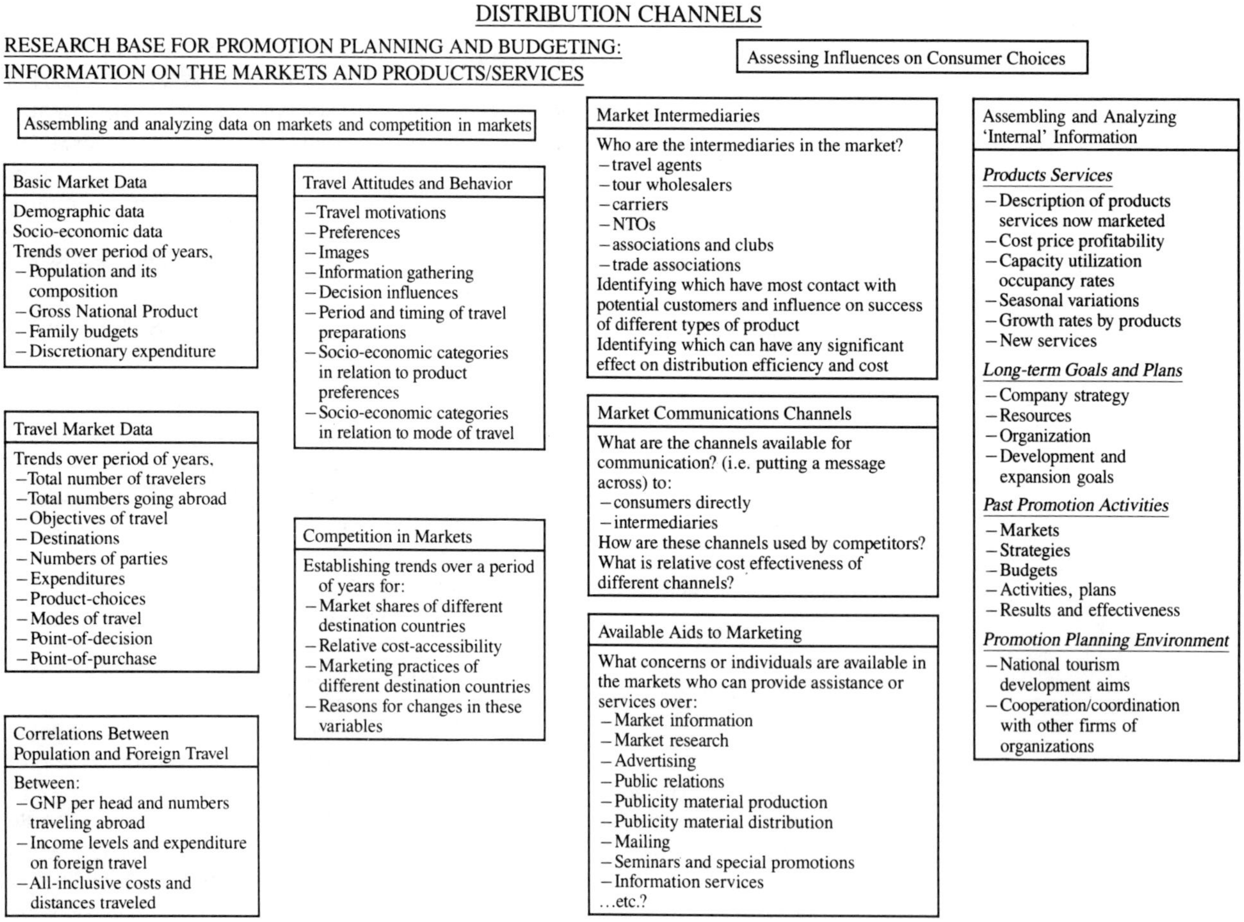

Figure 13-1 Source: Paul G. Hall, "Trends and Opportunities for Research in the Tourist Industry," U.S. Travel and Tourism Administration.

proper research tools, to identify research organizations and people who can assist in it, and to maintain proper information retrieval for reference and use.

To define the problem it is first necessary to identify and state the objective of the research; in other words, to have a proper understanding of the task. Several examples can illustrate this. The U.S. Travel Data Center completed an in-flight survey of international air travelers in 1987 (see Table 13-1). The purpose of the survey was to provide more accurate, detailed, and timely information on the characteristics and travel behavior of United States residents traveling abroad. The need for more accurate data has been growing in recent years, as international tourism has increased, and competition for the foreign traveler has become more heated and sophisticated.[2]

The United States has one of the largest tourist trades in the world. More information is needed to determine strategies for its continuance, or to increase the United States' share which will help the balance of trade payments problem. Before any action can be taken, or plans established to pursue the improvement of tourist trade in the United States, more information is needed about current travel patterns to and from the United States and between the states.

Douglas C. Frechtling, former director of the U.S. Travel Data Center, indicated that some major objectives for state travel research were:

1. To determine the role of travel in your state's economy.
   a. What is travel's contribution to the state economy?
   b. Who are those who benefit from travel's economic contribution?
   c. What are the costs associated with travel in your state?
2. To determine characteristics of your state's market.
   a. What is your current market—the profile of current travelers in your state?
   b. What is your potential market—those residing in major metropolitan areas and surrounding states who do not travel in your state?
3. To describe your product.
   a. What natural, scenic, and historic attractions does your state have?
   b. What business establishments serve and attract travelers?
   c. What kind of travel experience does your state offer?
4. To determine how the economic impact of travel, your market, and your product change over time.
   a. What annual and seasonal changes are taking place?
   b. What factors influence travel in your state?
   c. What does the future hold for travel in your state?[3]

Once the question is defined, the requirements of the research task can be directed. The definition of the problem

TABLE 13-1 PROFILE OF U.S. RESIDENTS TRAVELING TO OVERSEAS DESTINATIONS

Purpose of Trip		Mean Total Trip Expenditures	$2,037
Business	28.4%	Mean International Air Fare	$1,033
Attend Convention	4.0	Type and Size of Travel Party	
Vacation, Holiday	60.9	Traveling Alone	35.3%
Visit Relatives/Friends	31.4	Family Group	46.7
Study/Other	2.9	Business Group	7.5
Overseas Visits in Lifetime		Mixed Family/Business	13.3
One Visit	10.2%	Sex and Age of Visitor	
More than one Visit	90.8	Male	57.4%
Means of Booking Air Trip		Female	40.6
Travel Agent	71.4%	Annual Household Income	
Self	14.0	Mean Income	$54,204
Company Travel Dept.	8.0	Median Income	$55,136
Travel Club	2.2	Nights Away from Home	
Other	4.5	Mean Nights	20.9%
Use of Prepaid Package		Median Nights	11.0
Yes	24.5%	Types of Accommodation	
No	75.5	Hotel/Motel	73.9%
Type of Airline Ticket		Private Home	35.3
First Class	6.5%	Other	7.4
Executive/Business	15.2	Number of Countries Visited	
Economy/Tourist	75.3	One Country	70.7%
Other	3.0	Two Countries	17.5
		Three Countries or More	11.9

Source: *In-Flight Survey of international air travelers*, 1987, U.S. Travel Data Center.

identifies the informational needs of an organization and the process of how to go about obtaining those informational elements; it also includes the processing of the data collected. In the case of the research suggested by Douglas Frechtling, the major objective of a state's research is to determine how much travel activity contributes to the state's economy, and how much that activity contributes to the state's economy, and how much that activity will cost the state. Assessment of the economic impact on the community entails identifying the business related to tourism and understanding the return on investment of travel-related businesses, in order to obtain further investments. It also ascertains if areas needing economic stimulus can be affected by tourism-related investments.

RESEARCH PROCEDURES AND METHODS

Once the objectives of a research project are defined, the next task is to identify the exact information needed to reach those objectives. The first step is to cull existing sources of data to find if information is available pertaining to those objectives. There are a number of methods for collecting travel data. Some studies require minimal information that can be collected from the various industry segments that have direct contact with the tourist (e.g., hotel, national border, and attractions personnel), while others may require a greater depth of information specifically from the traveler. Some of the standard methods of collection are

Frontier control—This accounts for arrivals and departures into and out of a country. This can be an accurate count of the number of tourists coming and going. Today however, there is a movement to reduce these controls. Some regions, such as Scandinavia (Sweden, Norway, Denmark) count only the country of first contact, thus much international data lists only the total numbers for Scandinavia as a whole, rather than separate data for each country. In North America, citizens from the United States can enter border cities in Canada and Mexico without contact with a border official. Countries with visa control and a few border crossings do have an accurate count of the visitors and residents who cross their borders.

Surveys at frontiers—These are conducted to increase the information about the visitors, their trips, and the amount of money they spend; and to estimate the number of visitors to a country or state that does not have frontier officials. These are time consuming and sometimes difficult to handle, if large numbers of travelers are crossing the border. Some organizations give a questionnaire to people as they cross the border, and request that they complete it and return it in a preaddressed, prepaid envelope.

In-flight and on-board surveys—These are conducted if information is desired on fliers. The Hawaiian Visitors' Bureau has been gathering information for years on air travel to and from the islands. Other island countries, or destinations, are also able to conduct this type of research. A major problem with these surveys is that often the flight personnel, either lack the training to answer questions passengers might ask concerning the questionnaire, or they

don't care to see that the questionnaire is correctly completed. Several flight attendants, when passengers have asked about surveys, indicated that the completion of the survey was optional. Better trained flight attendants would have been able to obtain better results.

Census returns—These are gathered from accommodation establishments, and are sometimes used where border formalities are lacking, and the country (or company) wants to obtain information pertaining to the distribution of visitors within a given region or country. This is commonly done by the Organization for Economic Cooperation and Development (OECD). Countries that require some form of licensing and reporting in lodgings and campsites can obtain information about visitors, but there are many travelers who stay with friends and relatives, or in other locations. This is a major weakness of this type of survey. In the United States, to ensure an accurate census count, it would be necessary to know the people with friends and family living in major destination regions. Of course this is impossible! Even in Socialist countries, this form of counting is difficult. It was estimated at an international conference on tourism in the Soviet Union, that the city of Sochi, a popular Black Sea resort, had 100,000 visitors visiting friends and family, in addition to the 100,000 beds that were available for other tourists during peak times.

Household surveys—These are used to canvass people on their home ground about their travel patterns and experiences. The data gathered is more general than that discussed earlier, since it either deals with departure rather than arrival or is concerned with a local area. Surveys of households can be conducted by mail and by phone. Mail surveys have a lower response rate, while the phone survey has to be limited to a relatively short time period. The U.S. Travel Data Center and the U.S. Center for Transportation conducted these kinds of surveys to find out about the habits and characteristics of American travel. In spite of the problem of time, a phone survey conducted by the U.S. Travel Data Center is an excellent source of information. The U.S. Travel Data Center provides a special subscriber service for clients; specific research questions are included in their surveys. They contract with various states to help government officials gain a better understanding of their own travel market.

Census-taking and surveys conducted at attractions assist in identifying the number of visitors to specific attractions. Surveys enable researchers to gain a greater understanding of the visitors, and to determine the effectiveness of the advertising. These surveys also determine if the attraction is meeting the expectation of the visitors. Surveys at attractions must be short since visitors have little desire to answer long complicated questionnaires.

Diaries of travelers—These are sampled to ascertain the particular patterns of specific visitors. When the information in these diaries is correlated, general patterns emerge. Usually only a few diaries are sampled because the method is both time consuming and cumbersome.

Monetary flow—The flow of money into and out of a region can be assessed through the banking system; this helps to identify the economic impact tourism will have on a community. In addition to information about the flow of money, linkages with other regions can be determined from this data.

Tariff and brochure analysis—This gives some information about marketing strategies, and market targets, of organizations and regions which produce the information.

Surveys—Data concerning numbers, origins, sex, and similar statistics, provides some information about the market and types of tourists, but tourism research generally requires a deeper understanding of the visitor to assist in understanding the nature of existing patterns and likely growth areas than this information gives. Of all the previously discussed methods of research in the travel field, surveys are used the most. There are four major survey techniques—a personal interview, a handout questionnaire, an immediate mail questionnaire, and a delayed mail questionnaire. The U.S. Forest Service conducted a survey using the same questionnaire for all four methods to determine the effectiveness of results versus the expense of each. They were concerned with finding an alternative to the time consuming, thus expensive, personal interview to obtain needed and accurate information. The subject of the questionnaire was the sociological characteristics of campers, their purpose for camping, camping expenditures, investment patterns, income, and attitudes about various campground environmental conditions and administrative procedures.

As in all research, once the purpose was identified, the experimental design was developed. The first step of the experimental design was to determine the surey techniques, which in this case was to compare the four forms of surveys using the same questionnaire for all four. The second stage was to establish a sampling procedure that would be statistically sound; all visitors were to be randomly chosen to complete a certain survey which was also chosen randomly. Upon completion of the data gathering and analysis of the results, it was concluded that the delayed-mail results were most similar to the personal interview. The result of the research indicating that data could be obtained less expensively, and in less time, by the delayed-survey method, was significant. It showed that people tend to remember their vacations well, and that their impressions of pertinent facts surrounding the recreation experience and their attitudes towards them did not change noticeably after a three- to five-month period.

Two steps in research procedure have been illustrated in the discussion of the Forest Service study. They are, first, selection of data gathering tools and types of questionnaires; second, research design (the manner in which the survey will be conducted, and the sample selected to be the target group).

The final step in research is to analyze the data, consider the results, and formulate recommendations. This is discussed later in the chapter.

RESEARCH TOOLS

A number of tools are available to assist the researcher in organizing and analyzing data. They range from hand calculators to sophisticated computer programs. Computers have not only made information easier to store and organize but also to analyze. Computer programs have been developed to perform a variety of statistical calculations. A researcher needs only to enter the data compiled and provide a few basic commands. The computer program will then generate the requested statistical analysis. The interpretation, however, is made by the researcher using skill and commonsense.

Many companies have need of independent research skills. Large corporations may need specialized information pertaining to a given topic or a segment of their market, thus requiring a research supplier. Other times, organizations may want an independent view of a matter causing concern. Small organizations normally do not have the financial resources to maintain their own researcher or research team, and it becomes necessary for them to seek outside help. A number of organizations, such as the U.S. Travel Data Center and WTO, provide data that can be used by others in research. Research suppliers are familiar with data resources available. A number of research firms specialize in a certain segment of the tourist industry, such as marketing (Robinsons), hotels (Pannell, Kerr, Forster), or airlines (Lloyd's Aviation in London); while some are broad-based, handling a wide range of research topics. A major source of tourism research is conducted by university professors in a variety of fields, each using their particular skills on a segment of the industry. Research suppliers will either contract with an organization for a specific topic that is needed by the organization, or will follow an interest and publish the results in journals and magazines of interest to the tourist industry. See Appendix B for a listing of trade journals and magazines.

It is important for researchers to know how to retrieve information. They need to know sources, trends, and how to access the information for their particular research topics. Many organizations publish data with little interpretation of it, much of it can be useful in tourism research. Professional researchers can access the information and, using statistical methods of analysis, add to the body of knowledge pertaining to the phenomenon of tourism.

FORECASTING

A primary purpose of travel research is measuring and forecasting to arrive at an educated opinion. Two kinds of data can be generated, that which is quantitative in nature and that which is qualitative. Qualitative data are data for which there is little or no distinct number. Surveys frequently ask several qualitative questions. Occupation, sex, home state, or home country, are all qualitative subjects giving rise to questions which will elicit qualitative responses. Figure 13-2 and Table 13-2 from the USTTA in-flight survey are examples of this type of data.

Quantitative data are usually shown on a continuum. Each response has a specific number to represent a point (data), such as the number of flights each day of the year between New York and Paris, or the number of people in hotels in Rome during July for the past ten years.

A number of methods, from summaries to graphs, are

PURPOSE OF TRIP–ALL OVERSEAS TRAVELERS TO THE U.S.

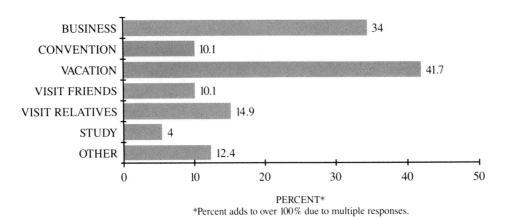

PERCENT*
*Percent adds to over 100% due to multiple responses.

Figure 13-2 Source: U.S. Travel and Tourism Administration.

used to analyze data. The in-flight survey conducted by USTTA, and other sophisticated statistical models are examples. Forecasting, which is the purpose of much research, requires maximum interpretation of the data collected. Theoretical forecasting tends to be quantitatively oriented. The most commonly-used quantitative approach is called *linear regression analysis* and is used to develop multivariable regression demand models and to make future projections. It is a statistical method for calculating the relationship between two or more related variables. Selecting the variables requires the use of specific data. For example, information may be available on the number of people who went abroad in a given year and their per capita income. In theory, it is assumed that income is a key determinant of tourism. Hence, if we plot a graph with income as the independent variable and departures as the dependent variable over a period of time, we should be able to test for a statistically significant correlation. This suggests that if income rises then the number of tourists traveling overseas will also rise; alternatively, if income (independent variable) falls then the number of tourists (the dependent variable) will decline. Thus, predictions about income will lead to predictions about travel. Not only does income help account for people taking trips, but it may influence other things related to travel as well. Consequently, researchers try to determine those variables that will improve forecasting the future of tourism. Major changes may occur in the independent variables, and they may require a new model of study. In other words, the relationships may change with trends in tourism and changing world conditions and the resulting analysis should only be used for short two- or three-year periods.

A variation of multivariate regression demand (forecasting) models are gravity and trip generation models. These are becoming quite complex. The purpose here is to introduce the concept and hope it is recognized as one of many methods used in tourism research. These two models, gravity and trip generation, use regression analysis, but their theoretical bases are a little different. Multivariate regression models are basically hypotheses stating that demand

for tourism has several variables. Gravity model analysis is derived from the physical science. The term gravity is the central concept here—the pull of gravity is determined by the mass of two bodies and the distance between them. *Gravity modeling* is a technique for predicting tourism demand using such factors as the size of related communities and the distances between them. Atlantic City receives more visitors than Las Vegas because Atlantic City is closer to a large population base. People from Chicago are more likely to go to New York than to Albuquerque.

The flow of people from their origin to specific destinations can be explained as a *trip generation model,* a function of variables, such as size of population in the zone of origin, the number of people in the destination area, and the distance between the origin and destination zones. This is an extension of the gravity idea. If it is assumed that the people in a given society make a certain number of trips a year, then it may be assumed that the proportion of trips from the zone of origin which will terminate in the destination area will be the same as the ratio of the population of the destination area to the society's total population. From this basic premise, additional calculations can be added covering factors that impede travel, such as cost, distance, and available means of transportation. Further requirements of basic population figures can also be made to seperate the data by income, age, sex, occupations and combinations of these. In effect, this technique can forecast such aspects of tourism demand as passenger traffic flows, retail shopping patterns, number of visitors to a specific resort, etc.

An additional quantitative technique is that of *linear systems analysis.* The theoretical assumption underlying this technique is that the flow of travelers is like an electric current; the origin is the current source, which flows through a path offering the least resistance, until grounded at the point of destination. A series of equations is then developed. For example, the first equation could be to calculate the flow of tourists from a given origin by determining the population's propensity to travel versus their resistance to travel. The second equation would define their resistance

TABLE 13-2 PROFILE OF OVERSEAS VISITORS TO THE U.S.A. FIRST QUARTER OF 1983

		Total percent Overseas Visitors
Residence:	Europe	40
	France	5
	Germany	6
	Netherlands	2
	U.K.	14
	Caribbean	7
	S. American	17
	Venezuela	8
	C. America	4
	Africa	1
	Oceania	4
	Far East	23
	Japan	19
	Middle East	5
Purpose of Trip:	Business	34
	Attend convention	10
	Vacation, holiday	42
	Visit friends	10
	Visit relatives	15
	Study	4
	Other	12
U.S.A. Trip Experience:	First time visitors	14
	Repeat visitors	86
Means of Booking Air Trip:	Travel agent	74
	Self	14
	Company travel dept.	11
	Travel club	1
	Other	5
Means of Booking Lodging:	Travel agent	28
	Self	14
	Company travel dept.	7
	Other	16
Information Sources:	Airline	19
	Travel agency	61
	U.S. government	2
	Friends, relatives	21
	Newspapers, magazines	7
	Other	12

Source: U.S. Travel and Tourism Administration.

as a function of distance, speed of travel, and cost. Lastly, their flow is defined to a specific destination as a function of attractiveness and propensity to take vacations to that place. Linking the equations gives a model predicting tourist flows from an origin to a specific destination. This is a fairly new approach to forecasting tourism demand. A problem with this approach is the need to quantify (give a number to) qualitative factors such as "attractiveness."

Using multivariate regression techniques, models have been built to forecast tourist outflows from one country to another. Variables used in the model include income levels in the sending country, cost of travel, and consumer costs in both the origin and destination countries. Remember, all of the techniques suggested here are based on the assumption that the interrelationship between the independent variables will remain reasonably constant. Beyond one

to two years, this assumption weakens; for longer term forecasts it has been found useful to supplement rigorous analysis with subjective opinion and informed judgment.

These opinions and informed judgments are termed *intuitive*. One of these intuitive techniques is the *Delphi model*. Originally developed by the Rand Corporation, this method involves research of the area to be forecasted, development of questionnaires, selection of a panel of experts, and analysis of the replies. The first task is to define the area of study, to identify a likely sequence of events, and to research what information has been developed pertaining to the area of study. From this, a questionnaire can be created to elicit the kind of opinions and judgments from which the forecast is to be made. Next, it is necessary to select a panel of experts, people who are believed to possess in-depth knowledge of the area under study. Anonymity of reply is necessary. The first round of replies to the questionnaire is edited, and summaries are prepared showing their range and distribution. The panelists are asked to reevaluate their responses from round one in light of the summaries of responses, and to indicate the reasons behind any given reply which varies significantly from the general distribution. These responses are again edited, and new summaries developed which are sent out as round three to the panelists. A final editing and analysis of the last round results in a listing of future events as predicted by the panel, with probabilities assigned to the events listed.

Essentially, the Delphi model applies statistical survey techniques to a panel of people whose experience give credibility to their subjective opinions. The value of the result depends on the quality of the background research and design of the questionnaire, as well as the quality of the panel. Since each expert presumably brings to bear a wide array of judgments on nonquantitative variables, this is a method of balancing personal idiosyncrasies and prejudices over a wide enough base to neutralize or isolate the more extreme opinions. It is still an intuitive approach, and while perhaps offering more reliability over longer periods of time, it is no better than the opinion of the people answering the questionnaire and just as vulnerable to unexpected future events as any other forecasting technique.

Another intuitive technique is *scenario writing*, in which a hypothetical sequence of events is constructed in order to examine the causal factors and to identify decision points. The purpose is to attempt to forecast a likely stream of events and to decide what steps, if any, may be required either to achieve desired goals or to prevent unwanted developments. Let's assume that a tourist project developer wants to assure adequate demand for a facility. A scenario could be written which would start with an analysis of target populations, competitive tourist attractions' cost, ease of transport, and likely growth of demand. The steps required for the specific project to attract and serve an adequate volume of visitors would then be laid out. This is a relatively new technique. There appears to be some question as to its validity in the absence of any rigorous analytical framework. Many people can write plausible scenarios, but assigning probabilities to them and justifying them with data can be difficult.

A form of scenario writing using a panel of experts might occur at a symposium or seminar where a series of scenarios can be exposed to "brainstorming" with probabilities assigned to each. While this broadens the number of people who contribute to the assessment, it presents the problem of dealing with one or more participants who may dominate the proceedings and skew the results from a more objective consensus. To avoid this problem, the Delphi method seems more reliable.

MANAGEMENT INFORMATION SYSTEMS

The generation of data helps both the government and private organizations formulate plans, policies, and programs. The requirements of the multi-billion dollar tourism industry for data and data manipulation, for forecasting, decision support, and understanding the industry, are large. All levels of government collect data in one form or another. Each private organization collects data from the simplest to the most complex.

The application of recommendations made as a result of analyzing data differs from organization to organization depending upon its needs. Governments use data to provide information, to assess current programs, and to indicate future programs to maximize tourist revenue and, in many cases, to minimize their costs. Organizations use collection and analysis techniques to determine the effectiveness of current programs, and to look ahead to the future of tourism as it relates to their own companies.

Governments disseminate their data in the form of reports, which are used, not only by them, but also by professional researchers and corporations involved in travel. Some private research or quasi-private organizations, such as the U.S. Travel Data Center, publish their results and distribute them for a fee to any potential user. The purpose of all research is to provide additional knowledge and understanding of some segment of the travel field, which, in turn, will help in understanding the field as a whole.

RESEARCH AND REVIEW

1. What are two major goals of research?

2. Describe the three steps necessary to create a marketing plan.

3. Discuss the advantages and weaknesses of five different methods of collecting data.

4. What are the four major survey techniques?

5. Discuss the question "Why do research?"

ENDNOTES

1. Paul G. Hall, "Trends and Opportunities for Research in the Tourism Industry," unpublished paper (U.S. Travel & Tourism Admin.), p. 5.
2. U.S. Travel Data Center, *In-Flight Survey of international air travelers*, p. 1.
3. Douglas C. Frechtling, "A Model State Continuing Travel Research Program," unpublished paper (Columbus, OH: Discover America Travel Institute, 1975).

CHAPTER 14

POLICY
AND
REGULATION

Tourism, in most cases, crosses local, national, or international boundaries, thus creating an interaction between people of the host area and people from the area of origin. In addition, tourism can have an effect within these units. As a result, governments set and enforce legislation and regulations.

Some legislation and regulations that affect the travel industry are part of the normal processes of government to protect the health and general welfare of the public, including tourists.

These regulations have usually been an outgrowth of legislation. However, the tourist system is properly the concern of government at all levels. Examples of regulations follow:

Accommodation Establishments
Classification and grading/rating of hotels and other establishment types
Fire safety regulations and codes.
Health safety regulations and codes
Building and zone codes
Issuance of operating and liquor licenses and other regulations of terms and conditions of operation
Liability laws with respect to guests and their belongings
Labor and taxation legislation

Travel Agents, Tour Wholesalers, and Operators
Regulation and licensing of travel agents, tour wholesalers, and operators.
Definition of responsibilities and limitations
Regulation of promotions
Labor and taxation legislation

Airlines, Railways, Buses, Ships, and Other Carriers
Control of fares and tariffs
Licensing of carriers
Regulation of safety procedures
Control of route entry and exit
Limitation of weights and capacities
Negotiation of services
Subsidization of routes
Labor and taxation legislation[1]

Tourism has traditionally been viewed from the economic perspective; it has been considered an implicit export and a job generator. It has been defined in terms of the numbers of visitors to a country and the number of dollars those visitors generate in the economy. At the end of World War II, tourism was used to help revitalize the war-ravaged economies of Europe. During the United Nations development decade of the 1960s, the idea of using tourism to help reconstruct Europe was expanded into using tourism as a means to further development in Third World countries. It was during the postwar era that statistics were first gathered specifically for tourism.

Traditionally, the economic approach to tourism has been to quantify tangible tourism outputs rather than to measure the quality of these outputs. An examination of vacation habits of a number of countries suggests that, in broad terms, the highest participation in tourism is found in countries with a relatively high standard of living and where a large proportion of the population is urbanized.

A high standard of living manifests itself in high disposable incomes, which tend to be accompanied by fewer hours of work and increased vacation time. A high standard of living means a high level of car ownership, which in itself is conducive to travel. With the growth of the industry in the 1960s and early 1970s, new destinations were established, and many places were no longer as isolated as they had once been.

In the 1970s concern for the tourist environment began to be felt. Government officials and residents in and near major resorts and cities began to question the claims that tourism would benefit the area; terms such as "pollution" "golden horde," etc., were coined. It was recognized that a tourist attraction itself might be destroyed by the very tourists visiting it and, in fact, many have closed their doors to the public.

In March, 1977, over 250 delegates from thirty countries gathered in Washington, DC for the International Symposium on Tourism and the Next Decade, sponsored by George Washington University, the Organization of American States, U.S. Forest Service, the U.S. Travel Service, and the U.S. Man and the Biosphere Committee of UNESCO. The purpose of this symposium was to provide a forum for the interchange of ideas and the development of alternative strategies for tourism planning, marketing, and management. The symposium recommendations regarding tourism management and marketing are listed below:

—Develop a mechanism to facilitate two-way communication between information users and information generators.

—Conduct an international assessment of census models to assist developed and developing countries to obtain planning data needed.
—Evaluate the relative supply of, and need for, different kinds of data.
—Obtain more appropriate information required in local, regional, and national planning, including input from industry.
—Conduct international multidisciplinary research studies to predict the impact of tourism on groups or communities with similar profiles. Present a petition to the United Nations for the recognition of the WTO.
—Develop standardized definitions used throughout the world for reporting and data retrieval systems.
—Establish a program for assessing research data needs: who has what; who needs what.
—Develop improved methods for socioeconomic forecasting in tourism.

POLICY NEEDS AND PROCESSES

The tourism policy decision-making process by nature is interdisciplinary in its approach and application. It should take into account the economic benefits and important principles of human welfare and the quality of life.[2]

The policy development process is complex, interrelated, and focused on serving the public interest now and in the future through appropriate governmental and private sector actions at all levels. Policy issues and requirements differ at the various levels of government. The local level is certainly not concerned with the political problems of entry and exit, or broad national concerns of foreign policy. It is more likely to be concerned about the quality of life and the bread-and-butter issues of tourism—jobs, revenue (private and public), and other local issues.

INTERNATIONAL CONCERNS

At the international and national levels, governments are involved in policy formation in order to establish procedures pertaining to the entry and exit of travelers (both foreign and domestic). Tourism is an export industry; thus it affects the economic relationships between countries. It has an effect on the total environment of a country in areas such as history, scenery, culture, and archeology. Consequently, it is possible that, while wishing to attract a foreign market, the physical or cultural environment may be lost.[3]

When in Vienna, President Ronald Reagan stated to Soviet Secretary General Mikhail Gorbachev, "Imagine how much good we could accomplish, how the cause of peace would be served, if more individuals and families from our respective countries could come to know each other in a personal way. . . I feel the time is ripe for us to take bold new steps to open the way for our peoples to participate in an unprecedented way in the building of peace."

Manila Declaration
International organizations have recognized the importance of international policy development to enhance

the opportunity for residents of the various nations to travel. The organization that acts on behalf of international tourism is the WTO. At their meeting held at Manila, Philippines in 1980, which was attended by 107 delegations of the nations of the world, an effort was made to clarify the nature of tourism and its aspects and role in a dynamic and vastly changing world. They were trying to consider the responsibility of the various nations for the development and enhancement of tourism in a larger sense than purely economic. The basic principles agreed upon are known as the Manila Declaration. The major conclusions and agreements were:

1. Tourism is an essential life activity in that it directly affects social, cultural, educational, and economic activities of each nation.
2. Tourism is interrelated with other human activities.
3. Tourism is dependent upon paid vacations.
4. A basic universal declaration of human rights is the right to use leisure time and holidays to travel.
5. Tourism barriers and constraints should be recognized and overcome in order to allow freedom of travel.
6. Tourism's economic impact makes it a major factor in world development.
7. Domestic tourism is an important method to redistribute national income.
8. Economic return should not be the sole criterion for tourism. It should include an understanding of the individual's environment, nationality, and culture.
9. Free time is important to all individuals.
10. Social tourism should also reflect the need of less privileged individual's right of rest.
11. Tourism can facilitate social stability.
12. Tourism creates new employment.
13. Tourism promotes mutual knowledge and understanding among diverse cultures.
14. International cooperation in tourism requires respect of the integrity of individual states.
15. Bilateral and multilateral technical assistance and financing constitutes a pooling of resources, ultimately beneficial to all.
16. Tourism should be a part of the formal and informal education process.
17. Youth tourism should be encouraged and facilitated.
18. The spiritual elements such as fulfillment, education, equality, dignity, identity, respect, and moral heritage should take precedence over technical and material elements.
19. The WTO is the body that should bring about international cooperation in the field of tourism.

The importance of the Manila Declaration is that so many nations of the world agreed on the importance of tourism, both domestic and international, and leisure time to their respective citizens. The first step in strengthening and increasing interaction between nations of the world comes from such statements of agreement. Until this meeting tourism had been viewed in marginal and restrictive terms that, for many years, limited and distorted its expansion. The conference brought out tourism's true potential and revealed the many facets of its activities at the service of mankind, showing it to be a force for the enhancement of the quality of human life in both a national and international context and in social, cultural, educational, political, and economic areas.

International Organizations

There is a need for international organizations to work together in an effort to create policy favorable to international tourism. The WTO has little control over international policy. Through its members from various countries and other organizations, it tries to facilitate programs and policies. The tourism officials of individual countries may then apply these programs in making their own government's policies.

A number of organizations that have affected tourism either directly or indirectly are described below.

International Monetary Fund (IMF)

The IMF influences exchange rates and controls and financial policy on a global scale. Currency exchange and controls imposed by governments can be considerable obstacles to tourist-related business and trade. Delays in currency conversion from credit cards can cause serious problems for companies providing service to tourists within a country. In 1978, Lufthansa discontinued its service to Kinshasa and closed its office in Zaire because of its inability to convert the local money into hard currency.

International Civil Aviation Organization (ICAO)

The ICAO consists of about 150 member countries. It recommends practices dealing with safety, the regularity and efficiency of air navigation, and customs and immigration procedures.

Customs Cooperation Council (CCC)

The Customs Cooperation Council in Brussels consists of more than ninety countries. It considers issues relating to customs; procedures, classification, and valuation of goods; and harmonization and simplification of practices.

Organization for Economic Cooperation and Development (OECD)

This organization, similar to a number of others established to handle regional concerns, adopted a new tourism policy for its twenty-four member countries to encourage the exchange of tourists between nations.

National Policies and Agreements

In addition to international organizations affecting policy and regulations, agreements between two nations can set policy between them. In 1986, the United States and Israel signed a ten-point "Memorandum on Tourism." In this agreement both parties:

1. Affirmed the importance of the unhindered flow of tourists between their respective countries;

2. Expressed their resolve to analyze the ways and means of removing obstacles to the flow of tourism and to explore practical measures to produce more open trade;

3. Welcomed each other's nationals to visit the other's territory;

4. Expressed the hope that the citizens and organizations of both countries would enter into sister city and other cooperative relationships that would encourage bilateral tourism;

6. Encouraged efforts to facilitate bilateral tourist traffic;

7. Acknowledged the importance of exchanges of information in the different areas of tourism such as investment development of projects, promotion, and tourism services;

8. Recognized the necessity to improve the reliability and comparability of tourism statistics;

9. Commended efforts to raise the standards of training and education in the field of tourism;

10. Recognized the role of national tourist offices in developing tourism between the two countries.[4]

One of the major problems in the international exchange of tourism is the barriers that are created by nations. Today, tourism is increasingly being considered by nations as a part of international trade. Governments are beginning to accept this point of view, even though for years they have considered it an import or an export. It had never been a major issue in trade circles until the 1986 meeting of the General Agreement on Tariffs and Trade (GATT). The participants were urged to include tourism as a trade in service. They were also invited to become involved in the effort to reduce national barriers (both tariff and nontariff) to improve trade. It was felt that the value of tourism would be even greater if there were fewer nontariff restrictions affecting travel and tourism services. The *Travel & Tourism Analyst* stated

The problems confronting international tourism are many and varied. Some are peculiar to individual aspects of tourism, such as customs regulations, documentation formalities, and regulations affecting transportation, lodging and travel agencies. Some are more general in nature and apply to several aspects of tourism, such as market access and operation of subsidiary companies. Most of the problems do not lend themselves to quick solutions, particularly when actions are required by national legislatures or other deliberative bodies.[5]

Some restrictions are illustrated in Table 14-1. The problems and reasons for restrictions are well set out in *Travel & Tourism Analyst*. They are

Government monetary and financial policy goals often operate to the disadvantage of foreign-owned travel and tourism business. Exchange controls and restrictions on remittance of earnings tend to

discourage the establishment of businesses by foreigners. Investment laws which require minimum ownership by local nationals are intended to promote domestic economic development. Restrictions on the use of foreign-made promotional and advertising materials also are intended to stimulate local business enterprise. Discrimination against the activities of non-established businesses often is designed to encourage inward investment and employment of local nationals. In some countries, tourism promotion offices are established as government monopolies and private foreign companies are excluded to assure full control of the business.

Tourism involves many different businesses which are subject to a wide variety of laws and regulations. Many of these regulations are not necessarily designed specifically to afford competitive advantages to the businesses of local nationals, although they may have that effect. The government motivations cited in this section are intended merely to illustrate how international tourism businesses are affected; they do not represent an exhaustive listing of the reasons behind regulations or restrictions.[6]

Problems such as these can be addressed by the various international organizations discussed above and, where possible, they can create policy to increase tourist interchange between countries. Policy then, is a set of guidelines that sets forth the specific objectives and actions that should be followed to meet the needs of those in both the destination region and the region of origin.

NATIONAL CONCERNS

All countries can benefit from domestic and international tourism; it is felt that the people of each country should be offered off-the-job recreational opportunities. The foundations for such a policy are that:

1. Tourism and recreation are important to a country, not only because of the numbers of people they serve and the vast human, financial, and physical resources they employ, but because of the great benefits tourism, recreation, and relaxed activities confer on individuals and on society as a whole.

2. Government can encourage tourism and recreation implicitly in their statutory commitments to the shorter work year and to passenger transportation systems, and explicitly in a number of legislative enactments to promote tourism and support development of outdoor recreation, cultural attractions, and historic and natural heritage resources.

3. Disposable incomes and leisure time can be expected to increase in cyclical patterns in developed and developing countries. As economic and political systems develop more complex global relationships,

TABLE 14-1 CHECKLIST OF TYPES OF OBSTACLE TO INTERNATIONAL TOURISM

I. Obstacles affecting the individual intending to travel
 1. Imposed by the home country:
  a) Currency restrictions imposed upon residents;
  b) Conditions and procedures for issue of travel documents;
  c) Customs allowances for returning residents;
  d) Restrictions on overseas travel.
 2. Imposed by the host country:
  a) Currency restrictions imposed upon visitors;
  b) Entry visas, identity documents, limitations on duration of stay;
  c) Formalities concerning entry of motor vehicles, pleasure boats or other craft;
  d) Formalities concerning applicability of drivers licenses, car insurance, etc.;
  e) Restrictions on acquisition of property by non-nationals (e.g. holiday flats);
  f) Taxes on international travelers.

II. Obstacles affecting companies providing services to facilitate travel (e.g. travel agents, tour operators)
 3. Limitations on foreign investment/equity participation.
 4. Restrictions on the establishment of foreign owned entities (branches and subsidiaries).
 5. Requirements for qualifications for operating professionally which are either directly discriminatory or more difficult for non-nationals to acquire.
 6. Restrictions on non-national personnel and employment (e.g. visas, work permits).
 7. Difficulties in obtaining licenses to operate.
 8. Relevant restrictions on transfer of funds in and out of the country (not covered under I above).
 9. Restrictions upon the ability of non-established foreign companies to solicit, advertise or sell direct to clients without locally established intermediaries.
 10. Distinction in EEC countries between EEC and non-EEC nationals with regard to the above items.

III. Obstacles affecting companies providing transportation (e.g. airlines, railways, coach operators, cruise liners)
 11–18. Categories as under II (3–10).
 19. Restrictions on non-national airlines, coach operators or cruise liners.
 20. Limitations on movements of passengers by foreign airlines or cruise ships.
 21. Discriminatory landing dues, taxes or port charges.
 22. Lack of reciprocal recognition of qualifications (e.g. air crew, site guides, coach drivers).
 23. Requirements for government employees to use national airlines/ferry services.
 24. Discriminatory access to special terms from state enterprises (e.g. airlines, railways), including differential commissions.
 25. Limitations on access to reservation systems.

IV. Obstacles affecting companies providing reception facilities (e.g. hotels, resorts, car hire firms)
 26–33. Categories as under II (3–10).
 34. Restrictions on imports of essential goods.
 35. Requirements for placing of contracts (e.g. for site development) with local enterprises.
 36. Discriminatory tax regimes for foreign entrants (including tax holidays not available to nationals).
 37. Restrictions on ownership by non-nationals (e.g. leasing only permitted) and problems related to security of tenure or repatriation of investments.
 38. Limitation on access to reservation systems.

V. Other obstacles
 39. Discriminatory regulations on health inspection/consumer protection, etc.
 40. Compulsory use of centralized governmental/municipal organizations or middlemen.

Source: Tourism Policy and International Tourism in OECD Countries in 1983, OECD 1984.

tourism and recreation will become ever more important aspects of our daily lives.

4. The existing and potential government involvement in tourism, recreation, and other related activities needs to be better coordinated to effectively respond to the national interest in tourism and recreation and, where appropriate, to meet the needs of local governments and the private sector.

Therefore, it is in the best interest of the citizens of all countries to develop a national tourism policy to:

—optimize the contribution of the tourism and recreation industries to economic prosperity, full em-

ployment, and the international balance of payments of the host country;

—make the opportunity for tourism and recreation, in the host country, universally accessible to all and to insure that present and future generations are afforded adequate tourism and recreation resources;

—contribute to personal growth, health, education, and intercultural appreciation of the geography, history, and ethnicity of the host country;

—encourage the entry of individuals traveling to and from the host country, in order to enhance international understanding and goodwill, consistent with immigration laws, the laws protecting the public health, and laws governing the import and export of goods and services;

—eliminate unnecessary trade barriers to the host country and to the tourism industry operating throughout the world;

—promote the continued development and availability of alternative personal payment mechanisms that facilitate national and international travel;

—promote quality, integrity, and reliability in all tourism and tourism-related services offered to visitors to the host country;

—preserve the historical and cultural foundations of the host country as a part of community life and development, and insure future generations an opportunity to appreciate and enjoy its rich heritage;

—insure the compatibility of tourism and recreation with other national interests in energy development and conservation, environmental protection, the judicious use of natural resources, and similar issues;

—assist in the collection, analysis, and dissemination of data that accurately measure the economic and social impact of tourism to and within the host country in order to facilitate planning in the public and private sectors; and

—harmonize, to the maximum extent possible, all governmental activities in support of tourism and recreation with the needs of the general public and the host countries, local governments, and the tourism and recreation industry, and to give leadership to all concerned with tourism, recreation, and national heritage preservation in the host countries.

Tourism and Foreign Policy

At the national level, tourism policy affects both the international community as well as the residents in the country. Many times, the policies are interwoven. Tourism policy at a national level has two uses, (1) as a tool of foreign policy, and, (2) as a general guideline to tourism development by and for the residents of that nation.

Foreign policy implications are broad. A strong case for government policies concerning tourism was made by Cord D. Hansen-Sturm in testimony before a senate committee in 1982. His testimony clearly and concisely indicated the essential character of tourism's role in foreign policy.

Von Clausewitz in the past, and legions of present day foreign policy theoreticians, have preoccupied themselves with war as an extension of foreign policy. However, few foreign policy experts have developed the more useful idea that tourism is at the very heart of the successful foreign policy of democracies. The international tourism industry forms the basic infrastructure of peace. Educational, scientific, cultural, political and commercial exchange among nations takes place in proportion to the ability of the international tourism industry to provide transportation, lodging and sustenance for international travelers. Foreign policies impact on tourism trends, and, even more importantly, changes in the tourism infrastructure alter foreign policies.

The international network of transportation routes, hotels, and restaurants, and its complex marketing and financial support system, make possible the movement of people across borders without which foreign policy as we know it would not exist. The principal elements of this world tourism network are also the principal symbols of international eminence of a nation; more visible and powerful in their effect on minds than are I.C.B.M.'s. Airline offices abroad with names such as Pan American, United, and Trans World; the American Express offices; the Sheraton and Marriott hotel chains; Olson Tour Buses in Europe; the Hilton cruise ships on the Nile, the Visa card and Citibank travelers checks—to cite a few prominent examples—symbolize to world citizens each day the power and influence of our nation.

. . . To summarize, the United States needs to incorporate tourism policy more effectively into its overall foreign policy as a prerequisite for tapping the enormous remaining potential of international travel to the United States from the industrial democracies. The United States cannot expect other developed countries to voluntarily dismantle their profitable national tourism plants which compete as destinations with the United States. A significant change in United States' tourism industry and government attitudes in the direction of a national view must take place before the federal government becomes an effective coordinator and promoter of United States' tourism exports.[7]

For some nations, tourism policy is a major part of their foreign policy. Most countries that have policies created by a centrally-planned government involve tourism in their foreign policy issues. For guests from other countries, the policy is designed to illustrate the benefits of the political system. This is strongly emphasized in the Soviet Union and China, where tour directors quickly and proficiently report the great strides society and the economy have made under socialism. The range of government involvement, and depth of policy from country to country, is considerable. Some, such as many of the centrally-planned economies, are fully involved in tourism while others, such as the United States, are less involved because they have no national policy.

The Case of United States Tourism Policy

United States policy is almost a policy to have no policy. The extreme under Ronald Reagan was to submit a budget for 1986 which would have eliminated the U.S. Travel and Tourism Administration. In 1973, a two-year study by the Tourism Resource Review Commission concluded that (1) the government's tourism efforts were in confusion and disarray. Over one hundred programs were found in more than fifty agencies that had direct concern with some aspect of tourism and that coordination of those agencies and further study of the programs were essential. (2) It recommended (and subsequent studies agreed) that a national tourism organization be established to execute a national policy on tourism.

The federal government partially recognized its role in tourism in 1940 when it passed the Domestic Travel Act, which was designed to encourage travel within the United States rather than internationally because of turbulent world conditions. After the Second World War, with mass tourism becoming internationally significant and the United States sending more visitors abroad than it was receiving, little was done to reverse this trend. President Eisenhower rejected a proposal for the federal government to become involved in a tourism program. Finally, under the Kennedy administration, the U.S. Travel Service was created with the 1961 International Travel Act to promote international travel to the United States. During both the Kennedy and Johnson administrations, some effort was made to increase the nation's programs, but little support was received. Members of Congress established a tourism caucus of 123

members in the House of Representatives; it grew to 255 members. Their specific areas of interest were energy, national tourism policy, improving transportation services, and federal tax policy as it related to travel and tourism.

One function of the caucus was to provide a steady flow of information, relevant to tourism, to Congress, the administration, and other appropriate federal agencies. By January, 1980, the group had persuaded President Carter's chief domestic policy advisor, Stuart Eizenstat, to support the travel industry. The Department of Energy appointed a high-ranking official to work with the industry, giving it a channel of communication with a federal agency that would make critical decisions affecting the availability of fuel.[8] Even with this new found support in the Carter administration, President Carter "pocket vetoed" a bill in 1980 that would have created a new independent agency and an advisory board dominated by industry. Shortly after President Reagan took office, the National Tourism Policy Act was passed and signed somewhat reluctantly by him; his budget director favored the elimination of the U.S. Travel Service. This changed the name of the U.S. Travel Service to the United States Travel and Tourism Administration (USTTA) and established it at the under-secretary level. However, under the Reagan administration the office has been in jeopardy; it has been saved only by strong

America's oldest theme park, Knott's Berry Farm in California. Photo courtesy of Anaheim Area Visitor & Convention Bureau.

action from the Congress. Linda K. Ritcher expressed the problem of this lack of support:

> . . . Still, given the alarming U.S. balance of trade deficit, it must seem bizarre that the Reagan administration begrudges the U.S. Travel and Tourism Administration not only a mere $12 million, much of which goes for overseas promotion, but indeed its very existence. Foreign tourists, on the other hand, contribute $14 billion to the American economy, spending per capita far more than their American counterparts. As the tourism slogan for the current National Tourism Week states: "Tourism Work$ for us."

Comparisons with other country's spending levels are misleading, Ritcher continues, because there are

> . . . key differences in the industry structure in the USA as opposed to many other nations. For one thing, the USA does not have a national airline, has only limited jurisdiction over a scanty rail system, and only loosely regulates the bus system. Nor does it own hotels as many countries like Mexico, India, Spain and Portugal, and most socialist countries do. Thus, the vast bulk of American tourism promotion is under the primary control and direction of the private sector.[9]

David Edgell, points out that

> Tourism policy in the United States is in its infancy and needs to be nurtured, understood, and supported. Only recently are we seeing travel and tourism courses and programs of study increasing at colleges and universities. A field of inquiry becomes a serious subject for policy analysis and research only when there [is] interest and recognition. . . tourism policy will find its place in the hierarchy of this nation's goals and objectives only through creative leadership, innovative research, academic inquiry, industry cooperation and governmental support. This interest and recognition of tourism must take place today; tomorrow may be too late.[10]

Further, Edgell made ten suggestions:

1. The United States must recognize it has a "comparative advantage." It does little to take advantage or use that advantage to lower the tourism deficit in the balance of trade payments. A first step was the "visa waiver" provision in the new Immigration Reform Act of 1986. But more must be done to make it easier to visit the United States.

2. The states, territories, and private sector need to recognize an opportunity exists for expanding and developing their tourism potential to its fullest by cooperating and assisting in sharing information and technology.

3. Policy needs to be developed to address the problem of seasonality. Seasonality causes under-employment and under-utilization of facilities.

4. Policy needs to be developed to resolve the problems of overcrowding and misuse of the environment.

5. There must be increased management capability to assure a successful industry.

6. Programs will be needed to deal with more sophisticated consumers and greater array of specialized travel services.

7. Policy issues for national and international organizations should always include health, security, and safety.

8. Plans need to be developed to handle or deal with long-term problems, such as terrorism, Chernobyl-type accidents, hostage-taking and hijackings, earthquakes and storms, and so on.

9. Trade negotiations should focus on tourism.

10. Recognize the importance of increasing worldwide contact and understanding between people.[11]

Linda Ritcher suggested that ninety-nine percent of the United States tourist-industry businesses are classified as small businesses. The industry is composed of many small travel agents, lodging and tour facilities, all of which would benefit from an increase in foreign tourism. Current concerns of the industry are expressed in *TRAVEL/LOG*, an official publication of the Travel and Tourism Government Affairs Council. They are USTTA funding, international visitor facilitation through visa waiver and overturning the customs user fees, energy usage taxes that may be expressed in an oil import fee, and an increased budget for the National Park Service.

Tourism Policy in Developing Nations

While the overwhelming majority of travel is among the developed nations, there is still considerable travel to the developing nations, bringing them a steady flow of money (hard currency) for use in foreign trade. Additionally, many of the jobs in travel are low skilled and labor intensive; many developing nations see this as a benefit. One problem facing developing nations has been the capital costs for construction of the buildings and the infrastructure needed for tourism.

Another problem facing these nations is their strong dependence upon the market. Economic changes in the tourists' countries of origin can have serious consequences on the economies of the host developing nation. For example, the former Commonwealth nations of the Caribbean were totally dependent on foreign carriers. It was estimated that in peak season, even if all the planes allocated to the region were full, they would still have a thirty percent vacancy rate on beds.[12] Thus, Air Jamaica, British West Indies Airways, and Caribbean International were created.

Government policy in developing nations has to be more extensive than for developed nations due to the limited nature of private investment funds. They need to work either with multinational corporations or make direct economic investment in tourism. C. L. Jenkins, stated

There are obvious reasons why governments in developing countries should positively intervene in tourism. When funds are required to support investment in tourism, the government is often the only agency able to raise or guarantee the loan. At the macro level, the government has ultimate responsibility for the allocation of funds and resources for specific sectors. It is a government responsibility to decide on regulations and loans which can affect tourism (e.g., foreign-exchange regulations, fiscal incentives for developments, vocational training for tourism, physical planning, land-use allocations).[13]

STATE OR PROVINCIAL CONCERNS

The next major level of government, after the national government, which is highly involved in tourism, is the state or provincial government, and for much the same reasons. They receive tourists from other countries, states and/or provinces. Tourism is far too important to be allowed to develop without policy direction and planning. In the United States and Canada, tourism ranks as one of the top three generators of jobs and income. For many, it is first in importance. Decisions made by state agencies and legislatures can have an affect on

—The rate of growth of the tourist sector
—The location of tourist facilities
—The quality of tourist services
—Public attitudes toward, and treatment of, tourists
—The seasonal demand of tourism

In order to meet these obligations, the states have established organizations. There are three basic types: travel development within another department; a public or quasi-public travel commission (bureau); and an independent or semi-independent travel development department.

California and Montana are examples of the first type. In California tourism is part of the department concerned with economic development for the state. In 1986, California began to take a more active role in promoting visitors to the state, and asking residents to vacation within the state. In Montana, tourism is organized as a Travel Promotion Unit within the Department of Highways.

Hawaii, Utah, New Mexico, and Michigan are examples of the public travel bureau. Michigan, Utah, and New Mexico have organizations that are under public control and leadership. In Michigan, the travel bureau is within the Department of Commerce. It has a board of directors referred to as the Michigan Travel Commission, made up of representatives of convention bureaus, the state travel bureau, and consumer representatives appointed by the governor.

The state of Tennessee is an example of the independent tourism office. It is set up on a cabinet level, directly under the governor. This is helpful because the tourism office has direct communication with the governor, and closer contact with the legislature during the budget-making process.[14]

LOCAL CONCERNS

Almost all sizable cities and urban counties have organizations concerned with tourism. An organizational chart prepared by *Tourism USA* to help local communities establish tourism councils was presented in Chapter 9.

The suggested organizational model (see Figure 9-1) provides for a tourism council that is responsible for establishing tourism philosophy and policies, and sets the overall goal for development of tourism. This proposal uses citizen committees that are involved in a variety of planning functions and serve as a source of information and opinion on which decisionmakers rely when selecting programs for implementation. In this organization, a director of tourism carries out the policies of the council, and is responsible for the basic functions of research, data collection, and marketing and promotion.

Mill and Morrison suggested that at the local level, a tourism organization evolves first as a small, informal group of people who get together to seek additional help from governmental or community agencies. When agencies become aware of how much the community is affected by tourism, they may form a subcommittee on tourism as part of the chamber of commerce or city council. Next, when people realize that certain jobs can best be accomplished by people who share the same priorities, associations can form. At the final stage, a full-time executive director may be hired to direct the organization's work.[15]

Because of the economic and social importance of tourism, the public has to be represented and take an active role in it. The degree of involvement will depend on many factors, such as the political philosophy of the government and residents, and the maturity of the destination area as a tourist attraction.

REGULATION

With the formulation of tourism policy, the next step in the process is some form of regulation. At the multinational level, most regulations affecting the travel industry have occurred by agreements. Most are concerned with air travel, governmental restrictions such as visa control, and trade issues with tourism as an element of trade.

Most of the airline agreements have been an outgrowth of the International Civil Aviation Conference in Chicago in 1944. These are referred to as the five freedoms, which were not fully agreed upon by all nations and never ratified, and became the basis for a number of international air agreements, many of which were discussed in Chapter 9. Currently, two of the most serious problems for airlines are the deregulation of the United States airlines, and foreign governments maintaining their controls.

Some countries such as Canada, Switzerland, West Germany, and the United States, believe that little regulation is the best regulation. The main function of their official national tourism offices is promoting tourism to their respective countries.

State and local municipal governments legislate laws that affect tourism. One of their most important functions relating to tourism is the regulation of land use through zoning and municipal master plans. Another state level concern is consumer protection legislation, which covers many areas.

COORDINATION

As we've said, in the United States there are over fifty governmental agencies involved in tourism. There is little coordination between them and no overall policy. In addition, what federal legislation there is, seldom considers the impact upon tourism.

There are a number of regulatory agencies in the United States directly or indirectly concerned with tourism. They are

Federal Aviation Administration (FAA):
—Regulates the manufacturing, operation, and maintenance of aircraft
—Maintains air traffic control centers
—Determines and certifies the proficiency and physical fitness of flight crews
—Certifies airports
—Inspects air navigation facilities
—Concerned with flight safety
Federal Highway Administration (FHA):
—Develops highway safety standards
—Identifies and monitors locations where serious accidents have occurred
—Involves itself in highway design, construction, and maintenance
—Investigates common carrier accidents
—Reviews commercial driver qualifications
—Inspects common carrier terminals and vehicles for safety
—Conducts safety education programs
Federal Maritime Commission (FMC):
—Regulates common carriers in domestic offshore commerce and U.S. flagships in foreign commerce
Federal Trade Commission (FTC):
—Controls and prevents deceptive advertising

Interstate Commerce Commission (ICC):
—Regulates bus lines, railroads, water carriers, and express agencies in both interstate and foreign commerce
National Highway Traffic Safety Administration (NHTSA):
—Regulates vehicle safety standards
—United States Coast Guard (USCG)
—Polices coastal and inland waters and navigable rivers
—Sets uniform standards for safety and inspects recreational boats for compliance
—Educates small boat operators in safe operation
—Controls traffic
Department of Transportation
—Regulates air safety standards
—Investigates air accidents

In addition, there has been little coordination between the federal government and states, or among the states themselves. What coordination has developed has been joint advertising to attract visitors to a region rather than a specific state. Certainly, much more can be done.

RESEARCH AND REVIEW

1. What are three policy issues important at the international level?
2. Discuss the importance of the Manila Declaration.
3. Identify four international organizations and describe their role in tourism.
4. Why do governments develop national tourist offices?
5. How does tourism policy affect the residents of a country and the international community, as a whole?
6. What role can tourism play in a country's foreign policy?
7. Outline the history of U.S. tourism policy.
8. What are some important considerations for the U.S. to consider with respect to its tourism policy?
9. Discuss the problems tourism policy must resolve in the developing nations.
10. What are the three basic types of state tourism organizations? Give examples of each.

ENDNOTES
1. Mill and Morrison, pp. 271–272.
2. David L. Edgell, "The Formulation of Tourism Policy—A Managerial Framework," in *Travel, Tourism and Hospitality Research* (NY: John Wiley & Sons, 1986), pp. 23–32.
3. Mill and Morrison, p. 242.
4. "Tourism Agreements," *Israel Travel News*, Aug./Sept. 1986.
5. Bernard Ascher and David L. Edgell, "Barriers to International Travel: Removing Restrictions to Trade in Service and Tourism," *Travel & Tourism Analyst* (London: Economist Publications, Oct. 1986), pp. 3–13.
6. Ibid., p. 9.

7. Cord D. Hansen-Sturm, testimony before the Senate Committee on Commerce, Science, and Transportation, 1982.
8. Bernetta Hayes, "The Congressional Travel and Tourism Caucus and U.S. National Tourism Policy," *International Journal of Tourism Management* (June 1981), pp. 121–137.
9. Linda Ritcher, "Fragmented Politics of U.S. Tourism," *Tourism Management,* Vol. 6, No. 3 (Sept. 1985), pp. 161–173.
10. David L. Edgell, *International Tourism Prospects 1987–2000* (Washington, DC: U.S. Dept. of Commerce, 1987), p. ii.
11. Ibid., pp. 35–41.
12. C. L. Jenkins, "Tourism Policies in Developing Countries: A Critique," *International Journal of Tourism Management* (Mar. 1980), p. 26.
13. Ibid., p. 27.
14. Mill and Morrison, p. 258.
15. Ibid., pp. 263–264.

CHAPTER 15

PLANNING

Planning is a process of decision-making concerning the future of a destination area or attraction. It is a dynamic process of determining goals, systematically considering alternative actions to achieve those goals, implementing the chosen alternative, and evaluating that choice to determine if it is successful. The planning process views the environment—which includes political, physical, social, and economic elements—as interrelated and interdependent components, which all need to be taken into account when considering the future of a destination area or attraction.

Tourism planning is recognized as vital. A major reason for the stagnation and decline of a destination or attraction, as discussed earlier, results from either the lack of planning, or poor planning. However, it appears that tourism will continue to increase both domestically and internationally, since it is so deeply enmeshed within the economy of most countries. Certainly, one of the great lessons learned from tourism is of the danger of uncontrolled development, which can lead to misuse of land, a complete unwanted change in the environment, and serious stress between cultures. The important concern today is how to attract as many tourists as possible, while minimizing the negative impact on an area or country. This raises a number of questions that a government must answer in attempting to ascertain the effectiveness of its tourism program in attaining these goals. They are:

—How large should the tourist industry be?
—What level of dominance should it have in an area or country?
—Should it be spatially concentrated or dispersed?
—How much foreign capital will it draw?

—What impact will tourism have on the environment?

—Will it be helpful in bringing technological skills to the area?

—Will it provide the country with desirable foreign exchange?

—What effect will it have on the local population?

—Will undesirable elements of other societies invade the country?

The answers to these and other questions are important in assisting countries trying to determine the role that the tourist trade will play, and to what degree it will take part. The nature of the three most important changes—social, economic, and environmental—will be discussed in the following chapters. It suffices to say, at this point, that proper planning should serve to emphasize the nature of the effect the planners want tourism to have on the country. This desired impact will, of course, differ between developed and undeveloped countries.

The major types of formal planning practiced today include

—Economic development planning

—Physical land use planning (city, urban, and regional)

—Social facility planning (educational, medical, and recreational)

—Comprehensive planning integrating economic, physical, infrastructure, and social elements

—Corporate planning

TOURISM PLANNING IN DEVELOPED COUNTRIES

Depending upon the political characteristics of a country, planning for tourists is less difficult in developed countries than it is in developing ones. Whatever the country, planning is important and should provide a quality environment for both tourists and residents. The planning process for tourism development involves the same general planning concerns as do city and regional planning. Most problems involve policy decisions on alternative land uses for the health and welfare of the citizens. In those countries with less control over the economic sector, guidelines and ordinances can restrict private development to prescribed areas, while in others, all development can be directed by the central government.

The stimulation of tourism is an important part of the role of government organizations. Through research and market analysis, target countries or states can be identified as potential tourist generators. Government assistance in direct advertising to attract people is well within the realm of proper planning.

In developed economies, planning and construction of the infrastructure is also important, particularly in areas that do not have one already present. For regions that have an existing infrastructure, the planning process should include alternatives to improve or further develop it.

TOURISM PLANNING IN DEVELOPING COUNTRIES

Tourism is important in bringing in much needed foreign money to developing countries. Mexico and Spain, for instance, have benefited considerably from tourism. For a number of other countries such as Cyprus, Jordan, Malta, Mauritius, Morocco, and Tunisia, tourism receipts account for a significant share of the national income. Two other advantages are increased employment opportunities, and the development of a much needed infrastructure. Roads, water, and sewage systems provided for tourists also help local industries. Government involvement in tourism planning is particularly important, not only to develop the needed infrastructure, but also to determine the cultural impact tourism will make on the environment and people.

If international tourism is allowed to expand without any regulation or plan, then problems can be expected in Africa and Latin America, similar to those already developing along the Spanish coast. Some Caribbean islands and Bali already feel the problems of poorly-planned tourist development. An ill-planned tourist industry will create problems of visual monotony, uniformity, and dull leveling of the landscape. It is, therefore, necessary for governments to be involved in all stages of tourism, from preliminary planning to market promotion. When private investment is lacking, the state needs to become involved. In many cases, private investments are in areas of high potential income and may serve to localize the tourism industry. In 1973, the United Nations Conference on Trade and Development drafted a document outlining the elements of tourism policy for developing countries. They indicated governments should:

1. Conduct general research and studies concerning tourism, including the collection of statistics that are indispensable both for research and policy formulation;

2. Undertake or sponsor studies of the tourism market associated with this research with a view to determining the country's potential;

3. Survey the country's tourist assets and attractions;

4. Draw up a general strategy of the development, including such matters as land use and physical planning, which areas of the country should enjoy priority in the location of resources of tourism, and provision for guidance as to which type of tourism is desirable;

5. Assess, in the general planning context, the probable requirements for accommodations and other facilities (including infrastructure) corresponding to the expected demand;

6. Carry out marketing and publicity campaigns with a view to promoting tourism from other countries;

7. Provide and support vocational training programs;

8. Regulate and control the various components of the tourist industry to whatever extent is considered necessary in the general public

interest, the interest of the industry itself, and that of domestic and foreign tourists;

9. Provide basic infrastructure service which any growth of tourism necessitates.[1]

Further, planning in developing nations must also account for tourism's cultural impact. Many times the culture may be so fragile that tourism can bring about considerable change. This is not generally true of developed countries. The presence of millions of tourists in England and other European countries affects the physical environment with the construction of hotels and other tourist-related facilities, but has little direct impact on changing the culture. In a developing society, the people tend to adopt the lifestyle of the tourists and are quick to change their clothing, foods, and other customs. In this way, the local culture becomes considerably altered.

THE PLANNING PROCESS

The planning procedure is best understood as a series of steps for the proposed development.

Step 1. Taking inventory and describing the social, political, physical, and economic environment.
Step 2. Forecasting or projecting trends for future development.
Step 3. Establishing goals and objectives.
Step 4. Identifying and considering the alternative plans of action to reach the goals and objectives.
Step 5. Selecting preferred alternative(s).
Step 6. Developing a strategy for implementing the plan.
Step 7. Implementing the plan.
Step 8. Evaluating the plan.
Step 9. Reviewing and revising the plan.

Planning is an on-going process that must keep up with the changing character of the world and of the destination or attraction itself.

This process can best be illustrated by a study, completed by Salah Wahab in 1979, of the planning for the coastal areas of Egypt. In the late 1970s, the government felt that tourism to Egypt was congested for both the international as well as domestic tourist. International tourism had been concentrated in a limited number of centers such as Cairo, Luxor, and Aswan. This gave rise to many problems resulting from large numbers of tourists visiting the unique archeological sites during the main tourist season. Domestic tourism was concentrated in the well-established and traditional summer resorts in Alexandria and Port Said. That also caused problems related to crowds, congestion, and pressure on the infrastructure during those peak months. Therefore, the government established a policy to create new tourist regions. The Mediterranean northwest coast, the Red Sea coast, the Sinai, and Lake Nubia are regions that Egyptian authorities felt had the potential for devel-

opment. They chose the North Coast, and began the planning process to ascertain its viability, and the alternatives available for development.

Step one was the inventory and description stage. The physical characteristics, economic features, and infrastructure in the proposed development area were identified. The physical characteristics are both topographic and climatic. The climate is Mediterranean; it is characterized by mild winters with some rain and plenty of sunshine, and a bearable hot, dry summer, cooled by a pleasant, mild sea breeze. The soils, vegetation, and water resources were identified. The infrastructure existed. There was sufficient water for present use. The natural mineral resources, such as gypsum and limestone, were few. They were used for industrial purposes, and agricultural and animal products. These industries accounted for more than eighty percent of the total employment in the area. Tourism did not exist.

Step two is the forecast stage. For example, the importance of agriculture was indicated, and the report also included a statement about the area's future as an agricultural area.[2]

Goals and objectives, step three, were formulated in light of the analysis of regional resources and constraints, as well as national priorities. Wahab reported that data was compiled and evaluated in terms of regional, national, public, and private objectives, with several alternatives given for each level of the project (steps four and five).

Step six, was to develop a plan to implement the strategy. The physical planning was done in two phases. The first was a conceptual plan of the development, and the second was a detailed land use, urban design plan, and allocation of resources for the development program. The plan for the West Coast was to develop the area for domestic tourism, with distinct areas for foreigners. As part of the detailed plan, the area was divided into four zones, each with a unique blend of attractive topography and interesting geological formations. Each zone was projected to reach a certain size, and the requirements for a master plan were given.[3]

At the time of the report, the plan had not been implemented (step seven) and is still to be completed. To adequately develop this area, the Egyptian government will not only need to finish the process, but continue the research and planning as an on-going program.

Mill and Morrison have identified five basic purposes of planning as it relates to tourism. They are

1. *Identifying alternative approaches to:*
    Marketing
    Development
    Industry organization
    Tourism awareness
    Support services and activities
2. *Adapting to the unexpected in:*
    General economic conditions
    Energy supply/demand situations
    Values and life-styles
    Fortunes of individual industries
    Other factors in the external environment

3. *Maintaining uniqueness in:*
   Natural features and resources
   Local cultural and social fabric
   Local architecture
   Historical monuments and landmarks
   Local events and activities
   Parks and outdoor sports areas
   Other features of the destination area
4. *Creating the desirable, such as in:*
   High level of awareness of the benefits of tourism
   Clear and positive image of the area as a tourism destination
   Effective industry organization
   High level of cooperation among individual operators
   Effective marketing, signage, and travel information programs
   Other objectives
5. *Avoiding the undesirable, such as in:*
   Friction and unnecessary competition among individual tourism operators
   Hostile and unfriendly attitudes of local residents toward tourists
   Damage or undesirable, permanent alteration of natural features and historical resources
   Loss of cultural identities
   Loss of a share in the market
   Stoppage of unique local events and activities
   Overcrowding, congestion, and traffic problem
   Pollution
   High seasonal use.
   Other factors [4]

Clearly, the purpose of planning is to enhance the area to provide for the tourist, and to avoid the negative physical, human, marketing, organization, and other impacts that can occur in tourism without planning.

GOAL FORMULATION

After identifying the assets and resources, and having some idea of the future of tourism in the area, the goals and objectives need to be set within a realistic and achievable framework. Often, the observed goals in most tourism plans are

—To stimulate employment, income, and economic development
—To improve communication systems
—To minimize degradation of the environment
—To increase the average length of tourists' visits

By and large, issues covered by tourism goals should include statements of what tourism is expected to contribute to the general goals of the region. Some of these are

—Community development
—Heritage and environmental conservation

—Enhancement of cultural identity
—Provision of leisure opportunities
—Population and demographic change
—Social welfare
—The provision and maintenance of amenities. [5]

Goals should be set specifically for the many segments of the industry. They should be consistent with the policies of the destination area.

TOURISM DEVELOPMENT

With the completion of the planning process, the next stage is the development of the destination area or attraction. Development occurs in three stages. First is the analysis of tourism projects, suggested in the planning process as suitable for the area. This is often referred to as the prefeasibility and technical study phase of the development. The second stage identifies the financing and investment strategies necessary to determine the economic feasibility. Last, the construction and operation phase, which, for some large projects, may not begin for some time after step two; in some cases, perhaps up to ten years later.

ANALYSIS OF TOURISM PROJECTS

In 1978, the OAS prepared a report on preinvestment studies of tourism projects. They indicated that the main purpose of a preinvestment study is to provide the planners and/or potential investors with the analytical framework for formulating and appraising investment potential early in the decision-making process. Thus, they conclude that a preinvestment study should show whether

a. *The project seems to (1) meet the minimum standards for the economy, (2) be technically feasible, and (3) be functional of priority within the tourism sector; or*
b. *The project is marginal, and/or critical parameters cannot be determined with certainty; or*
c. *The project fails to meet minimum standards by a wide margin.* [6]

The purpose is to arrive at one of the conclusions as quickly as possible to avoid costly mistakes.

Objective of the Project

The OAS recommended that all lending agencies require a statement of purpose, and a review of current literature on the project. The objectives relevant to both the direct and indirect impact of the area need to be stated in a clear, precise manner. An objective frequently stated by tourism studies concerns the preservation and/or development of a natural resource.

The OAS pointed out that:

1. *An attraction. . . will motivate people to travel at their leisure to see or enjoy it;*

2. *The superstructure (tourism facilities) to accommodate visitors (hotels, lodges, motels, bungalows, etc., restaurants, discotheques/night clubs, and travel agent and guide services) [should] directly serve the tourist.*
3. *The infrastructure to service airports, airlines, ports, highways, trains, ferries, etc., also urban services, such as potable water systems, sanitary and storm sewage systems, solid waste removal, electrical power, and telecommunications). . . . directly serves superstructure and attractions.*[7]

The alternatives to be considered—such as deciding whether the water needed for the tourism project would be better used for increasing irrigation for agriculture—are basic. At this stage, the study should identify the factors that will justify the project, but not include data or an indepth analysis. The justification of most projects should include a statement of the degree to which the project is critical to both the tourism sector and the national development plans; the target coverage; the efficiency of the project; the social benefits; the risk and flexibility of the options.

Demand for Tourism
Demand and supply are the two major components of market analysis. They relate to world and regional trends, major flows, causative factors, means of transportation, activities at the destination, types of accommodations, and facilities demanded. Most of this information can be obtained from secondary sources such as the WTO, or statistical publications of IATA, or the International Civil Aviation Organization, etc.

Demand analysis at the country level should include

—total number of visitors
—visitor expenditures
—length of stay
—motive for visit
—visitor country (and in some cases city) of origin
—visitor's last vacation or tourism trip
—means of arrival
—lodging demand
—activity and internal transport preferences in the country of the project
—form of tourism sales
—personal socioeconomic characteristics
—seasonal use

The demand characteristics associated with the reasons for travel such as pleasure, business, visits to friends and relatives, ethnic ties, religion, study, and health can be isolated for further analysis.

Tourism Supply
The tourism supply statement should be brief since the situation in the destination region and in competing destinations would have been described in the tourism plan; thus, a complete description is unnecessary in the prein-

vestment study. The preinvestment study may raise problems which would hamper the development of the supply situation.

Market Projection
Market projection should cover the precise type of attraction or facility, numbers of tourists expected, and their length of stay, the prices tourists would be willing to pay to pay, and some projection of the distribution of expenditures.

The supply projection will include both an inventory of the supply and the competition:

Training
In some small and/or developing countries with an immature tourism industry, training will need to be provided. The main elements of a training program should consider

—the manpower resources required by the project,
—those manpower resources available in the country,
—those who might be trained, and
—those who should be contracted from abroad for an initial period of time

While a full labor study is usually not needed, a minimum amount of data would include the number of employees required by class of hotel, restaurant, etc., by geographic location, by sex and by level of training or education; and the type of skills required, age, sex, education and other pertinent information such as seasonal employment, previous employment, salary, etc.

Tourism Sector Plan and Government Priorities
After having established the project objectives and deciding upon a project proposal

the study should indicate the manner in which the project idea serves plan objectives and identifies any outstanding policy issues. The range of possible issues of a policy nature which might affect tourism projects are numerous; they could relate to land use policy, policy toward indigenous communities, transportation strategy, archeological sites, regional development, to cite only a few examples. Where the concept of the project requires a policy decision, or an extraordinary budget allocation, it is not too early to seek at least a tentative decision in the course of the preinvestment study. . . .[8]

Project Technical Description
While the definition of the project would describe the project in general, the technical description provides the details (the prime components) of the project. It should

—Provide a discussion and an analysis of the main technical alternatives

—List the economic, technical, and safety standards required for the components and subprojects
—Describe the role of each component
—State the quantities and types of materials, equipment, and human or natural resources needed
—Indicate the inputs required for operation and maintenance
—Indicate the possible constraints or difficulties likely to be encountered by the project and their potential resolution and/or consequence
—Include a work plan including the major steps required
—Describe the capacity of the subproject

Investment Costs

Usually the cost estimates are separated into unit parts such as land, labor, materials and equipment, and professional services (including administration, technical assistance, and training). Each of these must be evaluated.

Operating Costs

These are the recurring costs needed for both operating and maintaining the project once it is completed. This estimate should be made for both the project and subproject, taking into account that the life expectancy of subprojects and projects are not the same. This will mean that the rate of depreciation, the scrap or residual value of the investment, and capital replacement requirements must be determined.

These costs are usually compared as a ratio to the total cost, as a ratio to total sales, or as a ratio of the overall operation of the project to the overall industry to determine the relative profitability of the project and subprojects.

Benefits

The development plans should also include the benefits, the income derived from the tourists' expenditures. Other economic benefits are considered elsewhere. This is done by pricing the components of the project, and applying the prices to the quantities of goods and services projected in the technical description of the project.

Financial Analysis

This includes profit and loss statements as well as capital recovery time, and financial planning (which indicates the source of investment capital). Loan and equity, foreign and domestic sources, and the terms of each, require weighty decisions of the financial planners, and should be clearly distinguished. In other words, a full financial statement, including the source of funding, must be prepared.

Sensitivity and Risk

An analysis must be made to determine if the project is vulnerable to failure; to see if improving the design of the project will increase the value; and to improve understanding of the nature and workings of the project. Sensitivity analysis enables risks to be identified, and suggests methods of redesigning that would reduce risk.

Socio/Economic Evaluation

Governments must not only consider the financial profitability of a project, but also its value to the national economy. One important element of the project is its availability to the local residents. In addition, this analysis takes into account factors such as income distribution—the income derived from providing goods and services to the project versus other projects, and some form of social cost/benefits analysis.

FINANCING AND INVESTMENT STRATEGIES

Financing for destination development projects is carried out by both private and governmental agencies. As the size of projects grow, they become more difficult to fund without some form of government assistance. The private sources include major institutional lenders such as savings and loans, insurance companies, credit unions, banks, and trust companies. Lending institutions require:

1. Adequate collateral or security, in many cases the land or other assets of the project.
2. Appropriate equity capital be invested by the developers.
3. A history of successful management experience in projects of a similar nature.
4. A study indicating evidence of the feasibility of the project.
5. Evidence of the viability of the tourism market as a long-term project.

Today, economic growth is of such importance to governments at all levels, that each level is willing to assist in the development of a project, either directly through low interest loans, through land swaps or donations, or indirectly through tax policies. Mill and Morrison suggested some types of financial incentives government agencies may provide to assist developers:

—Nonrefundable grants
—Low interest loans
—Interest rebate on interest costs of the project
—Forgivable loans
—Loan guarantees
—Working capital loans
—Equity participation
—Training grants
—Infrastructure assistance
—Leaseback
—Land grants or consolidation for purchase
—Tax deferrals or holidays such as sales tax rebates
—Special taxing districts to reduce property tax
—Tax reductions
—Issuance of bonds[9]

COST-BENEFIT ANALYSIS

One acceptable method of determining the feasibility of a project is the cost-benefit analysis. This is a method of balancing costs against benefits to show the estimated net effectiveness of the project. Cost-benefit analysis can be used for either income-generating projects or governmental projects. The analysis will weigh both the quantifiable and unquantifiable costs and benefits of a tourism project against each other and against alternative projects. Certainly, if it is a revenue-generating commercial project, positive economic cost-benefits are critical to financing and development. *Tourism USA* discusses how a cost-benefit analysis is accomplished.

Once financing is complete, construction can begin. This may be a long time for large projects which are often completed in stages. Finally, the project becomes operational. The following is the plan process with calculations for a model town, which are illustrated in Tables 15-1 and 15-2.

Range of Costs and Benefits

Before developing a tourism plan or deciding whether to add facilities which would increase tourist potential, you need to ask the question, "Is it

worth it?" The cost-benefit technique is a way to balance costs against benefits to show the estimated net effect of the plan. The cost-benefit study may be very comprehensive like those prepared by the U.S. Army Corps of Engineers for water resource projects or they may be of a rough-and-ready type often used by smaller communities. It is our intent in this section to show you how to develop a rough-and-ready cost-benefit study for your tourism actions.

Method

First, list the benefits applicable to your community. Next, do the same with costs. A portion of benefits and costs will be known with reasonable accuracy, some will be "guesstimates," and others may be unmeasurable. You will need several ingredients to estimate benefits and costs.

—Your inventory of support services gives the present range and capacity of support facilities. If the capacity does not meet present or future

TABLE 15-1 ESTIMATED BENEFITS AND COSTS OF PROPOSED TOURISM DEVELOPMENT PROGRAM—ANYTOWN, U.S.A., 1986–1990

	Benefits per year	Costs per year
1. Local Income		
wages	$110,000	
business profits, interest & rents	64,000	
Subtotal =	$174,000	
2. Local tax revenues		
bed tax	1,400	
property tax	0	
Subtotal =	1,400	
3. Support Services		
parking lot expansion		500
restrooms		4,000
patrol car		3,000
police officer		15,000
street repair		500
Subtotal =		23,000
4. Development of Plan		5,000
Subtotal =		5,000
5. Preservation of Mexican Heritage	500(+)	500
Subtotal =	500(+)	500
6. Environmental Impact		(−)
Subtotal =		(−)
7. Congestion at Local Park	(−)	(−)
Subtotal =	(−)	(−)
TOTALS	175,900	28,500

Net Benefits = Benefits per year − Costs per year
= $147,400
Benefit − Cost Ratio = 175,900/28.5 = 6.17
"Unmeasurables" = Check the appropriate box
☐ Pluses outweigh the minuses
☐ Too close to call
☐ Minuses outweigh the pluses

Source: *Tourism USA*, U.S. Travel and Tourism Administration.

TABLE 15-2 CALCULATIONS, SOURCES OF INFORMATION TOURIST DEVELOPMENT PROGRAM, ANYTOWN, U.S.A.

Item	Calculations	Sources of Information
1. Local Income $174,000	Tourist Expenditure × county income multiplier $290,000 × 0.6 = $174,000	State Economic and Business Research Division or your own estimation
2. Tourist Expenditure $290,000	Anticipated number of visitors, 10,000 by type a. overnight; 30% or 3,000 b. day visitors; 70% or 7,000 Anticipated expenditures by type of visitor per visit a. overnight; $50 per visit b. day visitor; $20 per visit Overnight expenditures; 3000 × $50:$150,000 7000 × $20:$140,000 Total $290,000	Section on Estimating Demand and Usage Travel Survey or average figures for your region
3. Wages	Employment by type of worker a. full-time; 5 b. part-time; 12 × prevailing wage rates a. full-time; $10,000/per year b. part-time; $5,000/year Wages: $10,000 × 5:$ 50,000 5,000 × 12: 60,000 $110,000	Inventory of support services and labor supply
4. Business profits, interest and rental income—$64,000	Local incomes − wages $174,000 − 110,000:$64,000	

Source: *Tourism USA*, U.S. Travel and Tourism Administration.

demands, expansion of those facilities in short supply will cost money and must be taken into account as a cost of tourist development. . . Do not forget to ask whether public services . . . will be expanded.

—A projection of the expected number of visitors to your area.

—An estimate of the expenditures tourists will make in your community. Multiply the anticipated increase in types of tourists (day visitor, overnight or camper) by the expenditures expected for each type, and sum. This will allow you to estimate the increase in sales as a result of your tourist actions.

Benefits most commonly associated with tourism are increased incomes and employment for the community. Your community may receive additional benefits as well.

—Tax revenues might increase which then may be used to provide additional public services or tax relief to local residents.

—Tourism may provide a means of diversifying the economic base. This is particularly important in areas dominated by one industry.

—Tourists also may be important for cultural or social reasons. The Pennsylvania Dutch are a major tourist attraction in Lancaster County. Tourism development has aided their community's economy enabling their culture to flourish.[10]

RESEARCH AND REVIEW

1. Define tourism planning.
2. Why is planning important?
3. Compare and contrast planning in developing and industrialized countries.
4. Describe the planning process.
5. What are some goals of tourism planning?
6. What statistics are needed for demand analysis?
7. What are the four major elements of a training program?
8. What is the purpose of sensitivity analysis?
9. Identify five items of lending institutions require before committing funds.
10. Describe cost-benefit analysis.

ENDNOTES

1. United Nations Conference on Trade and Development, "Elements of Tourism Policy in Developing Countries" (NY, 1973), p. 37.
2. Salah Wahab, "Tourism Planning of the Mediterranean Coast of Egypt (Rainbow Coast)" (Aix-en-Provence, Centre Des Hautes Etudes Touristiques, 1979), pp. 14–15.
3. Ibid., p. 39.
4. Mill and Morrison, pp. 289–290.
5. Donald Getz, "Models in Tourism Planning," *Tourism Management* (March 1986), pp. 21–32.
6. OAS, "Methods for Tourism Project Pre-Investment Studies," Research and Bibliography Series No. 4 (Washington, DC, 1978), p. 2.
7. Ibid., p. 5.
8. Ibid., p. 33.
9. Mill and Morrison, p. 341.
10. *Tourism USA*, p. 61.

CHAPTER 16

MARKETING

A deceptively simple sounding definition of marketing states that it is any activity involved with the sale or rental (or exchange) of a product or service in exchange for something of value. Historically, the market was the place where buyers and sellers met to exchange goods or services for something else of value (other goods, services, or money). The marketing emphasis was to sell the goods and service to a consumer. First there was an idea for a product or service, then the establishment of an outlet such as a neighborhood grocery store, then some form of advertisement, such as a sign on a building, an announcement posted on a door, or an advertisement in the local newspaper. This led to the culmination of the marketing experience, the actual sale of goods and services. The owners would then be "in business."

As the world industrialized, this has become only a small part of marketing. The definition of marketing has changed. Robert Reilly suggested that it now embodies all those activities necessary to bring a product or service from the manufacturer or creator to the end user. These activities include

—the product and/or service itself
—the methods of distribution
—the methods of pricing
—the methods of promotion
—the form of selling
—the form of advertising[1]

There is a wide range of products in the travel field, all offered to give service at a wide range of prices. This variation in products, likewise, creates a variation in each of these activities. For example, Thomson, a large tour operator in Great Britain specializing in low-cost, mass-produced tours to such places as Spain, Greece, and Italy, distributes its product through travel agencies in Wales, Scotland, and England. These agencies handle the details and a customer's time-consuming questions. The travel agent becomes a screening agent in handling the shoppers. Thus, Thomson only becomes involved once a decision is made to purchase a specific vacation. The agent handles future contacts and questions from the client. Thomson's staff is left free to continue selling, keeping costs low, to provide more low-cost, mass-produced tours. Promotion and advertising are handled in two ways: first, through national advertising, which keeps the company name in public view, and, second, through brochures detailing all that the company offers.

The success of Thomson is illustrative of the change in marketing. While historically, marketing dealt with the product and its sale, it is now focused on consumers and their needs, and in developing a product to meet those needs. Salah Wahab emphasized this when he stated: "Marketing is usually construed to (a) define markets, (b) study and analyze consumer needs and tastes, (c) re-orient and re-adapt the product accordingly, (d) develop means to relate the consumer needs to the product and even create those needs, (e) satisfy consumers through product perfection."[2]

The consumer is the focus of this concept of marketing. Thomson has done exceptionally well at keeping its focus sharp. A consumer's needs and tastes are determined, then a product or service is found to meet that need. Lastly, a program is developed to sell it to the public.

UNIQUENESS OF TOURISM SERVICES

While the theory and methods of marketing tourism are the same as for most products, it does have some unique qualities. Tourism is not a product; it is a service. A consumer does not buy a bed or a beach, but purchases a night's lodging in a hotel at the seashore. A manufactured item can be produced, stored, sold, shipped, and delivered. The inventory for tourism is a seat on a plane, a hotel room, and a number of intangibles such as a nice beach, a beautiful view, and an excellent ski slope. Unlike manufactured goods, if the inventory is not sold, the sale is lost forever. Manufactured goods can be stored and, while sometimes perishable, they generally are not lost if not sold on a given day. However, if an airplane from San Francisco to New York has twenty-five seats that remain unsold, that potential income is lost forever. This means that market forecasting and research are extremely important. This is not to suggest that product market forecasting and research are not critical for other products, only that in tourism the margin of error appears to be smaller than in many other industries.

A second significant characteristic of tourism is that the service provided is usually composed of several components (e.g., transportation, lodging, eating, entertaining, and other activities). The degree of success of any one component influences the success of all other components. Travelers who have a poor experience on an airline to a particular destination may well choose a different airline next time, or suggest to friends and relatives that the trip was not worthwhile, or the destination not worth visiting. It is a source of frustration to be vulnerable not only to the whims of the traveler, but also to the service offered by someone else.

The third characteristic of the tourism product is that travel intermediaries are a necessity. Since services are located around the world, potential visitors must be well informed before they leave home. There are many organizations that can bring consumers and services together. Organizations like Thomson and American Express are well known examples of these travel intermediaries. They exercise most influence over the services offered, dictating to whom, when, and at what price they are sold.

The fourth characteristic of tourism is that its demand is highly elastic, seasonal in character, and vulnerable to changes in taste and fashion. There are a number of options available to consumers to satisfy a wide variety of tastes. Sun, sea, and sand, for example, can be found in many places around the world. They offer many choices to the prospective traveler.[3]

TOURISM MARKETING DEFINED

As it relates to tourism, marketing is the systematic process by which an organization tries to optimize the satisfaction of tourist demand through research, forecasting, and the selection of tourism products and services to meet that demand. The elements of tourism marketing include:

(a) *A philosophy of management, [which leads to change]:*
   —*in organization structures, methods and attitudes. . . the whole organization should revolve around the marketing function and all other activities will become various phases of that marketing function.*
   —*in management techniques . . . it is a systematic search for action depending on demand studies and continuous amelioration of the internal environment (planning and co-ordination).*
   —*in a continuous evaluation of marketing results in the light of objectives already set on the one hand, and market realities on the other.*
(b) *It is a coordinated set of techniques to achieve a certain planned result, e.g.,:*
   —*Research techniques,*
   —*Forecasting techniques,*
   —*Selection (choice of objectives, selection of markets, of segments, of distribution channels, of media, of messages, etc.),*
   —*Planning*
(c) *It is oriented toward consumer satisfaction through the suitability of the tourist supply to the demand.*[4]

THE STRATEGIC MARKETING PROCESS

A strategic marketing process can be divided into three elements—market planning, target market selection, and the marketing mix selection.

Market Planning Process

In market planning the objectives are stated and the methods of attaining those objectives are identified. According to Wahab, the purpose is to determine the current situation, decide the goals for a set future time, and then establish a program to reach those goals.

There are seven steps in the market planning process:

1. *Data Collection:* As we've seen, data can be collected in two ways: first from secondary sources—organizations involved in collecting tourism data; second, by collecting primary data for the specific purposes of the organization. The second method is time consuming and costly. Many organizations do not have the skill to do market research planning, and they usually turn to other organizations or people that specialize in it.

2. *Data Analysis:* Data analysis organizes and interprets the data. This, too, requires a considerable amount of skill and understanding. Computers help shorten the process of organizing and applying the statistical measures necessary to interpret and study the data.

3. *Identification of Alternative Strategies for Reaching the Stated Goal:* There are, in most cases, more than one way to arrive at a desired goal. For instance, an airline company that wants to increase the percentage of seats occupied without having an impact on its current market, has a number of alternatives available. First, they can create a special fare with certain restrictions, such as the seven-day advance purchase. Second, they can create a special fare based on age, such as those under twenty-one fly for less. Several airlines that fly between the United States and Europe offer special flights to Europe that are good for up to one year. Third, special contracts with groups for surplus seats may be arranged.

4. *Cost-Benefit Analysis:* The cost-benefit analysis of the various methods for reaching the goals would indicate which of the alternatives or combination of them would be best from a financial standpoint. Some elements, however, such as the goodwill a program can generate, are not quantifiable. Frequent flyer or customer programs, such as those that airlines or hotels offer, are quantifiable, since free rooms or discounts for other services (a number of night's lodging or a specific amount of mileage flown) can be computed. This generates additional use of the seats, or rooms. However, some benefits or programs are only partly quantifiable (free newspapers, free shoe shines, and free wine). The product or item can be computed if the cost is known, but the goodwill and improved attitude towards the company that it brings are less quantifiable.

5. *Selecting Alternatives and Plan Formation:* Once the variables are identified, and the cost-benefit for each is identified, then the decision is made as to which one the organization should pursue. A plan of action, including the responsibility of the members of the organization, can then be established.

6. *Control Procedures:* These are methods that provide management reports analyzing the progress made toward achieving the stated goals.

7. *Plan Implementation:* Putting the plan of action into effect, and supervising it.[5]

According to Wahab, a market plan is a written document detailing seven points:

1. *Plan Objectives:* These are the stated objectives of the written plan. The marketing plan for Discover America stated

> *It is estimated that Americans spent $155 billion on traveling within their own country on vacation trips in 1984. While trips declined somewhat, spending grew at the compound rate of 9.6 percent a year between 1979 and 1984. . . .*
>
> *It is feasible for the domestic market plan to reach one-half of the American public with market-building messages by the end of the decade. If only one-half of these people took one or more vacation trips than they would have otherwise, we would increase U.S. domestic vacation person-trips by nine percent over what would have occurred without any such plan by 1990. . . .*
>
> *This goal of a $27 billion increase in domestic vacation travel spending in 1990 is consistent with $8 billion in additional payroll income for 550,000 new jobs. While it is virtually impossible to forecast tax rates that will prevail in 1990, at today's average rates this additional spending would generate more than $3 billion in additional tax revenue for federal, state, and local governments.*
>
> *Therefore, the major objective of this plan is to increase U.S. domestic vacation travel spending by 11.4 percent a year until 1990, or 1.8 percentage points above its trend rate. This would increase the domestic vacation travel market to nearly $300 billion. We expect that in the early years of the plan, the increase would be somewhat less, and in the later years, somewhat more than this rate.[6]*

2. *Methods of Achieving the Objectives:* The Travel Industry Association of America, in an effort to achieve these objectives developed several programs such as Discover America at McDonald's, a Discover America Month, increased public relations activities, and a Discover America photo and essay contest.

3. *Cost-Benefit Analysis:* In this example, the role of the Travel Industry Association of America was to coordinate the work and get other government and private organizations to carry out the details. Each element of the various methods was analyzed for cost and benefits, to determine whether to pursue the proposal or not.

4. *Responsibilities:* In order to carry out the program properly, the Travel Industry Association of America anticipated that there would be a number of public and private organizations involved. It was necessary to identify their responsibilities. The plan is complex, and a number of organizations are needed to carry it out. Suggested methods are given to achieve the objectives.

5. *Time Limits:* There are two types of costs associated with time. The first is lost opportunity cost when the goals are not reached, thus, keeping the organization from advancing towards other goals during the same time period. The second is the absolute loss of money caused by failing to reach the stated objectives. Large resort developments may take several years from conception of the idea to the actual completion date when sales begin. For these reasons, time is an important element and needs to be part of the plan.

6. *Funding:* Funds are required to meet the objectives of a stated plan. In the case of Discover America, the funds came from both private and public contributions.

Developing countries have financial help available from a number of sources. Some are individual countries giving grants through such organizations in the United States as Aid for International Development, and international organizations such as

—World Bank
—U.N. Economic Commission for Africa (ECA)
—U.N. Economic Commission for Latin America (ECL)
—U.N. Development Plan (UNDP)
—Organization of American States (OAS)
—Inter-American Development Bank
—Asian Development Bank
—African Development Bank

These and other organizations usually provide funds for capital investment in tourist infrastructure and superstructure, research and feasibility studies, and experts for advice and training.

7. *Controls:* All organizations need control over the project. The purpose of control is to see if the forecast is being met, and to identify reasons for differences if there are any.

TOURISM MARKET SELECTION

One certain way to fail is to try to please everyone. Not everyone is an avid tourist and, therefore, not everyone is equally important as a potential tourist. Markets can be defined in a number of ways. The concept of segmentation was introduced earlier, and various types of people were described to illustrate a number of segments. Geographic segmentation, for example, lets tourism promoters know where to focus their attention. They concentrate their efforts

TABLE 16-1 DISCOVER AMERICA POTENTIAL MARKET

Percentage	Characteristics (The Segments Overlap)
47	Couples market: two or more adults, no children
46	Multiwage earner: two or more employed
37	Family market: adults with children at home
33	Middle years; ages 35–54
32	College graduates
27	Maturity market; ages 55 and over
25	Early years: ages 25–34
25	Singles market; adults never married
16	Retired market; no longer working
15	Youth market: 18–24
14	Professional, managerial occupations
14	Blue collar occupations
13	Affluent market: family incomes $50,000 and up

Source: Discover America and U.S. Travel Data Center, National Travel Survey.

on a particular location. Similarly, the age of tourists, or, perhaps, the stage in the family lifecycle may provide a very good basis for market segmentation. By examining past research, you might find that a heavy incidence of travelers at a particular site are families with children in the six to fifteen year-old category. Or else, you might find that few unmarried people under the age of twenty-five visit that particular site.

Table 16-1 is the market segmentation for domestic travel in America, which indicates the potential types of advertisements and programs that have been adopted. The rational behind the decision to promote Discover America together with McDonalds can be seen in this figure. Note that the family market accounted for thirty-seven percent of the travel and that the youth market accounted for another fifteen percent. Combine this segment of the market and the large number of McDonalds, and you can see that the program can certainly be brought to the attention of the American public.

Other segmenting bases are available that may even be superior. However, it is vitally important to locate good market descriptors so that a few specific markets can be actively cultivated. Budgetary resources are seldom so abundant that promotion can use a shotgun approach to

TABLE 16-2 CHARACTERISTICS FOR IDENTIFYING TARGET MARKETS

Geography		Behavior	
	Psychographics	Demographics	
Place of residence	Motivations	Age	
Traffic patterns	Values	Marital status	
	Interests	Number of children	
	Activities	Age of children	
	Lifestyle	Stage in lifecycle	
		Education	
		Family income	
		Occupation	
		Disabilities and health considerations	

Source: *Tourism USA,* 1986, p. 78.

Kentucky Derby being run at Churchill Downs, Louisville, KY.

market development. Since it is virtually impossible to write advertising copy that will motivate everyone, it is more effective to study major market segments or specific targets that have good potential.

Tourism USA, 1986, suggested that studying the target market raises the following questions:

—What attractions do you have to offer?
—What is your "marketing program"?
—What are your objectives?
—How easily can they travel to your area?
—What attractions do you have to offer?
—What is your "marketing program?"
—What are your objectives?

These questions are divided into two major groups. The first is geographic; the questions are concerned with where the tourists live and their normal traffic patterns. The second concerns tourist behavior, which refers to their psychological and demographic characteristics. These are illustrated in Table 16-2. While this program, suggested by

Tourism USA, is designed for governments at local, regional, or national levels, adapting it to the private sector is not very difficult, since the pattern is very similar.

Visitor characteristics affect several decisions the community must make regarding tourism. The geographic location of a commmunity will influence the size of the potential target market, and the area from which that market will be drawn. Location may govern the size of an attraction needed to draw the desired market, the services necessary to support that attraction, and the promotional efforts necessary.

Geographic Factors

Travel distances, times, and cost are important factors to consider. Many people are concerned about the psychological and physical effort required to make a trip. People take into account the cost of a trip. Consumers want attractions to be as accessible as possible.

While travel time and distance can be barriers to travel, the area's attractions act as a pull force to offset them. Hawaii, although a long way from the mainland of

---

POSITIONING YOUR HOTEL IN THE MARKET

by Roger Dow

To position a hotel in the market is to identify those characteristics that distinguish it from the competition. To communicate these distinctions to target audiences requires the development of themes that project an image.

Consider, for example, the historic campaign devised several years ago for the Tuscany Hotel in New York. Management decided that the hotel's distinctions were its smallness and its masculine comforts. Advertising embodied the two distinctions in a single image-making headline:

BIGGEST LITTLE HOTEL IN NEW YORK

Supporting data in the ad copy listed Barcaloungers, butler's pantries, electric shoe polishers and large Irish towels among other conveniences. Occupancy rose 10 to 15 points above the city average in traceable response to the campaign.

A current campaign by the Pontchartrain of New Orleans is based on three distinctions defined in the hotel's positioning: (1) the hotel has been operated by the famous Aschaffenberg family for three generations; (2) it is a homelike small hotel in a major city; and (3) its food reputation is international. Note how all three segments of the positioning are embraced in a single advertising theme:

THE ASCHAFFENBERG HOME HAS 74 BEDROOMS AND A GREAT KITCHEN

Source: *Lodging* (October 1986).

North America, exerts strong influences on travel. A place that offers a large variety of interesting attractions, such as Southern California or Central Florida, exerts more influence on travel than places sometimes closer to the potential tourist. Accessibility and barriers have been discussed in an earlier chapter, but are also relevant here.

Target Markets

Tourism USA suggested four steps that should be taken to identify target markets. The first step is to estimate the lure of an area's attractions. This includes the degree of interest a tourist would have in the area, and the length of time a tourist will spend there visiting the attraction. A Disney-type theme park would produce considerably more interest than an alligator farm; visitors would stay longer at the former than the latter. A large world's fair would create more interest than a state fair. A three-day festival would be more important than a one-day festival.

For the second step there is a need to estimate the distance in both travel time and travel costs. The greater the attraction the longer the distances potential customers will travel.

Third, identify the potential target markets geographically by locating those population clusters within the maximum distance determined from the estimated travel time and drawing power of the attraction.

Fourth, identify real and potential competition in the target market. Attractions in direct competition, that are located closer to the identified population clusters, will be more likely to draw people to them than the area under study, unless there are other factors that will attract the potential visitors.

Behavioral Characteristics

The behavior of potential travelers is an important component for identifying target markets. Various people have different reasons for travel. Some people like museums, monuments, and other historical or cultural activities; others may prefer gambling, sporting events, or entertainment; while still others may prefer the sun, sea, and sand. Therefore, once the target markets have been defined, the segments must be studied to discover why these people travel, and why they travel to a specific location. Again, it is best not to use a shotgun approach with too many appeals targeted at a specific segment. People who choose to visit historical attractions or restored older buildings are not motivated in the same way as those who travel to man-made attractions offering athletic activities, gambling casinos, or musical shows.

The objective of marketing is to sell the mystique of any particular location; to tell potential visitors why it is unique. People travel to experience new environments. Modern hotel facilities may be appreciated and even play a vital part in a tourism site; however, they are not the magnets that attract the visitor. The impetus for travel must remain focused on the benefits offered by the core attractions.

As suggested in Table 16–2, a person's age, sex, mar-

TABLE 16-3 COMPARISON BETWEEN PROMOTION AND MARKETING

Promotion	Marketing
1. Promotion departs from the "product" and is concerned with raising its sales possibilities.	1. Emphasis in marketing is on the demand as tourism should be understood as consumption rather than production of services, and therefore the tourist "consumer" is the most important element to start with.
2. Promotion is usually conducted through (a) advertising (b) publicity (c) public relations.	2. Marketing operations and strategies encompass (a) product policy (b) price policy (c) points of distribution (d) promotion (e) marketing research, communication outlets, publicity, public relations, advertising.
3. Promotion is not sufficient, as it is mainly concerned with disseminating information and increasing sales in a rather fragmented way.	3. Marketing is a policy of management with forecasting a necessary element.
4. Promotion does not represent an all-embracing policy as it cannot provide coherent feedback to improve the product.	4. Marketing is all-embracing and provides feedback on the "product." Moreover, it helps to develop a system of constant communication.
5. Promotion covers all planned activities that involve distribution messages (advertisements, films, brochures, guidebooks, posters, etc.) through a variety of channels (press, cinema, radio, TV, mail, etc.) to actual and potential tourists, mainly foreign, with the aim of transmitting information and influencing them favorably toward a tourist destination or service.	5. Marketing not only lends itself to promotion, but it extends to a fourfold function: (a) Definition and study of actual and potential markets. (b) Communications: attract tourists by persuading them that the destination, with its existing attractions, facilities and services, matches their tastes better than any other alternative. (c) Development: to plan and develop new and existing tourist attractions and services. (d) Control: to evaluate, assess and measure what the yields of promotional activities are, the results of efficient utilization, and whether the marketing budget is sufficient to bring about a worthwhile return or not.

Source: Reprinted by permission of Tourism International and Salah Wahab.

---

ital status, and number and ages of children have an influence on travel patterns. Research and studies can identify the behavioral target markets that would most likely be suited for the particular product. Then all that is left is matching the attractions with those who are most likely to enjoy them, and to let tourists know of their existence through promotion and advertising.[7]

DETERMINING A MARKETING STRATEGY

There are six steps in the target market selection that bring the process together.

1. Identify the market segment. This is the key variable.
2. Determine the preferences of the segment identified.
3. Determine what influences the segment most—price, product, image, sales persuasion, customer service, product availability, and so on.
4. For countries, or regions, it is important to realize that there are two clients, the traveler and the travel intermediary (travel agent or tour operator).
5. Determine the marketing mix that will influence the segment identified.

6. Establish a price policy that will maximize profits by balancing the number of tourists with attraction capacity.

Marketing mix is the combination or mixture of elements (product, pricing, promotion, and distribution channels) that interact and complement each other to achieve the objectives of the market plan. Part of this mix to achieve the desired sales level is expressed in "Positioning Your Hotel in the Market." Another good example of the marketing process is given at the end of the chapter in the discussion of packaging, which involves many of the issues central to this chapter.

Promotion, which was treated in depth in Chapter 10, is the method by which sales are stimulated and, as such, is a component of marketing. Table 16-3 compares tourist promotion and tourist marketing.

RESEARCH AND REVIEW

1. Define and explain marketing.
2. What are the three elements of tourism marketing?
3. Describe the seven steps in the market planning process.

4. Create a mythical state and establish a set of objectives for its tourism market plan.

5. How can these objectives be achieved?

6. How important is market segmentation?

7. How do travel time and distance influence vacation decisions?

8. What are the four steps *Tourism USA*

suggested should be taken in order to identify target markets?

9. What is the process for determining a marketing strategy?

10. What is market mix?

11. What is the difference between promotion and marketing?

ENDNOTES

1. Robert T. Reilly, *Travel and Tourism Marketing Techniques* (Wheaton, IL: Merton House Publishing Co., 1980), p. 2.

2. Wahab, *Tourism Management* (London: Tourism International Press, 1975), pp. 102–103.

3. Mill and Morrison, pp. 357–358.

4. Wahab, pp. 105–106.

5. Wahab and Crampon pp. 137–138.

6. *Discover America: A National Domestic Travel Marketing Plan* (Washington, DC: Travel Industry Assn. of America), p. 11.

7. *Tourism USA,* 1986, pp. 78–82.

CHAPTER 17

EDUCATION
AND TRAINING

As indicated throughout this text, tourism is a big industry and indications are that it will become even bigger. In 1979, the famed futurist, Herman Kahn, predicted that tourism would be the world's largest industry by the year 2000. Eight years later, Somerset Waters, editor of *The Big Picture*, stated that tourism worldwide exceeded $2 trillion, directly and indirectly, generating 64.3 million jobs.[1] He concluded that tourism *is* the world's largest industry today.

A trend in the changing economy and employment structure of the western world began in the 1980s, and will continue into the 1990s. The service sector has become, and will continue to become, the fastest growing sector of the economy; in the 1990s it will be the major employer. This has a number of implications for tourism. First, tourism jobs are in the service sector and will most likely continue to be a major factor in tourism employment. Second, many of the service positions are low paying and this will mean less demand for travel jobs. However, with a decreasing labor market for younger people, these jobs should become more important and the wage scale is likely to increase. Third, many of the new service positions are well-paying professional ones in such fields as computers, insurance, and law. In addition to the higher salaries, people in the service-related professions are more flexible when they vacation because many are self-employed and more in control of their free time. Fourth, it is suggested by educators that a significant percentage of future employment opportunities may not even have been thought of today.

THE PRESENT SITUATION

The educational characteristics of the travel industry are changing rapidly. Abraham Pizam analyzed the relationship between society and the tourism industry. While he focused on unskilled and semiskilled employment in tourism, it does offer some view of a large segment of the industry. Figure 17-1 is his schematic assessment of the relationship between the work environment, society, and industry.

The industry has a number of problems in some segments of its employment opportunities. In the industrialized countries, these are mainly poor pay, a lack of advancement, and a high rate of turnover. In the developing countries, learning to be effective is still a major task. For many, the unskilled jobs in the tourism industry are a significant, if not major, contributor to the family income. Industrial society has become more leisure oriented with an increased movement to service industries and an increased emphasis upon tourism. Both factors, in turn, have increased the demand for tourism. Tourism is a provider of service for a leisure society. However, unlike other segments of service industries the unskilled and semiskilled nature of many tourism jobs does not provide self-actualization that other service industry positions do.

Pizam identified two other trends that enhance the growth of tourism but lead to job dissatisfaction for employees. Emphasis on immediate gratification and self-indulgence on the one hand has increased the demand for tourism, but on the other hand, many workers in the tourism field are not able to obtain the same degree of gratification or indulgence because of their low wages and the need to work nights, weekends, and holidays.

In many countries some of the service jobs, particularly those in hospitality and food service, have a poor image. There is a strong feeling in developing countries that service is equated with servitude; thus not a good career to pursue. This, combined with the increasing emphasis upon a college degree as a social statement of status, gives prospective employees in some countries a feeling that tourism jobs are beneath their status.

The tourism industry competes with other sectors of an economy for employees. Because of the poor entry-level salaries and the character of many positions, many able individuals do not choose tourism as a career.

The second major element Pizam illustrates is the characteristics of the industry. First, it is labor-intensive in that it employs a large number of workers; second, many of the unskilled and semiskilled positions cannot be replaced by automation; third, tourism products are perishable in that if they are not used the income is lost and cannot be recouped. Many facilities of the service industries are offered the year round and require a level of quality

TOURISM'S WORK ENVIRONMENT AND ITS DETERMINANTS

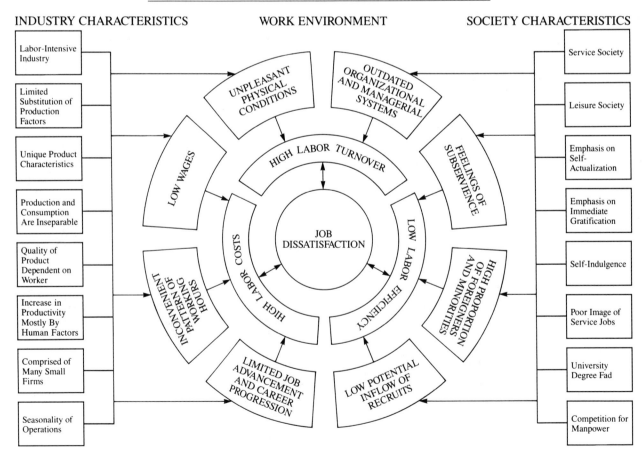

FIGURE 17-1 Source: Abraham Pizam. "Tourism Manpower: The State of the Art." *Journal of Travel Research* (Fall 1982).

that sometimes is difficult to sustain over long periods of time, encompassing an inconvenient pattern of working hours. Fourth, in the tourism industry production and consumption are inseparable and to control the quality and uniformity of service, management resorts to rigid controls and close supervision; fifth, the quality of service is dependent on the motivation and attitude of the employees even with extensive training; sixth, productivity can only be increased by improving the skills and expectations of the employees through training, rewards and a pleasant working environment; seventh, many tourism facilities and services are seasonal in nature, and in many countries employers compensate by hiring migrant workers, usually foreign nationals or minorities.

Often, unskilled and semiskilled jobs have unpleasant physical surroundings with no facilities for resting, eating, and personal hygiene. Outdated managerial systems are prevalent in many of the small and independent firms, discouraging employees and leaving them frustrated and apathetic. Some feel subservient which can manifest itself in negative attitudes. Also, the hospitality and food service sector in many industrial countries attract a large proportion of foreign and minority workers. According to Pizam this creates problems of cultural adjustment, conflicts, and discrimination. These characteristics of the work environment, combined with the low potential for advancement, low wages, and undesirable working hours presents a constant problem for the tourism industry. However, in the skilled and professional positions there appears to be improving opportunities.[3]

Emerging Professionalism

The WTO, in its general meetings in Manila, Acapulco, and New Delhi, indicated that true education is more than the transmission of technical information. It is the transformation of the character and, above all, the development of the true man. The WTO stated that the spiritual aspect was more important than the technical and material aspects, although they were important too. It strongly recommended that all nations should strive for

—The total fulfillment of the human being
—A constantly increasing contribution to education
—Equality of the destiny of nations
—The liberation of man in a spirit of respect for his identity and dignity
—The affirmation of originality of cultures and respect for the moral heritage of peoples[4]

Within this context, the WTO realized that education was more than the "skill training" that enables people to earn a living. It is that which deepens wisdom, foresight, and character, and enables people to live in cooperation and harmony. Being professional is more than "skill." The WTO asked:

"Travel, tourism, lodging and hospitality may be harmoniously planned, segmented and implemented, but what about the individuals who administer, work in, use and enjoy them?"[5]

Rapidly changing conditions in the world today are creating career opportunities to meet the diverse needs of the domestic and international traveler, the host communities, and service providers (e.g., airlines, hotels, travel agencies, car rental companies, bus companies, resorts, ski areas, campgrounds, retail stores, tour companies, cruise lines, restaurants, and others). Within these organizations and enterprises many of the specific jobs listed in Table 17-1 can be found. The list is descriptive of the types and diversity of positions available in the field of travel and tourism. (See also Appendix C.)

EDUCATION AND TRAINING IN DEVELOPED COUNTRIES

Historically, much of the education for those who want to make travel and tourism their profession has been in business or communications programs. Travel and tourism had not been taught as a specific degree program. It was the general belief of business schools, for example, to teach business principals and theory, then to let the students apply what they had learned to the segment of business in which they were eventually employed, whether it was transportation, retail, hotels, or development. As the industry developed, it was recognized that further education and training were necessary to complete the educational process of those in the travel field. The Institute of Certified Travel Agents (ICTA) has developed a program to provide management training for industry employees who have had at least three years of experience. After a part-time course of study, for approximately eighteen months, which is usually completed while working, a graduate receives the designation of Certified Travel Counselor. In some countries, such as the United Kingdom, people employed in tourism must have a license. This also encourages the development of certificate programs.

Many companies have some form of certification, but it is specific to the needs of their own companies and industry. Most major hotel organizations have management training programs for those employees who qualify after a certain period of entry-level work. The Walt Disney World College Program is designed to give students an opportunity to view the administration of a large commercial recreational facility through both practical hourly work experience and seminars. They provide a Leisure Time Business Management curriculum with a unique blend of academic theory and practical experience. This builds upon a college business program designed to provide students with general business and management theory.

Growth of Professional Programs

The early response to the need for large numbers of semiskilled and unskilled positions in the travel industry, has been met by technical and related forms of training. Proprietary schools, somewhat similar to technical schools, have been developing rapidly. Some proprietary and technical school programs are designed to enable a student to acquire the technical skills required at the entry level for hotels, restaurants, and travel agencies. An eight- to ten-week course is typical of such programs. The curriculum

TABLE 17-1 CAREER AND EMPLOYMENT OPPORTUNITIES IN THE TRAVEL INDUSTRY

Air Transportation		Ground Transportation	
Flight operations		*Bus*	
Pilot/Captain	Flight Dispatcher	Bus Operator (Driver)	Mechanic
Co-pilot/First Officer	Meteorologist	Dispatcher	Ticket Agent
Flight Engineer/Second Officer	Air Traffic Controller	Host/Hostess	Tour Representative
Flight Attendant	Airport Operations	Information Clerk	General Office
	Coordinator	*Car rentals*	
Ground operations		Mechanic	Sales Representative
Carpenter	Plumber	Rental Sales Agent	Utility Worker
Electrician/Electrical Engineer	Radio Technician	Reservation Agent	General Office
Line Maintenance Mechanic	Sheet Metal Mechanic	*Railroads*	
Machinist	Upholstery Mechanic	Conductor	Passenger Service
Maintenance Inspector	Welder	Engineer	Representative
Painter	Instrument Technician	Machinist	Reservation Clerk
In-flight catering		Signal Installer	Sales Manager
Baker	Food Service Porter	Track Worker	Station Agent
Cook	Commissary Personnel	Telegrapher/Telephone	General Office
Food Service Assistant	Quality Control	Operator	
	Ground Service		
		Water Transportation	
Office and sales		*Steamship and cruise lines*	
Accountant	Sales Representative	Captain	Entertainer
Auditor	Station Agent	Chief Officer	Refrigeration Engineer
Buyer	Stenographer	Second Mate	Electrician
General Clerk	Ticket Sales Agent	Third Mate	Firer
Communications Agent	Teletype Operator	Chief Engineer	Chief Cook
Computer Programmer	Tour Sales Agent	First Assistant Engineer	Chief Steward
Computer Operator	Marketing Analyst	Second Assistant Engineer	Tour Director
Customer Service	Passenger Service Agent	Third Assistant Engineer	Reservation Sales Agent
Representative	Personnel Officer	Radio Officer	Public Relations Officer
District Sales Manager	Public Relations Officer	Purser	Sales Representative
Employment Representative	Ramp Agent	Beautician	Marketing Analyst
Freight Sales and Operators	Reservation Sales Agent	Carpenter	Passenger Service Agent
Agent			

includes airline reservations and ticketing, fares, destination information, hotels, tour programs, documentation, car rentals, salesmanship, and a computer training segment. Although technical schools have added programs in tourism in the past ten years, they are designed mostly for travel agencies.

Many two year schools, including community and junior colleges, are now offering educational and training programs in tourism. They represent the first step in professional academic training. These two year schools offer an expanded education in liberal arts, but stress additional preparation in math, English, history, psychology, geography, public speaking, sales, and humanities.

College and University Programs

Colleges and universities have entered the travel field only in the past few years, even though universities have historically provided education in many of the pure disciplines or liberal arts/sciences which have been utilized in the development and management of tourism. Some components of tourism, such as hotel and restaurant management, and parks and recreation administration, are well developed in many universities. Programs in business admin-

istration, marketing, and urban and regional planning are also relatively plentiful. While these programs have served tourism and societal needs well, in the case of tourism, they have often created fragmentation, or a narrow and incomplete treatment of opportunities and problems.

University programs of study that integrate these and other fields in such a fashion that tourism is treated as a whole are hard to find. Simply speaking, tourism, as a field of academic study, is in its infancy. There are few models in the United States or elsewhere after which to pattern new programs. In cases where attempts have been made to develop such curricula, there is considerable disagreement concerning the basic foundation, the professional content, and the best balance between the applied or vocational versus theoretical or conceptual approach.

A search for tourism programs at the university level (Bachelor's degree and above) in the United States yields some interesting information. Most programs labeled as "tourism" are generally options or minors attached to an older, more traditional core curriculum in some other, yet related, curriculum; thus a strong bias or "flavor" of the root curriculum is maintained. These are generally found in hotel and restaurant management programs or parks and recreation programs. In these cases, the student is required

Tour Operations

Reservationist	Sales Representative
Operations Clerk	Tour Escort
Reservation and Traffic	Travel Scout
Coordinator	Corporate Travel Manager
Operations Supervisor	

Travel Agency

Commercial Counselor	Agency Manager
Domestic Counselor	Agency Owner
International Counselor	General Office
Group Sales Consultant	Outside Sales

Food and Beverage

Bakers/Cooks/Chefs	Menu Maker
Waiter/Waitress	Cashier
Host/Hostess	Chain Executive
Bartenders	Personnel Director
Restaurant Manager	Merchandising Supervisor
Assistant Manager	Director of Recipe
Food Production Manager	Development
Dietician	Food Service Supervisor
	Catering Director

Hotels and Motels

General Manager	Director of Marketing
Assistant Manager	Purchasing Director
Executive Housekeeper	Discotheque Manager
Food and Beverage Manager	Computer Programmers
Personnel Director	Front Office Manager
Sales Representative	Front Office Clerk
Sales Manager	Chief Engineer
Reservationist	Maintenance

Travel Related

Theme parks

Food Director	Operations Manager
Director of Group Sales	Games Manager
Purchasing Agent	Arcade Manager
Manager of Public Relations	Maintenance Director

Club management

Club Manager	Grill Manager
Office Manager	Golf Course Superintendent
Assistant Manager	Golf or Tennis Pro Shop
Food and Beverage Director	Manager

Journalism

Travel Editor	Travel Writer

Education

Teacher/Instructor	Curriculum Specialist
Researcher	

Recreation

Recreation Specialist	Park Manager
Program Coordinator	Manager of Recreation
Camp Counselor	Services

Government Agencies

Federal Aviation	Department of Transportation
Administration	Foreign Tourist Offices
Federal Maritime Commission	State and City Tourist Offices
Interstate Commerce	Department of Interior
Commission	Department of Commerce
U.S. Coast Guard	Tourism Bureau Manager
Information Office	Policy Analyst
Interpretive Specialists	Research/Statistical Specialist
(Museums, Crafts, Arts,	Economist
Destination Information,	Convention Center/Fair
etc.)	Manager

Adapted from: Chuck Y. Gee, Dexter S.L. Choy and James C. Makens, *The Travel Industry* (Westport, CT: AVI Publishing Co., 1984).

to complete a core of courses, and is given the opportunity to select a number of others that are designed to give the total curriculum a tourism orientation. Although these programs are good, and attempt to broaden the student's education, they do not necessarily provide a holistic treatment of tourism. Such traditional programs will, understandably, teach some content in that major field at the expense of content in tourism or other critically-related fields.

There appears to be no consensus on the appropriate academic or administrative location of tourism programs. Of fifty-three representative programs examined in the United States, there was near equal distribution within eight different academic areas. In actuality, the location of these programs appears to relate where the innovators of the tourism curriculum were located when it was developed.

It is safe to say that travel and tourism education at the university level in the United States is in the very early stages of evolution. Although there appears to be agreement among tourism educators and researchers that tourism is a multi- and interdisciplinary subject, there is little agreement on which disciplines are most important, the degree to which curricula should be distributed between general education and professional education, what professional or applied fields are most important, and whether emphasis should be placed on managerial, theoretical, and conceptual content or technical and applied skills.

The principles and guidelines of the George Washington University program are illustrative of the field today. They determined that tourism curriculum development should be founded on a set of fundamental principles.

—A holistic understanding of this complicated field is required, including the total range of touristic activities—economic, social, cultural, environmental, political, technological, and physical aspects.

—The graduate of a tourism program must be a broadly-educated person, with knowledge, skills, and awareness required by all educated people, with a professional specialization in tourism.

—The program should be designed so a graduate can secure an entry level position heading toward leadership and managerial roles in the tourism industry.

—The tourism program should be based on theoretical models of tourism which are dynamic, comprehensive, easily understood, and unifying. As student learning progresses, the models must provide a foundation around which the student can organize and synthesize knowledge and skills in this complex field.

Academic training in tourism should be founded on a philosophy and understanding of the field that is broad and all-encompassing. It should be treated in the context of a conceptual framework. This involves an approach to tourism which recognizes that it is made up of numerous parts, components, or functions that are interrelated. Unfortunately, tourism planning, development, and management has often been highly fragmented or extremely narrow. This condition has resulted in various negative impacts, poor development, lack of support, special interest conflicts, and less than optimum economic and social benefits.

Historically, tourism development has involved, or been perceived to involve, rather narrow or limited functions. While individual tourism businesses or special interest groups, such as hotels, airlines, attractions, or travel agencies, may have understandably narrow goals or operational functions, tourism education cannot respond to these needs alone. A professional must be prepared with knowledge and skill to understand the total field, the interrelationships involved, and the impacts created on people and economies. This leads to the conclusion that the theoretical model selected must be practical yet all inclusive. The fact that tourism, either directly or indirectly, touches the lives of everyone (tourists and hosts), increases the responsibility of the tourism educator. A leadership cadre is required that has a liberal education, supplemented with a broad professional understanding of tourism. While the nature of opportunities and problems in tourism are highly varied, any university education program, which does not consider all functions in tourism, will be simplistic and ineffective in providing well-educated and skilled professionals.

Any approach to the development of a conceptual framework for tourism should be responsive to the following guidelines:

1. The study of tourism requires an analysis of both the theoretical and practical considerations.

2. Tourism should be analyzed in terms of its global scope, relative to its stage of development in terms of tourism demand and supply in developed, newly-industrialized, and developing countries. Increasingly, tourism will be the means for bringing people in the world together, creating goodwill, understanding, and world peace.

3. Tourism should be treated as an emerging profession; evidence of this is characterized by professional societies and certification programs formed in order to establish a commonly-accepted code of ethics, building of a body of knowledge, and the formulation and validation of practice standards and procedures. Note the success of the following certification programs: Certified Hotel Sales Executives (CHSE), Certified Hotel Administrator (CHA), Certified Travel Counselor (CTC), Certified Corporate Travel

Executives (CCTE), Certified Meeting Planner (CMP), Certified Tour Professional (CTP), and the Travel Marketing Fellow designation of the Association of Travel Marketing Executives (ATME), which are serving as models for new professional recognition programs for tour operators, business travel managers, vacation property and resort managers, and campground operators.

4. The movement of people for touristic purposes should be particularly distinguished by cultural authenticity and hospitality presented by the host to the guest. The essence of tourism from antiquity to the modern era has been characterized by friendly and courteous treatment of the guest by the host. Due to the complexity of modern society, hospitality cannot be provided without management of the overall process at the macro and micro levels in order to reduce risk and conflict and to create conditions that will produce the best possible results for tourists, hosts, and their respective societies.

5. Tourism and hospitality education needs to be relevant to careers today and in the future. The aim of a professional education program should be to prepare students to meet the changing needs of the travel and tourism industry, while continuing to pursue the traditional principles of learning and research.

EDUCATION AND TRAINING IN DEVELOPING COUNTRIES

Tourism training in developing countries has centered on vocational and technical skills. Tourism for developing countries has been helpful in bringing considerable semi-skilled and unskilled employment. However, for developing countries, the basic skills, learned as a matter of course in industrial countries, must be taught. Moreover, with emphasis in the last twenty years on the environment, social, cultural, and political concerns, additional elements need to be introduced into the curriculum for developing nations. Tourism places two very different and contrasting cultures, operating with different assumptions, values, behavior and ideas, in close juxtaposition within the same environment.

David Blanton outlined a Kenyan training program created to address some of the problems posed by different cultures coming together in a developing host country. Kenya Utalii College in Nairobi trains some five hundred hotel and tourism students a year from mostly other sub-Saharan African countries. The "normal" tourism courses of tour guiding, service and sales, housekeeping and laundry, kitchen courses, and hotel management are taught. In addition, the college has developed programs to deal with host-guest relationships. This part of the curriculum is divided into four parts: First, they teach the culture and history of Africa, including settlement and cultural development of the continent. Second, studies of tourism and tourists include the history of travel, tourist motivation, and the cultural values and expectations of tourists. A series of "tourist profiles" are presented. Third, professional attitudes are stressed. Students are taught how to deal with stereotyped images guests have of Africa, prejudices, how to understand differing concepts of time, the significance of regular cash income, and basic economics. Lastly, students solve problems through case studies, drama, and by recognizing tourist expectations and behavior.[6]

While tourism education is rudimentary and technically oriented, it is needed to help the residents of developing countries gain an understanding of sophisticated principles of human interaction and self-awareness. There is also an increasing need for the same type of education developed countries have to create a skilled management level pool of talent for the tourism industry.

NEED FOR PROFESSIONALISM AND EDUCATED STUDENTS

The tourism industry, like tourism education, is going through an evolution. Many of the changes have been brought about by deregulation of the airline industry, changing society, and a changing economy. These changes have created, and will continue to create, an increased need for personnel; an increased need for the "educated person" rather than the technical; and an increased number of nontraditional career opportunities.

A *Business Week* article quoted Robert Longo, vice-president of personnel at Thomas Cook Travel: "Whenever you have a high-tech, high-growth, recently deregulated industry undergoing an incredible amount of change, you're going to need top college grads with management skills who are willing to learn the ropes from the bottom up. The travel industry can certainly provide that kind of opportunity."[7]

Further, Carol Walsh suggested that in a deregulated climate, large corporations with huge travel budgets will either want their own personnel in their offices, or will want to have their travel arrangements handled by sophisticated corporate travel agencies.

The increase in the service sector employment is in part due to the increase in the tourism industry demand. The U.S. Department of Labor has predicted that in the 1990s, nine out of every ten new jobs created in the United States will be in the service industry. The hotel industry, which already employs around 1.8 million, will need approximately 800,000 new workers by the year 2000, while the food-service industry, with 8 million employees as of 1986, will face a shortage of about 1.1 million by 1995.[8]

Both the hotel and the food-service industries have a high rate of turn over. In addition to the low pay, the American public's perception is that jobs in the lodging and restaurant industry are paths on the road to more permanent careers in "better fields." In Europe, on the other hand, both the lodging and food-service industries are looked upon as life-long, honored professions. Entrance to European professional schools for such occupations are expensive and in high demand.

The industry has done a number of things to overcome the American public's perception. In 1985, a number of industrial groups in the lodging and food-service industries researched and put together a program designed to convey a positive image of America's hospitality industry that they hoped would enhance the self-esteem of people currently employed in the industry; and also help recruit career professionals, since there is a considerable shortage of managers in both lodging and food-services. The "Ours is a Special World" theme was designed for both the current employees and the general public.

Other efforts (such as that by the Council on Hotel, Restaurant and Institutional Education, a leading organization for educators and industry professionals) are designed to improve the quality of hospitality and tourism education through research and communication between the educational field and the industry. Education helps to improve the public's image about fields of employment. Also encouraging is the tourism-related leadership in higher education of the Society of Travel and Tourism Educators (SOTTE), the Society of Park and Recreation Educators (SPRE), the Professional Conference Managers Association (PCMA), and the American Society of Travel Agents (ASTA).

Finally, the future of jobs, as already indicated, suggests that a significant number are yet to be created. (In California, a former travel agent has established himself in a new career, as a leisure time consultant. He sees his service matching that of other professionals, such as financial planners. He helps people find the best methods of using their leisure time.) The only way an individual can be prepared for the future envisioned by Herman Kahn, in his statement "we must not expect the expected," is through good education. The only way that segments of the industry can change their image and create professionalism is through well-designed educational programs.

RESEARCH AND REVIEW

1. How important is tourism in the world economy?

2. What decade had the most significant advances in tourism? Why?

3. As a nation becomes more service oriented what implication does that have on tourism?

4. Discuss the need for professional education and training in tourism.

5. Describe the different educational programs available.

6. Discuss the character of tourism education in colleges and universities.

7. What are the principles that a tourism curriculum should be based upon?

8. Identify the guidelines for a conceptual framework for tourism.

9. Describe tourism education in developing countries.

ENDNOTES

1. *Travel Industry World Yearbook—1987*, p. 11.
2. Abraham Pizam, "Tourism Manpower: The State of the Art," *Journal of Travel Research*, Vol. 21, No. 2 (Fall 1982), pp. 7–8.
3. Ibid.

4. WTO, "Determination of the Elements Required For Defining Training Programmes Tailored to the Specific Needs of Countries" (Madrid, 1985), pp. 9–10.
5. Ibid., p. 11.
6. David Blanton, "Tourism Training in Developing Countries: The Social and Cultural Dimension," *Annals of Tourism Research,* Vol. 7, No. 1 (1981), pp. 116–133.
7. Carol A. Walsh, "Travel Your Way to Success," *Business Week's Guide To Careers* (Spring/Summer 1985), pp. 73–75.
8. Sharon W. Walsh, "Service Jobs—Apply Within," *Washington Post* (Aug. 29, 1986), pp. E7–E8.

PART IV

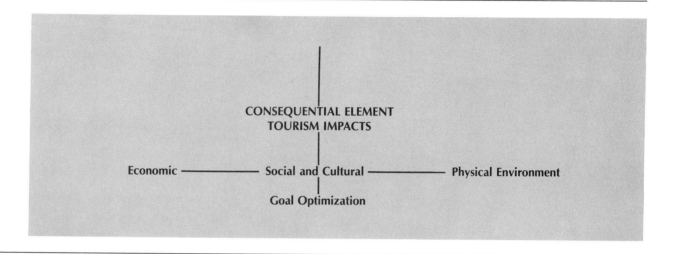

CONSEQUENTIAL ELEMENT
TOURISM IMPACTS

Economic ————————— Social and Cultural ————————— Physical Environment

Goal Optimization

CONSEQUENTIAL ELEMENT: TOURISM IMPACTS

CHAPTER 18

ECONOMIC IMPACTS

Economic growth and development is always a primary goal of government, from the local level to the international level. When discussing the economic impact of tourism, it is important to understand trade payments and tourism multipliers. These concepts, usually used at the international level, are equally important at all levels of governments.

BALANCE OF TRADE PAYMENTS

The balance of trade payments is an accounting of the flow of goods, services, and funds in and out of a country during a given period. If a country pays, or agrees to pay out, more money than it receives, it has a deficit in its balance of payments. If it receives more money than it sends, or exports, it has a surplus in its balance of payments.

There are three types of payment and receipts in international accounts: visible balance of trade, which include import and export goods; invisible items; and capital transfers. The visible balance of trade is most familiar, and we hear a great deal about it. The United States exports a considerable quantity of agricultural products and manufactured items to other countries; in turn, it imports raw materials from South America, cars from Japan and Germany, and oil from the Middle East and South America as part of its visible balance of trade. Capital transfers are payments from one country to another for reasons other than the exchange of goods and services. Foreign aid and World Bank grants are good examples of capital transfers. Tourism is part of the invisible export in the balance of payments. It is referred to as invisible because the exact amount of money being exchanged from one country to another is not directly known until the tourist expenditures flow through the banking system. Commodities and manufactured goods can be measured because a direct exchange is made. While tourists can be counted, the amount of money they will spend cannot be ascertained directly. In some countries (e.g., Spain, Austria, Yugoslavia, Greece, Ireland, Mexico), tourism is an important source of income. Table 18-1 lists the tourist receipts for some countries.

Travel expenditures in countries like the United States and West Germany (although they have large numbers of tourists in both other countries and their own) are not a major part of their balance of payments. In recent years, however, the tourism account is becoming more important in the United States, which is currently showing huge deficits in its balance of trade. These deficits take the United States from the world's largest creditor to the world's largest debtor nation. United States tourists traveling abroad, spent over $24.5 billion in 1986, which was offset by foreign tourists spending over $16 billion in the United States. This left a deficit of $8.5 billion.[1] An increase in the number of foreign tourists to the United States will help the balance of trade payments for the United States. The only year there was a surplus in the travel account was 1981.

Tourism Multipliers

The second principle to understand is tourism multipliers. They are generally referred to as additional income and employment that is created in a state, region, or nation as a result of new money being spent there. The income multiplier involves tourist spending and the changes it causes in the level of income in the area. The employment multiplier relates to the amount of employment created by tourism, and is generally expressed by some unit of tourism expenditure. In some areas, $10,000 spent by tourists will create one new job.

The nature of the multiplier effect can be explained as follows. Tourists spend money in a region buying their meals, for example. In order for restaurants to provide the meals, they need to hire people to cook, serve, clean, manage, and keep track of the money. They also have to buy food, tableware, paper supplies, electricity, furnishings, laundering services, and, in some cases, entertainment. The people who receive money from the restaurant in return for goods and services will, in turn, spend it to maintain themselves. This pattern will be repeated in a chain reaction. Thus, money spent by tourists is used several times, and is spread throughout the entire economy. Each time that the money changes hands, it provides "new" money to the region; this is the multiplier effect illustrated in Figure 18-1. Not all the money that changes hands stays in the region. Some companies purchase materials and services outside the area, allowing some of the money to leak from the region. The amount of purchases made outside the region will reduce the multiplier effect. Thus, money spent in regions that are more advanced and self-supporting than others will have a greater effect upon those regions than that spent in less-advanced places, where many goods and services must be purchased outside the region. Table 18-2 includes some estimated tourist or travel multipliers from a number of sources. Because they are from different studies, and in some cases different methods were used to gather the information, a direct comparison cannot be made. However, it does offer some indication of the differences between areas.

The multiplier indicates the amount of additional income generated for each dollar spent by the tourist in the region. Those areas with the highest multiplier effect provide more support for the tourist industry than areas with lower scores. The Caribbean, for example, is a low multiplier and has to import much of the goods and materials it needs to meet the demands of tourists. The United Kingdom, at the other end of the scale, provides much of its own support goods and materials. When China opened its doors to the world in 1978 and began to accept tourists again, it began developing rapidly to support a growing number of tourists. However, since it was so undeveloped, it had to import cars, buses, manufactured material, and technology from developed nations. This created considerable leakage in the multiplier; thus, for the first few years of expanding tourism, the multiplier was small. While the United States is an industrial economy and generally has a high multiplier effect, some regions within the United States have a lower multipliers than others.

The type of transportation and accommodations that a visitor chooses will also affect the income multiplier effect. Camping and caravans (camping vans) generate the least income to an area. Campers carry their own food or, if they purchase food, buy it in a grocery store or other retail outlets that are not as costly as restaurants, carfeterias, or pubs. The sleeping accommodations, quite naturally, cost less than they would if the campers were staying in a hotel, guest house, or bed-and-breakfast. Many French people prefer to camp when traveling. Consequently, some of the countries close to France, such as Spain and Portugal, do

TABLE 18-1 RECEIPTS AS A PERCENT OF TOTAL EXPORTS IN BALANCE OF PAYMENTS

Country	1985
European	
Austria	16.8
Denmark	5.5
Finland	3.0
France	5.2
Germany	2.7
Greece	20.1
Iceland	3.5
Italy	8.5
Netherlands	1.7
Norway	2.5
Portugal	14.2
Spain	21.1
Sweden	3.0
United Kingdom	3.5
Non-European	
Australia	4.0
Canada	3.5
Japan	0.5
New Zealand	3.8
United States	3.3

Source: Organization for Economic Cooperation Development, *Tourism Policy and International Policy in OECD Member Countries,* 1987, p. 79.

MULTIPLIER EFFECT
HOW TOURISM SPENDING FLOWS INTO THE ECONOMY

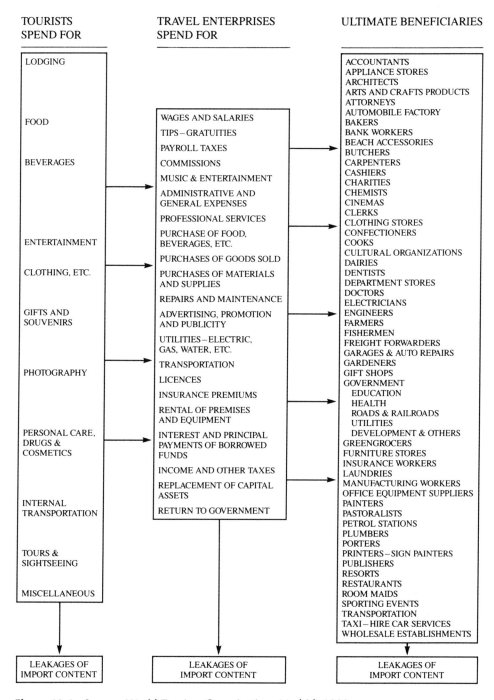

Figure 18-1: Source: World Tourism Organization, Madrid, 1982.

not receive as much income from their large numbers of French visitors as they do from visitors from other countries. Interestingly, whether it was intentional or not, when Spain decided to allow gambling in certain important tourist destination cities, the first two selected were cities with high numbers of French visitors. It may have been an effort to increase the income from these visitors, who like to both camp and gamble.

Bed-and-breakfast places, called pensions in Europe, are generally small, family run, and operate with a low capital outlay. Many people reserve a few bedrooms in their houses for visitors. Some of the old, large houses have

TABLE 18-2 TOURISM INCOME MULTIPLIER

Country or Region	Multiplier
Pacific and Far East	3.2 to 4.3
Hawaii	0.9 to 1.3
Greece	1.2 to 1.4
Pakistan	3.3
Ireland	2.7
Lebanon	1.2 to 1.4
Caribbean	0.58 to 0.88
U.S. Virgin Islands	0.57; 0.89
St. Lucia	0.80
Bahamas	0.89
Bermuda	0.86; 1.10
Eastern Caribbean	1.07
Antigua	0.88
Bahamas	0.78; 0.89; 1.36
Cayman Islands	0.65
British Virgin Islands	0.58

Source: Organization of American States: Department of Economic and Social Affairs. "Labor Market Issues in the English Speaking Caribbean Countries." Vol. 3, 1984, p. 19.

been renovated as bed-and-breakfast establishments. They usually have a few bedrooms, a parlor for watching television, and an eating area, and they are run by a family. There is a higher multiplier for those tourists who stay at these bed-and-breakfast establishments than in other types of accommodations. This is true because bed-and-breakfasts are much more labor-intensive. In other words, they have a higher ratio of employees per tourist than other accommodations. The residents (or employees) of these establishments will quickly spend the money for living expenses and to provide services for their guests. This keeps the money flowing through the area. Larger establishments, such as chain or multinational hotels, have a lower ratio of employees per tourist, and tend to have more leakage out of the local economy. Hotel owners or investors may not live in the area. They have a large profit margin and management fees that take money out of the local economy. In general, leakage can take several forms:

1. Payments abroad in the form of:
   (a) profits and capital remittances by foreign tourist companies;
   (b) wage remittances by expatriate workers;
   (c) interest payments on foreign loans;
   (d) management royalties and other fees, e.g., for franchised hotels;
   (e) payments due to foreign travel agents and tour operators.
2. The foreign exchange costs of capital investment in tourist facilities.
3. Promotion and publicity abroad.
4. The costs of imported goods and services used by tourists (e.g. imported fruit or whiskey).
5. Overseas training of personnel.
6. Extra expenditure on imports resulting from consumption by residents who have earned income from the tourist industry or whose

consumption patterns have altered due to the demonstration effects of tourism.[2]

Tourists who use public transportation create more income for an area than those who travel by car, and generally require only gasoline and some repairs. Public transportation requires the assistance of drivers and equipment maintained in the local area.

Although the general pattern is for tourists to travel from developed economies to developing economies, the lower multiplier effect in the developing countries indicates smaller dollar impact per tourist.

The second aspect of the multiplier effect is in employment. The tourist industry, in and of itself, is a valuable labor-intensive business. It employs large numbers of people by providing a wide range of jobs, from the unskilled to the highly specialized. Employment opportunities range from a diversity of unskilled jobs for maids, porters, gardeners, and cleaning people, to more skilled people such as entertainers, accountants, etc. In addition to the direct employment encouraged by tourism, there are many jobs created that, although not directly serving the tourists, exist because of tourism.

In the United States, travel expenditures generated 5.3 million jobs, paying well over $50 billion in wages and salaries.[3] In Britain, it has been estimated that for every hundred jobs created directly by tourism, approximately sixty others are created indirectly in other industries.

There is more indirect employment than direct employment generated in developing nations. For every hotel job created directly, there are three to four additional jobs created indirectly. This increase in indirect employment is strongest in nations that can produce agricultural commodities of the type demanded by hotels.

BENEFITS

General Income

The previous discussion shows two major benefits of the balance of trade payments and the tourist multiplier effect. Nations, wanting to increase their income, have used tourism as a means for reasonably quick growth. It takes less time to increase income from tourists than from manufactured goods or other available options. Mill and Morrison addressed this problem in the development of the manufacturing sector when they suggested that

The processing of raw materials—in increase local value-added—is related directly to the base amount available in the area, and possible projects are likely to be few for all but the most richly endowed nations.

For industries aimed at import substitution, the relatively small size of many domestic markets restricts growth.

Developing countries are characterized by a chronic shortage of skilled labor.

For export-oriented industries, their products will have to face full international competition, in terms of price and quality, as well as in terms of marketing techniques used.[5]

Tourism is both an income generator and an income redistributor. Over the past five years, world tourism growth has slowed. The receipts from 1980 to 1984 increased by an annual average of less than one percent, with 1982 and 1983 receipts falling below their 1981 level. However, in 1985 and 1986, receipts increased 6.9 percent and 5.0 percent respectively (see Chapter 1). Moreover, more of the receipts are going to the developing nations of the world.[6]

Much of this increase in developing nations has been in East Africa and the Pacific, principally as a result of China opening up to world tourism. The flow of capital from one country to another has been of concern to many nations resulting in some limit on the amount of currency nationals may take abroad for foreign travel. Spain has had a limit on the currency that can be taken out of the country, and will not allow transfers of money by check to other countries for payment of services rendered. During periods of large tourist deficits, Great Britain and France have limited foreign purchases of their citizens.

Donna F. Tuttle, the Deputy Secretary of Commerce, indicated the problem the United States faces when trying to increase the number of foreign tourists. She pointed out that in many countries the "allowance" is established in such a way that the traveler is encouraged to visit non-United States destinations. She cited an example of countries that limit the amount of currency that may be taken out of the country when visiting the United States, yet travelers to other countries are permitted to take any amount they choose.[7] Yet, in spite of these problems, the United States is the top earner of travel income in the world.

In addition to the benefits of additional income to a nation, tourism as a foreign exchange is becoming more important, since it is more stable than any other element of foreign trade. There is far more fluctuation in traditional commodity exports than in tourism.[8] The constancy of tourism receipts, because of the increasing demand for international travel, helps stabilize income flow to a country, and therefore, creates a greater dependency on tourism receipts than other commodities in the balance of trade payments.

In addition, the importance of tourism as a segment of international trade can be demonstrated by the fact that tourism produced foreign exchange earnings equal to or greater than world exports in raw materials, iron and steel, other semimanufactured goods, textiles, other consumer goods, clothes, nonferrous metals and minerals. For the past twenty years, tourism receipts have fluctuated around five percent of world exports. Throughout the world, travel and tourism has absorbed a rising proportion of consumer income.

Travel within the United States contributes enormously to its economy. In 1986, it was estimated that Americans spent $270 billion while traveling. The large states, led by California, received the most money; the small western states received the least. Some states, generally considered tourist states, such as Hawaii, Alaska, and Nevada, receive considerably less income than the large ones. However, tourism and travel are significant to these states' economies. Since they have small populations, it takes a smaller amount of gross income to be proportionately significant for them. These states also have well-defined tourist attractions, including many national parks and scenic areas. The larger states, such as New York, California, and Texas, have more diversified economies and, although they draw more total travel dollars, tourism is relatively less important to them.

The importance of tourism to individual states as a vital element of their economic growth has been well documented. One such study by Moheb Ghali, indicated that tourism in Hawaii had outstripped their traditional major money makers such as sugar, pineapple, and defense spending. The tourist trade had grown so well there that by 1974, for example, over 2.8 million visitors stayed at least one night in Hawaii, spending $1.07 billion.[9] By 1984, the income had grown to over $4.5 billion.[10]

For individual states and territories, there is a strong linkage with tourism and the other sectors of the economy. McElroy and Tinsley demonstrated the relationship between air arrivals and the value of construction permits from 1960 to 1979. The number of tourists arriving by air increased from 124,000 in 1960 to 826,813 in 1979, while construction permits increase from $7.5 million in 1960 to $73.1 million in 1979.[11]

Business Income

Much of the income, indicated above, at the international, national, and state level, is business income, going to operate organizations buying and selling goods and services to tourists. While the organizations are both small and big businesses, all the receipts are large. The total world airline passenger revenue in 1985 was $90 billion and is projected to reach $109.4 billion by 1990, an average annual increase of four percent. The total worldwide accommodations revenue was $123 billion in 1985; it is projected to be $149.6 billion in 1990.[12]

An advantage tourism offers developing countries is the range of businesses needed to provide for tourists. They include

—Local food, drinks, and flowers for the resort areas
—Local crafts for the tourists to buy
—Local cafes and restaurants
—Tour guides and interpreters
—Local travel services
—Local cultural events
—Decorative materials for the resort area
—Shops for tourist needs (for newspapers, film, drugstores, swimsuits, etc.)
—Specialized local housing (pensions, small inns)

Employment

As is the case with income, employment is an important benefit of tourism at all levels, from local to national. Generally, the tourist industry offers more employment opportunities than does any other economic sector; thus, generating employment is perhaps the single most important effect that tourism can have on a developing economy. Tourism employs people from population groups generally the most severely impacted by unemployment (women and youths). The three largest sectors, food and beverage, gifts and apparel, and services represent sixty-four percent of the total direct tourism employment.

World employment for 1984 was 64.3 million jobs generated by tourism (Table 18-3). It can be noted that more employment is generated per monetary unit for the developing nations. Thus, income generates employment faster for the developing nations than for the developed ones. Additionally, in the service sector, tourism employees in developed nations are usually paid at less than the average wage for the country, while in developing countries the opposite is true. In the United States, 13.7 million tourist jobs account for 12.7 percent of America's civilian work force.[13] This figure represents both the direct and indirect labor force.

The U.S. Travel Data Center indicated that travel expenditures for domestic trips alone directly generated 4.5 million jobs in 1984. Food service, the largest employer, accounted for nearly half the total. Within the United States, Nevada is the most dependent on travel for its jobs, with more than thirty percent. Only two other states have a double-digit share of total employment attributable to travel. They are Hawaii and Vermont. On the other hand, three states, Alabama, Connecticut, and Rhode Island, had less than three percent of their total employment payroll attributable to United States travel spending in 1984. The importance of travel to the economies of the states is borne out by the fact that in thirteen states, employment generated by domestic travel generated more jobs than any other private industry, and was among the top three employers in thirty-nine states.[14]

There are three types of employment generated by tourism; direct, indirect, and induced employment. Direct employment is considered employment generated as a result of providing goods and services directly to tourists in hotels, restaurants, bars, nightclubs, and so on. Those positions that are associated with other tourism-related activities, but used by both the local resident and the tourist (e.g., taxis, shops, and food wholesalers), are considered to be indirect employment. Induced employment refers to people working in positions only peripherally related to tourism, but generated because of it. A few examples of these jobs would be construction trades, professionals (doctors and accountants) who service the employees working directly in tourism-related positions, and merchants. This is the multiplier effect and is the basis for *Travel Industry World Yearbook*'s figure of 13.6 million jobs generated by tourism in the United States.

Government Receipts

Another economic benefit to all levels of government, is the amount of taxation brought in by tourist expenditures. Like any other sector, tourism is subject to taxes to generate revenue for whatever is deemed necessary by that state. Governments obtain these taxes from income tax, supplementary tax on wealth, capital gains tax, turnover tax, expenditure tax, and other indirect taxes.

Personal Income and Corporation Taxes

Two of the most direct forms of taxation are personal income tax and corporation tax. These taxes are based on the capacity to pay; nearly all countries have income taxes (individual and corporate) with varying schedules, structures, and methods of collection. In developed countries, a substantial portion of total revenues are gained in this manner, sometimes equaling more than fifty percent of all revenue. Other countries, particularly the developing ones, simply assess a poll tax (an indicative tax based on external signs of wealth).

In those countries where the degree of control by the public sector on economic activity is great, income transfer to the state is in a different form. Thus, it is not easy to draw parallels from one system to another, but some form of taxation always occurs. In centrally-planned economies, taxation of the individual is generally referred to as a tax on the population and varies according to the taxpayer's occupation and the specific country. Government enterprises, or corporations in capitalist countries, retain part of the income and pay taxes on the rest.

Turnover taxes are taxes on consumption; two major types are the sales tax and value added tax. Basically, the government levies a tax on goods and services that is passed directly on to the consumer. In many cases, tourists pay these taxes without knowing the precise amount, since it is included in the price of the goods and services. While sales tax is common in the United States, it is used less in other developed countries where it has been replaced by the value added tax (VAT). VAT is an indirect tax on goods and services. Table 18-4 shows the VAT rates for various European countries. The normal rate is the general level for most goods and services; the rest of the table indicates the rates applicable to tourists.

In many countries, in an effort to encourage production of goods, the VAT is refunded or deducted for tourists on items produced within that country, where additional sales would stimulate the economy through added employment and income. These goods, then, are considered an export item, since tourists will carry the goods from the

TABLE 18-3 EMPLOYMENT GENERATION BY TOURISM

Area	1984 Spending for Tourism Services ($ billions)	Jobs Generated (millions)
United States	411	13.6
Europe	427	14.1
Canada and Pacific	213	7.0
Rest of World	593	29.6
TOTAL WORLD	1,644	64.3

Source: *Travel Industry World Yearbook: The Big Picture—1987.*

TABLE 18-4 EUROPEAN VALUE ADDED TAX RATES

Rates	Germany FR	Belgium	Denmark	France	Ireland	Italy	Luxembourg	Norway	Netherlands	United Kingdom
Normal	13.0	17.0	22.0	17.6	25.0	15.0	10.0	20.0	18.0	15.0
Hotels - food	13.0	...	22.0	7.0	15.0	8.0	5.0	20.0	4.0	15.0
Hotels - lodging	13.0	6.0	22.0	17.6	15.0	8.0	5.0	(e)	4.0	15.0
Restaurants	13.0	17.0	22.0	17.6	15.0	8.0	5.0	20.0	4.0	15.0
International passenger traffic										
Air transport	0.0	0.0	(e)	0.0	(e)	0.0	0.0	(e)	0.0	0.0
Sea transport	0.0	0.0	(e)	0.0	(e)	0.0	0.0	(e)	0.0	0.0
Rail transport	6.5	6.0	(e)	0.0	(e)	0.0	0.0	(e)	4.0	0.0
Road transport	6.5	6.0	(e)	17.6	(e)	0.0	0.0	(e)	4.0	0.0
Theatre	(e)	6.0	22.0	7.0	10.0	8.0	5.0	20.0	18.0	15.0
Other public performances	6.5	6.0	22.0	17.6	10.0	8.0	5.0	20.0	18.0	15.0
Bus excursions	13.0	6.0	(e)	17.6	10.0	15.0	10.0	20.0	18.0	0.0
Tobacco	13.0	6.0	22.0	33.3	10.0	18 and 8	2.0	20.0	(7.4 to 14.7)	15.0
Books	6.5	6.0	22.0	7.0	10.0	2.0	5.0	4.0		4.0

Note: (e) exempt
Source: World Tourism Organization.

country. Thus, it is said that their purchases should not be taxed as domestic items. Travel-related businesses bring tax revenues directly to the country.

Expenditure Taxes

Expenditure taxes are luxury taxes paid on specific forms of consumption. Almost all tax systems impose such taxes on certain goods. They are often referred to as excise duties paid on items such as alcohol, tobacco, and petrol. This is done to control the production and consumption of such goods within the country (e.g., the increased social costs incurred by the consumption of alcohol). However, in order to promote international tourism, some countries provide some exceptions, usually in the form of duty-free sales for travelers at major ship and airplane terminals. Most countries have specific taxes on luxury goods because it is assumed that the purchaser can afford the increased costs.

Customs duties are import and export taxes, even though the tourists carry their purchases. Within this category are those taxes that are specific tourism taxes. They are justified and levied because tourism exists. Some are placed on the attractions, such as beach resorts or sports facilities. The justification is that tourism requires investment to construct those facilities, that financial resources must be obtained for this purpose, and thus the user should assist in paying for the development. In Switzerland these taxes are referred to as "taxes de sejour," in Federal Republic of Germany and Spain as "poliza de turismo," in Bulgaria, Poland, French Polynesia as "planning levy," in Peru as "consumption levy," and in Colombia as "impuesto turistico." [15] In the United States, a common tourist tax is the hotel room tax. The revenue is usually used to assist in promoting the local area.

Other Indirect Taxes

There are a variety of other indirect taxes such as fines, estate taxes, and income taxes paid by employees in tour-ism-related employment that are collected by the various levels of government.

The tax revenue resulting from tourism represented 2.1 percent of the total tax revenue collected in the United States. The tax revenue resulting from tourism was slightly more important to the states, accounting for 3.1 percent of their tax revenue.

COSTS

While most countries encourage tourism for the benefit it provides their economies, there are some negative economic aspects to tourism.

General Costs

Income derived from tourism is not always constant since tourists are transient. Political and other forces can

Variety of items that visitors may choose while shopping in Thailand. Photo courtesy of the Tourism Authority of Thailand.

rapidly change the flow of tourists and their money. *Travel Industry World Yearbook* estimated that Europe lost $1.2 billion in United States spending in 1986 because of terrorism, or the perceived unsafe travel environment. Currency fluctuation also effects income. The dollar dropping almost forty percent in value dramatically increased the flow of international tourists to the United States in 1987.

The increased demand for local products and land in some areas results in inflation, thus having a negative influence on local residents. One of the greatest markets in the world, Chichicastenango, Guatamala is a major attraction for tourists. However, the increased demand for goods and services by the tourists have driven prices up so high that a number of changes are occurring. First, local people no longer wear traditional clothing because it commands a high price on the local market; the inflated price benefits the person who controls the market but no one else. Consequently, local people purchase the cheaper western styles made of mass-produced material. Second, the increased costs for produce has forced some local people to travel great distances to other markets, thus increasing their costs for goods and services.

In some countries, the demand for hard currency is so high that a strong black market has developed. This is particularly true in socialist countries that need hard currency to pay for their imports from the western industrial countries. This is seen in the Soviet Union, where in spite of rather rigid controls by the authorities, the black market flourishes.

Not only is employment affected by the ebb and flow of tourist numbers, but also on its seasonal nature of tourism. To overcome this problem, Mallorcan officials imposed a tax on hotels which goes to unemployed hotel workers during the low season.

Two other important economic costs that are often associated with tourism are leakage of income from the area or country (as discussed in the sections on the balance of trade payments and the multiplier effect) and economic over-dependence on tourism. Leakage generally occurs through importing goods and services, the remittance of profits and wages to outside sources, promotion to encourage tourists, and inflation. Economic dependency occurs when a region becomes highly dependent upon tourism and subsequent changes in the flow of tourists to that region dramatically affect the area.

Private Sector Costs

Tourism is both a labor intensive and capital intensive industry, and requires a large expenditure of money to develop. The peaks and valleys of the seasons create fund flow problems that require access to short-term loans and banking support. Many projects require great amounts of capital investment but, in developing areas, the capital is not available to support the development. Even in industrial countries, local areas may want to benefit from the development of tourist-related facilities, but be unable to. In an effort to encourage development, governments have a number of methods to assist them. In general, governments reduce the cost of tourism investment by

(a) *granting exemption from taxes on the cost of capital goods and other productive inputs (skilled manpower, technological manpower, training of professionals, and technicians, etc.)*

(b) *granting public subsidies which reduce investment costs*

(c) *changes in the basis of taxation such as:*
   —*Tax incentives which treat interest on capital investments as tax-deductible, especially interest paid on foreign capital;*
   —*Allowing losses to be written off for purposes of tax levied on tourist activities which in many cases enables returns to be reduced and thus less tax to be paid;*
   —*Forms of depreciation allowable for tax purposes, e.g. incentives such as accelerated depreciation, extraordinary depreciation or excess depreciation. The aim is for the present value of depreciation allowed for tax purposes to be greater than present value arising from straight-line depreciation.*

(d) *tax incentives for foreign investment in tourism*[16]

Tax incentives appear in a number of forms. Most tax exemptions are given for a specific number of years. Allowances are deductions, which enable investors to reduce their basic liability, in the form of an accelerated depreciation. Tax deductions reduce or eliminate taxes so that consumer prices are lower and consumption by tourists, presumably, higher. A moratorium on payment puts off the date the tax payment must be made. Tax refunds on important items are necessary for development. Reduced tax rates are the same as tax credits. Nonliability for taxation is the exclusion of certain taxable tourist activities.[17]

Public Sector Costs

Loss of revenue is the public cost engendered by the tax collection method. However, this may be offset by increased employment and indirect revenue generated by that employment and income. In some cases, direct government investment is necessary for development to occur; this takes a reallocation of funds from other needed items.

IMPACT CONTROL MEASURES

There are a number of ways that the economic impact can lessen the negative aspects and optimize benefits to the area. Edward Inskeep, a consultant for WTO has suggested the following:

1. Develop tourism gradually, so that local residents have sufficient time to adapt to it and understand it, and the government can properly plan, organize and monitor tourism.

2. Maintain a scale of tourism development that is appropriate for the local environment and society and, where possible, develop other economic sectors so that there is a balanced economy and employment structure.

TABLE 18-5 ECONOMIC IMPACT MODEL

Benefit Factors	Cost Factors
Primary	*Private Costs*
1. Business receipts	1. Capital investment
2. Income	2. Operating capital
a. Labor or proprietors' income	3. Funds flow—cash, profitability, etc.
b. Corporate profits, dividends, interest and rent	*Public Costs*
3. Employment	1. Direct
a. Private	a. Services (public, fire, sanitation, facilitation)
b. Public	b. Investments—infrastructure, incentives (tax holidays, etc.)
c. Nonprofit	2. Indirect
4. Government receipts	a. Services
a. Federal	b. Investments
b. State	
c. Local	
Secondary	*General*
1. Business receipts	1. Creates overdependence on foreign tourism receipts and income.
a. Indirect*	2. Requires foreign imports which reduce net balance of foreign exchange earnings
b. Induced**	
2. Income	
a. Indirect	
b. Induced	
3. Employment	
a. Indirect	
b. Induced	
General	
1. Distribution or redistribution of benefits	
2. Stimulates exports which contribute to surplus balance of payments nationally	
3. Creates linkages with other economic sectors which utilize surplus goods and services produced domestically	

*Benefits generated by primary business outlays, including investment.
**Benefits generated by spending of primary income.
Source: After Douglas Frechtling, former Director, U.S. Travel Data Center.

In some areas, small-scale and dispersed forms of tourism are more suitable than concentrated mass tourism development.

3. Involve residents and their spokespeople in the decision-making process of planning and developing tourism, so that they can participate in determining the future of this sector.

4. Use tourism to help justify and financially support the preservation and maintenance of archeological and historic sites, conservation and revitalization of traditional dance, music, drama, arts, and handicrafts unique to the area, development of museums and cultural centers, and the organization of cultural events.

5. Where appropriate, apply the concept of tourism development zones so that any negative socioeconomic impacts are limited.

6. Make certain that residents have easy access to tourist attractions, facilities, and services, including reduced admission fees if necessary, and that important amenity features have public access and are not preempted by tourism.

7. Provide incentives for local ownership, management, and operation of hotels and other tourist facilities and services so that residents can receive direct economic benefits.

8. Develop strong linkages between tourism and other economic activities, such as agriculture, fisheries, handicrafts, and manufacturing, to help develop those sectors, reduce leakage of foreign exchange through import substitution, and spread the economic benefits of tourism.

9. Plan, develop, and organize tourism so that no area becomes too congested with tourists and residents can easily use community facilities and services.

10. Train local people to work effectively in all levels of tourism including managerial and technical positions in order to reduce the number of imported employees and to lessen possible misunderstandings between tourists and local employees.[18]

SUMMARY

Economic impacts discussed in this chapter can best be summarized in a model (see Figure 18-5). This model indicates the various components of both the economic benefits and costs of tourism. It illustrates the interrelated nature of economic activities between the government and private sectors and the various segments of the tourist industry, and serves to suggest that to benefit fully from tourism, a city, region or nation must achieve a balance.

RESEARCH AND REVIEW

1. Define balance of trade payments and describe three types.

2. Why is tourism an invisible export or import?

3. Compare and contrast the multiplier effect on developing nations and the developed nations of the world.

4. Why are multipliers higher for family-owned-and-operated establishments than for large multinational companies?

5. Describe four kinds of leakage in the balance of trade payments.

6. Discuss the economic benefits of tourism.

7. Give some examples of direct and indirect taxes.

8. What are some negative economic aspects of the costs of tourism?

9. What are four control measures that a government can take to reduce the negative impact of tourism?

10. What is a value added tax?

ENDNOTES

1. *Travel & Leisure's World Travel Overview 1987/1988,* pp. 31–32.
2. IUOTO (now WTO), "The Impact of International Tourism on the Economic Development of the Developing Countries" (Geneva, 1975).
3. *World Travel Overview 1987/1988,* p. 45.
4. Robinson, p. 129.
5. Mill and Morrison, p. 222.
6. Donna F. Tuttle, "The 'Visit USA' Program After 25 Years: Changing Markets, Growing Competition and New Challenges Ahead," *Business America* (Washington, DC: U.S. Dept. of Commerce, Feb. 17, 1986), p. 5.
7. Ibid.
8. WTO, "Economic Review of World Tourism" (Madrid, 1982), p. 63.
9. Moheb Ghali, "Tourism and Regional Growth: An Empirical Study of the Alternative Growth Paths for Hawaii," *Studies in Applied Regional Science* 11 (Leiden: Martinue, 1977), p. 35.
10. *Travel Industry World Yearbook—1987,* p. 98.
11. Jerome L. McElroy and John F. Tinsley, "United States Virgin Islands," *Tourism in the Caribbean* (Ottawa: International Development Center, 1982), p. 35.
12. *Travel Industry World Yearbook—1987,* p. 11.
13. Ibid., p. 15.
14. U.S. Travel Data Center, "Impact of Travel on State Economics, 1984" (Washington, DC, 1986), pp. 28–29. The U.S. Travel Data Center and *Travel Industry World Yearbook* have differing statistics because the U.S. Travel Data Center considers only domestic travel, thus omitting the nearly $13 billion in foreign travel, and they indicate only direct employment, while *Travel Industry World Yearbook* indicates both direct and indirect employment.
15. WTO, p. 19.
16. Ibid., pp. 25–29.
17. Ibid., pp. 29–32.
18. Edward L. Innskeep, *WTO Interdisciplinary Study Cycle—Granada: Socioeconomic Consideration in Tourism* (Spain, 1987), pp. 3–7.

CHAPTER 19

SOCIAL AND CULTURAL IMPACTS

Although the desire for cultural experiences has always been an important motivator for travel, it became much more important in the 1980s. This can be seen in tour offerings that include visits with families in private homes, an evening with a Bedouin family in their tent, or attendance at a series of lectures on education, health, agriculture, or history from local professionals.

TOURISM AND CULTURE

Culture is defined as a combination of the values, beliefs, symbols, and technology of a group of people, or the learned behavior associated with a common group; it includes symbolic language, architectural styles, clothing styles, food preferences, technology, legal systems, the role people play in social groups, political systems, race relations, and so on. Culture is expressed both in the landscape, and in the way of life of a group of people within a given area. Ritchie and Zins identified the following twelve elements of culture that are attractions for tourists:

1. Language
2. Traditions
3. Handicrafts
4. Food and eating habits
5. Art and music
6. History of the region (oral, written, and landscape)
7. Work and technology
8. Religion (expressed orally and in the landscape)
9. Architectural characteristics of the area
10. Dress
11. Educational systems
12. Leisure activities[1]

221

Mathieson and Wall suggested that cultural attractiveness centers around three major forms of culture:

1. *Forms of culture which are inanimate or which do not directly involve human activity. Tourists visiting places of unique architecture and art, historical buildings and monuments, and purchasing traditional arts and crafts are notable examples;*
2. *Forms of culture reflected in the normal daily life of a destination. Visiting "foreign" peoples to observe their normal social, economic and leisure activities in an attempt to understand their lifestyles, ideologies and customs is a common tourist motivation;*
3. *Forms of culture which are especially animated and may involve special events or depict historic or famous occurrences. Examples include musical festivals, carnivals, festivals reflecting old traditions and behavior, reenactment of battles and displays of old machinery.*[2]

Much has been written about the social and cultural impact of tourism on people. There are those who suggest tourism is a plague on the world, particularly on developing societies.

Two attributes of tourism have been to increase the acculturation process and cultural convergence of peoples. Acculturation is defined as those changes that occur in a culture through borrowing from other cultures; changes may include technology, language, and values. Cultural convergence is the tendency of world cultures to become more alike. For example, as other people are exposed to European culture and technology, particularly those in urban areas of less developed countries, they adopt many European ways.[3] This has occurred most rapidly in the past one hundred years since developing nations have increased their contact with western developed nations, and are proceeding to industrialize themselves.

One characteristic of the world is that its urban areas are becoming more and more alike. Modernization and change from an agriculture society to an industrialized one brings changes in people's attitudes, their way of life, and beliefs. Part of this change occurs through contact with tourists. In fact, tourism causes more interaction between peoples; it is the prime force in acculturation. Those people changing the least are the isolated ones; those who live in regions of extreme environmental conditions—deserts, jungles, or polar regions. Acculturation is a process that would occur without tourism, but tourism accelerates the process. In some cases, tourism may be blamed for a process that is inevitable.

These issues may appear, to officials in developing nations, to be manufactured by the industrialized nations to maintain their economic advantage. For example, at a meeting of The International Geographic Union Commission on Tourism, a participant reported on the negative attributes of high-rise hotels and other such tourism facilities. A representative from an African country rose and suggested that the negativity of western professionals was a ploy to keep developing countries from gaining the benefits of modernization. In a paper given by Mike Ashman at the Regional Development Planning Seminar of the East-West Center Technology Institute, two opposing incidents were reported. He reported one experience he had while visiting Honolulu. He met a group of Micronesian elected leaders in front of the big, Ala Moana Hotel. In conversation, after hearing their positive comments about having similar hotels to this one on their tiny islands, he asked if they would like to have their sons and daughters working in a place like that. A positive response was given based on the fact that waitresses and bellboys were smiling and seemed to be happy. Later, in Spain, some college-educated young people who had been to college away from home, presented a petition against the development of a proposed seven-story hotel. The petition was not accepted by the older residents because they felt the hotel was a sign of the progress they wanted.[4] Tourism does have its problems; it can cause some undesirable behaviors and patterns which can be avoided through awareness and proper planning.

HOST-VISITOR INTERACTIONS

In part, the process of understanding the social-cultural impact tourists have on an area comes from an understanding of the characteristics of various types of visitors. Valene Smith developed a typology of tourists in which she outlines her views of the intensity of interaction between the visitors (guests) and the local residents (hosts). Her classification is as follows:

Explorers: The character of this type of visitor is similar to that of an anthropologist—interested in being an active participant-observer among the host population. The explorer easily accommodates to local lifestyles, and does not need special "tourist" accommodations.

Elite: This type of tourist is few in number, and can afford to pay well for unusual vacations. Elite tourists are well-traveled, and usually referred to as the "jet-set." They differ from explorers in their attitude. Their arrangements can be made by any travel agent and be preplanned. Though they are willing to be adventurous and sample the local lifestyle, they require some degree of comfort.

Off-Beat: These tourists seek to get away from the tourist crowds, or to do something beyond the norm of a "typical tourist." They adapt well to simple accommodations and services provided for the occasional visitor.

Unusual Tourists: These tourists will leave an organized tour for brief visits to out-of-the-way locations. They tend to seek exotic cultural sites, the unusual or "primitive," as long as they can quickly and safely return to their more familiar surroundings and group.

Incipient Mass Tourists: These are the people who arrive in an area in a steady flow, either separately or in small groups. These tourists like the amenities of Western societies, the hotels and other travel-related facilities. They are a mixture of both pleasure-seeking and business visitors.

Mass Tourists: These are mainly middle class. They arrive at a destination in large numbers expecting all the

amenities of a well-developed industry, including a solicitous staff and multilingual employees in the hotels and
restaurants. There is a diversity of tastes among them and
their attitude is basically, "you-get-what-you-pay-for."

Charter Tourists: These tourists come *"en masse,"* creating an extremely high amount of business, and receiving
a high degree of standardization in services and products.
The interaction between the visitors and the hosts are limited and impersonal.[5]

The level of interaction between the hosts and guests
is illustrated in Table 19-1 for each type of tourist. Impact
and stress increases with each level of tourist. The explorers
and elite tourists, because of their limited numbers, usually
make little impact upon local culture, since few services
and simple hotels are required. The off-beat and unusual
tourists generally use the same hotels and services as do
local travelers. With the increase in number, greater expectations, and demand for special facilities and services,
there is a concomitant change in the local area.

Against this background it is possible to discuss the
different ways tourists make an impact on a locale. The
costs and benefits are summarized in Table 19-2.

BENEFITS

Social Change and Cross-Cultural Understanding

There are those who consider that one of the most
promising benefits of tourism is the bringing of culturally
diverse people together to help them understand one another. Pope Pius XII touched on this aspect of tourism when
he spoke of "subjecting oneself, joyfully or sorrowfully, to
the inconveniences, great and small, which can with difficulty be avoided, even on best-organized tours, making
contact with habits, traditions, convictions and prejudices
which are completely foreign to one's ordinary mentality."
Tourism, then, can become a tool for promoting understanding among peoples and cultures by causing them to
reconsider their traditional stereotyped images of different
cultures. This, certainly, is one of the objectives of socialist
governments.

China, in the late 1970s and early 1980s, provided
many opportunities for a group of touring diplomats to meet
local residents of all segments of society. Visitors were
taken to schools, factories, stores, health centers, hospitals,
and residential areas to visit local residents and observe
their lifestyles. The objective of these visits, and similar
ones in other socialist countries, was to demonstrate that
socialists are people with feelings, who work for a living,
and have an established way of life, attempting to human-
ize the local residents in the eyes of the visitors.

Thus, although governments might differ and each
might think of the other as an "evil empire," the visitor/
host interchange might create a cross-cultural understanding that on the "other side" there live folk "just-like-us."
Governments have felt that the young would be more ame-
nable to cross-cultural understanding, since they often like
to travel to less well-known locales, are also less demand-
ing in the type of facilities they are offered, and establish
personal relationships with the local populace. The WTO
has concluded that "The strong interest of governments in
the development of youth tourism appears to be attributable
to two factors; firstly, the fact that youth tourism at the
present time is an important factor in world integration and
education for peace; it is through youth tourism that basic
values may be exchanged. Secondly, the future shape of
tourism for adults is dependent upon the present profile of
youth tourism."[6]

The WTO recognizes this fact. It considers that tourism
is an encounter between a person and a destination in its
natural setting, with its historic and contemporary culture.
Above all, the WTO believes it is an exchange or encounter
between individual groups of people, as well as between
social groups; as such, it becomes an encounter between
nations and an exchange of values and of cultures.[7]

The impact of this exchange is significantly different
between industrialized nations and developing agricultural
nations. The WTO concluded that the more isolated the
country visited, the more significant are the likely social
and cultural changes to be.

The WTO outlined the positive social effects of tourism
as follows:

1. Social Structure:
   a) transition from employment in agriculture to
      the service sector;
   b) modernization of agriculture;
   c) decline in gaps between income levels;
   d) decline in differences in educational
      opportunities;
2. Modernization of the family:
   a) new status of women in the traditional peasant
      family;
   b) more liberal standards applied by parents to
      their children;
3. Broadening of outlook of residents of the
   receiving areas:
   a) changes in ethnic attitudes;
   b) diminution of prejudices.[8]

TABLE 19-1 FREQUENCY AND TYPES OF TOURISTS AND THEIR
ADAPTATION TO LOCAL NORMS

Type of Tourist	Number of Tourists	Adaptations to Local Norms
Explorer	Very limited	Adapts fully
Elite	Rarely seen	Adapts fully
Off-beat	Uncommon but seen	Adapts well
Unusual	Occasional	Adapts some-what
Incipient mass	Steady flow	Seeks Western amenities
Mass	Continuous influx	Expects Western amenities
Charter	Massive arrivals	Demands West-ern amenities

Source: Valene L. Smith, *Hosts and Guests: The Anthropology of Tourism*
(Philadelphia: Univ. of Pennsylvania Press, 1977), p. 9.

TABLE 19-2 SOCIAL AND CULTURAL IMPACTS OF TOURISM

Benefits	Costs
1. Creates a new medium for social change and multicultural understanding.	1. Physical presence of tourists—saturation, competition for limited resources.
2. Demonstration effects—encourages adaptation to realities of modern life and works toward improving the host country's environment and lifestyle options.	2. Demonstration effects—inappropriate alien commodities/lifestyles; hosts model themselves after tourist behavior, which is temporary and lacks normal constraints, builds unreasonable economic expectations, youth susceptibility; changes structure of rural life; encourages migration; changes in social structure, roles of women, community cohesion, demographics, and institutional membership.
3. Promotes knowledge and use of foreign languages.	3. Resentments due to expatriate presence—e.g., technology, alien food/drink tastes, foreign managers, specialists, etc.
4. Improves motivation and conditions necessary for better health, disease control, and sanitation.	4. Increase in socially disruptive behavior—i.e., crime, prostitution, alcohol and drug abuse, hawking, etc.
5. Stimulates cultural awareness and exposure through first-hand observation and participation (e.g., handicrafts, gastronomy, the arts, history, technology, architecture, social institutions, dress, leisure lifestyles, etc.).	5. Disguised form of colonialism and imperialism—e.g., economic dependency, multi-national control and manipulation, misuse of local residents.
6. Opportunity for intercultural communication.	6. Promotes immoral behavior—i.e., sexual liberties, hedonistic behavior, gambling, loosening of religious traditions.
7. Renaissance of native craftsmanship, art forms, distinctive lifestyles.	7. Native language changed or used less.
8. Produces personal benefits for the tourists—i.e., —Psychological —Physical —Interpersonal (between tourists and tourist/hosts) —Cultural —Business and professional development.	8. Tourists induce pollution and transmit disease to the host community.
9. Provides unlimited opportunities to develop authentic attractions, thus enhancing pride in the host's ethnic, racial, artistic, and similar cultural origins.	9. Inappropriate cultural changes—adoption/homogenization of "weak" to "strong" culture—i.e., strong materialistic, culture drift.
10. Attracts permanent residents to a destination for employment or retirement reasons, thus providing a more stable population base.	10. Disappearance of traditional art and craft forms by replacement with mass produced replicas.
	11. Reduces host culture to commodity status, violates host's cultural rights, and creates contrived attractions.
	12. Promotes cultural arrogance—e.g., manipulate authentic host traditions and events to conform to tourist time schedules, tastes etc.; use of foreign design/furnishings in hotels, restaurants and public spaces.

Source: Compiled by the authors.

This was expressed again and clarified in the WTO General Assembly in New Delhi, in 1983. First, the quality of life improves where tourism is being developed in rural areas by bringing both the urban infrastructure (water, housing, and sewerage) and population benefits (medical care, social assistance, schools, and cultural institutions) together. Second, the changes that occur in occupation and income patterns create a middle class with its resulting different attitudes, values, and social concerns. Third, increased social mobility follows educational improvements that result in new employment opportunities in tourism. Fourth, changes occur in family relations. Changing employment patterns from an agricultural society to a service society increases the family income rather substantially,

and decreases the dependency of family members upon one person. It introduces new positive and negative values to the family. The positive ones are the importance of education, health, and knowledge. In 1982, the OAS suggested that the potential social impacts of tourism could be categorized as those affecting the individual person, the family, and the community.

There are three ways in which tourism can affect individual people. They are first, that tourism can change inferior feelings that residents of developing countries sometimes have, by showing that economic wealth does not always bring security; the myth of a superpower foreigner is exposed.[9] Second, studies have indicated that tourism reinforces cultural traditions. Third, many cultural traditions and practices create an ethnic identity for the needs of the host population rather than for tourist consumption.[10]

Tourism can lead to the strengthening of the family by increasing the availability of jobs and opportunities that bring greater income; it can also improve the status of women in the family. Augustin Reynoso y Valle and Jacomina P. de Regt stated that women's employment outside the home in Ixtapa-Zihuatanejo has challenged the traditional machismo of the Mexican male.[11] Andronicou in "Tourism in Cyprus" suggested that tourism strengthened the family when he said:

> There is little doubt that the development of tourism created new jobs. Women in particular were hired not only for the low-paid jobs of cleaning and washing, but also as receptionists, managers, and tourist guides. The improved financial status of females did not create conflicts between parents and children or husbands and wives, nor did it challenge the authority of the parents or husbands. The ambition of every parent in Cyprus is to offer his children a good education and secure for them jobs which will establish them as decent citizens. The financial benefits accruing from tourism in fact enabled family members to share these financial burdens and encouraged savings that are used by the children to create their own homes and live more comfortably.[12]

The key to having tourism have a positive impact on the family lies first in developing a proper attitude concerning the importance of education.

Frank E. Manning indicated that tourism has had a positive impact on Bermudian communities. In an article, entitled "Tourism and Bermuda's Black Clubs: A Case of Cultural Revitalization," he wrote (after observing the custom of Bermudians to smile, wave, or extend a word of greeting to tourists):

> In this type of culture Bermudians came to present themselves to visitors as a society not of waiters and bellhops but of social directors and public relations artists. . . . hence, unlike other societies. . . where the encounter has become associated with colonial servitude and racial subordination, Bermuda has evolved a set of symbols that define amiable interaction with tourists as an essential expression of social identity and cultural character.[13]

Finally, a summary of the benefits of tourism to a society as a whole increases the sociocultural integration at the national level. The differences in outlook, lifestyles, and customs are diminished, and they are exposed to new values, customs, and traditions. Second, the linking created by domestic tourism helps people learn about their own country; decreasing regionalism in a nation brings about national unity. This is an important goal of domestic tour-

ism in the Soviet Union where tourists from the various regions and republics are encouraged, even by being given financial assistance, to visit Moscow and become familiar with other parts of Russia. It serves as a form of Russification, an acculturation process. Third, domestic tourism is important as a means of increasing educational diversification, knowledge of other areas, national values and, consequently, developing a respect for them. Fourth, tourism, in its contact with others, promotes progress and modernization through exposure to other attitudes and values. Fifth, domestic tourism improvements bring about improvements in other facilities and services, and increase both the quality of the leisure experience and the quality of life.[14]

Foreign Language Use

Foreign language use brings people in contact with those of other language groups. The need and desire to communicate increases interest by both the host and guest to learn another language. In Europe, because of the considerable amount of interaction which takes place, most central and western Europeans speak two or three languages. People can change from one language to another quite easily.

The English and southern Europeans are less skilled in languages. Only when the residents in those regions receive many tourists from another language group, will they develop skills in that language as a means of improving their own economic conditions. Around resort and other tourist enclaves in developing countries such as Mexico, Spain, and Italy, taxi drivers, hotel clerks, maids, waiters, waitresses, and others have picked up English, French, or German, depending upon the language most prevalent among tourists.

Visitors to destinations will, after a tour, often want to learn a language to improve the quality of future experiences. They may want to attend a school, or rent tapes and buy books to assist them in learning the language. In many of the popular tourist destinations, a number of short-term language courses have been developed to assist visitors.

Improved Health Conditions and Disease Control

For the tourist, physical and mental health are prime motivators for traveling. The desire for a high-quality public health facilities can contribute to the maintenance and improvement of those facilities in destination areas, and provide additional sources of revenue, which, in turn, can be invested in upgrading water and sewage disposal facilities.

Through tourism, local residents can become aware of both health problems and good hygiene. Thus, both the incentive and the financial capacity to develop a health infrastructure, and an awareness of good hygiene, will assist in affecting change in a destination. The WTO indicated that the presence of tourists, and their desire to avoid waterborne illnesses, requires local authorities to establish standards for chlorination of drinking water and treatment of waste water. They concluded that without tourism these measures would probably not be taken so promptly. Improvements in one community then acts as an impetus for improvement throughout the region, into areas that have little contact with tourists.

Renaissance of Native Culture

Tourism may be important to the host country or area to remind its peoples of its history and culture. In both eastern and western Europe, many traditional folk costumes and customs are perpetuated for the benefit of tourists, and folk culture festivals are organized to attract visitors and their money. Model cultural centers, in both the developed and developing nations, have been very successful and highly profitable and in some groups, have helped sustain interest in their cultures.

Traditional art forms have been through a renaissance in a number of countries. In the United States it has been particularly evident among the Indians. The Cherokee, in Tennessee, established an arts and crafts center, and, in cooperation with the local school district, has arranged a released time program for Indian students to receive instruction in traditional arts and crafts. L. I. Deitch, in a study of the Indians of the Southwestern United States, indicated that the increased demand for Indian arts and crafts encouraged the increased manufacture of traditional Indian rugs, pottery, jewelry, and baskets. This demand also led to the refinement of art forms by improving the quality and sophistication of the projects.[15] Deitch's study, and others of the Southwest Indians and the Canadian Inuit (Eskimo), found that the Indians were able to use their skills and traditional methods to produce additional souvenirs. Their talents and traditional skills were maintained and developed, both to revitalize traditional art forms and to create an impetus for new designs.[16]

Outside the United States, the impact has been the same. Eliam Tanirono, considering the impact of tourism on the Solomon Island culture, reported that tourism may have stimulated a movement for the preservation of traditional art including traditional songs and dances. During European attempts to "Christianize" the natives, and the process of acculturation to western culture, some traditional culture was lost—traditional songs and dances, for example, became taboo. As European attitudes changed and tourism grew, a return to traditional dances, songs, and art was encouraged. Tanirono was concerned that the young dancers might be interested only in the economic value gained from performing rather than maintaining cultural traditions associated with the dances and songs.[17]

Dr. Philip McKean, studying the positive impact of tourism on Balinese culture, indicated that with the opening of an airport, in 1969, thousands of tourists poured into the country to enjoy Balinese temple dancing and religious rites. In addition, tourists purchased handicrafts, paintings, and carvings. They took part in the ritual performances, and contributed to the economic well-being of the community in general.[18]

Ngahuia Te Awekotuku, indicated that tourists were alleged to be responsible for conserving traditional arts and crafts in the Rotorua, New Zealand area. The New Zealand Maori Arts and Crafts Institute depends entirely upon tourist

revenue for financing. The Institute, housed in a large building on the grounds of the national park, not only produces traditional Maori carvings, but trains apprentices at the Institute and conducts a traveling program to teach basic weaving skills and traditional garment production. The typical Maori articles—carvings, piupui (kilts), baskets, taniko weaving, jade ornaments—are collectors' items, and although some modification in their design has occurred, the essential Maori flavor is not compromised. The smaller, mass produced plastic curiosities, sold in abundance, are not a good representation of the culture, but are sold because they are what tourists "want."[19]

This trend to make cheap, inferior copies of classic art is common throughout the world. However, some areas have been able to adapt traditional art forms to the needs of the tourists, and produce them at a price tourists can afford. The American Indian doll, Kachina, is such an example. Tourist interest in the art has helped to preserve cultural artistic values by reviving the local population's interest. In many areas, as in Haiti with Haitian painting, tourist interest has contributed to the preservation of dying art forms. It fosters diversification of creative arts and crafts and employs local artisans. Sometimes, imported designs and materials were used to erect buildings that did not always blend with local architectural styles. Most recently, large-scale developments have tried to remedy this by merging hotel architecture with the local environment. The use of local materials and architectural styles not only maintained the local identity, but also reduced monetary leakage from the country.

The establishment of model culture villages (living museums) have contributed significantly to the renaissance of native traditions and crafts. Model culture villages are planned developments, creating historical and ethnic environments, designed to perpetuate tradition and stimulate awareness of the local area. Max Stanton stated the creation of the Polynesian Cultural Center in Hawaii was designed

> to keep alive (even revive) traditional art forms and practices, giving the guest a chance to view some limited historical aspects of lifestyle as it once was. . . As a cultural model or living museum the Center used a thematic approach which concentrates on certain dynamic and tangible aspects of culture. In an effort to make the visit more meaningful, each of the villages has developed some specific activity such as husking a coconut, learning to use a certain percussion instrument, involvement in a game of skill, or performing a dance that encourages tourist participation—all are popular with visitors.[20]

There are one or two purposes for cultural model villages. The first is to provide a location where visitors may observe and participate in a particular culture without disrupting the everyday lives of the people who live in the area; second, the model village is designed to portray the past history of the area. Living museums that represent the historical past include Williamsburg, Virginia and Old Sturbridge Village, Massachusetts, the Norwegian Folk Mu-

Fifes and drums of Colonial Williamsburg perform during the Christmas holidays. Photo courtesy of the Virginia Division of Tourism.

seum, and the Welsh Folk Museum, near Cardiff, Wales. Historical museums are common in many countries of the world. Some museums designed to display culture are the Bangkok's Rose Gardens, Fijian Orchid Island, and Nana Museum of the Arctic at Kotzebue, Alaska.

Folk festivals and fairs are other events that result in the preservation of traditional values and cultural awareness. At the Pennlsylvania Dutch Festival in Kutztown, a play on the theme of cultural conflict within an Amish family living in a modern world is performed nightly. The history of the Amish people forms the background of the play. Each summer night, Cherokees at the Cherokee village in Tennessee present "The Trail of Tears," a representation of their history. Local and state fairs exhibit local handicrafts. These maintain interest in, and stimulate continued exhibitions of older forms of handicrafts.

COSTS

While tourism has enabled different people to restore and maintain interest in their own cultures, or to strengthen the social structure, mass tourism has not only controlled the direction of this rejuvenation as illustrated above, but brought with it problems and costs.

Social Saturation

Cultural stress caused by tourism varies according to a country's stage of development. Tourism among the most developed countries, with their similar civilizations and well-developed infrastructures, creates little stress—at least until the competition of tourism for goods and services inconveniences residents.

This has occurred in England. Decreased air fares have attracted record numbers of tourists. British public transportation is so crowded with tourists, at times there is hardly any room for local residents. Shops are full of travelers, forcing natives to change shopping patterns. Subways and streets are full of visitors resulting in traffic jams. Westminster Cathedral hardly seems like a church because so many tourists flock to see it, not to worship. There is a growing feeling that tourism in London must not continue to increase. The vignette, "London Regroups After Tumultuous Tourist Season" illustrates this point.

There is greater concern about tourism's impact on developing nations, however. When an area exceeds its social carrying capacity, the nature of the area changes completely. The nature of tourist saturation and its impact on a community was illustrated in the London Sunday Times (1972), in a report showing a change that occurred in Lloret, a Spanish town.

They say it used to be a fishing village . . . but the village itself has disappeared beneath an appalling welter of hotel blocks, fish-and-chips shops, pubs, souvenir shops, discotheques and slot-machine arcades. In the height of summer Lloret is a quite dreadful place . . . Perhaps the most obnoxious feature is the smell of cooking oil—the product of

LONDON REGROUPS AFTER TUMULTUOUS TOURIST SEASON

by James O. Jackson

London—School is back in session, autumn's pleasant nip is in the air, and the mess of the "Lakerville" cheap-seat airline queue is cleared away.

It is possible again to find a seat on an Oxford Street bus, and English once again can be heard outside Selfridge's. Not so many growling, smoking tour buses clog Picadilly Circus, and the crowd at the changing of the guard is no more than 10 deep.

A stunned, stupefied, London is beginning to wonder if another tourist invasion like this year's should be allowed.

Despite the shower of dollars, yen, deutschemarks, and rials, Londoners are growing more hostile to foreigners. They are beginning to doubt if the game is worth the effort.

Normally polite citizens are growing surly as foreigners ignore the once-strict rules of bus lines and public manners. Sarcasm creeps in where suffering once reigned. . . .

Some Londoners are advocating nastiness as a means of driving the foreigners from their midst. Playwright John Osborne declared that Britain should ask two questions of their unwanted foreign guests.

The first: "Why are you here?"

The second: "When are you leaving?"

. . . Some critics of the tourist boom dispute the contention that the foreign visitors leave so much money behind. The critics rail against the daily jam of buses from France and Germany, bearing hordes who have paid for their package to a tour operator in Frankfurt or Lyon.

They despise the "backpackers," bright-eyed, mostly American youths who stagger through Regent Street and Picadilly beneath brightly colored loads of sleeping bags and spare jeans, spending their little money at McDonald's. . . .

More and more, that is what Londoners are choosing to do. They do their shopping in vast, U.S. style suburban shopping centers at Brent Cross or Croydon. They rent or sell their in-town apartments at hugely inflated prices to Americans and Arabs, and move to a quiet place in the country where the tourists cannot find them.

In the heart of summertime London, the tourist may be unlikely to encounter any genuine Britons at all except for greasy, shifty-eyed ticket touts, pickpockets, porn dealers, and enterprising street vendors daily dreaming up new ways to separate foreigners from their money.

Some central restaurants have taken to giving camera-laden tourists a "special" menu with shamefully inflated prices, and unscrupulous cart vendors frequently charge the equivalent of $2 for a Coca-Cola or $1.50 for an ice-cream cone.

The government itself has considered getting in on the act. There have been proposals, all rejected so far, to slap a special tourist tax on hotel bills, ostensibly to raise money for improving tourist facilities.

More constructively, tourist authorities are striving to get visitors to spend more time outside London and to visit Britain in the off-season when the pressure is easier and the natives are less restless.

. . . Next year could bring 15 million visitors . . . again pressing London's facilities and patience to the limit.

hamburgers, *deep-fried chips, deep-fried chicken . . . [which] on hot summer nights drifts around the alleys and lanes, merging with other smells from broken sewers or spilt beer. The odd thing is so few people care. "Lloret is finished," says a Spanish waiter with a shrug . . . but thousands of tourists who pour into Lloret every summer from Britain, Germany, Holland, Scandinavia, and Belgium seem to disagree with that verdict.*[22]

The same cultural stress from tourism occurs in many Spanish and Mexican coastal cities. In fact, advertisements in newspapers ask for help, but add that if applicants speak only Spanish they should not apply. In some of these cities, very little if any Spanish is heard. An Australian lady moved from Marabella, on the Costa del Sol, to Malaga so she could learn Spanish. She did this because in her interactions with people on the street she could use only French or her native English.

J. A. Walter referred to another type of carrying capacity, that is the point at which a site becomes ruined for the visitor. He suggested that there are certain perceptual expectations people have for a destination which, if shared with other visitors, would spoil these destinations.[21] Some forms of travel, such as for religious events at special times of the year, exemplify this. Colin Turnbull, in an article entitled "Christmas in Jerusalem," captured the concept when he wrote:

The Christmas spirit was quickly dampened the next day. Setting off early with the enthusiasm of a pilgrim, and with my rediscovered identity as a Christian, I found that within the walls of the old city the stores were as colorful and bright with tinsel as any New York department store—and just as full of junk being sold at ludicrous prices to Christmas shoppers (tourists) who seemed consumed by a compulsion to buy something or everything. I began to feel less Christian. Both the Christian and the Christmas spirit were further dispelled in the one place I thought might possibly revive them—the tomb of the Holy Sepulcher—partly because of the behavior of my fellow tourists who seemed to manifest a blatant lack of respect for the sacred by their flagrant use of cameras, despite signs prohibiting them. . . Other tourists pushed and shoved in a very un-Christian way, using shoulders and elbows to force a way through the narrow entrance to the sepulcher itself. Occasionally, a minor fight broke out, accompanied by swearing and gestures that were anything but sacred.[23]

As unpleasant as this may seem, it has little impact on tourism unless the destination becomes so "touristy" that it begins to act as a deterrent to further tourists, causing the region to decline, and ruining it for both visitors and hosts.

Changes in the Social Structure, Behavior, and Roles
The WTO indicated that social effects of tourism are as follows:

1. *Polarization of the population*
   a) *Disproportionate growth of incomes;*
   b) *Those who are involved with transforming the traditional economy and the provisions of services for tourists get rich quickly;*
   c) *Increased concern for making money without acquiring skills*
2. *Breakdown of the family*
   a) *More divorce;*
   b) *Excessive sexual freedom*
3. *Development of the attitudes of a consumption-oriented society; incidence of phenomena of social pathology:*
   a) *prostitution*
   b) *drug-abuse*
   c) *alcoholism*
   d) *delinquency.*[24]

Tourism changes the traditional forms of employment resulting in side effects, such as lowering the status of the agricultural workers, encouraging migration of the population, and the breaking up of families. These, and other family changes, were recognized to be occurring in Tonga by Lata'akau'ola, Lupe 'Llaiu, and 'Asinate Samate in the book *Pacific Tourism*. In addition to moving into towns, staying with relatives or friends in poor housing, thus overburdening them, many young people demanded freedom from their parents. They also disregarded social norms such as respect for their elders, and lost their close family bonds. Young women in Tonga, in entering the work force, have changed their traditional dress to light, tourist-type clothing. Work has given them freedoms granted previously only to men. Tongan women are no longer confined to the boundaries of the home, but can be found in pubs and dance halls. Prostitution, while small scale in Tonga, attracts an increasing number of young men and women, by offering a quick way of obtaining money.[25]

Tourism in some areas leads to other social problems in the family. Dr. Frances Cottington, a psychiatrist, illustrated these problems as they related to Hawaii. Wives hired as waitresses and maids in luxury hotels, made much higher salaries than their husbands. In addition, their improved dress and grooming often caused their husbands to accuse them of interest in other men. This led to ulcers in the women, and a higher divorce rate on the main island of Hawaii.[26]

This disruption in the kinship system also reduces cohesiveness in the entire community, so changing the population characteristics.

Community Problems
If prostitution of both sexes does not already exist, it will probably be introduced. Many young men, for example, flock to Spain's coastal resorts in hopes of meeting young Swedish, German, or English girls for "amorous adventures." Mathieson and Wall suggested reasons for the increase in prostitution in destination resorts:

1. *The process of tourism has created locations and environments which attract prostitutes and their clients;*
2. *By its very nature, tourism means that people are away from the puritanical bonds of normal living, anonymity is assured away from home, and money is available to spend hedonistically. These circumstances are conducive to the survival and expansion of prostitution;*
3. *As tourism affords employment for women, it may upgrade their economic status. This, in turn, may lead to their liberalization and eventually, to their involvement in prostitution to maintain or acquire new economic levels;*
4. *Tourism may be used as a scapegoat for a general loosening of morals.*[27]

The use of erotic pictures and suggestive slogans in an

advertisement leads some tourists to anticipate sun, sea, sand, and sex as part of their vacation experience.

Increasing tourism brings about new ways of relieving tourists of their money, both legally and illegally. V. L. Lin and P. D. Loeb identified the following three factors in the relationship between crime and tourism:

1. Population density during the tourist season increases, creating the availability of large numbers of targets and congestion.
2. The differences in income between hosts and tourists encourage robbery.
3. The location of resorts in close relation to an international border may attract undesirable migrants, resulting in increased expenditures for law enforcement, and monetary losses for businesses that become targets.[28]

Probably less important, but still creating an undesirable climate, is the increase in number of hawkers, shills, and other unwanted types. In many areas developed for tourism, these people are not a part of the traditional culture and, as such, bring an element of social change considered undesirable by the local community.

Negative Demonstrative Effects

Negative demonstrative effects are considered inappropriate social and economic tourist behaviors. One of the major outgrowths of negative demonstrative effects is the polarization of the hosts from the tourists. This occurs in a number of ways. First, tourists often demand commodities and tourist facilities beyond the economic capacity of local residents. High-living tourists frequently eat in fine restaurants and live in splendid hotels in areas of hunger, unemployment, and limited economic opportunity. This disparity has led, in some cases, to militant revolutionary action, such as occurred in the Bahamas. Second, the social norms that are so different from the local customs, sometimes give rise to social problems such as prostitution (discussed previously). Also, the values and materialism of young traveling westerners are copied, as much as possible, by young local people. Tourism might subject the local area to nude bathing, inappropriate dress, and irresponsible behavior. A third factor initiating polarization is the importation of foreign workers from more developed countries. These workers, more highly skilled than the local people, generally fill the better-paying jobs and are, in many cases, supervisors of less-skilled native citizens. These foreign workers are also able to compete more favorably than the natives for goods and services. The natives then begin to resent the foreigners. The opposite is true in some of the developed countries. Here comparatively less-skilled immigrants take the lower-paying jobs, so forming a lower social and economic group. This association sometimes creates social problems, since the immigrants don't have the standards and norms of the host country.

There are changes in consumption patterns in some cultures. Kentucky Fried Chicken, McDonald's, Burger King, German beer halls, or English fish-and-chips parlors can now be found in numerous tourist areas. In some places, the importation of foreign foods has had little impact on the culture, while in others a considerable change has occurred. Niddrie stated

Tourists on holiday in the Caribbean seldom eat the local foods. Every island seeking this trade must therefore allow considerable quantities of frozen, tinned or fresh food and Scotch whiskey to be imported. Since these are also displayed in the local retail shop, they become part of the islander's regular purchases. . . Puerto Rico has almost abandoned its "native" foods in favor of those imported from Miami in ever-increasing quantities.[29]

Even industrial societies are influenced by tourism. H. Robinson suggested that the rapid increase in wine consumption in Britain over recent years may, in part, be attributed to the increasing large number of continental visitors attracted by the devaluation of the pound sterling.[30] Tourism is an exporter of western lifestyles and culture. In other words, tourism stimulated the acculturation and cultural convergence process. This is shown in the increasing change from native clothing and material in many developing societies to the less expensive mass-produced western wear.

Loss or Deterioration of Traditional Art and Culture

Tourism, at times, leads to the destruction of a country's works of art. Natives resent tourists who think they have a right to their country's art, whether bought or stolen. Jaques Bugnicourt writes

It is perhaps in the sphere of the arts that the harm caused or accentuated by tourism is most marked. The fact that in most African countries, for example, tourists keep to a few specific places and do no stray far from the beaten track conceals certain indirect destructive effects which tourism entails. Whether the works of art are Berber jewelry, Bambara head-dress, daggers from Rwanda, of Bibles written on parchment in Amharic, the process does not differ greatly. Those who tout these objects for sale outside the international hotels constitute the final link in a chain of collectors which reaches deep into the interior of the country, prevailing upon peasants, frequently up to their eyes in debt, to part with traditional objects which may have been used for generations and which were originally fashioned for reasons other than money-making. . . This same greed for money which induces people to part with family heirlooms explains the plundering of archaeological sites or the desecration of monuments in Egypt, Bali, India or Central America. Thus tourism is an incitement to the pillage of national works of art.[31]

It is not an unfamiliar scene for a tourist to be met near an archeological site by a native selling artifacts he has just discovered (or made that morning). Shortly after China opened its doors to Western tourism, farmers could be observed on the Great Wall selling coins from the Ming Dynasty that they uncovered in the fields. This was in spite of the fact that China has a law against the exportation of cultural artifacts.

In addition to the loss of artifacts, the increased demand for them has led to changes in the form and function of art objects. They may no longer be representative of their traditional art. A number of factors account for these changes. Mathieson and Wall identified four. They have suggested that (1) because of the increased demand, which causes a need to increase production, either the products are mass produced as is the case in Tunisia, or the careful, precise workmanship is lost; (2) the impersonal nature of the tourist market has decreased the spiritual relevance of the artist's work; (3) art is produced according to the tastes of the tourists which, in Africa; means carving animals, grotesqueness, gigantism; and (4) the increased demand has led to the misrepresentation of the age or authenticity of objects, resulting in large numbers of fakes.[32]

Even model cultural villages may be encouraging cultural loss. Tourists, wanting to keep their schedules, as well as entertainment, require activities to be short, and therefore less authentic. Consequently, the entertainment loses its value as an example of cultural heritage. Cultural villages, and large hotels giving floor shows, may manipulate authentic host traditions and events to conform to tourist's time schedules, tastes, and such. This effort to turn folklore, religious or secular ceremonies, and artistic productions to material advantage show the local population making concession to commercialization, which transforms their values into merchandise.

While religion has been a powerful motivational force for travel to Jerusalem, Rome, Mecca, Medina, and other places, it has also changed the traditional forms of religion and created problems. The Balinese, for example, have always considered their land as sacred. Their way of life is integrated with their religion and beliefs. Tourism, and the resulting commercialization, is having a profound effect on Balinese life as it was.[33]

One additional change occurring in the host region is language. Rex Nettleford suggested that language is the basis for the inferiority complex of many Caribbean peoples who have been led to believe that their Caribbean English (syntax, vocabulary, and accent) is inferior to that of their English-speaking visitors. Therefore, waiters have adopted the speech habits of the tourists in an effort to please and be accepted by the people they serve. In addition to the economic aspect, local aspirations to be like the visitors leads to hosts replacing their own language with that of the tourists. Finally, the direct contact between hosts and guests has a greater impact on developing cultures, partly because of their inferiority complex.[34]

IMPACT CONTROL MEASURES

A number of control measures can be adopted to decrease the negative change in an area. Some of these are to:

1. Ration the contact between hosts and guests by limiting the carrying capacity of the destination, and by regulating the tourist flow, as does Bermuda and the Soviet Union.
2. Develop programs focusing on enhancing tourism's contribution to intercultural communication and interaction (e.g., matching tourist types with destination characteristics; host programs offered by local residents, goodwill "ambassador" tourist education).
3. Expand human resource development and training programs in all components of the tourism system to include social skills (interpersonal relations, intercultural communications, and networking/referral tactics).
4. Design community education programs and citizen involvement programs centered on tourism development, policy, and regulatory issues.
5. Separate the tourists and the hosts within tourist enclaves and by other methods.

Valene Smith illustrated this last point by using Nome, Alaska as an example. There tourists are housed in a discrete village unit and bused to the Eskimo village for their visit, which usually includes seeing craft demonstrations, blanket tosses, and ceremonial dances. The residents attend the dances and join in spontaneously; both tourists and hosts enjoy the interaction. She compared this with Kotzebue, where the tourists, mingling on the beaches to watch the midnight sun, interfere with Eskimo hunters returning to butcher their kill. She reports

Eskimos wearied of answering repetitive questions and complained about tourists who took muktuk and fish from drying racks, smelled it, and threw it on the ground as if it were garbage. Above all, the many Eskimo passengers aboard airplanes that included tour parties overheard the departing visitors brag about the "pictures I got," and interpreted the remarks as ridicule, which cuts deep into native ethos. In response, Eskimo women began to refuse would-be tourist photographers, then erected barricades to shield their work from tourist eyes, and some finally resorted to hiring a taxi to haul seals and other game to the privacy of their homes for processing.[35]

RESEARCH AND REVIEW

1. Define culture in the tourism context.
2. Discuss the following terms:
   a. Cultural attractiveness
   b. Golden horde
   c. Acculturation
   d. Cultural convergence
3. Compare and contrast cultural change resulting from tourism in a developed nation versus a developing nation.
4. Describe the impact that the seven different tourist types have on a host area.

5. How would you respond to the statement "Tourism mostly reinforces people's existing perception of a country." Do you agree or disagree? Why?

6. What are the social benefits of tourism?

7. Describe the benefits to a family that can occur in developing societies resulting from tourism.

8. How can an individual be affected by tourism?

9. What are some examples of a renaissance of native culture?

10. Discuss the negative attributes of tourism.

11. Why does crime increase in tourist areas?

12. What are five characteristics of tourism that generate a negative effect?

ENDNOTES

1. J. R. Ritchie and M. Zins, "Culture as a Determinant of the Attractiveness of the Tourist Region," *Annals of Tourism Research*, Vol. 5 (1978), pp. 252–267.

2. Alister Mathieson and Geoffrey Wall, *Tourism: Economic, Physical and Social Impact* (London & NY: Longman, 1986), p. 159.

3. R. H. Jackson and L. E. Hudman, *World Regional Geography* (NY: John Wiley, 1985), p. 198.

4. Mike Ashman, "The Island Lifestyle: An Endangered Species," unpublished paper, 1976.

5. Valene L. Smith, *Hosts of Guests: An Anthropology of Tourism* (Philadelphia: Univ. of Pennsylvania Press, 1977), pp. 9–10.

6. WTO, "The Social and Cultural Dimension of Tourism" (Madrid, 1981), p. 23.

7. Ibid., pp. 17–23.

8. Ibid., p. 12.

9. Emanual de Kadt, *Tourism: Passport to Development?* (NY: Oxford Univ. Press, 1979), p. 144.

10. OAS, "Enhancing the Positive Impact of Tourism on the Natural Environment," Vol. 1 (Washington, DC: Dept. of Economic Affairs, 1984), p. 192.

11. Augustin Reynoso y Valle and Jacomina P. de Regt, "Growing Pains: Planned Tourism Development in Ixtapa-Zihuatanejo," in de Kadt, p. 130.

12. A. Andronicou, "Tourism in Cyprus," in de Kadt, p. 249.

13. Frank E. Manning, "Tourism: Passport to Development," in de Kadt, pp. 157–176.

14. WTO, "Appraisal and Social Value of Investments in Domestic Tourism" (New Delhi, 1983), pp. 7–13.

15. L. I. Deitch, "The Impact of Tourism Upon the Art and Crafts of the Indians of the Southwestern U.S.," in *Hosts of Guests*, pp. 173–184.

16. J. J. Brody, "The Creative Consumer: Survival, Revival and Invention in Southwestern Indian Arts," in N. H. Gradburn *Ethnic and Tourism Arts: Cultural Expression From the Fourth World* (Berkley, CA: Univ. of Calif. Press, 1976), pp. 70–84.

17. Eliam Tanirono, "The Impact of Tourism on Solomon Culture," in *Pacific Tourism* (Hawaii: South Pacific Social Sciences Annals, 1980), p. 109.

18. Philip McKean, "Tourism, Culture Change, and Culture Conservation in Bali," unpublished paper (Toronto: American Anthropological Assn., 1972).

19. Ngahuia Awekotuku, "Maori Culture and Tourist Income," in *Pacific Tourism*, p. 29.

20. Max Stanton, "The Polonesian Cultural Center," in Smith, pp. 193–203.

21. J. A. Walter, "Social Limits to Tourism," *Leisure Studies 1* (1982), pp. 295–304.

22. "Inside the Packages," *Sunday Times* (London), August 6, 1972.

23. Colin Turnbull, "Christmas in Jerusalem: The Tourist As Pilgrim," *Natural History*, Vol. 91, pp. 30–32.

24. WTO (Madrid, 1981), pp. 12–13.

25. Lata'akau'ola, Lupe Llaiu and 'Asinate Samate, "The Social and Cultural Impact of Tourism in Tonga," in *Pacific Tourism*, pp. 17–24.

26. F. Cottington, "Socio-psychiatric Effects of Luxury Hotel Growth and Development on a Rural Population," paper presented at American Psychiatric Assn. meeting (Honolulu, 1969) in Chuck Y. Gee, p. 111.

27. Mathieson and Wall, p. 149.

28. V. L. Lin and P. D. Loeb, "Tourism and Crime in Mexico: Some Comments," *Social Science Quarterly*, 58 (1977), pp. 164–167.

29. David L. Niddrie, "The Caribbean" in *Latin America: Geographical Perspectives*, ed. by H. Blakemore and C. T. Smith (NY: Methuen, 1971), p. 110.

30. Robinson, p. 139.

31. Jaques Bugnicourt, "Tourism: The Other Face," *Development Forum*, Vol. 5, No. 6 (Aug.-Sept. 1977), p. 8.

32. Mathieson and Wall, p. 168.
33. Colin M. Turnbull, "Bali's New Gods," *Natural History* (Jan. 1982), p. 26.
34. Rex Nettleford, "Cultural Impact—Some Reflections For the Young," Address to Regional Seminar on Tourism and its Effects, Bahamas, 1975. (Barbados: Caribbean Tourism Research Center, 1977).
35. Smith, p. 59.

CHAPTER 20

IMPACTS ON THE PHYSICAL ENVIRONMENT

It seems to be a characteristic of human nature to exploit opportunities for immediate gratification, without regard for the future consequences of that enjoyment. This characteristic is seen particularly in tourist areas where the environment is the chief attraction, although some change in attitude is occurring. Tourists cannot help being attracted to scenic harbors, cascading waterfalls, or large lakes surrounded by high mountain or volcanoes; but in enjoying these attractions, tourists, being human, threaten the environment by exploiting it. Unless we recognize this tendency to destroy, and develop effective plans to balance environmental problems with tourist pleasures, we will have nothing left to enjoy.

ENVIRONMENT AND CHANGE

The term "environment" is used rather loosely, and connotes both human and physical characteristics. Speakers and writers often refer to human environment, physical environment, or a combination of both. A term that describes the human and physical characteristics of an area is "preexisting forms." The chapter on social and cultural impacts dealt partly with the changes in the human environment that occur as a result of tourism. Therefore, only a few brief comments on the human environment will be made in this chapter. The emphasis of this chapter will be the physical environment. However, a few introductory comments on both are in order.

An excellent example of changing preexisting forms associated with the human environment, as well as the physical, is the development of coastal resorts and cities. In Spain, for example, several coastal villages have changed rather drastically in the past few years. In the past, travel posters usually highlighted sights characteristic of the area

234

before the tourism boom began. The scattered villages of Torremolinos, Benidorm, Lloret Del Mar, and others are no longer recognizable.

It can be expected that some change in preexisting forms will be necessary to accommodate mass tourism. However, tourism can either be carefully controlled by the government in order to take advantage of economic and employment opportunities, while reducing its social, cultural, and physical impact, or can it be changed in such a way as to enhance the physical environment and make it more attractive to both visitors and local residents.

Certainly an analysis of the positive and negative aspects of tourism indicates a need to pay attention to wise resource management (particularly of water and energy) and to the problems of pollution and noise, as well as the problems of litter and fire hazards, which may arise from tourist activities. The environmental benefits and negative impacts of tourism need to be recognized. The WTO recognizes these problems. They state this in the Manila Declaration on World Tourism (see Chapter 14).

BENEFITS

As with social and cultural impacts, a few tourists have little impact upon the environment. However, the impact becomes more noticeable and changes occur as the numbers increase. Tourism has created environmental awareness in two ways. First, contact with scenic areas has raised awareness of the earth's beauty, and led to the creation of ways to make it easier for more to see and enjoy it by channeling visitors into paths that provide orderly methods to observe the attraction with a minimum of damage. Second, environmental awareness has been heightened by mass tourism, which is the cause of its destruction.

There are over three hundred national parks and monuments in the United States created to preserve the natural, cultural, and recreational resources of the land for the enjoyment, appreciation, and education of present and future generations. Two acts of Congress, in the early twentieth century, established the philosophy behind the national parks system. They were the Antiquities Act of 1906, which established national monument preservation on public lands, and the National Park Act of 1916, which established the National Park Service. It was made clear that past development was for tourism, and that they were designed to be attractions. In 1917, the Park Service distributed 83,000 automobile guidebooks promoting tourism.[1] By 1920, nearly a million tourists visited the nation's national parks and monuments.[2]

The development of the parks was intended to open up areas for viewing, and also to control the flow of traffic within the park. Schmitt stated "They lived by the road, and they most enjoyed the wilderness as it was framed in their windshields. To offer scenic beauty without destroying the wilderness it was only necessary to build a limited but carefully designed road network between major park attractions."[3] The national parks in Canada were established in somewhat the same manner. Banff was established as a park for tourists, not to protect the landscape.[4]

The development of the National Trust (English Heritage) in Great Britain, or the National Trust for Historic Preservation in the United States, came about partly because tourism has provided a reason for the preservation of historical buildings and the creation of museums. Also, today many developing nations are realizing that their monuments mean tourists and income. People have an increased desire to preserve their national monuments. In developed countries, unspoiled natural attractions are becoming more and more rare. Consequently, people travel to the developing nations where nature is still unspoiled by the impact of visitors, or where the remnants of great ancient civilizations are located. Developing countries recognize that their historical sites or traditional towns and neighborhoods, untouched by "progress," are economic assets.[5] L. M. Alexander suggested that "Year-round inhabitants realize that among the area's greatest assets [is] the quaint charm of its villages. . . . Lighthouses, harbors, and fishing piers are ideal tourist attractions and many old houses and buildings were repainted and landscaped to catch the tourist's 'eye'."[6] P. J. Greenwood noted that in Fuenterrabia, Spain, an observable change took place after it was proclaimed a national historic community.[7]

Tourism has created appreciation of the environment by bringing the public's attention to scenic attractions. In Switzerland, mountain sports and vacations, both in winter and summer, are common as a result of the mountain railway development which themselves, result from rapid tourist growth.

On the other hand, all levels of government have recognized that an increase in tourism brings problems, so, in order to protect and preserve the environment, they have responded appropriately. The WTO said the following about tourism's contribution to protecting the environment:

> The protection, enhancement and improvement of the various components of man's environment are among the fundamental conditions for the harmonious development of tourism. Similarly, rational management of tourism may contribute to a larger extent to protecting and developing the physical environment and the cultural heritage, as well as to improve the quality of man's life.
>
> [We] seek to promote, establish and implement a strategy and a programme of concerted actions designed to ensure balance between the development of holiday and travel activities, which should be considered irreversible, and the protection of the environment, whose components constitute the common heritage of mankind.[8]

In Central America and the Caribbean, recognition of the need to protect and promote preservation led to the creation of the Eastern Caribbean Natural Area Management Programme, the Island Resources Foundation, and the inclusion of environmental topics in the Caribbean Tourism Research and Development Centre (CTRC) journal. In Mexico, FONATUR (Fondo Nacional de Fomento al Turismo), the agency responsible for developing new destinations, has devoted considerable effort to maintaining a quality environment to avoid problems like those that occurred in Acapulco.

Conservation

Conservation and preservation of the environment can be, and in some cases has been, an important benefit to the preservation of resources. Conservation and preservation are beneficial to both the local area and the future of tourism. First, the local residents benefit from the measures to preserve the area, and, second, tourism will continue to be important as the attraction continues to draw tourists. The purpose of the National Parks Service, with the inclusion of conservation, is much broader today than it was in the past. The national parks in East Africa, Kenya, and Tanzania were founded for the purpose of wildlife protection. A considerable amount of international attention on conservation has been focused on Kenya. Nairobi, its capital, is the headquarters of the United Nations Environmental Program. There are also a host of international and national organizations such as the African Wildlife Leadership Foundation, the New York Zoological Society, the East African Wildlife Society, and the World Wildlife Fund. While the parks were created to save animals from Arab and European hunters, trappers' and traders' current problems come from population growth, which has led to the development of settlements in rural areas. The recognition by Tanzania and Kenya of the importance of the game preserves to stimulate tourism has also increased the governments' desire to preserve the area. There is a drive to identify and protect additional areas within Kenya.

In some places, such as on the island of Mallorca, bird preserves are listed as one of the major attractions for the tourists seeking a change from sun, sea, and sand experiences. Natural trails and bird-watching areas have been established to help the traveler enjoy the area and to maintain the quality of the environment.

According to Clare Gunn, there are four factors which led to the conservation movement. The role of tourism in the conservation movement is clearly indicated.

1. *There was a social concern to which the park movement owes its beginnings. The growth of industry and commerce and their associated ills stimulated a demand for the parks and open space. The provision of public land was seen as an antidote to the immoral values of urban society and as an escape from the routine of work and urban living;*
2. *There was an emphasis on the efficiency of resource use, particularly of non-renewable resources. Early expressions stressed maximum utilization but with a minimum of environmental degradation;*
3. *Conservation also incorporates a notion of aesthetic enhancement. This is particularly significant in a recreational context. One major tourist activity is sightseeing which depends*

heavily on the qualities of the natural environment;
4. *More recently conservation has gained a scientific and ecological emphasis in which the maintenance of a balance between man and environment is of prime importance. The outcome of this perspective is the application of stringent controls to protect and preserve the natural environment from unsystematic and unplanned human manipulation.*[9]

In addition, Mathieson and Wall identified four ways that tourism has been important to conservation. These are

1. Stimulating the rehabilitation of existing historic sites, buildings, and monuments;
2. Stimulating the transformation of old buildings and locations into new tourist facilities;
3. Creating the impetus for the conservation of natural resources; and
4. Bringing about the introduction of administrative and planning controls necessary to maintain the quality of the environment to ensure a satisfying, rewarding experience for the tourists[10]

It can be concluded that in some cases tourism provides incentives and the economic means for conservation and preservation of natural and historic sites. Many monuments, historic houses, villages, old churches, etc. could not be maintained without the tourist income.

The fourth element, administration and planning controls (which appear to be instituted because of tourism's detrimental nature), requires some discussion. One characteristic (noted in Chapter 5) was the closing of many attractions to tourists because the attractions were wearing out from too many visitors. (Examples included Hadrian's Roman Wall, Canterbury Cathedral and Stonehenge in England, the Great Wall of China, and the Parthenon in Athens which can now only be enjoyed from the outside). The national parks in the United States and Kenya are also feeling the impact of too many tourists. As a result, tourism now, has created an impetus for conservation and preservation of both natural areas and important historic and archeological sites.

Attractions Development

All around the world, countries that have been or are now in favorable locations to attract tourists are identifying areas with that potential. The Languedoc-Roussillon coastal area in southern France is one such example. It was built to relieve some of the tourist stress on the Riviera.

In the Caribbean, near the island of St. Croix, the U.S. National Park Service has established and developed an underwater national park. The park service has marked an underwater path which a swimmer can follow, reading informational signs pertaining to the physical characteristics of the area and the types of fish that the swimmer can see.

Mont-Saint-Michel, one of France's outstanding medieval monuments.
Photo courtesy of Air France.

This rather unique site attracts snorklers and those interested in coral, helping to preserve the area, and creating an awareness of the character of coral reefs and the sea floor. This will help when future issues arise concerning conservation, because the knowledge gained will generate a more sympathetic population. In addition to the hotel development on or near outstanding natural attractions, the Caribbean islands, for example, have developed and are promoting a variety of natural attractions, including rain forests, wildlife, rivers, crater lakes, waterfalls, limestone caves, and other outstanding landscapes.[11]

High mountain areas, such as the Jungfrau in Switzerland, have been developed. The Jungfrau boasts of having the highest railway in Europe. The train leaves from Interlaken, connects with a cog railroad at Kleine Scheidegg, arriving at the Jungfraujoch station above the clouds several days later. The Salt Cathedral of Zipaquira, near Bogota, Colombia, is a combination of nature and man-made development. It is an ancient salt mine worked by the now extinct Chibcha Indians before recorded history.

Man-made attractions are of two kinds. First, there are archeological sites. Mexico and the countries of Central America are famous for the development and preservation of such sites. One such example is Tikal, in the Peten jungles of northern Guatemala. Tikal is the largest Mayan city discovered; it is in the process of being restored for tourism. Tikal covers at least twenty-five square miles and includes more than 10,000 structures, although only about six square miles have been cleared for visitors. Second, there are historical sites in both urban and rural areas. One of the most impressive examples is Mont-St.-Michel off the rocky west coast of France. The abbey's development as an attraction was insured when the French government made it a national shrine. The restoration of historically significant areas has happened as a result of tourism. Jamestown and Colonial Williamsburg in Virginia and Old Sturbridge Village and Plymouth Plantation in Massachusetts are excellent examples of the many historical sites that dot the landscape, not only in the United States, but throughout the world.

Historic Preservation

The development and rejuvenation of urban areas has become common throughout the world. In the United States, it seems that almost every town of any size has restored an area of historical significance to attract tourists. Certainly, the uniqueness of San Francisco, a major tourist city, is maintained by its old-fashioned trolley system and the development of stores and restaurants on the pier. In South Carolina, Old Charleston has come alive with Victorian houses, stately antebellum mansions, and other historic homes that have been restored. A visitor can walk along narrow cobblestone streets and past old brick houses with flowering gardens and wrought-iron gates. Restoration of areas in other countries is also worthy of note. "Nelson's Dockyard, Antigua" (see vignette) and the restoration of the harbor area in Sidney, Australia, where ships docked with their loads of prisoners banished to the new land, are but two. The list can go on and on, but this is sufficient to show that this restoration and rejuvenation process is occurring rapidly throughout the world, and serves as a major characteristic of an area intended to impress tourists.

NELSON'S DOCKYARD, ANTIGUA

Nelson's Dockyard was built in the 18th Century to accommodate, maintain and refit British
ships during the wars of that period. In 1951, restoration of historic buildings began under
the guidance of an organization called the Friends of English Harbour, with the main
intention of promoting local and tourist attractions in the Dockyard by emphasizing its
historical importance. It became a major yachting centre, visitor use increased consistently,
and slow but effective gains were made in restoration work.

A more aggressive and comprehensive approach to restoration and development of the
area was adopted in the past five years with good results. A technician with a feel for
conservation needs and appropriate economic uses was put in charge of the effort; an historic
architect was provided by the Commonwealth Fund for Technical Cooperation (CFTC) to
assist with the restoration of buildings; appropriate uses were identified for specific buildings
and restoration planning was geared to those uses; based on proposed uses, projects were
developed, showing benefits to be derived, including jobs, revenue and cultural appreciation,
and grant funding received from CIDA, BDD and other donors; concessions were given to
individuals or companies for ventures such as the operation of a hotel whose interior design,
furnishing and initial operation was supported by a loan from the CDB (as a result several
more jobs were created); and both local and tourist interest in the history of the Dockyard
is increasing.

Legislative changes were also introduced, as the Friends of English Harbour was considered too limited in scope to achieve the overall objectives for conservation and development of the Dockyard. In its place will be the Nelson's Dockyard Foundation, whose
capacity to raise funds will be strengthened by, among other things, tax free status for
contributions to its efforts. The Foundation will be run by a Board of Governors, who will
supervise various commercial concessions and charge a royalty, which will be used to further
conservation and development of the Dockyard and other surrounding historic resources,
which along with the Dockyard will be included in a national park.

Source: OAS, "Enhancing the Positive Impact of Tourism on the Built and Natural Environment,"
Vol. 5 (U.S. Dept. of Economic Affairs, 1984).

Resident Rewards

While it would seem that in most cases the hordes of
tourists would be in conflict with the local residents, there
are some benefits accruing to local residents as a result of
tourism. First, as suggested earlier, tourism brings economic growth to an area. Secondly, the results of conservation and preservation can be enjoyed by the local community as well as by tourists. The creation of 337 national
parks and monuments in the United States provides considerable open space and quick access to a variety of nature's wonders and outdoor activities. In Kenya, native land
was taken to create the national parks. In an effort to resolve
the problem this action created, Amboseli National Park
(near the base of Mount Kilimanjaro) was formed. A program was instituted, which identified the most important
area for conservation and tourism and water resources for
the Masai tribe. This allowed the Masai to graze their cattle
along with the wildlife in non-park areas. The Masai were
also paid for "losses resulting from limiting the availability
of land." This money came from tourist revenues. The ra-
tionale was to relieve the pressure on the park, and to
redistribute some of the tourist benefits.[12] While the Masai
have some questions about the benefits gained to this point,
the park may provide the tribe with some long-term benefits, such as preventing the wildlife (game) from becoming

extinct and providing a stable income. Climatic variations
always affected agriculture to such an extent that the Masai
economy was unstable. The parks may help stabilize the
economy and reduce the rate at which parts of Africa are
becoming desert.

Another type of benefit accruing from tourism development can be seen in coastal areas. The enclosure of
beaches for industrial development often means the public
no longer has access to them. The planned development
of a coastal resort, which allows free access for tourists and
local residents, can be a benefit to both groups. In this
sense, it is beneficial for the community to have tourism
create such a conflict. Without the help of this powerful
protagonist (tourism), local residents probably would not
have the weight needed to gain access to their beaches.
Tourism development assigns natural resources to a determined use, and ensures that more harmful, and, perhaps,
polluting, industrial development does not occur.[13]

COSTS

Fundamental to the concept of cost is the fact that when
the carrying capacity and saturation levels of an area are
exceeded, there will be a number of negative effects on
that area. The term *carrying capacity* is the degree of de-

velopment that can take place without there being detrimental effects on the resources or, in this case, the environment. The WTO suggested that benefits progressively decrease when the number of visitors reaches a threshold in terms of:

> The Tourism Image (*the loss of quality of the attraction to tourists*): *The capacity or number of visitors that are compatible with the image of the tourist product and the type of environmental experience that the visitor is seeking. If the tourist development becomes saturated, the very attractions visitors come to see may be destroyed and the destination [will] decline in quality and popularity.*

> The Indigenous Environment (*damage to the physical, cultural and social environment*): *The capacity that can be achieved without physical damage to the natural and man-made environment, social/economic damage to the local community and culture or prejudicing the proper balance between development and conservation. Saturation may lead to permanent damage to the indigenous environment, as well as transient social/economic and cultural problems.*[14]

Saturation levels and the type of environment between developed and developing countries are different. Some environments for which there are considerable differences at the saturation level are wilderness, rural, coastal, mountain, urban, and developed versus developing. The differences between developed and developing lie in the cultural dissimilarities and the measure of control used to handle the development. In developing societies, the control measures are lacking because of cultural differences as are the technical skills and financial resources needed to create and implement plans. In an industrial urban area, the development of coastal areas with the resulting high-rise hotels will probably fit into the landscape unnoticed by anyone other than crowds on the beaches. The city's water and sewerage system must be designed to handle the tourist facilities as well as the other normal city facilities. In developing countries the development may be sporadic and insensitivity to local culture can change the character of the area considerably.

Archeological and other similar sites can also reach a saturation level. The famous Altamira Caves at Santander, Spain are an example: The large numbers of sight-seers created problems because their breath and perspiration were ruining the paintings.

Tourism can produce excessive demand on the infrastructure—particularly the roads, sewage disposal, and water supply. This is particularly true of developing countries, since they have fewer resources to meet the tourist demands. In developed societies, the demand is less because they have more capital and technical material available. In developing societies, the demand for water by tourists is greater per capita than for the residents. Resort development requires water for drinking, laundries, fire fighting, cooling and heating, street cleaning, irrigation,

swimming, and bathing. This demand is generally much greater for visitors from the developed nations than for local residents. Not only is there a higher demand for the quantity of water but also for quality water at tourist resorts. It is rather easy in the coastal areas of developing nations for the capacity of the sewage treatment plant to be outstripped, thus polluting the water around the resort and urban area.

Environmental Conflicts

One of the major issues in many countries today is the quality of the environment. Much has been written concerning its problems. They have affected the vegetation, the quality of the air and water, and wildlife. Tourism is part of this concern. Vegetation is one of the primary attractions of tourism; it adds to the quality of the environment. The destruction of the vegetation partly occurs because of the sheer numbers of tourists. Mathieson and Wall identified five tourist activities that affected the vegetation:

1. The species composition in an area changes as a result of the collection of flowers, plants, and fungi by tourists.
2. Fires caused by tourists in forested areas have caused serious conflagrations.
3. The age structure of the plant community has been changed because of the removal of younger trees for firewood and poles.
4. The ecology is damaged because of the dumping of garbage and debris.
5. There is excessive destruction and trampling of vegetation from pedestrian and vehicular use as well as camping and picnicking.[15]

In California's Yosemite National Park, more than 10,000 people visit during one day in summertime. In the course of that day, through many of their activities, tourists trample on the vegetation and pollute the water. The indiscriminate collection of plants compounds the effect of trampling when the animals that feed on those plants are affected. In many parks, campers have cut branches off trees, and completely cut down small trees, creating an eyesore. In areas such as oceanfronts and islands, both construction and visitors going to and from the area destroy the vegetation cover, changing natural habitats for birds and animals, in some cases, even affecting the temperature of an area. Sometimes, the loss of vegetation leads to soil erosion and further degradation of the environment.

Air pollution and a number of related problems result from the use of automobiles, taxis, buses, and aircraft. Air pollution is probably less of a problem for the travel industry than for other industries, yet those locations with a number of conveyances to move people will suffer from some pollution. Two national parks, Yosemite and Shenandoah, have had problems with congestion causing air pollution and damage to vegetation.

Most studies on pollution have focused on the discharge of untreated waste from resorts or boats into seas, lakes, rivers, and springs. The lack of an effective sewerage system on Tarawa (one of the Gilbert and Ellis Islands), for example, has led to the widespread pollution of its inshore waters, making fish consumption inadvisable and swimming unhealthy. Mediterranean pollution, partly due to tourist develoment, is considered a real threat to swimming. In addition, such diseases as cholera, typhoid, viral hepatitis, and dysentery can be traced to seafood from polluted waters.

Noise pollution is a third form of pollution associated with traffic congestion on land and in the air. Also, many recreational vehicles—motorcycles, motorboats, snowmobiles, and aircraft—cause a lot of noise.

Wildlife

Problems associated with wildlife changes result from the killing of animals or birds, and the disrupting of normal habits of feeding and breeding. The competition over territory between bears and humans in Yellowstone Park has led to removing much of the bear population.

The creation of Cancun, Mexico as a major resort led to lagoons being filled in and the mangrove trees removed. Two years after the changes, one lagoon began to show signs of deterioration; algae began blooming and two small wildlife sanctuaries were inundated with sea water. In order for tourists to see the native birds, an aviary was created, but doing so forced the birds to eat unfamiliar foods.[16] This is a direct negative impact of tourism, which resulted from the disruption of the traditional feeding and breeding areas, a common error of many resort developers. The concentration of many tourists in an area such as Yellowstone National Park in the United States or Serengeti, Tsavo, or Mount Kenya in Kenya was so disruptive that it changed the breeding habits and living patterns of much of the wildlife; the animals then had to move to a less traditional habitat.

Another impact on animals can also occur from tourism. One of the principal ones is the killing of elephants for tusks, zebras for hides, antelopes for the heads, lion claws for necklaces, monkeys for skin throw-rugs, gazelles for hoof key-rings, and so on. The creation of national parks and game reserves has encouraged the proliferation of certain species at the expense of others, destroying the natural balance.[17]

Geological Conflicts

Tourism has had an effect on geological formations; some tourists collect minerals, rocks, and fossils. In caves, the natural formations are vandalized. In the Caribbean, along the Great Barrier Reef and other coastal areas, coral collecting by tourists has become a serious problem.

A number of ecosystems have serious problems resulting from tourism.

Coastlines

The strong attraction of sun, sea, and sand has resulted in beaches receiving the full force of mass tourism. As discussed earlier, some areas of Spain have become so saturated, that not only have ecosystems been destroyed, but so has the original charm of the small villages. The sand

dunes are destroyed either from the development of hotels and campsites or trampling by the tourists. The loss of dune vegetation has led to a "blow-out," causing the dunes to expand rapidly due to natural weathering processes.

The presence of people may cause the disappearance of sensitive animals (e.g., sea birds), or the disruption of their breeding habits with a subsequent decline in breeding success. At a resort in Australia, the evening migration of penguins from the sea to the shore has proved such a popular tourist attraction that the introduction of the associated activities, such as arc lights and viewing stands, has prevented the penguins from breeding successfully. In other coastal areas, rock climbing on cliff faces may prevent sea birds from nesting successfully.

Ecological damage also results from the exploitation of virgin coasts for infrastructure development. Swamps, salt marshes, and mud flats are often prime targets for dumping rubbish or for land reclamation sites for airports, hotels, curio shops, and marina development. Such areas are among the most important to wildlife habitats. They serve as staging posts for many migratory species of birds. They sometimes support valuable fisheries. With many tourist developments, all or part of the ecosystem is lost.

The use of motorboats and other forms of water-borne recreational vehicles, not only has a detrimental effect on beaches, but on marine life as well. Tropical marine ecosystems are particularly susceptible to the oil pollution seeping from motorboats. Complex and delicate coral reefs are being physically removed to facilitate water skiing and speedboat activities. This is further exacerbated by souvenir trade in shells, shell jewelry, and pieces of coral. The British Virgin Islands has declared black coral an endangered species. Traiton shellfish feed on crown starfish. The removal of traiton may be a contributing factor in the spread of crown starfish on coral reefs. The starfish feed on the reef causing it to die. Thus, the reef loses its typical fauna and flora, and the area loses its tourist attraction. Further physical changes cover the beaches with mud, and the land behind is left open to erosion.

Mountains

Mountains, with steep slopes in extreme climatic regions are fragile; they have low resistance to mass tourism. Their carrying capacity is low and environmental damage takes years to correct. Landslides, mud slides, rockfalls, and avalanches often increase due to tourism development. The ski lifts, cable cars, power lines, accommodations, and access roads can also create a negative visual impact.

Mountain ecosystems are also very fragile. Mountains provide homes for a large variety of wildlife that live in different zones of the mountains according to the climate, which varies with the height of the mountain. The forests on the lower slopes are home to animals that are driven out as ski runs are built. Areas the animals use during adverse weather conditions are drastically reduced too.

Deserts

Like mountains and coastal regions, deserts have fragile ecosystems. The increased development in the south-

View of the beach of Javea, Spain. Photo courtesy of the National Tourist Office of Spain.

western United States poses a challenge to that area. Extremely damaging to the desert ecosystem is the popular use of off-road vehicles. They destroy flora and disrupt the life of the fauna creating an imbalance in the system, thus changing the quality and character of the area.

Islands

Islands in subtropical environments are extremely popular tourist attractions. They include some of the ecosystems already discussed. In addition, land is scarce on islands, and the need to provide large airports as well as other infrastructure requirements means the loss of large tracts. The scarcity of fresh water supplies on some islands is another very serious problem.

Decay of Man-Made Environments

Three major environments are considered man-made for tourism. First, as resorts are developed, they change the structure and spatial organization of existing villages or towns. Second, some "virgin" (previously untouched) areas have been developed as major tourist destinations (Cancun and other major Mexican resorts are examples). In both instances, as the resorts age and other areas become more fashionable, and these deteriorate. Third, many older resorts may go through a decline, requiring some form of reconstruction and a review of the market. In some cases, the declining resort brings social and economic problems to the area, and leaves decaying structures on the landscape which degrade the environment.

Resident Conflicts

A number of conflicts frequently occur between residents and tourists or tourist developers. In cities, hotels are sometimes built at the expense of residential accommodations. The increase in land values often forces residents to move away from the area. Hotel development also brings traffic congestion and further air pollution. In areas of hunting and fishing, the increased demand creates problems for local hunters and fishermen who now compete with the tourists as well as each other.

Some tourists conflict with the local residents by creating litter, vandalism, traffic congestion, and visual blight, all of which lower the quality of an area. In rural areas, the damage to crops, farm buildings, and livestock are a common complaint of farmers, as are the increased land values, competition for labor, and land erosion.

IMPACT CONTROL MEASURES

The increased interest in the problems of the environment has been well-documented and studied. There has been considerable growth in the movement to administer proper control of tourism development to counteract the destruction that tourism creates. To date, two measures have been identified which will reduce the negative impact of tourism and create a quality environment for both residents and tourists. They are, first, general protective measures and, second, regulation and control of tourist development. The protective measures are designed to protect the various aspects of the environment, from endangered animals and plants, beaches, and forests, through the creation of national parks and wilderness areas.

Conservation and Protection

The man-made environment is included in the conservation and restoration of historical or archeological monuments, and valuable buildings and neighborhoods. These measures are two-fold; one, to protect the environment; and, two, to continue its attractiveness as a tourist destination. This has been the most common method of conservation and protection in both the developed and developing nations. The second, regulation and control, is more common in developed nations. These may win issues of zoning and land use, which either exclude or include tourism development in some areas; limitations on the facilities being built as to height, appearance, open space, and overall design, etc. This is rather rigidly done in Switzerland, where builders must adhere to certain architectural styles before permission is given for development. This is designed to limited growth and unsightly tourist development. In Micronesia, which has few measures of control, there have been some occasions where a builder constructs a building with little or no indication as to its purpose. When completed, the "hotel" turns out to be a boxlike concrete building, totally incompatible with its surroundings, in a poor location for tourists, with bare light bulbs hanging from the ceilings.[18]

This generally will not occur in developed countries, since they have long histories of protective and regulative measures. However, in both the developed and developing nations, the public sectors need to assume a more active role in all measures enacted to conserve, preserve, and restore both natural and man-made environments. The private sector, strong and active in tourism, generally takes a short-term approach to development. Since environmental impacts occur over the long term, the private system does not, because of its short-term focus, have the necessary monitoring systems to identify changes in the quality of the environment. In many cases, the preservation of fragile ecosystems, unique landscapes, and ancient sites and monuments, is beyond the resources of the private sector.

Information and Education

The states should inform tourists, tour operators, and local populations of the need and the means to preserve and enhance the environment and of the effort required on the part of each to insure the results. In many situations and in some countries, the philosophy concerning pollution is that the "polluter pays." It is felt that the possibilities and methods of applying this principle to tourism should be examined. However, experience has shown that financing environmental protection through tourist taxes does not work since it may hinder tourism development.

Standards and Regulations

Standards should be set for protection of the environment, (e.g., pure air, clean drinking water, and clean sea water). This should be accomplished by both the national and local governments working cooperatively. The control

of land use should reflect modern city planning principles to benefit both visitors and local residents.

Carrying Capacity Control

To date, no country has set limits on the number of tourists relative to the impact they have or might have on a destination. Some limits are set, but mostly because of the lack of facilities to house the tourists. The WTO stated that capacity and saturation problems arise in three tourist zones:

> *The Tourist Generating Zone—saturation caused by failure to stagger departures due to climate, employment conditions, school holidays, etc. or concentration of demand at particular times on certain types of tourism (sun/sea/sand, snow, cultural);*
> *Transit Zone—saturation (or a bottleneck) of the means of transport (air, sea or land) from the generating zone to the destination zone;*
> *The Receiving or Destination Zone—saturation to a level which damages the overall environment of the destination (in physical, social or economic terms) and/or destroys the tourist image and leads to visitor dissatisfaction.*[19]

The saturation level, suggested by the WTO, is that point at which (1) the physical environment exceeds the acceptable level of visual impact; (2) ecological damage occurs; (3) wildlife and marine life become threatened; (4) a level of tourism that will help maintain monuments and cultural facilities and traditions without detrimental effects is achieved; (5) further development would exceed the availability of public utilities (e.g., water); (6) there is noticeable pollution; aesthetically and hygienically, resulting in an area losing its attractiveness.

The reason to evaluate and establish the capacity of an area is twofold. First, it will enable governments to plan ahead to maintain a quality environment for both residents and visitors. Second, to help overcome the disadvantages where saturation already exists, or is approaching, by recognizing adjustments that need to be made to reduce the problems.

Concern for the environment and its carrying capacity is necessary. As tourism increases and the pressure increases, there is a danger of negative reactions; as saturation is reached, the quality of environment declines for both residents and visitors. Market forces do not generally deal with long-term solutions since they are concerned with the short-range elements of development.

Integrated Development Planning

There are many large international companies that have realized the importance of a proper and fully-integrated planning approach to resort development. They have both the financial and technical ability to accomplish such a task. They have come to recognize that good development is good business but, unfortunately, there are too few companies with the ability and even those may be somewhat myopic in their decisions. Therefore, a balanced policy for tourism that implies both sustained long-term effort and the development of measures which take into account the environmental consequences are important to all levels of government. This planning cannot be restricted to one sector, but must be integrated into an overall plan. Tourism and the quality of the environment are so closely linked that it is necessary to integrate them by means of comprehensive studies and plans to regulate the development of tourism and the protection of the environment. The purpose of these studies and plans, according to WTO, is to maintain a quality environment that both visitors and residents can appreciate. This is done

> —by avoiding long-term overburdening of the available space with amenities which are too concentrated, heavy or voluminous, in preference to light weight, airy and evolutionary designs (of the type used on camping or residential sites);
> —by limiting any pollution or environmental nuisance caused by the development, resulting from a more detailed knowledge of the true effects of these activities on their surroundings, as well as improved knowledge of the effects of measures to compensate for the development and amenities (control over the number of visitors, undeveloped zones, "soft" energy systems, specially-adapted equipment such as small purification plants);
> —by drawing up a scale of environmental sensitivity to the tourism and leisure activities;
> —by offering the development and tourism planning staff sufficient data for them to take more positive account of environmental protection constraints. Preservation of the environment, particularly in the case of open air accommodation, cannot be restricted to simple "camouflage," as is frequently the case;
> —by measuring, in the specific field of tourism and leisure, the relevance of present parameters used for general analysis of the environment and, if necessary, by constituting new and specific indicators;
> —by defining a simplified impact study methodology so that, if the results of the legally-required main study prove inconclusive, a diagnosis can be made to reduce the financial risks which constitute a brake in development of the infrastructure required;
> —by preserving the natural countryside (especially wooded areas), the traditional types of housing and local attractions;
> —by safeguarding the cultural inheritance—local values, traditions, and personality.[20]

Land Use and Zoning

Land use and zoning are common tools used by developed countries for control of environment, but they are little used by developing countries for a number of reasons. Most developing societies are eager to have any type of development and so have few restrictions on either what is built or where. Guatemala City, for example, had only height restrictions because of proximity to the airport. In developed countries, land use and zoning restrictions are usually adhered to at the local level because the impact of new development is felt directly by local residents. They are used to keeping undesirable development from certain areas. Fragile areas are zoned for limited use or no development in an effort to preserve the environment.

Remedial Measures

A number of remedial measures can be taken to reduce the impact of tourism on the environment:

1. Market/product match those who are most likely to appreciate the area and react favorably to it as the targeted market.
2. Traffic control in areas such as deserts and mountainsides where off-road vehicles can do extensive damage. Traffic control would limit the number of vehicles in a particular region to reduce the pollution, erosion, or marring of the landscape.
3. Visitor quotas, based on an area's saturation level, to restrict the number of visitors.
4. Taxation policies that would tax tourist facilities; the money to be used for environmental protection.
5. Removal of financial incentives to discourage development.
6. Land reclamation to reduce damage in fragile areas that have suffered from erosion in the past.
7. Government involvement in the politics of preservation and control of the environment.

Conclusion

It has become obvious that tourism expansion cannot be unlimited and that government policy makers and planners need to recognize this fact. Eric Cohen has written that those in the decision-making process need to "reorient their major concern from planning the environment for tourism to defending the environment from the tourist impact, even at the expense of a curtailment in the number of tourists or in certain types of tourist use to which an area is subjected."[21] However, the difficulty here is that the developing nations on which tourism will have the greatest impact will also have the least ability to develop policies and finance control of development to maintain or enhance their environment.

RESEARCH AND REVIEW

1. Discuss the following statement: "We often destroy that which attracts us."

2. Describe the nature of change associated with the term "preexisting forms."

3. Describe the environmental benefits of tourism.

4. Discuss the role of tourism in preservation, conservation, and protection of the environment.

5. What four factors led to the conservation movement?

6. Name some outstanding examples of historical preservation.

7. What are two major consequences to the environment resulting from too many visitors?

8. Is there such a thing as a saturation level in tourism? Discuss your answer.

9. How is vegetation impacted by tourism?

10. What forms of pollution are associated with traffic congestion?

11. Discuss the problems associated with tourism development on coastlines.

12. What kind of conflicts may occur between residents and tourists?

13. What are two reasons to evaluate and establish the capacity of an area?

14. What are some methods for development control?

ENDNOTES

1. Peter J. Schmitt, *Back to Nature: The Arcadian Myth in Urban America* (NY: Oxford Univ. Press, 1969), p. 160.
2. Frank C. Brockman, *Recreational Use of the Wildlands* (NY: McGraw Hill, 1959), p. 113.
3. Schmitt, p. 163.
4. John A. Jakle, *The Tourist* (Lincoln, NE: Univ. of Nebraska, 1985), p. 82.
5. Eric Cohen, "The Impact of Tourism on the Physical Environment," *Annals of Tourism Research,* Vol. 2 (1976), pp. 215–237.
6. L. M. Alexander, "The Impact of Tourism on the Economy of Cape Cod, Massachusetts," *Economic Geography,* Vol. 29 (1953), p. 323.
7. P. J. Greenwood, "Tourism as an Agent of Change: A Spanish Basque Case," *Ethnology,* Vol. 11, No. 1 (1972), pp. 80–91.
8. WTO and the UNEP, "Workshop on Environmental Aspects of Tourism" (Madrid, 1983), p. 2.
9. Clare A. Gunn, "Needed: An International Alliance for Tourism—Recreation —Conservation," *Travel Research Journal 2* (Madrid, WTO, 1978), p. 3.
10. Mathieson and Wall, pp. 98–100.
11. OAS, "Enhancing the Positive Impact of Tourism on the Built and Natural Environment," Vol. 5 (Washington, DC: Dept. of Economic Affairs, 1984), p. 5.
12. "The Hidden Places of Keyna," *The New York Times* (Sept. 12, 1982), p. 144.
13. WTO, "Risk of Saturation of Tourist Carrying Capacity Overload in Holiday Destinations (Madrid, 1983), pp. 10–14.
14. Ibid., p. 2.
15. Mathieson and Wall, p. 102.
16. Fred Bosselman, *In the Wake of the Tourist* (Washington, DC: The Conservation Foundation, 1978), pp. 52–53.
17. Mathieson and Wall, p. 109.
18. Ashman, pp. 6–7.
19. WTO, p. 1.
20. WTO and the UNEP, p. 86.
21. Cohen, p. 235.

CHAPTER 21

THE FUTURE: GOAL OPTIMIZATION

In this book, we have stressed that tourism is a dynamic, evolving field. To attempt to predict what's going to happen in the travel industry next month, next year, or twenty-five years from now is at best difficult. There are so many variables, particularly economic, that may influence travel. Changes occur rapidly and many are very dramatic. A quick look back can demonstrate this change.

Not long ago the concept of a bucket shop, or consolidator, was just beginning in Great Britain and still unheard of in the United States. Bucket shops or consolidators obtain discounted tickets from airlines and sell them through travel agents with certain restrictions. A few years ago, less than forty percent of all travel agencies were automated. As recently as the early 1970s, the industry was hoping for an industrywide reservation system. The rapid change that has occurred in the past few years gives emphasis to greater visions of the future. People are more willing to dream dreams they would never have thought possible only a few years ago.

There are some things we do know. We know some of the characteristics of the population. In the United States, for example, it is an aging population with greater education and wealth. A third of today's American population is part of a generation referred to as "baby boomers," children born following the Second World War. The first of this group is in their early forties. With better education and, in many cases, both spouses working and increasingly smaller families, more travel opportunities exist. Those of, or near, retirement age are wealthier due to pension programs and are healthier than ever before. By 1990 thirty-three percent of the population will be retired. They have and will have a higher income, be free of mortgage payments, and be free from supporting their children.[1]

The future, based on these and other indicators, is

bright for the industry. This chapter is devoted to visions of the future as many in the industry see them.

TOURISM COMES OF AGE IN THE 1980s

With tourism becoming the largest industry in the world, more and more people from all economic and educational sectors are becoming aware of its importance. Its future does, indeed, seem bright. The academic community has also recognized the importance of the changes that are taking place in tourism and tourism development. Scholars are studying tourism's impact, both the good and the bad. Historically, most levels of governments looked upon tourism as an economic stimulus and made their decisions solely on that basis. However, that is no longer true as both government and private organizations have come to realize that the balance of quality of product (visitor satisfaction) and economic rewards (profit) to the developer, while important, must be placed in the context of providing a service or product that is socially and politically worthwhile. Many individuals and organizations have come to realize that preservation and quality planning will not only maintain an excellent environment, but enhance the capacity to attract tourists. This is particularly true in developing nations where change can have a significant impact. Quality experiences by both the host and guest will increase the desire for further interaction between them. The best possible consequence is both a growth of tourism and a strengthening of the local environment to benefit both the resident and the visitor.

Professor John Hunt, in a presentation to the North Dakota tourism industry, identified a number of trends pertaining to the future of domestic travel in the United States. Some of the trends he has recognized are:

1. "Travelers will tend to increase length of stay in fewer destinations." This trend was discussed earlier in this book in connection with the multiwage-earning family and the increasing "empty nest" characteristics of an older population. Residents of the United States are becoming more destination oriented and prefer a broader range of recreational and travel services when they get to their destination.

2. "Sales of recreational vehicles and some recreational equipment will witness dramatic changes and fluctuations." The jump in gasoline prices in the 1970s reduced this demand for a while, but with gasoline prices stabilizing and people becoming used to paying the higher prices, RV purchases are increasing. Other important factors in their increased popularity are the fear of terrorism abroad, the fluctuation of the dollar, and the aging of our population.

3. "Travelers will elect to use multiple accommodations." Travelers are using a mixture of accommodations from motels along paths, or RVs and camping in parks, to luxury resorts once a destination has been reached. The pattern seems to be developing whereby people will stay at relatively inexpensive motels on the way to a destination, then expect to be pampered once they arrive.

4. "Mass transportation will grow in popularity as a mode of transportation to recreation areas and for vacation travel." Two factors are important to point out in Hunt's prediction here. First, as indicated, the two wage-earning families will take more vacations and need to travel quickly to and from the destination. Second, older people become less adventuresome and are more comfortable in motorcoach tours as a means of travel.

5. "Deregulation will have a lasting effect on the overall nature on travel and the tourism industry." While, to date, the traveler has benefited from competition and lower air fares, the future remains cloudy. However, deregulation does allow for the ability to implement cost-saving packages and discounts. It will provide a greater variety of options to the traveler.

6. Successful marketing and management of tourism services will become more market segmented. Tourism services will become more skilled at identifying their potential users and market specifically to that segment of the population.

7. "Travelers will seek more back-to-nature and personally enriching experiences." The trend toward physical fitness and health has already led hotels to provide services for their travelers. The high-powered urban world will also increase the demand upon state and national parks.

8. "The willingness to pay for public recreation opportunities will increase." The trend in government has been to introduce a user fee. Public recreation agencies and the public have come to realize that the increasing cost of recreation development and maintenance will require some form of funding.

9. Public and private organizations will compete less in providing tourist services and accommodations. Better service can be provided by public and private agencies by identifying common areas of concern and working together.[2]

Economic conditions are among the more important factors affecting the outlook for international tourism in the United States. Some of these are

1. The health of the world economy—the events in the latter part of 1987 in stock markets around the world focused attention on the world economy and its interrelated problems.

2. The continued weakening of the U.S. dollar will increase the number of incoming tourists and will have a positive influence on the balance-of-trade payments. However, many Americans will still travel abroad; first, because of low-cost transatlantic and transpacific air fares; and, second, the potential deregulation of European air carriers will increase the pressure for lower air fares.

3. A merger mania among the European airlines will create stronger companies and competition will keep air fares low. This will encourage travel both ways across the Atlantic and, combined with the weakening dollar, bring more Europeans to the United States.

4. The United States will increase its promotion

abroad further encouraging and attracting more visitors to the United States.

5. The baby boomers are reaching prime age for international travel.

There are, however, some trends that are cause for concern. Among these are:

1. The strained capacity of the United States airport network. If we are continuing to evolve into shorter, destination-oriented travel patterns, the hub system, which has already created bottlenecks, may put limits on the growth of air travel. One way this can be overcome is for the airlines to begin offering more direct flights. It will also be necessary to create secondary hubs in a region to relieve some of the congestion.

2. The continuing devaluation of the dollar will increase the number of tourists to the United States. If there is no large dramatic devaluation, Americans will not be deterred from traveling abroad. Following the downturn in 1986 (resulting from fears of terrorism) many began to flock to Europe despite the devaluation at that time. Low air fares will somewhat offset the lowering value of the dollar.

3. Urban deterrents—cities in the United States are viewed as unsafe. Little change in this perception can be made as the situation is not likely to improve.

THE CHANGING AMERICAN VACATION: A WORLD TREND

Many of the socioeconomic characteristics of the United States are occurring in the other industrialized nations of the world. Thus, many of the travel patterns in the United States will be similar to those of the other industrialized countries. However, in some cases the United States is following the European pattern. Joyce Kuh discussed these changing patterns. Excerpts from this report based on a study conducted by Marriott Hotels follows:

THE CHANGING AMERICAN VACATION

by Joyce Kuh

Americans are taking more vacations each year for shorter periods of time. A recent study commissioned by Marriott Hotels and Resorts and conducted by Audits & Surveys has shown that the traditional two-week vacation in the United States is giving way to shorter trips taken more frequently. . . .

—Two-thirds of Americans took pleasure trips in 1986, spending at least one night away from home.

—73% of all pleasure trips taken during 1986 were from one to three days long.

—59% of the shorter trips were taken over weekends.

—Americans who took pleasure trips in 1986 took an average of 4.7 trips during the year. . . .

The increase in more frequent, shorter pleasure trips seems to be directly attributable to the increase in dual-career households. . . . Homes with multiple paychecks had 60% of the spendable discretionary income available for luxuries like pleasure trips.

Among the age group 23–44 which constitutes one-third of the population, two-thirds of the households include working wives.

The Marriott survey notes: "The increased time pressures in the households where two adults are employed most likely requires those Americans to take shorter trips at mutually convenient times. Weekends are probably the most appropriate time when two working adults can find the time to get away together.". . .

Age as well as income, affects the incidence of pleasure travel. . . . The highest number of pleasure travelers (75%) fell into the group of 55 to 64. Not only does this age group fall within the group having the most discretionary income, but within this group, men have been taking early retirement in record numbers. It is estimated that by 1990, one third of the men in this age group will be retired. This may also explain why the preponderance of longer trips occurs among this group. . . .

Among all short trips, 43% were taken on weekends and 30% were trips of one to three days taken during the week. The latter are more likely to be taken by persons over 65 years-old; this group is freer to travel during mid-week when destinations are less crowded. And longer trips are taken most by the group that takes the most trips: 55–64; 34% of this group took long vacations. The ponderance of weekend travelers falls within that age group containing the largest percentage of wives working outside the home.

Source: *Travel & Leisure's World Travel Overview 1987/1988* (NY: American Express Publishing Corp., 1987), pp. 124–126. Reprinted by permission.

Given the changing characteristics as the population ages, the greater percentage of two-income households, fewer children per family, more frequent and shorter vacations will continue to grow in importance. For the younger, smaller families Peter Francese predicts that there will be a greater demand for child-oriented activities with flexible scheduling and hassle-free accommodations.[3] The early retirement of baby boomers in the next decade will not only increase the number of short weekday trips, but also increase their distance and length of stay, as they will have both the time and money. The use of package tours increases with age, particularly for women. In addition, this group will choose more cruises. With a better educated traveler, the trend of combining trips with education will also increase. A number of universities offer both special programs at their campuses during the off-season and educational trips, such as marine biology in St. Croix and whale watching off the Mexican coast, which are very popular.

WORLD TRENDS

World trends are similar to those in the United States. The length of time spent on the average trip is shortening at the same time as there are more trips taken. Better air service, at reasonable prices, has increased the average trip's distance, while reducing the travel time to major destinations.

Tourism markets have become broader, with the increased prosperity of the Pacific Rim countries. However, countries in North America, Western Europe and Japan are still the major market for international tourism. The product has improved, with a much greater quality available at the destinations and more destinations available for world travelers to choose from.[4]

Somerset Waters reviewed the growth of tourism in 1987 and had a generally positive outlook for the future.

The World's economy entered 1987 on a generally upbeat note. Inflation in the industrialized countries (members of OECD) was at the lowest level in 22 years. Interest rates were the lowest in six years. Oil prices fell by one-half in 1986. . . .

These favorable economic trends have produced a growth in real disposable income in most of the world. Tourism always grows as there is an increase in the national economy. Since most tourism spending is for domestic travel, the year 1986 set new records for the volume of travel and spending for tourism. Even international travel, despite terrorism, Chernobyl and other setbacks, showed a worldwide increase of 2.1% in arrivals and a 5% increase in tourism receipts.

There are, of course, economic problems of currency instability, third-world debt, trade frictions and continued high unemployment. For the sixth year in succession, more than 30 million people are jobless in the rich industrialized nations. And countless tens of millions remain unemployed in the developing countries.

The developing nations have been squeezed by weak commodity prices. Non-fuel commodity prices are at the lowest "real" levels since World War II.

Strange as it may seem, these negative developments in the past few years have often been beneficial for the tourist industry. Weak commodity prices have caused a number of developing countries to turn to tourism as a way of earning much needed foreign exchange. Official tourism agencies have been raised to higher levels within the bureaucracies in a large number of countries. Many have eased restrictions on the entry of foreign airlines.

High unemployment has been another factor that has produced new interest in government circles in stimulating the domestic tourism business as a way to generate jobs. States, provinces and cities throughout most of the world have been more active in developing their tourism resources.

The decline in oil prices may have weakened the economies in nations and states that produce oil, but cheaper fuel has been helpful to tourism interest everywhere by reducing the cost of transportation. . . .

The world's economy, while continuing to grow, has been climbing at a slower pace. . . . While growth has been at a modest rate, it has lasted over an unusually long period of time, and has raised the standard of living of millions of people throughout the world. . . .

The continued year-after-year increase in world travel has encouraged both private investors and governments to rapidly expand facilities for transporting, housing, feeding and entertaining travelers. Today in many regions of the world, there is an over-supply of airline capacity, hotel rooms, rental cars, cruise ships and other facilities. This had created enough competition to be beneficial to travelers by holding prices at reasonable levels. Suppliers of tourism services in many countries, however, need a pause in their rush to expand capacity in order to let demand catch up with supply. . . .

The growth of spending for domestic and international tourism to the estimated $2 trillion [in 1986] makes this industry the largest in the world. This spending amounts to $5.5 billion a day. Total spending for tourism is larger than the gross national product of any country in the world except the United States. It is more than double the $900 billion spent by the world's military establishments.[5]

This suggests several important clues to the future. First, the state of the economy is an important indicator. Second, and related to the first, while tied to the state of the economy, countries and regions are realizing the importance that tourism can play in improving their economy. Therefore, unless there is global economic disaster, tourism will continue to grow. Third, in spite of regional conditions that influence tourism such as terrorism, Chernobyl, and the continuous fall in the dollar, tourism will continue, although the destination may shift. Governments have recognized tourism is important to their economic well-being. This suggests that the future will continue to be positive barring world economic collapse. Given that there will probably be growth, real changes will occur in the product and the marketing of tourism.

THE AIRLINES

The future of airlines and the impact of deregulation was discussed by John Maldutis:

> In order to examine the forces and issues that will shape the industry in the future, let me offer a few observations about the recent past.
> Deregulation is now almost ten years old—that is, from a legal perspective. However, in my opinion, deregulation really did not commence until 1983. . . .
> What have been the effects of deregulation? I believe that everyone is familiar with the massive consolidation that the airlines have experienced. Prior to 1978, there were 36 carriers. . . In the 1978–86 period, 198 new carriers were certificated, totaling 234. However, in the past several years, the industry has experienced the loss of about 160 companies. Thus, there are 74 airlines, and the number, rather than increasing, is shrinking. . . .
> The most significant part of this consolidation process has been the massive merger movement in the past two years. . . .
> Under the current administration, we have had, and I believe that all will agree, quite liberal merger guidelines. . . .
> By buying another airline, it was easy and an inexpensive way to buy into markets or market share, given the congestion and lack of facilities at the major airports.
> Many of us on Wall Street are beginning to realize that it will be years before the profits from some of these mergers pay off the costs associated with the acquisition. In fact, two carriers that made acquisitions are experiencing quite serious problems.
> Recent explosion of service problems can, in large part, be blamed on the multitude of airline mergers. Thus, the growing political backlash from deteriorating airline service and the inequality of airline fares, make this and the next Administration less prone to approve any more airline combinations. Similarly, there will be no more "new" airlines for years to come. The reasons are simple.
> There are no more niches or hubs left. In fact, there are some 40 hub airports in the United States. Carriers now boast that some have three, four, five, and as many as six hubs.
> Airport facility constraints in terms of gates, or landing slots, make it prohibitive—if not exclusionary—for any new airlines to be formed.

> The capital markets are closed, and I mean closed. The capital markets will not finance the formation of any new companies. The losses to equity investors who financed People Express, Air One, Air Atlanta, just to name a few, have been prohibitive. . . .
> We are at, I believe, the sunset, or the twilight zone, of the industry's deregulation experience. Aside from one or two companies whose future is still unclear, the industry appears to be headed in a new and different direction. . . .
> Demands for reregulation are becoming more and more vocal. Congress has ten bills under consideration. . . . While airline service problems are the motivating force for reregulation, in my judgment, it is the price discrimination that exists today. . . . namely, two different consumers being charged two different prices for the same product. . . .
> This price discrimination is always the causal factor for regulation of an industry. As long as this price discrimination exists, the pressures for economic regulation of the airline industry will be there and will be exacerbated in direct proportion to the pricing differentials.
> Regulation may also return via the back door. The national airways system is congested, and the chairman of the National Transportation Safety Board (NTSB) is demanding restrictions on airline operations. I am concerned that the next aviation incident will produce excruciating political demands for the FAA to step in and impose flight restrictions at 7 or 8 more airports. . . .
> The airline industry has really become a "mass transit" industry. Intercity travel is only possible by airplane. I expect air travel to grow by 6%–7% annually for the next decade.
> My estimate is much higher than the prevailing ones, because by the middle of the next decade, there will be some 85 million Americans who are 45 years of age and over. These older Americans do more air travel than any other group—some 43% of all air travel. They also generate some 48% of all the discretionary travel. Therefore, I expect airline traffic growth to continue at a high pace. Furthermore, the structural change in the demand side of the air travel market is making the industry less and less dependent on the business traveler. Today, business travel constitutes only 45% of all air travel, whereas a decade ago, it represented some 55%. Consequently, with the ever-declining dependence of the airlines on the business traveler, the industry will become less and less cyclical.
> More important, those that have argued that the consolidation of the industry will lead to an oligopolization and much higher fares, fail to realize that given the industry's dependence on the discretionary traveler, it will always have to keep airline fares low. From time to time, airlines will

raise fares during the seasonal period. . . . but these increases will be only temporary, and airline fares will remain relatively flat and low. . . .

Airline managements should seriously rethink their current pricing strategies, whereby they keep trying to raise the fare levels, while restrictions are almost non-existant.

Some carriers still have made few, if any, advances in understanding the new pricing regime. However, a few of the airlines have developed new pricing techniques to solve the age old problem of "no-show passengers.". . .

In a recent discussion of airline developments with a Canadian official, I was rather startled to hear a statement that, "We in Canada started deregulation four years later, and we have finished it four years sooner." Canada, in contrast, is now left with three major airline systems. Within the liberalization movement, the globalization of airlines is also taking place. Joint marketing relationships and eventually dual designations portend the much stronger financial relationships that will emerge.

I believe that we are at the leading edge of full or partial ownership between international airlines. . . . I foresee a situation over the next several years in which major foreign carriers hold equity positions in U.S. airlines, and similarly, U.S. airlines will take equity positions in foreign airlines. In effect the world aviation community is drawing closer together. The joint experiments and experiences of deregulation are now leading to a joint experiment in marketing and operating relationships. We are in the earliest stages of full or partial ownership of air transport companies.

Overall, I have always been an optimist and remain so. I believe that the industry's fundamentals are positive for the long term. The prospect of strong airline traffic growth will result from the changing population demographics.

We have ever-increasing pricing sophistication on the part of airline managements so that airline fares, which were once regulated and static and unresponsive to market needs, are now more flexible and will remain in line with the demands of the marketplace. . . .[6] (Reprinted with permission of Julius Maldutis, PhD, Director Solomon Brothers, Inc.)

Deregulation has created five huge, supercarriers, United, American, Texas Air (Continental, Eastern, Frontier, Peoples), Delta, and Northwest which account for over seventy percent of industry revenues. Michael Derchin identified the common characteristics of this consolidation:

1. *Dominant hub positions in four or five domestic/international cities;*
2. *Sophisticated computerized reservation systems.*
3. *Lots of liquidity (cash).*
4. *Smart, aggressive managements, and*

5. *If not low costs, progress in reducing labor costs through bargaining/confrontation.*[7]

Derchin identifies six reasons that further illustrate why, even in what he refers to as "sloppy economic conditions," travel is becoming more important:

—*The airlines are offering very attractive air fares.*
—*The post-World War II baby boomers are entering the 35–55 age bracket—the primary age for air travel.*
—*Because of the weak dollar, there has been an influx of foreign citizen travel in the United States for business and pleasure reasons.*
—*Terrorism is keeping U.S. citizens closer to home. Since the cost of a European trip is three times the cost of domestic travel, we're seeing more multiple U.S. trips.*
—*Finally, underlying business travel demand remains strong. Perhaps marketing people are on the road drumming up business.*[8]

TRAVEL AGENCIES

Deregulation has changed the character of the travel agency business. The future will continue to be an evolutionary process for the distribution system. The following report from *Travel Weekly* presents one view of the future:

Agencies who take the "general store" approach to their businesses will be dwarfed or wiped out in the future by burgeoning mega-agencies, predicted Peter Sontag, chairman of Washington-based USTravel Systems.

The travel agencies that survive will be those that specialize, he said. . . .

"By 1997, you will have three international mega-agencies that are doing $3 billion-plus in sales," he said.

"There will be six domestic mega-agencies with $2 billion each in sales and four dozen regional dominants with 40% of market share."

Sontag predicted the remainder of the market share will be held by 6,000 travel agency "boutiques" that sell special-interest travel.

Sontag likened the situation to the food business: supermarkets wiping out mom-and-pop groceries, and specialty shops such as cookie and "gourmet popcorn" boutiques springing up to augment supermarkets' offerings.

"The reason boutiques will survive is that they have product definition," said Sontag. . . .

"If you are a full-service agency, you have to make the transition to defining your product."

"If you're going to be in the general store business, you'll have to be very big if you're not going to start defining your market."

Sontag also suggested that agencies specializing

in corporate travel think of differentiating themselves by providing special services. . . .

Sontag said travel agencies today are working in dangerous times because of the high numbers of agencies, all promising essentially the same thing: good service.

"I ask many purchasing agents in corporations, 'When agents walk in, what do they tell you about being different?'

"The most common answer is 'good service.' Their eyes glaze over, because everyone gives good service."

Sontag said customers are price sensitive and that agencies that compete on price—and many will have to—must focus on operations and costs.

"If your objective is to compete on costs, figure out how to drive your costs into the ground."

"Segment your customer base, get rid of the cradle-to-grave business that most agencies are running, have special services desks, queue things around."

The agency's objective, he said, should be to differentiate its product but still operate effectively in a market that's sensitive to prices.

"Once you develop uniqueness you can start charging a little more," he said.

The ultimate goal—and most businesses never reach it—is a product that is so unique customers are willing to pay almost anything for it, he said.[9]

TECHNOLOGY

Automation in the travel industry is here to stay. Computerization will affect the industry most in three areas:

Communications: Business travelers frequently alter their itineraries to suit their changing requirements. Considerable time today is lost in making alternative arrangements via vendors or distributors from pay phones, hotel rooms, or secretaries' phones. Portable Communication Data Units (PCDUs), a portable telephone/computer, will allow a business travelers to communicate with any travel entity from anywhere (including airplanes) and consequently rearrange or reconfirm their travel plans.

Interactive CRTs: We've seen the first application of interactive television in some cities, and within a few years we'll see much more. For example, it is quite possible that much of the order placement process will be shifted to interactive television. Specific order parameters and order forms can be programmed into a data base that can be accessed by any number of users.

If calls are cut to one-third by interactive CRTs, travel counselors should be reaching productivity levels of $2.5 million to $5 million per annum each. Consequently, the cost of getting a traveler on an airplane, into a hotel or a car is considerably reduced and profitability of the distribution system as well as cost to the traveler is optimized.

Elimination of tickets: In conjunction with the above, there no longer will be a need for the traveler to carry an actual document for an airplane seat or a hotel reservation.

Visualize the following: On a relaxing Sunday evening you plan a trip for the following Thursday. You place the order on your interactive television, and you insert your travel card into the appropriate slot on the side of the console. After all arrangements and confirmations have been made, the computer magnetically codes your card. You arrive at the airport, go to the appropriate gate, and as you enter the airplane, right before you hang up your carry-on bag, there is a slot into which you simply stick your card. If the response is positive, you press a button and, as in a parking lot, exit; a receipt will pop out of the wall.

One of the biggest problems faced by agents today is finding the most efficient way to deliver the traveler's documents. The elimination of tickets will make the single biggest impact on the distribution system because the fiduciary role of the agent is eliminated. Consequently, the order-taker-only agent will also be eliminated.[10]

CHANGES IN TOURISM PRODUCTS AND MARKETS: THE FUTURE

Airlines

Little change is anticipated by the industry, except that by 2008 airplanes will be larger, quieter and use less fuel. Supersonic flight will improve; it, too, will be faster, quieter, use less fuel, and it will have a much greater range and payload.

However, as discussed above, most change will be in automation and information technology. Paperwork will decrease and become more efficient. Teleconferencing will not advance air travel, but decentralization will likely lead to more.

Cruises

As in other industries, baby boomers are arriving at the age when they are prime market targets for cruises. The new generation of cruise vessels is larger and more spacious. Distribution will remain with travel agencies, but there will be greater in-agency computerization. Probably more cruises will offer packages in connection with education or learning opportunities.

Hotels

Most hotel leaders are very optimistic over the future. Jim Evans suggests that in future there may be a Hyatt Regency Moon. We will have more people with more wealth and personal freedom, who will be taking more trips, both for therapeutic and educational purposes. Resort hotel development will continue to expand all around the world. Evans suggests:

Hotels will become community centers. . . We will have to create events, seminars and activities to sell, as well as rooms, food and beverages and meeting space. . . .

We will see increased use of technology in hotels. Wider acceptability of teleconferencing, not as a meeting substitute but as a meeting enhancement, will be common.

We will see the creation of full-scale communications centers in hotels where telephone messages. . . will be extinct because, instead, a memo will be transmitted instantaneously.

A videoconference will be possible in a private terminal. . . You will be able to meet with employees in various parts of the country during a convention coffee break. Computer terminals by hotel beds and airline seats will become common, so that traveling businessmen can plug in their hand-held computers and send information back into the base computer at the home office. We may see robots in the housekeeping departments of hotels, but even though it will be possible, never at the front desk. Service, in an industry where service is a large part of what we sell, can never be replaced.[11]

The use of technology in the hotel industry is illustrated in the vignette on "The Future."

Car Rental

The car rental industry has consistently outstripped air travel growth and will probably do so in the future. While the industry has grown the car has become more luxurious, efficient, and smaller. Jim Philion envisions the future:

[The traveler] will arrive at a modern airport center and possibly be shuttled to what might be called a carport on a generic bus, a bus that doesn't contain the name of any car rental company on its side, but

provides basic transportation to the carport where all rent-a-car companies are located if they wish to be represented.

At that carport, a traveler will ask for the reservation which will be guaranteed through the use of a major credit card and received via totally automated systems. . . .

The traveler may or may not be met by a live body. Warmth and personality are important in the car rental business because first and foremost, it is a service business—an aspect we hope will dictate the future.[12]

Summary

The common elements that can be extracted from these various views are, first, computer technology is changing and will dramatically change the way the product is sold and serviced. Second, tourism is a service industry and will remain so. As such, human interaction and contact will always be important. Third, tourism is an expanding industry that is becoming more important in the lives of the people of the world. Fourth, the tourism product will be easier to access, more comfortable, more pleasurable, and more cost effective.

A THIRD GENERATION OF TOURISM THINKING

L. J. D'Amore discussed tourism in a global perspective. It is a summary of the future of tourism and ties the past and present into the future.

Hyatt Regency Scottsdale. Scottsdale, Arizona.

THE FUTURE

by Larry Chervenak

You make your reservation at the convention hotel by telling your wrist communicator (WC) the number of the hotel's central reservation computer. When you put your index finger on the face of the display screen, the computer recognizes your fingerprint and calls up your data file. . . .

When nearing the convention hotel, you speak into your wrist communicator to notify the hotel's computer of your pending arrival. The computer flashes back your room number, verbally describes your accommodations, and asks if they are satisfactory. You agree and are automatically checked in. Your fingerprint will unlock the door when you arrive.

Your luggage will be transferred from a central staging point via an electronic "dumb waiter" to your room's built-in receiving compartment, where you also receive room service orders. The telecommunication system in the room allows you to see your family when you call home. When you are out of the room, callers can reach you directly on your WC.

Your food service is automatic as your eating habits have been tracked according to food preferences and consumption habits. Food preparation is the function of automated equipment in which large quantities of the menu ingredients are stored and which produce entrees according to verbal instructions.

You agree with your colleagues that increased longevity and the 24-hour work week caused by the advance of automation have changed the role of the lodging industry substantially. Most hotels are not only recreational and social centers, but also educational centers where guests stay in a comfortable environment to keep up with changed skills needed for their present jobs, prepare for new careers, and learn about social and cultural areas that are in no way job-related.

At convention's end, you put your luggage in the electronic dumbwaiter. To check out, you call up your guest bill on the video screen, and as soon as you approve it, a copy of your folio is automatically transferred to your home computer file and your bank account is debited for the amount of your bill.

Source: *Lodging,* June 1985, p. 80.

The three most serious threats facing humanity are the continued build-up of military and nuclear arms and on-going warfare in various parts of the world; the growing disparities between the poorest nations of the world and the world's affluent nations; and the continued desecration of our environment.

A third generation of tourism will acknowledge these global issues, and as the world's largest industry will set an example as the world's most responsible industry .

There is no better way to promote understanding, respect and trust among people than through tourism. Tourism can be a vehicle for the exchange of ideas, learning and appreciation of different cultures, and the bringing together of persons who, though from different cultures, share common aims.

Tourism can also be a vehicle for economic and social development. Several of the world's disadvantaged countries have tourism potential but require assistance in developing that potential in a manner which is sensitive to the local social and cultural context.

Tourism can also play a key role in increasing our awareness and knowledge of environmental issues and the promotion of an environmental ethic. This should be the central purpose of a tourism—national parks partnership.

This is a beginning vision of a Third Generation of Tourism. This is the beginning of a "creative conspiracy" that we can work together to achieve.[13]

RESEARCH AND REVIEW

1. Why is the future of tourism difficult to predict?

2. What are three goals upon which tourism development must be predicated?

3. What are the trends in tourism identified by John Hunt?

4. What are some recent patterns in American vacations?

5. How is changing technology affecting the travel industry?

6. Discuss the future of the four major types of transportation.

7. What reasons does Somerset Waters suggest for the continued growth of tourism?

8. Discuss L. J. D'Amore's vision of future tourism. Do you agree with his views?

ENDNOTES

1. Peter Francese, "Travel Markets: Fighting the Stereotype," *1987 Outlook for Travel and Tourism,* U.S. Travel Data Center (1986), pp. 77–86.
2. John D. Hunt, "Trends in Tourism Development and Marketing: An Overview," unpublished paper, 1987.
3. Francese, pp. 81–82.
4. Jeanne V. Beekhuis, "World Travel Overview: An Analysis of Travel and Tourism Worldwide," *Travel & Leisure's World Travel Overview 1987/1988* (NY: American Express Publishing Corp., 1987), pp. 8–9.
5. *Travel Industry World Yearbook—1987,* pp. 4–6.
6. Julius Maldutis, "The Airlines: The Twilight Zone," paper presented at National Passengers Traffic Assn., Atlanta, 1987.
7. Derchin, p. 90.
8. Ibid., p. 93.
9. Laura del Rosso, "Sontag: Specialization Is Key for Agencies Future," *Travel Weekly* (May 11, 1987), p. 9.
10. Peter M. Sontag, "Industry Predictions," *Travel Weekly's 25th Anniversary* (1983), pp. 318–320.
11. Jim Evans, "Industry Predictions," *Travel Weekly's 25th Anniversary* (1983), pp. 321–323.
12. Jim Philion, "Industry Predictions," *Travel Weekly's 25th Anniversary* (1983), pp. 324–327.
13. L. J. D'Amore, "A Third Generation of Tourism Thinking," unpublished paper, 1987.

APPENDIX A

NATIONAL TOURISM OFFICES

Note: This listing is for the convenience of North American information users. A list of national tourism offices' headquarters may be obtained from the World Tourism Organization.

Afghan Tourism Organization
c/o Bakhtar Afghan Airlines
535 Fifth Avenue
New York, NY 10017

Andorra Bureau for Tourism and Information
1923 West Irving Park
Chicago, IL 60613

Anguilla Tourist Board
1208 Washington Drive
Centerport, NY 11721

Antigua Tourist Board
610 Fifth Avenue
Suite 311
New York, NY 10020

Argentine Consulate
25 S.E. Second Avenue
Miami, FL 33131

Aruba Tourist Bureau
1270 Avenue of the Americas
Suite 2212
New York, NY 10020 or

399 N.E. 15th Street
Miami, FL 33132

Australian Tourist Commission
2121 Avenue of the Stars
Suite 1200
Los Angeles, CA 90010-2480 or

489 Fifth Avenue
New York, NY 10111

Austrian National Tourist Office
500 Fifth Avenue
New York, NY 10110 or

500 North Michigan Avenue
Suite 544
Chicago, IL 60611 or

11601 Wilshire Boulevard
Suite 2480
Los Angeles, CA 90025

Bahamas Tourist Office
150 East 52nd Street
New York, NY 10022 or

1950 Century Boulevard N.E.
Suite 26
Atlanta, GA 30345

Barbados Board of Tourism
800 Second Avenue
New York, NY 10017

Belgian National Tourist Office
745 Fifth Avenue
New York, NY 10151

Bermuda Department of Tourism
310 Madison Avenue
Room 201
New York, NY 10017 or

235 Peachtree Street, N.E.
Suite 2008
Atlanta, GA 30303

Bhutan Travel Service
120 East 56th Street
New York, NY 10022

Bolivian Tourist Institute
Plaza Venezuela
P.O. Box 1868
La Paz City, Bolivia

Bonaire Tourist Information Office
275 Seventh Avenue
19th Floor
New York, NY 10001-6788

Brazilian Tourism Authority-EMBRATUR
551 Fifth Avenue
Room 421
New York, NY 10176

British Columbia Ministry of Tourism
100 Bush Street
Suite 400
San Francisco, CA 94104

British Tourist Authority
40 West 57th Street
New York, NY 10019 or

World Trade Center
Suite 450
350 South Figueroa Street
Los Angeles, CA 90071

British Virgin Islands Tourist Board
370 Lexington Avenue
New York, NY 10017

Bulgarian Tourist Office
161 East 86th Street
New York, NY 10028

Burma Hotel and Tourist Corporation
104 Strand Road
Rangoon, Burma

Cameroon, General Delegation for Tourism
Amadou Ali, General Delegate for Tourism
Yaounde, Cameroon

Canadian Consulate General Tourism Section
1251 Avenue of the Americas
16th Floor
New York, NY 10020 or

300 South Grand Avenue
10th Floor, Suite 1000
Los Angeles, CA 90071 or

One Maritime Plaza
11th Floor
San Francisco, CA 94111 or

CSTFT Canada
235 Queen Street
Ottawa, Ontario K1A OH6

Cayman Islands Department of Tourism
9999 Richmond Avenue
Suite 131
Houston, TX 77042 or

250 Catalonia Avenue
Suite 604
Coral Gables, FL 33134

Chile, Tourist Office of
c/o Lan-Chile Airlines
630 Fifth Avenue
Suite 809
New York, NY 10111 or

510 West Sixth Street
Suite 408
Los Angeles, CA 90014 or

Servicio National de Turismo
P.O. Box 14082
Catedral 1165
Santiago, Chile

China National Tourist Office
60 East 42nd Street
Suite 3126
New York, NY 10165 or

333 West Broadway
Suite 201
Glendale, CA 91204

Colombia Government Tourist Office
140 West 57th Street
New York, NY 10022

Costa Rican Tourism Bureau
630 Fifth Avenue
New York, NY 10111

Curacao Tourist Board
400 Madison Avenue
Suite 311
New York, NY 10017 or

330 Biscayne Boulevard
Miami, FL 33132

Cyprus Tourist Office
13 East 40th Street
New York, NY 10016

Czechoslovak Travel Bureau-CEDOK
10 East 40th Street
New York, NY 10016

Danish Tourist Board
655 Third Avenue
New York, NY 10017

Dominica Tourist Board
P.O. Box 73
Roseau, Dominica

Dominican Republic Tourist Information Center
485 Madison Avenue
New York, NY 10022

Ecuador
Ecuatoriana Airlines
1290 Avenue of the Americas
New York, NY 10014

Egyptian Government Tourist Office
630 Fifth Avenue
New York, NY 10111 or

323 Geary Street
San Francisco, CA 94102 or

2425 Fountain View No. 280
Houston, TX 77057

El Salvador Tourist Information Office
Radio City Station
46 Park Avenue
New York, NY 10016

Ethiopian Tourism Organization
P.O. Box 2183
Addis Ababa, Ethiopia

Fiji Visitors Bureau
G.P.O. 92
Suva, Fiji Islands

Finnish Tourist Board
655 Third Avenue
New York, NY 10017

French Government Tourist Office
French West Indies Tourist Board
610 Fifth Avenue
Suite 222
New York, NY 10020 or

9401 Wilshire Boulevard
Suite 840
Beverly Hills, CA 90212 or

645 North Michigan Avenue
Suite 430
Chicago, IL 60611 or

1 Hallidie Plaza
Suite 250
San Francisco, CA 94102

Gabon Tourist Information Office
Leggesse Travel & Tourism Consultants
300 Madison Avenue
New York, NY 10017

Galapagos, Inc.
7800 Red Road
South Miami, FL 33143

Gambia
Permanent Mission of Gambia to the U.N.
19 East 47th Street
New York, NY 10017

German National Tourist Office
747 Third Avenue
New York, NY 10017 or

444 South Flower Street
Suite 2207
Los Angeles, CA 90071

Ghana Tourist Board
P.O. Box 3106
Accra, Ghana

Gibraltar Government Tourist Office
Arundel Great Court
179 The Strand
London, England WC2R 1EH

Greek National Tourist Organization
Olympic Tower
645 Fifth Avenue
Fifth Floor
New York, NY 10022 or

31 State Street
Boston, MA 02109 or

611 West Sixth Street
Suite 1998
Los Angeles, CA 90017

Grenada Department of Tourism
141 East 44th Street
Suite 701
New York, NY 10017

Guadeloupe. *See* French West Indies Tourist Board

Guatemala, Consulado General De
57 Park Avenue
New York, NY 10016

Haiti Government Tourist Bureau
630 Fifth Avenue
Suite 2109
New York, NY 10111

Honduras Tourist Bureau
P.O. Box 591, Murray Hill Station
18 East 41st Street
New York, NY 10117 or

1138 Freemont Avenue
South Pasadena, CA 91030

Hong Kong Tourist Association
548 Fifth Avenue
New York, NY 10036 or

333 North Michigan Avenue
Chicago, IL 60601 or

421 Powell Street
Suite 200
San Francisco, CA 94102

Hungarian Travel Bureau-IBUSZ
630 Fifth Avenue
New York, NY 10111

Iceland National Tourist Board
655 Third Avenue
New York, NY 10017

India Tourist Office
30 Rockefeller Plaza
North Mezzanine
New York, NY 10112 or

230 North Michigan Avenue
Chicago, IL 60601 or

3550 Wilshire Boulevard
Suite 204
Los Angeles, CA 90010

Indonesia Tourist Promotion Office
3457 Wilshire Boulevard
Los Angeles, CA 90010

Iraq
Permanent Mission of Iraq to the U.N.
14 East 79th Street
New York, NY 10021

Irish Tourist Board
757 Third Avenue
New York, NY 10017 or

230 North Michigan Avenue
Chicago, IL 60601

Israel Ministry of Tourism
350 Fifth Avenue
New York, NY 10118 or

6380 Wilshire Boulevard
Suite 1700
Los Angeles, CA 90048 or

5 South Wabash Avenue
Chicago, IL 60603 or

3514 International Drive N.W.
Washington, DC 20008 or

220 Montgomery Street
Suite 550
San Francisco, CA 94104 or

4151 Southwest Freeway
Houston, TX 77027 or

420 Lincoln Road
Miami Beach, FL 33139

Italian Government Travel Office-ENIT
630 Fifth Avenue
New York, NY 10111 or

500 North Michigan Avenue
Chicago, IL 60601 or

360 Post Street
Suite 801
San Francisco, CA 94108

Jamaica Tourist Board
866 Second Avenue
New York, NY 10017 or

36 South Wabash Avenue
Chicago, IL 60603 or

3440 Wilshire Boulevard
Suite 1207
Los Angeles, CA 90010

Japan National Tourist Organization
630 Fifth Avenue
New York, NY 10111 or

624 South Grand Avenue
Suite 2640
Los Angeles, CA 90017 or

360 Post Street
Suite 401
San Francisco, CA 94108

Jordan Information Bureau
2319 Wyoming Avenue N.W.
Washington, DC 20008

Kenya Tourist Office
424 Madison Avenue
New York, NY 10017 or

9100 Wilshire Boulevard
Suite 111
Beverly Hills, CA 90212

Korea National Tourism Corporation
460 Park Avenue
Suite 400
New York, NY 10022 or

510 West Sixth Street
Suite 323
Los Angeles, CA 90014 or

230 North Michigan Avenue
Suite 1500
Chicago, IL 60601

Lebanon, Consulate of
7060 Hollywood Boulevard
Hollywood, CA 90028

Liberia Consulate
5201 16th Street N.W.
Washington, DC 20011

Luxembourg National Tourist Office
801 Second Avenue
New York, NY 10017

Macau Tourist Information Bureau
3133 Lake Hollywood Drive
Los Angeles, CA 90068

Malaysia Tourist Information Center
818 West 7th Street
Suite 804
Los Angeles, CA 90017 or

Transamerica Pyramid Building
600 Montgomery Street
San Francisco, CA 94111

Mali, Embassy of the Republic of
2130 R Street N.W.
Washington, DC 20008

Malta Consulate
249 East 35th Street
New York, NY 10016 or

5428 East Beverly Boulevard
Los Angeles, CA 90022

Mauritius Tourist Information Service
401 Seventh Avenue
New York, NY 10001

Mexican Government Tourist Council
405 Park Avenue
Suite 1002
New York, NY 10022 or

10100 Santa Monica Boulevard
Los Angeles, CA 90067

Monaco Government Tourist Office
845 Third Avenue
New York, NY 10022

Moroccan National Tourist Office
20 East 46th Street
Suite 503
New York, NY 10017

Netherlands Board of Tourism
355 Lexington Avenue
New York, NY 10017 or

605 Market Street
Suite 401
San Francisco, CA 94105 or

225 North Michigan Avenue
Suite 326
Chicago, IL 60601

New Zealand Government Tourist Office
630 Fifth Avenue
Suite 530
New York, NY 10111 or

10960 Wilshire Boulevard
Suite 1530
Los Angeles, CA 90024 or

Citicorp Center
1 Sansome Street
San Francisco, CA 94104

Nigerian Information Service
575 Lexington Avenue
New York, NY 10022 or

369 Hayes Street
San Francisco, CA 94102

Northern Ireland Tourist Board
680 Fifth Avenue
2nd Floor
New York, NY 10019

Norwegian Information Service
825 Third Avenue
New York, NY 10022

Pakistan Display Center, Commercial Division
747 Third Avenue
16th Floor
New York, NY 10017

Panama Government Tourist Bureau
2355 Salzedo Street
Suite 201
Coral Gables, FL 33134

Papua New Guinea Embassy
1140 19th Street N.W.
Washington, DC 20036

Paraguay, Consulate General of
2901 Ponce de Leon Boulevard
Coral Gables, FL 33134

Peru National Tourist Office
50 Biscayne Boulevard
Miami, FL 33132

Philippines Ministry of Tourism
556 Fifth Avenue
New York, NY 10036 or

30 North Michigan Avenue
Suite 1111
Chicago, IL 60602 or

3460 Wilshire Boulevard
Suite 606
Los Angeles, CA 90010 or

447 Sutter Street
Suite 409
San Francisco, CA 94108 or

1617 Massachusetts Avenue N.E.
Washington, DC 20035

Polish National Tourist Office
500 Fifth Avenue
New York, NY 10110

Portuguese National Tourist Office
548 Fifth Avenue
New York, NY 10036

Puerto Rico Tourism Company
1290 Avenue of the Americas
New York, NY 10104

Romanian National Tourist Office
573 Third Avenue
New York, NY 10016

Saint Lucia Tourist Board
41 East 42nd Street
Suite 315
New York, NY 10017

Saint Maarten/Saba/Saint Eustatius Tourist Office
275 Seventh Avenue
New York, NY 10001

Saint Vincent and the Grenadines
East Caribbean Tourist Association
801 Second Avenue
21st Floor
New York, NY 10017

Scandinavian National Tourist Offices
655 Third Avenue
New York, NY 10017

Senegal, Embassy of the Republic of
2112 Wyoming Avenue N.W.
Washington, DC 20008

Seychelles Tourist Board
P.O. Box 33018
St. Petersburg, FL 33733

Singapore Tourist Promotion Board
342 Madison Avenue
Suite 1008
New York, NY 10173 or

8484 Wilshire Boulevard
Suite 510
Beverly Hills, CA 90211 or

251 Post Street
Suite 308
San Francisco, CA 94108

South African Tourist Board
747 Third Avenue
New York, NY 10017 or

9465 Wilshire Boulevard
Suite 721
Beverly Hills, CA 90212

Spanish National Tourist Office
665 Fifth Avenue
New York, NY 10020 or

Sandiente Plaza Building
8383 Wilshire Boulevard
Beverly Hills, CA 90211

Sri Lanka Tourist Board
609 Fifth Avenue
Suite 704
New York, NY 10017 or

2148 Wyoming Avenue N.W.
Washington, DC 20008

Surinam, Embassy of the Republic of
2600 Virginia Avenue N.W.
Washington, DC 20037

Swiss National Tourist Office
608 Fifth Avenue
New York, NY 10020 or

250 Stockton Street
San Francisco, CA 94108

Syrian Embassy
2215 Wyoming Avenue N.W.
Washington, DC 20008

Tahiti Tourist Promotion Board
12233 West Olympic Boulevard
Suite 110
Los Angeles, CA 90064

Taiwan Visitors Association
3325 Wilshire Boulevard
Suite 515
Los Angeles, CA 90010

Tanzania Tourist Corporation
205 East 42nd Street
New York, NY 10017

Thailand, Tourism Authority of
5 World Trade Center
Suite 2449
New York, NY 10048 or

3440 Wilshire Boulevard
Suite 1101
Los Angeles, CA 90010

Togo Information Service
1706 R Street N.W.
Washington, DC 20009

Trinidad and Tobago Tourist Board
400 Madison Avenue
Suite 712–14
New York, NY 10017 or

200 S.E. First Street
Miami, FL 33131

Tunisian Embassy of Tourism
1515 Massachusetts Avenue N.W.
Washington, DC 20005

Turkish Government Tourism and Information Office
821 United Nations Plaza
New York, NY 10017

Turks & Caicos Tourist Board
P.O. Box 592617
Miami, FL 33159

United States Travel and Tourism Administration
U.S. Department of Commerce
Washington, DC 20230

United States Virgin Islands
Department of Commerce
1270 Avenue of the Americas
New York, NY 10020

Uruguay Consulate
747 Third Avenue
37th Floor
New York, NY 10017 or

1918 F Street N.W.
Washington, DC 20006

USSR Intourist
630 Fifth Avenue
Suite 868
New York, NY 10111

Yugoslav National Tourist Office
630 Fifth Avenue
Suite 280
New York, NY 10111

Zaire, Embassy of the Republic of
1800 New Hampshire Avenue N.W.
Washington, DC 10009

Zambia National Tourist Board
237 East 52nd Street
New York, NY 10022

Zimbabwe Tourist Office
1270 Avenue of the Americas
Suite 1905
New York, NY 10020

SELECTED INTERNATIONAL TRAVEL ORGANIZATIONS

Caribbean Tourism Association
20 East 46th Street
New York, NY 10017

East Asia Travel Association
630 Fifth Avenue
New York, NY 10111

European Travel Commission
630 Fifth Avenue
New York, NY 10111

Pacific Area Travel Association
1 Montgomery West Tower
Suite 1750
San Francisco, CA 94104

World Tourism Organization
Captan Haya 42
Madrid 16, Spain

APPENDIX B

Part 1: Periodicals

Air Transport: Developments and Economic Conditions (quarterly), Geneva, Switzerland: International Air Transport Association.

Annals of Tourism Research, (quarterly) Elmsford, NY: Pergamon Press.

ASTA Travel News (monthly), NY: Communications International.

Canada Travel Survey, Ottawa, Ontario: Statistics Canada.

Canadian Travel News (biweekly), Don Mills, Ontario: Southam Communications.

Digest of Statistics, Montreal, Quebec: International Civil Aviation Organization.

Economic Review of World Tourism (every two years), Madrid: WTO.

Eurotrends, Middle East and Africa Trends, London Trends, in series "Outlook in the Hotel and Tourism Industries," London: Pannell, Kerr, Forster.

ICTA Journal (biannual), Wellesley, MA: Inst. of Certified Travel Agents.

International Journal of Hospitality Management (quarterly), Oxford: Pergamon Press.

International Tourism Quarterly (quarterly), London: The Economist Intelligence Unit.

Journal of Leisure Research (quarterly), Alexandria, VA: National Recreation and Park Assn.

Journal of Travel Research (quarterly), Boulder: Business Research Dept., College of Business, Univ. of Colorado.

Leisure Sciences (quarterly), NY: Crane, Russak.

Leisure Studies, (3 times yearly), London: E. & F. N. Spon.

263

Lloyd's Aviation Economist (monthly), London: Lloyd's of
    London Press.
National Travel Survey (annual), Washington, DC: U.S.
    Travel Data Center.
PATA Annual Statistics, San Francisco, CA: Pacific Area
    Tourism Assn.
Recent Management (monthly) San Diego, CA: Western
    Speciality Publications.
Revue de l'Academe Internationale du Tourisme
    (quarterly), Saint Gallens, Switzerland: AIEST.
Statistical Yearbook (annual), NY: U.N. Statistical Office.
Tourism Management (quarterly), England: Butterworth
    Scientific.
*Tourism Policy and International Tourism in OECD
    Member Countries* (annual), Paris: Organization for
    Economic Cooperation and Development.
Tourist Review (quarterly), Berne, Switzerland: AIEST.
Travel Business Analyst (monthly), Hong Kong.
Travel Industry World Yearbook: The Big Picture (annual),
    NY: Child & Waters.
Travel Outlook Forum (annual proceedings), Washington,
    DC: U.S. Travel Data Center.
Trends in the Hotel Industry, International Edition
    (annual), Houston, TX: Pannell, Kerr, Forster.
Trends in the Hotel Industry, USA Edition (annual),
    Houston, TX: Pannell, Kerr, Forster.
U.S. Lodging Industry (annual), Philadelphia: Laventhol
    and Horwath.
World Air Transport Statistics (annual), Geneva,
    Switzerland: International Air Transport Assn.
World Travel Overview (annual), NY: American Express
    Publishing Corp.
World Wide Lodging Industry (annual), NY: Horwath and
    Horwath International.
Yearbook of Tourism Statistics (annual), Madrid: WTO.

Part 2: Trade Publications and Associations

Adventure Travel Society
6301 Newbury Drive
Bethesda, MD 20816

Air Transport World
1030 15th Street N.W.
Washington, DC 20005

Airline and Travel Food Service
665 La Villa Drive
Miami Spring, FL 33166

Airline Economics Inc.
2011 Eye Street N.W.
Suite 200
Washington, DC 20006

Airline Executive
6255 Barfield Road
Atlanta, GA 30328

Air Transport Association of America
1709 New York Avenue N.W.
Washington, DC 20006–5206

American Bus Association
1025 Connecticut Avenue N.W.
Washington, DC 20036

American Hotel & Motel Association
1201 New York Avenue N.W.
Suite 600
Washington, DC 20005

American Recreation Coalition
1331 Pennsylvania Avenue N.W.
Suite 726
Washington, DC 20004

American Resort and Residential
Development Association
1220 L Street N.W.
Suite 510
Washington, DC 20005

American Society of Travel Agents
P.O. Box 23992
Washington, DC 20026–3992

Association of Travel Marketing Executives International
P.O. Box 43563
Washington, DC 20010

Amusement Business
14 Music Circle East
Nashville, TN 37203

Aviation Week
1777 North Kent Street
Suite 710
Arlington, VA 22209

Banamex
Department of Economic Research
Socorro Corea Avenue
Medero 21 2nd Floor
Mexico D.F. 06000

Business Traveler's Report
10076 Boca Entrada Boulevard
P.O. Box 3007
Boca Raton, FL 33431–0907

The Cornell Hotel and Restaurant Administration
Cornell University
327 Statler Hall
Ithaca, NY 14853

Corporate & Incentive Travel
488 Madison Avenue
New York, NY 10022

Corporate Meetings & Incentive Magazine
747 Third Avenue
New York, NY 10017

Council for Hotel, Restaurant and Institutional Education
1200 17th Street N.W.
7th Floor
Washington, DC 20036

Cruise Lines International Association
17 Battery Place
New York, NY 10004

Cruise Travel Magazine
1020 Church Street
Evanston, IL 60201

Economic Research Association
680 Peach Street #370
San Francisco, CA 94109

Euromonitor Publications Limited
18 Doughty Street
London WC1N 2PM, UK

Horwath & Horwath International
919 Third Avenue
New York, NY 10022

Hotel & Motel Management Magazine
7500 Old Oak Boulevard
Cleveland, OH 44130

Hotel & Resort Industry
488 Madison Avenue
New York, NY 10022

Hotels and Restaurants International
1350 East Touhy
P.O. Box 5080
Des Plaines, IL 60018

Hotel Sales and Marketing Association International
1400 K Street N.W.
Washington, DC 20005

Incentive Travel Manager Magazine
825 Barrington Avenue
Los Angeles, CA 90049

Industry Week Magazine
1111 Chester Avenue
Cleveland, OH 44114

International Association of Amusement Parks
and Attractions
4230 King Street
Alexandria, VA 22302

International Association of Convention
and Visitor Bureaus
702 Bloomington Road
Champaign, IL 61820

International Association of Scientific Events
in Tourism (AIEST)
Varnbuelstrasse 19
CH-9000 St. Gallen, Switzerland

International Travel News
2120 28th Street
Sacramento, CA 95818

Jax Fax
Travel Marketing Magazine
280 Tokeneke Road
Darien, CT 06820

Lodging-Hospitality Magazine
1111 Chester Avenue
Cleveland, OH 44114

Meeting News
1515 Broadway
New York, NY 10036

Meetings and Conventions International
340 East 64th Street
New York, NY 10021

Meeting and Convention Magazine
1 Park Avenue
New York, NY 10036

National Campground Owners Association
11307 Sunset Hills Road
Suite B7
Reston, VA 22090

National Restaurant Association
311 First Street N.W.
Washington, DC 20001

National Tour Association, Inc.
P.O. Box 3071
Lexington, KY 40596

National Trust for Historic Preservation
1785 Massachusetts Avenue N.W.
Washington, DC 20036

Recreation Vehicle Industry
1896 Preston White Drive
P.O. Box 2999
Reston, VA 22090

Resort & Hotel Management
2431 Morena Boulevard
San Diego, CA 92110

Restaurants and Institutions Magazine
1350 East Touhy Avenue
Des Plaines, IL 60018

Runzheimer Report on Travel Management
555 Skokie Boulevard
Suite 245
Northbrook, IL 60062

Society for the Advancement of Travel
for the Handicapped
26 Court Street
Brooklyn, NY 11242

Society of American Travel Writers
1120 Connecticut Avenue N.W.
Room 940
Washington, DC 20036

Special Events Report
213 West Institute Place
Suite 303
Chicago, IL 60610

Successful Meetings
633 Third Avenue
New York, NY 10017

Tourism Canada
235 Queen Street
Ottawa, Ontario
Canada K1A OH6

Tourism Industry Association of Canada
130 Albert Street
Ottawa, Ontario
Canada, K1P 564

Tourist Attractions and Parks
Kane Communications, Inc.
401 North Broad Street
Suite 226
Philadelphia, PA 19108

Traffic World
1335 G. Street, N.W.
Suite 900
Washington, DC 200

Travelage East
888 Seventh Avenue
New York, NY 10106

Travelage Midamerica
2416 Prudential Plaza
Chicago, IL 60601

Travelage Southeast
888 Seventh Avenue
New York, NY 10106

Travelage West
100 Grant Avenue
San Francisco, CA 94108

Travel Agent
2 West 46th Street
New York, NY 10036

Travel and Tourism Research Association
P.O. Box 8066
Foothill Station
Salt Lake City, UT 84108

The Travel Business Manager
90 West Montgomery Avenue
Suite 184
Rockville, MD 20850

Travel Business Report
P.O. Box 889
Midtown Station
New York, NY 10018

Travel Digest
342 Madison Avenue
New York, NY 10017

Travel Industry Association of America
2 Lafayette Center
1133 21st Street N.W.
Washington, DC 20036

Travel Trade
6 East 46th Street
New York, NY 10017

Travel Management Daily and
Travel Management Newsletter
888 Seventh Avenue
New York, NY 10106

Travel Weekly
1 Park Avenue
New York, NY 10016

Universal Federation of Travel
Agent Associations (UFTAA)
30 Avenue Marniz
B-1050 Brussels, Belgium

United States Tour Operators
211 East 51st Street
New York, NY 10022

APPENDIX C

PART 1: COMPOSITE LIST OF STANDARD INDUSTRIAL CLASSIFICATION CODES THAT COMPRISE THE TRAVEL AND TOURISM INDUSTRY—UPDATED 1987

Old Codes	Name	New Codes
152	*General Contractors*	152
40(pt)	*National Rail Passenger Corp (AMTRAK)*	4011(pt)
412	*Taxicabs*	412
413	*Intercity Bus*	413
414	*Local Bus Charter*	4141
4142	*Intercity Bus Charter*	4142
4171	*Bus Terminals*	4173
44(pt)	*Water Transport of Passengers, Deep Sea*	4481
4469	*Water Transport, NEC**	4489
451	*Certified Air (now Scheduled Air)*	4512
452	*Non-Certified Air (now Non-scheduled Air)*	4522
458	*Air Services*	458
4722	*Arrangers of Passenger Transportation*	472
	Travel Agencies	4724
	Tour Operators	4725
	*Arrangers, NEC**	4729
4784	*Road Toll Facilities*	4785
	*Trans Services, NEC**	4789
53	*General Retail*	53
55	*Auto Dealers*	551
554	*Service Stations*	554
555	*Boat Dealers*	555
556	*Recreation & Utility Trailers*	556
58	*Eating & Drinking Places*	58

5948	*Luggage Retail*	5948
59	*Miscellaneous Retail, Other*	5995
701	*Hotels, Motels*	701
703	*Camps, Trailer Parks*	703
7032	*Recreation Camps*	7032
7033	*RV Parks & Campsites*	7033
704	*Membership Hotels*	704
7512	*Auto Rental w/o Driver*	7514
783	*Motion Picture Theatres*	783
792	*Bands, Orchestras & Entertainment*	7929
794	*Commercial Sports*	794
7996	*Amusement Parks*	7996
7999	*Amusements, NEC**	7999

*NEC = Not Elsewhere Classified

PART 2: THE TOURISM SYSTEM: PROFESSIONAL OCCUPATIONS

The Travel Trade and Distribution Outlet Sector

Travel Agency & Tour Promoters/Operators — Travel Agent (owner/manager), General Sales Agent (consultant), FIT/DIT Specialist (technician), Group Sales Specialist, Commercial Account Specialist, Ticket Agent, Reservation Agent (wholesale), Account Executive (wholesale), Group Desks (wholesale), Operations Manager Sales Promotion/Travel Writer, Guides (sight-seeing, tour escorts)

Travel Service-Promotion — Media Specialist, Print Media (travel writers, editors), Publication Design & Research (technician), Public Relations (consultant), Communications Specialist

Travel Management for Private Companies — Tour Arrangers Corporate Travel Manager, Incentive Travel Manager

Government (federal, state, county, municipal) — Director of Tourism, Director of Industry Development

Government (federal, state, county, municipal) continued — Director, Research and Development; Economist/Research Officer; Planning & Development Officer; Policy Planning Director; Industrial Relations Director; Information Services Director; Director of Marketing; Director of Meetings & Conventions; Director of Advertising & Promotion; Market Research Analyst

The Transportation Sector

Air Transportation — Airport Manager, Manager of Tariffs, Reservation Agent, Passenger Service Agent, Ticketing Agent, Airline Tours Agent, Airline Sales Representative, Sales Manager, Manager of Flight Operations, Manager of Operations, Manager of Purchasing, Manager of Marketing, Manager of Training, Public Relations Representative, Flight Attendant & Steward

Road/Bus/Rail Transportation — Transit Operator/Tour Operator, Auto Rental-Counter Representative, Passenger Train Conductor, Passenger Service Agent, Ticketing Agent, Reservation Agent

Marine — Passenger Attendant, Social Director, Boatline Tour Operator

The Accommodations Sector

Hotels, Motels; Resorts; Campgrounds; Institutional Camp — General Manager, Personnel Manager, Convention/Banquet Manager, Sales Representative

Convention Centers
Railroads
Steamship Companies
Special Lodging (guest
  ranches, fishing
  lodges, B & Bs)

Front Office Manager
Desk Clerk
Information Clerk
Building Superintendent
Housekeeping Manager
Social Director

Food and Beverage Sector
Restaurants
Fast Food Services
Catering Services

Manager
Food Services Supervisor
Maitre d'Hotel
Food & Beverage Control
  Clerk
Food and Beverage Analyst
Dietician
Food Technologist

Attractions, Events and Entertainment Sector
Amusement Parks, Theme
  Parks
Casinos
Night Clubs
Circuses
Wildlife & Game Reserves
Expositions
Tournaments
Museums
Historical Sites
Special Exhibits & Events
Outdoor Recreation
  Complexes (ski,
  equestrian centers)
Productions-Performing
  Arts

Concession Operator
Manager
Ticket Clerk
Reservation Clerk
Facility Operator
Researcher, Consultant
Events Promoter
Booking Agent
Road Manager

BIBLIOGRAPHY

Ahmed, Sadrudin A. "What Attracts Tourists to Sri Lanka? An Empirical Analysis of Sri Lanka's and Tourists' Belief." Ottawa: Univ. of Ottawa. Working Paper 83–69, undated.

Air Service Agreement—United States and United Kingdom. Bermuda: Dept. of State Publications No. 2565, Treaties and Other International Acts, Series 1507. Feb. 11, 1946.

Alexander, L. M. "The Impact of Tourism on the Economy of Cape Cod, Massachusetts." *Economic Geography.* Vol. 29.

Amory, Cleveland. *The Last Resorts.* Baton Rouge, LA: Greenwood Press, 1952.

Ascher, Bernard and David L. Edgell, "Barriers to International Travel: Removing Restrictions to Trade in Service and Tourism." *Travel and Tourism Analyst.* London: Economist Publications, Oct. 1986.

Ashman, Mike, "The Island Lifestyle: An Endangered Species." Unpublished Paper. Kona, HI: Pacific Area Travel Assn. Workshop, Apr. 1976.

Awekotuku, Ngahuia. "Maori Culture and Tourism Income in Pacific Tourism." in *Pacific Tourism.* Hawaii: So. Pacific Social Sciences Assn., 1980.

Bale, Dennis E. "Motels." *Motels.* June 1985.

"Barriers to International Travel: Removing Restrictions to Trade in Service and Tourism." *Travel & Tourism Analyst.* London: Economist Publications, Oct. 1986.

Bates, E. S. *Touring in 1600.* Boston and NY: Houghton Mifflin, 1911.

Beekhuis, Jeanne V. "World Travel Overview: An Analysis of Travel and Tourism Worldwide." *Travel & Leisure's World Travel Overview 1987/1988.* NY: American Express Publishing Corp., 1987.

Bell, Charles W. "Vacation Blues Syndrome Strike." *Salt Lake Tribune.* July 1, 1979.

Blanton, David. "Tourism Training in Developing Countries: The Social and Cultural Dimension." *Annals of Tourism Research.* Vol. 7, No. 1, 1981.

Bohan, Gregory T. "Resorts." *Lodging.* June 1985.

Bosselman, Fred. *In the Wake of the Tourist.* Washington, DC: The Conservation Foundation, 1978.

Brockman, Frank C. *Recreational Use of Wildlands.* NY: McGraw Hill, 1959.

Bruce, Margaret. "New Technology and the Future of Tourism." *Tourism Management.* June 1987.

Bryden, John M. *Tourism and Development.* Cambridge: Cambridge Univ. Press, 1973.

Brymere, Robert A. *Introduction to Hotel and Restaurant Management.* Dubuque, IA: Kendall/Hunt Publishing Co., 1984.

Bugnicourt, Jaques "Tourism: The Other Face." *Development Forum.* Vol. 5, No. 6, Aug.–Sept. 1977.

Burkart, A. J. and S. Medlik. *Tourism Past, Present and Future.* London: Heinemann, 1981.

Casson, Lionell. *Travel in the Ancient World.* London: George Allen & Unwin Ltd., 1974.

Chadwick, Robert A. "Concepts, Definitions and Measures Used in Travel and Tourism Research." in *Travel, Tourism and Hospitality Research: A Handbook for Managers and Researchers.* Ed. J. R. Brent Ritchie and Charles R. Goeldner. NY: John Wiley & Sons, 1986.

Chrvenak, Larry. "Technology: Achieving Inroads." *Lodging.* June 1985.

Cohen, Eric. "The Impact of Tourism on the Physical Environment." *Annals of Tourism Research.* Vol. 5, No. 2, 1978.

Cook, Robert L. and Ken W. McCleary. "Redefining Vacation Distances in Consumer Minds." *Journal of Travel Research.* Vol. 22, No. 2, Fall, 1983.

Cottingham, Jane. "Sex Included." *Development Forum.* June 1981.

Crompton, John L. "A Systems Model of the Tourists Destination Selection Process with Particular Reference to the Roles of Image and Perceived Constraints." Dissertation. Texas A&M Univ., 1977.

Crompton, John L. "Motivations for Pleasure Vacation." *Annals of Tourism Research.* Vol. 6, No. 4, 1979.

"Cruising." *Travel Agent.* Apr. 19, 1971.

Curran, Patrick J. T. *Principles and Procedures of Tour Management.* Boston, MA: CBI Publishing, 1978.

D'Amore, L. J. "A Third Generation of Tourism Thinking." Unpublished Paper, 1987.

Daniele, Daniel W. "The U.S. Budget Lodging Industry Yesterday, Today and Tomorrow." *U.S. Budget Lodging Industry.* Philadelphia: Laventhol and Horwath, 1982.

Del Rossa, Laura. "Sontag: Specialization is Key for Agencies Future." *Travel Weekly.* Vol. 46, No. 23. Apr. 16, 1987.

de Kadt, Emanuel. *Tourism: Passport to Development?* NY: Oxford Univ. Press, 1979.

Derchin, Michael. "1987 Outlook for Airlines." *1987 Outlook for Travel & Tourism.* Washington, DC: U.S. Travel Data Center and the Travel & Tourism Research Assn., 1987.

Discover America: A National Domestic Travel Marketing Plan. Washington, DC: Travel Industry Assn. of America.

Dorsey, Leslie and Janile Devane. *Fare Thee Well.* NY: Crown Publishers, 1964.

Dulles, Foster R. *A History of Recreation: America Learns to Play.* NY: Appleton-Century-Crofts, 1940.

Economic Analysis of the American Campground Industry: 1982. Washington, DC: National Campground Owners Assn., 1982.

Edgell, David L. *International Tourism Prospects 1987–2000.* Washington, DC: U.S. Dept. of Commerce, 1987.

————— . "The Formulation of Tourism Policy—A Managerial Framework." in *Travel, Tourism and Hospitality Research.* Ed. J. R. Brent Ritchie and Charles R. Goeldner. NY: John Wiley & Sons, 1986.

Ehemann, Jane. "What Kind of Place is Ireland: An Image Perceived Through the American Media." *Journal of Travel Research.* Vol. 16, No. 2, 1977.

"Elements of Tourism Policy in Developing Countries." U.N. Conference on Trade & Development, NY, 1973.

Evans, Jim. "Industry Predictions." *Travel Weekly's 25th Anniversary.* Vol. 42, No. 46. May 31, 1983.

Feifer, Maxine. *Tourism in History: From Imperial Rome to the Present.* NY: Stein and Day, 1986.

Ferguson, Jay. "Competition Heightens for Car Rental Market." *Travel Weekly's 25th Anniversary.* Vol. 42, No. 46. May 31, 1983.

Ferrario, Franco F. "Inventories as a Tool in Regional Tourism Development." Paper presented at the XIV Travel and Tourism Research Assn., Banff, Canada, 1983.

Francese, Peter. "Travel Markets: Fighting the Stereotypes." *1987 Outlook for Travel and Tourism: Proceedings of the Eleventh Annual Travel Outlook Forum.* Washington, DC: U.S. Travel Data Center, 1986.

Frechtling, Douglas C. "Travel Trends in 1986." *1987 Outlook for Travel and Tourism: Proceedings of the Twelfth Annual Travel Outlook Forum.* Washington, DC: U.S. Travel Data Center, 1987.

————— . "A Model State Continuing Travel Research Program." Paper for Discover America Travel Institute. Columbus, OH, 1975.

Fredrick, John H. *Commercial Air Transportation.* 5th ed. Homewood, IL: Richard D. Irwin, 1961.

Gearing, Charles E., William W. Stuart and Turgut Var. *Planning for Tourism Development: Quantitative Approaches.* NY: Praeger, 1976.

Gee, Chuck Y., Dexter J. L. Choy and James C. Makens. *The Travel Industry.* Westport, CT: The AVI Publishing Co., 1984.

"Get into Something Great." Washington, DC: National Assn. of Motorbus Owners, 1974.

Getz, Donald. "Models in Tourism Planning." *Tourism Management.* March, 1986.

Ghali, Moheb. "Tourism and Regional Growth: An Empirical Study of the Alternative Growth Paths for Hawaii." *Studies in Applied Regional Science* 11. Leiden: Martinue Mijhoff Social Sciences Division, 1977.

Gradburn, N. H. *Ethnic Tourism: Cultural Expressions From the Fourth World.* Berkley, CA: Univ. of California Press, 1976.

Gray, Peter H. *International Travel—International Trade.* Lexington, KY: D.C. Heath, 1970

Greenwood, P. J. "Tourism as an Agent of Change: A Spanish Basque Case." *Ethnology.* Vol 11, No. 1, 1972.

Grossman, Peter Z. *American Express: the Unofficial History of the People who Built the Great Financial Empire.* New York: Crown Publishers, 1987.

Gunn, Clare A. "Needed: An International Alliance for Tourism, Recreation, Conservation." *Travel Research Journal.* Vol. 2.

———. *Tourism Planning.* NY: Crane Russak, 1979.

———. "Getting Ready for Megatrends in Travel Attractions." *Tourism Management.* June 1985.

Hall, Paul G. "Trends and Opportunities for Research in the Tourism Industry." Unpublished Paper for Market Research Analyst. U.S. Travel and Tourism Admin.

Hawkins, Donald E., "Tourist Holiday Options: Timeshare Versus Competition." *Tourism Management.* Dec. 1985.

Hayes, Bernetta. "The Congressional Travel and Tourism Caucus and U.S. National Tourism Policy." *International Journal of Tourism Management.* June 1981.

Haywood, Michael K. "Can the Tourist–Area Life Cycle be Made Operational?" *Tourism Management.* Sept. 1986.

Hazerjian, Margie. "Planner Salaries Rise 8.3%; Average Pay Hits $33,909." *Meeting News.* Nov. 1985.

Henry, Richard. "Conventions and Meeting Facilities." Unpublished Paper.

"The Hidden Places of Kenya." *New York Times.* Sept. 12, 1982.

Horwath and Horwath International. "15th Annual Report on International Hotel Operations." *1985 Worldwide Lodging Industry:* NY: 1985.

Hudman, Lloyd E. "The Travellers' Perception of the Role of Food and Eating in the Tourist Industry." *The Impact of Catering and Cuisine Upon Tourism.* Vol. 27. St.-Gall (Suisse): AIEST, 1986.

Hughes, Ann. "Incentive Travel: Tailored for Individuals." *Successful Meetings.* Dec. 1984.

Hunt, John D. "Trends in Tourism Development and Marketing: An Overview." Unpublished Paper. ND: Conference on Tourism, 1987.

"The Impact of International Tourism on the Economic Development of the Developing Countries." Geneva, International Union of Travel Organizations (now WTO): 1975.

Innskeep, Edward L. "Interdisciplinary Study Cycle: Planning of Cultural Tourist Attractions." Granada, Spain: WTO, 1987.

Jafari, Jafar and J. R. Brent Ritchie. "Towards a Framework for Tourism Education: Problems and Prospects." *Annals of Tourism Research.* Vol. 8, No. 1, 1981.

Jakle, John A. *The Tourist.* Lincoln, NE: Univ. of Nebraska, 1985.

Jarvis, Feliz. "All Suite Hotels." *Lodging.* June 1981.

Jenkins, C. L. "Tourism Policies in Developing Countries: A Critique." *International Journal of Tourism Management.* Mar. 1980.

Jud, G. Donald. "Tourism and Economic Growth in Mexico Since 1950." *Inter-American Economic Affairs.* Vol. 28, 1 (1974).

Kaynak, Erdener. "Developing Market Strategy for a Resource-Based Industry." *Tourism Management.* Sept. 1985.

Kestigian, Mark. *U.S.A. Today.* Feb. 25, 1985.

Kosters, Martinus. "Holland and Tourism in the Next Decade." in *Tourism Planning and Development Issues.* Ed. Donald E. Hawkins, et. al. Washington, DC: George Washington Univ., 1980.

Krause, Walter, Donald G. Judd and Hyman Joseph. *International and Latin American Development.* Austin, TX: Univ. of Texas, 1973.

Krippendorf, Jost. "Tourism in the System of Industrial Society." *Annals of Tourism Research.* Vol. 13, No. 4, 1986.

Kuh, Joyce. "The Changing American Vacation." *Travel & Leisure's World Travel Overview 1987/1988.* NY: American Express Publishing Corp., 1987.

Kyle, W. T. "Changes in the Channels of Distribution in Travel." *The 80s: Its Impact on Travel and Tourism Marketing.* Salt Lake City: The Travel Research Assn., 1977.

Lanquar, Robert. "The Organizational Development of the World Tourism Organization: A Case Study." *The Travel Journalist.* Vol. 31. Jan. 1985.

Lata'akau'lola, Lupe Llaiu and 'Asinate Samate. "The Social and Cultural Impact of Tourism in Tonga." in *Pacific Tourism.* Hawaii: So. Pacific Social Sciences Assn., 1980.

Lattin, Gerald W. *The Lodging and Food Service Industry.* East Lansing, MI: The Educational Institute, 1985.

———. "Hotels." *Lodging.* June 1985.

Lazar, William. "A Note on Maslow's Theory of Motivation." *Marketing Management: A System Perspective.* NY: John Wiley & Sons, 1971.

Lesure, John D. "1910–1985 Years of Economic Impact." *Lodging.* June 1985.

Lewis, David L. *The Public Image of Henry Ford.* Detroit: Wayne State Univ. Press, 1976.

Lichorish, L. J. and A. G. Keshaw. *The Travel Trade.* London: Practical Press, 1958.

Lin, V. L. and P. D. Loeb. "Tourism and Crime in Mexico: Some Comments." *Social Science Quarterly.* Vol. 58, 1977.

Liu, Juanita C. and Jan Auyong. "The Attractiveness of Hawaii Tourism." *Travel and Tourism: Thrive or Survive.* Salt Lake City: Travel and Tourism Research Assn., 1987.

Louden, David and Albert J. Della Bitta. *Consumer Behavior: Concepts and Applications*. NY: McGraw-Hill Book Co., 1979.

Loukissas, Philippos J. "Tourism Regional Development Impacts: A Comparative Analysis of the Greek Islands." *Annals of Tourism Research*. Vol. 9, No. 4, 1982.

Lundberg, Donald E. *The Tourist Business*. NY: Van Nostrand Reinhold Co., 1985.

Maddox, R. Neil. "Measuring Satisfaction with Tourism." *Journal of Travel Research*. Vol. 23, No. 3, 1985.

Maldutis, Julius. "The Airline: The Twilight Zone." Unpublished Paper for National Passenger Traffic Assn: Atlanta, 1987.

Manning, Frank E. "Tourism and Bermuda's Black Clubs: A Case of Cultural Revitalization." in *Tourism: Passport to Development*. Ed. Emanuel de Kadt. NY: Oxford Univ. Press, 1979.

Maslow, A. H. "A Theory of Human Motivation." *Psychological Review*. Vol. 50, No. 4. July 1973.

Mathieson, Alister and Geoffrey Wall. *Tourism: Economic, Physical and Social Impacts*. London & NY: Longman, 1986.

Mayo, Edward S. and Lance P. Jarvis. *The Psychology of Leisure Travel*. Boston: CBI, 1981.

McElroy, Jerome L. and John F. Tinsley. "United States Virgin Islands." in *Tourism in the Caribbean*. Ed. Shirley B. Seward and Bernard K. Spinrad. Ottawa: International Development Research Center, 1982.

McIntosh, Robert W. "Definitions." Unpublished Paper, 1979.

McIntosh, Robert W. and Charles R. Goeldner. *Tourism: Principles, Practices, Philosophies*. NY: John Wiley & Sons, 1986.

McKean, Philip. "Tourism, Culture Change, and Culture Conservation in Bali." Unpublished Paper. Toronto: American Anthropological Assn., 1972.

McLellan, Robert W. and Kathryn Dodd Foushee. "Negative Images of The United States as Expressed by Tour Operators From Other Countries." *Journal of Travel Research*. Vol. 22, No. 1, 1983.

Mead, William. *The Grand Tour in the Eighteenth Century*. NY & Boston: Houghton Mifflin, 1914.

Mill, Robert Christie and Alastair M. Morrison. *The Tourism System: An Introductory Text*. Englewood Cliffs, NJ: Prentice-Hall, 1985.

Miller, Jeffrey R. *Legal Aspects of Travel Agency Operation*. Wheaton, IL: Merton House, 1982.

Muster, Bill. *Traveler's Almanac*. Chicago: Rand McNally & Co., 1978.

Nanninga, Nico J. and Ruud J. Reuland. *Hotel and Tourism Training in Developing Countries*. The Hague: School of Hospitality Management, Hague Hotel School, 1985.

Neulinger, John. *The Psychology of Leisure*. Springfield, IL: Charles C. Thomas, 1974.

Nolan, Howard J. "Tourist Attractions and Recreation Resources Providing for Natural and Human Resources." in *Tourism Planning and Development Issues*. Ed. Donald E. Hawkins, et al. Washington, DC: George Washington Univ., 1980.

Organization of American States. "Methods for Tourism Project Pre-Investment Studies." Research aned Bibliography Series, No. 4. Washington, DC: Dept. of Economic Affairs, 1978.

_____ . "Socio-Cultural Impact of Tourism in the Americas." Vol. 9, 1982.

_____ . "Enhancing the Positive Impact of Tourism on the Built and Natural Environment." Vol. 1, 1984.

Papson, S. "Tourism—World's Biggest Industry in the Twenty-First Century?" *Futurist*. Aug. 1979.

Pearson, Jim. "Great Moments in Lodging." *Lodging*. June 1985.

_____ . "The Economics of the Lodging Industry." *Lodging*. Sept. 1985.

Peppelenbosch, P. G. N. and G. J. Tempelman. "Tourism and the Developing Countries." *Tijdschrift voor Economics en Social Geografie*. Vol. 64, No. 1, 1973.

Peters, Michael. *International Tourism*. London: Hutchinson, 1969.

Philion, Jim. "Industry Predictions." *Travel Weekly's 25th Anniversary*. Vol. 42, No. 46. May 31, 1983.

Phillips, S. Gordon. "Organizing a Tourism System: The Ontario Example." in *The Tourism System: An Introductory Text*. Ed. Robert Christie Mill and Alastair M. Morrison. Englewood Cliffs, NJ: Prentice-Hall, 1985.

Pimlott, John A. R. *The Englishman's Holiday*. Salem, NH: Faber, 1947.

Pisarski, Alan and Donald E. Hawkins. *United States Outbound Travel Statistics Sourcebook*. Northbrook, IL: Runzheimer International, 1988.

Pizam, Abraham, "Tourism Manpower: The State of the Art." *Journal of Travel Research*. Vol. 21, No. 2, 1982.

_____ , Yoram Neuman and Arie Reichel. "Dimensions of Tourist Satisfaction with a Destination Area." *Annals of Tourism Research*. Vol. 4, No. 3, 1978.

Plog, Stanley C. "Why Destination Areas Rise and Fall in Popularity." *Cornell Hotel and Administration Quarterly*. Vol. 14, No. 4. Feb. 1974.

Reilly, Robert T. *Handbook of Professional Tour Management*. Wheaton, IL: Merton House, 1982.

_____ . *Travel and Tourism Marketing Techniques*. Wheaton, IL: Merton House, 1980.

Reynoso y Valle, Augustin and Jacomina P. de Regt. "Growing Pains: Planned Tourism Development in Ixtapa-Zihuatanejo." in *Tourism: Passport to Development?* Ed. E. de Kadt. NY: Oxford Univ. Press, 1976.

Richardson, Evelyn K. and Ernest J. Donehower. "Tourism Marketing Research and Its Applications—The Hawaii Case." Report of Proceedings. Sixth PATA Travel Research Seminar. Honolulu, HI: Pacific Area Tourism Association, 1978.

Ritcher, Linda. "Fragmented Politics of U.S. Tourism." *Tourism Management*. Vol. 6, No. 3. Sept. 1985.

Ritchie, J. R. Brent. "Roles of Research in Tourism Management." in *Travel, Tourism, and Hospitality Research: A Handbook for Managers and Researchers*.

Ed. J. R. Brent Ritchie and Charles R. Goeldner. NY: John Wiley & Sons, 1986.

———— and M. Zins. "Culture as a Determinant of the Attractiveness of Tourist Region." *Annals of Tourism Research.* Vol. 5, No. 2.

Robinson, H. *A Geography of Tourism.* London: Macdonald & Evans, 1976.

Rubin, Karen. "People Power II." *Travel Agent.* Apr. 29, 1985.

Rudney, Robert. "The Development of Tourism on the Cote d Azur: A Historical Perspective." in *Tourism Planning and Development Issue.* Ed. Donald Hawkins, et al. Washington DC: George Washington Univ., 1980.

Schmitt, Peter J. *Back to Nature: The Arcadian Myth in Urban America.* NY: Oxford Univ. Press, 1969.

Schmoll, G. A. *Tourism Promotion.* London: Tourism International Press, 1977.

Seward, Shirley B. and Bernard K. Spinrad. *Tourism in the Caribbean: The Economic Impact.* Ottawa: International Development Research Center, 1982.

Sessa, Alberto. *Elements of Tourism Economics.* Rome: Catal, 1983.

Shafer, Elwood L. and John F. Hamilton Jr. "A Comparison of Four Survey Techniques Used in Outdoor Recreation Research." Research Paper for U.S. Forest Service. NE-86. Upper Darby, PA: 1967.

Sheth, Jagdish N. "A Psychological Model of Travel Mode Selection." *Advances in Consumer Research.* Vol. 3. 1975.

Sims, J. Taylor, J. Robert Foster and Arch G. Woodside. *Marketing Channels: Systems and Strategies.* NY: Harper & Row, 1977.

Singh, Tej Vir and Jagcish Kaur. *Studies in Wildlife Parks Conservation.* New Delhi: Metropolitan, 1982.

Smith, Valene L. *Hosts of Guests: An Anthropology of Tourism.* Philadelphia: Univ. of Pennsylvania Press, 1977.

Sontag, Peter M. "Industry Predictions." *Travel Weekly's 25th Anniversary.* Vol. 42, No. 46. May 31, 1983.

Taneja, Nawal K. *Airlines in Transition.* Lexington, MA: Lexington Books, 1981.

Tanirono, Eliam. "The Impact of Tourism on Solomons Culture." in *Pacific Tourism.* Hawaii: So. Pacific Social Sciences Assn., 1980.

Toohey, William D. *Travel: An Engine of Employment.* Washington, DC: Discover America Travel Organization, 1977.

"Tourism Agreements." *Israel Travel News* #4. Vol. 7. Aug./Sept. 1986.

"Tourism as a Factor in National and Regional Development." Occasional Paper No. 4. Peterborough, Canada: Dept. of Geography, Trent Univ., 1975.

"Tourism Policy and International Tourism in OECD Member Countries, 1976." Paris: Organization for Economic Cooperation and Development, 1977.

Tourism USA. "Guidelines for Tourism Development." Washington, DC: U.S. Department of Commerce, U.S. Travel and Tourism Admin., 1986.

Travel & Leisure's World Travel Overview 1987/1988. NY: American Express Publishing Corp., 1987.

"Trends: 20 Top Trends for 1987." *Restaurant and Institutions,* Vol. 97, No. 1, Jan. 1987.

Turnbull, Colin. "Bali's New Gods." *Natural History.* Jan. 1982.

————. "Christmas in Jerusalem: The Tourist as Pilgrim." *Natural History.* Vol. 91.

Tuttle, Donna F. "The 'Visit USA' Program After 25 Years: Changing Markets, Growing Competition and New Challenges Ahead." *Business America.* Washington, DC: U.S. Dept. Of Commerce, Feb. 17, 1986.

"Twelve-Point Plan." U.S. Dept of the Interior, National Park Service. Washington, DC: Arizona Memorial Museum Assn., 1985.

U.S. Travel Data Center. "1982 National Travel Survey." Washington, DC: U.S. Dept. of Commerce.

————. "Impact of Travel on State Economics, 1984." Washington, DC: U.S. Dept. of Commerce, 1986.

U.S. Travel Service. *Planning for Tourism.* Vol. 2, "Development." Washington, DC, 1978.

"The Visitor Industry in Hawaii's Economy, A Cost Benefit Analysis." *Mathematica.* 27–29, 1970.

Wahab, Salah. *Tourism Management.* London: Tourism International Press, 1976.

————. "Tourism Planning of the Mediterranean Coast of Egypt (Rainbow Coast.)" Aix-en-Provence: Centre Des Hautes Etudes Touristiques, 1979.

———— and Salah Eldin. *Elements of State Policy on Tourism.* Turin, Italy: Ital Graffica, 1974.

————, L. J. Crampon and L. M. Rothfield. *Tourism Marketing.* London: Tourism International Press, 1976.

Walsh, Carol A. "Travel Your Way to Success." *Business Week's Guide To Careers.* Spring/Summer 1985.

Walsh, Sharon W. "Service Jobs—Apply Within." *Washington Post.* Aug. 29, 1986.

Waters, Somerset R. *The Travel Industry World Yearbook: The Big Picture—1985.* NY: Child & Waters.

————. (1987).

————. (1988).

————. "Three Periods of Change Show Industry's Growth, Resiliency: Twenty-five Years of the Jet Age." *Travel Weekly's 25th Anniversary.* Vol. 42, No. 46. May 31, 1983.

Weinberger, Bill Jr. "Marketing for the Premium Gaming Customers—Caesar's Palace Experience." Paper at XII Travel and Research Assn., 1981.

"What Do 42 Wars Add Up To?" *Washington Post,* Apr. 27, 1986.

WTO. "Acapulco Document." Madrid, 1982.

————. "The World Tourism Organization in 1981." Madrid, 1985.

————. "1976 Research Program: Distribution Channels." Madrid, 1976.

————. "Appraisal and Social Value of Investments in Domestic Tourism." New Delhi, 1983.

————. "Concept and Production Innovations of the Tourism Product." Madrid, 1983.

————. "Determination of the Elements Required For Defining Training Programmes Tailored to the Specific Needs of Countries." Madrid, 1985.

————. "Domestic and International Tourism Contribution to State Revenue." Madrid, 1982.

————. "Guidelines for the use of National Resources in

the Building and Maintenance of Tourist Plant." Madrid, 1981.

——— . "Manila Declaration." Manila, 1980.

——— . "Report on the Development of the Accomodation Sector." Madrid, 1983.

——— . "Report on the Working Party on Tourism and Health." Madrid, 1985.

——— . "Risk of Saturation of Tourist Carrying Capacity Overload in Holiday Destinations." Madrid, 1983.

——— . "The Social and Cultural Dimension of Tourism." Madrid, 1981.

——— . "Study on Tourism's Contribution to Protecting the Environment." Madrid, 1983.

——— and the U.S. Environment Programme. "Workshop on Environmental Aspects of Tourism." Madrid, 1983.

Wynegar, Don. "Outlook for International Travel Markets." *1987 Outlook for Travel and Tourism.* Proceedings of the Twelfth Annual Travel Outlook Forum. Washington, DC: U.S. Travel Data Center, 1987.

Young, George. *Tourism: Blessing or Blight?* Middlesex, England: Penguin, 1973.

Zamora, Mario D., Vinson A. H. Sutlive and Nathan Altshuler, eds. *Tourism and Behavior.* Williamsburg, VA: William and Mary, 1978.

INDEX

AAA. *See* Automobile Association of
  America
AAA Tour Book, 92
Acapulco, 45, 81, 83, 135, 236
accommodations. *See* hotels, lodging
  industry
acculturation, 222, 225, 230
advertising, 29, 30, 46, 54, 55, 56, 71,
  73, 92, 97, 105, 106–107, 125, 126–
  128, 131, 165, 194. *See also*
  promotion
advertising, types of: brochures, 97, 127,
  145, 157, 158; direct mail, 127;
  magazines, 127; newpapers, 126–127;
  news releases, 128; outdoor, 127;
  point-of-sale, 127; radio, 127;
  television, 29, 127; theme parties, 109;
  travel destination films, 128; yellow
  pages, 127. *See also* promotion, types
  of
Africa, tourism in, 57, 185, 206, 230, 231
African Travel Commission, 112
African Wildlife Leadership Foundation,
  236
Ahmed, Sadrudin A., 56
Aid for International Development, 196
Air Jamaica, 180
Airline Deregulation Act, 139, 140
airline industry, 73, 74, 122, 130, 136,
  138–141, 152, 247, 249–250, 251
airline passenger revenue, 215
airport development, 143–144, 240, 241
airports, transportation to/from, 102
Alabama, tourism in, 216
Alaska, tourism in, 53, 65, 66, 142, 215
Alaskan Rockies, 52
Ala Moana Hotel, 222
Albuquerque, 63, 101
Alexander, L. M., 235
Alexandria, 186

Alps, 65
Altamira Caves, 69, 239
Amalfi Drive, 65
Amboseli National Park, 238
amenities, 25, 86–87
American Airlines, 19, 43, 140, 160
American Express, 94, 152–153, 157,
  194
American Hotel Protective Association,
  76
American Sightseeing, 93
American Society of Travel Agents (ASTA),
  16, 121, 207
American Trail, 130
Amish country, tourism in, 62, 63, 64,
  69, 227
Amsterdam, 143, 144
Amtrak, 137, 138
amusement parks. *See* theme parks
ancient Assyria, travel in the, 10
ancient Egypt, travel in, 10,12
ancient era, travel in the, 9–10
ancient Greece, travel in, 11
ancient Persia, travel in, 10
ancient Polynesia, travel in, 9
ancient Rome, travel in, 9, 11–12, 75
animals, observation of, 65, 236, 240.
  See also safaris
Antigua, 237
Antiquities Act, 235
Appomattox Courthouse, 62
Arc de Triomphe, 62
Argentina, 53
Arizona, 65
arts and crafts, traditional, 63, 226, 227
arts festivals, 63, 226
Ashman, Mike, 222
Asia Minor, history of travel in, 12
association meetings, 100. *See also*
  conventions

Association of Travel Marketing Executives
  (ATME), 121
ASTA. *See* American Society of Travel
  Agents
Athens, influence on travel of, 11
Athens, tourism in, 143
Atlanta, 102
Atlantic City, tourism in, 14, 40, 54, 66,
  76, 81, 170
Atlantic Conference, 112
attractions: achitecture as, 63, 93;
  classification of, 62–67; cuisine as, 66;
  enhancement of, 67; entertainment as,
  66; hallmark events as, 65; historical
  sights as, 62, 138, 198, 235, 237, 242;
  industrial archeology as, 62; limiting
  access to, 69; management of, 72;
  music and dance as, 64; overload of,
  52, 69; religious, 41, 62–63, 64, 93,
  231; scenery as, 65; wildlife as, 65,
  236, 238, 239, 240; uniqueness of, 69;
  vegetation as, 65
attractions development. *See* destination
  development
Australia, tourism in, 58, 65, 73, 240
automobile, influence on tourism, 77,
  136, 137–138
Automobile Association of America (AAA),
  80
automobile rental industry, 42, 93, 138,
  143, 158, 252
average length of stay, 57
Awekotuku, Ngahuia, 226

Baden, 66
Bahamas, tourism in, 64–65, 230
balance of trade, 211–212
balance-of-trade payments, 211, 214,
  215, 218, 246
Bali, 135, 185, 226, 231

277

PHOTO CREDITS

The publisher and authors gratefully acknowledge the following for the photographs reproduced in this text:

Formal gardens of the Louvre in Paris. Courtesy of Air France. Page iii.

Temple of Karnak at Luxor, Egypt. Courtesy of the Egyptian Ministry of Tourism. Page 3.

Traditional Samoan house used by campers. Courtesy of the Samoan Office of Tourism. Page 18.

Red Square, Moscow. Courtesy of Intourist. Page 37.

Nice, queen of the Riviera. Courtesy of the French Government Tourist Office. Page 50.

Chichen Itza, Mexico. Courtesy of FONATUR. Page 61.

Estoril, the fashionable seaside resort on Portugal's Costa del Sol. Courtesy of the Portuguese National Tourist Office. Page 75.

Amsterdam's Museum Boat picks up passengers at the Tourist Information Center and makes stops at the city's most prominent museums. Courtesy of the Netherlands Board of Tourism. Page 91.

Las Vegas Convention Center. Courtesy of Las Vegas Convention and Visitors Authority. Page 100.

City Hall in Hannover. Courtesy of the German National Tourist Office. Page 111.

The medieval walled city of Carcassonne. Courtesy of the French Government Tourist Office. Page 123.

The Shinkansen Bullet Train passing Mount Fuji. Courtesy of the Japan National Tourist Organization. Page 134.

Charter bus. Courtesy of Gray Line Tours. Page 149.

River rafting on Riviere Rouge, Quebec. Courtesy of the Canadian Government Tourist Office. Page 165.

Playing roulette in Las Vegas. Courtesy of the Las Vegas Convention and Visitors Authority. Page 173.

Loggia della Signoria in Florence. Courtesy of the Italian Government Travel Office. Page 184.

Skiing the Magic Mile on Mount Hood in the northern Oregon's Cascade Mountains. Courtesy of the Oregon Economic Development Department. Page 193.

Passengers relaxing on the *Fairsea*. Courtesy of Sitmar Cruises. Page 201.

Torremolinos. Courtesy of the Portuguese National Tourist Office. Page 211.

The Viking Ship Hall of Roskilde, Copenhagen. Courtesy of the Danish Tourist Board. Page 221.

Delicate Arch in Arches National Park (Canyonlands). Courtesy of the Utah Travel Council. Page 234.

Space shuttle Atlantis, Kennedy Space Center, FL. Courtesy of NASA. Page 245.

Appenzellerland in Eastern Switzerland. Courtesy of the Swiss National Tourist Office. Page 255.

Suzdal, an ancient Russian town. Courtesy of Intourist. Page 263.

The Maritime Museum in Oslo. Courtesy of the Norwegian National Tourist Office. Page 267.

The Berlaymont, EEC headquarters in Brussels. Courtesy of the Belgian Tourist Office. Page 271.